New Approaches to Down Syndrome

New Approaches to Down Syndrome

Edited by

Brian Stratford and Pat Gunn

CASSELL

Cassell
Wellington House
125 Strand
London WC2R 0BB

127 West 24th Street
New York
NY 10011

First published 1996

British Library Cataloguing-in-Publication Data

A catalogue record for this book is available from the British Library.

ISBN 304–33350–6

Typeset by Keystroke, Jacaranda Lodge, Wolverhampton

Printed and bound in Great Britain by Redwood Books, Trowbridge, Wiltshire

Contents

Contributors

Göran Annerén, is a Senior Physician and Associated Professor in the Department of Clinical Genetics, Uppsala University Children's Hospital, Sweden. He is responsible for a Down Syndrome Clinic and his main field of research is medical concerns in Down syndrome. He has published about 90 papers in this field and was invited visiting assistant professor to the University of California in San Francisco 1985–86.

Adrian Ashman is Director of the Fred and Eleanor Schonell Special Education Research Centre, University of Queensland. He is a graduate of the University of New South Wales, Australia and the University of Calgary, Canada. He has published many books and papers in the areas of educational psychology, special education and intellectual disability.

Gordon Ashton is a District Judge at Preston and Blackpool who graduated in law at Manchester University, qualified as a solicitor in 1967 and practised in Cumbria before judicial appointment in 1992. He is also a Chairman of the Social Security Appeal Tribunal. He writes and lectures widely on the legal implications of mental incapacity and his books include *Mental Handicap and the Law* (1992) *The Elderly Client Handbook* (1994) and *Elderly People and the Law* (1995). He has a son with severe learning disabilities.

Gillian Bird is Research Fellow and Deputy Director of the Sarah Duffen Centre, Department of Psychology at the University of Portsmouth, where she has worked for the past ten years. She is currently engaged in an action research project working with 40 schools that have children with Down syndrome fully included in mainstream classes.

Martin E. Block is an Assistant Professor and Director of the Masters Program in Adapted Physical Education at the University of Virginia. He is past Chair of the Adapted Physical Activity Council of the American Alliance of Health, Physical Education, Recreations and Dance, and his particular expertise is integration of children with disabilities in physical education.

Roy I. Brown is Foundation Professor and Dean of the School of Special Education and Disability Studies, The Flinders University, Adelaide, and Professor Emeritus in the Department of Educational Psychology, University of Calgary. As a practitioner and researcher, he has published extensively on quality of life and disabilities across the life span and has developed professional education projects in a variety of countries.

Sue Buckley is Professor of the Psychology of Developmental Disability and Director of the Sarah Duffen Centre at the University of Portsmouth She is the author of a number of books and papers on Down syndrome and is the editor of *Down's Syndrome: Research and Practice.*

Angela Byrne is a Research Student at the Sarah Duffen Centre, University of Portsmouth. She is investigating the literacy, language and memory skills of 24 children with Down syndrome and their mainstream peers.

Alan D.B. Clarke CBE is Emeritus Professor, Department of Psychology, University of Hull, and Visiting Professor, University of Hertfordshire. He worked in the NHS from 1951 to 1962 and during this period jointly edited and contributed to the first edition of *Mental Deficiency: the Changing Outlook* (1958). The fourth edition was published in 1985. He was appointed CBE in 1974 for services to teachers of the mentally handicapped, and with Ann Clarke received the AAMD Research Award (1977) and the IASSMD Distinguished Achievement Award for Scientific Literature (1982). As co-founder of the latter association (1964), he is now its Honorary Life President. The Royal College of Psychiatrists elected him to an Honorary Fellowship in 1989. Research interests lie in the field of life-span development.

Ann M. Clarke is Emeritus Professor of Educational Psychology, School of Education, University of Hull. She worked in the NHS from 1951 to 1962, editing and contributing to the first edition of *Mental Deficiency: the Changing Outlook* (1958) during this period. The fourth edition was published in 1985. She received a joint Research Award (1977) from the AAMD, and a joint Distinguished Achievement Award for Scientific Literature (1982) from the IASSMD. Her main research interests lie in the field of normal and abnormal life-span development, with special reference to factors relating to outcomes.

Mary Crombie is an educational psychologist and school guidance officer. She has also been a college lecturer and university tutor in courses concerned with learning disabilities and assessment in special education. Her doctoral thesis was a longitudinal study that investigated the long term effects of early intervention for children with Down syndrome.

Monica Cuskelly is an educational and developmental psychologist who is a Lecturer at the Fred and Eleanor Schonell Special Education Research Centre, University of Queensland. Her interests include the development of individuals with Down syndrome and the way in which families, and their individual members, respond to having a child with Down syndrome in the family.

Bethan Davies is a Consultant in Audiological Medicine at the Cromwell Hospital in London and was previously for 19 years a Consultant at Charing Cross Hospital in London. Her main professional interests are in the assessment of hearing in children who are difficult to test because of physical or mental handicap or disturbed behaviour. She has been particularly interested in the early identification of hearing impaired children, and particularly in the study and management of auditory disorders in Down syndrome.

John Elkins is Dean of the Faculty and Head of the Graduate School of Education in the University of Queensland. He is a member of the Board of Directors of the International Reading Association. He is co-editor with Adrian Ashman of Australia's most widely used textbook on special education and the author of many research publications in the fields of reading and disability.

Margaret Farrell is a support teacher (learning difficulties) and an Associate Lecturer in the Fred and Eleanor Schonell Special Education Research Centre, University of Queensland. She has a special interest in teaching reading to children with Down syndrome.

Ann Gath is a Consultant Child Psychiatrist at the Child Health Centre, Bury St Edmunds. She has a particular interest in developmental disability and was formerly Professor of Developmental Psychiatry, University College, London. She has published in the field of the family and psychiatric aspects of learning disability.

Joan F. Goodman is a Professor in the Graduate School of Education, University of Pennsylvania, with many years experience as a clinical psychologist and as Director of a Preschool Treatment Programme for children with multiple handicaps. She has a special interest in early intervention for pre-schoolers with developmental delays.

Pat Gunn is a psychologist and remedial teacher who is an Honorary Research Consultant at the Fred and Eleanor Schonell Special Education Research Centre, University of Queensland. She has been involved with research into the development of people with Down syndrome for many years.

David Gibson is Emeritus Professor of Psychology at the University of Calgary, Alberta, Canada. He was formerly Chief of Psychological Services at the Rideau Regional Center and founding Director of the Vocational and Rehabilitation Research Institute (Canada). His research interests include the syndromic bases of atypical development, management systems accountability, and the behavioural genetics of mentally limiting conditions.

K.A. Hallidie-Smith completed her chapter in spite of severe illness. We report with sadness that she died in September 1995. She was an Honorary Consultant Paediatric Cardiologist at Great Ormond Street Hospital for Children and a contributor to *Current Approaches to Down's Syndrome*. Hallidie-Smith had lectured to Down Syndrome Association members and to other groups, both in the

UK and overseas, on many aspects of the diagnosis and management of cardiac defects in Down syndrome.

Christopher J. Hammond is an Ophthalmology Registrar at the Western Eye Hospital, London and has a special interest in neuro-developmental and paediatric ophthalmology.

James Hanrahan is Associate Dean (Academic) in the Faculty of Education, McGill University. He is currently conducting research into the area of arithmetic for developmentally delayed children.

Alan Hayes is Associate Professor of Developmental Psychology within the Fred and Eleanor Schonell Special Education Research Centre, The University of Queensland, Australia, where he is a Director of the Down Syndrome Research Program, which currently focuses on family issues, development and self-regulation.

Anne Jobling is a Lecturer at the Fred and Eleanor Schonell Special Education Research Centre, The University of Queensland. She is Vice-President of the Australian Sport and Recreation Association for People with intellectual disabilities (AUSRAPID) and a member of the National Advisory Panel on Sport and Recreation for the Australian Down Syndrome Association.

Jane McCarthy is a Lecturer in Developmental Psychiatry at University College London Medical School. She was formerly a Senior Registrar in the Department of Psychiatry of disability at St George's Hospital Medical School. Her research interests include ageing and learning disability and the families of people with learning disability.

Roy McConkey is Director of Training and Research with the Brothers of Charity, Borders Region, Scotland. He has worked in many developing countries on projects sponsored by UNESCO, the Leonard Cheshire Foundation International, British Council, Canadian International Development Agency and Irish Foreign Aid.

Elisabeth A. Millis is Associate Specialist at Paddington Green Children's Unit, St Mary's Hospital, London. The hospital includes a children's developmental assessment unit as a special part of the paediatric opthalmology department.

Tina Newman is a doctoral student in the Department of Educational and Counselling Psychology, Faculty of Education, McGill University. Her research interests include arithmetic for Down syndrome children and writing for learning disabled children.

Trevor R. Parmenter is a Professorial Fellow in the School of Education, Macquarie University. After 21 years as teacher and principal in special schools he joined the foundation special education staff at Macquarie University in 1974. Here he developed the Unit for Community Integration Studies, which has extensive research interests in community living, vocational training, transition, ageing and policy development. He chairs a residential programme Board of Directors and is the President-Elect of the International Association for the Scientific Study of Intellectual Disability.

Siegfried M. Pueschel worked at the Developmental Evaluation Clinic of the Children's Hospital in Boston from 1967 to 1975. There he became Director of the first Down Syndrome Program and provided leadership to the PKU and Inborn Errors of Metabolism Program. In 1975 Dr Pueschel was appointed Director of the Child Development Center at Rhode Island Hospital in Providence, Rhode Island. He continued to pursue his interest in clinical activities, research, and teaching in the fields of development disabilities, biochemical genetics and chromosome abnormalities. He is certified by the American Board of Pediatrics and is a Diplomate of the American Board of Medical Genetics. His academic appointments include Lecturer in Pediatrics, Harvard Medical School and Professor of Pediatrics, Brown University. Dr Pueschel has authored and co-authored 15 books and over 200 articles in the field of handicap.

Greg Reid is Professor and Chair, Department of Physical Education, McGill University, Montreal, Quebec, Canada. His research is in the areas of physical activity programming, developmental disabilities, including Down syndrome, autism and physical awkwardness. He is also the editor of the journal *The Adapted Physical Activity Quarterly*.

Vivienne Riches is a Research Fellow in the Unit for Community Integration Studies, School of Education, Macquarie University. She has a background in secondary school teaching, clinical psychology and research in special education and disability issues. Her interests include transition, social interaction skills, vocational assessment and training and anger control strategies for youth with disabilities.

Jonathan Steele has been involved in research into Down syndrome for over a decade, and has a particular interest in incidence, prevalence and the size of the Down syndrome population. He has published in major scientific journals in Britain, Europe and America as well as having written articles for parents. His other professional interest lies in the education of children with severe learning difficulties. He is currently Headteacher at The Loyne School, Lancaster.

Brian Stratford KSG is Senior Research Fellow/Professor at Loughborough University Department of Education. He has held posts as Visiting Professor at a number of universities in many parts of the world, including the University of Queensland, Australia, and the State University of Bucharest, Romania, and is regarded as an international authority on Down syndrome. He is Principal Adviser to the Hong Kong Down Syndrome Association and holds a number of senior advisory positions in the area of rehabilitation of handicapped people in the People's Republic of China. He was created a Knight of the Illustrious Order of

St Gregory the Great in 1986 by His Holiness Pope John Paul II, for services to handicapped people. Dr Stratford is also the author of a number of books and scientific papers on the development of children and adults with Down syndrome. He is currently seconded to China where he is Director of a Research and Development Centre in the Guangdong Province, dedicated to the training of multi-disciplinary professional staff.

Merete Vigild is Associate Professor, Department of Community Dentistry and Graduate Studies, Copenhagen. Her research activities have been in the fields of oral health status, attitudes and behaviour, oral health care among handicapped children and institutionalized elderly, and the evaluation of oral health care programmes. She has more than 40 publications in international and national scientific journals and textbooks.

Jennifer G. Wishart is a Senior Research Fellow/Reader at the University of Edinburgh. Over the last ten years her research has focused on learning difficulties in young children with Down syndrome. She is an adviser to the European Down Syndrome Association, the Down Syndrome Association (UK) and the Scottish Down Syndrome Association.

Jacek Zaremba is Professor and head of the Department of Genetics at the Institute of Psychiatry and Neurology, Warsaw, Poland. He is a specialist in neurology and human genetics. His main interests are the aetiology of mental retardation, clinical genetics, genetic counselling and prenatal diagnosis.

Acknowledgements

Many people with Down syndrome, both children and adults, together with their families, have taken part in the research projects discussed in this book. We would like to thank them all very much for their co-operation as it is through such participatory research that we acquire the most insightful knowledge about Down syndrome.

We are also indebted to our authors for their willingness to contribute their knowledge and expertise. We thank Pam Tupe of the University of Queensland and Paula Cross of the University of Loughborough for helping to keep the lines of communication open between the UK and Australia. We give a special word of thanks to Pam Dix, a most patient and understanding literary agent. Pam has been highly efficient in adjudicating and negotiating, and in ensuring that deadlines were met.

Finally, we thank Maureen and Morris because they have not yet divorced us.

Preface

In recent years, there have been dramatic changes in the lives of many individuals with Down syndrome who live in western societies. Children are reared at home instead of facing life in institutions while adults are encouraged to greater independence within their own communities. Advances in medical treatment are overcoming many health problems and reports around the world have indicated longer and healthier lives.

These changes have been documented in a number of books written for parents or by parents about their child with Down syndrome. Other books have been directed to a specialized audience, often in the biomedical field. *New Approaches to Down Syndrome* has a somewhat different aim as it is intended for a multi-disciplinary readership. It follows the principles espoused by David Lane and Brian Stratford when they edited *Current Approaches to Down's Syndrome* a decade ago viz., to present the most up-to-date information from leading world authorities; to make this knowledge available to the widest possible readership amongst those professionals working in the field; and to present this in a language which can be understood by all professionals and students, regardless of discipline.

The need for multidisciplinary communication is as strong as ever but whereas *Current Approaches* reflected the predominant research role then played by medicine, this book reflects the increasing role of other professions. There is a thread running through the topics, however, which can trace its origins to the earlier publication. Medical advances continue to impact on the well-being of those with Down syndrome and this has led to a new emphasis on preventive care. The right to treatment for infants with Down syndrome was an important legal-medical issue a decade ago and the rights of citizens with Down syndrome continue to be important issues in law, medicine and education. The chapters on education show that the possibility of acquiring a few academic skills has been overtaken by integration into ordinary classrooms and an expectation that academic learning can extend beyond the acquisition stage. Similarly, the discussion on vocational programmes has broadened to include programmes that monitor the transition from school and a consideration of the elements which lead to a fulfilled life as a citizen in the community.

In the last few years, a number of western countries have passed legislation intended to expand the opportunities for individuals with disabilities. These have been underpinned by the recognition that functional limitations are not solely characteristics of the individual but are dependent on the opportunities offered to that individual. If we focus on the disability, we ignore the possibility of changing the environment (or society) so that the individual can participate more freely in the life of the community. Worse, as McConkey argues in his final chapter, if we concentrate solely on treating the disabilities (or the syndrome) we will not succeed in improving the quality of life for people with Down syndrome because that is determined primarily by relationships with others. And building these relationships is a challenge for both developed countries and developing countries.

Finally, we note that because the contributors come from many parts of the world, there are some differences in terminology. One example is reflected in the title of the book where Down syndrome is used instead of Down's syndrome. Another concerns the use by some contributors of the term mental retardation where others prefer intellectual disabilities or learning disabilities. We acknowledge that every change in label has been initiated by those who would like to improve the status of the person with a disability, although we are not convinced that changing the label forces a change in attitudes. Since our ultimate goal is to communicate knowledge which will benefit the lives of individuals with Down syndrome, we have accepted each author's terminology in the belief that arguments about language would distract from the main goal.

Brian Stratford
Pat Gunn

Historical Aspects

1 In the Beginning

Brian Stratford

During the course of an interview I was once asked, 'How old is Down syndrome?' A simple question, but not all that easy to answer. It is easy enough to give a rough timing to the genesis of such conditions as asbestosis or travel sickness, but records do not reveal when the first case of Down syndrome was diagnosed as a distinct clinical entity. Langdon Down, who gave his name to the condition, assumed it to be well known already when he wrote his now famous paper in 1866. Edouard Seguin refers to the condition in a description which can be none other than Down syndrome in 1846, but again with the assurance that the condition would be familiar. Chambers referred to 'idiocy of the mongolian type' in a book published in 1844. It certainly appears in a two-volume medical dictionary written by Esquirol and published in Paris in 1838. But Down syndrome, or the particular arrangement of chromosomes which signals Down syndrome, must have been part of the human constitution well before these nineteenth-century references. Indeed, it must have been established very early, even in the beginning of man's history.

The scientific chapters of this volume will make it clear how Down syndrome arises from a genetic 'error' which occurs at or around the moment of conception. And it does this quite regularly in the human race; at a rate of somewhere between one in seven to one in nine hundred live births, (Steele and Stratford, 1995). It is also remarkable that this figure remains fairly constant in all parts of the world and is not influenced by race, creed, colour, climate, poverty or wealth. Consequently Down syndrome is as old as mankind.

Of course the environment does have an influence on the survival of babies born with this condition. In the past, when living conditions were much harsher, or even today, in countries of the Third World where medical care and social welfare is not so advanced as in richer nations, the survival into childhood, let alone adulthood, is a gamble where the odds are unfavourable. This can give rise to a misunderstanding about the presence of Down syndrome in different parts of the world. The difference is between incidence (number of live births) and prevalence (number of babies surviving), (Stratford and Steele, 1985; Steele, Chapter 4 in this volume).

ATTITUDES

However, it is not always useful to measure life in terms of its length, nor even in terms of intellectual, commercial or material success. Life is perhaps best perceived in terms of the quality of relationships, of relative contentment, of a sense of relative achievement. Such a state of affairs can only be attained through acceptance, first of all by the immediate family and then by the community in which one lives. Throughout the ages attitudes to people with Down syndrome have varied considerably, even within families. There have been very different, sometimes contradictory and often fluctuating attitudes to handicapped people. It would be reassuring and gratifying to believe that attitudes to mentally handi-capped people have gradually improved with time and sophistication, but it would not be true. The earliest reference to people with Down syndrome, for example, is not a written one but it is very positive, later ones are sometimes inhuman.

IN ANCIENT MEXICO

Throughout history it has always been plain that people needed to explain minorities, those who were in some way or another different, or deviated from the norm. The Olmecs were a tribe who lived around what we now call the Gulf of Mexico from about 1500 BC to AD 300. Though no writing survives from this period, these people left sufficient evidence about their attitude to those who were handicapped through wall reliefs, sculptures and other artefacts. Many of these take the form of idealizations of various handicapping conditions. Hunchbacks figure frequently (a high incidence of spinal tuberculosis has been reported in this area at the time) as does 'club foot', a hereditary condition (present in one dynasty lasting only 60 years in the rulers of Palenque in the neighbouring Mayan region) and other physical deformities. However, what interests us here is the presence of carvings, sculptures and figurines of children and adults with Down syndrome. There can be no mistaking these representations as they do not resemble 'natural' figures of the normal Olmec type of which there are many examples. A number of historians and anthropologists are in agreement that these artistic depictions of handicapped people represent a mystical attitude and have religious significance, found as they are, around the temples, (Comas, 1942; Covarrubias, 1946, 1957; Greene-Robertson, *et al.*; 1974; Milton and Gonzalo, 1974; Reich 1979; Wicke, 1971).

A series of wall reliefs seem to suggest that the Olmec explanation for the presence of children with Down syndrome was the result of mating between senior women of the tribe with the jaguar, the sacred totem of the Olmecs. The child with Down syndrome therefore was regarded as a god-human hybrid, the 'natural' offspring of this close union with the gods. This is not mere wild speculation, since there is other evidence. A number of cave paintings at Oxtitlan depict sexual relations between a jaguar and a human. It seems therefore that these children were singled out for special treatment because a) they were more frequently born to older and therefore more senior members of the tribe, b) only a few would survive which would give them something of a rarity value, and c) they had the striking physical and facial features which represent Down syndrome, a phenomenon which called for reason. These characteristics were accommodated into the community and the differences regarded as sacred, giving people with Down syndrome religious or superhuman significance. This may be an attitude common in ancient eastern communities. Until only a hundred years ago microcephalics (small-headed mentally handicapped people) were maintained at a shrine in the Punjab. It was considered that they brought grace to the shrine and its visitors. In some parts of India this kind of regard for the handicapped is preserved to this day and they are still venerated at the shrines as they have been for centuries.

THE GREEKS

In European society handicapped people were not regarded so highly, indeed, they were lucky to survive at all. Obviously recognizable handicapped babies (those with Down syndrome would be a case in point) were put out on the hillsides to starve or to be taken by wild animals. Greek culture did not admit the handicapped any more than did the Spartans. Any sign of weakness might reduce the physical and moral strength of the community. To support the barbaric practices it was assumed into Greek philosophy that these handicapped creatures were not human but were 'monsters' belonging to a different species. Aristotle counselled differently and said that they did belong to the natural order, but gave no suggestion as to cause or any explanation for their existence. Even Aristotle however, joined forces with those who preferred to be rid of those who might damage good Greek culture and practice. The fortunate few who did manage to survive into adulthood were certainly not allowed to take part in public life, but on the other hand neither were slaves or women. 'Democracy' only extended to 'the public people', a minority of the 40,000 or so people who lived in fifth century Athens, all of whom were men. The three groups comprising the majority, slaves, women and the handicapped, were 'the private people'; in Greek 'the idiots'. This Greek word, innocent in itself, became associated with the weak and despised and remained so for many centuries. In fact 'idiot' was still being used as a medical description of severely mentally handicapped people well into the 1960s, and even in 1995 I have seen abandoned babies with no known name being cared for under the institutional name 'Genetic Idiot'.

It is perhaps this poor beginning and total lack of regard for the handicapped in the 'civilization' and 'democracy' which comes to us from the Greeks that accounts for the later attitudes and subsequent abuses of mentally handicapped people, described in the next chapter by the Clarkes, and could also account for some of the more extreme attitudes to minority groups which still prevail today. And this does not only apply to the handicapped. Demosthenes (384–22 BC), the Athenian orator, highly regarded by the Greeks of his time for his patriotism and sound reasoning, was to sum up the position of women in Greek society: 'We have courtesans for our pleasure, concubines for our comfort and wives to give us legitimate children.' For the Athenian, his wife was merely the first of his servants.

The ancient Greek attitudes to women have prevailed until the very recent revolution which has not even yet granted full equality to women in the West, let alone world-wide. As to the mentally handicapped, there was the confusion between the mentally ill (the 'madmen' who might do things contrary to good

Greek custom) and the mentally handicapped who might pass on their condition. The difference is not even yet clear to the press, which frequently substitutes the usefully shorter word 'ill' in its headlines as though it were interchangeable with 'handicap'. This, in spite of the fact that the difference is made clear in one of the very first legal statutes of England, as the Clarkes point out in the next chapter.

The Laws of Lycurgus countenanced the neglect and abandonment of handicapped babies from motives of eugenics, (Castle, 1961). No one who has a memory of attitudes leading up to the Second World War and the atrocities committed by the Nazis will dismiss the proposal that these same laws gave comfort, authority and reassurance to those responsible for acts of genocide. Even if the Nazi leaders knew nothing of the Greeks or the Spartans, they were still heirs to history's worst legacy.

THE MIDDLE AGES

The Middle Ages are not principally known for their loving kindness and humanity, and certainly not for their benevolence to the unfortunate. Even Martin Luther, a sixteenth-century example of social reformation, did not carry his charity to the handicapped nor to their families. He called for the burning of the child and of the mother, for consorting with the devil; how else could a deformed child have been conceived? (It is worth comparing this with the Olmecs belief that the mother had consorted with their gods.) It is indeed odd that Martin Luther could not accept transubstantiation but could readily defend the incarnation of the devil in the body of an innocent baby.

It had already been well established by the early Christian church, taking its canonical attitudes conveniently 'off the peg' from the Greeks and the Romans, that the birth of a handicapped child was associated with sin of some kind. Fortunately all ages have had their 'intellectual anarchists', those who look on conventional wisdom and see its shortcomings. The ninth century was no exception. St Augustine was at great pains to point out in many letters to troubled clergy, that the sins and peccadilloes of parents are not in any way responsible for the birth of handicapped children. If sin is involved at all, said St Augustine, it is in the realm of original sin, which is responsible for all the ills of the world. It is an interesting but unfortunate fact that this early attitude, like many others, still reaches out from the past – if ever it actually went away – to torment parents today. I am constantly hearing the cry from anguished new mothers of children with Down syndrome who are grieving for the child they have 'lost' and have not yet come to terms with a new set of facts, 'What did I do wrong?' I can only answer, in the same way as did St Augustine did nearly six centuries ago, without his authority but with his equal lack of general success, 'You did nothing wrong. But, whoever selects mothers to have children with Down syndrome does so nearly always quite at random. What always amazes me is the way these children almost without fail are born to the most appropriate and "right" families for them'. Of course, personal abuse through smoking, excessive drinking or taking drugs will not help to produce a healthy infant, but however undesirable the mother's behaviour during pregnancy, it will have no effect whatsoever in the event of a child being born with Down syndrome. Such prenatal behaviour will however have an effect on whether the baby with Down syndrome is relatively healthy or an even weaker child with Down syndrome. Down syndrome has already been determined at conception.

Saint Augustine must have been essentially practical as well as theoretical because he seems to have influenced more than a few monasteries to care for handicapped children. There had been one such monastery situated at Breedon-on-the-Hill in the county of Leicestershire, UK, which was being excavated by archaeologists in the 1950s. A skull was found that was later proved beyond doubt to be that of a 9-year-old child with Down syndrome, (Brothwell, 1960). Naturally, though this is the only tangible evidence of Down syndrome from that time, it is not an isolated instance of evidence of such care of the handicapped. It was a well-known fact that communities of mentally handicapped people would gather around the large monasteries in northern France and be cared for by the religious order. Some of the more able would be taken in to work in the monastery as lay brothers. These large communities of mentally handicapped people came mainly from the mountainous regions of Switzerland where similar communities lived together. Much later it was discovered that the cause of so many of these people from the same part of the world, suffering from similar conditions, was the lack of iodine in the mountain water, thus creating hypothyroidism. The people who lived in the villages around the monasteries used to refer to these communities living around the monastery walls as the 'Christians'. Of course as this was France the word was 'Cretien', a word which as a result of travel became 'cretin'. Some of the early descriptions of Down syndrome refer to 'a bran-like' cretinism, meaning perhaps a softer kind of cretinism, (Weihs, 1977).

It is one of the paradoxes of the world of human creatures that unquestioning kindness and all-embracing care can live almost side by side with enormous, seemingly senseless cruelty.

THE RENAISSANCE

The Renaissance is of course dominated by the arts; a new interest in music, architecture and fine painting. Art is no less fine because it frequently depicts the grotesque or the unusual. The dwarf, for example, appears often in works of art. Even representations of disease and physical deformity can be found in works of art from ancient Greece to the Impressionists. The paintings of Brueghel (1525–69) for example, abound with the lame and the deformed. Artists of all periods have been impressed by the unusual, hence the surviving artefacts of the Olmecs of ancient Mexico which give us such detailed information about attitudes to handicapped people in that period.

Andrea Mantegna (1431–1506), considered to be a link between early mysticism and the later Renaissance, was, if not the first, certainly one of the first artists to employ actual living people as models for his paintings. He also, through the influence of one his mentors, Donatello, acquired an aptitude for scrupulously precise drawing and, exceptional for his time, accurate representation of what he saw. Through an interest in art I happened to know these facts, gathered from somewhere and pushed into the dustbin of one's mind. They came to the surface however one hot day in Florence when I visited an exhibition of the painter's work in the Uffizi Gallery. My subconscious attention was drawn to one painting of a Madonna and Child hanging alongside many similar paintings. It was this one which appealed to my professional eye. Here was a child with Down syndrome representing the infant Jesus and here also, unless I was very much mistaken, was his natural mother. I knew that Mantegna was at the time of this painting the Court Painter to the rich and powerful Gonzaga family of Mantua. In this kind of household and in the softer climate of Italy, this child had not only survived but had been loved and admired sufficiently for him to be depicted as the Christ child.

I subsequently wrote an article about this painting and its subjects which was published in the *Journal of Family Medicine* (Stratford, 1982) and as a result I was to learn more about the people involved. Through the use of modern computers and the way these search the literature, my medical article had been picked up by a history professor from Rome. She confirmed my submission but told me that the child was quite probably one of the Gonzagas, a son of Barbara di Brandenburgo. The history professor also knew that the child had some kind of sickness but did not know what it was. Sadly, in spite of sending to Venice for the best available doctors, the child died at the age of four. The Madonna was either Mantegna's wife or his mistress; more likely to be his wife Nicolosa Bellini. A further interesting fact to emerge was that one of the 14 of Mantegna's own children had the same 'sickness', an influence in Ludovico Gonzaga's decision to invite Mantegna from his native Padua to be his Court Painter. A further possibility then is that the child in the picture belonged to Nicolosa Bellini and Andrea Mantegna. Certainly the Madonna has an obvious goitre and until quite recently hyperthyroidism was associated with Down syndrome births, only later to be dismissed as coincidence. One or the other, this shows not only what must be the first Down Syndrome Association in the history of the world, but also reveals another kind of attitude to Down syndrome, and when the rich and powerful take this stance, their attitude carries a great deal of influence in a wider population; note the influence of the Kennedy family in modern times. It would be fascinating to know what the popular attitude to mentally handicapped children actually was in the Mantua of the mid-fifteenth century.

There are other examples of the influence that children with Down syndrome had on Renaissance artists. A paediatrician friend from Dublin, Dr Patricia Sheehan, (who in 1983 noted an unusual cluster of Down syndrome births in Dundalk after a nuclear accident in 1957 at what was then Windscale, where a radioactive cloud was reported to have passed over a school attended by the girls who later gave birth to the children with Down syndrome – but that's another story and 'unusual' clusters are being reported all the time and are naturally, if unscientifically, blamed on local environmental causes) showed me some reproductions of paintings by the Carmelite Friar, Fra Filippo Lippi (1406–69). We were both interested in a picture where the angels surrounding a *Madonna della Humilita* painted around 1437 have some of the unmistakable characteristics of babies with Down syndrome. I am of the opinion that they are not painted from models. The bodies are far too chubby and muscularly well developed to match the typical hypotonic baby with Down syndrome. Yet, there is something more than mere artistic autographic style about these baby angels. Lippi, a contemporary of Mantegna under the patronage of the Medici was far from being a model monk, his son Filippino (1457–1504) is known to have become a pupil of Botticelli. I mention this so that the two Lippis are not confused because one of them did visit Mantegna but it is never made clear which one it was. For the sake of continuity in the study of Down syndrome I hope it was the father, but if not, he was surely on speaking terms with his son.

Fra Lippi spent his early years in an orphanage where there must have been many infants with Down syndrome who had been rejected and abandoned by their families and placed in the orphanage. Equally, given the times and resources, many of them would not have survived for very long. A sensitive young man like Lippi could not have lost the significance of so many children leaving the world so young and this experience would have made a lasting impression on him. He would surely have remembered their facial characteristics; he was an artist. Even at the time he might possibly have thought of them as angels; after all he did become a monk in later life. It was this memory, real or subconscious, which emerges in the paintings of his angels.

The Flemish painter Jacob Jordaens (1593–1678) includes his wife Catherine van Noort and their daughter Elizabeth, who had Down syndrome, in a number of religious paintings including his famous *Adoration of the Shepherds* painted in 1618. Because Jordaens painted his daughter Elizabeth a number of times there are many opportunities to examine the features. Consequently there is little doubt of the Down syndrome. Elizabeth figures prominently in the secular painting 'The Peasant and the Satyr'.

It is however, important to treat any suggestion that a painting depicts a child with Down syndrome with caution, especially if the provenance is difficult to obtain. The majority of pictures which have been pointed out to me as representing Down syndrome are merely stylish characteristics of the artist and can be found in all the children he paints. As very young children have little or no cartilage, making the upper part of the nose distinct from the space between the eyes, it is easy to imagine the epicanthic folds which are so characteristic of Down syndrome. As an illustration of this mistaken identity it is worth examining a painting by Sir Joshua Reynolds (1723–92). In 1774 he painted a portrait of *Lady Cockburn and Children*. The child looking over his mother's shoulder has from time to time been pointed to as a child with Down syndrome. What makes it extremely unlikely that this child had Down syndrome is that he later became an Admiral of the Fleet in the British Royal Navy and was knighted as Sir George Cockburn. He was to become the Commander of the ship which transported Napoleon to exile on St Helena. If Sir George had Down syndrome, it certainly beats any stories of children with Down syndrome passing one or two GCSEs.

BACK TO ATTITUDES

The general theme of this chapter has been the way in which Down syndrome, or indeed any other mental handicapping condition might be approached; how it has been approached in former times and how we might ask ourselves if we have learnt anything from the past, or does each age have to start again from scratch?

I have raised the question elsewhere (Stratford, 1989) as to how we might look at the handicapped; who is the person with Down syndrome? And I raise the same principles again for further examination here.

I have an old piano which has not been tuned for 20 years, many of the keys, though present, do not strike any strings, some keys are missing altogether whilst others are no longer coated with ivory. I am lucky enough to have Mitsuko Uchida as a guest and so I ask her to play some Mozart for me. She does her best but the resulting sound is not very good. Do I now conclude that Mitsuko Uchida is a very poor pianist? I think it is more likely that I will conclude that she is a very good pianist but that she has been given a very inferior instrument to play on. I like to think of the handicapped people I know as being very good at all kinds of things but unfortunately they have been provided with a rather inadequate 'instrument' on which to display their talents.

I think about Down syndrome with its extra chromosome and I think again about Mitsuko Uchida, but this time she is playing a concerto and she needs the backup of an orchestra. She has an orchestra of perfect players, but an extra and totally unnecessary trombone player has been engaged. He also plays his score twice as fast as everyone else. This will certainly cause some differences in the concerto even though the overall theme is still recognizable; it is not as good as it should be. And then this trombone has a solo. He produces those themes we are so familiar with, the flattened bridge of the nose, the epicanthic folds and narrow palpebral fissures, Brushfield spots, the small earlobes, the square neck, the open mouth and the protruding tongue, the incurved little fingers. the space between the toes, and all the other 'solos' which make up the Down syndrome score. Uchida is a great musician (the central nervous system) and holds it all together. It is not the concerto we expected but it is not without its own unique interest.

How do I see a person, a child, an adult, a boy or a girl with Down syndrome? It is a pity that it is more than likely that I will first see the Down syndrome. But now let me think about how I see myself. When I say 'I' about myself, who do I mean? Do I mean my body for example? Well I can hardly mean my body can I because I am never wholly at one with my body, it is either too lazy or too fat or too painful. And anyway, my body is always changing. I am the same 'I' as I was when I said 'I' to myself when I was 10, 20 and 30 years old; the 'I' hasn't changed. So. I am more than my body. I cannot mean the other person's body either because I do not love a fat person more because there is more of that person; I do not love a person less if they lose an arm or a leg. So the actual body is fairly insignificant, in other words, I do not say 'I' to my body. Do I mean my thoughts then when I say 'I'. Well that can hardly be true either, because I am often ashamed of my thoughts if they be of anger or envy or avarice or anything else which causes me to feel ashamed. Who then is ashamed? I suppose that the nearest I can get to answering the question, 'Who am I?' is to say that I am my conscience, my ego, my soul, depending on my psychological, religious or philosophical allegiance. But I then must accept that the same 'I' of the most seriously handicapped child is just as perfect as mine.

I have to conclude that no person is handicapped within the scope of their own existence. Any person is only handicapped in so far as the demands which are made on them by the society in which they live. If we can see a person with Down syndrome in some way as I have described then both the person with Down syndrome and we too will be much better off. Perhaps this book about Down syndrome will help to make us more aware of the parameters of the condition, lead us to a better understanding making us a little bit wiser, but I do hope it will not contribute to making us feel in any way superior.

REFERENCES

Brothwell, D.R. (1960) A possible case of mongolism in a Saxon Population. *Annals of Human Genetics*, **24,** p. 141.

Castle, E.B. (1961) *Ancient Education and Today*, London: Pelican.

Chambers, R. (1844) *The Vestiges of the Natural History of Creation*, London: Churchill.

Comas, J. (1942) El problema de la existencia de un tipo racial olmeca. *Sociedad Mexicana de Antropologia Reninones de Mesa Redonda, Mayas y Olmecas*, pp. 69–70.

Covarrubias, M. (1946) El arte 'Olmec' o de la Venta. *Cuadernos Americanos*, **4,** pp. 153–79.

Covarrubias, M. (1957) *Indian Art of Mexico and Central America*, New York: Knopf.

Down J.L.H. (1866) Observations on an ethnic classification of idiots. *London Hospital Clinical Lectures and Reports*, **3,** p. 259.

Esquirol, J.E.D. (1838) *Des Maladies sous les Rapports Medicale, Hygienique et Medico-legal*, 2 vols, Paris: Bailliere.

Greene-Robertson, M., Rosenblum-Scandizzo, M.S. and Scandizzo, J.R. (1974) Physical deformities in the ruling lineage of Palenque and the dynastic implications. In M. Greene-Robertson (ed.), *The Art Iconography and Dynastic History of Palenque, Part III: The Proceedings of the Segunda Mesa Redonda de Palenque*, pp. 59–86, Pebble Beach: Robert Louis Stevenson School.

Milton, G. and Gonzalo, R. (1974) Jaguar Cult – Down's Syndrome – Were – Jaguar. *Expedition*, 16, pp. 33–37.

Reich, S.G. (1979) Pathology in Olmec Art. Degree thesis, Tulane University.

Seguin, E. (1846) *Le Traitement Moral, l'Hygiene et l'Education des Idiots*, Paris: Bailliere.

Sheehan, P.M.E., and Hillary, I.B. (1983) An unusual cluster of babies with Down's syndrome born to former pupils of an Irish boarding school. *British Medical Journal*, **287,** pp. 1428–29.

Steele, J. and Stratford B. (1995) United Kingdom population with Down syndrome: present and future projections. *American Journal of Mental Deficiency*, **99,** pp. 664–82.

Stratford, B. (1982) Down's syndrome at the Court of Mantua. *Journal of Family Medicine: Maternal and Child Health*, **7,** pp. 250–54.

Stratford, B. (1989) *Down's Syndrome*, London: Penguin.

Stratford, B., and Steele, J. (1985) Incidence and prevalence of Down's syndrome. *Journal of Mental Deficiency Research*, **29,** pp. 95–107.

Weihs, T.J. (1977) *In Need of Special Care*, Leeds. University of Leeds.

Wicke, C.P. (1971) *Olmec: an Early Style of Pre-Columbian Mexico*, Tucson: University of Arizona Press.

2 The Historical Context

A.D.B. Clarke and Ann M. Clarke

It goes almost without saying that one cannot fully comprehend the present without some understanding of the past. In this chapter it is our aim to provide a brief historical context for current views on mental retardation, both in their scientific and their humane aspects. We will stress that the treatment of the retarded at any one point in time reflects some major ideology in society. Since those with Down syndrome constitute the largest identifiable group among the more severely retarded, this wide review is likely to be of relevance to them.

TERMINOLOGY

Table 2.1 indicates some of the generic terms for those whom, in this chapter, we will term mentally retarded, in accordance with long-established international usage. In Britain, between 1913 and 1959, 'mental deficiency' was the official description of this field, then yielding to what at the time was seen as a less preju- dicial term 'subnormality'. From then on, changes in terminology have accelerated, each being superseded by a more politically correct description. There is no reason to suppose that this process has been completed with current 'learning disabilities', 'learning difficulties', 'special needs' or 'intellectual disabilities', just to name recent examples. Indeed, some argue that the first term is far too wide, embracing as it does many other conditions than mental retardation.

Most generic terms allow a subdivision according to levels of functioning. They have in common an agreement that an IQ of around 50 marks an important water- shed, below which virtually all owe their condition to the effects of particular genes,

Table 2.1 Generic Terminologies

Fatuus naturalis	Idiocy	Oligophrenia
Feeble-mindedness	Amentia	Mental deficiency
Mental subnormality	Mental retardation	
Mental handicap	Mental impairment	
Intellectual disability	Learning disability/	
	Learning difficulties	

Note: These changing terminologies in recent years have represented attempts to soften the image of what in this chapter we have termed mental retardation, the internationally accepted description. These generic terms are usually subdivided to represent differing levels of retardation. Sometimes, too, such subdivision relates to educational provision.

chromosome aberrations, injury, maternal infections, poisonings or trauma, for example. Their general level of functioning is poor or very poor, their prospects of real independence almost non-existent, and their physical health often impaired. Although above this figure, roughly IQ 50, a sizeable minority (perhaps 30 per cent) owe their condition to similar organic or pathological factors already noted, but to a lesser degree, the majority have a 'familial' aetiology. Here one can distinguish two groups. The first requires no special mechanism to account for its presence; it represents the tail-end of the normal genetic distribution. Parents who are themselves somewhat limited in ability may produce similar children, or brighter or less bright. The latter may fall into the mildly retarded range. The second group owes its condition to an interaction between somewhat poor heredity and adverse conditions of upbringing. Should there be a radical change into a better environment, these individuals may have reasonable prospects. In any event, they can, with luck, achieve a modicum of independence, especially under conditions of full employment.

Throughout the whole of history, and no doubt, prehistory, it is probable that retarded persons have been recognized as such, with differing interpretations applied to them, sometimes as 'les enfants du bon Dieu' and sometimes as objects of superstition, leading to infanticide. In England, statutory mention of these people dates as far back as the reign of Edward II (1284–1327) when. for the first time[1] a distinction was made between the 'born fool' and the 'lunatic'. This allowed arrangements for the disposal of property to be made. For the latter, the Crown took possession of belongings only during the period of illness. For the former, the property reverted permanently to the Crown, subject only to an obligation to provide for the individual's personal needs.

In later centuries, the distinction between retardation and lunacy disappeared. Indeed, in the early nineteenth century 'idiocy' was seen as a form of psychosis. However, in England the Idiots Act of 1866 made a clear distinction, and by 1870 the Education Act subdivided the whole range, the criterion being the educability or trainability of the various grades of 'defect'.

1859 AND ONWARDS

Darwin's (1859) *The Origin of Species* represented the major biological advance of the nineteenth century, with enormous implications for the understanding of the human condition. The notion of 'survival of the fittest' against natural pressures was rapidly applied to human society. As Brent (1981) indicates, the keystone to Darwin's proposition was his belief in variation; organisms produce offspring marginally different from themselves, enabling natural selection to exert its leverage. Where such differences were disadvantageous, descendants would ultimately disappear. It is small wonder, then, that Darwin's cousin, Francis Galton (who later founded the study of individual difference, and consequent statistics), wrote in 1869 (352, 356)

> The wisest policy is that which results in retarding the average age of marriage among the weak, and in hastening it among the vigorous classes, whereas unhappily for us,

the influence of various social agencies has been strongly and banefully exerted in precisely the opposite direction ... Its effect would be such as to cause the race of the prudent to fall, after a few centuries, into an almost incredible inferiority of numbers to that of the imprudent ... [it would] bring utter ruin upon the breed of any country. It may seem monstrous that the weak should be crowded out by the strong, but it is still more monstrous that the races best fitted to play their part on the stage of life, should be crowded out by the incompetent, the ailing and the desponding.

Darwin himself (1871: 149) followed his cousin's message, arguing that

With savages, the weak in mind or body are soon eliminated ... We civilized men, on the other hand, do our utmost to check the process of elimination; we build asylums for the imbecile, the maimed, and the sick ... Thus the weak members of civilized society propagate their kind. No-one who has attended to the breeding of domestic animals will doubt that this must be highly injurious to the race of man ... excepting in the case of man himself, hardly anyone is so ignorant as to allow his worst animals to breed.

Langdon Down (1866) was the first accurately to describe the syndrome which bears his name. Strongly influenced by Darwin, he appeared to regard the retarded as evolutionary throw-backs or 'atavistic regressions' to inferior races, hence his 'ethnic classification' of idiots'. Thus he named his famous syndrome 'mongolism' because of the superficially mongoloid appearance of the eyes. He also claimed to have identified 'negroid' types, and microcephalics were thought to be connected with an Aztec race. A Malayan type was also suggested. At the time Langdon Down's article was written, correlates were often mistaken for causes. Thus alcoholism and tuberculosis were seen as major aetiological agents, with the latter being regarded by Langdon Down as a cause of 'mongolism'.

The stage was set for a general alarm about the breeding rates of 'the lower orders'. Their fertility was such that, in the context of an over-simple understanding of genetics, national degeneracy was the future prospect. Goddard (1912) attempted an intergenerational study of the 'Kallikak' family, claiming that the descendants of a liaison between Martin Kallikak and a feeble-minded tavern girl, during the American War of Independence produced 143 feeble-minded persons, 46 said to be normal and the rest, some 291, of unknown status. Martin's later marriage to a girl of good family produced 496 descendants, none of whom were mentally retarded, and in general these were of high social and economic status. One notes first, the huge sample loss, and second, the confounding of heredity and environment in both families. These points were not appreciated at the time, and the impact of this and other studies was very large, reflected in Great Britain in parliamentary discussions prior to the passage of the Mental Deficiency Act 1913. This included the three established levels of retardation, idiot, imbecile and feeble-minded, but added a fourth, moral defective, those who showed vicious and criminal propensities. The feeble-minded, wrote one American writer at the time, are a parasitic and predatory class, never capable of self-support or of managing their own affairs. The women 'are almost invariably immoral and if at large become carriers of venereal disease, or give birth to children who are as defective as themselves ... Every feeble-minded person ... is a potential criminal ...' (Fernald, 1912, quoted in Davies, 1930).

The solution to the menace of mental deficiency, reflected in the 1913 Act, was well expressed by E.R. Johnstone (1904), the then President of the American Association on Mental Deficiency, the foremost society with interests in this field. Noting that the 'unsexing' of these persons did not find favour with the public, he wrote that 'There is one method of elimination upon which we may all agree . . . that is permanent institutional care . . . It will appeal to the great public who stand back of us . . . it shocks no-one's ideas of propriety, humanity and Christianity' (Sloan and Stevens, 1976, p. 55). In this connection it is of interest that, among those who showed 'arrested or incomplete development of mind', one of the criteria enabling the person to be 'subject to be dealt with' (i.e. incarcerated), was having given birth to an illegitimate child while in receipt of Poor Relief. The eugenic overtones are again obvious. While in the late twentieth century one is shocked at such legislation, one must be reminded that those concerned were acting on the basis of the imperfect knowledge then available.

One of the major influences which buttressed social policy was the development from 1904 onwards of intelligence testing. Galton had already drawn attention to the wide range of individual differences in most human characteristics, and the initiation of compulsory education had endorsed such findings. Many pupils were failing, hence the Ministry of Public Instruction in Paris asked Alfred Binet to develop a method to distinguish those who for environmental reasons were backward, from those who were congenitally retarded. He did so by producing scales of short tests, posing problems which seemed to him to be culture fair and uninfluenced by the rote learning characteristic of schooling at the time. He emphasized that his measures would describe the child's functioning at the time of test, and would have no necessary bearing upon prognosis. Indeed, he explicitly rejected the notion of intellectual constancy. His tests were used – and misused – to identify those lacking intelligence, with the common assumption 'once a defective, always a defective'. Later, when it was discovered that some of the mildly retarded improved into dull normality, it was concluded that the first diagnosis must have been wrong, they must have been 'pseudo-feeble-minded'.

The first textbook on mental deficiency which attempted to be both comprehensive and scientific was that of Tredgold (1908), recently reassessed by Day (1993). It ran to eight editions and was highly influential. As Day indicates, these successive revisions spanned the birth of clinical genetics, improvements in public health, epidemiological studies, compulsory education for retarded children, intelligence testing, the rise and fall of the eugenics movement, the growth of specialist asylums, the initiation of the first State institution for criminal defectives, the passing of the 1913 Act, in operation until 1959. Tredgold recognized that Down syndrome arose as a 'primary amentia', that is, a 'defective development of germ cells', arising from 'a specific alteration in the germ chromosome', but he discounted the association with maternal age. Believing in 'morbid heredity' as a prime cause, he was a strong supporter of the eugenics movement, but in many ways was forward looking in his belief in treatment, training and care (Day, 1993).

The London County Council appointed Cyril Burt in 1913 as the first educational psychologist in the world. He began to survey various groups of backward or retarded children. These were important in exploding a number of myths. For example, he noted that the children of the mentally retarded tended to be brighter than their parents, and that the dull are usually backward, but the backward are not necessarily dull. Moreover, a brief follow-up of retarded children indicated that constancy of IQ was 'but imperfectly realized'.

The pessimism which in the early years of the century had suggested institutionalization as the solution to the problem of mental retardation lightened here and there in the 1920s and 1930s notably in the work of the Iowa School. These researches were primarily concerned with service issues, and with the more mildly retarded. Their orientation was humane, and their bias environmental. Their methodologies were either rather weak or clearly unsound. Nevertheless, the work of such people as Skeels, Skodak and Wellman clearly indicated that adverse social factors could override genetic potential. If such children were moved to better circumstances, many showed a degree of 'catch-up', reverting towards or into normality.

The Colchester Survey of an institution was published by Penrose in 1938. It revealed a strong social class correlate, depending upon level of retardation. The more severely retarded were to be found equally in all parental social classes, but the milder grades were strongly biased towards the lower social groups. Moreover, reanalysis of an earlier, cruder survey showed that prevalence varied according to age, with official numbers declining markedly in mid-adolescence. In turn, this indicated that a large proportion of those who, at school age, were regarded as retarded, later were no longer so classified; that is, administratively identified mental retardation was a self-curing condition in such cases. Research two decades later was to throw some light upon the causes of these findings (Clarke *et al.*, 1958) which applied primarily to the mildly retarded.

THE POST-WAR YEARS

In the immediate post-war period, several influences combined to accelerate scientific advances. First, the spirit of optimism and humanism characteristic of those times, caused many to become more aware of the disadvantaged, to be attracted to these fields and to seek preventive or ameliorative measures. Second, the belief that scientific methodology has much to offer became more widespread, and its successes more obvious. Third, the parents of the more severely retarded began to initiate pressure groups and to influence the relevant laws and practices. Hospitals at the time were low-cost Dickensian institutions, breaching the conditions promoting mental health, and doing little more than 'occupying' the severer grades of patient. Already, by 1952, family pressures allowed short-stay individuals to enter hospital without legal certification, so that parents might take holidays.

In 1949, Penrose's *The Biology of Mental Defect* (1949) proved to be a landmark in recording the already considerable advances in the biomedical field. A less impressive book by S.B. Sarason (1949), *Psychological Problems in Mental Deficiency*, offered a mainly descriptive account of the field, but staked a claim for what later became an acknowledged role for psychologists. The situation a decade later had altered almost beyond recognition. The first quite comprehensive general text in the post-war years was published by Hilliard and Kirman (1957). Although medically oriented, it included contributions by a psychologist and a speech therapist In the following year, a multi-authored text, almost entirely by psychologists, devoted seven chapters out of 18 to education, training and other forms of treatment (Clarke and Clarke, 1958).

In 1959 came the major breakthrough, applying to Down syndrome but ultimately with much wider repercussions. The identification of the extra chromosome led to the whole field of prenatal diagnosis and the possibility of diagnosing a whole range of genetic disorders. Indeed, it began to be recognized that the earlier view ascribing causes of severe retardation to acquired characteristics (accidents, diseases, injuries promoting brain injury) must give way to a realization that rare genetic effects, including chromosome aberrations, might be prime agents.

In the USA at about the same time, President Kennedy's personal interest in mental retardation provided an enormous boost to government and other involvement. The President's Committee on Mental Retardation, which still exists, issues statements and advice from time to time, sometimes unwisely. So intoxicated were its members with scientific progress that in 1972 they believed that current techniques in the biomedical and behavioural sciences could reduce the prevalence of retardation by 50 per cent by the end of the century. This general optimism continued, reflected later by President Johnson with his vision of a Great Society. Thus, in the mid-1960s a nation-wide preschool programme, Head Start, was initiated with the expectation that cycles of intergenerational disadvantage would be broken. Such optimism reflected the spirit of the times.

All scientific disciplines which have a bearing upon the human condition have achieved major advances, some of which are especially relevant to the field of mental retardation. Their progress tends to show periods of great acceleration, followed by consolidation and plateau. For the behavioural sciences, for example, the 1950s and 1960s were times of unexpected increments in knowledge. In the last two decades, however, it is the biomedical sciences which have developed most markedly. Elsewhere in this book reference is made to research with a particular relevance to Down syndrome. Here we will merely pick out a few examples of work which has had a major impact on social or medical policy.

The work initiated by the late Jack Tizard was pre-eminent in influencing the changing attitudes to the more severely retarded. He showed that these people responded to incentives, could exhibit impressive perceptual-motor learning, retaining it over time, and transfer skills to other problems. Equally important was his Brooklands experiment. He drew attention to the lamentable conditions in institutions, where the most elementary principles of mental health were ignored. Lacking personal possessions, herded through the day, often without even nominal education, these children showed behaviour disorders reminiscent of those in eastern European orphanages of today. Tizard arranged for the removal of a small group of severely retarded children from a particularly disadvantaged hospital. They were then housed in a residential unit, distant from it, where they lived in small groups, learned informally through play and through close contact with normal adults, and possessed their own clothes and toys, in stark contrast with a matched control group that remained in the hospital. The former gained in verbal intelligence over a two-year period, and showed a reduction in anti-social behaviour compared with the controls. All this underpinned the notion of de-institutionalization and community care, both anticipated in the 1959 Mental Health Act at about the same time. For an account of Tizard's life and work, see Clarke and Tizard (1983).

The changing outlook in both Britain and the USA is nowhere more clearly apparent than in the field of education. Categories of pupils requiring special educational treatment in England and Wales were defined in the Handicapped Pupils and Special Schools Regulations, 1959, as amended. Definitions of ten types of disability relating, for example, to vision, hearing, maladjustment and various physical handicaps were offered. Educationally subnormal pupils were those who, by reason of limited ability or other conditions resulting in educational retardation, require some specialized form of education wholly or partly in substitution for the ordinary education given in ordinary schools. At that time there was also a category of children excluded from school altogether on the grounds of ineducability. From 1971 the law was altered to establish a new category of schools, Educationally Subnormal (Severe), distinct from Educationally Subnormal (Moderate).

Increasing concern about rigid categorization and labelling, as in the USA, led to a committee being set up under Lady Warnock. This reported in 1978 and suggested some very important changes. Categorization, it believed, perpetuates a sharp distinction between groups of children – the handicapped and the non-handicapped, a distinction it was determined to remove. Instead, among other things, it recommended that 'children with learning difficulties' should now be the chosen term, with levels ranging from mild, moderate to severe. The Education Act 1981 followed quite closely the Warnock arguments, a child having 'special needs' if he or she has a 'learning difficulty'. It also provided a number of important safeguards for the child, the parents and local education authorities. The emphasis is now on integrating as many children as possible in normal schools, and devising special programmes to facilitate individual development in a variety of socially relevant skills.

The development of behaviour modification techniques for the mentally retarded, from the 1960s onwards, has been one of the most pervasively useful (if sometimes controversial) movements. The essential notion behind these powerful techniques is the analysis of complex behaviour into small components which are taught by manipulating the contingencies of reinforcement. It is known that the consequences of a particular behaviour may increase or decrease the likelihood of its recurrence, depending on whether the reinforcement is positive or negative. Rewards are favoured over punishment which may be associated with fear, and these rewards may vary widely according to individual desires. Experts acknowledge the dangers of over-enthusiastic use of behaviour modification by those lacking an understanding of its complexity. Nevertheless, these techniques underlie the majority of successful programmes for creating new skills in the retarded (see Carr, 1980; Carr and Collins, 1992; Coupe-O'Kane, 1991).

Prospective longitudinal studies are especially important in the field of mental retardation, and have been used in the evaluation of various programmes of intervention or in evaluating the natural outcome of various conditions. In the latter connection, the research on Down syndrome by Janet Carr (1992) is exemplary. In the report cited, one of several, she sketched the methodological necessities for both types of investigation. Her own 21-year study tracked development from birth of Down syndrome babies, outlining their natural histories to adulthood, and yielding some important and in some cases surprising findings. Of these, the most salient are the wide range of abilities for this group, some 60 IQ points, equivalent to the difference between border-line mildly retarded people and those of superior intelligence (IQ 70 to 130). Second, there was a degree of consistency between early 'easy' behaviour and later, and 'difficult' behaviour across time. Third, there was ample documentation of the deceleration in early childhood of intellectual growth with increasing age. See also Carr (1994).

While the behavioural sciences have been primarily concerned with the amelioration of handicapping conditions, and with social influences upon causation, the biomedical sciences have been highly successful in revealing biological causative factors which in turn are aimed at more effective prevention. We have already referred to the 1959 breakthrough when the extra chromosome in Down syndrome was discovered, ultimately leading to, among many other things, the discovery of the second largest clinical group, the fragile-X syndrome (Lubs, 1969). Meanwhile the Human Genome Project continues apace, and the location of particular genes is being established almost monthly. Moreover, genetic engineering is likely to make a major impact upon prevention and treatment. Various forms of brain scan (CAT, NMR and PET) have opened up new fields for understanding normal and abnormal brain function, and there is now increasing interest in the behavioural phenotypes of particular genetic conditions.

Epidemiology is of supreme importance in helping to identify causal agencies, in tracking the natural history of disorders and in predicting service needs (Fryers, 1993). For example, Nicholson and Alberman (1992) have forecast increasing numbers of Down syndrome persons in England and Wales up to the year 2000, using demographic projections of maternal age structure, age-specific fertility rates, and the availability, detection and take-up rates of prenatal diagnosis and termination. The much smaller risk of Down syndrome pregnancies below the current screening age of 38 is more than outweighed by the very much greater number of pregnancies below this age. The authors argue that observed live birth prevalence will rise to levels higher than those seen in the last 20 years. Together with increased survival and longevity, the prevalence of Down syndrome through-out the next century will be higher than ever before. There are obvious service implications.

In tandem with changing attitudes, services have evolved in many ways, and current trends will be reviewed elsewhere in this volume. Mention must be made, however, of the Normalization movement. Characteristic of the advanced social welfare systems of Denmark and Sweden, this movement was initiated in the 1960s. It has advocated, as a general principle, that retarded people should be enabled to lead as normal a life as possible. Such an approach links with the philosophy of integration in schools and in the community, community care and de-institutionalization. In the USA, however, under the influence of, among others, Wolfensberger (1983), a more radical influence has emerged, normalization being seen as 'using culturally valued means to enable people to lead culturally valued lives'. This is the Social Role

Valorization Model, a moralistic stance with an allegedly scientific basis. Yet some lone voices have cast doubt upon this latter aspect (e.g. Rapley, 1990) and earlier Rose-Ackerman (1982) had shown the inconsistencies in the normalization philosophy. The problems relate both to economic factors and to the 'not-in-my-backyard' syndrome, to the preparedness or otherwise of retarded people for community living, and to the community's acceptance. Costs and resource needs have often been underestimated, and.only in Scandinavian countries where taxation is exceedingly high are services likely to approximate to the philosophy (see Pedlar, 1990). It may well be that the necessity for an increasing use of the term 'challenging behaviour' arises from the stressful demands placed upon some of the retarded by living in the community, and their poor socialization arising from lack of appropriate training and lack of sensitivity to social expectations (Boucherat, 1990; Clarke and Clarke, 1991; McCool *et al.*, 1989).

PROSPECTS

We have attempted to trace some of the historical links between changing ideologies, changing perceptions, advances in research and changing practices in supporting the mentally retarded. While there have always been challenging voices, there have been dominant ideologies which have had both immediate and long-lasting impacts. From the latter part of the nineteenth century onwards, eugenic alarms held sway, although increasingly attenuated towards the 1950s. Then came the burst of optimism, over-optimism and humanitarian ideals characteristic of the 1960s and 1970s. Thereafter these developed even more radically alongside notions of positive discrimination, community care and normalization, often being unrealistic, and sometimes inconsistent in the context of limited resources, not only financial but, perhaps especially, human.

Predicting future trends is obviously much more uncertain than analysing the past. It is clear, however, that biomedical advances will continue apace, with considerable implications for prevention. Increasingly the evaluation of cost-effective services will prove necessary (Barnett and Escobar, 1987), and the limits to effective intervention will be established. In this connection, most intervention methods have either lacked intensity or duration, or both. It is of little use to provide, for example, a two-year period of special help early in life, and expect this necessarily to have long-term effects, unless such an approach sets in train ongoing enriched training. There is, (Clarke and Clarke, 1989) of course, an increasing place for voluntary services, and this is to be commended. An extreme example, however, is provided by village communities run in the main by voluntary helpers (and incidentally opposed to the main integration movement!). One such excellent village reported that despite the efforts of everyone to be as self-supporting as possible, they still have to rely on friends to find the extra £18 per week for each villager (£78 per month), over and above local authority grants which do not meet the full costs of running the village.

The most immediate need is to apply in practice what is already known about prevention and amelioration of handicapping conditions, all in the context of limited resources. This is easily said, but difficult to do. One can foresee unfortunate conflicts of interest between the various groups which have to rely upon the public purse.

NOTE

1. *De praerogitiva*, 1325.

REFERENCES

Barnett, W.S. and Escobar, O.M, (1987) The economics of early intervention. *Review of Educational Research*, **57**, pp. 387–414.
Boucherat, A. (1990) Normalization in mental handicap – acceptance without questions? *Bulletin of the Royal College of Psychiatrists*, **11**, pp. 423–25.
Brent, P. (1981) *Charles Darwin: 'a Man of Enlarged Curiosity'*, London: Heinemann.
Carr, J. (1980) *Helping Your Handicapped Child*, London: Penguin.
Carr, J. (1992) Longitudinal research in Down syndrome. *International Review of Research in Mental Retardation*, **18**, pp. 197–223.
Carr, J. (1994) Annotation: Long-term outcome for people with Down's syndrome. *Journal of Child Psychology and Psychiatry*, **35**, pp. 425–39.
Carr, J. and Collins, S. (1992) *Working towards Independence*, London: Jessica Kingsley.
Clarke, A.M. and Clarke, A.D.B. (eds) (1958) *Mental Deficiency: The Changing Outlook*, London: Methuen.
Clarke, M. and Clarke, A.D.B. (1989) Editorial: the later cognitive effects of early intervention. *Intelligence*, **13**, pp. 289–97.
Clarke, A.D.B. and Clarke, A.M. (1991) Research on mental handicap: past, present and future. In S. Segal and V. Varma (eds), *Prospects for People with Learning Difficulties*, ch. 1. London: David Fulton.
Clarke, A.D.B. and Tizard, B. (1983) *Child Development and Social Policy: the Life and Work of Jack Tizard*, Leicester: British Psychological Society.
Clarke, A.D.B., Clarke, A.M. and Reiman, S. (1958) Cognitive and social changes in the feebleminded – three further studies. *British Journal of Psychology*, **49**, 144–57.
Coupe-O'Kane, J. (1991) Teaching and learning: retrospect and prospect. In S. Segal and V. Varma (eds), *Prospects for People with Learning Difficulties*, ch. 2. London: David Fulton.
Darwin, C. (1859) *The Origin of Species*, London: John Murray.
Darwin, C. (1871) *The Descent of Man*, London: John Murray.
Davies, S.P. (1930) *Social Control of the Mentally Deficient*, London: Constable.
Day, K. (1993) Books reconsidered: *Mental Deficiency (Amentia)*, A.F. Tredgold. *British Journal of Psychiatry*, **163**, pp. 702–04.
Feruald, W.E. (1912) The burden of feeblemindedness. Journal of Psycho-Asthenics, **17**, pp. 90–4.
Fryers, T. (1993) Epidemiological thinking in mental retardation: Issues in taxonomy and population frequency. *International Review of Research in Mental Retardation*, **19**, 97–133.
Galton, F (1869) *Hereditary Genius*, London: Macmillan.
Goddard, H.H. (1912) *The Kallikak Family*, New York: Macmillan.
Hilliard, L.T. and Kirman, B.H. (1957) *Mental Deficiency*. London: J. and A. Churchill.
Johnstone, E.R. (1904) President's Address, American Association of the Study of the Feebleminded. *Journal of Psycho-Asthenics*, **9**, p. 237.
Langdon Down, J. (1866) Observations on an ethnic classification of idiots. *Clinical Lectures and Reports of the London Hospital*, **3**, pp. 259–62.

Lubs, H.A. (1969) A marker-X chromosome. *American Journal of Genetics*, **21,** pp. 231–44.

McCool, C., Barrett, S., Emerson, E., Toogood, S., Hughes, H. and Cummings, R. (1989) Challenging behaviour and community services: 5, structuring staff and client activity. *Mental Handicap*, 17, June, British Institute of Mental Handicap.

Nicholson, A. and Alberman, E. (1992) Prediction of the number of Down's syndrome infants to be born in England and Wales up to the year 2000, and their likely survival rates. *Journal of Intellectual Disability Research*, **36,** pp. 505–17.

Pedlar, A. (1990) Normalization and integration: a look at the Swedish experience. *Mental Retardation*, **28,** pp. 275–82.

Penrose, L.S. (1938) A clinical and genetic study of 1280 cases of mental defect. *Special Report Series*, Medical Research Council, No. 229. London: HMSO.

Penrose, L.S. (1949) *The Biology of Mental Defect*, London: Sidgwick and Jackson.

President's Committee on Mental Retardation (1972) *Entering the Era of Human Ecology*, Washington, DC: Department of Health, Education and Welfare, Publ. No. (OS) 72–7.

Rapley, M. (1990) Is normalization a scientific theory? *Clinical Psychology Forum*, pp. 16–20 [occasional publication].

Rose-Ackerman, S. (1982) Mental retardation and society: the ethics and politics of normalization. *Ethics*, **93,** pp. 81–101.

Sarason, S.B. (1949) *Psychological Problems of Mental Deficiency*, New York: Harper.

Sloan, W. and Stevens, H. (1976) *A Century of Concern*, Washington, DC: American Association on Mental Deficiency.

Tredgold, A.F. (1908) *Mental Deficiency (Amentia)*, London: Ballière Tindall.

Wolfensberger, W. (1983) Social role valorization: a proposed new term for the principle of normalization. *Mental Retardation*, **21,** pp. 234–239.

Developments in the Law

3 An Overview of the Law

Gordon Ashton

This chapter seeks to provide an overview of the law and its procedures in so far as they relate to people with Down's syndrome in England and Wales. Scotland has its own legal system and where appropriate any variations are mentioned, whereas Northern Ireland tends to follow the English system.[1] There is no special law for people with Down's syndrome, but some aspects of our general law need to be modified or enhanced to deal with certain of their disabilities. In most respects they are as different from each other as people who are not disabled, but the underlying problem that they present to lawyers is an inability, to a greater or lesser extent, to make or communicate their own decisions. This failing is shared by people with other forms of learning disabilities, mental illness or brain damage and must be faced by society and its legal system.[2] Another problem that they may have in common with other people is physical disability, and in this respect they share entitlement to any benefits or services that are available. In consequence of these problems they are unlikely to be financially self-supporting so some form of income supplement is usually needed as well as continuing care or supervision.

ROLE OF THE LAW

In a civilized society the law must take into account the interests of its more vulnerable members. It should seek to protect them from abuse and exploitation but also to empower and support them, and it may need to protect other members of society from them. In doing so the law must first identify those members who deserve special treatment, but there is a growing realization that people should not be categorized and then treated according to the general category into which they fall. That is why we do not say 'This person has Down's syndrome therefore we treat him or her accordingly'. Everyone should be acknowledged as an individual whose particular needs and abilities are taken into account. Whilst the physical appearance of Down's syndrome may raise questions as to whether special treatment is appropriate, this label should not be carried in society or attached by the law.

Protection may take the form of control, supervision or restrictions upon personal powers. Empowerment means enabling the individual to exercise personal rights that could not be exercised without assistance. Support may come in the form of services such as day, residential or respite care and physical aids, or may be of a financial nature such as state benefits. Although support may be welcomed, there is a tension between protection and empowerment which must take into account the interests of other members of society. You cannot protect without taking away some of the powers of self-determination that you seek to preserve, and you cannot empower without subjecting the individual to some risk. A balance appropriate to the individual and acceptable to society is difficult to achieve and there can be conflict between parents, professionals and the public as to where it should lie, but the views of the individual must not be overlooked when considering this balance merely because of difficulty in eliciting them, hence the role of the personal advocate. In addition to this underlying tension there is competition for the limited support available from the local authority to those in need.

The necessity to identify people who are to receive special treatment presents great challenges. If we are considering detaining a mentally disordered person in a hospital a restrictive test must be applied so that interference with personal freedom only takes place when absolutely necessary. At the other extreme, if a new weekly incapacity benefit is introduced by the social security system it should be adequately targeted and an unduly restrictive test of entitlement is inappropriate. Equally, the criteria for a benefit based upon care needs will be different from one based upon financial needs. Further controls may be appropriate in regard to entitlement to services because these are expensive to provide and resources are not limitless. It follows that our law is littered with rules and regulations that regulate entitlement to support or impose restrictions, and lawyers argue as to their interpretation. Those concerned for the welfare of people with Down's syndrome should be alert to these gateways or barriers and know how best to open or traverse them. This is potentially fertile ground for lawyers but few have shown an interest and many aspects of the law have not yet been developed.

PROTECTION

Under this heading we consider restrictions on capacity which are intended to protect the individual from abuse, the powers of organs of the State to intervene and also what happens when the individual is in trouble with the police. Some aspects of empowerment and support which are considered later in this chapter could also be interpreted as providing protection. The general law does not prevent discrimination against disabled people, and although there has been recent legislation this is likely to relate more to those with physical disabilities.[3] Contrary to popular belief, parents and other carers have no legal rights of control over a mentally disabled adult nor are they empowered to make decisions for that person, although they frequently do so with the acquiescence of all concerned. Whilst paternalism is to be discouraged, the individual may in consequence be vulnerable because no one is entitled to take the initiative. It is therefore important that concerned people should 'blow the whistle' when abuse is believed to be taking place and that there should be someone to listen who has power to intervene.

Limitations on capacity

Financial abuse is controlled by the law requiring that an individual has mental capacity to enter into any transaction, and this depends upon understanding and the ability to make a choice. However, in England the transaction will only be set aside if the other party knew (or should have been aware) of the lack of capacity, whereas in Scotland such knowledge is irrelevant. A person who is 'incapable by reason of mental disorder of managing his property and affairs' is deprived of all such capacity once someone has been appointed to handle these finances (see below) even though competent to handle small transactions. Civil court proceedings can only be commenced by or against such a person if a suitable representative is appointed.[4] In these situations delegation tends to be an 'all or nothing' business with no duty to involve or consult the incapacitated person though it is good practice to do so.

Physical abuse may be controlled by the criminal law or by civil proceedings, and injunctions can be obtained to prevent such conduct. Sexual abuse is sexual activity without the consent of one of the parties or when one party appears to be exploited. Statute makes certain activities unlawful, generally where a person is severely mentally handicapped or the other party is in a position of trust (e.g. a carer).[5] These limitations upon the capacity of people with learning disabilities to consent to such activity take no account of the fact that they may be quite capable of consenting, and there may be an offence even without exploitation.[6] Conversely, when such a person has been sexually abused it may not be possible to prosecute the offender because of the difficulty in producing evidence acceptable to a court. The law is not clear as to the extent to which such a person may be given a sex education, but merely giving advice on birth control or providing contraceptives is likely to be too remote from any act of sexual intercourse to constitute an offence.

Intervention

The aim of intervention may be to improve the quality of life or prevent abuse and neglect, but the balance between necessary protection and unjustified interference is difficult to achieve. Authorities should be placed under a clear duty to intervene in specific circumstances but they need adequate and well-defined powers of investigation, assessment and intervention as well as guidance as to how and when to use them. At present both the duty and the powers are lacking.

Local authority responsibilities

Local authorities are responsible through their social services departments for protecting vulnerable individuals as well as providing services for those in need. They may need to intervene when help and support is refused by an individual who cannot live in the community without this, or where a 'carer' refuses access to or services for such an individual. Conflicts do arise between social workers and parents as to the manner in which their adult son or daughter with Down's syndrome should be brought up, and abuse can take place in a family environment. There is also abuse in institutional settings which may need to be investigated and controlled, and a system of registration and inspection has been set up for residential care and nursing homes.[7]

A local authority may apply to a magistrates court for power to remove persons to suitable premises for the purpose of securing necessary care and attention if (*inter alia*) being infirm or physically incapacitated they are living in insanitary conditions and unable to devote to themselves, and are not receiving from other persons, proper care and attention.[8] This does not provide a power of entry to investigate the need for such intervention.

Mental health legislation

There are powers to intervene where a person who is believed to suffer from a mental disorder is causing a problem or is a cause for concern.[9] The person may be removed by a police constable from a public place to a place of safety, or may be removed from specific premises on the authority of a magistrate following application by an approved social worker if being neglected, ill treated or not kept under control. The place of safety might be residential accommodation or a hospital, and detention there is limited in time but should be for the purpose of assessment and possible treatment. Further powers of compulsory admission to hospital for assessment or treatment are unlikely to apply to a person with Down's syndrome because they depend upon 'abnormally aggressive or seriously irresponsible conduct' or the need for treatment in hospital which is likely to alleviate the condition. These powers are designed to be used in respect of people who are mentally ill and there are various safeguards against their excessive use.

A form of statutory guardianship is available when the individual suffers from a mental disorder and displays abnormally aggressive or seriously irresponsible conduct.[10] It is of limited application to persons with Down's syndrome because of these criteria[11] and is little used because of the limited powers of the guardian and the reluctance of social workers to adopt an authoritarian role, but it can assist in resolving disputes about personal arrangements. The guardian cannot authorize medical treatment and merely has power to require that the individual live at a specific place and attend for medical treatment, occupation, education or training at specified times and places, and that access be given to doctors and certain other people.

Criminal law

An individual with Down's syndrome may find him or herself in trouble with the police, perhaps because he or she is an easy target and or inappropriate behaviour has been misunderstood although it might be that he or she has done something wrong. People who are not capable of understanding or obeying the rules should not be punished and there are safeguards that apply when someone with learning disabilities becomes involved with the criminal justice system.[12] There are serious concerns about recognizing the people to whom these safeguards should be applied but this is unlikely to be a problem in the case of Down's syndrome.

In the first instance a Code of Practice must be followed by the police when they are questioning someone.[13] Notes for Guidance contain specific provisions dealing with mentally handicapped people which apply if the officer is told or has any suspicion of this condition. A third party, known as an appropriate adult, must then be brought in to safeguard the rights of that person. This will be a relative or carer of the detained person, or someone other than a police officer who has experience of dealing with mentally handicapped people. Failure to comply with the Code can result in evidence being rejected, and the police complaints procedure is available where there is misconduct.

Where an offence has been committed consideration should be given to whether prosecution is appropriate taking into account alternatives such as cautioning, admission to guardianship or to hospital, or informal support in the community by the social services department. The overall aim is to divert mentally disordered people from the criminal justice system and the policy is that they should not be prosecuted unless it is in the public interest.[14] If prosecution is thought necessary the individual may be found unfit to plead if unable to understand the proceedings and until recently would have been detained in a hospital until fit, so the person with learning disabilities could have been detained indefinitely on mere suspicion of an offence. Recent legislation provides for a 'trial of the facts' so that the accused has the chance of being acquitted.[15]

Finally, alternatives to prison should be considered for a person with severe learning disabilities either whilst awaiting trial or after conviction. The courts now have a wider range of disposal options and there is more co-operation with health, probation and social services to ensure that appropriate support is provided. Heavy reliance may be put on medical reports and social assessments placed before or obtained by the court.

EMPOWERMENT

Empowerment means enabling the exercise of personal choices (e.g. where and with whom to live, how to spend money, what medical treatment to accept). Delegation to another person may be necessary if the choices are to be made at all, but so far as possible these should be the choices of the individual rather than of parents or carers, although their legitimate needs must be taken into account. Different types of decisions should not be treated in the same way, and the significance of the decision and degree of risk involved is relevant. Decisions may be classified as personal, financial or medical and although for children our law is preoccupied with personal matters, in respect of adults it currently only provides for delegation of financial decisions.[16] This demonstrates a mistaken view of priorities which is especially unfortunate for people with learning disabilities because they seldom have any savings and are much more dependent upon personal decisions. In practice 'he who controls the purse controls the person' sometimes with unfortunate results.

Incompetence

An individual who is incapable of making or unable to communicate a decision is treated as incompetent, but it should not be assumed that communication difficulties are synonymous with incapacity and every effort should be made to overcome these. There is a presumption of capacity which is not overturned by status such as old age, residence in a care home or a diagnosis of Down's syndrome, though the existence of these factors may cause it to be questioned.[17] Nor should it be thought that an individual is incapable simply because his or her choices appear foolish to others – we are all entitled to be eccentric. A function test based on understanding and ability to make an informed choice should be applied to the particular decision at the time it is to be taken because capacity may vary from time to time. The test of capacity to marry is thus different from that to make a will or enter into a financial transaction. No one should be assumed incapable of all decision-making powers, and the general principle is that such personal autonomy as the individual has should be respected (although the law does not always conform to this). There are specific rules that apply to civic duties such as voting and jury service but these do not necessarily address the issue of capacity.

Whether a person is incapable of making a decision is ultimately a matter for the courts based upon the available evidence of which the views of a doctor merely form a part. The evidence of a carer, teacher, nurse or family member may also be of value. When someone expresses a view as to capacity it is necessary to consider whether they have applied the correct legal test, and it is remarkable how often they have not. A typical example of the inappropriate application of a status test is 'He cannot possibly do this because he has Down's syndrome'. The question is not whether he has a particular disability but what his abilities are.

Personal decisions

We all make and act on our own decisions and have to live with the consequences. Many of these decisions only affect us in the short term, but others have long-term implications and some have a serious and perhaps irreversible impact on the quality of our lives. We may in practice allow other people such as a spouse to make decisions for us, but there are some decisions that only we can take for ourselves, including whether to get married or have a relationship (sexual or otherwise). Even when we delegate our decisions, we have to decide to do so or later to adopt the decisions made for us. If an individual cannot make personal decisions a procedure is needed for these to be made and this usually involves delegation to another person. At present there is no legal basis for this to be done in England,[18] but the courts have had to face situations where there is a dispute as to what decision should be acted upon or a decision has to be made which no one can make.

One approach is adult guardianship with a specified relative assuming the power to decide, but whilst this may reflect what happens in many cases it is generally considered to be too paternalistic. Parents do not necessarily know what is best for their children and cannot always be relied upon to act in the best interests of a disabled son or daughter as distinct from their own interests. Other children grow up and assert their independence so why should the child with Down's syndrome be treated otherwise? Enhancing personal autonomy is now seen as important and the role of the personal advocate is increasing, but parents may continue to provide personal care at great cost to themselves both financially and in terms of their own way of life, so it is difficult to balance their needs with the autonomy of the individual.

Even if an acceptable delegated decision-maker can be found, on what basis should decisions be made for the incompetent individual? A preference has emerged for adopting the choice that the individual would have made if able (substituted judgement) as distinct from that which the decision-maker considers best for the individual (best interests), but in the case of learning disability there may be no previous pattern of personal decision-making to follow. Too rigid an approach should not be adopted because we all make decisions that we know to be foolish but from which we gain pleasure. Any preferences that are perceived should be followed where possible (an individual whose wishes are never taken into account will cease to express them after a while) and failure to involve the individual may lead to behaviour problems which, if treated in other ways, can result in an escalation of those problems. Where a choice is offered this should be a real choice, not artificially restricted so as to achieve one of the options preferred by the decision-maker especially when another option might have been preferred by the individual.

Financial affairs

Legal procedures are available for the management of financial affairs and, although these are designed to meet the needs of the elderly who may have acquired substantial assets before losing capacity, they should not be overlooked when considering someone with Down's syndrome. The usual approach of parents and carers, which is to find a procedure that works and use it regardless of legality, is understandable and should not necessarily be discouraged. Many small transactions take place on this basis as a practical response to the failure of the law to provide a simple and inexpensive procedure, but problems do arise. Thus an account may have been conducted at a local bank or building society based upon personal contact, but as financial institutions become less personal this might be questioned.

Most individuals with Down's syndrome will be eligible to claim one or more weekly State benefits. An agency procedure enables these benefits to be collected on behalf of a claimant who, although mentally competent, is unable or unwilling to cope with the payment procedure but the money must then be handed to the claimant. An appointee may be appointed to collect and spend state benefits for a claimant who is unable to deal with financial affairs. This must be done for the claimant's own benefit, but there is little supervision and the appointee will usually be a close relative or personal carer thus able to exercise financial control and deny independence. Where the only financial resources of the individual are State benefits these procedures will be all that is required. There are also a few other facilities that may be useful: for example, income tax can be reclaimed by the next of kin of a mentally incapacitated person up to specific financial limits and certain relatives may register on the person's behalf for interest to be paid without deduction of tax. The National Savings Bank allows deposits and withdrawals on an account in the name of an incapacitated person.

When the individual has capital resources, for example from an inheritance or a damages claim, involvement with the Court of Protection is usually required.[19] This is a special court empowered to deal with the financial affairs of patients, being people who by reason of mental disorder are incapable of managing and administering their property and affairs.[20] It is under the direction of a Master but much of the work is dealt with by correspondence and administered by the Public Trust Office. The Court needs to be satisfied that it has jurisdiction, so forms must first be completed and submitted by any interested person, including a medical certificate and a statement of 'family and property'. If the estate is simple and straightforward, or less than £5,000, a short order may authorize the patient's assets to be used in a specified way for his or her benefit. Thus a parent who applies might be given authority to spend the money with little or no supervision or the patient may be enabled to enter into a tenancy. In other cases the Court appoints a receiver with power to take specified actions under supervision. The receiver acts on behalf and in the name of the patient under the authority of orders issued by the Court which may be in general terms (e.g. to spend the annual income for the benefit of the patient) or for specific purposes (e.g. to sell a house and invest the proceeds). Whilst this is the most secure procedure, suitable for large sums where professional assistance would be required in any event, it involves a large amount of paperwork (including annual accounts) with consequent delays and is expensive because fees are charged by the court.

In response to the demand for a procedure of choice available to those who lose mental capacity during their lifetime, the Enduring Powers of Attorney Act 1985 was passed for England and Wales.[21] This provides a practical, inexpensive way in which the elderly and infirm can anticipate incapacity by appointing an attorney who may deal with their financial affairs even after they become incapable. A special form is used and this must be registered after incapacity has arisen, with notice being given to specified relatives, but there is little supervision even though the attorney may be given wide powers over financial affairs. There is some scope for those with Down's syndrome to use this procedure because the court has held that you may sign the form if you understand that you are delegating your affairs to someone of your choice even if not capable of managing those affairs yourself (the power will then need to be registered immediately).[22]

Medical treatment

No medical treatment should be given without consent and a doctor cannot compel a patient to accept treatment, however convinced he or she may be that it is in the patient's best interests. Although the medical profession still uses the word 'consent' and seems obsessed with having a bit of paper signed, the real question is whether the patient chose to have the treatment after considering all available options, and a signature is neither essential nor conclusive though it may be evidence.[23] Consent may be implied, as when a patient presents him or herself for treatment, and basic nursing care such as cleaning up a protesting patient may be excusable in the absence of consent, but intrusive medical treatment will not. The consent must be real, which means that the patient understood in broad terms what he or she was consenting to, though it tends to be for the doctor to decide how much to explain to the patient. Every risk need not be mentioned, but any questions should be answered and the patient must not be misled.[24] The consent must also be to the treatment actually given and the doctor should not normally go beyond this.

A patient is competent to give consent who has sufficient understanding and intelligence to comprehend the nature, purpose and likely consequences of undergoing or refusing treatment as well as the ability to communicate to the doctor a decision in relation to the particular treatment.[25] The implications or severity of the proposed treatment may affect the degree of understanding required, so an individual may be able to decide whether to have a tooth extracted but not whether to have a hysterectomy. A person with Down's syndrome may never be competent to give consent but should not be denied all treatment, so by whom and in what circumstances may treatment be authorized? The general position is that no one may give consent on behalf of a patient unless the latter is a minor, in which event the parent or other person with parental responsibility may consent or the Court may do so under its inherent jurisdiction.[26] In the case of an adult the Court in England does not have an inherent jurisdiction and there are no procedures whereby the personal power to consent to or refuse medical treatment may be delegated to others.[27] In an emergency the doctor responsible for a patient unable to give or refuse consent to treatment (e.g. because unconscious) may act in accordance with good medical practice and give treatment which is designed to preserve the life of the patient, assist recovery or ease suffering.[28] Short-term incompetence is of less significance than long-term incompetence because the minimum necessary treatment can be given until the patient recovers and can express wishes in regard to further or more drastic treatment. In 1989 the House of Lords in the well known case of *Re F* held that a doctor when considering whether to sterilize a young mentally handicapped woman must act in her best interests and in conformity with a responsible body of medical opinion.[29] This enables a doctor to give treatment without consent, but how is he or she to decide what are the patient's best interests unless these are restricted to best *medical* interests, which is surely too narrow? The simple answer is that the doctor consults relatives and carers, not for the purpose of obtaining consent but to ascertain the attitudes and likely wishes of the patient.[30]

A person who is likely to remain permanently incompetent is entitled to more than minimum treatment, but there may be doubt or disagreement as to what this should be. To deal with this the High Court in England has developed a procedure whereby a 'declaration' is made that the action the doctor proposes to take would not be unlawful[31] and this has become common for controversial or irreversible treatments, but ordinary medical treatment is still a problem. The doctor can hardly be expected to apply to the Court every time he proposes to give non-essential but nevertheless desirable treatment, and disagreements do arise between professionals and parents as to how a mentally incapable person should be treated. There is a danger that beneficial treatment that the rest of us request and take for granted may be denied to a person with Down's syndrome simply because there is no one empowered to take an overall view of that person's medical needs. Much may depend upon the attitude of the medical practitioner concerned, but in a society that is becoming more litigation conscious a conservative approach is likely to be adopted.

SUPPORT

Support for an individual with Down's syndrome will come from the immediate family, the local authority, the Department of Social Security (DSS) and the health authority. It is important to ensure that this support is co-ordinated so that the best possible care package is provided and support from one source does not preclude another.

Community care

Care in the community is not a new concept. For many it has been the reality for years, but has meant being cared for by family with little support from the state in an indifferent society. Advantage might be taken of any services available but these were not structured to meet personal needs and when family could no longer cope institutionalized care was the only alternative. The need to reduce institutional care coupled with pressure to recognize the rights of the individual have found expression in community care policies, but these mean more than just the provision of a home in the community for former hospital patients; a whole range of support and services must be provided for all persons needing care, including those already living in their own family homes. A series of reports[32] resulted in legislation in 1990[33] which was designed to create a change of approach and has been supplemented by government guidance and circulars, and by directions issued by the Secretary of State.[34] Whilst the new policies may appear reassuring to families with a Down's syndrome member, implementation has been inhibited by a lack of funding and there are few legal remedies available to the individual.

The 1990 Act relies on earlier legislation[35] rather than creating rights to new services but imposes new duties upon local authorities which must draw up Community Care Plans in consultation with other authorities and the voluntary sector. The lead role is given to social services departments which are under a duty to assess the needs of persons ordinarily resident in its area who appear to need care services, and then to decide what services (if any) are to be provided. Instead of providing services itself the authority is encouraged to arrange for them to be provided by the private sector, which includes both commercial undertakings and 'not-for-profit' organizations. There is thus scope for the development of voluntary organizations which may be set up as charities thereby obtaining tax concessions and funding advantages. The emphasis is upon partnership between all concerned to secure packages of care appropriate to the needs of individuals.

Services are not restricted in nature and may be for the benefit of the disabled person or the carer. They are generally classified as domiciliary which are provided inside the home, day which are provided outside the home and residential which means the provision of a place in a residential care or nursing home either on a short-term or a long-term basis. There may also be assistance for physically disabled people with aids and appliances. Although money cannot be provided, some authorities have introduced voucher schemes to encourage greater independence. Local authorities fund services through their social services budgets but are expected to charge users according to their capacity to pay and are free to determine the basis on which they do so.[36] Disability benefits are increasingly being taken into account under means-testing procedures, but the parents or carers of a service user cannot be assessed.

Although it may appear that a local authority is obliged to provide services this is not necessarily so. A distinction must be drawn between a power to provide a service and a duty to do so, and also between a general duty to provide services and a duty to an individual. The duties imposed upon local authorities tend to be of a general nature and it can be difficult for an individual to enforce the provision of any particular service. Where the authority is not under a duty to the individual it has a discretion and action may only be taken if it does not exercise that discretion at all or in a proper manner. Each case must be dealt with on its merits and the authority cannot fetter its discretion by imposing a blanket policy, but lack of resources may be a factor to take into account. It is only where the authority is under a duty to provide a service to an individual that it cannot decline to do so because of lack of resources. However, failure by the service user to pay an assessed contribution does not justify withdrawal of the service and any arrears can only be collected as a civil debt.

A new social services complaints procedure has been introduced[37] and this may be used where the obligation to assess needs and consider the provision of services has not been fulfilled. In extreme cases an application may be made to the High Court for judicial review. Anyone who considers that they have suffered injustice due to maladministration by a local authority may be able to have a complaint looked into by the Commissioner for Local Administration (ombudsman) but usually all existing remedies or rights of appeal must first be used. The Secretary of State also has supervisory powers so a complaint may be made direct to the minister if the authority has not complied with directions or other guidance issued by the government.

Disabled persons

Specific services for disabled people have been available for years[38] and these now merge into the general provision of community care services, although there remain some differences. In particular the authority may be under a duty to provide any of these specific services that are assessed as needed although the absence of time limits makes this ineffective. The definition of disability is based upon being 'handi-capped by illness, injury or congenital deformity or suffering from mental disorder of any description' so Down's syndrome is likely to be included. Local authorities are under a duty to keep a voluntary register of disabled persons in their area although entitlement to services does not depend upon being on the register.[39]

Residential care

Care 'in the community' is now preferred to residential care in 'institutions' but it has been found that the provision of care in ordinary houses is not a cheap option and can bring its own problems. A range of options is to be encouraged and small communities run by charitable organizations continue to flourish and may be of particular interest to people with Down's syndrome. All residential care homes are subject to a system of registration and inspection by the local authority in whose area they are situated, but this should not be used to impose that authority's own care policies.

The method of funding new residents in registered homes was changed upon the full implementation of community care policies in April 1993. It now depends upon the willingness of the local authority in whose area the potential resident resides to provide a top-up for the care element of the fees based upon an assessment of need. No longer can the full weekly fees be automatically covered by income support upon admission to a home, although there are preserved rights for those who were already in care homes. The means test applied to the resident by the local authority is now similar to that for income support[40] and effectively denies such residents any substantial savings or assets other than personal possessions, although provision is made for a weekly personal expenses allowance. There is scope for families to fund the top-up but homes are reluctant to admit a resident without local authority sponsorship because of the risk that family funding will cease during the lifetime of the resident.

Education

A suitable education is of great importance to people with Down's syndrome and they are entitled to have their special educational needs (SEN) assessed and provided for up to the age of 19 years.[41] They should not merely be provided with the educational facilities that the local education authority (LEA) has available or can afford, and wherever possible subject to the views of parents they should be educated in mainstream schools.[42] Unfortunately there has been a failure by LEAs to discharge their duties due to a lack of resources and this has caused great stress to families. Recent legislation in England[43] strengthens the assessment and 'state-menting' procedures by imposing time limits, places duties on schools and makes an independent appeal procedure available to parents.[44] The emphasis is again upon partnership, with each school publishing annually information on its SEN policies and these being monitored by inspectors. Parents may express a preference as to their child's school which must be followed unless the LEA can establish one of three statutory grounds of objection.[45] It is expected that schools, LEAs, health services, social services, voluntary organizations and other agencies will work closely with each other and with parents, and a 'named person' must be notified by the LEA to give advice and information to parents. Concern is felt that this legislation is primarily aimed at encouraging schools to opt out of LEA control, and only time will tell whether it results in less legal challenges to the procedures and policies of LEAs.

Financial

A person with Down's syndrome is unlikely to be financially self-supporting so needs to be provided with a personal income. This will come from state benefits or from the family and needs to be managed by others to a greater or lesser extent.

State benefits

Everyone in Great Britain is entitled to an income for personal maintenance.[46] Those with disabilities which render them unable to earn a living are provided with a weekly income and the more profound the disability the greater this is likely to be. Those with insufficient income for their needs are provided with a supplement. In each case it is paid by the DSS through the Benefits Agency; procedures for claimants who cannot manage their own affairs have already been considered. The individual with Down's syndrome is unlikely to build up a personal record of National Insurance contributions, so will depend upon certain non-means-tested, non-contributory disability benefits which may be topped up by one or more means-tested benefits. The former include severe disablement allowance and disability living allowance (with separate care and mobility components) and the latter comprise income support and perhaps housing benefit which is administered by the local authority. Disability working allowance is available for those who can engage in some remunerative employment, and a voluntary carer may be entitled to invalid care allowance. Various loans and grants may also be available from the social fund. The entitlement criteria constantly change and space does not permit a further explanation here.[47]

Family provision

The biggest anxiety of parents of a Down's syndrome child is what will happen after they have died. They should make care plans for the future which avoid the prospect that overnight the child may lose not only a parent who has been a carer for life but also a home and a whole way of life. They should also make wills containing special trust provision for their worldly wealth. It is important to realize that a will can only deal with money and cannot provide personal care for a child in a suitable environment. Whilst such care can be bought it is extremely expensive and most parents do not leave enough money to fund this for a few years let alone for life, especially if they have other children to share the estate. Failure to make a will is a disaster: not only will there be no one appointed to deal with the estate, but the disabled child will inherit a share (or the whole estate if an only child) on intestacy yet be unable to cope with this and also be vulnerable to reduction or withdrawal of State benefits and charges for community care or residential services. Parents usually wish to provide extras and a contingency fund in case of difficulty, and are unwilling to contemplate their money being used to replace benefits or pay for services that would otherwise have been available without charge. All these complications may be avoided by making a will, appointing trustees and creating a trust.

Parents may put money 'in trust' either under their wills or during their life-times.[48] This means that the money is held by trustees, on the terms of the particular trust created by the provider. If the money is held for the individual absolutely it will be means-tested as part of personal resources, so it is usually better to create discretionary trusts giving the trustees maximum flexibility over what they may do with the money. This has the disadvantage that the individual has no entitlement and is denied the personal autonomy that the rest of us seek, but you cannot have it both ways! It may be more effective to support the carers or a charity which provides care services than the individual, or to invest in a home or assets that can be used by the individual, but the trustees must be given adequate powers if they are to do this.

The difficulty is that the trust provision may only take effect on the death of the parents yet is intended to continue for the lifetime of the disabled 'beneficiary'. The needs and circumstances of this person are likely to change during that time in ways that cannot be anticipated, as are the forms of care provision that are available and the means-testing provisions that apply. There is an element of crystal-ball gazing that makes this kind of financial provision rather complicated, but precedents written by this author have now been published and these should be referred to for a more detailed explanation of the strategies that can be adopted.[49] The old strategy of leaving all the money to other children in the hope that they will support their disabled sibling is no longer acceptable, and may be challenged by a local authority that takes on the care role.[50]

THE FUTURE

The Children Act 1989 introduced major reforms and is generally considered to provide an effective regime for the upbringing and protection of children whether or not they are disabled.[51] This ceases when they attain the age of majority, and the law in respect of mentally incapacitated and vulnerable adults has recently been examined by the Law Commission and found to be fragmented, complex and out of date. Having previously published four consultation papers,[52] in March 1995 the Commission published a final report containing recommendations and annexing a Mental Disability Bill intended to make comprehensive provision for people over 16 years of age.[53] It is proposed that a code of practice be prepared after full consultation to give guidance on the implementation of the legislation.

Of particular relevance to people with Down's syndrome and their families and carers it is recommended that:

- the fundamental concepts of lack of capacity and best interests be clarified and defined (as set out in the report);
- carers have a general authority to act reasonably in doing anything for the personal welfare or health care of an incapacitated person (subject to certain qualifications set out in the report);
- there be power for the individual (if capable) to make advance statements about health care, and independent supervision of certain medical and research procedures;
- continuing powers of attorney be introduced to enable an individual to delegate personal and medical decisions (as well as financial decisions) in the event of subsequent loss of capacity (subject to safeguards set out in the report);
- the Court should have power to make a declaration in relation to the capacity of a person and either make a decision or appoint someone (a manager) to be responsible for making a decision on behalf of a person who lacks capacity to make it (the report indicates how this power should be approached);
- there be extended powers for a local authority to provide protection to vulnerable people who are at risk, and a duty to do so (the report spells this out);
- there be a new structure for dealing with these matters in a Court of Protection with nominated judges at all levels and cases being dealt with at an appropriate level, and with powers to obtain reports on the individual concerned.

CONCLUSION

Community care policies may be a step in the right direction but they are being frustrated by ignorance and discriminatory attitudes on the part of the public as much as by lack of funding. It takes a generation or more to change attitudes but the law can play a part in encouraging such change rather than merely reflecting changes that have already taken place. Legislation to prohibit discrimination against disabled people now should follow that which has been enacted in respect of discrimination on grounds of race or sex, and it is hoped that the proposals of the Law Commission will soon be carried into effect. Until then our law and its procedures merely re-enforce the handicap already encountered in society by disabled people and in particular those with Down's syndrome.

Editors' note

Although this chapter has focused specifically on UK law, similar laws can be identified in most other counties. Jurisprudence and the central issues relating to the care and treatment of mentally handicapped and other disabled people are equally relevant and important worldwide.

NOTES

1. More detailed consideration will be found in the writer's book *Mental Handicap and the Law* (London: Sweet and Maxwell, 1992).
2. By far the largest potential category is the elderly who are more vulnerable to mental illnesses such as senile dementia or Alzheimer's disease.
3. Disability Discrimination Act 1995.
4. In England this will be a next friend or a guardian *ad litem* (see Rules of the Supreme Court, Order 80 and County Court Rules, Order 10), and in Scotland it will be a curator or a tutor.
5. See generally Sexual Offences Acts 1956 and 1967 (England); Mental Health (Scotland) Act 1984.
6. In practice prosecutions in these circumstances will be rare.
7. Registered Homes Act 1984 and regulations made thereunder; there are also Codes of Practice. A similar system exists in Scotland under different legislation.
8. National Assistance Act 1948, s. 47. There is also a duty to protect the property of the individual under s. 48.
9. Under the Mental Health Act 1983 and the Mental Health (Scotland) Act 1984. Guidance is found in the Code of Practice under the Act in England. There are some variations in Scotland.
10. Mental Health Act 1983, ss. 7–10.
11. They do not apply in Scotland where many people under guardianship are mentally handicapped – Mental Health (Scotland) Act 1984, Part V.
12. These safeguards also exist in Scotland in general terms but are not so well developed as in England.
13. Under the Police and Criminal Evidence Act 1984 (PACE). There is no Code in Scotland but similar safeguards are recommended in guidance notes by the Scottish Office to the police.
14. Home Office Circular 66/90 *Provisions for Mentally Disordered Offenders*. See also the Code for Crown Prosecutors. In Scotland the Procurator-fiscal decides whether to prosecute and may adopt a similar approach.
15. Criminal Procedure (Insanity and Unfitness to Plead) Act 1991. This does not apply in Scotland.
16. In Scotland a tutor-dative may be appointed by the court with powers to make a range of personal decisions for an incapacitated person.
17. There are now few instances where status results in loss of capacity, the most obvious being the status of a minor.
18. In Scotland personal decisions may be delegated to a tutor-dative appointed by the court.
19. This Court does not have jurisdiction in Scotland but other procedures are available including the appointment of a curator or a tutor.
20. Mental Health Act 1983, Part VII.
21. In Scotland any Power of Attorney may now survive the incapacity of the person who signs it, and none of the English safeguards apply – Law Reform (Miscellaneous Provisions) (Scotland) Act 1990, ss. 71(1).
22. *Re K, Re F* [1988] 1 All ER 358.
23. The onus is on the patient to prove lack of consent if this is alleged – *Freeman v Home Office (No 2)* [1984] 1 All ER 1036, CA.
24. *Sidaway v Board of Governors of the Bethlem Royal and the Maudsley Hospital* [1984] 1 All ER 1018, CA; [1985] 1 All ER 643, HL.
25. *Glllick v West Norfolk and Wisbech AHA* [1985] 3 All ER 402, HL.
26. There have been inroads into the status test for minors in recent years. They may give consent if *Gillick* competent, but refusal of consent may be overridden by the consent of a person with parental responsibility or the Court – *Re R (a minor) (wardship: medical treatment)* [1991] 4 All ER 177, CA.

27. The only statutory exception to this is provided by the Mental Health Acts which allow treatment of certain types to be given to detained patients. In Scotland a tutor-dative may be appointed with power to make medical treatment decisions.
28. This is based on the principle of necessity. See *Bolam* v *Friern Hospital Management Committee* [1957] 2 All ER 118.
29. *F* v *West Berkshire HA* [1989] 2 All ER 545; also reported as *Re F (Sterilisation: Mental Patient)* [1989] 2 FLR 376.
30. *Re T (Adult: Refusal of medical treatment)* [1992] 4 All ER 649, CA.
31 *Re F* (supra); *Airedale NHS Trust* v *Bland* [1993] 1 All ER 821, HL. In Scotland the court can give express approval under the tutor-dative procedure.
32. In particular *Community Care: Agenda for Action* (1988) and the White Paper *Caring for People: Community Care in the Next Decade and Beyond* (1989).
33. National Health Service and Community Care Act 1990; Part III applies to England and Wales and Part IV to Scotland.
34. Copies of the key circulars may be obtained from DH Store, Health Publications Unit, No 2 Site, Manchester Road, Heywood, Lancashire OL10 2PZ.
35. National Assistance Act 1948 (Part III), Health Services and Public Health Act 1968, Chronically Sick and Disabled Persons Act 1970, Housing Act 1985, National Health Service Act 1977, Disabled Persons Act 1981, Mental Health Act 1983, Health and Social Services and Social Security Adjudications Act 1983, Disabled Persons (Services Consultation and Representation) Act 1986.
36. *Discretionary Charges for Adult Social Services*, Advice Note for use by Social Services Inspectorate, January 1994.
37. Local Authority Social Services (Complaints Procedure) Order 1990; Complaints Procedure Directions 1990; *The Right to Complain: Practical Guidance on Complaints Procedures in Social Services Departments* (London: HMSO, 1991).
38. National Assistance Act 1948 s. 29, Chronically Sick and Disabled Persons Act 1970, Disabled Persons (Services, Consultation and Representation) Act 1986.
39. A separate voluntary register is maintained by the Department of Employment for the purpose of employment.
40. National Assistance (Assessment of Resources) Regulations 1992. See also DoH Circular LAC (92)19 *Charges for Residential Accommodation*, DoH Circular LAC (93)8 and *Charging for Residential Accommodation Guide* (CRAG) with amendments in Circular LAC (94)1.
41. Until 1971 severely mentally handicapped children were excluded from the education system. The Education Act 1981 created a framework for all children with special educational needs but with inadequate enforcement procedures.
42. Some parents still prefer 'special schools' and fight to keep these open.
43. Education Act 1993; see Part III and the *Code of Practice on the Identification and Assessment of Special Educational Needs*. A separate system applies in Scotland.
44. The Special Educational Needs Tribunal with a legally qualified chairman, replaces the appeal committee previously set up by the LEA which could merely make a recommendation.
45. Basically that the school is not suitable for the child, the child is not suitable for the school or inefficient use of resources.
46. The primary legislation is Social Security Contributions and Benefits Act 1992 and Social Security Administration Act 1992. There is a similar system in Northern Ireland under different legislation.
47. The *Disability Rights Handbook* is published annually by the Disability Alliance ERA, Universal House, 88–94 Wentworth Street, London E1 7SA. It is a valuable source of information as are the publications of the Child Poverty Action Group.
48. It may be convenient to create a lifetime 'settlement' containing the desired trusts. Any money for the disabled individual may then be left by will to the trustees of that settlement, and this avoids the need for each donor to set up separate trusts.
49. *Butterworths Wills Probate and Administration Service* (Butterworths: London)

and *Encyclopaedia of Forms and Precedents, volume 42* (Butterworths: London). This topic is also covered in *Mental Handicap and the Law* (London: Sweet and Maxwell, 1992).

50. An application may be made to the court in England and Wales in the name of the disabled child for provision under the Inheritance (Provision for Family and Dependants) Act 1975.

51. It does not apply in Scotland.

52. No 119 *Mentally Incapacitated Adults and Decision-Making: An Overview* (1989);
No 128 *Mentally Incapacitated Adults and Decision-Making: A New Jurisdiction* (February 1993);
No 129 *Mentally Incapacitated Adults and Decision-Making: Medical Treatment and Research* (April 1993);
No 130 *Mentally Incapacitated and Other Vulnerable Adults: Public Law Protection* (May 1993).

53. Report No 231 *Mental Incapacity*. A separate consultation process has been undertaken by the Scottish Law Commission (Discussion Paper No 94: *Mentally Disabled Adults*, September 1991) and a final report is awaited which is also expected to include a draft Bill.

Developments in Medical Research and Treatment

4 Epidemiology: Incidence, Prevalence and Size of the Down's Syndrome Population

Jonathan Steele

Establishing the size of the population with Down's syndrome is clearly important in planning the appropriate range of medical, educational and social services for this group of people. It was well over a decade ago when I was informed by a special school teacher that there was no point making long-term plans for the educational needs of the population with Down's syndrome, as prenatal diagnosis meant that there would soon be no children growing up with this condition. Time has shown that nothing could be further from the truth.

Yet this prediction was made thoughtfully, after an assessment of the situation as it was presented to this teacher, through the press, media and some professional journals. However, it also reflected the confusion between incidence (rate of affected births) and prevalence (rate of affected persons in the general population) and how clear changes in these rates, particularly incidence, could have less clear effects on the actual size of the population with Down's syndrome.

In this chapter I consider briefly the size of the Down's syndrome population, factors that affect it and how some estimation of the future population can be made.

BACKGROUND AND ATTITUDES

An account of the biological cause of Down's syndrome may be found elsewhere (Stratford and Steele, 1989; Zaremba, 1985). Obviously the mechanism for arriving at the situation where a human embryo has effectively three, rather than two number 21 chromosomes is not new. Therefore we must presume such conceptions have happened from time to time throughout the history of mankind. However, the harsher living conditions of early history and the lack of medical intervention must have meant that the prognosis for such unborn children was poor (see Chapter 1, this volume). Even if a child with Down's syndrome was born, the generally poor prospects for infant and child survival would have selected against those who had any medical weakness. The well documented susceptibility to infection or heart conditions among children with Down's syndrome would have constituted such a weakness.

During this last half-century, medical science and technology has developed rapidly. There is now the possibility of greatly improved pre- and post-natal survival for babies with Down's syndrome. There has also been much important work done on the integration of people with Down's syndrome into society, with an emphasis on respecting and valuing each individual. Such progress may, however, misleadingly indicate that compassion and respect towards those with Down's syndrome is a relatively modern phenomenon. This is not the case.

Of course, this is not to suggest that attitudes in the past have always been positive. For example, the prevalence of Down's syndrome in 1930s Germany (Dioxiades and Portius, 1938) was only half what would be expected compared to other European studies (e.g. Penrose, 1949) and, prior to the 1970s, British people with Down's syndrome were not considered educable.

Hence, before embarking on a discussion about incidence and prevalence of Down's syndrome and the factors that can affect it, the importance of attitudes must be acknowledged. With developments in medical science and technology come not only additional opportunities for choice and greater freedom, but much greater responsibilities. At present this is particularly so in the area of prenatal diagnosis.

Clearly, as scientists, we would wish developments to be made. However, it is also important that we are aware of philosophical issues, such as the values and attitudes that may be encouraged by the simple existence of new technology.

INCIDENCE OF DOWN'S SYNDROME

Studies of incidence

As with many studies of this type, complete ascertainment of Down's syndrome births can often be a problem. Most studies have been retrospective and usually rely on obtaining information from a number of different sources. Such sources vary in number and nature depending on the individual study, but as the number of sources checked increases, so the reliability of the data may be expected to increase. Some studies introduce an element of correction to their data to offset the effect of under-ascertainment (Hook and Chambers, 1977; Huether and Gummere, 1982). A few studies have attempted a prospective method, by following a number of consecutive births (Harlap, 1973; Rantakallio and Von Wendt, 1986), although under-ascertainment at birth could still be a problem.

British studies

Malpas (1937) presented some early figures on incidence from Liverpool Maternity Hospital in his general paper on birth defects. Although the small number of Down's syndrome births makes this essentially of historical interest now, a maternal age effect is clearly visible from his data.

Carter and MacCarthy's 1951 study of maternity hospital records from the south of England acknowledged some degree of under-ascertainment; this is particularly

Table 4.1 British incidence studies (incidence rates per 1,000 births)

Period of study	15–19	20–24	25–29	30–34	35–39	40–44	45+	Total 15–45+	Down's syndrome births
[1]1923–32	0.95	0.48	0.49	0.76	5.11	4.38	21.28	1.29	18
[2]1943–49	0.00	0.28	0.29	1.72	3.52	14.18	26.32	1.51	100
[3]1961–79	0.66	0.52	0.80	1.27	4.25	15.74		1.39	319
[4]1980–85	0.51	0.63	0.89	0.97	4.40	9.01	27.77	1.05	74

Maternal age bands (years)

[1]Malpas (1937); [2]Carter and MacCarthy (1951); [3]Owens *et al.* (1983); [4]McGrowther and Marshall (1990)

apparent in the under 30-year-old maternal age groups (Table 4.1). The authors also included stillbirths in their figures, unlike other studies where 'births' were taken to mean live births. Comparisons with other studies is therefore further complicated. Carter and MacCarthy reported a higher incidence among professionals due to their increased maternal age.

Owens *et al.* (1983) conducted a search of the Liverpool Congenital Malformations Registry with secondary searches through paediatric cardiology and neonatal surgery units; ascertainment was therefore likely to be more reliable. The maternal age bands below 40 years certainly do seem to be fairly closely aligned to McGrowther and Marshall's 1990 study.

Studies from outside Britain

Collmann and Stoller's (1962) Australian study took information from an extremely wide variety of sources, covered a large number of Down's syndrome births and was updated in 1965 (Stoller and Collmann, 1965). Their incidence rates are therefore considered very reliable for the period covered and have been referred to extensively. Sutherland *et al.* (1979) identified births through public institutions that may have had contact with people with Down's syndrome and by advertising in the medical press. Chromosome analysis was obtained for almost all the Down's syndrome births identified and regression analysis used to produce incidence figures by single years of maternal age. Mulcahy (1979b) used a similar methodology, but presented incidence in five-year maternal age bands.

Table 4.2 Australian incidence studies (incidence rates per 1,000 births)

Period of study	15–19	20–24	25–29	30–34	35–39	40–44	45+	Total 15–45+	Down's syndrome births
[1]1942–57	0.43	0.62	0.83	1.15	3.50	9.93	22.0	1.45	1134
[2]1960–77	0.41	0.57	0.80	1.32	3.34	12.79	31.51	1.19	447
[3]1966–76	0.57	0.61	0.75	1.25	4.80	14.55	20.01	1.14	231
[4]1976–85	*0.55	0.64	0.74	1.52	4.43	21.43		1.18	446

Maternal age bands, in years

*under 20 years old
[1]Collmann and Stoller (1962); [2]Sutherland *et al.* (1979); [3]Mulcahy (1979b); [4]Bell *et al.* (1992)

Interestingly, a more recent Australian study (Bell *et al.*, 1992) shows broadly similar age-specific incidence rates and overall incidence rates. It is not surprising, therefore that their analysis shows no variation due to year of birth throughout their study period. Bell *et al.* (1992) conclude that they find no changes in incidence that cannot be explained by changes in maternal age distribution.

Three of the four American studies covered large populations and produced incidence rates of a broadly similar nature (Table 4.3), the greatest variations occurring in the 45+ age band. Both Hook and Chambers (1977) and Huether and Gummere (1982) applied corrections for under-reporting of Down's syndrome on birth certificates. Adams *et al.* (1981), however, had a narrow geographical focus in Atlanta and a smaller, though still considerable, population. Adjustment for age distribution did seem to bring the overall incidence rate into line with other studies, although their 35–39 rate does seem quite low.

A Swedish study was conducted between 1969 and 1970 (Hook and Lindsjö, 1978; Lindsjö, 1974), again gaining information from a variety of sources to produce maternal age-specific incidence rates within the range seen in the more recent British and Australian studies. Interestingly, Lindsjö (1974) suggests that differences in incidence rates between areas may be due to differences in ascertainment. Whilst this may well be the case, the argument is lost as Lindsjö presumes that there is no variation in maternal age-specific incidence in his calculations of differences in ascertainment. Hence the argument becomes circular; observed variations in incidence being due to differing ascertainment, presuming that there is no real variation in incidence.

A large Canadian study was conducted by Lowry *et al.* in 1976. Whilst the majority of age-specific incidence rates were within ranges already discussed, the incidence to mothers under the age of 19 was 0.80/1,000 – higher than many studies. This may suggest a possible increase in incidence to younger mothers; this is discussed later.

The early Danish study (Oster, 1956) is notable because it identifies a 27 per cent rate of under-diagnosis of Down's syndrome around the time of birth. As the area covered has a well-established history of recording congenital abnormalities through the Copenhagen University Institute for Human Genetics, this demonstrates the ascertainment difficulties experienced in less recent studies

Hence, considering the incidence studies above, it would appear that underlying age-specific incidence rates may be expected to be broadly the same throughout most populations, with any major differences being explained by methodological aspects of individual studies. However, there does seem to be one notable exception. A prospective study in Jerusalem followed some 42,000 births and identified 103 infants with Down's syndrome between 1964 and 1970 (Harlap, 1973), giving an overall incidence of 2.4/1,000 births. This high rate cannot be explained by increased child-bearing age in the Jerusalem population, because incidence is raised in individual maternal age bands, particularly between the ages of 25 and 39 years (Table 4.4).

Harlap reports that these raised rates seem to be confined to women born in Israel, North Africa or the Middle East, particularly orthodox Jewesses. No definitive explanation has been offered for this, although the possibility that it is related to infection has been suggested (Harlap, 1973; Sharav, 1985). If this was the reason, the effect would of course be environmental rather than racial.

Table 4.3 American incidence studies (incidence rates per 1,000 births)

Period of study	15–19	20–24	25–29	30–34	35–39	40–44	45+	Total 15–45+	Down's syndrome births
				Maternal age bands (in years)					
[1]1959–65	–	*0.64	*0.80	*1.30	*4.36	*14.68	*49.48	–	1250
[2]1963–74	0.64	0.64	0.96	1.39	4.37	13.44	43.25	1.44	933
[3]1968–76	0.66	0.61	0.78	1.54	2.63	14.29	34.19	0.99	229
[4]1970–79	0.63	0.74	1.01	1.63	5.02	15.80	59.09	1.23	1010

*Averages of single year rates
[1]Hook and Fabia (1978); [2]From Hook and Chambers (1977) data; [3]Adams *et al.* (1981); [4]Huether and Gummere (1982)

Table 4.4 Incidence rates in Jerusalem, per 1,000 births

Period of study	15–19	20–24	25–29	30–34	35–39	40–44	45+	Total 15–45+	Down's syndrome births
				Maternal age bands (years)					
1964–70	1.08	0.73	1.50	2.17	5.79	17.95	15.08	2.43	103

Sex ratios

There is some disagreement in reported sex ratios in Down's syndrome births. However, whilst some studies report ratios not significantly different to those found in the general population; i.e. a slight excess of males being born (e.g. 1.05:1 from Collmann and Stoller, 1962; 1.06:1 from Sutherland *et al.*, 1979), the majority report a greater excess of male births than would be found in the general population (e.g. 1.27:1 from Iselius and Lindsten, 1986).

Changes in incidence through time

Some consistency has previously been noted in underlying maternal age-specific incidence rates from different areas. It may also be reasonable to expect that age-specific conceptions rates have altered little through time (Stratford and Steele, 1985), although harsher living conditions in the distant past will have lead to fewer Down's syndrome pregnancies surviving to term. However, more recent age-specific incidence figures do not seem to show any clear increase with time.

Yet this must not be confused with changes in the *overall* incidence of Down's syndrome; i.e. the rate calculated from mothers of all ages grouped together. In Britain such changes do seem to have occurred; a reduction in overall incidence rates has been observed in the 1960s and 1970s (Fryers, 1984; Owens *et al.*, 1983; Richards, 1967), with some indication of a stabilization in the 1980s (McGrowther and Marshall, 1990; Stone *et al.*, 1989). In most situations, closer examination reveals that changes to the overall incidence rate may be explained by changes in the age distribution of child-bearing women. A number of studies have been published from other European countries reporting this sort of effect (Koulischer and Gillerot, 1980; Lindjö, 1975; Oster, 1956). American, Canadian and Australian studies also report a changing overall incidence rate that may be explained by a shifting distribution of child-bearing ages (Bell *et al.*, 1992; Collmann and Stoller, 1969; Goodwin and Huether, 1987; Lowry *et al.*, 1976; Rothman and Fabia, 1976).

There have been a few isolated smaller areas or groups where age-specific incidence rates seem to have changed. Iselius and Lindsten (1986) noted an increase in age-specific incidence to their youngest mothers and Koulischer and Gillerot (1980) noted an increase in all their five-year age groups between the ages of 20 and 35. However, a large increase in age-specific incidence in New York initially reported in the 1970s (Hook and Cross, 1981) was later found to have disappeared or have been a methodological artefact (Hook *et al.*, 1983).

Some seasonal or cyclical variations in incidence have been reported by a few studies (Collmann and Stoller, 1962, 1969; Harlap, 1974). Harlap (1974) had suggested infections may have a part to play in such peaks and troughs in incidence; however conclusive evidence for the existence of seasonal variations is not available.

Factors affecting incidence

These may be divided into factors that are basically environmental, or exogenous (e.g. prenatal diagnosis, radiation, etc.) and factors that are basically endogenous (e.g. maternal ageing).

Maternal age

The relationship between advanced maternal age and increased risk of Down's syndrome was suggested over a century ago (Fraser and Mitchell, 1876; Shuttleworth, 1909) and has been well demonstrated in all the incidence studies previously noted. The most likely explanation for this effect is that all the undeveloped eggs are present in the ovaries from birth; they therefore age with the woman. Hormonal changes later encourage maturation and they are then released on a monthly basis until menopause. The eggs of a 40-year-old are therefore much older than the eggs of a 20-year-old. This is not the case with sperms, which are produced on an on-going basis once puberty is reached. Hence no clear paternal age effect has been reported (Cross and Hook, 1987; Stene *et al.*, 1987). However, with increasing age, eggs seem to be more likely to undergo the process of non-disjunction, whereby an extra chromosome 21 is retained at the initial cell divisions of the developing embryo. This results in Down's syndrome. Further details of this process are described by Steele (1990) and Stratford and Steele (1989).

About a third of the incidence studies reviewed by Steele (1990) also showed a slightly increased incidence risk to teenage mothers. Low numbers of Down's syndrome births in this group make significant results difficult to obtain and pooling all 15–19 data may hide any effect occurring at the younger end of this age band. Whilst the explanation of this effect is obscure, it could be that there is a greater predisposition to non-disjunction in a female reproductive system that is still undergoing some development.

The large maternal age effect makes it important to consider changes in child-bearing age in the population. If there is a trend to older child bearing, the overall incidence of Down's syndrome will increase. Likewise, movement to younger child-bearing will decrease the overall incidence.

Prenatal diagnosis

Different prenatal diagnostic procedures and their possible effects on the population with Down's syndrome have been extensively discussed elsewhere (Steele, 1990, 1991, 1993); hence only a brief overview is presented here. Procedures for examining foetal cells have now been available for some time, through amniocentesis and chorionic villus sampling.

Amniocentesis involves the removal of a small sample of the amniotic fluid surrounding the foetus. Foetal cells are present in this fluid which can then be cultured and their chromosomes examined. Whilst this technique was used in the 1950s to determine foetal sex (Fuchs and Riis, 1956), it was not until the late 1960s that it was sufficiently refined to detect human chromosome disorders (Jacobson and Barter, 1967; Steele and Breg, 1966). It is now a well-established method of testing for Down's syndrome. However, there is a small risk of miscarriage (1–1.5 per cent; Tabor *et al.*, 1986), although this risk has been shown to decline as the operator's experience increases (MRC, 1977).

Whilst amniocentesis is a well-established prenatal diagnostic procedure, developments continue to be made, particularly with the speed of obtaining results (e.g. Bryndorf *et al.*, 1994; Pertl *et al.*, 1994). However, the uptake of amniocentesis has not been hugely successful in preventing Down' s syndrome births; a fact that is reflected in the fairly steady age-specific incidence rates that have been noted. This would seem to be due to the low uptake of amniocentesis among women over 35, where risk is high, combined with the lack of availability of the procedure to younger women. It must be remembered that the increased risk of Down's syndrome in older mothers is far outweighed by the much greater number of all births to younger mothers. Hence the majority of Down's syndrome births are to women under 35.

The low uptake of amniocentesis has provoked some discussion (Bell *et al.*, 1986; Ferguson-Smith, 1983; Kuliev *et al.*, 1985; Steele, 1993) and may be due to moral, cultural, economic and educational factors, as well as the attitudes of prospective parents and physicians towards Down's syndrome.

Retrospectively establishing the effect of prenatal diagnosis on the size of the population with Down's syndrome is fraught with difficulty, whilst proposing a possible future effect is much easier. Several studies have tried to quantify the effect of amniocentesis, but often the very real methodological difficulties raise doubts about their conclusions. For instance, whilst Lowry *et al.* (1976) found a reduction in the proportion of Down's syndrome births to older mothers following the introduction of amniocentesis, there was no appreciable change in incidence.

The reduction simply reflected a general reduction in all births to older mothers. Mulcahy (1983) did find a reduction in the overall incidence of Down's syndrome following amniocentesis introduction. He established that the incidence before the introduction of amniocentesis was not significantly different from the underlying incidence (i.e., including prenatally diagnosed cases) after its introduction. The prenatally diagnosed cases were then excluded to reveal a difference. However, Mulcahy did not account for the fact that 25 per cent of the prenatally diagnosed cases would not have been born anyway, due to natural spontaneous abortion (Hook, 1979, 1981). The extent of the effect of amniocentesis introduction was therefore exaggerated.

Noting such difficulties, yet accepting the need to consider the possible effect of amniocentesis, information from four different studies is presented in Table 4.5. The Danish situation followed considerable publicity and probably represents the maximum possible effect. Therefore it would realistically seem that the age-related method of recommending amniocentesis would only be likely to reduce the Down's syndrome population by about 10 per cent.

Chorionic villus sampling is a later development, described by Mohr in 1968 and used in China for sex determination in the mid-1970s (Anshan Department of Obstetrics and Gynaecology, 1975). In the early 1980s it started to be used for chromosome analysis. Chorionic villus sampling can be used between the eighth and eleventh week of pregnancy, hence giving parents an earlier opportunity to decide how to react to a positive diagnosis. It involves taking a villus sample from the developing placenta and examining the chromosomes from these cells. Like amniocentesis there is a small risk of miscarriage following the procedure. Whilst some authors (Leschot *et al.*, 1987) report a greater risk (between 2 per cent and 3 per cent) for chorionic villus sampling, it must be remembered that there is a higher risk of natural miscarriage in a ten-week pregnancy than a 16-week pregnancy. When this factor is accounted for some authors consider there to be little difference in risk (e.g. Canadian Collaborative CVS-Amniocentesis Clinical Trial Group, 1989; Jahoda *et al.*, 1985). However, there has been some suggestion

Table 4.5 Reported effects of the introduction of amniocentesis on Down's syndrome births to older women (from Steele, 1993)

Year	% Down's syndrome births to women > 35 years		Location of study	% Reduction in Down's syndrome population
	If no prenatal diagnosis	With prenatal diagnosis		
[1]1972–73	20.0	–	British Columbia	–
[2]1977–81	[a]24.6	[b]14.5	Western Australia	[c]10.8
[3]1979–80	[a]30.7	[b]16.0	Denmark	18.2
[4]1981–83	[a]31.5	[b]27.5	Queensland	[c]5.0

[a]Calculated as: {(no. DS births to > 35s)+(75% PND[d] cases)} × 100 / (total no. DS births)+(75% PND[d] cases)
[b]Calculated as: (no. DS births to > 35s) x 100 / (total no. DS births)
[c]As estimated by authors.
[1]Lowry *et al.* (1976); [2]Mulcahy (1983); [3]Mikkelsen *et al.* (1983); [4]Bell *et al.* (1986)

that the risk of limb defects is raised with early chorionic villus sampling (Mastroiacova and Botto, 1992).

Chorionic villus sampling is an alternative to amniocentesis, generally offered to the same age group. Hence Down's syndrome births should not undergo an additional significant reduction due to the introduction of this procedure.

Over the last ten years there have been considerable developments in maternal blood tests for Down's syndrome. However, it must be remembered that these tests to not give a definitive answer through analysis of foetal cells, but indicate the level of risk of having an affected pregnancy through establishing the levels of certain proteins in the mother's blood. If a high risk is established then a more definitive test such as amniocentesis may be recommended.

The advantage of this development is that younger women, where the majority of Down's syndrome births occur, may now access a prenatal screening procedure. Hence the possibility of significantly affecting the incidence of Down's syndrome would appear to be greatly increased. It therefore seems appropriate to briefly consider the developments in this area.

Low levels of maternal serum alpha-fetoprotein (MSAFP) and maternal serum unconjugated oestriol (uE_3) in pregnancy have been linked to increased risk of Down's syndrome (Cuckle *et al.*, 1984; Cuckle, *et al.*, 1988). Conversely, raised levels of human chorionic gonadotrophin (hCG) or free beta-human chorionic gonadotrophin (ßhCG) and maternal serum pregnancy specific $ß_1$-glycoprotein (SP-1) have also been linked to increased risk of Down's syndrome (Bartels and Lindemann, 1988; Bogart et al., 1987; Spencer *et al.*, 1992). Whilst the individual levels of these proteins do have some predictive power, their screening potential is much improved when considered together and in conjunction with maternal age (Wald *et al.*, 1988). Such testing is more accurate than age alone in establishing which pregnancies have a high risk of Down's syndrome. This high-risk group could include women of any age, but would exclude low-risk pregnancies in older women. Demand for amniocentesis need not be increased, as low-risk older women would not be referred; hence making more efficient use of existing cytogenetic facilities.

Using a risk of 1 in 250 or higher to define the 'high-risk' group, Wald *et al.* (1988) suggested that 60 per cent of affected pregnancies could be detected, reducing the number of Down's syndrome births in the UK from 900 to 350 per year. However, this presumes that all affected pregnancies would be terminated and that low-risk women over 35 years old would accept not being referred for amniocentesis.

With well under half the women entitled to amniocentesis undergoing the procedure, it remains to be seen how much the Down's syndrome population is reduced by the introduction of maternal blood tests. Whilst this is mere speculation, experience seems to indicate that the actual effect of new procedures on incidence is much less than the possible theoretical effect. Such speculation would seem to be held out by recent research indicating that by the end of 1992 only 56 per cent of health authorities or boards in England and Wales would be offering some form of combined blood tests 'in all or part' of their area (Wald *et al.*, 1992). This research also notes a 76 per cent uptake of blood tests in the areas it is offered. These figures would therefore suggest that the absolute maximum reduction in births would be around 25 per cent; i.e. from 900 to 670 per year. This would be between the two most optimistic estimates calculated by Nicholson and Alberman (1992). However, despite this Mutton *et al.* (1993) report a 38 per cent prenatal diagnosis rate for 1991, based on data obtained by the national Down syndrome cytogenetic register. Either the uptake of screening tests has exceeded expectations or there is a selectively lower rate of referral of postnatally diagnosed cases to this register. In either case, caution is needed in extrapolating the theoretical effects of such developments into clinical practice.

When considering the impact of prenatal diagnosis it would therefore seem particularly important to distinguish between what is *possible* and what is *probable*. It is also important to remember that incidence refers to *birth* rate. People already living in our community with Down's syndrome will still need services, and no procedures will realistically be able to reduce incidence to zero.

As the possibility of more frequent prenatal detection increases, so parents' opportunity to make choices increases. With this responsibility comes greater stress, so the need for support and a clear understanding of the information available becomes even more important. Research has now identified problems in this area; 80 per cent of a sample of obstetric consultants noted that patients found difficulty in understanding the function of the blood tests (Green, 1994). Prospective parents may perhaps confuse such screening tests with definitive diagnostic tests, such as amniocentesis, chorionic villus sampling or other blood tests for different conditions. This leads to a high anxiety level for the 'false positive' patients; hence several reports have noted the urgent need for both pre-test and post-test counselling (Dennis *et al.*, 1993; Green, 1994; Stratham and Green, 1993).

Clearly, no one would wish a child to be affected by Down's syndrome and developments in prenatal diagnosis enable parents to exercise much greater choice now. Yet we must be careful how information is presented. Some parents may wish to have tests irrespective of the risks of conceiving a child with Down's syndrome, and may wish to follow positive results with termination. Others may not want any tests, or may wish not to follow positive results by termination. We must also consider the effect that emphasis on prenatal testing may have on affecting parents' attitudes and decision-making. It may be that such an emphasis could be distressing to existing parents or people with Down's syndrome, or could encourage negative attitudes towards neighbours who happen to have Down's syndrome.

With this greater choice, it may be that individual parents' personal or ethical viewpoints become the major determining factors in incidence, rather than the limitations of medical technology. These views must be acknowledged and respected by professionals.

Other exogenous factors (radiation and use of oral contraceptives)

The possibility that radiation could affect the incidence of Down's syndrome was first considered around 1960 (Lunn, 1959; Uchida and Curtis, 1961). Stratford *et al.* (1988) review studies in this area, noting that four out of ten studies reported some significant increase in Down's syndrome births to maternal groups exposed to X-rays, although the dose required and the magnitude of the effect is much less clear. Massive doses of radiation, such as those encountered from atomic explosions, would seem to depress the incidence of Down's syndrome. Maternal physical and mental health together with greatly increased gene or chromosome damage in such a situation may well have increased miscarriage rate. Both these factors could select against any abnormal foetus. Overall, the effect of radiation through X-rays would seem to be much less than that of maternal age. Hence Stratford *et al.* (1988) note that their review does not justify anything other than the continued careful use of X-rays in its important role of medical diagnosis and therapy.

Use of the contraceptive pill has also been investigated by several authors. Unfortunately there is again no clear picture. For example, Lejeune and Prieur's (1978) sizeable study found an excess of pill users among 30 to 38-year-old mothers of Down's syndrome children, when compared to a control group of mothers who had babies with non-chromosomal problems. Janerich *et al.* (1976), however, actually found an insignificant deficiency of pill users among their Down's syndrome group. Harlap and Eldor (1980) found no difference in incidence of Down's syndrome between three groups ('all Jerusalem Perinatal Study', 'oral contraceptive failure' and 'other pill users'). However, the oral contraceptive failure group was younger than the other groups, suggesting that there should have been a lower incidence in this group than the others. Hence the lack of difference between groups could be taken as an indication that oral contraceptive failure was associated with increased incidence of Down's syndrome.

PREVALENCE OF DOWN'S SYNDROME

Mortality and its effect on prevalence

Clearly, anything that affects the birth rate of Down's syndrome (i.e. incidence) will have an effect on the rate that Down's syndrome occurs in the general population (i.e. prevalence). Yet prevalence can also be affected postnatally by the higher mortality rates present in the Down's syndrome population.

Unfortunately, closer examination of mortality studies becomes more complex, as methodology varies considerably. Some studies compare numbers of years survived in an age band by a Down's syndrome population with a matching general population (e.g. Thase, 1982). Others compare the number of deaths between the two populations by age band (e.g. Balarajan *et al.*, 1982). Other studies present non-comparative results that are independent of mortality rates in the general population. These studies give the probability of death or cumulative survival by age band in a Down's syndrome population (e.g. Baird and Sadovnick, 1987; Carter, 1958; Collmann and Stoller, 1963a; Masaki *et al.*, 1981).

The comparative studies have the advantage of reflecting mortality that is purely Down's syndrome specific; accounting for any mortality changes that apply to the whole population. However, results from non-comparative methods are more easily used in population projections; studies showing such cumulative survival are shown in Figure 4.1.

Whilst this type of cross-study comparison is a somewhat crude measure of temporal changes, as different studies may be subject to different effects due to

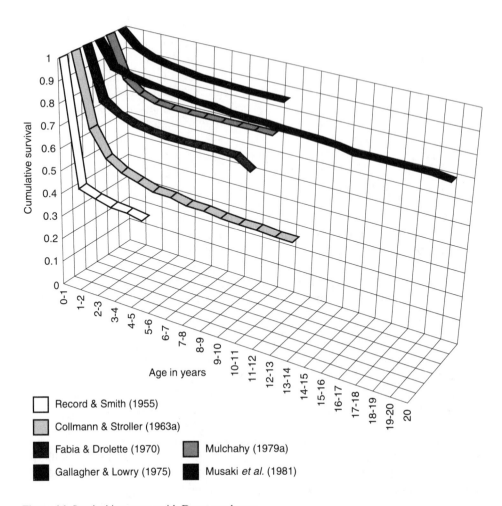

Figure 4.1 Survival in persons with Down syndrome

their individual population location or size, there seems little doubt that survival has increased greatly in recent years. This is also demonstrated within several individual studies (Carter, 1958; Collmann and Stoller, 1963a; Masaki *et al.*, 1981; McGrowther and Marshall, 1990). Certainly improved treatment of infection generally and respiratory disease specifically will have had an effect as these have been shown to be particular problems in Down's syndrome (Balarajan *et al.*, 1982). A degree of immune deficiency seems apparent (Sassaman, 1982; Zaremba, 1985). However, as congenital heart diseases is present in 30 to 45 per cent of babies born with Down's syndrome (Pueschel, 1987), survival should be considered with and without such heart problems (Figure 4.2).

The much worse survival rates for those with congenital heart disease is clear from Figure 4.2 and many other studies (e.g. Masaki *et al.*, 1981; McGrowther and Marshall, 1990; Mulcahy, 1979a). The greatest increase in risk of death is clearly

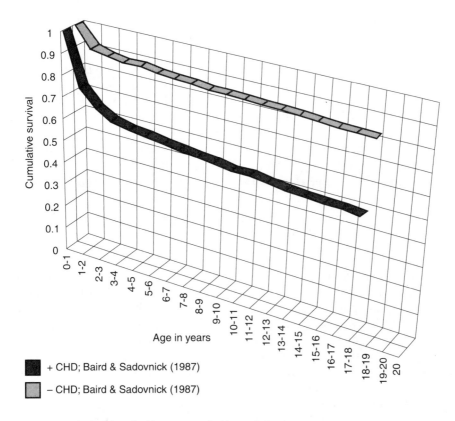

Figure 4.2 Survival with and without congenital heart defects

with younger children, particularly under the age of 4 or 5 years, although mortality may still be slightly raised beyond this age. Again making crude cross-study comparisons through time suggests that improved survival is particularly marked among the Down's syndrome population with congenital heart disease. However, when considering individual studies (Baird and Sadovnick, 1987; Masaki *et al.*, 1981) this improvement is less marked. It may be that cross-study comparisons exaggerate improvements in survival if recent studies have specifically better ascertainment of 'healthier' individuals with heart problems. Yet Baird and Sadovnick's (1987) results were unusual as they showed no improvement in survival from 1952 to 1981. However, there is a possibility that deaths may have been missed by presuming that individuals with Down's syndrome did not move out of the study area. This would raise survival figures, particularly in the more distant time periods and therefore mask improvements, although the effect would probably be small.

Improvements in survival are often explained by the development of more advanced medical techniques. However, this may be an over-simplification. It may be that attitudes towards intervention have changed markedly in recent years. Fryers (1986) considered attitudinal change to be an important factor affecting survival in Down's syndrome, although the greater attention given to all vulnerable babies, with or without Down's syndrome, has a part to play.

As the population with Down's syndrome becomes older, so neurological disorders become more relevant. Whilst they do not feature highly on tables of causes of death (Balarajan *et al.*, 1982) they have a significant effect on the care required. The Alzheimer-like condition and its relationship with Down's syndrome (Lott, 1982; Schweber, 1987; Scola, 1982) must become more important as survival improves.

In summary, a combination of more effective treatment of congenital heart disease, changes in attitudes and better ascertainment of healthy individuals is probably responsible for the increased survival seen among the Down's syndrome population.

Studies of prevalence

As has been noted, prevalence is the rate of occurrence of Down's syndrome in the general population. It therefore describes the frequency of Down's syndrome across the whole population age range, not just at birth. There are, of course, considerable problems in establishing accurate prevalence figures; Steele and Stratford (1995) note four main areas. First, defining the Down's syndrome population may not always be as easy as expected; chromosomal analysis would not be expected in most prevalence studies and several studies only include people whose IQ is below 50. This is further complicated by the fact that, from an aetiological point of view, the Down's syndrome population is made up of several different groups (trisomies, familial translocations and *de novo* translocations) which may respond to the same biological or environmental change in different ways.

Secondly, different methods of identifying individuals with Down's syndrome may be used:

1. Direct survey, where researchers personally identify all individuals with Down's syndrome. Whilst close monitoring of each individual identified is possible, it would be impractical for any other than a small, geographically discrete study.
2. Indirect survey, where social service and health authority registers are referred to. This has the advantage of being able to cover large geographical areas, with registers usually having a wide variety of sources in order to ensure reasonable ascertainment. However, there is obviously a great reliance on those responsible for administering the registers.
3. Application of birth incidence figures to general population births, followed by imposition of mortality rates.

Clearly, the method used can affect the result.

The third area is the accuracy of the general population data which will obviously affect prevalence figures, because prevalence is a rate. Figures from the Office of Population Censuses and Surveys are probably the most accurate for United Kingdom studies. Whilst the census years will provide the most reliable data, the degree of inaccuracy introduced by using intercensal estimates is probably small when compared to other problems, such as under-ascertainment.

Finally it is important to present prevalence data in standardized five-year age bands, to allow comparisons to be made. As will be seen later, total prevalence rates are fairly meaningless, particularly when an age breakdown of the study population is not provided.

Bearing these factors in mind, results from past British prevalence studies giving complete age-banded information for children and/or adults are presented in Table 4.6. As can be seen, the complete age-range studies have used the indirect survey methodology; reflecting its practicality in such situations. However, considerable differences between studies are apparent and warrant some consideration. Clearly, Penrose's (1949) early work would seem to have particularly low prevalence rates, probably due to under-ascertainment. However, Murdock's (1982) study would also seem to have unusually low rates beyond the age of 9 years. Murdock used general practitioners as his single source of information, whose records would not normally be computerized at that time. Hence questionnaires would have been completed from personal recall, introducing the possibility of error. Later studies use more than once source of information, hence probably reducing the degree of under-ascertainment.

More recently Steele (1990) used the indirect survey method to consult 30 health and social service registers that had multiple sources of information. A study population of over seven million people was covered, whose age distribution matched that of the general population fairly well. The youngest prevalence rates were refined to take account of obvious under-ascertainment, which was identified through comparing ratios of 0 to 4 prevalence to total prevalence for each register. It is therefore argued that these data represent reasonably accurate rates for the UK. Male prevalence rates were higher than female rates. Although an excess of male births may possibly explain this, the difference between male and female prevalence in the 0 to 4 age band was small and gradually increased up to the 15 to 19 age band, suggesting that the increased mortality among females may be a more fitting explanation. However, a gradual reduction of the difference between male and female mortality over the last 20 years would also explain this finding.

Prevalence generally seems to increase towards the 20- to 24-year-old group. As the Down's syndrome population has mortality rates in excess of the general population, a steady decrease in prevalence with increasing age may be expected. Such trends in prevalence are apparent from other studies in Table 4.6 but have usually been explained by age-specific under-ascertainment. However, bearing in mind the extensive nature of this study and the likelihood that ascertainment is good in school-aged children, age-specific under-ascertainment up to the age of 24 would seem an unlikely explanation. Further clarification of this point is provided in the second part of Steele's (1990) study (where prevalence was calculated using Method C – an incidence and mortality-based method).

Both Collmann and Stoller (1963b) and Steele (1990) have built up a theoretical Down's syndrome population by Method C. Incidence figures were applied to preceding years' general population births to give numbers of Down's syndrome births. These figures were then reduced by mortality rates to give the expected

Table 4.6 Prevalence of Down's syndrome in Britain per 10,000 general population

Age bands	[1]1948	[2]1861	[3]1969	[4]1981	[5]1983	[6,7]1987*(M/F)	[6,7]1987
0–4	0.7	6.0	4.8	7.9	6.3	7.5 (7.6/7.3)	9.3
5–9	3.1	10.2	14.2	6.0	7.1	7.2 (7.6/6.8)	8.2
10–14	4.6	7.0	10.0	4.8	6.9	7.3 (7.9/6.7)	8.7
15–19	3.0	13.1	10.4	4.1	8.6	7.3 (8.4/6.2)	8.7
20–24	3.1	8.5	9.0	(15–24)	9.1	8.8 (10.0/7.7)	8.9
25–29	1.8	(20–29)	6.8	4.2		7.9 (8.9/7.0)	10.0
30–34	(25–34)	4.9	7.5	(25–34)	5.0	6.8 (7.5/6.1)	
35–39	0.8	(30–39)	3.6	2.7	(25–44)	7.1 (7.9/6.2)	
40–44	(35–44)	2.2	4.5	(35–44)		7.0 (7.4/6.6)	
45–49		(40–49)	3.0			4.1 (4.4/3.9)	
50–54		1.5	0.7		2.0	3.5 (3.8/3.2)	
55–59	0.0	(50–59)	1.1	0.5	(45–64)	1.8 (2.0/1.5)	
60–64	(45+)	0.1	0.4	(45+)		0.9 (1.1/0.8)	
65+		(60+)	0.01		0.1	0.2 (0.2/0.3)	
Total	1.8	5.0	5.3	3.0	4.6	5.4 (6.1/4.7)	N/A
Study Method: (a)/(b)/(c)	(b) Indirect survey	(b) Indirect survey	(b) Indirect survey	(b) Indirect survey	(b) Indirect survey	(b) Indirect survey	(c) Appl[n] of incidence and mortality rates

[1]Penrose, (1949); [2]Ross, Innes and Kidd, (1967); [3]Midwinter (1972); [4]Murdock, (1982); [5]Stratford and Steels, (1985); [6]Steele, (1990); [7]Steele and Stratford (1995)
*(m/F) Male/Female prevalence shown in parenthesis

population at the time of the study. Collmann and Stoller (1963b) applied a total incidence figure to the general population births, hence did not account for any change in maternal age distribution. Mortality rates were also presumed to remain constant from the 5 to 9-year-old age band. This presented two possible areas for improvement in such studies. Hence the UK study (Steele, 1990; Steele and Stratford, 1995) applied age-specific incidence rates to corresponding numbers of births from 1956 onwards. Age-specific mortality rates could also be applied (from McGrowther and Marshall, 1990) up to the age of 29, to give numbers of people alive with Down's syndrome at a point in time. Such a theoretical Down's syndrome population could then be compared with the general population, by age band, at that time to provide the prevalence rates shown in Table 4.6.

Prevalence still increases from the 5 to 9 age band using this theoretical method. Clearly this increase cannot be due to differential ascertainment as the population has been calculated rather than counted. Collmann and Stoller (1963b), however, had noted a steady decrease in prevalence with age, using their total incidence rate. It would therefore seem that increases in prevalence with age are due to changes in the maternal age distribution of births rather than under-ascertainment. In other words, there was a greater proportion of births to older women among the mothers of the 25 to 29-year-old group than the mothers of the 5 to 9-year-old group.

Again, this strongly emphasizes the need to carefully consider the maternal-age effect and changing maternal-age distribution of all births when discussing the prevalence of Down's syndrome.

Geographical differences in prevalence

Geographical differences in occurrence of any condition will promote interest, particularly in questioning the existence of some underlying or environmental effect. In terms of birth incidence, Sheehan and Hillary (1983) provoked considerable interest by reporting a cluster of Down's syndrome infants born to mothers who attended an Irish boarding-school during an influenza outbreak, around the time of the Windscale Nuclear Power Station accident. However, total numbers were low (six) and it is difficult to draw any definitive conclusions.

On the other hand, high prevalence rates (i.e. rates of Down's syndrome in the general population) may be due to simple population movement. The existence of special communities for people with severe learning difficulties may draw a selective age group of people with Down's syndrome into an area. However, this type of effect was not apparent in the United Kingdom study although high prevalence rates were noted in some areas covered by this study. Raised prevalence was particularly noticeable in the Western Isles of Scotland and the Orkneys (Table 4.7), although numbers of persons with Down's syndrome were not particularly high (35 and 18 respectively).

However consultation with the Chief Medical Officer for the Orkney Health Board revealed that the average maternal age for Down's syndrome births was 40.6 years at that time; considerably more that the 31 years reported by the Office of Population Censuses and Surveys (1983). Therefore increased prevalence was probably due to this raised maternal age, although a genetic predisposition towards

Table 4.7 Prevalence of Down's syndrome in the Western Isles and Orkneys per 10,000 general population

Age band in years	Area of study	
	Western Isles	Orkneys
0–4	5.6	17.3
5–9	9.4	15.7
10–14	8.4	7.7
15–19	16.7	14.6
20–24	5.1	7.5
25–29	22.4	8.0
30–34	16.0	0.0
35–39	29.2	14.2
40–44	10.5	14.3
45–49	17.2	15.9
50–54	30.2	28.9
55–59	0.0	0.0
60–64	6.0	0.0
65+	0.0	0.0
Total	11.3	9.3

a reduced loss of affected foetuses has been suggested (Roberts *et al.*, 1991). Interestingly, the highest prevalence was in the 50 to 54-year-old age band, despite the effects of mortality. Although individual numbers are low, this could suggest a particularly high average child-bearing age in these areas during the early 1930s; a position not apparent in any other of the United Kingdom areas studied.

THE SIZE OF THE UK POPULATION WITH DOWN'S SYNDROME

Whilst changing incidence and prevalence may be important indicators of changing medical, biological or social factors, it must be remembered that the actual numbers and distribution of the population with Down's syndrome are most important statistics from a service provider's point of view. As both incidence and prevalence can change independently, they may be misleading indicators of the size of the Down's syndrome population.

The UK study identified around 3,800 individuals in a general population of just over 7 million. Applying age-specific prevalence values to total general population figures indicated that there were around 30,100 individuals in the UK with Down's syndrome at the time.

The age distribution of both general and Down's syndrome population is shown in Figure 4.3. Despite the issue of changing child-bearing age with time and its effect on the Down's syndrome population, the two distributions seem broadly

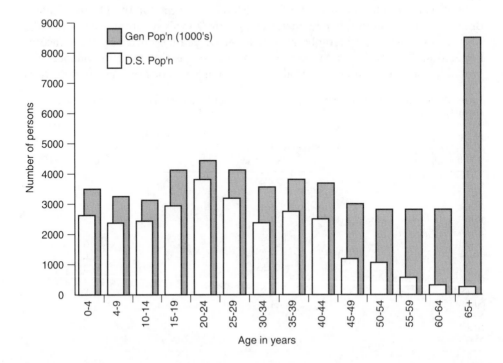

Figure 4.3 Age distribution of the UK Down syndrome and general populations

similar across the younger end of the spectrum. However, far fewer people with Down's syndrome were identified in the over 45-year-old bands, reflecting the group's much higher mortality at more advanced ages.

The distributions of both Down's syndrome and general populations are not as expected; i.e. the greatest numbers at the younger end, gradually declining due to mortality. Clearly this is due to variations in the numbers of births to different years. For example, there was a trough in births in the 1970s and early 1980s, producing a smaller population in the under 14-year old quinquennia than in many other older age bands, despite the fact that mortality will have decreased numbers in these age bands.

Future Down's syndrome populations

Projections based on total prevalence

Future Down's syndrome populations may be projected in several way. The simplest method of applying a total prevalence rate to total general population numbers has considerable drawbacks. No account is taken of changes in age distribution of the population or changing average maternal ages. Furthermore the information provided is of limited value to service providers as there is no breakdown by age of the population with Down's syndrome. However, accepting these problems, Stratford and Steele (1985) predicted a future *rise* in the numbers of people with Down's syndrome from around 26,000 in 1981 to 27,500 in 2021 applying a static 4.6/10,000 total prevalence rate to an increasing general population.

Projections based on age-specific prevalence

The need for greater precision provoked further work (Steele, 1990; Steele and Stratford, 1995). Age-specific prevalence rates were applied to projected future general populations by five-year age bands, to give the Down's syndrome population shown in Figure 4.4 (data sorted into broad age bands). A peak in the 1987 15 to 19-year-old population can be seen to move through the age bands with time, creating a peak in the 30 to 44-year-old population 15 years later, and a smaller peak in the 45 to 64-year-old population in 2016. Whilst the overall population remains fairly stable, such changes in age distribution can have important consequences for educational, medical and social services.

However, total numbers do give a different picture from the 1985 work, with the larger initial population of around 29,400 persons decreasing to 29,000 by 2021, and total prevalence falling from 5.31 to 4.89. Hence total prevalence is predicted to decrease by around 8 per cent with only a 1.4 per cent fall in numbers of persons with Down's syndrome. This effect is due to an increasing general population, particularly in the older age bands, where the numbers of persons with Down's syndrome are low. Again, the danger of planning services without considering actual numbers is emphasized.

A reduction in numbers of all births with a trend towards older child bearing

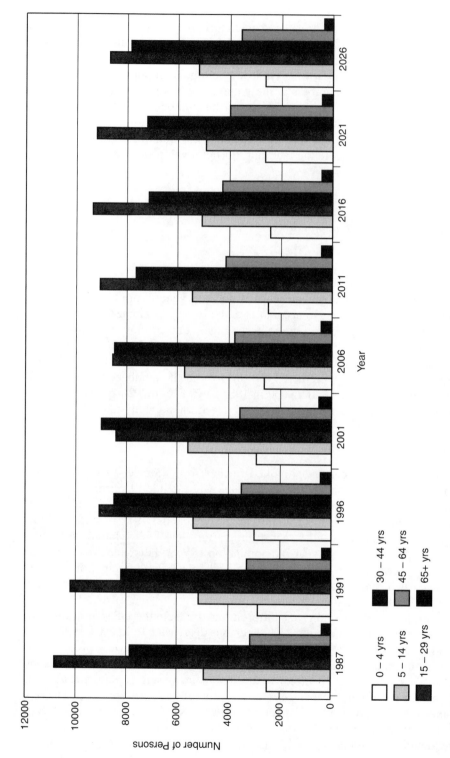

Figure 4.4 Future UK population with Down syndrome by age-band, projected from prevalence rates

could also cause such an effect. However, as Figure 4.4 is based on population prevalence rather than birth incidence data, this is not a reasonable explanation in this particular situation.

Projections based on incidence, mortality and general population projections

The third method of population projection in the UK study (Steele, 1990; Steele and Stratford, 1995) involves building up a theoretical population based on applying age-specific incidence figures to general population births from 1956 to 2026. The resultant Down's syndrome births were then reduced by mortality rates to provide a 0 to 29-year-old population over the period 1981 to 2026.

Nicholson and Alberman (1992) also used this system to predict numbers of birth from 1992 to 2000, but used mortality rates to follow this 0 to 9-year-old cohort through to 2060, rather than constructing a complete population in future years.

Such projections based on age-specific incidence have the advantage of accounting for changes in maternal age distribution over time, which could affect age-specific prevalence rates. For example, if a particularly high proportion of births is

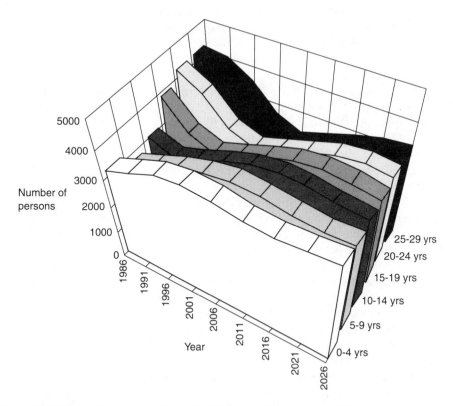

Figure 4.5 Down syndrome population, projected from incidence and mortality rates

expected from the 35+ maternal age group in year (X), prevalence in the 0 to 14 year age band could be high in year (X+5). However, it would not be reasonable to apply this 0 to 4 prevalence rate to other time periods unless they had a similar maternal age distribution. Using projections of births by maternal age and applying maternal age-specific incidence values helps to overcome this problem.

A population built up in this fashion is shown in Figure 4.5. A trough in numbers of 5 to 9-year-olds is apparent in 1986, which can be seen to move up the age bands with time. This is due to the low numbers of Down's syndrome births calculated for the late 1970s, resulting from a reduction in total number of general population births and a reduction in the proportion of these births to the 35+ age group.

It would clearly be tempting to attribute this type of population change (i.e. a reduction in number of Down's syndrome births, particularly among the 35+ age group) to the effect of the introduction of prenatal diagnosis. However, as these effects were noted whilst applying *static* maternal age-specific incidence rates, this could not be the case.

Comparing projections

Clearly using age-specific prevalence or incidence and mortality data provides a fuller and more accurate picture than simple projections using total prevalence rates. However, limitations still exist. Even when using this more sophisticated projection method, no account is taken of possible future changes in these incidence or mortality rates. Mortality is more than likely to reduce in the future, and the possibility that age-specific incidence may be further affected by prenatal diagnosis cannot be discounted.

However, given these problems it is interesting to compare the 0 to 29-year-old population projected from incidence and mortality rates (Figure 4.5) with that projected from prevalence data (Figure 4.6). Steele (1990) notes that the total numbers of persons in the two population projections are not significantly different, hence concluding that using incidence and mortality rates may be reasonably accurate. There is also a trough in numbers that moves up the age bands of both populations with time. However, Figures 4.5 and 4.6 do show some interesting differences. All age bands, with the exception of 20 to 24-year-olds, are smaller in the prevalence based population (Figure 4.6). Age-specific under-ascertainment seems an unlikely explanation, as there seems little reason to presume that 20 to 24-year-olds would be better known to services. Furthermore, Figure 4.6 shows increases in population groups as they move through time; a situation that is not possible. For example, in 2011 there is a much greater number of 20 to 24-year-olds that there were 15 to 19-year-olds years earlier. This is not so with Figure 4.5, where population groups slowly decline due to mortality.

Hence it would seem that changes in maternal age distribution that have been predicted for future years will change age-specific prevalence rates, introducing inaccuracies into projections based on prevalence.

However, age-specific prevalence around 1986 should be reasonably sound, being based on known numbers of persons at that time. Hence the 1986 data in Figure 4.6 may well be accurate. Yet the 1986 25 to 29-year-old population is much

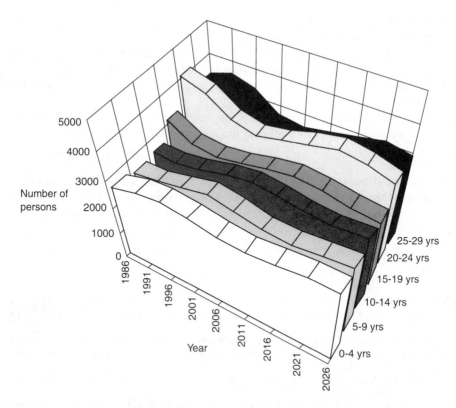

Figure 4.6 Down syndrome population, projected from prevalence data

lower than that projected from incidence and mortality rates. An explanation of this effect must therefore be based on inaccuracies introduced by using either static age-specific incidence rates or static mortality rates. One explanation could be an unusually high mortality rate being experienced by the youngest age band in the late 1950s, although this is speculation.

What does seem clear is that there are different problems associated with whichever projection method is used. For example, variations in mortality rates due to the effect of an epidemic would probably introduce inaccuracies into the most sophisticated methods of projection. Hence the use and comparison of different methodologies would give a less definitive, but probably more accurate, picture.

CONCLUSIONS

In conclusion, several points are worthy of emphasis:
- The maternal age effect on the incidence of Down's syndrome is probably the strongest and most important effect to consider when studying epidemiological issues.

- Other factors may affect incidence, although the magnitude of this effect is much less than maternal age.
- The effect of parental choice and viewpoint will become an increasingly important factor as the opportunities for prenatal diagnosis broaden.
- Population projections based on static rates should only be used for broad estimates.
- It is important to consider a combination of actual numbers, prevalence rates and incidence rates when making judgements on population activity.

Yet the most important conclusion is suggested at the start of this chapter:

- There will be a population with Down's syndrome in our communities for many years to come. These people will not only need the support of the educational, social and medical services, but are entitled to a valued role in society.

REFERENCES

Adams, M.M., Erikson, J.D., Layde, P.M. and Oakley G.P. (1981) Down's syndrome: Recent trend in the United States. *Journal of the American Medical Association*, **246,** pp. 758–60.

Anshan Department of Obstetrics and Gynaecology, (1975) Foetal sex prediction by chromatin of chorionic villi cells during early pregnancy. *China Medical Journal (England)*, **1,** pp. 177ff.

Baird, P.A. and Sadovnick, A.D. (1987) Life expectancy in Down syndrome. *Journal of Pediatrics*, **110,** pp. 849–54.

Balarajan, R., Donnan, S.P.B. and Adelstein, A.M. (1982) Mortality and cause of death in Down's syndrome. *Journal of Epidemiology and Community Health*, **36,** pp. 127–29.

Bartels, I. and Lindemann, A. (1988) Maternal levels of pregnancy-specific ß$_1$-glycoprotein (SP-1) are elevated in pregnancies affected by Down's syndrome. *Human Genetics*, **80,** pp. 46–48.

Bell, J., Hilden, J., Bowling, F., Pearns, J., Brownlea, A. and Martin, N. (1986) The impact of prenatal diagnosis on the occurrence of chromosome abnormalities. *Prenatal Diagnosis*, **6,** pp. 1–11.

Bell, J.A., Pears, J.H. and Norrie, M.A. (1992) The incidence of Down's syndrome in Queensland: a ten-year total population study, 1976–1985. Pre-publication copy of paper.

Bogart, M.H., Pandian, M.R. and Jones, O.W. (1987) Abnormal maternal serum chorionic gonadotrophin levels in pregnancies with fetal chromosome abnormalities. *Prenatal Diagnosis*, **7,** pp. 623–30.

Bryndorf, T., Sundberg, K., Christensen, B., Philip, J., Yokobata, K. and Gaiser, C. (1994) Early and rapid prenatal exclusion of Down's syndrome. *Lancet*, **342,** p. 802.

Canadian Collaborative CVS–Amniocentesis Clinical Trial Group, (1989) Multicentre randomised clinical trial of chorion villus sampling and amniocentesis. First report. *Lancet*, **2,** pp. 1–6.

Carter, C.O. (1958) A life-table for mongols with the causes of death. *Journal of Mental Deficiency Research*, **2,** pp. 64–74.

Carter, C.O. and MacCarthy, D. (1951) Incidence of mongolism and its diagnosis in the new-born. *British Journal of Social Medicine*, **5,** pp. 83–90.

Collmann, R.D. and Stoller, A. (1962) A survey of mongoloid births in Victoria, Australia, 1942–1957. *American Journal of Public Health*, **52,** pp. 813–29.

Collmann, R.D. and Stoller, A. (1963a) A life table for mongols in Victoria, Australia. *Journal of Mental Deficiency Research*, **7,** pp. 53–59.

Collmann, R.D. and Stoller, A. (1963b) Data on mongolism in Victoria, Australia: Prevalence and life expectation. *Journal of Mental Deficiency Research*, **7,** pp. 60–68.

Collmann, R.D. and Stoller, A. (1969) Shift of childbirth to younger mothers, and its effect on the incidence of mongolism in Victoria, Australia, 1939–1964. *Journal of Mental Deficiency Research*, **13,** pp. 13–19.

Cross, P.K. and Hook, E.B. (1987) An analysis of paternal age and 47, +21 in 35,000 new prenatal cytogenetic diagnosis data from the New York State Chromosome Registry: no significant effect. *Human Genetics*, **77,** pp. 307–13.

Cuckle, H.S., Wald, N.J., Barkai, G., Fuhrmann, W., Atland, K., Brambati, B., Knight, G., Palomaki, G., Haddon, J.E. and Canick, J. (1988) First trimester biochemical screening for Down's syndrome. *Lancet* **2,** pp. 851–52.

Cuckle, H.S., Wald, N.J. and Lindenbaum, R.H. (1984) Maternal serum alpha fetoprotein measurement: a screening test for Down's syndrome. *British Medical Journal*, **297,** p. 876.

Dennis, J., Sawtell, M. and Rutter, S. (1993) Counselling needed after screening for Down's syndrome. *British Medical Journal*, **307,** p. 1005.

Dioxiades, I. and Portius, W (1938) Zur atiologie des mongolismus inter besonderen beruck-sictigeung der sippenbefunde. *Z. Konst. Lehre*, **21,** p. 348.

Fabis, J. and Drolette, M. (1970) Life tables up to age 10 for mongols with and without congenital heart disease. *Journal of Mental Deficiency Research*, **14,** pp. 235–42.

Ferguson-Smith, M.A. (1983) Prenatal chromosome analysis and its impact on the birth incidence of chromosome disorders. *British Medical Bulletin*, **39,** pp. 355–64.

Fraser, J. and Mitchell, A. (1876) Kalmic idiocy: report on a case with autopsy, and notes of 62 cases. *Journal of Mental Science*, **22,** p. 169.

Fryers, T. (1984) *The Epidemiology of Severe Intellectual Impairment*, London: Academic Press.

Fryers, T. (1986) Survival in Down's syndrome. *Journal of Mental Deficiency Research*, **30,** pp. 101–10.

Fuchs, F. and Riis, P. (1956) Antenatal sex determination. *Nature*, **177,** p. 330.

Gallagher, R.P. and Lowry, R.B. (1975) Longevity in Down's syndrome in British Columbia. *Journal of Mental Deficiency Research*, **19,** pp. 157–63.

Goodwin, B.A. and Huether, C.A. (1987) Revised estimates and projections of Down syndrome births in the United States, and the effect of prenatal diagnosis utilisation, 1970–2002. *Prenatal Diagnosis*, **7,** pp. 261–71.

Green, J.M. (1994) Serum screening for Down's syndrome: experiences of obstetricians in England and Wales. *British Medical Journal*, **309,** pp. 769–72.

Harlap, S. (1973) Down's syndrome in West Jerusalem. *American Journal of Epidemiology*, **97,** pp. 225–32.

Harlap, S. (1974) A time-series analysis of the incidence of Down's syndrome in West Jerusalem. *American Journal of Epidemiology*, **99,** 210–17.

Harlap, S. and Eldor, J. (1980) Births following oral contraceptive failures, *Obstetrics and Gynecology*, **55,** pp. 447–52.

Hook, E.B. (1979) Spontaneous deaths of fetuses with chromosomal abnormalities diagnosed prenatally. *New England Journal of Medicine*, **229,** p. 1036–3.

Hook, E.B. (1981) Down syndrome. Frequency in human populations and factors pertinent to variation in rates. In F. De La Cruz and P.S. Gerald (eds), *Trisomy 21 (Down Syndrome) Research Perspectives*, pp. 3–67, Baltimore: University Park Press.

Hook, E.B. (1992) Prevalence, risks and recurrance. In D.J.H. Brock, C.H. Rodeck and M.A. Ferguson-Smith (eds), *Prenatal Diagnosis and Screening*, pp. 351–92, London: Churchill Livingstone.

Hook, E.B. and Chambers, G.M. (1977) Estimated rates of Down Syndrome in live births by one year maternal age intervals for mothers aged 20–49 in a New York State study: implications of the risk figures for genetic counseling and cost-benefit analysis of pre-natal diagnosis programs. In D. Bergsma and R.B. Lowry (eds), *Numerical Taxonomy of Birth Defects and Polygenic Disorders, Birth Defects: Original Article Series*, vol. 13, no. 3A, pp. 123–41.

Hook, E.B. and Cross, P.K. (1981) Temporal increase in the rate of Down syndrome live births to older mothers in New York State. *Journal of Medical Genetics*, **18**, pp. 29–30.

Hook, E.B., Cross, P.K. and Schreinemachers, D.M. (1983) Chromosome abnormality rates at amniocentesis and in live-born infants. *Journal of the American Medical Association*, **249**, pp. 2034–38.

Hook, E.B. and Fabia, J.J. (1978) Frequency of Down syndrome in livebirths by single-year maternal age interval: results of a Massachusetts study. *Teratology*, **17**, pp. 223–28.

Hook, E.B. and Lindsjö, A. (1978) Down syndrome in live births by single year maternal age interval in a Swedish study: comparison with results from a New York State study. *American Journal of Human Genetics*, **30**, pp. 19–27.

Huether, C.A. and Gummere, G.R. (1982) Influence of demographic factors on annual Down's syndrome births in Ohio, 1970–79, and the United States, 1920–79. *American Journal of Epidemiology*, **115**, pp. 846–60.

Iselius, L. and Lindsten, J. (1986) Changes in the incidence of Down syndrome in Sweden during 1968–1982. *Human Genetics*, **72**, pp. 133–39.

Jacobson, C.B. and Barter, R.H. (1967) Interuterine diagnosis and management of genetic defects. *American Journal of Obstetrics and Gynecology*, **99**, pp. 796–807.

Jahoda, M.G.J, Vosters, R.P.L., Sachs, E.S. and Galjaard, H. (1985) Safety of chorionic villus sampling. *Lancet*, **2**, pp. 941–42.

Janerich, D.T., Fink, E.M. and Keogh, M.D. (1976) Down's syndrome and oral contraceptive usage. *British Journal of Obstetrics and Gynaecology*, **83**, pp. 617–20.

Koulischer, L. and Gillerot, Y. (1980) Down's syndrome in Walonia (South Belgium), 1971–1978: cytogenetics and incidence. *Human Genetics*, **54**, pp. 243–50.

Kuliev, A., Model, B. and Galgaard, H. (1985) *Perspectives in Fetal Diagnosis of Congenital Disorders. Serono Symposium Review No. 8*, Rome: Serono.

Lejeune, J. and Prieur, M. (1978) Contraceptifs oraux et trisomie 21. Etude rétrospective de sept cent trente cas. *Annales de Genetique*, **22**, pp. 61–66.

Leschot, N.J., Wolf, H., Verjaal, M., Van Prooijen-Knegt, L.C., De Boer, E.G., Kanhai, H.H.H. and Christianens, G.C.M.L. (1987) Chorionic villi sampling: cytogenetic and clinical findings in 500 pregnancies. *British Medical Journal*, **295**, pp. 407–10.

Lindsjö, A. (1974) Down's syndrome in Sweden: an epidemiological study of a three-year material. *Acta Paediatrica Scandinavia*, **63**, pp. 571–76.

Lott, I.T (1982) Down's syndrome, ageing, and Alzheimer's disease : a clinical review. *Annals of the New York Academy of Sciences*, **396**, pp. 15–27.

Lowry, R.B., Jones, D.C., Renwick, D.H.G. and Trimble, B.K. (1976) Down syndrome in British Columbia, 1952–73: incidence and mean maternal age. *Teratology*, **14**, pp. 29–34.

Lunn, J.E. (1959) A survey of mongol children in Glasgow. *Scottish Medical Journal*, **4**, pp. 368–72.

McGrowther, C.W. and Marshall, B. (1990) Recent trends in incidence, morbidity and survival in Down's syndrome. *Journal of Mental Deficiency Research*, **34**, pp. 49–57.

Malpas, P. (1937) The incidence of human malformations and the significance of changes in the maternal environment in their causation. *Journal of Obstetrics and Gynaecology of the British Empire*, **44**, pp. 434–54.

Masaki, M., Higurashi, M., Iijima, K., Ishikawa, N., Tanaka, F., Fujii, T., Kuroki, Y., Matsui, I., Iinuma, K., Matsuo, N., Takeshita, K. and Hashimoto, S. (1981) Mortality and survival for Down's syndrome in Japan. *American Journal of Human Genetics*, **33**, pp. 629–39.

Mastroiacovo, P. and Botto, L.D. (1992 Safety of chorionic villus sampling. *Lancet*, **340**, p. 1034.

Midwinter, R.E. (1972) Mental subnormality in Bristol. *Journal of Mental Deficiency Research*, **16**, pp. 48–56.

Mikkelsen, M., Fischer, G., Hansen, J., Pilgaard, B. and Nielsen, J. (1983) The impact of legal termination of pregnancy and of prenatal diagnosis on the birth prevalence of Down syndrome in Denmark. *Annals of Human Genetics*, **47**, pp. 123–31.

Mohr, J. (1968) Foetal genetic diagnosis: development of techniques for early sampling of cells. *Acta Pathological et Micribiologica Scandinavia*, **73**, pp. 73–77.

MRC Working Party on Amniocentesis (1977) An assessment of the hazards of amnio-centesis. *British Journal of Obstetrics and Gynaecology*, **85:** Suppl 2, pp. 1–41.

Mulcahy, M.T. (1979a) Down's syndrome in Western Australia: mortality and survival. *Clinical Cytogenetics*, **16,** pp. 103–08.

Mulcahy, M.T. (1979b) Down's syndrome in Western Australia: cytogenetics and incidence. *Human Genetics*, **48,** pp. 67–72.

Mulcahy, M.T. (1983) The effect of prenatal diagnosis on the incidence of Down's syndrome in Western Australia. *Australian and New Zealand Journal of Obstetrics and Gynaecology*, **23,** pp. 197–98.

Murdock, J.C. (1982) A survey of Down's syndrome under general practitioner care in Scotland. *Journal of the Royal College of General Practitioners*, **32,** pp. 410–18.

Mutton, D.E., Ide, R., Alberman, E. and Bobrow, M. (1993) Analysis of national register of Down's syndrome in England and Wales: Trends in prenatal diagnosis. *British Medical Journal*, **306,** pp. 431–32.

Nicholson, A. and Alberman, E. (1992) Prediction of the number of Down's syndrome infants to be born in England and Wales up to the year 2000 and their likely survival rates. *Journal of Intellectual Disability Research*, **36,** pp. 505–17.

Office of Population Censuses and Surveys (1983) Down's syndrome. *Series MB3, No. 1: Congenital Malformation Statistics. Notifications 1971–80*, pp. 69–71. London: H.M.S.O.

Øster, J. (1956) The causes of mongolism. *Danish Medical Bullitin*, **3,** pp. 158–64.

Owens, J.R., Harris, F., Walker, S., McAllister, E. and West, L. (1983) The incidence of Down's syndrome over a 19-year period with special reference to maternal age. *Journal of Medical Genetics*, **20,** pp. 90–93.

Penrose, L.S (1949) The incidence of mongolism in the general population. *Journal of Mental Science*, **45,** p. 685.

Pertl, B., Yan, S.C., Sherlock, J., Davies, A.F., Mathew, C.G. and Adinolfi, M. (1994) Rapid molecular method for prenatal detection of Down's syndrome. *Lancet*, **343,** pp. 1197–98.

Pueschel, S.M. (1987) Maternal α-fetoprotein screening for Down's syndrome. *New England Journal of Medicine*, **317,** pp. 376–78

Rantakallio, P. and von Wendt, L. (1986) Mental retardation and subnormality in a birth cohort of 12,000 children in northern Finland. *American Journal of Mental Deficiency*, **90,** pp. 380–97.

Record, R.G. and Smith, A. (1955) Incidence, mortality, and sex distribution of monogoloid defectives. *British Journal of Preventive and Social Medicine*, **9,** pp. 10–15.

Richards, B.W. (1967) Mongolism: the effect of trends in age at childbirth on the incidence and chromosomal type. *Journal of Mental Subnormality*, **13,** pp. 3–13.

Roberts, D.F., Roberts, M.J. and Johnston, A.W. (1991) Genetic epidemiology of Down's syndrome in Shetland. *Human Genetics*, **87,** pp. 57–60.

Ross, H. S., Innes, G. and Kidd, C. (1967) Some observations on the prevalence of Down's syndrome. *Scottish Medical Journal*, **12,** pp. 260–63.

Rothman K.J. and Fabia J.J. (1976) Place and time aspects of the occurence of Down's syndrome. *American Journal of Epidemiology*, **103,** pp. 560–64.

Sassaman, E.A. (1982) Immunology. In F De La Cruz and P.S. Gerald (eds), *Trisomy 21 (Down Syndrome) Research Perspectives*, pp. 229–33. Baltimore, University Park Press.

Schweber, M. (1987) Interrelation of Alzheimer's disease and Down syndrome. In S.M. Pueschel and J. Rynders (eds), *Down Syndrome. Advances in Biomedicine and the Behavioural Sciences*, pp. 135–44. Cambridge MA: The Ware Press.

Scola, P.S. (1982) Neurology. In S.M Pueschel and J. Rynders (eds), *Down Syndrome. Advances in Biomedicine and the Behavioural Sciences*, pp. 219–25. Cambridge, MA: The Ware Press.

Sharav, T. (1985) High-risk population for Down's syndrome: Orthodox Jews in Jerusalem. *American Journal of Mental Deficiency*, **87,** pp. 559–61.

Sheehan, P.M.E. and Hillary, I.B. (1983) An unusual cluster of babies with Down's syndrome born to former pupils of an Irish boarding school. *British Medical Journal*, **287,** pp. 1428–29.

Shuttleworth, G. E. (1909) Mongolian imbecility. *British Medical Journal*, **2**, pp. 661–65.
Spencer, K., Coombs, E.J., Mallard, A.S. and Milford Ward, A. (1992) Free beta human chorionic gonadotrophin in Down's syndrome screening: a multicentre study of its role compared with other biochemical markers. *Annals of Clinical Biochemistry*, **29**, pp. 506–15.
Steele, J. (1990) Investigation into the incidence and prevalence of Downs syndrome. Unpublished PhD thesis, University of Nottingham.
Steele, J. (1991) Prenatal diagnosis and Down's syndrome. Part 1. A review of possible procedures. *Mental Handicap Research*, **4**, pp. 155–79.
Steele, J. (1993) Prenatal diagnosis and Down's syndrome. Part 2. Possible effects. *Mental Handicap Research*, **6**, pp. 56–69.
Steele, J. and Stratford, B. (1995) Present and future possibilities for the UK population with Down's syndrome. *American Journal on Mental Retardation*, **99**, pp. 664–82.
Steele, M W. and Breg, W R (1966) Chromosome analysis of human amniotic-fluid cells. *Lancet*, **1**, pp. 383–85.
Stene, E., Stene, J. and Sengel-Rutkowski, S. (1987) A re-analysis of the New York prenatal diagnosis data on Down's syndrome and paternal age effects. *Human Genetics*, **77**, pp. 299–302.
Stoller, A. and Collmann, R.D. (1965) Pattern of occurance of births in Victoria, Australia, producing Down's syndrome (mongolism) and congenital anomalies of the central nervous system: a 21-year prospective and retrospective study. *Medical Journal of Australia*, **1**, pp. 1–4.
Stone, D H., Rosenberg, K. and Womersley, J. (1989) Recent trends in the prevalence and secondary prevention of Down's syndrome. *Paediatric and Perinatal Epidemiology*, **3**, pp. 278–83.
Stratford, B. and Steele, J. (1985) Incidence and prevalence of Down's syndrome: a discussion and report. *Journal of Mental Deficiency Research*, **29**, pp. 95–107.
Stratford, B. and Steele, J. (1989) Appendix: the biological basis of Down's syndrome. In B. Stratford, *Down's Syndrome: Past, Present and Future*, pp. 156–79. London, Penguin.
Stratford, B., Steele, J. and Albertini, G. (1988) Down's syndrome and ionizing radiation. Possible effects of ionizing radiation on the incidence and prevalence of Down's syndrome. *Journal of Paediatric Neurosciences (Rome)*, **4**, pp. 129–43.
Stratham, H. and Green, J (1993) Serum screening for Down's syndrome: some women's experience. *British Medical Journal*, **307**, pp. 174–76.
Sutherland, G.R., Clisby, S.R., Bloor, G. and Carter, R.F. (1979) Down's syndrome in South Australia. *Medical Journal of Australia*, **2**, pp. 58–61.
Tabor, A., Philip, J., Madesen, J., Bang, J., Obel, E.B. and Norgaard-Pedersen, B. (1986) Randomised controlled trial of genetic amniocentesis in 4,606 low risk women. *Lancet*, **1**, pp. 1287–92.
Thase, M.E. (1982) Longevity and mortality in Down's syndrome. *Journal of Mental Deficiency Research*, **26**, pp. 177–92.
Uchida, I.A. and Curtis, E.J. (1961) A possible association between maternal radiation and mongolism. *Lancet*, **2**, pp. 848–50.
Wald, N.J, Cuckle, H.S., Densem, J.W., Nanchahal, K., Royston, P., Chard, T., Haddow, J.E., Knight, G.J., Palomaki. G.E. and Canick, J.A. (1988) Maternal serum screening for Down syndrome in early pregnancy. *British Medical Journal*, **297**, pp. 883–87.
Wald, N.J., Wald. K. and Smith, D. (1992) The extent of Down's syndrome screening in Britain in 1991. *Lancet*, **340**, p. 494.
Zaremba, J. (1985) Recent medical research. In D. Lane and B. Stratford (eds), *Current Approaches to Down's Syndrome*. London: Holt, Rinehart & Winston.

5 Medical Aspects

Jacek Zaremba

THE MOLECULAR GENETICS OF CHROMOSOME 21 AND DOWN SYNDROME

The entire complement of genes in man (the human genome) is composed of 23 different individual chromosomes in its haploid form, where there is one representative of each pair. Together, these chromosomes contain around 50 to 100 thousand genes.

During the last decade there has been steady but rapid progress in investigations into the molecular structure of chromosomes. This has been mainly due to the development and application of new molecular and cytogenetic techniques.

Progress has been made on several fronts, in cytogenetics the development of a high resolution banding technique[1] and *in situ* hybridization techniques[2] (ISH) have helped. Progress in molecular biology has made it possible to use restriction enzymes for cutting DNA into predictable pieces, to propagate the fragments of interest in microbial cells and to store them in the microbial hosts – that is to say, to establish the so-called recombinant DNA libraries. The fragments of known origin (belonging to the well-defined regions of particular chromosomes) may be used as probes for identification of different parts of chromosomes and genes. Polymerase chain reaction (PCR) – the way of amplifying target pieces of DNA into millions of copies – is a technique which has revolutionized molecular genetics. These and many other sophisticated methods have enabled hundreds of genes to be identified and their positions on different chromosomes established.

Moreover many genes have been sequenced, i.e. the ordered arrangements of nucleotides within them have been established. In fact, The Human Genome Project is a world-wide endeavour to map and sequence the entire human genome[3] – a goal which should be reached at the turn of the century.

Chromosome 21 gene map

In Down syndrome, there is a triple, rather than double, dose of chromosome 21 genes. However, not all genes located on chromosome 21 (Figure 5.1) are necessarily responsible for specific phenotypic features of Down syndrome when present in three, instead of two, copies. Some of them, like AML-1 oncogene, may be related to the considerably increased risk of acute myeloid leukaemia in Down

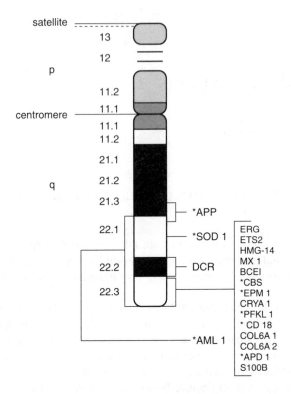

Figure 5.1 Gene map of chromosome 21; G (Giemsa) banding pattern of chromosome staining, p = short arm, q = long arm. As one can see most genes mapped so far to chromosome 21 are clustered within band q22.3.

For some genes the exact location is not known. In such cases a segment to which a gene has been assigned is provided, e.g. gene AML 1 has been assigned to the extensive region q22. DCR (Down syndrome chromosome region) is superimposed upon the gene map. Full names of the genes and respective disorders are provided in Table 1. (Terminology and location according to McKusick, 1994).

syndrome. Another, APP the gene of amyloid beta precursor protein, is relevant to one of the familial forms of Alzheimer disease and seems to be connected with presenile dementia, common in Down syndrome. A map of the genetic disorders which have been mapped to specific sites of chromosomes is called 'the morbid anatomy of human genome', and chromosome 21 has its own morbid anatomy.

Chromosome 21 phenotypic mapping of Down syndrome

It has been believed for a long time that the phenotypic features of Down syndrome is caused by trisomy 21, i.e. by the presence of the third, extra copy of chromosome 21. There are, however, rare cases of partial 21 trisomies – usually the unbalanced products of chromosomes rearrangements, such as unbalanced translocations in which only parts of the extra 21 chromosome are present. Niebuhr (1974) described a case in which Down syndrome phenotype seemed to be caused by only one extra

Table 5.1 Location symbols and disease phenotype (if known) of the 17 out of 30 known genes mapped to chromosome 21

Symbol	Location	Title	Disorder (if known)
*APP	21q21.3–q22.05	Amyloid beta (A4) precursor protein	Amyloidosis, cerebroarterial, Dutch type Alzheimer disease, one form
*SOD 1	21q21.1	Superoxide dismutase	Amyotrophic lateral sclerosis
*AML 1	21q22	AML-1 oncogene	Acute myeloid leukemia
ERG	21q22.3	Oncogene EGR	
ETS 2	21q22.3	Oncogene ETS-2	
HMG-14	21q22.3	Nonhistone chromosomal protein HMG-14	
MX 1	21q22.3	Myxovirus (influenza) resistance-1	
BCEI	21q22.3	Breast cancer estrogen-inducible segment	
*CBS	21q22.3	Cystathionine beta-synthase	Homocystinuria
*EPM 1	21q22.3	Epilepsy, progressive myoclonic 1	Epilepsy progressive myoclonic
CRYA 1	21q22.3	Crystallin, alpha polipeptide 1	
*PFKL	21q22.3	Phosphofrucktokinase, liver type	Hemolytic anemia
*CD 18	21q22.3	Integrin beta-2	Leucocyte adhesion deficiency
COL6A1	21q22.3	Collagen 6, alpha-1 polypeptide	
COL6A2	21q22.3	Collagen 6, alpha-2 polypeptide	
*APD 1	21q22.3	Autoimmune polyglandular disease, type 1	Autoimmune polyglandular disease, type 1
S100B	21122.3	S100 protein, beta polypeptide	

*Symbols of genes whose disease phenotypes are known. Terminology and location according to McKusick, 1994.

band, namely 21q22.2. Further investigations of rare cases with partial 21 trisomy seemed to provide some evidence that small regions, i.e. 21q22.1, q22.2, q22.3, were responsible for different characteristics, such as mental deficiency, heart anomaly, facial dysmorphic features. Cytogenetic studies of partial trisomics, i.e. rare cases in which only small parts of the extra 21 chromosome were present, have been reviewed by different authors (e.g. Epstein, 1986). In some patients only a proximal part of long arm of chromosome 21 was found (i.e. without a 'pathogenic segment') and the features of Down syndrome were not present (e.g. Park *et al.*, 1987).

Introduction of more sophisticated cytogenetic methods and molecular techniques enabled some authors to establish the location on chromosome 21 of DNA sequences from cell lines containing different parts of chromosome 21, i.e. to construct a physical map of chromosome 21. By correlating the presence of the phenotypic features of people with different extra portions of chromosome 21, a phenotypic map of Down syndrome could then be created. Such a map was published by Korenberg in 1991 and was based upon 17 cases of partial trisomies.

In a more recent paper (Delabar *et al.*, 1993) molecular mapping of 24 physical features of Down syndrome was presented. The authors 'analysed phenotypically and molecularly' ten patients with partial trisomy 21 and defined six minimal regions on chromosome 21 for 24 physical features of Down syndrome. Most of

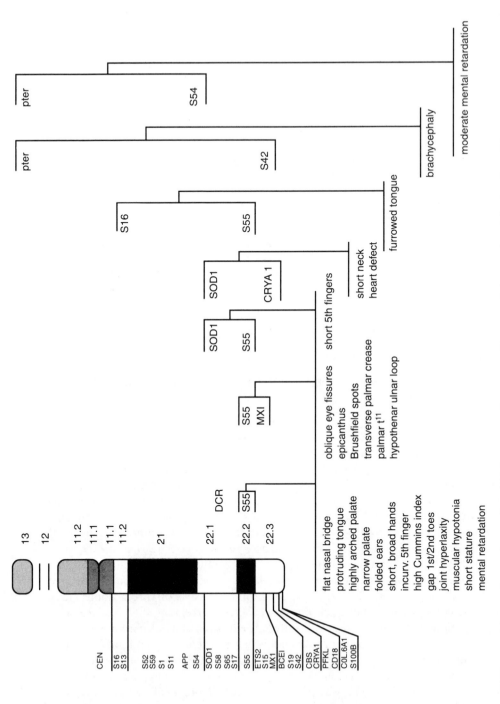

Figure 5.2 Down syndrome phenotypic mapping of 24 features on chromosome 21. For each feature the minimal region of chromosome 21 was defined as the region which was triplicated (trisomic) in every patient revealing that feature. The symbols and location of the applied probes are provided on the left (for full names see Table 5.1). Those marked with S1 to S65 represent so called anonymous probes (cloned fragments of DNA of unknown function/expression). Note that DCR (Down syndrome chromosomal region) corresponds to band q22.2 and to the fragment S55. Adapted from Delabar *et al.*, 1993).

the features could be correlated with the so-called Down syndrome chromosome region (DCR) corresponding to the cloned segment S55, which maps within the band 21q22.2 (Figure 5.2). The authors' conclusion is that Down syndrome 'may in large part result from the overdose of only one or a few genes within the DCR, or within the region between markers S55 and MX1', i.e. within sub-bands 21q22.2 and q22.3. No gene has yet been identified in DCR, and four genes belong to the S55-MX1 region, namely: oncogenes ERG, ETS2, nonhistone chromosomal protein HMG-14 and myxovirus resistance-l (MX1) (see Figure and Table 5.1).

Overdose (three instead of two copies) of these genes, or other genes yet to be discovered in this region may be a cause of Down syndrome. However, some important elements of the clinical picture seem to be 'situated' outside the critical region. If, for instance overdose of the amyloid beta precursor protein gene (APP) causes Alzheimer-like presenile dementia in Down syndrome, then the region 21q21.3–q22.05 to which the APP gene is mapped, should be also considered very important for the clinical picture of Down syndrome. Therefore the phenotypic maps, like those of Delabar *et al.* (1993) (Figure 5.2) and Korenberg (1991), although very interesting, should be interpreted with caution. Such caution is needed because of the well-known variability of the clinical picture in Down syndrome, as well as the scarcity of partial 21 trisomy patients, upon whom the phenotypic maps created so far have been based. However, despite these problems, molecular analysis of chromosome 21 is bringing a new understanding of Down syndrome. The major progress in molecular genetics[4] has led us to the verge of elucidating the etiopathogenesis of the most frequent cause of low-grade mental deficiency.

PREMATURE AGEING IN DOWN SYNDROME

The life span of individuals with Down's syndrome, although remarkably longer than in the past (Richards and Siddiqui, 1980; Steele, 1995), still remains much shorter than that of the general population. A broad discussion with survival rates and particular reference to congenital heart disease is presented elsewhere in this book (Steele, 1995). One of the other main reasons for raised mortality is the high incidence of neurological disorders. According to Øster *et al.* (1975) there is a fivefold increase in mortality due to senility and strokes. Richards and Siddiqui (1980) found that death rates of Down syndrome and other mentally retarded patients were virtually the same between age 10 and 30 years. Following the age of 30, however, there was a significant increase of mortality among individuals with Down syndrome.

As early as 1876 Fraser and Mitchell had described 'premature senility' in some of their patients with Down syndrome. After this, many authors began to report premature ageing, regression and dementia in Down syndrome. Some of the earlier reports are those of Bertrand and Koffas (1946), Jervis (1948), Rollin (1946), and more recent ones are those of Miniszek (1983), Ropper and Williams (1980) and Roeden and Zitman (1995).

In the study of Thase *et al.* (1982), 45 per cent of individuals with Down syndrome aged 45 or more had a full-blown syndrome of dementia, as compared to only 5 per cent in age-matched mentally retarded controls.

Histological changes associated with precocious ageing become apparent as early as in the thirties. In Down syndrome they were noticed for the first time by Struwe (1929), and later described by Bertrand and Koffas (1946), Jervis (1948) and many other investigators.

These changes are identical to those characteristic of presenile dementia known as Alzheimer's disease. This disease is a progressive dementia developing usually between the fiftieth and sixtieth years of life. Among its clinical signs are a progressive loss of memory, particularly for recent events, psychotic symptoms, disorientation, and confusion; in later stages of the disease focal neurological signs may be present. Aphasia (inability of expression by speech and/or understanding spoken or written language), dysarthria (disturbances of articulation) and apraxia (loss of ability to carry out purposeful movements but with an absence of paralysis) are not uncommon. Pathological examination usually reveals symmetrical atrophy of the cortex, most marked in the frontal lobes, and general shrinkage of the brain (Corsellis, 1976). Three main histological lesions present in the grey matter of the brain are: senile (or neuritic) plaques, neurofibrillary degeneration (also known as neurofibrillary tangles) and granulovascular degeneration of nerve cells.

In so far as the histology of the brain is concerned, Alzheimer's dementia and dementia in Down syndrome are difficult to distinguish. In fact the pathological changes characteristic of Alzheimer's disease appear to be present in most cases of Down syndrome over, the age of 35 years, although they do not always correlate with clinically demonstrable dementia (Ropper and Williams, 1980).

During the last ten years impressive progress has been made in research on the pathogenesis of both Alzheimer's disease and Down syndrome. It was found that beta-amyloid peptide is a major constituent of the neuritic plaques (Masters *et al.*, 1985b); it is also present in neurofibrillary tangles and in blood vessels (Masters *et al.*, 1985a). This peptide is derived from the amyloid beta-precursor protein (APP) (Kang *et al.*, 1987). The evidence has been accumulating that beta-amyloid plays a causal role in pathogenesis of Alzheimer's disease and Down syndrome. As has been noted earlier, the APP gene is located on chromosome 21q21 (Robakis *et al.*, 1987; Zabel *et. al.*, 1987) (see Figure 5.1 and Table 5.1) and mutations of this gene have also been detected in some families with Alzheimer's disease (Chartier-Harlin *et al.*, 1991, Goate *et al.*, 1991). It has been assumed that these mutations might interfere with the function of protease, which normally splits the APP protein. As a result APP, or strictly speaking its metabolite – beta-amyloid protein – is accumulating in the brain, forming the neuritic plaques (Hardy, 1992). It is interesting to note that another mutation of the same gene has been described, resulting amyloid depositions in blood vessels and causing cerebral haemorrhage (Levy *et al.*, 1990) (Figure 5.1 and Table 5.1; Amyloidosis, cerebroarterial Dutch type). This is a good example of pleiotropy, i.e. the quality of the gene to manifest itself in more than one way.

The presence of neuritic plaques in Down syndrome is due to the extra copy of chromosome 21 and to the resulting overdose of APP gene. The evidence for this was provided by Rumble *et al.* (1989) who found that the serum concentration of

APP was increased 1.5 fold in persons with Down syndrome when compared to controls and patients with Alzheimer's disease. The concentration of APP in the brain tissue was also higher than in controls and in a group of patients with Alzheimer's disease.

Experiments on animals have shown that depositions of beta-amyloid are neuro-toxic (Kowall *et al.*, 1992) – causing degenerative changes and loss of neurones – one of the principle features of Alzheimer's disease. There have been attempts at producing transgenic animals[5] expressing beta-amyloid deposits in the brain. The most recent ones were the most successful; transgenic mice were produced that express a high level of human mutant APP and reveal most pathologic brain lesions typical of Alzheimer's disease (Games *et al.*, 1995; LaFerla *et al.*, 1995). This is an excellent animal model of Alzheimer's disease, which may soon bring a real break-through in research on pathogenesis and possibly also therapy of Alzheimer's disease and of Down syndrome.

In fact the problem of Alzheimer's disease is further complicated, as it has been found that three other genes may be involved in pathogenesis of the disease. These are:

1. *The gene for Apolipoprotein E (ApoE)*, which is on chromosome 19q13.2. ApoE has its specific polymorphism determined by the presence of three alleles designated as varians E2, E3 and E4, the differences between them are determined by single substitutions of amino acids in the respective gene products, for instance E4 differs from E3 by substitution of one amino acid – Cysteine 112[6] with Arginine(Cys112→Arg). The polymorphism brings about six different phenotypes of ApoE: three heterozygotes – E3/E2, E4/E2, E4/E3 – and three homozygotes – E2/E2, E3/E3 and E4/E4. ApoE is known to have a special relevance to the nervous tissue, it plays an important part in the mobilization and redistribution of cholesterol in repair, growth and main-tenance of myeline[7] and neuronal membranes (Poirier *et al.*, 1993). ApoE has different properties, one of them being the ability to bind and to form complexes with beta-amyloid. Therefore it constitutes a component of neuritic plaques and neurofibrillary tangles. ApoE is an important suscebility factor in Alzheimer's disease and also in Down syndrome.

   Of the three variants, E2, E3 and E4, the latter was found to reveal special association with Alzheimer's disease (Poirier *et al.*, 1993; Van Duijn *et al.* 1994). The risk of a homozygote E4/E4 being affected by Alzheimer's disease was found to exceed 90 per cent; also heterozygotes with one gene E4 are at significantly increased risk (Scott, 1993). Observations of Pickering-Brown *et al.* 1994) indicate that the variant ApoE4 is also a risk factor in other diseases and, in particular, may contribute to the development of Alzheimer's pathology in Down syndrome. On the other hand, there are some data which suggest that Alzheimer's pathology develops more slowly in the presence of E2; this is also true for Down syndrome. In the material of Hardy *et al.* (1994), who analysed age at death of individuals with Down syndrome, the longest surviving person (76 years at death) was a homozygote E2/E2.

2. *The gene located on chromosome 14q24.3.* In some families, particularly those with early onset of Alzheimer's disease, the gene responsible was located on

chromosome 14q24.3 (Schellenberg *et al.*, 1992). Only very recently that gene was identified and called S182 (Sherrington *et al.*, 1995).

3   *The gene located on chromosome 1q31–42.*

The last gene to be identified and called STM2, – so far detected only in some Volga German families affected with Alzheimer's disease – is located on chromosome 1q31–42 (Levy-Lahad *et al.*, 1995).

The structure of the latter two genes, i.e. of S182 and STM_2 is similar, and so is the structure of their protein products. These products are known to be present in cell membranes, but their role remains yet to be discovered.

Thus Alzheimer's disease is a heterogeneous condition, and at least four genes may be involved in its causation – those located on chromosomes 21, 19, 14 and 1. The gene APP located on chromosome 21, if present in three instead of two copies, is most probably responsible for the Alzheimer's type pathology in Down's syndrome. The gene ApoE located on chromosome 19 may also be involved but in an indirect way; the allele E4 perhaps being responsible for a greater degree of Alzheimer's type pathology in Down's syndrome (Pickering-Brown *et al.*, 1994). On the other hand, this type of pathology may be induced more slowly in the presence of E2 variant, and in this way E2 may play a protective role, i.e. it may provide better prospects for longer survival in Down syndrome (Hardy *et al.*, 1994). Mutations in the remaining two genes, namely those present on chromosomes 14 and 1, do not seem to be involved in the pathology of Down's syndrome.

Alzheimer's pathology is not the only possible cause of dementia in Down's syndrome. Recently Collacott *et al.* (1994) observed a multi-infarct dementia in a 55-year-old woman with Down syndrome; she had evidence of cerebrovascular disease (multicerebral infarction is the second commonest cause of dementia in the general population). According to these authors, persons with Down syndrome may be more vulnerable to multi-infarct dementia than the rest of the population because of the higher prevalence of emboli (originating in them from congenital heart disease) and of hypercholesterolemia. Congenital heart disease is known to be common in Down syndrome, and hypercholesterolemia (high level of cholesterol in blood serum) may also be a feature, particularly as individuals with Down's syndrome often suffer of hypothyroidism which is associated with hypercholesterolemia. Collacott *et al.* (1994) point out that life expectancy in individuals with Down syndrome is increasing, so a greater number survive to an age when multi-infarct dementia is more prevalent.

However, it is also worth noting that a reversible pseudodementia, of differing aetiology, may resemble Alzheimer's disease. Thase (1982) describes such a situation in a 38-year-old person with Down syndrome and hypothyroidism.

In conclusion it is hoped that the developments made in these aspects of medical research will lead to a greater understanding of some of the problems faced by people with Down syndrome.

NOTES

1. Staining chromosomes in late prophase (called prometaphase), when they are not fully contracted; during metaphase only about 400 Giemsa bands may be seen in the whole human karyotype; in prometaphase they split into 850 or more sub-bands.
2. Application of probes (cloned pieces of natural or synthesized DNA of known origin or sequence), which are able to bind (hybridize) to the complementary segments of chromosomes. Normally DNA is double stranded; it must be converted to single strands with heat or alkali before hybridization can occur). Two single strands (of a chromosome and of a used probe) bind together (hybridize) only if their nucleotides' sequences are complementary. Probes for ISH must be labelled, for instance with fluorochrome, and a fluorescence microscope must be used for visualization of the results – hence the term FISH (fluorescence ISH).
3. Total DNA present in haploid set of 23 human chromosomes composed of about 3 million nucleotides. Only a small proportion of them – probably 3 per cent – constitutes so-called coding sequences, within the genes, which are transcribed into messenger RNA and translated into proteins (the gene products).
4. For readers who would like to be better acquainted with some problems and approaches of molecular biology the author of this chapter recommends the book of K. Davies and A. Read: *Molecular Basis of Inherited Diseases*, (1992) Oxford, New York, Tokyo: Oxford University Press, and a series of articles on molecular medicine by N. Rosenthal published recently in the *New England Journal of Medicine*, (1994) **331**, 39–41, 315–17, 599–600.
5. By inserting a segment of DNA of one species into the genome of other species, e.g. inserting a mutated human gene of APP into the genome of a mouse.
6. Amino acid located on one hundred and twelfth position in the polipeptide protein chain.
7. White substance composed of lipids and protein forming a sheath around certain nerve fibres (myelinated nerve fibres).

REFERENCES

Bertrand, I. and Koffas, D. (1946). Case d'idiotie mongolienne adulte avec nombreuses plaques seniles et concretions calcaires pallidales. *Revue Neurologique* **78**, 338–45.
Chartier-Harlin, M., Crawford, F., Houlden, H. and Warren, A. (1991). Early-onset Alzheimer's disease caused by mutations at codon 717 of the ß-amyloid precursor protein gene. *Nature*, **353**, 844–6.
Collacott, R.A., Cooper, S-A. and Ismail, I.A. (1994). Multi-infarct dementia in Down's syndrome. *Journal of Intellectual Disability Research*, **38**, 203–208.
Corsellis, J.A.N. (1976). Ageing and the dementias. In Blackwood, W. and Corsellis, J.A.N. (eds), *Greenfield's Neuropathology*, 3rd edn, pp. 796–817. London: Edward Arnold.
Delabar, J.M., Theophile, D., Rahmani, Z., Chettouh, Z., Blouin, J.L., Prieur, M., Noel, B. and Sinet, P.M. (1993). Molecular mapping of twenty-four features of Down syndrome on chromosome 21. *European Journal of Human Genetics*, **1**, 114–24.
Epstein, C.J. (1986). *Consequences of chromosome imbalance: principles. mechanisms and models*. New York: Cambridge University Press.
Fraser, J. and Mitchell, A. (1876). Kalmuc idiocy: report of a case with autopsy; with notes on sixty-two cases. *Journal of Mental Science*, **22**, 161, 169–79.
Games, D., Adams, D., Allessandrini, R. *et al.* (1995). Alzheimer type neuropathology in transgenic mice overexpressing V717F ß-amyloid precursor protein *Nature*, **373**, 523–7.
Goate, A., Chartier-Harlin, M.-C., Mullan, M. *et al.* (1991). Segregation of a missence mutation in the amyloid precursor protein gene with familial Alzheimer's disease. *Nature*, **349**, 704–6.
Hardy, J. (1992). Framing ß-amyloid. *Nature Genetics*, **1**, 233–4.

Hardy, J., Crook, R., Perry, R., Raghavan, R. and Roberts, G. (1994). ApoE genotype and Down's syndrome. *Lancet*, **343**, 979–80.

Jervis, G.A. (1948). Early senile dementias in mongoloid idiocy. *American Journal of Psychiatry*, **105**, 102–106.

Kang, J., Lemaine, H.-G., Unterback, A. *et al.* (1987) The precursor of Alzheimer's disease amyloid A4 protein resembles a cell-surface receptor. *Nature*, **325**, 733–6.

Korenberg, J.R. (1990). Molecular mapping of the Down syndrome phenotype. In Patterson, D. and Epstein, C.J. (eds), Molecular genetics of chromosome 21 and Down syndrome. *Progress in Clinical and Biological Research*, **360**, 105–15. New York: Wiley-Liss.

Korenberg, J.R. (1991). Down syndrome phenotypic mapping. In Epstein, C.J. (ed), The morphogenesis of Down syndrome. 43–52. *Progress in Clinical and Biological Research*, **373**, 43–52. New York: Wiley-Liss.

Kowall, N., McKee, A., Yankner, B. and Beal, F. (1992). In vivo neurotoxicity of ß-amyloid (ß1–40) and the ß (25–35) fragment. *Neurobiology of Aging*, **13**, 537–42.

LaFerla, F.M., Tincle, B.T., Bieberich, C.J., Hudenschild, C.C. and Jay, G. (1995). The Alzheimer's A ß peptide induces neurodegeneration and apoptotic cell death in transgenic mice. *Nature Genetics*, **9**, 21–30.

Levy, E., Carman, M., Fernandez-Madrid. I. *et al.* (1990). Mutation of the Alzheimer's disease amyloid gene in hereditary cerebral hemorrhage, Dutch type. *Science*, **248**, 1124–6.

Levy-Lahad, E., Wasco, W., Poorkaj, P. *et al.* (1995). Candidate gene for the chromosome 1 familial Alzheimer's disease locus. *Science*, **269**, 973–7.

McKusick, V.A. (1994). *Mendelian Inheritance in Man: Catalogs of Autosomal Dominant Autosomal Recessive. and X-linked Phenotypes* (11th edn). Baltimore: Johns Hopkins University Press.

Masters, C.L., Multhaup, G., Simms, G., Pottgiesser, J., Martins, R.N. and Beyreuther, K. (1985a) Neuronal origin of cerebral amyloid: neurofibrillary tangles of Alzheimer's disease contain the same protein as the amyloid of plaques cores and blood vessels. *EMBO Journal*, **4**, 2757–63.

Masters, C.L., Simms, G., Weinman, N.A., Multhaup, G., McDonald, B.L., and Beyreuther, K. (1985b) Amyloid plaque core protein in Alzheimer disease and Down syndrome. *Proceeding of the National Academy of Sciences of the United States of America*, **82**, 4245–9.

Miniszek, N.A. (1983). Development of Alzheimer disease in Down syndrome individuals. *American Journal of Mental Deficiency*, **87**, 377–85.

Niebuhr, E. (1974). Down's syndrome: the possibility of a pathogenic segment on chromosome No 21. *Humangenetik*, **21**, 99–101.

Øster, J., Mikkelsen, M. and Nielsen, A. (1975). Mortality and life-table in Down's syndrome. *Acta Paediatrica Scandinavica*, **64**, 322–6.

Park, J.P., Wurster-Hill, D., Andrews, P.A., Cooley, W.C. and Graham, J.M. (1987). Free proximal trisomy 21 without the Down syndrome phenotype. *Clinical Genetics*, **32**, 342–8.

Pickering-Brown, S.M., Mann, D.M.A., Bourke, J.P., Roberts, D.A., Balderson, D., Burns, A., Byrne, J. and Owen, F. (1994). Apolipoprotein E_4 and Alzheimer's disease pathology in Levy body disease and in other ß-amyloid-forming diseases. *Lancet*, **343**, 1155.

Poirier, J., Davignon, J., Bouthillier, D., Kogan, S., Bertrand, P. and Gauthier, S. (1993). Apolipoprotein E polymorphism and Alzheimer's disease. *Lancet*, **342**, 697–9.

Richards, B.W. and Siddiqui, A.Q. (1980). Age and mortality trends in residents of an institution for the mentally handicapped. *Journal of Mental Deficiency Research*, **24**, 99–105.

Robakis, N.K., Wisniewski, H.M., Jenkins, E.C. *et al.* (1987). Chromosome 21q21 sublocalization of gene encoding ß -amyloid peptide in cerebral vessels and neuritic (senile) plaques of people with Alzheimer's disease and Down's syndrome. *Lancet*, **1**, 384–5.

Roeden, J.M. and Zitman, F.G. (1995). Ageing in adults with Down's syndrome in institutionally based and community-based residences. *Journal of Intellectual Disability Research*, **39**, 399–407.

Rollin, H.R. (1946). Personality in mongolism with special reference to the incidence of catatonic psychosis. *American Journal of Mental Deficiency*, **51**, 219–37.

Ropper, A.H. and Williams, R.S. (1980). Relationship between plaques, tangles, and dementia in Down syndrome. *Neurology*, **30**, 639–44.

Rumble, B., Retallack, R., Hilbich, C. *et al.* (1989). Amyloid A4 protein and its precursor in Down's syndrome and Alzheimer's disease. *New England Journal of Medicine*, **320**, 1446–52.

Schellenberg, G., Bird, T., Wijsman, E. *et al.* (1992). Genetic linkage evidence for a familial Alzheimer's disease locus on chromosome 14. *Science*, **258**, 668–71.

Sherrington, R., Rogaev, E.J., Liang, Y. *et al.* (1995). Cloning of a gene bearing missense mutations in early-onset familial Alzheimer's disease. *Nature*, 375, 754–60.

Scott, J. (1993). Apolipoprotein E and Alzheimer's disease. *Lancet*, **342**, 696.

Steele, J. (1996). Epidemiology. In B. Stratford and P. Gunn (Eds) *New Approaches to Down's Syndrome*. London: Cassell.

Struwe, F. (1929). Histopathologische Untersuchungen uber Entstehung und Wesen der senilen Plaques. *Zentralblatt für die gesamte Neurologie und Psychiatrie*, **122**, 291–307.

Thase, M.E. (1982). Reversible dementia in Down's syndrome. *Journal of Mental Deficiency Research*, **26**, 111–13.

Thase, M.E., Liss, L., Smeltzer, D. and Maloon, J. (1982). Clinical evaluation of dementia in Down's syndrome: a preliminary report. *Journal of Mental Deficiency Research*, **26**, 239–44.

Van Duijn, C.M., de Knijff, P., Crusts, M., Wehnert, A., Havekes, L.M., Hofman, A. and Van Broeckhoven, C. (1994). Apolipoprotein E E4 allele in a population-based study of early onset Alzheimer's disease. *Nature Genetics*, **7**, 74–8.

Zabel, B.U., Salbaum, J.M., Multhaup, G., Masters, C.L., Bohl, J. and Beyreuther, K. (1987) Sublocalization of the gene for the precursor of Alzheimer's disease amyloid A_4 protein on chromosome 21. *Cytogenetics and Cell Genetics*, **46**, 725–6.

6 The Heart

K.A. Hallidie-Smith

There have been dramatic changes in both the approach to and practical management of congenital heart disease in Down syndrome over the past decade. First, there has been a fundamental change in attitude towards the overall management of the Down syndrome child with multiple handicaps, in whom a major congenital heart defect unfortunately occurs so commonly. It is now accepted that a policy of endeavour to diagnose and effectively treat such defects may not only save life but also substantially improve the quality of life. Such efforts also help to ease the burden of management on parents of these multiply handicapped infants and children. Secondly, because of advances in surgical techniques and postoperative management, particularly in the infant age group, there is now the practical possibility of achieving successful corrective surgery of major congenital heart disease before the end of the first year of life. Thirdly, with the development of sophisticated two-dimensional ultrasound and Doppler techniques, it has become possible to make early and accurate non-invasive diagnosis of congenital heart defects.

The evolution and implications of these major advances is here discussed and attention drawn to additional ongoing areas of cardiological interest in Down syndrome.

INCIDENCE OF CARDIAC DEFECTS

The high incidence of congenital heart disease in Down syndrome of approximately 1 in 2 live births contrasts with the incidence of 1:120 to 1:140 live births in the general population. There is no convincing evidence that the incidence of congenital heart disease in Down syndrome is changing; however, an interesting report (Khoury and Erickson, 1992) demonstrates an incidence of 20 per cent in the early 1970s, whereas the incidence was 50 per cent in the late 1980s in Down syndrome infants born in the same identically assessed population area. The seemingly significantly increased incidence may, in fact, reflect improved diagnostic skills coincident with more aggressive management policies dependent on early diagnosis.

Major cardiac defects predominate in Down syndrome compared with the general population. While ventricular septal defects occur commonly in both groups, the majority are large in Down syndrome and small in normal children.

Patent ductus arteriosus, tetralogy of Fallot and multiple defects are shared by both groups, and secundum atrial septal defects account for approximately 10 per cent of all defects in both Down syndrome and normal children. However, whereas atrioventricular canal represents only approximately 2.8 per cent of cardiac defects in the normal population (Wilson *et al.*, 1993), it is the most common cardiac defect in Down syndrome, accounting for up to 50 per cent of all single defects, and may also be combined with tetralogy of Fallot. By contrast, it has long been recognized that other cardiac defects, common in the general population, are rare in those with Down syndrome. Such defects include aortic stenosis, coarctation of the aorta, muscular ventricular septal defect, isolated pulmonary valve stenosis and transposition of the great arteries (Lo *et al.*, 1989; Marino, 1993; Pinto *et al.*, 1989). Pinto *et al.* found that female Down syndrome patients have a significantly higher incidence of congenital heart disease than males in comparison with the normal population. Atrioventricular septal defect was the dominant lesion in the Down syndrome patients studied but there were no instances of the defects normally predominating in males, specifically, aortic stenosis, coarctation of the aorta and transposition of the great arteries. They suggest that the molecular determinants of Down syndrome positively influence the preponderance of atrioventricular canal in females while acting negatively concerning those congenital heart defects usually showing male prevalence. Marino favoured further investigation into the role of adhesiveness of trisomy 21 cells and into neural crest anomalies as a way forward in the understanding of the presentation and distribution of these assumed genetically determined cardiac defects in Down syndrome.

A great deal of interest and scientific activity has been focused on the region of the atrioventricular canal involving the development of the endocardial cushions. In the normal development of the heart there is fusion of the endocardial cushions following proliferation and migration of cushion tissue cells along an extracellular matrix, resulting in the complete division of the atrioventricular canal (Duff *et al.*, 1990). In Down syndrome the endocardial cushion area may show poorly differentiated and immature valves (Okado, 1991). Earlier studies of defect-free Down syndrome hearts showed enlargement of the membranous septum (Rosenquist *et al.*, 1974) and an absence of commissure between anterior and medial leaflets of the tricuspid valve (Rosenquist *et al.*, 1975). As the predominant cardiac defect in Down syndrome, it seems reasonable to hypothesize that the increased dosage of chromosome 21 located gene may be causally related to the atrioventricular canal defects. However, two recent careful studies of autosomal dominant atrioventricular canal defects excluded chromosome 21 as the genetic location for these defects in the families (Wilson *et al.*, 1993; Cousineau *et al.*, 1994) and would suggest that a different gene is involved in atrioventricular canal formation. Nevertheless, it is by no means clear that the situation pertaining in autosomal dominant atrioventricular canal defect families and that in Down syndrome are analogous and, given the complexity of atrioventricular canal embryology, it is certain that many genes contribute to its development in a complex, multifactorial manner, including, probably, some genes on chromosome 21.

Collagen type VI is known to be expressed in vascular endothelium and the heart and may play a role in the fusion of septa. Davies *et al.* (1993) suggested that genetic

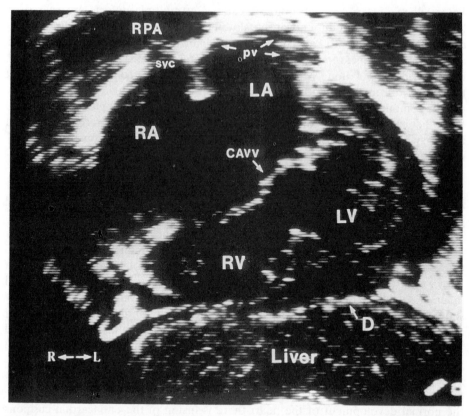

Figure 6.1 Two-dimensional echocardiogram (4-chambered view) of Down syndrome infant with complete atrioventricular canal. The gap between the two atria demonstrates the large primum atrial septal defect. The gap between the two ventricles demonstrates the large ventricular septal defect. The echocardiogram in this view is comparatively easy to obtain and clearly portrays the exact cardiac anatomy.

LA = left atrium   RPA = right pulmonary artery
RA = right atrium   SVC = superior vena cava
LV = left ventricle   pv = pulmonary vein
RV = right ventricle   D = diaphragm
CAVV = common atrioventricular valve

variation in the COL6A1 gene region may contribute to the pathogenesis of congenital heart defects in Down syndrome. Kurnit *et al.* (1985) drew attention to the increased adhesiveness of endocardial cushion cells in trisomy 21 and suggested that this results in the stunted growth and lack of fusion of the endocardial cushions. However, it is generally felt that it is unlikely that this offers the entire explanation. Ferencz *et al.* (1989) suggested that endocardial cushion defects occurring with or without Down syndrome in three families might imply inheritance of a defect which affects cellular migration. Miyabara *et al.* (1989) related migration of neural crest cells and extracellular matrix to endocardial cushion defects in trisomy 21, associated with loose nuchal skin.

There is much active and complex ongoing scientific work in this vital area concerning the selective presentation of cardiac defects in Down syndrome. It seems credible that geneticists will effectively solve the outstanding questions in the foreseeable future.

DIAGNOSIS

Paediatric cardiology is a very specialized subject which is comparatively rarely taught in depth to medical students and paediatricians in training. Neonatal discharge examinations are usually carried out by busy junior paediatric staff and it is not surprising that a major cardiac defect in an acyanotic newborn can be frequently missed, mainly because of an absence of heart murmur. Thus, many Down syndrome infants over past years have had delayed recognition of a major cardiac defect which was, in fact, adding considerably to their difficulties of feeding and growth and challenging their parents with the unappreciated extra problem.

Fortunately, two-dimensional echocardiogram and Doppler studies can now give precise and accurate cardiological detail and are available on an outpatient

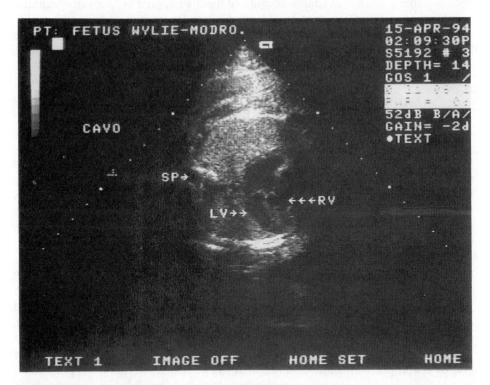

Figure 6.2 Foetal echocardiogram recorded at 23 weeks gestation. There is a common atrioventricular orifice and valve. The atria communicate through a large atrial septal defect. The ventricles communicate through a large ventricular septal defect.

RV = right ventricle; LV = left ventricle; SP = spine; CAVO = common atrioventricular orifice.

basis at specialized paediatric cardiac centres. Since major congenital heart defects are so common in Down syndrome and since it is important that the parents and professional staff concerned know at an early stage whether or not a cardiac defect is present so that a management plan can be agreed, it is essential that the cardiac status of every newborn Down syndrome infant should be known as soon as possible. Although the specificity of an expert clinical examination with chest X-ray and electrocardiogram is acknowledged, this is not always immediately available and the undoubted valuable diagnostic accuracy given by a good two-dimensional echocardiogram cannot be overestimated (Hoe *et al.*, 1990; Rosenberg *et al.*, 1994; Tubman *et al.*, 1991). Because of the anatomical accuracy of two-dimensional echocardiography and the helpful physiological information given by Doppler studies, the indications for diagnostic cardiac catheterizations in Down syndrome as in other infants have greatly diminished.

We should make it current policy that a routine cardiac echocardiogram should be arranged for every newborn Down syndrome infant during the neonatal period, whether or not a cardiac defect is suspected.

Foetal cardiac echocardiography has advanced over the past decade but remains confined to a comparatively few specialized centres. It seems unlikely that it will become more generally available because of the high degree of necessary technical training and skills required. Accurate cardiac studies may be expected from 18 weeks of intrauterine life onwards. This facility is usually available for mothers who have a positive triple test or amniocentesis, so that the presence or absence of a major cardiac defect can be ascertained and management plans facilitated.

THE HEART IN DOWN SYNDROME IN THE OLDER CHILD AND ADULT

Recent fundamental rethinking of the management of cardiac defects in Down syndrome in infants and young children must stimulate increasing interest in the steadily increasing numbers of long-term survivors of cardiac surgery in infancy and early childhood, in those who have survived this age group with major cardiac defects without the benefit of surgery, and those Down syndrome patients who have grown up diagnosed as having a normal heart in childhood.

Up until 20 years ago approximately 40 per cent of Down syndrome infants with heart defects failed to survive the first years of life and less than 56 per cent survived beyond 4 years of age (Mulcahy, 1979). The survivors of a large systemic/ pulmonary communication (notably ventricular septal defect, atrioventricular canal and large patent ductus arteriosus) do so after an infancy marred by heart failure, repeated chest infections and failure to thrive and an ability to increase their pulmonary vascular resistance. Such individuals eventually become increasingly cyanosed and polycythaemic because of reversal of their shunts from pulmonary to systemic side (Eisenmenger syndrome). Despite some physical restriction to be expected as cyanosis increases, survival into adult life can be achieved with a tolerable day-to-day quality of life. However, others will be lost from right heart failure or pulmonary complications before adult life, and the onset of puberty seems to be a particularly exacting time. Those Down syndrome individuals with secundum atrial septal defects may reach adult life without symptoms, as should the comparatively small numbers with minor cardiac defects if protected from endocarditis.

Regarding Down syndrome individuals thought to have normal hearts in childhood, a recent finding has been the development of mitral and aortic incompetence, the former being due to mitral valve prolapse. A 14 per cent incidence of mitral valve prolapse has been found in adult Down syndrome examined clinically (Goldhaber *et al.*, 1986) and a 58 per cent incidence using two-dimensional echo and Doppler studies (Goldhaber *et al.*, 1987). The comparable incidence of aortic incompetence was 8 per cent and 11 per cent respectively. Valvar calcification was noted in 14.3 per cent of Down syndrome individuals aged 20 to 46 years of age (Hamada *et al.*, 1993) and some years ago Sylvester (1974) described fenestration in aortic valve cusps of Down syndrome adults, increasing in prominence with age. The findings are probably accounted for by connective tissue abnormalities in Down syndrome (Malcolm, 1985) though the effects of premature ageing also have to be considered. There is no known documentation that surgical management has been required for the valvar incompetence described, though Barnett *et al.* (1988) point out the possible risks of endocarditis.

Premature ageing is well described in Down syndrome, the increase in mortality after 44 years (Baird and Sadnovick, 1988) being attributed to the development of Alzheimer's disease (Lai and Williams, 1989). There has been a limited amount of work looking towards premature ageing in Down syndrome. Usually, dietary factors are normal, there is a below average consumption of tobacco and alcohol, and groups studied have been normotensive or had below average blood pressures for their age (Richards and Enver, 1979; Ylä-Herttuala *et al.*, 1989). We have little information as yet concerning myocardial performance in the Down syndrome adult.

Down syndrome is associated with atherogenic lipid profiles, yet autopsy studies show little evidence of significant atherosclerosis. The explanation for this paradox is not clear. An autopsy study on five adult Down syndrome individuals aged 40 to 66 years carried out by Murdoch *et al.* (1977) showed an absence of atheroma throughout the cardiovascular system and raised the question as to whether Down syndrome and Alzheimer's disease provide atheroma-free models (Hughes, 1977). Subsequent studies have documented the presence of atheromatous changes in Down syndrome, though the extent of the changes noted, specifically in the left coronary artery, was much less than that found in other mentally handicapped and normal individuals of the same age group (Ylä-Herttuala *et al.*, 1989).

Lipid studies fail to provide an answer. Fasting lipid analyses have consistently shown reduced levels of HDL cholesterol; apo A1 and HDL cholesterol/total cholesterol ratios are low in individuals with Down syndrome (Dorner *et al.*, 1984; Pueschel *et al.*, 1992). These results would, in fact, favour an increased rather than a decreased risk of coronary artery disease.

Brattstrom *et al.* (1987) have suggested that a high activity of cystathione-ß-synthetase, of which the gene is located on chromosome 21, may protect against atherosclerosis. It is known that gene expression for enzymes acting as free radical scavengers are increased in individuals with Down syndrome by the gene dosage effect, whereby increased levels of these enzymes are produced in the trisomy as compared with the diploid state. Soluble Cu, Zn-superoxide dismutase (SOD-1) and glutathione peroxidase (GSH-Px) are two such enzymes. Fibroblasts from trisomy 21 individuals show an increased activity of these enzymes (Anneren and Epstein, 1987) and the gene for glutathione peroxidase is located to chromosome 21 (Scoggin and Patterson, 1982). These enzymes protect against activated oxygen radicals and compounds and may influence atherogenesis by reducing lipid peroxidation and thereby preventing vascular endothelial injury, the first stage of the widely held response-to-injury hypothesis of atheroma. Some workers have found that SOD-1, coded for on chromosome 21, may paradoxically increase lipid peroxidation by way of H_2O_2 formation, a highly reactive intermediary in free radical metabolism (Sinet *et al.* 1979). In spite of this, it is generally believed that increased levels of these enzymes reduce lipid peroxidation and protect lipid membranes from damage. Intact endothelial surfaces protected in this manner are likely to have a high resistance to atheroma formation. However, exact details of the control of lipid peroxidation and atheroma remain unclear in both the normal and Down syndrome population.

The exact mechanisms influencing the probable retardation of atherosclerosis in Down syndrome and freedom from coronary artery disease are unclear and likely to be multifactorial, involving environmental, immunological, haematological, endocrine and metabolic processes. There is no doubt that we shall learn more precise facts in the future relating to this fundamental subject and to other aspects of cardiac performance in the Down syndrome adult as experience and interest in this age group steadily increase.

PULMONARY HYPERTENSION AND PULMONARY VASCULAR DISEASE

It is generally accepted that Down syndrome individuals are prone to develop pulmonary hypertension. There has been less than complete agreement as to the effect of pulmonary hypertension on the pulmonary vascular bed and whether any changes develop more rapidly in Down syndrome than in a normal individual with a comparable cardiac defect.

Airways obstruction in Down syndrome on account of a crowded pharynx, decreased pharyngeal muscle tone, possible small trachea (Aboussouan *et al.*, 1993) and airways secretions all add to the possibility of sleep apnoea, hypoxia and pulmonary hypertension. Even with a normal heart, pulmonary hypertension has been recognized and a specific case history with sleep apnoea and pulmonary hypertension has been recently documented (Bloch *et al.*, 1990).

Cooney *et al.* (1988) described the structural changes in the lungs in Down syndrome. The two striking differences from normal are the persistence of a double capillary network in the alveolar walls and, probably more importantly, failure of acinar alveolar multiplication in the immediate postnatal period. This is microscopically evident by four months of age and the appearances do not change. The resultant Down syndrome lung shows dilated alveoli in reduced numbers and thus a significant reduction in total cross-sectional area of the capillary vascular bed, presenting as alveolar hypoplasia (hypoplastic lung) (Cooney and Thurlbeck, 1982; Tarroch *et al.*, 1989).

The overwhelming weight of clinical and physiological data suggests that the Down syndrome child develops progressive pulmonary vascular disease more rapidly than a comparable non-Down syndrome child. Over the last decade this view has been strengthened by haemodynamic studies in infant Down syndrome with major cardiac defects. Clapp *et al.* (1990) in a review of Down syndrome with atrioventricular canal and non-Down syndrome patients with the same defect found that the Down syndrome patients studied during the first year of life had both a higher pulmonary vascular resistance and more rapid progression to fixed pulmonary vascular obstruction than the comparable group with normal chromosomes. In 1:8 Down syndrome patients there was fixed pulmonary vascular obstruction by 1 year old, a situation not found in the comparable normal group. Hals *et al.* (1993) found a fixed pulmonary vascular resistance in 112 Down syndrome patients with AVSD at less than one year, the youngest being 5 months of age.

Detailed histological studies of the lungs in Down syndrome with major cardiac defects reviewed at autopsy or at lung biopsy have failed to completely substantiate the clinical and haemodynamic findings. These studies have been based on a long-established and well-accepted histological classification of pulmonary vascular disease (Heath and Edwards, 1958). More recently, greater attention has been drawn to pulmonary histology in infants and young children and it has been suggested that this grading may not be entirely appropriate for this age group (Haworth, 1987). Yamaki *et al.* (1993) looked at the pulmonary histology in 67 patients with atrioventricular canal (mean age 19 months). They noted that thinning of the media of small pulmonary arteries was established by 6 months of age and most noticeable in the Down syndrome patients, in some of whom there was acute fibrous proliferation obstructing the lumen.

There seems no doubt that infants with Down syndrome and large systemic/ pulmonary communications, such as atrioventricular septal defect, develop progressive pulmonary vascular disease which may be well established by six months of age. There are probably multiple factors of which the structural changes in the pharynx, upper airways and lungs have been outlined. Reduction in the alveolar surface area demonstrated by Cooney *et al.* (1988) may also favour the precocious development of pulmonary vascular disease. A possible additional contribution may be that there is impaired biosynthesis of prostaglandins in Down syndrome due to over-expression of copper zinc superoxide dismutase gene dosage in human trisomy 21 (Minc-Golomb *et al.*, 1991). Prostaglandins are naturally occurring and one of their many functions is pulmonary vasodilation. They are often given therapeutically to try and control pulmonary hypertension.

The overwhelming evidence of the development of early pulmonary vascular disease in Down syndrome has very important practical implications. If corrective surgery is to be successful in the longer term, ideally it has to be attempted in the Down syndrome infant younger than 6 months of age. For this reason, as well as for other medical and social factors relevant to the best management of the Down syndrome infant, the case for early diagnosis is mandatory.

MANAGEMENT OF CARDIAC DEFECTS

The presentation of major cardiac defects with early lung damage and the establishment of pulmonary vascular disease, sometimes irreversible well before the end of the first year of life, explains the recent emphasis on the role of early surgery for these Down syndrome infants. It also explains the need for early exact cardiac diagnosis. The technical and practical realities of such an approach have, in their turn, helped to focus attention on the necessity for a close team of professional workers with fully informed parents from the earliest possible time, sometimes even in foetal life if a major cardiac defect is demonstrated by two-dimensional ultrasound in a diagnosed trisomy 21 foetus. After diagnosis of a major cardiac defect in a young Down syndrome infant, it is important that the parents meet the paediatric cardiologist soon afterwards. Discussion should be directed to the natural history, the general management principles, the role of surgery, the outlines of what this admission will entail for the infant and the family. The risks involved should also be evaluated as well as the likelihood of successful surgery being able to change the natural history. Since age and size of the infant is no longer a deciding factor in the timing of surgery, it is often possible to make a provisional surgical booking before 6 months of age, with the understanding that the date can be advanced if the baby develops intractable heart failure or multiple chest infections. An isolated large patent ductus arteriosus can be ligated as soon as possible after diagnosis. It is always essential to emphasize to parents that surgical correction can alleviate acute symptoms, help the baby to thrive and help towards the achievement of motor milestones. It can never change the basic intelligence of the child. However, early corrective cardiac surgery gives the infant an increased chance of responding to early training enterprises. In the interval between initial cardiac diagnosis and surgery, care of the Down syndrome child belongs primarily to the home and local paediatric teams.

Major cyanotic congenital heart disease is less common in Down syndrome than the normal population and usually presents as tetralogy of Fallot, sometimes in association with atrioventricular canal. Though surgical correction will now be arranged for these infants, the optimum timing is less clear and often dependent on symptoms. Episodes of severe cyanosis (blue spells) are dealt with on an emergency basis. Continued therapy with beta blockers is often advocated, but a surgical approach at any age is more effective and would consist of either a shunt to one or other pulmonary artery from the unilateral subclavian artery, using Goretex material, or correction, dependent on the age of the baby, anatomical details and the local surgical practice.

There is not universal agreement as to the indications for closure of secundum atrial septal defect which occurs equally commonly in Down syndrome and the normal child. Such defects do not usually cause major symptoms in infancy and childhood. The minority with symptoms need surgical closure, but when closure is recommended for the greater majority it is done so on the basis of the effects of chronic right heart overload continuing into adult life and the possible onset of arrhythmias or, more remotely, pulmonary hypertension in adult life. Indications for surgical closure and the optimum age at which this should be carried out, commonly early childhood, are debated for the normal population and could be extended to the Down syndrome child, with greater reluctance for a non-essential major operation. It could be that the next few years will see the closure of significantly large secundum atrial septal defects by umbrella-type devices become a practical and routine procedure.

A minor cardiac defect, though unusual in Down syndrome, should not affect the prognosis or long-term outlook for the infant in any way and cardiac follow-up visits should be infrequent. However, all cardiac defects are prone to endocarditis, particularly so in Down syndrome (Saxen and Aula, 1982), so all invasive dental work or surgical procedure should be covered by appropriate antibiotic cover recommended by the local paediatric cardiac unit and usually printed on locally available 'antibiotic cards', the usual standard antibiotic being a large single dose of amoxicillin.

Approximately one in every two Down syndrome infants born does not have a cardiac defect and once this is established by careful clinical examination, chest X-ray, electrocardiography, two-dimensional echocardiogram and Doppler study in early infancy, the parents should be strongly reassured and no further cardiac appointment made.

The potential of cardiac surgery to improve the welfare of Down syndrome children, their parents and their carers, has undergone dramatic change during the last decade. The major breakthrough for Down syndrome has come with the ability to repair atrioventricular septal defect in infancy. Although it was suggested that the added risk of a young age was neutralized by 1975 (Studer *et al.*, 1982), this initially applied to a few highly specialized paediatric cardiac units and it has taken time for more general acceptance, particularly when added to the intricacy of atrioventricular septal defect repair. The option of preliminary banding of the pulmonary artery to cut down pulmonary blood flow and reduce pulmonary artery pressure was often utilized in an attempt to cut down operative mortality and to prevent incurable pulmonary vascular disease. However, it involves two surgical procedures, the results are not completely predictable and it is an unsuitable procedure if there is significant AV incompetence (Frid *et al.*, 1991). Surgical repair of atrioventricular septal defect has carried a high mortality in many series relating to Down syndrome and non-Down syndrome patients. An illustrative series of primary repair of complete AV canal cites 33 patients operated on between 1979 and 1991 with a hospital mortality of 32 per cent (Garcia-Hernandez *et al.*, 1993). These results are linked with established pulmonary vascular disease and the high per centage of Down syndrome patients. The mean age at operation has been reduced from 19.5 months to 11 months since 1986. Perhaps surprisingly it has not been confirmed that a patient with Down syndrome carries a higher operative risk than a non-Down syndrome patient of the same age and with the same cardiological problems (Backiewicz *et al.*, 1989; Vet and Ottenkamp, 1989).

The necessity for early surgical repair, particularly in Down syndrome, is now well understood and becoming routine practice. As the practice increases, so the results improve. Operating on atrioventricular septal defect under the age of 2 years, a unit of excellence reported a mortality of 62 per cent from 1975 to 1977 and 17 per cent from 1978 to 1980 (Chin *et al.*, 1982). In the same year a mortality of 8 per cent was reported in atrioventricular canal operated on under the age of 1 year (Bender *et al.*, 1982). Metras *et al.* (1989) report a mortality of three out of 22 infants under 1 year who had atrioventricular canal repair, the youngest being one month of age. The numbers of atrioventricular septal defect presenting to each paediatric surgical unit is fortunately small, but the trend is certainly towards continued improvement in results. In our own experience, there were 14 repairs of complete atrioventricular septal defect in Down syndrome infants aged between 2 months and 10 months between January 1993 and December 1994 with one operative death. Though the numbers are small, the results are sufficiently encouraging to justify the current policy of repair of atrioventricular septal defect in Down syndrome infants under the age of 6 months, whenever practically possible.

Although there is no convincing evidence that Down syndrome constitutes a threat to operative survival, most centres feel that the infant with Down syndrome spends longer in the intensive care unit than the comparable non-Down syndrome patient, needing a longer period of ventilation and attendance to pulmonary problems (Moray *et al.*, 1986; Vet and Ottenkamp, 1989). Infants and children with preoperative pulmonary hypertension may develop pulmonary hypertensive crises in the immediate postoperative period (Wheller *et al.*, 1979) and recently the successful use of low-dose inhaled nitric oxide to a series of ten postoperative infants, including three with Down syndrome, is reported (Miller *et al.*, 1994). This therapeutic advance may prove of immense benefit in helping to reduce hospital mortality and morbidity in Down syndrome patients after cardiac surgery.

INTERVENTIONAL CARDIOLOGY

The last decade has seen the development of therapeutic measures carried out in the catheter laboratory by paediatric cardiologists. The basic principles involve closure of defects using umbrella-like devices and the stretching of narrowed valves and vessels by balloons or stents. Customarily, the appropriate device is introduced percutaneously from the femoral vein in the groin and occasionally an arterial approach is indicated. Although these procedures are usually carried out under general anaesthetic, they avoid a surgical thoracotomy and cardiopulmonary bypass if it would have been indicated, and radically transform and abbreviate the postprocedural period.

Because of the atypical presentation of cardiac defects in Down syndrome, the available procedures have a limited place in their management thus far. The single most helpful manoeuvre applicable to Down syndrome patients is patent ductus arteriosus occlusion by double umbrella technique. This was first described in 1987 (Rashkind *et al.*, 1987). It is now an established alternative to surgical ligation. It involves the insertion of two back-to-back umbrella-like structures, the poly-urethane foam covers being left behind to block off the patent ductus arteriosus. Until recently the procedure was limited to children and adults because of limitations in size imposed by the necessary instrumentation. In Down syndrome a patent ductus is usually large and needs ligating in infancy, so it is encouraging that we recently have a report of adaptation of technique which has made ductus occlusion feasible in small infants, and a series is described of 29 patients under the age of 2 years, including three Down syndrome infants, who had umbrella closure of their patent ductus (Rigby and Redington, 1994).

Isolated pulmonary valve stenosis is uncommon in Down syndrome, but pulmonary valvotomy by balloon dilation (Kan *et al.*, 1982) is now accepted as having replaced surgical pulmonary valvotomy except when a specific valve is deemed not to be amenable to the technique.

Closure of secundum atrial septal defects is now possible using adaptations of the umbrella technique (Rome *et al.*, 1990). Development of this technique, which entails circumferential or clam shell apposition of the umbrella around its margins, has been developed in the USA and is not as yet fully available in the UK. However, when an accepted and reliable modification is available, it is an appealing method to deal with significant atrial septal defect in Down syndrome for which closure is thought to be indicated, thus avoiding cardiopulmonary bypass, surgical incision and potential postoperative complications.

There is as yet no satisfactory method of closing a large ventricular septal defect by an occlusive device, but extensive modifications of currently available techniques may eventually make it a practical alternative to conventional surgery and such a possibility would, of course, be exciting for Down syndrome infants.

The stretching of pulmonary arteries, narrowed usually as a component of multiple defects or following correction of tetralogy of Fallot, is proving a valuable alternative to surgical repair. This technique involves the use of tubular stainless steel stents expanded across the narrow area by balloon dilation (O'Laughlin *et al.*, 1991). The specific use of this technique in Down syndrome patients is, however, limited.

The introduction of these techniques is a major step forward in the management of cardiac defects. Their development continues and they can also be utilized as appropriate for treating infants and children with Down syndrome.

LATE POSTOPERATIVE RESULTS

There is little available information on Down syndrome patients following successful surgical correction. Haneda *et al.* (1992) report 25 patients 1 to 17 years after repair of atrioventricular septal defect, of whom ten had Down syndrome. There was one late death and five patients with severe mitral regurgitation, of whom two underwent mitral valve replacement. Although pulmonary artery pressure and pulmonary resistance decreased, the changes were significantly less in Down syndrome patients. There were comparable haemodynamic findings in another series of 59 children, including 47 with Down syndrome, operated on between 1981 and 1989 with a 100 per cent two-year survival for non-Down syndrome patients and 77 per cent plus or minus 6 per cent of the Down syndrome patients (Morris *et al.*, 1992). It is too early to assess the long-term follow-up of Down syndrome with atrioventricular canal operated on successfully in infancy, but the extensive available literature and practical experience suggest that the optimum time for planned surgical intervention is before pulmonary vascular disease can be established, probably before 6 months of age. Surgical skills and postoperative care can now cope with the challenge of complex cardiac surgery in early infancy necessary for the survival and acceptable quality of life of a Down syndrome infant born with a major cardiac defect.

REFERENCES

Aboussouan, L.S., O'Donovan, P.B., Moodie, D.S., Gragg, L.A., Stoller, J.K. (1993) Hypoplastic trachea in Down's syndrome. *American Review of Respiratory Disorders* **147,** 72–5.

Anneren, K.G. and Epstein, C.J. (1987) Lipid peroxidation and superoxide dismutase-1 and glutathione peroxidase activities in trisomy 16 fetal mice and human trisomy 21 fibroblasts. *Pediatric Research,* **21,** 88–93.

Backiewicz, J.A., Melvin, W.S., Basilius, D., Davis J.T. (1989) Congenital heart disease in Down's syndrome patients: a decade of surgical experience. *Journal of Thoracic and Cardiovascular Surgery,* **37,** 369–71.

Baird, P.A. and Sadnovick, A.D. (1988) Life expectancy in Down's syndrome adults. *Lancet* ii: 1354–67.

Bender, H.W., Hammon, J.W., Hubbard, S.G., Muirhead, J., Graham, T.P. (1982) Repair of atrio-ventricular canal malformations in the first year of life. *Journal of Thoracic and Cardiovascular Surgery,* **84,** 523–4.

Bloch, K., Witztum, A., Wieser, H.G., Schmid, S., Russi, E. (1990) Obstruktives schalf-apnoe-syndrom bei einem kind mit trisomy 21. *Monatsschrift-Kinderheilkunde,* **138,** 817–22.

Brattstrom, L., Englund, E., Brun, A. (1987) Does Down syndrome support homocysteine theory of arteriosclerosis? *Lancet* i: 391–2.

Cooney, T.P. and Thurlbeck, W.M. (1982) Pulmonary hypoplasia in Down's syndrome. *New England Journal of Medicine 367:* 1170–73.

Cooney, T.P., Wentworth, P.J. and Thurlbeck, W.M. (1988) Diminished radial count is found only postnatally in Down's syndrome. *Pediatric Pulmonology,* **5:** 204–9.

Barnett, M.L., Friedman, D, Kastner, T. (1988) The prevalence of mitral valve prolapse in patients with Down's syndrome: implications for dental management. *Oral Surgery, Oral Medicine, Oral Pathology,* **66,** 445–7.

Chin, A.J., Keane, J.F., Norwood, W.I., Castaneda, M.D. (1982) Repair of complete atrio-ventricular canal in infancy. *Journal of Thoracic Cardiovascular Surgery,* **84,** 437–45.

Clapp, S., Perry, B.L., Farooki, Z.Q., Jackson, W.L., Karpawich, P.P., Hakimi, M., Arciniegas, E., Green, E.W., Pinsky, W.W. (1990) Down's syndrome, complete atrioventricular canal, and pulmonary vascular obstructive disease. *Journal of Thoracic Cardiovascular Surgery,* **100,** 115–21.

Cousineau, A.J., Lauer, R.M., Pierpont, M.E., Burns, T.L., Ardinger, R.H., Patil, S.R., Sheffield, V.C. (1994) Linkage analysis of autosomal dominant atrioventricular canal defects: exclusion of chromosome 21. *Human Genetics,* **93,** 103–8.

Davies, G.E., Howard, C.M., Gorman, L.M., Farrer, M.J., Holland, A.J., Williamson, R., Kessling, A.M. (1993) Polymorphisms and linkage disequilibrium in the COL6A1 and COL6A2 gene cluster: novel DNA polymorphisms in the region of a candidate gene for congenital heart defects in Down's syndrome. *Human Genetics* **90,** 521–5.

Dörner, K., Gaethke, A.S., Tolksdorf, M., Schumann, K.P., Gustmann, H. (1984) Cholesterol fractions and triglycerides in children and adults with Down's syndrome. *Clinica Chimica Acta* **142,** 307–9.

Duff, K., Williamson, R. and Richards, S.J. (1990) Expression of genes encoding two chains of the collagen type VI molecule during human fetal heart development. *International Journal of Cardiology,* **17,** 128–9.

Ferencz, C., Boughman, J.A., Neill, C.A., Brenner, J.I., Perry, L.W. (1989) Congenital cardiovascular malformations: questions on inheritance. *Journal of the American College Cardiology* **14,** 756–63.

Frid, C., Thoren, C., Book, K., Bjork, V.O. (1991) Repair of complete atrioventricular canal. 15 years' experience. *Scandinavian Journal of Thoracic and Cardiovascular Surgery*, **25,** 101–5.

Garcia-Hernandez, J.A., Caceres-Espejo, J., Soult-Rubio, J.A., Charlo Molina, T., Barrera, S.M., Cabello, L.R., Alvarez, M.A., Gil-Fournier, C.M., Romero, P.A. (1993) Evaluacion de la correccion quirurgica en los canales auriculoventriculares completos. *Revista Español Cardiologia*, **46,** 293–7.

Goldhaber, S.Z., Rubin, I.L., Brown, W., Robertson, N., Stubblefield, F. (1986) Valvular heart disease (aortic regurgitation and mitral valve prolapse) among institutionalized adults with Down's syndrome. *American Journal of Cardiology* **57,** 278–81.

Goldhaber, S.Z., Brown, M.P., St John Sutton, M.G. (1987) High frequency of mitral valve prolapse and aortic regurgitation among asymptomatic adults with Down's syndrome. *Journal American Medical Association*, **258,** 1793–5.

Hals, J., Hagemo, P.S., Thaulow, E., Sorland, S.J. (1993) Pulmonary vascular resistance in complete atrioventricular septal defect. A comparison between children with and without Down's syndrome. *Acta Paediatrica*, **86,** 595–8.

Hamada, T., Kuroda, M., Miyakoshi, M., Koshino, Y., Murata, T., Oomori, M., Murata, I. and Mishawa T. (1993) Echocardiographic study in adult patients with Down's syndrome. *Rinsho-Byori* **41,** 807–12.

Haneda, K., Togo, T., Sato, N., Ogata, H., Mohri, H. (1992) Late results after repair of complete atrioventricular canal. *Tohoku Journal of Experimental Medicine*, **166,** 201–8.

Haworth, S.G. (1987) Understanding pulmonary vascular disease in young children. *International Journal of Cardiology*, **15,** 101–3

Heath, D., Edwards, J.E. (1958) The pathology of hypertensive pulmonary vascular disease. *Circulation* **18,** 533.

Hoe, T.S., Chan, K.C. and Boo, N.Y. (1990) Cardiovascular malformations in Malaysian neonates with Down's syndrome. *Singapore Medical Journal*, **31,** 474–6.

Hughes, W. (1977) Atherosclerosis, Down's syndrome and Alzheimer's disease. *British Medical Journal*, **2,** 702.

Kan, J.S., White, R.I., Mitchell, S.E., Gardner, T.J. (1982) Percutaneous balloon valvuloplasty; a new method for treating congenital pulmonary valve stenosis. *Circulation* **75,** 583–92.

Khoury, M.J. and Erickson, J.D. (1992) Improved ascertainment of cardiovascular malformations in infants with Down's syndrome, Atlanta, 1968 through 1989. Implications for the interpretation of increasing rates of cardiovascular malformations in surveillance systems. *American Journal of Epidemiology* **136,** 1457–64.

Kurnit, D.M., Aldridge, J.F., Matsuoka, R., Matthysse S. (1985) Increased adhesiveness of trisomy 21 cells and atrioventricular canal malformations in Down syndrome. *American Journal of Medical Genetics*, **20,** 385–99.

Lai, F. and Williams, R.S. (1989) A prospective study of Alzheimer's disease in Down's syndrome. *Archives of Neurology*, **46,** 849–52.

Lo, N.S., Leung, P.M., Lau, K.C., Yeung, C.Y. (1989) Congenital cardiovascular malformations in Chinese children with Down's syndrome. *Chinese Medical Journal* **102,** 382–6.

Malcolm, A.D. (1985) Mitral valve prolapse associated with other disorders: causal incidence, common link or fundamental genetic disturbance? *British Heart Journal*, **53,** 353–62.

Marino, B. (1993) Congenital heart disease in patients with Down's syndrome: anatomic and genetic aspects. *Biomed Pharmacother* **47,** 197–200.

Metras, D., Kreitmann, B., Wernert, F., Montegna, P., Pannetier, A., Couvely, J.P., Garbi, O. (1989) Correction du canal atrio-ventriculaire complet avant l'age d'un an. *Archive des Maladies du Coeur*, **82,** 719–22.

Miller, O.I., Celermajer, D.S., Deanfield, J.E., Macrae, D.J. (1994) Very-low-dose inhaled nitric oxide: A selective pulmonary vasodilator after operations for congenital heart disease. *Journal of Thoracic and Cardiovascular Surgery*, **108**, 487–94.

Minc-Golomb, D., Knobler, H., Groner, Y. (1991) Gene dosage of CuZnSOD and Down's syndrome: diminished prostaglandin synthesis in human trisomy 21, transfected cells and transgenic mice. *EMBO Journal* (European Molecular Biology Organisation), **10**, 2119–24.

Miyabara, S., Sugihara, H., Maehara, N., Shouno, H., Tasaki, H., Yoshida, K., Saito, N., Kayama, F., Ibara, S., Suzumori, K. (1989) Significance of cardiovascular malformations in cystic hygroma: a new interpretation of the pathogenesis. *American Journal of Medical Genetics*, **34**, 489–501.

Moray, J.P., MacGillivray, R.M., Duker, G. (1986) Increased perioperative risk following surgical repair of congenital heart disease in Down's syndrome. *Anaesthesia* **65**, 221–4.

Morris, C.D., Magilke, D., Reller, M. (1992) Down's syndrome affects results of surgical correction of complete atrioventricular canal. *Pediatric Cardiology*, **13**, 80–4.

Mulcahy, M.T. (1979) Down's syndrome in Western Australia: mortality and survival. *Clinical Genetics*, **16**, 103–8.

Murdoch, J.C., Rodger, J.C., Rao, S.S., Fletcher, C.D., Dunnigan, M.G. (1977) Down's syndrome: an atheroma-free model? *British Medical Journal*, **2**, 226–9.

Okada, R. (1991) Pathology of the cardiac valves. *Journal of Cardiology* (Suppl) **25**, 35–43.

O'Laughlin, M.P., Perry, S.B., Lock, J.E. and Mullins, C.E. (1991) Use of encovascular stents in congenital heart disease. *Circulation* **83**: 1923–39.

Pinto, F.F., Nunes, L., Ferraz, F., Sampayo, F. (1990) Down's syndrome: different distribution of congenital heart diseases between the sexes. *International Journal of Cardiology*, **27**, 175–8.

Pueschel, S.M., Craig, W.Y., Haddow, J.E. (1992) Lipids and lipoproteins in persons with Down's syndrome. *Journal of Intellectual Disabilities Research*, **36**, 365–9.

Rashkind, W., Mullins, C., Hellenbrand, W., Tait, M. (1987) Nonsurgical closure of patent ducus arteriosus: clinical application of the Rashkind PDA occluder system. *Circulation* **75**, 583–92.

Richards, B.W. and Enver, F. (1979) Blood pressure in Down's syndrome. *Journal of Mental Deficiency Research*, **23**, 123–36.

Rigby, M.L. and Redington, A.N. (1994) Primary transcatheter unbrella closure of perimembranous ventricular septal defect. *British Heart Journal*, **72**, 368–71.

Rome, J., Keane, J.F., Perry, S.B., Spevak, P.J., Lock, J.E. (1990) Double umbrella closure of atrial defects. Initial clinical applications. *Circulation* **82**, 751–8.

Rosenberg, H.C., Jung, J.H., Soltan, H.C., Li, M.D., Sheridan, G. (1994) Cardiac screening of children with Down's syndrome. *Canadian Journal of Cardiology*, **10**, 675–7.

Rosenquist, G.C., Sweeny, I.J., Amsel, J., McAllister, H.A. (1974) Enlargement of the membranous ventricular septum: an internal stigma of Down's syndrome. *Journal of Pediatrics*, **85**, 490–3.

Rosenquist, G.C., Sweeny, I.J. and McAllister, H.A. (1975) Relationship of the tricuspid valve to the membranous ventricular septum in Down's syndrome without endocardial cushion defect: study of 28 specimens, 14 with a ventricular septal defect. *American Heart Journal*, **90**, 458–61.

Saxèn, L. and Aula, S. (1982) Periodontal bone loss in patients with Down's syndrome; a follow up study. *Journal of Periodontology*, 53, 158–62.

Scoggin, C.H. and Patterson, D. (1982) Down's syndrome as a model of disease. *Archives of Internal Medicine*, **142**, 462–4.

Sinet, P.M., Lejeune, J. and Jerome, H. (1979) Trisomy 21 (Down's syndrome) glutathione peroxidase, hexose monophosphate shunt and IQ. *Life Science*, **24**, 29–34.

Studer, M., Blackstone, E.H., Kirklin, J.W., Pacifico, A.D., Soto, B., Chung, K.T. (1982) Determinants of early and late repair of atrio-ventricular (canal) defects. *Journal of Thoracic and Cardiovascular Surgery*, **84**, 523–4.

Sylvester, P.E. (1974) Aortic and pulmonary valve fenestrations as ageing indices in Down's syndrome. *Journal of Mental Deficiency Research*, **18**, 367–76.

Tarroch, X., Rovirosa, M., Toran, N., Lozano, C. (1989) Hipoplasia e hipertension pulmonar en un sindrome de down: valoracion pronostica mediante la biopsia pulmonar. *Revista Español Cardiologia*, **42**, 348–50.

Tubman, T.R., Shields, M.D., Craig, B.G., Mulholland, H.C., Nevin, N.C. (1991) Congenital heart disease in Down's syndrome: two year prospective early screening study. *British Medical Journal*, **302**, 1425–7.

Vet, T.W. and Ottenkamp J. (1989) Correction of atrio-ventricular septal defect. Results influenced by Down's syndrome? *American Journal of Diseases of Children*, **143**, 1361–6.

Wheller, J., George, B.L., Mulder, D.G., Jarmakani, J.M. (1979) Diagnosis and management of postoperative pulmonary hypertensive crisis. *Circulation*, **60**, 1640–4.

Wilson, L., Curtis, A., Korenberg, J.R., Schipper, R.D., Allan, L., Chevenix-Trench, G., Stephenson, A., Goodship, J. and Burn, J. (1993) A large, dominant pedigree of atrioventricular septal defect (AVSD): exclusion from the Down syndrome critical region on chromosome 21. *American Journal of Human Genetics*, **53**, 1262–8.

Yamaki, S., Yasui, H., Kado, H., Yonenaga, K., Nakamura, Y., Kikuchi, T., Ajiki, H., Tsunemoto, M., Mohri, H. (1993) Pulmonary vascular disease and operative indications in complete atrioventricular canal defect in early infancy. *Journal of Thoracic and Cardiovascular Surgery*, **106**, 398–405.

Ylä-Herttuala, S., Luoma, J., Nikkari, T., Kivimaki, T. (1989) Down's syndrome and atherosclerosis. *Atherosclerosis*, **76**, 269–72.

7 Auditory Disorders

Bethan Davies

INTRODUCTION

In his Lettsomian lectures (1887) John Langdon Down described in detail the characteristics of his eponymous syndrome. He drew attention to the impaired hearing often found in Down's syndrome individuals and wrote at some length about their linguistic and phonological problems.

> Hearing is generally less acute, and this is often an important element in cases of delayed speech. We all know that absence of speech is often the outcome of complete deafness, but it is not sufficiently recognised that a very slight congenital defect of hearing, is sufficient to cause deferred and defective speech. (23)

This recognition of the effect of a mild hearing loss is most unusual for the time when he was writing.

> Delayed speech is universal, permanent absence less common. The lesion of speech in these cases is the outcome of several factors. The form of the mouth is, as I have shown, often abnormal. The high, narrow vaulted palate presents a formidable difficulty; this is apt to be intensified by the ill development of the lower jaw, the horizontal ramus forming too obtuse an angle with the ascending ramus so that labials are expressed with difficulty. In addition to this the tongue is large, flabby, and defective in its muscular movements, and these are ill co-ordinated. Again the congenital defective hearing I have referred to is another factor. (24–5)

So far as management is concerned Dr Down (83) recommended 'the defective speech is best overcome by a well arranged plan of tongue gymnastics, followed by a cultivation of the purely imitative powers, teaching at first monosyllable sounds which have concrete representatives'.

In spite of J. Langdon Down's careful description it was to be nearly a hundred years before it was realized that all Down's children needed careful audiological assessment and management, and assessment and intensive help from speech and language therapists. There was increasing awareness of the high incidence of auditory problems during the 1970s and 1980s. Meanwhile extensive work on the nature of the speech and language problems of Down's individuals proceeded so that there is now an increasing understanding of the nature and effects of hearing loss and speech and language problems on the development of the Down's Syndrome child. However, there remain many unanswered questions:

1. What differentiates the Down's syndrome child who has normal hearing and no middle ear problems?
2. What is the pathological process involved in the progressive sensori-neural hearing loss seen in older children and adults?
3. On the basis of present knowledge what is the ideal screening programme of hearing and speech and language in Down Syndrome children?
4. How should the hearing loss of Down's syndrome children be managed?

The need for careful audiological assessment to identify auditory problems in all children who present with developmental delay has been accepted for some 30 years. It is clear that a child with a severe learning problem and deafness, even of moderate degree, will often have great difficulty in using compensatory strategies which may be used by children of normal intelligence. The possible interaction between auditory deficits and the well-known linguistic difficulties of Down's children is an area which is being carefully researched. However, it is clear from clinical experience that an improvement in auditory function achieved by surgical intervention or by the use of hearing aids can dramatically improve auditory attention and can often greatly increase the rate of speech and language progress.

It is important to note the particularly severe synergistic effect of the combination of a visual and hearing problem in Down's children. Even in children of potentially normal intelligence, the combination of a moderate undiagnosed vision and hearing impairment, especially associated with hypotonia, can lead to a misdiagnosis of severe mental retardation. Such children may present with severe language retardation and disturbed behaviour. In a child with a severe learning problem, as may be the case with a Down's child, the additional presence of a combined visual and hearing problem, even in moderate degree, may result in the child appearing to be very much more severely retarded than is in fact the case. Occasionally such a child, once provided with corrective spectacles, hearing aids and appropriate management, may show a quite remarkable improvement in all aspects of development and especially in linguistic progress and behaviour.

LITERATURE REVIEW

There is an extensive literature on the various aspects of Down's syndrome although literature on hearing loss is very limited. In detailed medical overviews of the syndrome, including those of Breg (1977) and Smith and Berg (1976) there is usually very little information about hearing loss. However, a good deal of interest has been shown in the external ears in the syndrome. The characteristically small pinnae lying flat against the head with an angular folded helix and a small ear lobe with stenosed meata have been widely described (see Figure 7.1), and there are as many references in the literature to the abnormalities of the pinnae as there are to the nature of hearing loss in Down's Syndrome.

The early literature on hearing in the syndrome suggested widely disparate figures for the incidence of hearing loss, from as little as 8 per cent to as much as 95 per cent. The early studies of note are those of Rigrodsky *et al.* (1961) McIntire *et al.* (1965) and Glovsky (1966).

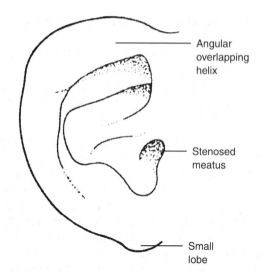

Angular
overlapping
helix

Stenosed
meatus

Small
lobe

Figure 7.1 Typical pinna in Down Syndrome

Fulton and Lloyd's (1968) study reported a 58 per cent incidence of significant hearing loss and among those affected they reported that 55 per cent had conductive hearing losses, 23 per cent sensori-neural hearing losses, and 23 per cent mixed hearing losses.

The first study of auditory function in Down's syndrome using both pure tone audiometry and tympanometry was carried out by Brooks *et al.* (1972). This was a study of 100 Down's syndrome individuals from age 12 months to 59 years, matched for age and sex with non-Down's individuals. Both populations were in residential care because of mental retardation. To summarize Brooks's findings, he reported that in his Down's syndrome group only 23 per cent had normal hearing and normal middle ear function, compared with 74 per cent in his control group. If one looked at middle ear function alone then 60 per cent of the Down's population were abnormal and only 17.5 per cent of the control group (Table 7.1).

There was a marked difference in the incidence of sensori-neural hearing loss between the two groups, with 21 per cent of the Down's individuals under 20 having

Table 7.1 Proportion of patients with middle ear dysfunction found by impedance measurements in different studies

Study	Proportion %	Population type
Brookes *et al.* (1972)	60	Mixed
Schwartz and Schwartz (1978)	73	Child
Balkany *et al.* (1979)	76	Mixed
Davies and Penniceard (1980)	70	Child
Nolan *et al.* (1980)	69	Mixed
Keiser *et al.* (1981)	50	Adult
Dahle and McCollister (1986)	65	Child
Davies (1988)	71	Child

a sensori-neural hearing loss and 15 per cent of the control group. However in the individuals aged over 21, 55 per cent of those with Down's syndrome had a sensori-neural hearing loss and only 10 per cent of the controls. Brooks therefore concluded that a sensori-neural hearing loss in Down's individuals may well be developing later in life and that the risk of developing such a loss is greater in Down's Syndrome than in retarded individuals without this condition.

Davies and Penniceard (1980) reported a comparison of middle ear function in a group of unselected Down's schoolchildren compared with normal controls and found 50 per cent of the Down's children had normal tympanograms and 50 per cent abnormal, i.e. Jerger type B or C (Jerger, 1970). The comparative figures for normal controls were 96 per cent normal and 4 per cent abnormal. In a further study, three years later, of the members of the Down's group who were still at school the tympanometric findings were remarkably consistent i.e. 55 per cent normal 45 per cent abnormal. In this case the children were matched with other severely retarded children without Down's syndrome and in these 100 per cent of the tympanograms were normal.

So far as hearing levels were concerned a significant difference was found between the levels in the Down's children and the controls at all frequencies. After three years had elapsed there was no significant difference in the thresholds of the Down's children at 250 Hz, 500 Hz and 1 kHz but there were significant differences at the 5 per cent level at 4 kHz and 8 kHz. There was also a difference at 2 kHz in the expected direction but the difference was not sufficient to reach statistical significance. It appeared therefore that there was evidence of an increasing high frequency hearing loss in this group of children.

The study also reported on findings in Down's children already attending audiology clinics for regular assessment. In a group comprising 73 ears, normal tympanograms were obtained in only 30 per cent and abnormal in 70 per cent. In this group of children, ranging in age from 12 months to 15 years there was no significant change in the incidence of abnormal tympanograms throughout the age range.

The clinic population had a higher incidence of middle ear dysfunction and a higher incidence of significant hearing loss than the school population. This is likely to be due to the fact that many of the clinic children had been specifically referred because of doubt about their hearing. By far the commonest audiological findings were of a moderate mixed hearing loss with a characteristic sensori-neural involvement at 4 kHz and 8 kHz.

Schwartz and Schwartz (1978) reported a study of tympanometry in Down's children and found that 26 per cent of the children had normal tympanograms and 63 per cent abnormal. Balkany *et al.* (1979) reported a study of children and adults with Down's syndrome in which 78 per cent showed a significant hearing loss. In 83 per cent of cases the loss was conductive and in 17 per cent sensori-neural. The tympanograms in this study were classified by Jerger's method and 76 per cent were abnormal and 24 per cent normal.

In the study of a group of Down's and non-Down's retarded individuals Nolan *et al.* (1980) reported the incidence of hearing loss in the Down's group as 69 per cent and middle ear dysfunction in 69 per cent. In the non-Down's group an incidence of hearing loss of 40 per cent and of middle ear dysfunction of 15 per cent was found. This study again confirms that the incidence of hearing impairment and middle ear dysfunction is much higher in Down's syndrome individuals than in retarded individuals without the syndrome. The English Picture Vocabulary Test (EPVT) was used to investigate receptive vocabulary and no significant correlation was found between the EPVT scores and hearing loss measured by pure tone audiometry in the non-Down's group. However there was a correlation significant at the 5 per cent level between the EPVT scores and hearing levels in the Down's group.

Davies and Penniceard (1980) also used the EPVT to look at verbal receptive vocabulary in their Down's and non-Down's groups. They found no significant difference in mean quotient for the two groups although they pointed out that the two groups were not matched for intelligence. It is of note that when the EPVT scores on the first test were compared with the scores achieved three years later by the Down's group there was a mean change in the recognition quotient of –3, a significant indicator of their very poor language progress.

Cunnningham and McArthur (1981) studied 24 Down's syndrome children aged 9 to 32 months using distraction techniques and impedance measurements, and reported that all the children failed the distraction test at screening level and 80 to 85 per cent were regarded as having a hearing loss of more than 40 dB(A). It is of note that 50 per cent of the sample had passed a routine screening of hearing at a local authority clinic. This would support the generally held view among paediatric audiologists that such children should be routinely assessed in a specialist audiology clinic which might be hospital or community based.

A further study of hearing in adult Down's was carried out by Keiser *et al.* (1981) reporting a 39 per cent incidence of abnormal tympanograms and a high incidence of sensori-neural hearing loss with 23 per cent in the 15- to 20-year age group. This study also identifies the characteristic loss at 4 kHz and at 8 kHz demonstrated by others.

Dahle and McCollister (1986) reported on a detailed study of hearing loss, tympanometric and otological findings in a group of 30 Down's schoolchildren matched with 30 non-Down's children at the same school. They confirmed the high incidence of middle ear problems in the Down's children with 65 per cent of the latter having Jerger Type B and C traces on tympanometry compared with only 20 per cent of the non-Down's children. In addition, their findings for hearing loss confirmed the high incidence of significant hearing loss in the Down's children of over 65 per cent compared with 9 per cent in the controls. The proportion of conductive and mixed losses in the Down's was 46 per cent compared with 7 per cent in the controls, sensori-neural loss 10 per cent in the Down's children compared with 2 per cent in the controls (Table 7.2). They also emphasized the high occurrence in the Down's children of impacted wax. They stressed the need for further investigation of the hearing problems in Down's children and the need for better monitoring and management of hearing problems in all retarded children.

Davies (1988) reported a study of 100 Down's syndrome individuals (aged 8 months to 22 years) attending an audiology clinic, analysing the results by use of the same criteria used by Brooks in 1972. She reported normal hearing and normal

Table 7.2 Type of loss (percentage of population studied)

Study	Normal	Conductive or mixed	Sensori-neural
Brooks *et al.* (1972)	27	56	17
Balkany *et al.* (1979)	22	65	13
Dahle and McCollister (1986)	35	46	10
Davies (1988)	38	58	4

middle ear function in only 16 per cent of the sample. Thirty-eight per cent had normal hearing and 57 per cent had a mild to moderate hearing loss and the number of severe to profound losses was the same as in Brooks's study, namely 5 per cent (Table 7.3). Middle ear function as judged by impedance testing was abnormal in 71 per cent.

Buchanan (1990) reported a study of Down's Syndrome subjects of mixed ages with non-Down's controls. He excluded from his study all the conductive and mixed losses and looked at only sensori-neural problems, and particularly at the possible deterioration in hearing with age. He came to the conclusion that the higher frequency losses were occurring as early as the second decade and described this as an early onset of presbyacusis suggesting that this was another manifestation of the possible precocious ageing in Down's subjects. Buchanan felt that the so-called presbyacusis in Down's develops 20 to 30 years earlier than in other mentally retarded individuals and 30 to 40 years earlier than in the normal population, and suggested that Down's individuals of over 40 years of age should be considered for amplification. This, of course, ignores the fact that in most Down's individuals the loss is mixed in nature and the need for amplification is in fact at a very much earlier age and many Down's children of preschool age are needing amplification. He reported an important warning that brain-stem evoked response levels have to be interpreted with caution in Down's individuals because of the possible presence of presbyacusis.

Bluestone and Klein (1988) discuss the parallels between the middle ear function seen in Down's syndrome and children with other cranio-facial malformations, and also with children having a cleft palate.

An important contribution to the literature on middle ear dysfunction in Down's syndrome was made by White *et al.* (1984) in an analysis of Eustachian tube function in children with Down's syndrome. They concluded that Down's syndrome individuals were a unique population doubly at risk from serous otitis because of two functional abnormalities of the Eustachian tube. They showed that the Eustachian tube does not dilate and that the middle ear is therefore subject to high negative pressures and middle ear effusion. They also showed that because of the

Table 7.3 Degree (percentage) of hearing loss in population

Study	Normal	Mild	Moderate	Severe	Profound
Brooks *et al.* (1972)	27	58	10	4	1
Davies (1988)	38	36	21	4	1

low resistance of the tube unwanted secretions from the naso-pharynx can spread to the middle ear space resulting in middle ear infection. These workers showed that the particular nature of the dysfunction of the Eustachian tube in Down's children is almost unique and the only comparable population group they have found were Native Americans.

Strome (1981) reported an interesting study of Down's syndrome from an ear, nose and throat (ENT) point of view. He found an increased incidence of middle ear effusion in those children with stenotic meata, and he also reports that in his series adenoidectomy had little effect on middle ear effusion, breathing problems or rhinorrhoea. He reported a trend towards the disappearance of rhinorrhoea with age, presumably due to anatomical changes, and this finding would be confirmed by most workers in the field. Strome considered that the indications for tonsillectomy in Down's children are very limited and emphasized the postoperative risks of this operation in these children. In the UK there is considerable conservatism regarding the indications for tonsillectomy in all children, whether or not they suffer from Down's Syndrome.

Selikowitz (1993) reported a study of the effect of tympanostomy tubes in Down's syndrome children compared with a control group of normal children. Using careful audiological follow-up he showed that the results in the Down's group were poor even in the short term, i.e. after 6 to 9 weeks, as judged by hearing levels. Impairment had recurred in 40 per cent of the Down's ears and in only 9 per cent of the control ears. He does not comment on the tympanometric findings but implies that blockage of the tympanostomy tubes was the main problem. He points out that parents need to know of the high failure rate before surgery takes place. Unfortunately this information is still not widely known among audiologists and ENT surgeons.

Ongoing research (Marcel, 1994) is reporting the typical audiological findings of other workers. In this work with Down's Syndrome young adults the study of the relationship between hearing loss and their linguistic difficulties is showing that the long-standing auditory dysfunction in these individuals may be producing much more complex effects on their cognitive processing than had previously been thought.

A considerable degree of agreement clearly exists between different workers looking at auditory problems in Down's Syndrome – both middle ear function and hearing levels. Unfortunately information about the actual pathological processes taking place is very limited. The number of temporal bone studies is very small and there is an urgent need for more studies of this type.

Krmpotic-Nemanic (1970) reporting on a study of the temporal bones in two Down's children, one stillborn baby and one 7-year-old child, noted changes in the whole spiral tract reminiscent of those seen in advanced presbyacusis. Harada and Sando (1981) reported on temporal bones from seven patients with Down's syndrome and did not feel that their findings increased the understanding of the pathology of the hearing loss. They did however demonstrate that the cochlea was small in many cases, with a reduced number of turns, but they found that the organ of Corti was always well developed. In four cases they found evidence of middle ear inflammation and they reported that a remnant of mesenchymal tissue obstructing the round window in most of their patients might be significant, although its implications are not yet clear. Igarashi *et al.* (1977) studied four cases of Down's Syndrome all of whom were babies. They reported significantly shorter cochlea spirals but no significant difference in the widths of the basal coils. There were no other significant inner ear abnormalities. Of the four, three had evidence of middle ear effusions. Balkany *et al.* (1979) have reported the presence of abnormalities of the ossicles in some Down's children. This could of course be due to chronic middle ear disease. They also suggest that there may be a higher risk of development of Cholesteatoma in Down's children with chronic middle ear disease than in normal children with this condition, an observation which has been confirmed in the author's experience.

It is possible that progressive sensori-neural hearing loss in older Down's children and adults may be secondary to long-standing middle ear disease. One can look here for a parallel with individuals who have cleft palates and in whom middle ear effusions are almost universal and in whom there is an increasing risk of sensori-neural hearing loss with age (Bennett *et al.*, 1968; Bennett, 1972; Loeb 1964; Yules, 1970). Alternatively the mechanism in Down's syndrome may be different and associated with an abnormally rapid ageing process in the cochlea. There is no doubt that the nature of the problem in older children and in young adults with Down's syndrome is a mixed one, combining a persistent conductive hearing loss with middle ear effusion and a high risk of a sensori-neural hearing loss particularly affecting the higher frequencies (4 kHz and 8 kHz). A full understanding of the pathological process which is occurring in these individuals remains to be achieved by further serial audiological studies and further pathological studies of temporal bones.

AUDIOLOGICAL ASSESSMENT

A full history is taken, especially in relation to the frequency of upper respiratory tract infections and any ear, nose and throat problems. The parents' opinions of the child's hearing should be sought together with a history of the child's speech and language development.

Audiological assessment of the Down's child is carried out using standard techniques of paediatric audiology. The tests used must always be appropriate for the child's mental age at the time of the assessment. In a clinic where a large number of Down's children are examined it is found to be possible to carry out threshold pure tone audiometry with headphones in a few Down's children at the age of 3 to 3½ years. In skilled hands a threshold audiogram can be obtained at a mental age of about 2½ years. However in the majority of Down's children a reliable pure tone audiogram will not be obtained until 4 to 5 years. Occasionally in a very severely handicapped older child techniques usually used only in babies will have to be attempted.

In babies, a distraction test using the Ewing technique is usually carried out and one expects to be able to identify reliable localizing responses to sound when the child is at a developmental level of 6 to 7 months of age, and occasionally a little below this. It is nevertheless worth while seeing Down's babies before they reach this developmental level as tympanometry can be carried out and the presence of a middle ear effusion identified. In addition the nature of the problem can be explained to the parents and they can be helped to understand why it is necessary for their baby to have regular hearing checks. Parents will often ask about the possibility of deterioration of hearing and a full understanding of the possibilities in terms of future management is invariably helpful for the parents and ensures their future co-operation.

If a child's mental age is around 2 years, attempts should be made to condition the child to sound using speech sounds (e.g. 'Go'). Successful approximate thresholds for 'Go' and subsequently for the sound 'SS' can then be obtained using play techniques. Later, one can proceed to condition the child to pure tones or warble tones using a free-field audiometer and suitable play material. Once the child is able to co-operate adequately in free-field testing one can proceed to carry out threshold audiometry using headphones. For those children unhappy to wear a headset testing can be by means of a single headphone.

Throughout the testing it is essential to maintain very close rapport with the child, and the parent(s) need to be close by to provide support if the child becomes anxious. It is essential also to have a wide variety of suitable materials available for the tests (stacking beakers, 2.5 cm bricks, large-sized-wooden pegs) to provide frequent changes of game and maintain the child's interest in the procedure. As in all paediatric audiological testing, unless the child's interest is sustained and he or she is enjoying the task reliable results will not be obtained. The testing of Down's children is no different from the testing of other children except that the procedure takes a little longer and requires a greater expenditure of energy by the tester. Most Down's children enjoy the tests but they may show certain characteristics of response which have to be observed. There may be a delay in response (both in a distraction test and performance test) and the timing of signals has therefore to be very carefully controlled. The child has to be encouraged to wait carefully for the signals in pure tone audiometry but some Down's children become impatient and need a good deal of persuasion. In distraction testing the length of signal must sometimes be increased for some babies before a response is obtained and as a result the timing of signal presentation requires considerable care.

An older Down's child with a severe previously undiagnosed hearing loss may be difficult to test as his auditory attention is usually poor. In these children the first attempt at pure tone audiometry may be difficult but often with adequate control of his or her responses, the child may prove much easier to test on subsequent occasions. Obtaining pure tone levels for air and bone conduction is essential but it is frequently difficult, or impossible, to use any masking procedures. Tympanometry requires a suitable impedance bridge and the child should be introduced to the machine in a way which is suitable for his or her mental age. In those children who are unhappy to accept tympanometry allowing the child to control the trace by pressing the buttons of the machine will often distract him or her from the unhappiness of having the probe in his or her ear. A child's thresholds for speech can usually only be explored using toy material (Kendall test or the McCormick test). Ability to perform in these tests will depend not only on auditory acuity but also on linguistic level. Despite the limitations of such tests and their inaccuracy compared with techniques used in older children and adults they will nevertheless provide useful information on the child's auditory function in relation to speech.

Many Down's children now use Makaton signing at school and will respond to the names of the toys in a toy test by signing the appropriate word instead of pointing to the object and this response is perfectly acceptable. In older Down's children and adults standardized word lists can be used (Manchester Junior Words or AB Word Lists) either in free field or through headphones as one would for normal children. Results may be difficult to evaluate because of scoring problems produced by phonological errors. Picture identification tests are a useful alternative.

It is rarely necessary to use evoked response techniques (brain-stem evoked responses) in Down's children. However, for a young child where there is a suspicion of a sensori-neural loss and behavioural testing is difficult such techniques can be used.

In some areas Down's babies may be included in a high-risk register (with other children with cranio-facial abnormalities) for brain-stem evoked response screening soon after birth. The relatively rare congenital sensori-neural loss would be identified by this technique but the very common auditory deficits will only develop later. Therefore if the new born Down's baby passes screening, it must be understood that it will still need careful audiological surveillance.

Techniques of testing using oto-acoustic emissions (Cope and Lutman, 1988) have not been found useful because of the very high incidence of middle ear effusions. On the other hand the techniques of visual response audiometry (VRA) as described by Bamford (1988) are proving very useful in many centres. Greenberg *et al.* (1978) a study using VRA in Down's children. In the UK the technique is found to be particularly useful in children of a developmental level of 14 to 15 months up to 2½ years, that is, it is especially useful in children who are too old for successful testing by distraction techniques and too young to co-operate successfully in a conditioning technique. There seems to be no doubt that VRA is a most useful technique both in normal children and in handicapped children given appropriate selection by developmental age.

The ENT examination will usually show the pinnae to be as described previously with stenosed meata which are often occluded with wax and desquamated epithelium. Full visualization of the tympanic membranes is often very difficult. There may be marked nasal and/or postnasal obstruction and it is common to find chronic rhinorrhoea with a purulent nasal discharge.

AUDIOLOGICAL FINDINGS AND DISCUSSION

(The findings discussed below are depicted among Figures 7.2a to 7.11b.)

Middle ear dysfunction with flat tympanograms and a conductive hearing loss is the most usual finding in young Down's children. The hearing loss is likely to be between 25 and 50 dB(H1), usually bilateral, and in young children is generally of an entirely conductive nature.

This varying hearing loss parallels the well known natural history of middle ear

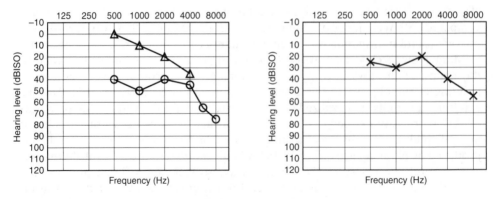

Figure 7.2 MF (M) 11 yrs
Typical mixed loss. Excellent hearing aid use and child in mainstream school

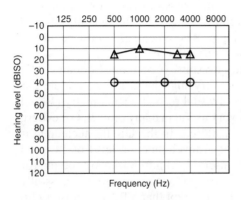

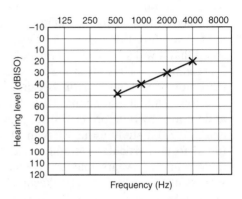

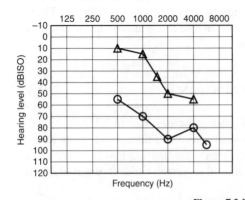

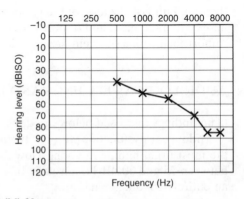

Figure 7.3 RC (M) 20 yrs
Typical progressive mixed loss with good hearing aid use
(a) at 7 years (b) at 20 years

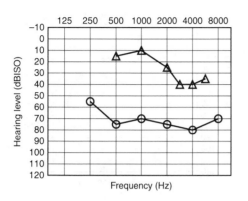
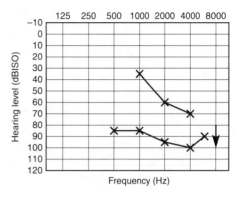

Figure 7.4 LE (F) 24 yrs
Typical mixed loss unchanging from age 14 to 24 years

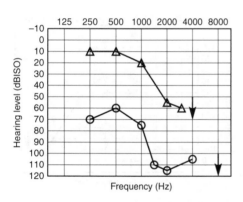
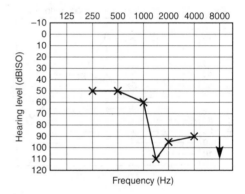

Figure 7.5 AR (M) 14 yrs
Late diagnosis (14 years) of typical mixed loss with bilinguality. Hearing aid use unsuccessful

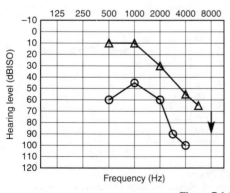
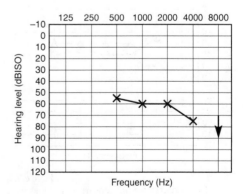

Figure 7.6 TB (M) 10.5 yrs
Late diagnosis (10.5 years) with severe behavioural disturbance. Good result of aiding.

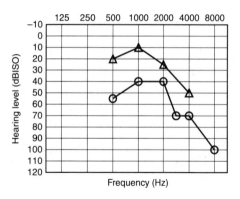
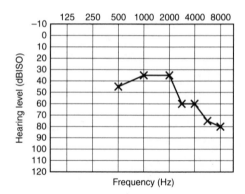

Figure 7.7 SR (M) 28 yrs
Typical mixed loss. No deterioration from 18 years to 28 years

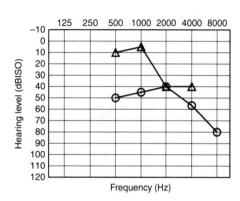
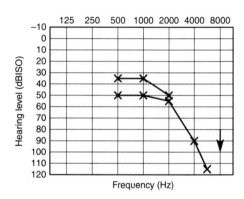

Figure 7.8 SK (F) 28 yrs
Slowly progressive mixed loss from 11 years to 30 years. No deterioration from 20 years to 30 years.

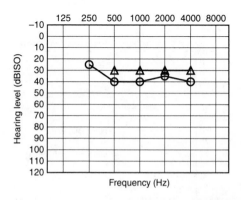
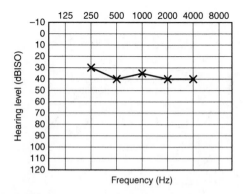

Figure 7.9 HR (F) 29 yrs
Rare progressive flat sensori-neural loss with no effusion. Reviewed from 14 years to 32 years
(a) at 14 years (b) at 29 years

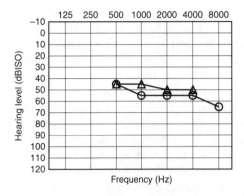
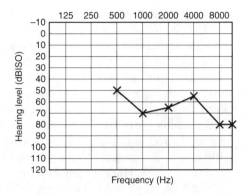

Figure 7.9 (cont'd) HR (F) 29 yrs
Rare progressive flat sensori-neural loss with no effusion. Reviewed from 14 years to 32 years
(a) at 14 years (b) at 29 years

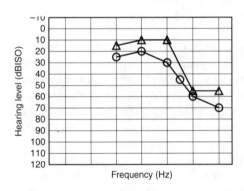
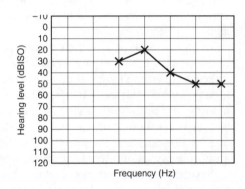

Figure 7.10 RI (F) 8 yrs
High frequency sensori-neural loss without effusion

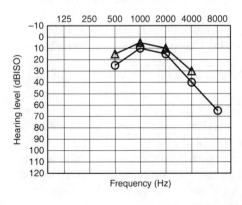
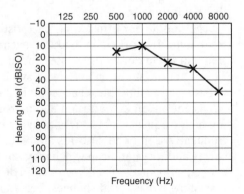

Figure 7.11 JM (M) 9 yrs
High frequency sensori-neural loss without effusion

effusion in normal children. However, the particular characteristics of the condition in Down's children is that the tympanogram rarely returns to normal, even when the child is going through a phase of having relatively good hearing thresholds. As the middle ear disease starts early in life and is so persistent and intractable it seems likely that this may well have considerable effects on the child's linguistic development. There is a considerable literature on the effects of mild conductive hearing loss in normal children and this is currently a topic of great interest to audiologists and psychologists. The long-term effects of mild to moderate conductive hearing loss in children are less well known. There is a very considerable literature on serous otitis media, in particular, the following studies: Chalmers et al., 1989; Bluestone and Klein, 1988; Haggard and Hughes, 1991; Lim *et al.*, 1984; Rapin, 1979.

It seems reasonable to extrapolate from work with normal children – in whom the effects of even mild hearing losses on linguistic progress and on educational progress are well known – to the situation in Down's children. They cannot use compensatory mechanisms so effectively as normal children and a conductive hearing loss of moderate degree may in their case produce severe problems of auditory attention, delay in linguistic development and delay in progress at school as well as behaviour changes.

In later childhood a high frequency sensori-neural hearing loss frequently develops at 4 kHz and at 8 kHz. This may be monaural at first but then usually affects both ears. There is then a tendency as the years pass for this loss to progress in severity and gradually to affect lower frequencies. Although the sensori-neural hearing loss commonly begins in later childhood it may occasionally start as early as four years. Long-term studies show that the progression of the loss often ceases at 18 to 20 years and the pure tone audiograms remain unchanged for many years and probably indefinitely (author's unpublished data).

Severe or profound congenital sensori-neural hearing loss is rarely seen in Down's babies and in the writer's experience is invariably associated with very severe levels of general retardation. A progressive sensori-neural loss affecting all frequencies without any conductive element is also an unusual occurrence.

In those children who have no middle ear effusion it is still important to monitor their hearing levels, as the progressive sensori-neural hearing loss often occurs in these children also.

The middle ear effusion characteristically persists in spite of rigorous surgical treatment. In normal individuals such effusions commonly become much less frequent as childhood progresses and are relatively unusual after the age of 9 years. This is not the situation in Down's syndrome where middle ear effusion frequently persists into adult life. The combination of a conductive hearing loss due to persistent middle ear effusion and a progressive sensori-neural hearing loss affecting high frequencies produces a highly characteristic audiometric picture which is frequently seen in adolescents and young adults. The effect of this is to produce a severe auditory handicap which may not be recognized in otherwise severely handicapped individuals. The Down's child or young adult whose hearing is deteriorating may show behavioural changes, becoming withdrawn and quiet and making poor educational progress.

MEDICAL MANAGEMENT

Down's children are particularly susceptible to frequent upper respiratory tract infections. The characteristic picture of chronic rhinorrhoea with a varying degree of nasal and postnasal obstruction is very common. Children presenting in this way will frequently be shown to be suffering from a middle ear effusion with a conductive hearing loss. In spite of a considerable amount of research it is still not clear why Down's children should have these particular problems. It may well be that the aetiology of their characteristic ENT difficulties is associated with deficiencies in their immune system (Breg, 1977; Smith and Berg, 1976), combined with structural abnormalities of the skull (Spitzer *et al.*, 1961) which militate against good middle ear ventilation.

A parallel can be drawn here with children who have a cleft palate in whom middle ear effusion is virtually universal and in whom the mechanism of failure of middle ear aeration is well understood. A Down's child who also has a cleft palate is, of course particularly at risk for severe middle ear problems. Unfortunately the middle ear effusion tends to persist even after repair of the palate.

The use of decongestants for the management of chronic upper respiratory catarrhal problems with middle ear effusion is widely debated. Although such decongestants are often used there is no research evidence to show that they are effective (Cantekin *et al.*, 1983). In clinical practice there are undoubtedly some children who show some benefit from the use of decongestants but their use in Down's children tends to be less successful than in other children. Some parents feel that the children's respiratory tract infections are less frequent when they are given large doses of Vitamin C but there are as yet no carefully controlled studies on this subject. Most ENT surgeons are not in favour of the use of decongestant nose drops on a long-term basis. There is no evidence as yet that there is likely to be an allergic element contributing to the upper respiratory problems of most Down's children. Clearly antibiotic treatment is not indicated for serous otitis media. However, in those Down's children with severe upper respiratory catarrhal problems with middle ear effusion there is sometimes improvement by the use of low-dose antibiotics, especially through the winter months.

SURGICAL TREATMENT

Those children who have persistent middle ear effusion with a severe conductive hearing loss are frequently subjected to surgery, i.e. myringotomies and the insertion of grommets, with adenoidectomy if indicated. If there is evidence of sinus infection, antral washout at the same time is clearly useful. The immediate results of surgery are sometimes good, often with improvement in hearing levels and sometimes a small leap forward in linguistic progress. In the author's practice over the last 20 years initially many Down's children seen were subjected to this surgery. However, the long-term results were so poor that this line of approach has largely been given up. If a child is to be subjected to surgery, the parents must be fully informed beforehand, i.e. they must be told that any improvement is likely to be temporary and that, although rarely improvement may last a year, in many cases the middle ear effusion recurs within a matter of weeks of surgery.

These children may present considerable problems to the surgeon as the meata may be so severely stenosed that it is impossible to insert grommets. It is of interest that the fluid removed at myringotomy in Down's children is often quite characteristic in nature. In normal children the viscosity of the middle ear fluid when removed at myringotomy is very variable from a thin serous-like fluid to a thick highly viscous material, hence the common name of 'glue ear'. In Down's children the fluid removed is invariably of a highly viscous nature and can be almost cartilaginous in quality. However despite this obvious difference in middle ear effusion in normal children and Down's children pathologists have not been able, so far, to demonstrate histological or biochemical differences between the effusions. Current research (Pearson and Hutton, 1994) on the nature of the Down's effusion may well elucidate this problem and perhaps lead to new ideas for treatment.

In view of the chronicity of the effusion, if a decision is made to perform myringotomy it is useful to insert T-tubes rather than grommets. These are of a wider bore than grommets and tend to remain patent and *in situ* for a longer period. They therefore improve the possibilities of maintaining good middle ear aeration for a longer period. However, both grommets and T-tubes in Down's children often become blocked (Selikowitz, 1993) and the problem then persists of dealing with a chronic middle ear effusion and its effects on hearing, and of making decisions about further anaesthesia for the removal and reinsertion of tubes. Most ENT surgeons are loath to insert grommets or T-tubes on more than three occasions because of the scarring of the tympanic membranes which may result.

If middle ear infection with a purulent otorrhea develops after surgery this must be rigorously treated with good aural toilet and topical antibiotics and systemic antibiotics if indicated. A compromise mode of treatment is to grommet one ear only so that if infection occurs in that ear and hearing aid use is indicated, one can fit a hearing aid to the ungrommetted ear. If the Down's child has a mixed hearing loss it is essential to explain to the parents that surgical intervention will not cure a sensori-neural element and it is important that parents and professionals concerned in the management of the child understand what degree of improvement is likely to occur. It is of course essential that for all Down's children who are going to be subjected to myringotomies careful audiological assessment is carried out beforehand so that both the surgeon and the parents know as precisely as possible what the effects of surgery are likely to be. This principle, of course, applies to all children being subjected to myringotomies but unfortunately careful audiological assessment prior to surgery is by no means universal.

The question of adenoidectomy for middle ear effusion is a subject of considerable debate in normal and Down's children. In some cases severe postnasal obstruction with enlarged adenoids presents a clear indication for adenoidal removal but without this indication myringotomies without adenoidectomy are usually carried out.

There must always be a careful assessment of a Down's child's fitness for anaesthesia, especially if congenital heart disease is present.

HEARING AIDS

Because of the intractable nature of the middle ear problem and the fact that it is frequently not resolved by surgical intervention, there is an increasing tendency to use hearing aids as an alternative to surgery. In the past there has been a dis-inclination to use aids in severely retarded children because of the alleged difficul-ties in getting the child to accept the aid. The fitting of suitable aids to a Down's child is now very much easier as miniature postaural aids are freely available in the UK through the National Health Service. It is also now possible to obtain well-fitting ear moulds as a wide variety of ear mould material is now available (Figure 7.12). Most practitioners in the field find that the majority of Down's children accept their aids very well. The first task of the prescriber is of course to explain to the parents why the aids are necessary because without their enthusiastic support the use of hearing aids is impossible.

The main problems in fitting postaural aids to these children are in finding an aid which is ergonomically suitable (because the pinna is usually so small) and to obtain a well-fitting ear mould. Stenosed meata present considerable problems but they can usually be overcome by using suitable techniques in taking impressions and by using soft material for the construction of the moulds. It is essential to clear

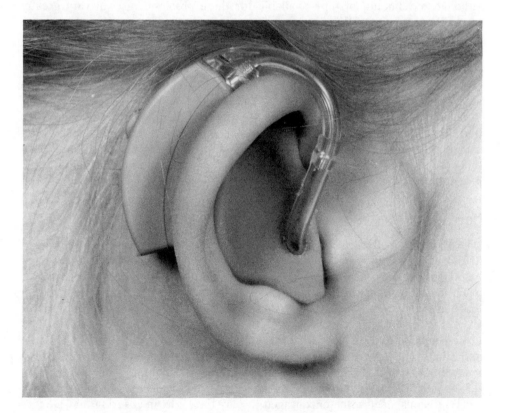

Figure 7.12 Well-fitting ear moulds are now readily available in a wide variety of materials.

the meata of wax and debris before taking an impression. The choice of aids will of course depend on the nature of the hearing loss. Because of the well-known risk of a deteriorating loss, regular assessment of hearing levels at, say six-monthly intervals is necessary as aids providing higher gain may well be needed as the child grows older. For a child to use aids effectively a teacher of the hearing impaired must be involved and in most cases this will be a peripatetic teacher visiting the child at home or at school. The teacher will be responsible for overseeing the use of aids and to work both with the parents and other involved professionals to help them to understand the implications of the child's hearing loss, and to teach them how to help the child to make the best use of his or her residual hearing, as well as to improve the child's auditory attention and linguistic progress.

The provision of a support service by teachers of hearing-impaired children for those children with a severe learning problem varies across the UK, and the amount of time teachers feel able to spend with such children will obviously depend on their own case loads. With an increasing number of Down's children in school provided with hearing aids, there is a need for a regular service from a peripatetic teacher and it is to be hoped that educational authorities will accept the need for such a service.

Special schools often have the services of a speech and language therapist although the amount of time available for these professionals will vary greatly from school to school. Where such a therapist is involved in organizing language programmes within the school, the teacher of hearing-impaired children and the speech therapist should work closely together. The audiological physician or the ENT surgeon concerned in managing the child's hearing problem must liaise regularly with the teacher of the hearing impaired, speech therapist and others who are involved in providing care for these children.

If hearing aids are to be used, there are emotional and practical difficulties for the parents in accepting that the child needs to use such equipment. However, usually the considerable advantage to the child soon becomes apparent and once this occurs the parents are allies with the professionals in trying to maintain the best auditory function in their child.

CONCLUSIONS

There is ample evidence, from the small but consistent body of research relating to auditory function in Down's children and adults, that all Down's individuals need careful audiological supervision from infancy and throughout their lives. Surgery, when indicated, and hearing aids and appropriate support services from the professionals concerned should be available to all Down's individuals. The implications for audiological services are considerable. More, adequately trained professionals are needed to carry out good audiological assessments of children and adults with severe learning problems and the training of doctors, scientists, teachers and speech therapists needs to be improved so that they can provide a better service for Down's children. Doctors, whether family doctors, paediatricians or ENT surgeons, need to be encouraged to play their part in ensuring that Down's children have as good an auditory function as it is possible to provide.

Parents of Down's children should be informed about the likelihood of hearing deficits and should be encouraged to ensure that this aspect of their child's development is carefully monitored and appropriate treatment given.

The questions posed at the beginning of this chapter are not yet answered:

1. We do not know why a few Down's children remain free of middle ear effusion and hearing loss, although it is clear that these children are invariably free of upper respiratory tract problems. Some of these children develop a sensorineural loss suggesting that the cause of this is not chronic serous otitis media.
2. The pathological process of the progressive high frequency loss is not understood, nor is it known why the deterioration often ceases in early adult life.
3. The ideal screening programme is undoubtedly that all Down's syndrome children under 1 year old should have careful audiological assessment by skilled paediatric audiologists. Follow-up intervals will depend on the findings, varying from three months to a year. All Down's syndrome individuals need audiological review at least annually.
4. Management should include:
   a) the best possible hearing aid service
   b) optimum support services by teachers of the hearing impaired and speech and language therapists.
   c) Close liaison between audiologists and speech and language therapists to attempt to elucidate further the effects of auditory deficits on linguistic progress.

Future research, both clinical and pathological, may lead to a greater understanding of the nature of the hearing deficits in Down's syndrome and may, as a result, lead to possible improvements in our management of these problems.

REFERENCES

Balkany, T.J., Down's, M.P., Jafek, B.W. and Krajicek, M.J. (1979) Hearing loss in Down's syndrome. *Clinical Pediatrics*, **18** (2), pp. 116–18.

Balkany, T.J., Mischke, R.E., Down's, M.P. and Jafek, B.W. (1979) Ossicular abnormalities in Down's syndrome. *Otolaryngology: Head and Neck Surgery*, **87**, p. 372.

Bamford, J. (1988) Visual reinforcement audiometry. In B.W. McCormick (eds.), *Paediatric Audiology 0–5 years*, London: WHURR, pp. 117–35,

Bennett, M. (1972) The older cleft palate patient. *Laryngoscope*, **82**, p. 1217.

Bennett, M., Ward, R.H. and Tait, C.A. (1968) Otologic and audiologic study of cleft palate children. *Laryngoscope*, **78**, pp. 1011–19.

Bluestone, C.D. (1978) Prevalence and pathogenesis of ear disease and hearing loss. In M.D. Graham (ed.), *Cleft Palate: Middle Ear Disease and Hearing Loss*, Springfield: Charles C. Thomas.

Bluestone, C.D., Klein, J.O. (1988) *Otitis Media in Infants and Children*, Philadelphia: Saunders.

Breg, W.R. (1977) Down syndrome: a review-of recent progress in research. *Pathobiology Annual*, **7**, pp. 257–303.

Brooks, D.N., Wooley, H. and Kanjilal, G.C. (1972) Hearing loss and middle ear disorders in patients with Down's syndrome. *Journal of Mental Deficiency Research*, **16**, pp. 21–9.

Buchanan, L.H. (1990) Early onset of presbyacusis in Down syndrome. *Scandinavian Audiology*, **19**, pp. 103–10.

Cantekin, E.L., Mandel, E.M., Bluestone, C.D., Rockette, H.E., Paradise, J.L., Stool, S.E., Fria, T.J., Rogers, K.D. (1983) Lack of efficacy of a decongestant-antihistamine combination for otitis media with effusion (secretory otitis media) in children: results of a double randomized trial. *New England Journal of Medicine*, **308**, pp. 297–301.

Chalmers, D., Stewart, I., Silva, P., Mulvena, A. (1989) *Otitis Media with Effusion in Children: the Dunedin Study*. Clinics in Developmental Medicine No 108, London: MacKeith Press.

Cope, Y., Lutman, M.E. (1988) Oto-acoustic emissions. In B.W. McCormick (ed.), *Paediatric Audiology 0–5 years*, London : WHURR, pp. 221–45.

Cunningham, C. and McArthur, K. (1981) Hearing loss and treatment in young Down's syndrome children. *Child: Care, Health and Development*, **7**, pp. 357–74.

Dahle, A.J. and McCollister, F.P. (1986) Hearing and otologic disorders in children with Down syndrome. *American Journal of Mental Deficiency*, 90, **6**, pp. 636–42.

Davies, B. (1988) Auditory disorders in Down's syndrome. In J.J. Barras and E. Borg (eds) Overview and evaluation of the hearing impaired child. *Scandinavian Audiology*, supp. 30. pp. 65–68.

Davies, B. and Penniceard, R.M. (1980) Auditory function and receptive vocabulary in Down's syndrome children. In I.G. Taylor and A. Markides (eds), *Disorders of Auditory Function III*, London: Academic Press.

Down, J. Langdon. (1887) On some of the mental affections of childhood and youth. (Lettsomian Lectures). In R.G. Mitchell (ed.), (1990) *Classics in Developmental Medicine*, (No 5), MacKeith Press.

Fulton, R.T. and Lloyd, L.L. (1968) Hearing impairment in a population of children with Down's syndrome. *American Journal of Mental Deficiency*, **73**, p. 298.

Glovsky, L. (1966) Audiological assessment of a mongoloid population. *Training School Bulletin*, **33**, p. 27.

Greenberg, D.B., Wilson, W.R., Moore, J.M. and Thomson, G. (1978) Visual reinforcement audiometry (VRA) with young Down's syndrome children. *Journal of Speech and Hearing Disorders*, **43**, pp. 448–58.

Haggard, M. and Hughes, E. (1991) *Screening Children's Hearing*, London: HMSO.

Harada, T. and Sando, I. (1981) Temporal bone histopathological findings in Down's Syndrome. *Archives of Otolaryngology*, **107**, pp. 96–103.

Igarashi, M. Takahashi, I. Alford, B.R. and Johnson, P.E. (1977) Inner ear morphology in Down's syndrome. *Acta Otolaryngologica*, **83**, p. 175.

Jerger, J. (1970) Clinical experience with impedance audiometry. *Archives of Otolaryngology* **92**, pp. 311–24.

Keiser, H., Montague, J., Wold, D., Maune, S. and Pattison, D. (1981) Hearing loss of Down's syndrome adults. *American Journal of Mental Deficiency*, **85** (5), pp. 467-72.

Krmpotic-Nemanic, J. (1970) Down's syndrome and presbyacusis. *Lancet*, **2**, pp. 670–71.

Lim, D.L., Bluestone, C.D., Klein, J.O., Nelson, J.D. (1984) *Recent Advances in Otitis Media with Effusion*, Philadelphia: Decker.

Loeb, W.J. (1964) Speech, hearing and the cleft palate. *Archives of Otolaryngology*, **79**, pp. 20–30.

McIntire, M.S., Menolascino, F.J. and Wiley, J.H. (1965) Mongolisms: some clinical aspects. *American Journal of Mental Deficiency*, **69** p. 794.

Marcell, M.M. (1994) Recent audiological and cognitive findings from a three year longitudinal study of adolescents and young adults with Down's syndrome. Verbal presentation. Royal Society of Medicine and Down's Syndrome Association Symposium, London.

Nolan, M. McCartney, E. McArthur, K. and Rowson, V.R. (1980) A study of the hearing and receptive vocabulary of the trainees of an adult training centre. *Journal of Mental Deficiency Research*, **24**, pp. 271–86.

Pearson, J.P. and Hutton, D.A. (1994) Glue: a physiological and molecular perspective. Verbal presentation. Royal Society of Medicine and Down's Syndrome Association Symposium, London.

Rapin, I. (1979) Conductive hearing loss: effect on children's language and scholastic skills: a review of the literature. *Annals of Otology, Rhinology and Laryngology* **88,** suppl. 60, pp. 3–12.

Rigrodsky, S., Prunty, F. and Glovsky, L. (1961) A study of the incidence, types and associated etiologies of hearing loss in an institutionalised mentally retarded population. *Training School Bulletin*, **58,** p. 30.

Schwartz, D.M. and Schwartz, R.H. (1978) Acoustic impedance and otoscopic findings in young children with Down's syndrome. *Archives of Otolaryngology*, **104,** pp. 652–56.

Selikowitz, M. (1993) Short-term efficacy of tympanostomy tubes for secretory otitis media in children with Down syndrome. *Developmental Medicine and Child Neurology*, **35,** pp. 511–15.

Smith, G.F. and Berg. J.M. (1976) *Down's Anomaly*, 2nd edn, Edinburgh: Churchill Livingstone.

Spitzer, R., Rabinowitch, J.Y. and Wybar, K.C. (1961) A study of the abnormalities of the skull, teeth and lenses in mongolism. *Journal of the Canadian Medical Association*, **84,** pp. 567–72.

Strome, M. (1981), Down's syndrome: a modern otorhinolaryngolical perspective. *Laryngoscope*, **91** (10), pp. 1581–94.

White, B. LeM., Doyle, W.J., Bluestone, C.D. (1984) Eustachian tube function in infants and children with Down's syndrome. In D.L. Lim, C.D. Bluestone, J.O. Klein and J.D. Nelson (eds) *Recent Advances in Otitis Media with Effusion*, Philadelphia: Decker, pp. 62–66,

Yules, R.B. (1970) Hearing in cleft palate patients. *Archives of Otolaryngology*, **91,** pp. 319–23.

8 Ocular Findings in Children

Christopher J. Hammond and Elisabeth A. Millis

INTRODUCTION

Ocular abnormalities are almost universally found in Down's syndrome, but many children are not referred to ophthalmologists routinely. Some of the features, which will be described in this chapter, have diagnostic significance but no functional importance: for example the epicanthic folds, broad nasal bridge, sloping eyelids and Brushfield spots. Other features have therapeutic importance because they may significantly affect the vision: keratoconus and corneal scarring, cataracts and refractive errors fall into this category.

Much of the older literature is concerned with describing the eye features and associations, but recently efforts have been directed at the more practical aspects of care for children with ocular complications of Down's syndrome. The first part of this chapter will detail the ocular anomalies including a literature review, and the second part will deal with management of the eye problems to deal with and prevent sight-threatening complications.

In a survey of mothers' health concerns about their children with Down's syndrome, visual problems (as well as hearing problems and respiratory infections) were perceived as the most common concerns (Turner *et al.*, 1990).

OCULAR MANIFESTATIONS

External ocular findings

'The eyes are obliquely placed and the internal canthi more than normally distant from one another. The palpebral fissure is very narrow.' This was how Langdon Down (1866, p. 259) described the ocular features which contributed so much to the characteristic facial appearance of a group of retarded children in his care. Indeed, he commented that the appearance was so typical that a group of unrelated children could be mistaken for siblings.

Down thought that the flat cheekbones and shape of the palpebral apertures suggested that these children looked 'mongolian' and he used this term to describe the disorder (ibid., ch. 1). In fact, the apertures are shorter, wider and more tilted than in the true Mongolian, where they are seen to be long, narrow and almond shaped. Despite this disparity, however, Down had succeeded in labelling a particular group of handicapped children, who show a variety of ocular abnormalities. Ormond (1912, p. 69) remarked that 'almost all have some ocular defect', citing blepharitis, distorted lids, squint, nystagmus and cataract as common problems.

Epicanthic folds

These folds of skin situated on either side of the nose, often overlying the medial canthi (Figure 8.1). They are usually bilateral, but may be asymmetrical. They are common in normal babies but disappear as the nasal bridge and face develop. In trisomy 21, the nasal bridge is flat and all babies have epicanthic folds: these may have led Langdon Down to conclude that the eyes were set further apart than in the normal baby. Although they are more marked in children with Down's Syndrome, they usually disappear as the child reaches teenage years.

The folds can give rise to an apparent squint ('pseudosquint'), especially when a child looks to one side: the eye tucks behind the fold of skin adjacent to the nose, giving an impression of turning too far. The apparent squint can be differentiated from a true squint by observing corneal reflections and by the cover test (see later).

Blepharitis

Blepharitis occurs commonly in Down's syndrome, resulting in red and irritable eyelids with dry flakes appearing at the base of the lashes. Chronic staphylococcal bacterial infection, abnormally sensitive skin and Demodex mites have all been implicated in the aetiology. It may cause irritation resulting in eye rubbing which could cause distortion of the eyelids; either entropion (turning in) or ectropion (turning out). Ingrowing eyelashes (trichiasis) which rub the cornea causing irritation may also result. In addition, the tear film is abnormal (Filipello *et al.*, 1992) which will also contribute to increased infections.

Keratoconus

Several investigators have reported cases of keratoconus (a conical protrusion of the central cornea). It is a degenerative bilateral disease in which there is generalized thinning of the cornea which causes marked astigmatism (irregular curvature of the cornea) which ultimately cannot be corrected with spectacles. It may cause hydrops, a rupture of the deep layer of the cornea (Descemet's membrane), causing corneal swelling (oedema) and scarring and loss of useful vision. Rados (1948) reported two cases in young adults. Later, Cullen and Butler (1963) examined 143 patients with Down's Syndrome aged 2 to 53 years and found keratoconus in 5.5 per cent of the series.

Keratoconus tends to occur around the time of puberty in these children. The acute form (hydrops) is more common in Down's syndrome than any other disorder. The aetiology is unknown, but other associated diseases (for example atopic eczema and vernal conjunctivitis) have been shown to have increased eye rubbing

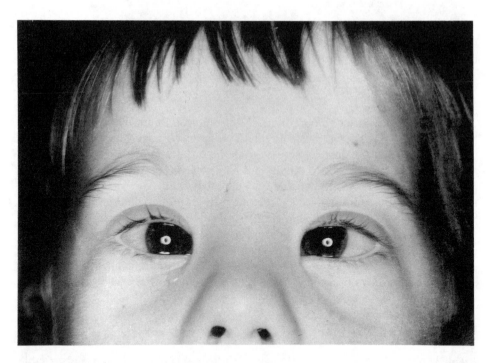

Figure 8.1 Epicanthic folds are broad folds of skin adjacent to the nose giving the appearance of a pseudosquint. In this child, the light reflex on the cornea in each eye is asymmetric, suggesting a true squint.

and this may well be a causative factor. The rubbing may release proteolytic enzymes which thin the cornea (Pierse and Eustace, 1971).

Iris anomalies

Brushfield(1924) included in his thesis on mongolism a brief review of the ocular features and noted pale-coloured spots on the iris which have continued to be known by his name (Figure 8.2). These spots are situated at the junction of the middle and outer thirds of the iris and are more easily seen in blue than brown eyes. Indeed, Brooke Williams (1981) could not demonstrate any nodules in the black children he examined. However, he did not use a slit-lamp microscope, and with sufficient magnification and illumination the nodules are visible on the dark-brown iris.

As with many features of Down's syndrome, the spots occur more frequently than in the normal population and are more likely to encircle the iris completely. Donaldson (1961) reported an incidence of 85 per cent as against 24 per cent in normal subjects. The nodules are condensations of the anterior stromal layer of the iris, and have no pathological significance. Brushfield spots have been reported in other syndromes with chromosomal anomalies, and Brooke Williams suggests that they may be an indicator of defective development of a foetus. Donaldson (1961) attempted to assess their significance but failed to find a correlation between spots, age or IQ.

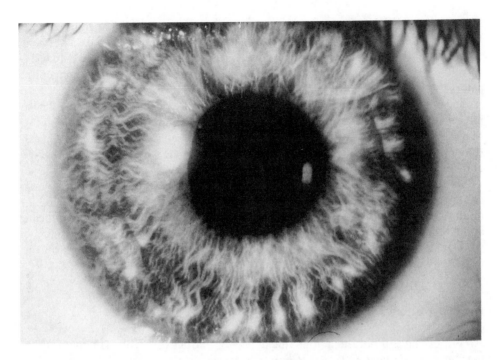

Figure 8.2 Brushfield spots are pale-coloured spots at the junction of the middle and outer thirds of the iris (the coloured part of the eye).

The pupils appear normal but they are abnormally sensitive to Atropine (Berg *et al.*, 1959), showing a more rapid and sustained dilatation. Although initial reports suggested a blue iris, this merely represented the studied population: Down's syndrome occurs in all ethnic groups and affected eyes can be blue or brown.

Cataracts

The most detailed survey of the ocular manifestations of the disease is, in the authors' opinion, that undertaken by Lowe (1949). In his well-illustrated account he described all the common features of the disease, with the exception of keratoconus and the more recently described abnormal retinal vessels. In particular, he described four types of cataract; arcuate, sutural, flake and congenital lens opacities. Nearly all studies remark on the presence of more than one type of cataract in any given lens, particularly in older children. They also agree that virtually all these children show some evidence of cataract by the time they are in their teens.

The incidence of cataract in Down's syndrome varies. Some investigators only included 'those cataracts which would seem dense enough to cause visual difficulty' (Eissler and Lognecker, 1962, p. 399), and not all investigators used a slit-lamp to examine the lens, particularly in children. However, the incidence is believed to be of the order of 50 per cent.

An incidence of congenital cataracts (cataracts present at birth) in children with Down's syndrome of 1 to 6 per cent has been reported, compared to 0.03 per cent in the general population. They may interfere seriously with vision and may be related to trisomy 21 or an unrelated cause; they appear similar to other congenital cataracts.

The most common form of cataract is the dot or flake opacity (Figure 8.3). These have an oil-drop appearance and usually occur initially in the lens periphery and so may be overlooked in an undilated pupil. Because they are small and peripheral, they rarely encroach on the visual axis and so do not affect vision, but in teenage and adulthood may coalesce and affect vision.

Sutural opacities develop within the foetal nucleus, deep in the lens (which continues to grow throughout life, adding layers). They are in the form of an anterior Y suture (Figure 8.4) or in the posterior inverted Y. They are often delicate and feathery and can only be seen with the slit-lamp.

Arcuate opacities are less common and seen as a small white arc deep in the lens. They are probably a sectoral form of zonular cataract.

Refractive errors

All series have reported a high incidence of refractive errors (Fanning 1971; Gardiner, 1967; Jaeger, 1980). Refractive errors consist of myopia (short sight),

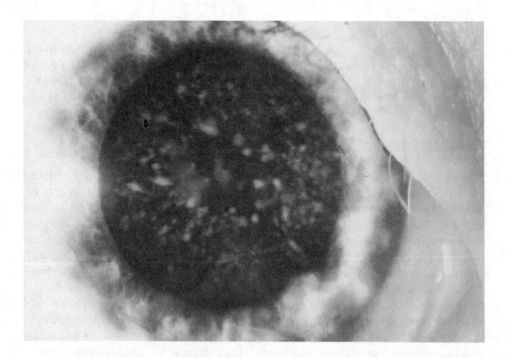

Figure 8.3 Congenital flake or dot cataract which may impair vision

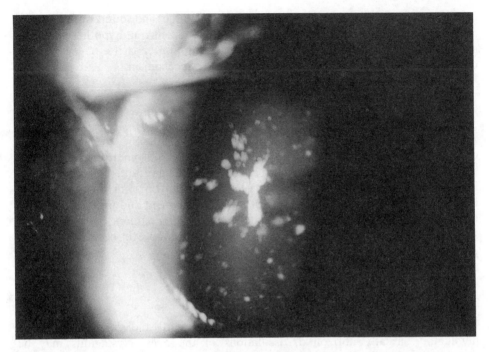

Figure 8.4 A sutural 'Y' cataract in the lens of a child with Down's Syndrome

hypermetropia (long sight) and astigmatism (unequal curvature of the cornea in vertical and horizontal meridians). Normal refraction is called emmertropia.

Children with myopia have reduced distance vision but can usually read unaided by holding a book close. Parents often suspect the condition when the child peers closely at objects. In most series some 30 per cent of the patients were myopic and there was an increased incidence of high myopia (children with an error greater than –6 dioptres), necessitating thick glasses.

Hypermetropia (hyperopia) is more common, but many manage well without a spectacle correction as the vision is less affected by long sight; the children can read books with relatively large print and their distance vision is not greatly affected. Therefore, they may not be keen to wear spectacles as they would notice relatively little improvement.

Squint (strabismus)

Strabismus, or squint, is reported by virtually all observers, and exists when the visual axes of the eyes are out of alignment so that only one eye is directed at the object (Figure 8.1). Its incidence varies widely; up to 89 per cent (Caputo *et al.*, 1989). This probably reflects a selected (symptomatic) group, but an unselected community study suggested 27 per cent (Roizen et al., 1994). The vast majority are convergent squints, in which the eyes turn inward (esotropia), but some children may be exotropic (divergent). Lowe thought that cataract and squint were the most important cause of squints, but Jaeger has outlined the current hypothesis that the squint is due to decreased fusional or visual resolution capacity, or a failure to develop an adequate accommodative convergence mechanism.

AMBLYOPIA

Amblyopia, or a lazy eye, develops as a result of either a squint or a large difference in the refraction ('power') of the two eyes (anisometropia), or due to something such as a cataract blocking a child's vision. The result is a lazy eye, which is irreversible beyond the age of about 8 years old. Amblyopia in Down's syndrome is surprisingly uncommon (12.5 per cent in Jaeger's series) and probably because most squints, in our experience, are alternating. The treatment of amblyopia is spectacle correction and occlusion (patching) of the good eye; occlusion is often poorly tolerated by handicapped children.

NYSTAGMUS

Nystagmus is derived from the Greek word 'to nod' and describes constant involuntary, usually horizontal, oscillations of the eyes. Nystagmus may be congenital or acquired, and the majority in Down's syndrome are congenital. It was first recorded by Sutherland in 1899, and in Lowe's series of 67 patients, only 9 (13 per cent) showed nystagmus. However, the movements may be very fine, and if carefully looked for nystagmus may be more common: Wagner *et al.*'s 1990 series of 188 consecutive patients found 56 patients with nystagmus, 41 of these with a convergent squint, but the majority having no obvious ocular pathology to account for it.

Typically, with congenital nystagmus near vision is affected less than distance as the nystagmus movements are dampened by convergence. Some children may adopt a compensatory head posture in order to minimize their nystagmus: they find a so-called 'null point' at which the eye movements are least. It is unwise to correct this posture.

Other anomalies

There have been other, more rare, ocular findings described in Down's syndrome. There are three reports of optic nerve hypoplasia (Awan, 1977; Catalano 1990). Williams *et al.* (1973) reported the presence of more retinal vessels crossing the disc margin in a spoke-like manner in Down's syndrome compared to the normal population.

Congenital glaucoma has been described in association with Down's syndrome (Traboulsi *et al.*, 1988), but this may be a chance concordance. However, the combination of infantile glaucoma, myopia and cataracts in Down's syndrome infants carries a poor visual outcome.

Syringoma, an epithelioma arising from sweat and meibomian glands around the eyelids, has been reported in 37 of 200 Down's syndrome patients by Butterworth *et al.* (1961), suggesting a higher incidence than in other types of mental deficiency. The significance is unknown.

MANAGEMENT OF CHILDREN'S EYE PROBLEMS IN DOWN'S SYNDROME

Many children with Down's syndrome are not routinely referred to ophthalmologists; 60 per cent of an unselected group of 77 children were found to have ophthalmic disorders in the study by Roizen – 35 per cent of these were felt to have no abnormality when examined by a paediatrician. Paediatric ophthalmologists and in particular orthoptists have considerable expertise at assessing the visual performance of affected children from an early age. In our experience, vision is not generally worse in children with hearing and other difficulties.

Visual acuity

In comparison with the extensive literature on ocular complications, relatively little is written about the most important aspect of the eyes from the parents' and child's view: that of the functional vision. Non-verbal methods of visual acuity testing have been used with considerable success in Down's syndrome children (Courage *et al.*, 1994, Parker *et al.*, 1994), the most popular being the Teller acuity card. This test uses the technique of preferential looking; children are presented with stimulus cards which contain a contrast grating on one side and a blank on the other side (Figure 8.5). If they can discriminate the grating they will reliably look at that side, and the gratings can be altered to a finer pattern until the child can no longer see them.

Data from these studies suggest that children with Down's syndrome have a significantly reduced vision (in the presence or absence of ocular complications), but that for the first six months to two years the vision parallels that in the normal population. After that it deviates, and this corresponds to the change in rate of cognitive development: Becker *et al.* (1986) showed a progressive atrophy of the dendritic tree, delayed myelination and other abnormalities in the developing neural system of children with Down's syndrome. In addition, there is evidence that there is reduced accommodation (the ability of the lens to change shape in order to focus on objects near) in Down's syndrome (Woodhouse *et al.*, 1993) which would further reduce vision, particularly in those methods testing near vision.

Visual acuity testing requires time and patience, but reproducible results can be obtained. For older children who have been taught the Makaton vocabulary, vision testing can be supplemented using this (Charnock, 1994).

Spectacles for Down's syndrome children

In young children and in the majority of handicapped children of all ages, it is necessary to test for a refractive error using cycloplegic eye drops. These dilate the

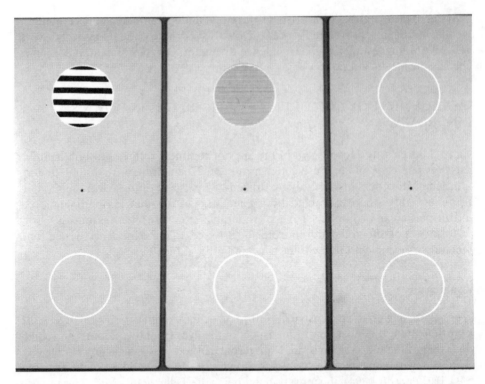

Figure 8.5 Preferential looking cards in which the child will look at the grating if they can discriminate it from the blank side of the card. Each card is tested separately.

pupils and temporarily paralyse the focusing. Drops used today include atropine which is very effective but can last up to a week (and is therefore used less often these days), or cyclopentolate, which only lasts 24 hours. The spectacle correction is assessed using the technique of retinoscopy.

Spectacles should be provided whenever they appear necessary. Most patients will wear their spectacles happily. For those less willing, it may be possible for the teacher at school to persuade them to wear them in class. Alternatively, at home, co-operation is often more easily obtained if spectacles are put on to watch a favourite television programme. The period of wear can then be gradually increased.

Fitting spectacles for these children is not easy. They tend to have broad heads with flat, wide nasal bridges and small, soft, low-set ears. All these factors pose problems for the optician. Spectacle frames need to have a narrow, conventional bridge and often fit better if the nose pads are reduced and splayed back. A round eye shape is preferred (Figure 8.6) so that the central part of the lens is less affected if the spectacle frame is bent. Short sides are needed by many Down's syndrome children. For very small children it is possible to obtain tie-on frames in either metal or plastic.

An accurate fit is important, particularly with strong lenses, as these require an accurate distance between eye and lens. Plastic lenses will help to reduce weight and are less likely to shatter. It is best to order two pairs of spectacles for each child: breakages are not uncommon and a spare pair avoids interruption.

Figure 8.6 Spectacles of a child with Down syndrome.

Squint (strabismus)

A simple assessment of the degree of squint can be made from the position of the corneal reflections. The test is carried out on the undilated pupil and the position of the corneal reflection compared to the pupil margin and iris is assessed. A squint is confirmed using the cover test. Each eye is covered and the other eye is observed to see if it makes a refixation movement. The orthoptist may use a prism cover test which is a very accurate method of measuring a squint.

Treatment of squint

If the refractive error is significant, then correction by wearing spectacles will provide a clear image and act as a stimulus to the child to straighten the eye. This is particularly the case in convergent (accommodative) squints when hypermetropic spectacles may reduce or eliminate the squint when the child attempts to focus on a near object.

To prevent amblyopia (a lazy eye, see earlier) and to improve vision in a lazy eye, occlusion treatment will sometimes be necessary. The eye with good vision is covered for part of each day with an adhesive patch, to stimulate the visual pathway in the squinting eye. This usually improves the vision, although getting adequate co-operation in many Down's syndrome children may not be easy! During this treatment, children are usually monitored fairly closely.

If spectacles and occlusion (if necessary) fail to straighten the eye, then surgical correction is considered. This involves realigning the muscles of the eye so that balance is restored. Usually surgery is performed on one or two muscles of the affected eye; sometimes on one muscle of each eye. If it is being performed to improve vision and gain binocular function, surgery is often performed early, but if the indication is simply cosmesis, then there is no urgency and indeed because of the risk of later divergence (particularly if the vision is poor) surgery may be deferred. Obviously the child's general health must be assessed when considering surgery, but provided this is satisfactory then the indications for surgery are the same as for the non-Down's syndrome population, and no special precautions are required apart from a sympathetic staff.

Cataract

If cataracts are felt to be significantly interfering with vision, then cataract extraction will be considered. This involves removal of the lens from the eye, and afterwards the child will require correction either with thick spectacles (which cause distortion and in effect tunnel vision) or contact lenses, which may be fraught with problems in a child with Down's syndrome, particularly if the eye is rubbed. Intraocular lens implants are used in adults and in older children these days, although if the cataracts require removal as an infant, then an intraocular lens is not possible currently. If cataract surgery has to be delayed, for example due to cardiac problems, then an eye drop which dilates the pupil may improve acuity.

Keratoconus

In the acute (hydrops) form this condition is not difficult to recognize as the child has a painful, red eye. Treatment is with ocular lubricants, padding the eye if possible and pain relief. It usually resolves over a period of a few days to weeks. Diagnosis of the usual asymptomatic form is difficult. Suspicions are aroused by an increasing astigmatism and the diagnosis confirmed by slit-lamp examination and keratometry – measurement of the corneal curvature.

If scarring remains, then corneal transplantation (a 'graft') may be required. Down's syndrome is no contraindication to this procedure, and there have been successful series published, although the incidence of complications is a little higher (Sharif and Casey 1991; Volker-Dieben *et al.*, 1993). It is a fairly major procedure, requiring frequent postoperative attendances and eye drops, but may make a large impact.

Blepharitis

Treatment of this condition to prevent recurrent red, irritable eyes is primarily based on lid toilet; keeping the lids clean and removing crusts from the lashes using warm water and cotton wool (or cotton buds). In the event of a flare-up, the crusts should be removed and an antibiotic ointment (with or without hydrocortisone) applied.

SUMMARY

Damage to the eyes, to a greater or lesser extent, is a feature of all children with Down's syndrome. Generally, both eyes are affected equally, although changes may occur in one eye earlier than another. In the past, the assessment and active treatment of Down's children have often been dismissed as practically impossible or not worth while. Modern methods have, however, made the task easier, and treatment is becoming more readily available.

Spectacles

Many Down's children benefit from wearing spectacles. These may be used to correct refractive error, to help treatment in cases of squint, or to aid vision after cataract extraction. They may even be ordered for babies if the refractive error is such that, if uncorrected, the vision is likely to be seriously affected.

Surgery

Surgery is required only for a minority of these children. It may be necessary to remove dense congenital lens opacities in order to obtain vision and encourage the visual development of the eye. In these cases, cataract extraction is undertaken as early as possible.

The surgical realignment of the eye by operation on one or more of the extra-ocular muscles may be indicated where spectacles and occlusion have proved insufficient to correct a squint. Squint surgery may also be performed when the child is older to improve his or her general appearance.

In cases of corneal scarring in both eyes as a result of keratoconus, corneal transplantation surgery may be required if sufficient compliance is possible.

Supervision and management

It is important that any child who is suspected of having an ocular problem should be seen by an ophthalmologist. Advice should be sought early, as those conditions which can affect vision do not resolve spontaneously, and the earlier treatment is started the better the result is likely to be. It is the authors' opinion that all Down's babies should be seen for a routine ophthalmic assessment within the first year of life. For those children with no immediate problem, a follow-up visit for a preschool assessment is made. At this visit, the parents can be advised if findings suggest that vision may cause problems at school.

Follow-up visits are also made for those children whose parents notice a squint, even if it is not present at the time of examination. Any refractive error is corrected and the child is kept under observation. Children with a family history of squint are often kept under observation. Children with intermittent or alternating squints are kept under observation to make sure the vision does not drop in one eye.

Further routine visits should be arranged as the children get older to monitor visual acuity, refractive error and cataract. In addition, in the secondary school age group, the possibility of keratoconus must be borne in mind. Because the incidence of cataracts is believed to increase with age, vision may deteriorate, so it is important that these children should not be lost to follow-up, and the purpose of visits is explained to parents so that they do not feel that time is being wasted.

ACKNOWLEDGEMENT

Photographs reproduced by kind permission of the Audiovisual Department, Western Eye Hospital, London.

REFERENCES

Awan, K.J. (1977). Uncommon ocular changes in Down's Syndrome. *Journal of Paediatric Ophthalmology, 19,* **14** (4), 215–6.

Becker, L.E., Armstrong, M.D., Chan, F. (1986). Dendritic atrophy in children with Down's Syndrome. *Annals of Neurology,* **20,** 520–26.

Berg, J., Brandon, M., Kirman, B. (1959). Atropine in Mongolism. *Lancet, 2*

Brooke Williams, R.D. (1981). Brushfield spots and Wolfflin nodules in the iris: an appraisal in handicapped children. *Developmental Medicine and Child Neurology,* **23,** 646–50.

Brushfield, T. (1924). Mongolism. *British Journal of Children's Diseases,* **21,** 241–58.

Butterworth, T., Strean, L., Beerman, H. (1961). Syringoma in Mongolism. *Archives of Dermatology,* **90,** 483–7.

Caputo, A.R., Wagner, R.S., Reynolds, D.R. Guo, S., Goel, A.K. (1989). Down syndrome. Clinical review of ocular features. *Clinical Pediatric,* **28,** 355–58.

Catalano, R.A. (1990). Down Syndrome. *Survey of Ophthalmology,* **34** 385–98.

Charnock, A. Down's Syndrome: methods of assessment. Personal communication.

Courage, M.L., Adams, R.J. Reyno, S., Kwa, P.-G. (1994). Visual acuity in infants and children with Down Syndrome. *Developmental Medicine and Child Neurology,* **36,** 586–93.

Cullen, J.F., Butler, H.G. (1963). Mongolism (Down's Syndrome) and keratoconus. *British Journal of Ophthalmology,* **47,** 321.

Donaldson, D. (1961). The significance of spotting of the iris in Mongoloids. *American Medical Association Archives of Ophthalmology,* **65,** 26.

Down, J., Langdon H. (1886). *Observations on an ethnic classification of idiots.* Clinical Lectures and Reports by the Medical and Surgical staff of the London Hospital 3, 259.

Eissler, R., Lognecker, P. (1962). The common eye findings in Mongolism. *American Journal of Ophthalmology,* **54** (3), 398–406.

Fanning, G.S. (1971). Vision in children with Down's Syndrome. *Australian Journal of Optometry,* **54,** 74–82.

Filipello, M., Scimone, G., Cascone, G., Zagami, A. (1992). Ferning test in Down's Syndrome. *Acta Ophthalmologica,* **70,** 274–7.

Gardiner, P. (1967). Visual defects in Down's and other mentally handicapped children. *British Journal of Ophthalmology,* **57,** 469–74.

Jaeger, E.A. (1980). Ocular findings in Down's Syndrome. *Transactions of the American Ophthalmological Society,* **78,** 808–45.

Lowe, R.F. (1949). The eyes in Mongolism. *British Journal of Ophthalmology,* 33(3), 131–74.

Ormond, A.W. (1912). Notes on the ophthalmic condition of 42 mongolian imbeciles. *Transactions of the Ophthalmological Society, UK,* **32,** 69–76.

Parker, M., Pakeman, V.H. Woodhouse, J.M., Fraser, W.I., Lobo, S. (1994). *Visual acuity and development in infants and young children with Down's Syndrome.* Paper presented conference of Medical Aspects of Mental Handicap, Rome, March.

Pierse, D., Eustace, P. (1971). Acute keratoconus in Mongols. *British Journal of Ophthalmology,* **55,** 50–54.

Rados, A. (1948) Conical cornea and Mongolism. *Archives of Ophthalmology (Chicago)* **80,** 618–21.

Roizen, N.J., Mets, M.B., Blondis, T.A. (1994). Ophthalmic disorders in children with Down Syndrome. *Developmental Medicine and Child Neurology,* **36,** 594–600.

Sharif, K.W., Casey, T.A. (1991). Penetrating keratoplasty for keratoconus: complications and long-term success. *British Journal of Ophthalmology,* **75,** 142–6.

Sutherland, G.A. (1899). Mongolian imbecility in infants. *Practitioner,* **63,** 632.

Traboulsi, E.I., Levine, E., Mets, M.B. *et al.* (1988). Infantile glaucoma in Down's Syndrome (Trisomy 21). *American Journal of Ophthalmology,* **105,** 389–94.

Turner, S., Sloper, P., Cunningham, C., Knussen, C. (1990). Health problems in children with Down's Syndrome. *Child: Care, Health and Development,* **16,** 83–97.

Volker-Dleben, H.J., Odenthal, M.T., DíAmaro, J., Kruit, P.J. (1993). Surgical treatment of corneal pathology in patients with Down's Syndrome. *Journal of Intellectual Disabilities Research,* **37,** 169–75 .

Wagner, R.S., Caputo, A.R., Reynolds, R.D. (1990). Nystagmus in Down's Syndrome. *Ophthalmology,* **97,** 1439–44.

Williams, E.J., McCormick, A., Tischler, B. (1973). Retinal vessels in Down's Syndrome. *Archives of Ophthalmology,* **89,** 269–71.

Woodhouse, J.M. Meades, J.S., Leat, S.J., Saunders, K.J. (1993). Reduced accommodation in children with Down Syndrome. *Investigative Ophthalmology and Visual Science,* **34,** 2382–7.

9 Oral Health

Merete Vigild

Perhaps the first record of the oral health of children with Down syndrome was made by Jones in 1889 (cited by Reuland-Bosma and van Dijk, 1986). Since then, there have been many reports documenting deviations from normal development with respect to the development of dentition, dental occlusion, periodontal disease and dental caries (Vigild, 1992 is a recent review).

CHARACTERISTICS OF CRANIAL MORPHOLOGY AND ORAL CAVITY

Some problems are associated with congenital anomalies in the cranial morphology. For example, the maxilla and the mandible are much smaller than usual in persons with Down syndrome (Cohen and Winer, 1965; Frostad *et al.*, 1971; Kisling, 1966). It has been reported that the dimensions of the palate are also smaller (Jensen *et al.*, 1973; Kisling, 1966) although Shapiro *et al.* (1967) indicated that the palate height is normal despite a shorter length and narrower width. There are also reports of cleft palate, poor lip seal, frequent tongue thrusting and a tongue that seems larger than usual (Ardran *et al.*, 1972; Cohen and Cohen, 1971; Schendel and Gorlin, 1974; Shapiro *et al.*, 1967). Some studies which have reported macroglossia have not distinguished between true macroglossia and tongue size relative to the oral cavity (Gullikson, 1973), but some Down syndrome individuals do have true macroglossia, which can complicate the airway, speech and mastication difficulties. (Ardran *et al.*, 1972; Becking and Tuinzing, 1991; Cohen and Cohen, 1971; Olbrisch, 1982; Sigal and Levine, 1993; Wexler *et al.*, 1986).

MALOCCLUSIONS AND FUNCTIONAL ANOMALIES

The term 'malocclusion' covers a number of different morphologic deviations from normal occlusion which may occur as single traits or in various combinations. Malocclusion can be either of dento-alveolar or skeletal (basal) origin as is the case with most malocclusions found in Down syndrome individuals. In persons with Down syndrome, the mandible (lower jaw) often protrudes significantly in relation to the cranial base and to the maxilla (upper jaw). The size of the upper jaw is much smaller than the lower jaw (Kisling, 1966), and it has been suggested that this is one of the reasons for a very high prevalence of malocclusions found in persons with Down syndrome (Cohen *et al.*, 1970; Cohen and Winer, 1965; Gullikson, 1973; Jensen *et al.*, 1973; Kisling, 1966; Vigild, 1985b). Vigild (1992) reported that individuals with Down syndrome, children as well as adults, have frequencies of mandibular overjet, frontal open bite, and crossbite that are significantly higher than observed in the general population.

One study found that children with Down syndrome who had severe mental retardation had the highest prevalence of, and often the most severe, malocclusions (Oreland *et al.*, 1987). Due to the frontal open bite and to the large or relatively large tongue, many persons with Down syndrome breathe through the mouth, causing dryness of the lips and oral mucosa; e.g. angular cheilitis (inflamed corners of the lips) (Borea *et al.*, 1990; Butterworth, 1960).

Although these malocclusions are associated with the anomalies in cranial morphology, functional anomalies of the tongue and hypotonia also play a role in the development of malocclusions. Habits such as finger-sucking and pressing the tongue against the lower front teeth are complicating factors which can have a marked effect on the relationship between the upper and lower teeth. Very poor occlusal conditions lead not only to cosmetic defects but also to reduced masticatory ability with greatly reduced tooth contact during chewing and occlusion (Borea *et al.*, 1990).

DENTITION

Morphological abnormalities in the dentition of persons with Down syndrome are common. These include peg-shaped incisors, slender-pointed molars, and microdontia (smaller teeth than usual) in the permanent teeth (Cohen *et al.*, 1970; Jensen *et al.*, 1973; Kisling, 1966; Prahl-Andersen and Oerlemanns, 1976). There are several reports of delays in shedding and eruption (Barkla, 1966; Cutress, 1971a; Le Clerch, *et al.*, 1986; Orner, 1973; Orner, 1975b; Roche and Barkla, 1964, 1967) and abnormal sequence in eruption (Barkla, 1966; Cutress, 1971a; Jensen *et al.*, 1973, Roche and Barkla, 1964; Swallow, 1964). There is also a high prevalence of congenitally missing teeth (Cohen *et al.*, 1970; Jensen *et al.*, 1973; Kisling, 1966; Orner, 1971; Roche and Barkla, 1967) and an increase in dental asymmetry (Barden, 1980).

PERIODONTAL DISEASE

Periodontal disease has been reported for young children with Down syndrome, and nearly all persons with Down syndrome are affected by the time they are adults (Brown, 1978; Cohen *et al.*, 1961; Johnson and Young, 1963; Miller and Ship, 1977; Modéer *et al.*, 1990; Reuland-Bosma, 1990; Reuland-Bosma and Van Dijk, 1986; Saxèn and Aula, 1982; Ulseth *et al.*, 1991; Vigild, 1985a). The disease involves gingivitis with loss of attachment of teeth and alveola bone loss.

It has been suggested that local factors such as a large tongue, abnormal tooth morphology, oral habits such as tongue thrusting, lack of masticatory function, differences in type and amount of microbes in the dental plaque and in saliva, and lack of lip seal are implicated in the onset of periodontal disease in Down syndrome (Cutress, 1971b; Reuland-Bosma and Van Dijk, 1986; Shapiro, Stabholz *et al.*, 1991; Shaw and Saxby, 1986).

Although some of these factors may affect oral hygiene, no direct link with periodontal tissue has been found. Of these factors, the most likely candidate is tooth morphology, as a shorter than normal root length may decrease the area for periodontal attachment (Reuland-Bosma and Van Dijk, 1986). Other possible ethiologic factors such as poor blood circulation, disorders in the connective tissue, differences in collagen biosyntheses, differences in the number of fibroblasts, macrophages, plasma cells, and mast cells in the periodontal tissue, malabsorption of vitamin A, and high concentration of cyclic amino-monophosphate have been investigated (Claycomb *et al.*, 1970; Cutress, 1976; Reuland-Bosma and Van Dijk, 1986; Reuland-Bosma *et al.*, 1988; Schaeffer, 1977).

However, there seems to be recent agreement that periodontal disease in Down syndrome is mainly related to immunological abnormality such as T cell deficiency, a functional defect in the polymorphonuclear leucocytes, a reduced number of mature T cells, and an increased incidence of auto-antibodies to thyroid, Barkin *et al.*, 1980a; Barkin *et al.*, 1980b; Dupont *et al.*, 1986; Reuland-Bosma and Van Dijk, 1986; Shaw and Saxby, 1986; Sigal and Levine, 1993; Thase, 1982; Ugazio *et al.*, 1978; Whittingham *et al.*, 1977).

Although good oral hygiene can minimize the disease, it cannot stop completely the onset and progression. As Vigild (1992: 85) concluded, 'Persons with Down syndrome constitute a special risk group with respect to periodontal disease'. Poor oral hygiene will result in an inflammation of the gingiva, and the tissue surrounding the tooth will start to break down resulting in periodontal disease and tooth loss. Another serious complication of poor oral hygiene may be a chronic bacteremia (Sigal and Levine, 1993) caused by the oral bacteria entering the systemic circulation directly through the inflamed tissue. Of course, it is also of utmost importance to minimize the loss of teeth due to periodontal diseases because the protruded mandible, the protruded and relatively large tongue, and the dry mouth make it difficult for the patient to wear full dentures. As a further complicating factor, many Down syndrome patients develop dementia of the Alzheimer's type as early as 40 to 50 years of age with loss of memory skills, a decrease in the ability to perform oral hygiene, and loss of motor skills, and many patients at this stage will be unable to co-operate with professional dental care (Sigal and Levine, 1993). Preventive care prior to the onset of dementia and maintenance of preventive programmes during the individual's cognitive decline is of utmost importance (Sigal and Levine, 1993). Traditional mechanical control of plaque should be supplemented by chemical means, e.g. chlorhexidine treatments (Chiktel *et al.*, 1991; Stabholz *et al.*,1991).

DENTAL CARIES

Whereas reports concerning periodontal disease have consistently shown high prevalence, there has been less consistency regarding dental caries. Some reports have tended to show lower prevalence than the norm (Barnett *et al.*, 1986; Creighton and Wells, 1966; Gullikson, 1973; Johnson *et al.*, 1960; Orner, 1975a; Steinberg and Zimmerman, 1978) and for many years there was some speculation that those with Down syndrome were resistant to dental caries. These results were explained as being due to conditions such as high concentrations of cyclic adenosine monophosphate in saliva (Schaeffer, 1977) and increased pH and sodium level in saliva (Cutress, 1972; Winer and Feller, 1972). However, other studies found no differences in caries prevalence between persons with Down syndrome and others (Cutress, 1971a; Kroll *et al.*, 1970; Shaw *et al.*, 1990; Ulseth *et al.*; 1991).

Many factors play a role in the development of dental caries. One important factor is the daily health behaviour, and the myth that individuals with Down syndrome are resistant to caries comes mainly from the results of studies carried out among institutionalized patients. Among the institutionalized, the consumption of sweets is lower and the diet more regular than among people living in the community, which explains the lower prevalence of dental caries among the institutionalized (Vigild, 1992).

Recent studies have strengthened the methodology (Vigild, 1992) and have included environmental factors such as living conditions, the number of teeth, and the time during which the teeth had been exposed to caries, concluding that persons with Down syndrome are not resistant to caries (Cutress, 1971a; Vigild, 1986). They do have a low frequency of approximal caries (Barnett *et al.*, 1986; Swallow, 1964; Steinberg and Zimmerman, 1978; Vigild, 1986), but this has been attributed to the increased spacing between the teeth (Jensen *et al.*, 1973) and a high frequency of peg-shaped incisors (Vigild, 1986). It is important to note, however, that persons with Down syndrome are not resistant to dental caries and that preventive measures should not be neglected (Randell *et al.*, 1992).

ORAL HEALTH CARE

The tongue appears to be larger than normal, usually because of the small oral cavity. This can make the cleaning of the teeth more difficult than usual. It is also common to find that the tongue is furrowed and it is therefore advisable to brush the tongue on the dorsal site daily to remove bacteria and remnants of food.

Because of the anomalies in the jaws and dentition, prosthodontic or orthodontic measures can be difficult. Traditional dental treatment also can be more difficult than usual and may require great patience because of the person's mental retardation and difficulties in controlling the tongue. This does not indicate, however, that general anaesthesia is necessary.

Due to the high prevalence of congenital heart disease and respiratory disease, dental treatment poses a risk if a general anaesthetic is required. However, whatever treatment and measures are employed, the dentist must make sure that the patient will benefit and informed consent (from the legal guardian, if necessary) should be obtained before starting treatment.

Vigild (1992) offered some of the following guidelines for dental care of patients with Down syndrome:

Dental visits should emphasise preventive activities and good dietary habits and be scheduled 3 to 4 times per year and start when the child is 18 to 24 month of age.

The aim is to prevent the onset of dental caries and to minimise the progression of periodontal disease. It is recommended that traditional mechanical control of plaque be supplemented by chemical means, e.g. chlorhexidine treatments. Caregivers should be trained in daily oral hygiene procedures.

Of utmost importance is a confident relationship and adequate coordination between the individual, the dentist and the caregivers. This will not be achieved overnight but must be carefully established over the course of time.

REFERENCES

Ardran, G.M., Harker, P. and Kemp, F.H. (1972) Tongue size in Down's syndrome. *Journal of Mental Deficiency Research*, **16,** pp. 160–66.
Barden, H.S. (1980) Fluctuating dental asymmetry: a measure of developmental instability in Down syndrome. *American Journal of Physical Anthropology*, **52,** pp. 169–73.
Barkin R.M., Weston W.L., Humbert, J.R. and Marie, F. (1980a) Phagocytic function in Down syndrome: I. chemotaxis. *Journal of Mental Deficiency Research*, **24,** pp. 243–50.
Barkin, R.M., Weston, W.L., Humbert, J.R. and Sunada, K. (1980b) Phagocytic function in Down syndrome: II. bactericidal activity and phagocytosis. *Journal of Mental Deficiency Research*, **24,** pp. 251–56.
Barkla, D.H. (1966) Ages of eruption of permanent teeth in mongols. *Journal of Mental Deficiency Research*, **10,** pp. 190–97.
Barnett, M.L., Press, K.P., Friedman, D. and Sonnenberg, S.M. (1986) The prevalence of periodontitis and dental caries in a Down's syndrome population. *Journal of Periodontology*, **57,** pp. 288–93.
Becking A.G. and Tuinzing D.B. (1991) Orthognathic surgery for mentally retarded patients. *Oral Surgeon* **72,** pp. 162–64.
Borea, C., Magi, M., Mingarelli, R. and Zambani, C. (1990) The oral cavity in Down syndrome. *Journal of Pedodontics*, **14,** pp. 139–40.
Brown, R.H. (1978) A longitudinal study of periodontal disease in Down's syndrome. *New Zealand Dental Journal*, **74,** pp. 137–44.
Butterworth, T. (1960) Cheilitis of mongolism. *Journal of Investigative Dermatology*, **35,** pp. 347–51.
Chikte, U.M., Pochee, E., Rudolph, M.J. and Reinach, S.G. (1991) Evaluation of stannous fluoride and chlorhexidine sprays on plaque and gingivitis in handicapped children. *Journal of Clinical Periodontology*, **18,** pp. 281–86.
Claycomb, C.K., Summers, G.W., Hall, W.B. and Hart, R.W. (1970) Gingival collagen biosynthesis in mongolism. *Journal of Periodontal Research*, **5,** pp. 30–35.
Cohen, M.M., Arvystos, M.G. and Baum, B.J. (1970) Occlusal disharmonies in trisomy G (Down's syndrome, mongolism). *American Journal of Orthodontics*, **58,** pp. 367–72.
Cohen, M.M. Blitzer, F.J., Arvystos, M.G. and Bonneau, R.H. (1970) Abnormalities of the permanent dentition in trisomy G. *Journal of Dental Research*, **49,** Suppl. 6, pp. 1386–96.
Cohen, M.M., Sr and Cohen, M.M., Jr (1971) The oral manifestations of trisomy G (Down syndrome), *Birth Defects*, **7,** pp. 241–51.
Cohen, M.M. and Winer R.A. (1965) Dental and facial characteristics in Down's syndrome (mongolism). *Journal of Dental Research*, **44,** pp. 197–208.
Cohen, M.M., Winer, R.A., Schwartz, S. and Shklar, G. (1961) Oral aspects of mongolism: Part I. Periodontal diseases in mongolism. *Oral Surgeon*, **14,** pp. 92–107.
Creighton, W.E. and Wells, H.B. (1966) Dental caries experience in institutionalized mongoloid and nonmongoloid children in North Carolina and Oregon. *Journal of Dental Research*, **45,** pp. 66–75.

Cutress, T.W. (1971a) Dental caries in trisomy **21**. *Archives of Oral Biology*, 16, pp. 1329–44.

Cutress, T.W. (1971b) Periodontal disease and oral hygiene in trisomy 21. *Archives of Oral Biology*, **16,** pp. 1345–55.

Cutress, T.W. (1972) Composition, flow rate and pH of mixed and parotid saliva from trisomic and other mentally retarded subjects. *Archives of Oral Biology*, **17,** pp. 1081–94.

Cutress, T.W. (1976) Vitamin A absorption and periodontal disease in trisomy G. *Journal of Mental Deficiency Research*, **20,** pp. 17–23.

Dupont, A., Vaeth, M. and Videbech, P. (1986) Mortality and life expectancy of Down's syndrome in Denmark. *Journal of Mental Deficiency Research*, **30,** pp. 111–20.

Frostad, W.A., Cleall, J.F. and Melosky, L.C. (1971) Craniofacial complex in the trisomy 21 syndrome (Down's syndrome). *Archives of Oral Biology*, **16,** pp. 707–22.

Gullikson, J.S. (1973) Oral findings in children with Down syndrome. *Journal of Dentistry for Children*, **41,** pp. 293–97.

Jensen, G.M., Cleall, J.F. and Yip, A.S.G. (1973) Dentoalveolar morphology and developmental changes in Down's syndrome (trisomy 21) *American Journal of Orthodontics*, **64,** pp. 607–18.

Johnson, N.P. and Young, M.A. (1963) Periodontal disease in mongols. *Journal of Periodontology*, **34,** pp. 41–47.

Johnson, N.P., Young, M.A. and Gallios, J.A. (1960) Dental caries experience of mongoloid children. *Journal of Dentistry for Children*, **27,** pp. 292–94.

Kisling, E. (1966) *Cranial morphology in Down's Syndrome. A Comparative Roentgencepholometric Study in Adult Males*. Copenhagen: Munksgaard.

Kroll, R.G., Budnick, J. and Kobren, A. (1970) Incidence of dental caries and periodontal disease in Down's syndrome. *New York Dental Journal*, **36,** pp. 151–56.

Le Clerch, G., Journel, H., Roussey, M. and Marec, B.L. (1986) La première dentition du trisomique 21 (Primary dentition in Down syndrome). *Annales de Pédiatrie*, **33,** pp. 795–98.

Miller, M.F. and Ship, I.I. (1977) Periodontal disease in the institutionalized mongoloid. *Journal of Oral Medicine*, **32,** pp. 9–13.

Modéer, T., Barr, M. and Dahllöf, G. (1990) Periodontal disease in children with Down's syndrome. *Scandinavian Journal of Dental Research*, **98,** pp. 228–34.

Olbrisch, R.R. (1982) Plastic surgical management of children with Down's syndrome: indications and results. *British Journal of Plastic Surgery*, **35,** pp. 195–200.

Oreland, A., Heibjel, J. and Jagell, S. (1987) Malocclusions in physically and/or mentally handicapped children. *Swedish Dental Journal*, **11,** pp. 103–19.

Orner, G. (1971) Congenitally absent permanent teeth among mongols and their sibs. *Journal of Mental Deficiency Research*, **15,** pp. 292–302.

Orner, G. (1973) Eruption of permanent teeth in mongoloid children and their sibs. *Journal of Dental Research*, **52,** pp. 1202–08.

Orner, G. (1975a) Dental caries experience among children with Down's syndrome and their sibs. *Archives of Oral Biology*, **20,** pp. 627–34.

Orner, G. (1975b) Posteruptive tooth age in children with Down's syndrome and their sibs. *Journal of Dental Research*, **54,** pp. 581–87.

Orner G. (1976) Periodontal disease among children with Down's syndrome and their sibs. *Journal of Dental Research*, **55,** pp. 778–82.

Prahl-Andersen, N.B. and Oerlemans, J. (1976) Characteristics of permanent teeth in persons with trisomy G. *Journal of Dental Research*, **55,** pp. 633–38.

Randell, D.M., Harth, S. and Seow, W.K. (1992) Preventive dental health practices of non-institutionalized Down syndrome children: a controlled study. *Journal of Clinical Pediatric Dentistry*, **16,** pp. 225–29.

Reuland-Bosma, W. (1990) Periodontal disease in Down's syndrome. *Nederlands Tijdschrift voor Tandheelkunde*, **97,** pp. 468–71.

Reuland-Bosma, W., Liem, R.S.B., Jansen, H.W.B., Van Dijk, L.J. and Wiele, L. (1988) Cellular aspects of effects on the gingiva in children with Down's syndrome during experimental gingivitis. *Journal of Clinical Periodontology*, **15**, pp. 303–11.

Reuland-Bosma, W. and Van Dijk, L.J. (1986) Periodontal disease in Down's syndrome: a review. *Journal of Clinical Periodontology*, **13**, pp. 64–73.

Roche, A.F. and Barkla, D.H. (1964) The eruption of deciduous teeth in mongols. *Journal of Mental Deficiency Research*, **8**, pp. 54–64.

Roche, A.F. and Barkla, D.H. (1967) The development of the dentition in mongols. *Australian Dental Journal*, **12**, pp. 12–16.

Saxén, L. and Aula, S. (1982) Periodontal bone loss in patients with Down's syndrome: a follow-up study. *Journal of Periodontology*, **53**, pp. 158–62.

Schendel, S.A. and Gorlin, R.J. (1974) Frequency of cleft uvula and submucous cleft palate in patients with Down's syndrome. *Journal of Dental Research*, **53**, pp. 840–43.

Shaeffer, L.A. (1977) Cyclic AMP in saliva, salivary glands and gingival tissue. *Advanced Cyclic Nucleotide Research*, **3**, pp. 283–93.

Shapiro, B.L., Gorlin, R.J., Redman, R.S. and Bruhl, H.H. (1967) The palate and Down's syndrome. *New England Journald of Medicine*, **276**, pp. 1460–63.

Shapiro, J., Stabholz, A., Schurr, D., Sela, M.N. and Mann, J. (1991) Caries levels, streptococcus mutans counts, salivary pH, and periodontal treatment needs of adult Downs Syndrome patients. *Special Care In Dentistry*, **11**, (6), pp. 248–51.

Shaw, L. and Saxby, M.S. (1986) Periodontal destruction in Down's syndrome and in juvenile periodontis. How close a similarity? *Journal of Periodontology*, **57**, pp. 709–15.

Shaw, M.J., Shaw, L. and Foster, T.D. (1990) The oral health in different groups of adults with mental handicaps attending Birmingham (UK) adult training centres. *Community Dental Health*, **7**, pp. 135–41.

Sigal, M.J. and Levine, N. (1993) Down's syndrome and Alzheimer's disease. *Journal of Canadian Dental Association*, **59**, pp. 823–29.

Stabholz, A., Shapiro, J., Shur, D., Friedman, M., Guberman, R. and Sela, M. (1991) Local application of sustained-release delivery system of chlorhexidine in Down's syndrome population. *Clinical Preventive Dentistry*, **13**, pp. 9–14.

Steinberg, A.D. and Zimmerman, S. (1978) The Lincoln dental caries study: a three-year evaluation of dental caries in persons with various mental disorders. *Journal of American Dental Association*, **97**, pp. 981–84.

Swallow, J.N. (1964) Dental disease in children with Down's syndrome. *Journal of Mental Deficiency Research*, **8**, pp. 102–18.

Thase, M.E. (1982) Longevity and mortality in Down's syndrome. *Journal of Mental Deficiency Research*, **26**, pp. 177–92.

Ugazio, A.G., Anzavecchia, A.L., Jayakar, S., Plebani, A., Duse, M. and Burgio, G.R. (1978) Immunodeficiency in Down syndrome. *Acta Paediatric Scandinavica*, **67**, pp. 705–08.

Ulseth, J.O., Hestnes, A., Stovner, J.L. and Storhaug, K. (1991) Dental caries and periodontitis in persons with Down syndrome. *Special Care in Dentistry*, **11**, pp. 71–73.

Vigild, M. (1985a) Periodontal conditions in mentally retarded children. *Community Dentistry and Oral Epidemiology*, **13**, pp. 180–82.

Vigild, M. (1985b) Prevalence of malocclusion in mentally retarded young adults. *Community Dentistry and Oral Epidemiology*, **13**, pp. 183–84.

Vigild, M. (1986) Dental caries experience among children with Down's syndrome. *Journal of Mental Deficiency Research*, **30**, pp. 271–76.

Vigild, M. (1992) Oral health conditions. In S.M. Pueschel and J.K. Pueschel (eds), *Biomedical Concerns in Persons with Down Syndrome*, Baltimore: Brookes.

Wexler, M.R., Peled, I.J., Rand, Y., Mintzker, Y. and Feuerstein, R. (1986) Rehabilitation of the face in patients with Down's syndrome. *Plastic and Reconstructive Surgery* **77**, pp. 383–93.

Winer, R.A. and Feller, R.P. (1972) Composition of parotid and submandibular saliva and serum in Down's syndrome. *Journal of Dental Research*, **51**, pp. 449–55.

Whittingham, S., Pitt, D.B., Sharma, D.L.B. and MacKay, I.R. (1977) Stress deficiency of the T-C lymphocyte system exemplified by Down syndrome. *Lancet*, **1**, pp. 163–66.

10 Preventive Medical Care

Göran Annerén and Siegfried M. Pueschel

INTRODUCTION

Persons with Down syndrome run an increased risk of developing disorders in various organs and of having multiple congenital malformations. However, better medical care and changing attitudes during the last 20 to 30 years have had a profound effect on the health of individuals with Down syndrome in many countries. Previously, most persons with Down syndrome died during childhood but with better medical care, the median life expectancy for persons with Down syndrome in the western world has increased to more than 55 years (Baird and Sadovnick, 1989).

Special programmes for intellectual and motor difficulties, and special medical care to prevent treatable disorders from remaining undiagnosed both benefit persons with Down syndrome. Medical check-ups are often given by physicians with different training who are not always aware of the special problems associated with Down syndrome. Consequently, problems such as hypothyroidism, impaired vision or auditory impairment may remain undiagnosed for long periods. For this reason, several medical care programmes for Down syndrome have been developed in different parts of the world (Annerén and Gustafsson, 1994; Chicoine et al., 1994). Most of these programmes are similar to each other. In order to create one common international acceptable programme for all individuals with Down syndrome, a group of experts from different parts of the world met in June 1994 in Sweden and a preventive medical care programme for Down syndrome was established. The guidelines from this programme are presented in this chapter.

ESTABLISHMENT OF THE DIAGNOSIS AND EMOTIONAL SUPPORT TO THE PARENTS

When, after delivery, a newborn infant is suspected to have Down syndrome, a thorough physical and neurologic examination should be carried out in order to establish the clinical diagnosis. A chromosomal analysis should be performed which will establish the karyotype and can be used for genetic counselling purposes. If the child with Down syndrome has regular trisomy 21, the recurrence risk is about 1 per cent. If the child has a Robertsonian translocation, the parents will have to undergo a chromosomal analyses since one of them might be a balanced carrier, with a much higher recurrence risk.

The initial counselling of parents of a newborn child with Down syndrome will have a significant influence on the parents' subsequent adjustment. The parents adjustment to the new situation will have importance for the future of the family and the child with Down syndrome. The parent should have one doctor, who is well informed about Down syndrome and whom they will meet several times during the neonatal period.

NEUROPSYCHIATRIC DISORDERS

Mental retardation is, apart from the chromosomal abnormality, the only feature which is present in most individuals with Down syndrome. There is a wide range of mental abilities, however, and the intelligence quotients (IQ) usually vary between 20 and 80. Berry *et al.* (1984) have shown that the mean mental age of the majority of children with Down syndrome before the age of 5 years is close to half the chronological age plus three months. This means that young children with Down syndrome have a higher IQ than the older children and adults. Girls with Down syndrome have a slightly higher IQ than boys. At the age of 1 year the mean IQ is about 70 and after the age of 3 years it is about 50 and there is virtually no further decline in IQ after the age of 5 years (Carr, 1988).

Behaviour and psychiatric disorders are observed more often in persons with Down syndrome (Myers and Pueschel, 1991). Autistic behaviour is not uncommon in children with Down syndrome and should be treated by a child psychiatrist (Ghaziuddin *et al.*, 1992). Depressive disorder, might be more common in adolescents and young adults with Down syndrome (Lund, 1988). The symptoms might be mistaken for dementia, but there are clinical differences. Sleep and eating disorder are common in depressed persons with Down syndrome, however, epilepsy and memory disorder are common symptoms in persons with dementia. If the person is younger than 40 years depression should be suspected and if the person is older than 50 years dementia is more probable. Depression may be due to loneliness, and one way to help this is by increasing the person's social contacts. Specific treatment with medication should be offered after the diagnosis has been established.

Epilepsy is less common during childhood (4 per cent), but infantile spasms occur more often in children with Down syndrome (Pueschel *et al.*, 1991). Seizure disorders are, however, more common in the third decade in Down syndrome and even more common in the fifth and sixth decade, mostly as myoclonic epilepsy (Collacott, 1993). It is important to recognize seizure disorders and provide appropriate treatment with anticonvulsant medications.

As mentioned above, adults with Down syndrome have been found to have an accelerated ageing process. Almost all older persons with Down syndrome (>35 years) have neurohistopathological changes, with tangles and amyloid plaques, nearly identical to those found in patients with Alzheimer disease (Kemper, 1988; Wisniewski *et al.*, 1985). The underlying causes might, however, be different in Down syndrome. The dementia in Down syndrome should be called Down syndrome dementia (DSD) and not Alzheimer disease. There is an increased risk of presenile dementia in Down syndrome, but it is uncommon with any clinical symptoms before the age of 40 years (<5 per cent). Signs of dementia is found in 20 to 25 per cent of persons with Down syndrome in their fifties (Wisniewski *et al.*, 1985). Other have reported that at the age of 54 years about 50 per cent of individuals with Down syndrome have developed signs of dementia (Johanson *et al.*, 1991; Kemper, 1988).

CARDIOVASCULAR SYSTEM

Congenital malformations of the heart are found in about 40 per cent of children with Down syndrome (Park *et al.*, 1977; Rowe and Uchida, 1961). The most common malformation is atrioventricular canal (AV defect), which occurs in about 60 per cent of the children with Down syndrome who have cardiac malformations. An AV defect should usually be corrected surgically before the age of 10 months, because of the increased risk in children with Down syndrome for early development of permanent pulmonary hypertension, which sometimes occurs before the age of 1 year (Chi and Krovetz, 1975). A cardiac examination, with electrocardiography and echocardiography, is recommended during the neonatal period. If this examination shows a normal heart, but with an open ductus arteriosus, it is prudent to perform a further examination at the age of 2 to 3 months. Depending on the findings, the pediatric cardiologist will decide upon the future treatment and follow-up.

Adult persons with Down syndrome have an increased risk of developing mitral valve prolapse with secondary insufficiency and also aortic regurgitation (Goldhaber *et al.*, 1987; Pueschel and Werner, 1994). This might be due to a collagen defect and has also been observed in previously cardiac healthy individuals. These insufficiencies usually do not give any clinical symptoms, but it is advisable to treat with antibiotics prophylactic to surgery and dental therapy, especially in case of mitral valve insufficiency.

AIRWAY OBSTRUCTIVE DISEASE AND SLEEP APNOEA

Upper airway obstruction leading to sleep apnoea are common problems in children with Down syndrome. Nasopharyngeal obstruction, caused by hypertrophic tonsils and adenoids and glossoptosis are usually causing the obstruction. Hypotonia of pharyngeal musculature and maldevelopment of other upper airway structures also contribute to this phenomenon. Sleep apnoea often results in reduced oxygen supply to the brain. Children with Down syndrome run an increased risk of developing cor pulmonale due to this obstruction (Macartney *et al.*, 1969). Upper airway obstruction should be treated in order to minimize clinical symptoms and secondary pulmonary hypertension.

GASTROINTESTINAL SYSTEM

Atresia of the gut is found in 8 per cent of newborn babies with Down syndrome, and these atresia have to be surgically corrected during the neonatal period (Levy,

1991; Pieper *et al.*, 1979). The outcome of this surgery is similar to that in chromosomally normal children (Drott *et al.*, 1985). Intestinal obstructions in Down syndrome are due to oesophageal, duodenal or anal atresia, or to Hirschsprung's disease. Postoperative treatment of the child with Down syndrome does not differ from that of chromosomally normal children with the same malformation. In view of the increased risk of atlantoaxial and atlanto-occipital instability in Down syndrome, the anaesthesiologist has to be careful when intubation is required (Pueschel *et al.*, 1984) (see below).

OCULAR SYSTEM

Eye examination to identify congenital cataract is recommended before 1 month of age, as 1 to 3 per cent of children with Down syndrome have congenital cataract. Congenital cataracts that are not corrected before the age of 3 months will result in permanent visual impairment. Among children with Down syndrome, nystagmus is found in 5 to 30 percent, strabismus in 23 to 44 per cent, blepharitis in 2 to 67 per cent, keratoconus in 5.5 to 8 per cent and refractive errors in 70 to 80 per cent (Mills, 1985). The refraction errors are often the cause of the nystagmus and strabismus. It is especially important to detect myopia at an early age. An ophthalmological examination, including slit-lamp examination is recommended at the age of 12 months or earlier. Tear-duct stenosis is common in Down syndrome, but probing of tear channels before the age of 9 to 12 months is generally not recommended. Mostly this problem resolves spontaneously along with the growth of the mid-facial bones. Follow-up ophthalmological examinations are decided by the ophthalmologist. After the age of 25 years regular eye examinations are recommended because of the increased risk (12 to 86 per cent) of developing cataract (Catalano, 1992; Jaeger, 1980).

DENTAL CARE

Although dental caries is not more frequent in children with Down syndrome, periodontal disease has been reported to be more prevalent in Down syndrome. Therefore, appropriate dental hygiene, fluoride treatments, good dietary habits and restorative care if needed, should be forthcoming to prevent dental problems, in particular periodontitis.

OTOLOGICAL SYSTEM

Otological manifestations are common in Down syndrome, and 60 to 70 per cent of individuals with this syndrome have impaired hearing, mostly caused by middle ear effusion (Brooks *et al.*, 1972; Davies, 1988). The auditory canals are narrow and frequently filled with wax. If excessive wax is present, using wax-removing eardrops five days in every month is recommended. In view of the frequent middle ear problems experienced in Down syndrome, yearly auditory examinations and examination two months after every ear infection are advised in children. A complete audiogram at the age of 4 years is recommended in all children with Down syndrome. High frequency hearing loss has been reported in adults with Down syndrome. Therefore, it is recommended that at least once every two years adults with Down syndrome undergo a hearing assessment. Sometimes a hearing aid may be necessary.

IMMUNE SYSTEM AND PRONENESS TO INFECTIONS

The susceptibility to infections in children with Down syndrome is well known (Björkstén *et al.*, 1979; Oster *et al.*, 1964). There are several reasons for this proneness to infections (Annerén *et al.*, 1990; Funa *et al.*, 1984; Levin, 1987), but no special preventive measure is recommended. The use of antibiotic therapy is recommended in children with Down syndrome who have bacterial infections. Auditory follow-up after upper respiratory infections is important, since middle ear effusions are extremely common.

Persons with Down syndrome have an increased risk to become persistent hepatitis-B carriers after a hepatitis-B infection. If there is an increased risk of catching hepatitis-B, vaccination is recommended. In some countries all children with Down syndrome will become immunized in the newborn period.

There are many indications of an abnormal immune response in Down syndrome, e.g. an increased incidence of autoimmune diseases. Elevated serum level of antithyroid autoantibodies and increased incidence of hypothyroidism are most well known (see below). Coeliac disease also seems to be more common in Down syndrome, and increased levels of gliadin antibodies are reported (Storm, 1990). If there are signs of malabsorption and growth retardation in a child with Down syndrome an investigation for coeliac disease is recommended.

NUTRITION COUNSELLING

During early infancy, feeding problems and poor weight gain may be observed, especially in those infants with congenital malformation of the heart. After the heart malformation has been surgically corrected, most children with Down syndrome thrive.

It is important to closely monitor growth. Growth retardation is a characteristic feature of the syndrome. Most children with Down syndrome are already small at birth. The growth velocity is markedly reduced between 6 months and 3 years of age, when mean height used to be shorter then −3SD compared to healthy children (Sara *et al.*, 1983). During puberty the growth spurt is reduced compared to healthy children (Arnell *et al.* 1995). Some children with Down syndrome, in particular during adolescence, have a tendency to gain weight more than would be ordinarily expected. Obesity should be avoided as much as possible. There are specific growth charts for children with Down syndrome (Cronk *et al.*, 1988), which are recommended.

There are many reports of trace element abnormalities in Down syndrome, but there is no clear-cut deficiency that could not be explained by the observed repeated infections (Annerén *et al.*, 1985; Annerén and Gebre-Medhin, 1987). Trace element supplementation is not recommended. It is important, however, to give children with Down syndrome a balanced diet.

ENDOCRINE SYSTEM

Congenital hypothyroidism is found in 1 per cent of children with Down syndrome, and thyroid screening in the neonatal period is important. About 20 per cent of the children with Down syndrome will develop thyroid dysfunction (Pueschel and Pezullo, 1985), mostly hypothyroidism, and in about 30 per cent of the children elevated levels of antithyroid autoantibodies are reported (Fialcow, 1970). Annual thyroid tests are recommended, especially when growth retardation is evident. Thyroid dysfunction occurs more often in adults with Down syndrome and it has been estimated that nearly 40 per cent of adults with Down syndrome have hypothyroidism.

Growth retardation in Down syndrome (Cronk *et al.*, 1988) responds to growth hormone treatment (Annerén *et al.*, 1986, 1993). Growth retardation might be due to a selective deficiency of insulin-like growth factor I, or resulting from hypothalamic dysfunction and partial growth hormone deficiency (Castells *et al.*, 1988). However, treatment with growth hormone is not recommended in Down syndrome since the long-term effects are unknown and there are ethical and economic concerns.

Most females with Down syndrome are probably fertile and contraception in adolescent females should be considered (Goldstein, 1988). Men with Down syndrome are generally infertile, although one man with Down syndrome has been proven to be a father (Scheridan *et al.*, 1989).

ORTHOPAEDIC PROBLEMS

Most of the orthopaedic problems in Down syndrome are found in adult individuals and 27 per cent of patients with Down syndrome develop orthopaedic symptoms which need surgical intervention (Diamond *et al.*, 1981). Few malformations of the skeleton have been reported and most of the orthopaedic problems result from joint laxity and muscular hypotonus. Dislocation of the patella and hips are common, as well as epiphysiolysis of the hips. The feet are broad and many adult patients have hallux valgus (Diamond *et al.*, 1981).

Physiotherapy and a motor training programme carried out by the parents, in order to increase the muscular tonus of the newborn infant with Down syndrome, might be important for the motor and possibly, for the intellectual development (Reed *et al.*, 1980). It is unclear whether this programme prevents muscular hypotonia, but there are data that suggest that early intervention programmes may lead to more rapid acquisition of milestones in affected children (Carr, 1988). There is,

Table 10.1 Programme of preventive medicine for children with Down syndrome (age 0 to 17 years)

Age		Recommended examinations and evaluations
Neonate	1	Clinical confirmation of the diagnosis
	2	Chromosomal investigation
	3	Emotional support during the traumatic crisis for the parents
	4	Cardiac examination including electrocardiographic and echocardiographic examinations
	5	Instructions on physiotherapy programme to improve muscular hypotonus are given to the parents
	6	Thyroid screening
1 month	1	Ophthalmological examination to check for congenital cataract and severe refractive errors
2–3 months	1	Re-evaluation of the heart, if an open ductus arteriousus was found in the neonatal period
6 months	1	Otological examination; if wax and narrow ear ducts, recommendation for wax-removing ear drops
	2	Evaluation by child dentist, preventive information
	3	Thyroid test if child shows growth retardation
12 month	1	Ophthalmological examination with slit lamp and examination for refractive errors, with recommendation for follow-up
	2	Thyroid tests
	3	Otological examination and evaluation of hearing capacity
1–10 years	1	Annual thyroid tests
	2	Otological examinations twice a year at 1–7 yrs and annual examinations to 8 yrs and an audiogram at 4 yrs
	3	Ophthalmological examinations as recommended
	4	Developmental evaluation before school entry
	5	In event of autistic behaviour, an admission to child psychiatric dept.
	6	Preventive dental treatment twice a year
	7	X-ray of cervical spine before intubation anaestesia (>2.5 yr) or if there is any suspicion of atlantoaxial instability
11–17 years	1	Annual thyroid tests
	2	Annual otological examinations
	3	Ophthalmological examinations as recommended
	4	Advice on contraception in adolescent females
	5	Vaccination against hepatitis B when leaving school or earlier if there is hepatitis B in the environment
	6	Child-psychiatric evaluation in the event of depression

however, a gradual increase of muscle tone observed in children with Down syndrome as they get older, which probably is due to a neurological maturation phenomenon. Physiotherapy should continue during childhood in order to promote correct movement patterns, which might prevent problems from the hips, knees and other joints in adulthood (Mercer, 1994).

Atlantoaxial dislocation is a well-known abnormality in Down syndrome (Pueschel *et al.*, 1984; Pueschel and Pueschel, 1987). It is known that 15 per cent of individuals with Down syndrome show radiographic signs of instability of the cervical spine (Jagjivan *et al.*, 1988). About 1 to 2 per cent of individuals with Down syndrome will have symptomatic atlantoaxial instability. X-ray examination of the cervical spine should be considered at about 3 years of age and should always be performed in persons who have pain in the neck or if any neurologic abnormalities referable to the cervical area are present. X-ray is required for all persons with

Down syndrome attending the Special Olympics. Anaesthesia before intubation is also recommended in children older than 2.5 years.

CONCLUSION

All physicians, who are responsible for the medical care of children and adolescents with Down syndrome, should be made familiar with the special needs in Down syndrome patients. The training programmes for children with Down syndrome concerning motor and speech skills have improved considerable in recent years. No training of a child will become meaningful, however, if for example, impaired vision, hearing problems or hypothyroidism has not been corrected.

The preventive medical care programme in Table 10.1 is based on the needs of the child and adolescent with Down syndrome. It is similar to the recommendations recently given by Rogers and Coleman (1992) in the USA. By following these recommendations, the child with Down syndrome will receive optimal medical care. The programme does not include any controversial aspects of therapy and, although the programme was designed for Sweden, it was intended to be useful in most other countries. It is believed that these guidelines will diminish the risk of treatable medical problems in children with Down syndrome remaining undiagnosed for long periods with subsequent effects on adult life.

REFERENCES

Anneren, G. (1987) A medical care and support program for families with multiple congenital anomalies-mental retardation syndromes (MCA/MR). *Upsala Journal of Medical Science*, Suppl. **44,** pp. 221–25.

Anneren, G. and Gebre-Medhin, M. (1987) Trace elements and transport proteins in serum of children with Down syndrome and of healthy siblings living in the same environment. *Human Nutrition and Clinical Nutrition*, **41C,** pp. 291–99.

Anneren, G. & Gustavson, K.-H. (1994) Medical management of Down's syndrome. In R.K. Puri, H.P.S. Sachdev, P. Choudhury and I.C. Verma (eds), *Current Concept in Pediatrics*, Jaypee and New Delhi: Jaypee Medical pp. 106–12.

Anneren, G., Gustafsson, J., Sara, V.R. and Tuvemo, T. (1993) Normalized growth velocity in children with Down's syndrome during growth hormone therapy. *Journal of Intellectual Disability Research*, **37,** pp. 381–87.

Anneren, G., Johansson, E. and Lindh, U. (1985) Trace element profiles in individual cells from patients with Down's syndrome. *Acta Paediatrica Scandinavica*, **74,** pp. 259–63.

Anneren, G., Magnusson, C.G.M. and Nordvall, S.L. (1990) Increase in serum concentrations of IgG2 and IgG4 by selenium supplementation in children with Down syndrome. *Archives of Disease in Childhood*, **65,** pp. 1353–55.

Anneren, G., Sara, V.R., Hall, K. and Tuvemo, T. (1986) Growth and somatomedin responses too growth hormone in children with Down's syndrome. *Archives of Disease in Childhood*, **61,** pp. 48–52.

Annell, H., Gustafson, J., Ivansson, S.A. and Annerin, G. (in press) Growth and pubental development in children with Down syndrome. *Acta Paediatrica*.

Baird, P.A. and Sadovnick, A.D. (1989) Life tables for Down syndrome. *Human Genetics*, **82,** pp. 291–92.

Berry, P., Gunn V.P. and Andrews R.J. (1984) Development of Down's syndrome children from birth to five years. In J.M. Berg (ed.), *Perspective and Progress in Mental Retardation Vol 1. Social, Psychological and Educational Aspects*, pp. 167–77. Baltimore: University Park Press.

Björkstén, B., Bäck, O., Hägglöf, B. and Tärnvik, A. (1979) Immune function in Down's syndrome. In F. Guttler, R.A. Harkness and J.W.T. Seakins (eds), *Inborn Errors of Immunity and Phagocytosis*, pp. 189–98. Lancaster: MTP Press.

Brooks, D.N., Wooley, H. and Kanjial, G.C. (1972) Hearing loss and middle ear disorders in patients with Down's syndrome. *Journal of Mental Deficiency Research*, **16**, pp. 21–32.

Carr, J. (1988) Six weeks to twenty-one years old: a longitudinal study of children with Down's syndrome and their families. *Journal of Child Psychology and Psychiatry*, **29**, pp. 407–31.

Castells, S., Torrado C., Bastian W. and Wisniewski K.E. (1992) Growth hormone deficiency in Down's syndrome children, *Journal of Intellectual Disability Research*, **36**, pp. 29–43.

Catalano, R.A. (1992) Opthalmological concerns. In S.M. Pueschel and J-K. Pueschel (eds), *Biomedical Concerns in Persons with Down Syndrome*, pp. 259–72, Baltimore: Brookes.

Chi, T.P.L. and Krovetz, J. (1975) The pulmonary vascular bed in children with Down syndrome. *Journal of Pediatrics*, **86**, pp. 533–8.

Chicoine, B., McGuine, D., Hebein, S. and Gilly, D. (1994) Development of a clinic for adults with Down syndrome. *Mental Retardation*, **32**, pp. 100–106.

Coleman, M. (1983) A program of preventive medicine for Down's syndrome individuals of all ages. *Papers and Abstracts for Professionals*, **6**, pp. 1–3.

Collacott, R.A. (1993) Epilepsy, dementia and adaptive behavior in Down's syndrome. *Journal of Intellectual Disability Research*, **37**, pp. 153–60.

Cronk, C.E., Crocker, A.C., Pueschel, S.M., Shea, A.M., Zackai E., Pickens G. and Reed R.B. (1988) Growth charts for children with Down syndrome: 1 month to 18 years of age. *Pediatrics*, **81**, pp. 102–10.

Davies, B. (1988) Auditory disorders in Down's syndrome. *Scandinavian Audiology*, suppl. **30**, pp. 65–73.

Diamond, L.S., Lynne, D., and Sigman, B. (1981) Orthopedic disorders in patients with Down's syndrome. *Symposium on Orthopedic Surgery in the Mentally Retarded, Orthopedic Clinics of North America*, **12**, pp. 57–71.

Drott, P., Anneren, G., Esscher, E., Esscher, T. and Olsen, L. (1985) Results of neonatal surgery in Down's syndrome: ethical considerations. In Thomasson, B. and A.M. Holschneider (eds), *Kongress berichter, XV Congress of the Scandinavian Association of Paediatric Surgeons*, pp. 18–21. Odense, 31 May– 3 June, 1984. Stuttgart: Hippokrates Verlag GmbH.

Fialcow, J.T. (1970) Thyroid autoimmunity and Down's syndrome. *Annals of New York Academy of Science*, **171**, pp. 500–11.

Funa, K., Anneren G. and Björkstén B. (1984) Abnormal interferon production and NK cell response to interferon in children with Down's syndrome. *Clinical Experimental Immunology*, **56**, pp. 493–500.

Ghaziuddin, M., Tsai L.Y. and Ghaziuddin N. (1992) Autism in Down's syndrome: Presentation and diagnosis. *Journal of Intellectual Disability Research*, **36**, pp. 449–56.

Goldhaber, S.Z., Brown W.D. and St John Sutton, M.G. (1987) High frequency of mitral valve prolapse and aortic regurgitation among asymptomatic adults with Down's syndrome, *Journal of the American Medical Association*, **258**, pp. 1793–95.

Goldstein, H. (1988) Menarche, menstruation, sexual relations and contraception of adolescent females with Down syndrome. *European Journal of Obstetric Gynecology Reproduction Biology*, **27**, pp. 343–49.

Jaeger, E.A. (1980) Ocular findings in Down's syndrome. *Transaction of the American Ophthalmological Society*, **78**, pp. 808–45.

Jagjivan, B., Spencer, P.A.S. and Hosking, G. (1988) Radological screening for atlanto-axial instability in Down's syndrome. *Clinical Radiology*, **39**, pp. 661–63.

Johanson, A., Gustafson, L., Brun, A., Risberg J., Rosén I. and Tideman A. (1991) A longitu- dinal study of dementia of Alzheimer type in Down's syndrome. *Dementia*, **2**, pp. 159–223.

Kemper, T.L. (1988) Neuropathology of Down Syndrome. In L. Nadel (ed.), *The Psychobiology of Down Syndrome*, pp. 269–89. Cambridge, MA: The MIT Press.

Lai, F. (1992) Alzheimers disease. In S.M. Pueschel and J.K. Pueschel (eds) *Biomedical Concerns in Persons with Down Syndrome*, pp. 175–96, Baltimore: Brookes.

Levin, S. (1987) The immune system and susceptibility to infections in Down's syndrome. In E.E. McCoy and C.J. Epstein (eds), *Oncology and Immunology of Down syndrome*, pp. 143–62, London: Alan R Liss.

Levy, J. (1991) The gastrointestinal tract in Down syndrome. In C.J. Epstein, (ed.), *The Morphogenesis of Down Syndrome*, pp. 245–56, New York: Wiley-Liss.

Lund, J. (1988) Psychiatric aspects of Down syndrome – *Acta Psychiatrica Scandinavica*, **78**, pp. 369–74.

Macartney, F.J., Panday J. and Scott, O. (1969) Cor pulmonale as a result of chronic nasopharyngeal obstruction due to hypertrophic tonsils and adenoids. *Archives of Disease in Childhood*, **44**, pp. 585–92.

Mercer, L. (1994). The active preschooler. In Y. Burns and P. Gunn (eds), *Down Syndrome: Moving through Life*. London: Chapman and Hall.

Myers, B.A. and Pueschel S.M. (1991) Psychiatric disorders in persons with Down's syndrome. *Journal of Nervous Mental Disorders* **179**, pp. 609–13.

Mills, E.A. (1985) Ocular findings in children. In D. Lane, and B. Stratford (eds), *Current approaches to Down syndrome*, pp. 103–19, London: Cassell.

Oster, J., Mikkelsen, M. and Nielsen, A. (1964) The mortality and causes of death in patients with Down's syndrome (mongolism). *International Copenhagen Cong Scientific Study of Mental Retardation*, **1**, pp. 123–33.

Park, S.C. Mathews, R.A., Zuberbuhler, J.R., Rowe, R.D., Neches, W.H. and Lenox, C.C. (1977) Down's syndrome with congenital heart malformation. *American Journal of Disease in Childhood*, **131**, pp. 29–33

Pieper, W.M., Rochels, R. and Schmid, F. (1979) Kinderchirugische Erkrankungen beim Mongolismus-Syndrom. *Zeitschrift für Kinderchirurgie*, **27**, pp. 93–101.

Pueschel, S.M., Annerén, G., Durlacc, R., Flórez, J., Sustrova, M. and Verma, I.C. (1995) Guidelines for optimal medical care and management for persons with Down syndrome. *Acta Paediatrica*, **84**, pp. 823–7 and in *Down Syndrome: A Seminar Report on Medical Family Issues*, pp. 9–24, Stockholm: International League of Societies for Persons with Mental Handicap.

Pueschel, S.M., Herndon, J., Gelch, M., Senft, K., Scola, F. and Goldberg, M. (1984) Symptomatic atlantoaxial subluxation in persons with Down syndrome. *Journal of Pediatric Orthopedics*, **4**, pp. 682–88.

Pueschel, S.M., Louis, S. and McKnight, P. (1991) Seizure disorders in Down syndrome. *Archives of Neurology*, **48**, pp. 318–20.

Pueschel, S.M., and Pueschel, S.R. (1987) A study of atlantoaxial instability in children with Down syndrome. *Journal of Pediatric Neuroscience*, **3**, pp. 107–16.

Pueschel, S.M. and Pezullo, J.C. (1985) Thyroid dysfunction in Down syndrome. *American Journal of Disease in Childhood*, **139**, pp. 636–69.

Pueschel, S.M. and Werner, J.C. (1994) Mitral valve prolapse in persons with Down syndrome. *Research in Developmental Disabilities*, **15**, pp. 91–97.

Reed, R.B., Pueschel, S.M., Schnell, R.R. and Cronk, C.E. (1980) Interrelationships of biological, environmental and competency variables in young children with Down syndrome, *Applied Research Mental Retardation*, **1**, pp. 161–74.

Rogers, P.T. and Coleman, M. (1992) *Medical Care in Down Syndrome. A Preventive Medicine Approach. Pediatric Habilitation*, vol. 8, New York, Marcel Dekker.

Rowe, R.D. and Uchida, I.A. (1961) Cardiac malformation in mongolism: a prospective study of 184 mongoloid children. *American Journal of Medicine*, **31**, 726–35.

Scheridan, R., Lierana, J. Jr, Matkins S., Debenham, P., Cawood, A. and Bobrow, M. (1989) Fertility in a male with trisomy 21. *Journal of Medical Genetics*, **26**, pp. 294–98.

Storm, W. (1990) Prevalence and diagnostic significance of gliadin antibodies in children with Down syndrome. *European Journal of Pediatrics*, **149,** pp. 833–34.

Wisniewski, K.E., Wisniewski, H.M. and Wen, G.Y. (1985) Occurence of neuropathological changes and dementis of Alzheimer's disease in Down's syndrome. *Annals of Neurology*, **17,** pp. 278–82.

*Developments in Educational
Research and Practice*

11 Precognitive and Cognitive Resource Profiles: an 'Abilities' Approach to Biobehavioral Remediation

David Gibson

REDISCOVERING MULTIDISCIPLINARY REMEDIATION RESEARCH AND APPLICATION

People with Down syndrome present a picture of physical and behavioural homogeneity that is both real and deceiving at the same time. Close inspection of the morphological and psychological stereotype for Down syndrome reveals inter- and intra-case variations. These are governed by aberrant chromosomal subtypes, extent and kinds of secondary structural and metabolic disorders, quality of health care and nurture, and age. Despite within-stereotype variability, the evidence is strong that Down syndrome children and adults are 'not like the others' (Gibson, 1991a and 1991b) because between-syndrome variation is more striking than are within-syndrome differences. It is this greater degree of biobehavioral homogeneity that furnishes us the opportunity to target remediation programmes more effectively to the assets/deficits profile characteristics of the syndrome.

Easier said than done! The emerging ability/disability maps for Down syndrome are weighted heavily on the deficit side where our research in bridging to practice is still scant. It is proposed here, therefore, to work initially with the less daunting biobehavioral and syndromic 'resource' indicators (assets, residuals, abilities) as a foundation for the development of multidisciplinary precognitive, cognitive and metacognitive intervention programmes. Accordingly, much of the present chapter is a 'resources' catalogue (Tables 11.1 and 11.2) supported by relevant studies and explanation where necessary. The catalogue is representative but hardly comprehensive, given the extent of the available research.

At the outset, it will be helpful to understand the origins of the growing biobehavioral approach to management. The honourable beginnings were in the pioneer work of Langdon Down, Itard and Seguin's Physiological Training Method, and in their perceptual training experiments. Then, too, there is Guggenbuhl's Abendberg marriage of health, sensori-motor and language enrichment for his Cretin (perhaps Down syndrome) patients (Kanner, 1964; Scheerenberger, 1983). Since these products of fertile medical minds yielded no great intellectual gains ('cures'), whatever the secondary benefits achieved, the care and protection model for mentally retarded persons became entrenched public policy. It was the largely successful enterprise of dealing with special learning disorders in children that pointed the way back to a discipline team approach to managing deficits in cognitive processing. Their diagnostic target population was the attention deficit and hyper-activity disorders (ADHD). The first full-blown treatment programmes were mounted by Strauss and Kephart (1947) and Strauss and Lehtinen (1955). Psycho-pharmacological support systems soon followed. Not all cures were complete, as Weiss and Hechtman (1986) and Wender (1987) remind us, but gains were sufficient for this enterprise to continue to flourish.

Surprisingly, our success with remediation programmes for classical learning disorders didn't soon or easily transfer to coping with learning disorder among developmentally handicapped children. The reasons were largely cultural, doctrinal and fiscal. It was only by 1971 that Belmont was able to assemble the first evaluative review of biobehavioral research in the field of mental retardation (MR) and so to spark new interest in study and practice built around specific psychological disorders often having unique needs patterns. Similar investigations of the Down syndrome population have been mounted by Anwar (1981), Gibson (1978, 1991a, b), Lane and Stratford (1985), Pueschel (1984), Pueschel *et al.*, (1987b). And not only for Down syndrome!

Biobehavioral patterns typical of Fragile-X syndrome have been comprehen-sively documented by Dykens *et al.* (1994b). The study of mental processing deficits and the atypical hemispheric specialization of Turner's syndrome subjects owes much to Netley and Rovet (1982) and Rovet and Netley (1982). These etiology-specific studies continue on an ever broadening base.

Turning finally the body of the chapter, Table 11.1 is a diary of the precognitive resources of the Down syndrome child and youth. These include mostly the psycho-motor and sensori-motor domains as the primary builders of the cognitive and metacognitive facilities. Table 11.2 asks the reader to consider the cognitive resources of Down syndrome persons as a key to structuring intervention tech-nologies for the metacognitive levels of functioning; evaluating, planning, projecting consequences and choosing. Remember however that these catalogues deal only with 'resource' indicators as the working material.

DEVELOPING SENSORIMOTOR RESOURCES AS AGENTS OF COGNITIVE GROWTH IN DOWN SYNDROME

Table 11.1 lists indicators of intervention opportunities derived from the research literature. The majority of these resource indicators will readily suggest their programme potentials. The Part A indicator list begins with grip strength, gross motor facility and eye-hand co-ordination as at or near normal levels in early life. These strengths can be harnessed to compensate for developmental shortfall in other sensori-motor subdomains. Advancing early psychomotor status, generally, contributes to stronger neural structures associated with cognitive and language growth.

Overall, the Part A indicators reveal a number of remediation programme building themes. Among these are that a) throughout the psychomotor subdomains,

Table 11.1 Developing sensori-motor resources as agents of cognitive growth in Down syndrome

Part A *Early motor signs assets as potential building blocks to ongoing development*

Down syndrome persons are claimed, typically, to exhibit the following comparatively 'positive' sensori-motor characteristics:

1. Gross motor performance often close to normal expectation in early childhood.
2. Grasp and eye following superior to mentally handicapped (MH) peers; especially in early childhood.
3. Near-normal eye/hand functioning and finer co-ordination in first few years of life.
4. Hypotonia reduces with advancing age; the reduction usually evident by CA 10 months.
5. And as hypotonia recedes, muscle strength increases.
6. Grip strength superior to MH peers.
7. Range of movement potential of the joints is in advance of MH peers.
8. Diminished resistance of the joints to passive movement compared with MH control subjects.
9. Postural training most effective if (a) initiated in first months of life and (b) of higher than usual intensity and frequency.
10. Respond most favourably to motor system training if given frequent rest periods: all ages.
11. Movement training gains are best if instruction is unidirectional in any one session.
12. Motor task performance can reach the norm for MH peers if not involving simultaneous sensory/proprioceptive inputs.
13. Psychomotor response to training is generally superior to symbol-based training; but with the spread between psycho-motor and symbol management potentials reducing significantly with advancing age. A timing-of-treatments challenge.

Part B *The remedial opportunities in sensori-motor and cognitive systems synergy*

1. More efficient tactile/form recognition learning if task is stationary: not involving turntable or other motion components.
2. Attention best sustained if material to be learned is limited to a single dimension or modality.
3. Least distraction effect if performance in a given single modality is cued from a different modality.
4. Down syndrome subjects can achieve normal motor response times *if* decision time is subtracted from the performance measure.
5. Competency on a visual-visual matching task is enhanced if the stimulus material does not necessitate handling by Down syndrome subject.
6. Display superior performance to MH peers on drawing straight lines, paper-folding and on various visual/motor tasks.
7. Display superior performance to MH peers on processing kinesthetically derived information (motor/tactile recognition as in to feel, trace, explore).
8. Display equal or better performance to MH peers on visual/stereognostic and visual/tactile discrimination tasks: an indicator of visual exploration potential.
9. Display slower than average self-regulation growth (to MH peers) initially but can accelerate past MH peers in later childhood.

Part C *Imitation 'abilities' expedite psychomotor to cognitive learning transfer*

1. Imitation behaviours is in advance of MH peers and non-MH subjects.
2. Locomotor agility is said to boost motor imitation facility.
3. Motor learning success is greater if based on imitation of movement rather than on directed learning of motor tasks: learning to walk backwards, for example.
4. Gestural communication superior to verbal; is said to be a by-product of imitation facility.
5. Tendency (most) to mimic rhythm, move to music and to enjoy acrobatics is significantly more advanced than MH peers.
6. An alleged propensity for motor expression and pantomime is associated with the imitation facility.
7. The foregoing item has been further interpreted as evidence of a 'creative' sense – as in acting (mimicry).

Note MH – mental handicap/mental retardation

early and intensive training is most potent for evolving a stronger central processing capacity, lateralization and the storage and retrieval of language symbols (Yessayan and Pueschel, 1984), b) similarly, early motor system strengthening oriented to resources rather than to deficits serves to extend the range of motor abilities, c) motor ability enhancement, in turn, can inhibit recession of cognitive functioning usually associated with advancing age, and d) the ability/disability equation for Down syndrome children and adults shifts with age so it is necessary that these elisions be factored into remedial programming. In this regard we learn that (Dubowitz, 1980) hypotonia is frequently in significant recession by 10 months of age and in concert with increasing muscle strength. Parenthetically, if circulatory system shortfall is not medically managed, muscle strength, psychomotor ability and cognitive function can deteriorate. As noted by Yessayan and Pueschel (1984), muscle tone is a reliable predictor of later competence in all domains.

The more complex resource particulars of Part A of Table 11.1 have been ably elaborated by Henderson (1985). Additional explanation (item 14) can be found in Cornell and Birch (1969), McNeill (1955), and Stedman and Eichorn (1964). Item 13 owes much to the work of Anwar (1981).

Part B of Table 11.1 attempts to identify more direct linkages between sensori-motor resources that might bear on cognitive process maturation and specialization. The first five, of nine, entries have in common superior (against peers with mental handicaps, MH) performance in various subdomains but only if other simultaneous stimuli are selectively controlled or excluded from a given learning/teaching procedure. These observations can be traced respectively to Silverstein *et al.*, 1982 (item 1); Cunningham, 1983 (item 2); Henderson, 1985 (item 3); Saqi, 1983 (item 4); Lewis and Bryant, 1982 (item 5). To a greater or lesser degree, all of the nine Part B resource indicators reflect the tendency for Down syndrome persons, on average, to fail initially to combine spatial and temporal inputs in task performance; a tendency not shared by MH peers (Cratty, 1974, Henderson, 1987). Intervention technology designers would need to be aware of the phenomenon as documented by Belmont (1971), Gibson and Fields (1984), Rohr and Burr (1978).

In the second half of the Part B series, items 6 to 9 indicate exploitable resources in visual/motor potential and in the motor/kinesthetic/tactile and stereognostic modalities. Guidance to practical exploitation of these indicators is evident in the work of Silverstein, *et al.*, (1982) (item 6); Anwar (1983) and Harris and Gibson 1988 (item 7). Anwar adds that best learning results are achieved if visual feedback is prevented, with only proprioceptive reafferent feedback in play. Item 8 is elaborated by Pueschel (1988). The final item on the evolution of self-regulation in Down syndrome children and adults owes much to Kopp (1983). Evidently, self-regulation for Down syndrome subjects starts below the norm for MH peers (being unable to delay or inhibit gratification) but accelerates with advancing age. Intervention curricula builders need to evaluate these growth trajectories in order to capitalize on maximum readiness periods.

Part (C) of Table 11.1 includes seven potentially useful resources, each centred on a claimed 'imitative' propensity for the syndrome. That claim is much debated: whether or not imitation in DS is unique, inherent, merely artifactual, useful and exploitable or a stereotypic novelty. All suggested origins have some clinical or data-based support. Langdon Down (1867) and, later, Crookshank (1924) favoured an atavistic explanation. Fennel (1904) had reduced this to the merely 'innate'. Barr (1904) opted for superior rote-memory and short-term recall as the basis of the imitation 'talent'. Benda (1946) implicated a prolongation and exaggeration in Down syndrome subjects of a similar but briefer childhood phase seen in non-handicapped children. Bilovsky and Share (1965) declared the prolongation to be compensation (inherent and fostered) for the auditory/verbal facility deficit characteristic of the syndrome. Variations on this theme include Øster's (1953) explanation that imitative behavior reflected a relatively strong Down syndrome visual/perceptual processing capacity. Blacketer-Simmonds (1953) preferred a perseveration or over-compensation explanation of the imitative advantage. Not so different is the view that mimicry in Down syndrome is a security device or attention gainer (Share, *et al.*, 1964). Finally, the drive/impulse characteristics of the syndrome must be acknowledged in any attempt to understand the origins of mimicry, modelling and imitation, however conceived (Blessing 1959; Sternlicht and Wander, 1962; Sternlicht, 1966).

While the debate on antecedents of imitative learning continues, Part C of Table 11.1 shows a practical face. The first item is derived from the Huffner and Redlin (1976) studies of mimicry, gestural behaviour, aerobics and pantomime claimed for members of the syndrome. The case for item 2, that improving motor agility, already comparatively advanced, will enhance the quality of motor imitation (LeBlanc, *et al.*, 1977) is nevertheless conjectural. Item 3 is attributable to Neeman (1971) in his 'Limitation of Movement' study where he reports that the use of motor imitation is superior as a teaching tactic to directed motor train. Item 4 makes the point that the extended use of gestural communication, in many Down syndrome individuals, should be tolerated and encouraged as part of training objectives, and primarily as a foundation for later motor/speech encoding in the cognitive systems (Gibson, 1978).

Rhythm, dance and musical response as components of the imitation propensity suggest a special creative sense for Down syndrome members (see items 5 to 7). De Grandement-Fortier (1983) views this array of talents, or stereotypes, as important to relevant pedagogy; providing the guidance is subtle and non-verbal. Penrose and Smith (1966) were of like mind. They cite Langdon Down's (1887) claim for Down syndrome people as having 'a strong sense of the ridiculous'. We are told of Down syndrome patients who converted their pillowslips into surplices, the better to play out their imitation in appearance, cadence and speech of the just departed clergymen. Belmont (1971) refers to this *joie de vivre* as a possible window for managed growth.

Overall, Table 11.1 supports a few plausible generalizations:

1. We will need to enrich our intervention programmes in the direction of greater sensitivity to both the biobehavioural particulars of syndrome and the maturational timing and trajectory of these particulars.
2. Intervention programmes are likely to be more easily mounted if they start with the ability side of the asset/deficit equation.

Table 11.2 offers additional support for these two propositions.

Table 11.2 From precognitive to cognitive and metacognitive resource inventories: learning and deciding

Part A *The psychometric approach to cognitive asset identification*

Down syndrome persons are claimed, typically, to exhibit the following comparatively 'positive' intellectual characteristics:

1. Mental test profiles are significantly more homogeneous than those for MH peers – a curriculum delivery advantage.
2. While WISC subtest scaled scores are slightly lower on average in Down syndrome populations than for etiologically exogenous MH peers, they tend to be significantly more stable in early adulthood thus facilitating more uniform services delivery.
3. Mental test items favouring Down syndrome subjects over etiologically undifferentiated MH peers include rote memory, psychomotor, visual/motor and non-conceptual performance tasks.
4. Cognitive assets favouring psychometric performance by Down syndrome subjects include test items requiring figural inputs (shapes in two and three dimensions) and visual/motor skills.
5. Competency scaling comparing Down syndrome subjects and MH peers rates Down syndrome samples superior for motor performance (hand use, ambulation, habit formation as in eating, dressing, etc.) and for behavioural status (as in self-injury, temper tantrums, etc.) from childhood to younger adulthood.
6. Comparative superiority is claimed for object grouping tasks; a possible expression of preference for symmetry in both the psychomotor and cognitive domains.
7. Down syndrome persons typically display a unique tendency to 'order reversal'; an idiosyncracy exploitable for teaching purposes.

Part B *Remedial implications of imbalance in the two cognitive system dichotomies, a) successive over simultaneous mental processing, and b) visual over auditory inputs in mental processing*

1. Down syndrome students respond best to highly structured and well differentiated learning environments.
2. If learning situations are relatively unstructured, Down syndrome students respond better to suggestion over direction.
3. Down syndrome students exploit learning opportunities less well (than MH peers) if in a 'free choice' situation.
4. Young Down syndrome adults respond more favorably to cognitive skills training than Down syndrome children or older Down syndrome adults.
5. Instruction in 'planning' skills is improved if the teaching method employs mainly the visual/motor and figural potentials of Down syndrome persons.
6. Visual cognitive encoding is superior to auditory cognitive encoding; compared with MH peers.
7. Teaching content will have greater instructional value if derived from non-symbolic than from abstract/conceptual foundations.
8. Mental encoding is stronger if instructional content is successive/sequential/linear in nature rather than being primarily simultaneous/configural and multidimensional in programme content.
9. The tendency to engage successive/sequenced cognitive tactics in information processing, storage and retrieval is enhanced if Down syndrome subjects are working exclusively within the visual modality.
10. *Appropriately timed* (test detectable) cognitive training for simultaneous configural mental coding is essential to mastering higher level planning and more complex problem-solving appropriate to age.
11. Programming through visual/motor circuits is an effective precursor to improving visual/verbal cognitive circuitry: building from auditory/motor to auditory/verbal performance is less successful and much slower to register gains (also age dependent).
12. When speed or time pressure on an auditory or visual/perceptual instructional demand is accelerated, there is evidence of increasing deficit in *both* modalities – another time and modality sensitive intervention concern for programme planning.

Part C *Windows to learning, relearning and the consolidation of learning: Attention as the instructional mediation*

1. The frame of spatial reference of Down syndrome persons is more intact if not disrupted by kinesthetic after-effects.

Table 11.2 (cont.,)

2. Comprehension of sequenced linguistic content suffered when only syntactic (grammatical) linguistic instruction was used. Attention and learning improved when a supporting extra linguistic context was also employed.
3. Attention to learning simultaneous/configural content is strongest if accompanied by visual and/or motor instructional cueing.
4. Down syndrome learners respond more readily to instruction on a parallel or related second task if first task teaching is suspended. Simultaneous demands in one session are mutually distracting.
5. Split attention tasks impede learning, compared to non-handicapped students who can attend to several demands at the same time.
6. Attention or intake focus can be strengthened if the task has a degree of animation (novelty) to drive interest and reduce the tendency to over-focus (perseverate).
7. Attention instability responds best to immediate rewards; assuming rewards are not themselves distracting. Ongoing reward schedules can be spaced in increments best suited to encourage postponement of gratification in individual cases.
8. Down syndrome subjects exhibit most learning flexibility (compared to MH control subjects) when faced with perceptual discrimination tasks.
9. Syntactical learning (see item 2) follows a stop-start pattern. Language training therefore should be more intensive when cognitive growth is in an accelerative phase; and later in the life of the Down syndrome learner than is usually supposed.
10. Cognitive limitations among Down syndrome students in retention, integration and generalization is arguably sustained by a deficit in consolidation facility. Training success in consolidation of learning is said to occur if a repeated or relearning strategy is used – however prolonged.
11. The relearning model is most effective on visual/motor tasks, initially, but provides a subsequent base for engaging other modalities as vehicles of instruction.

Note: MH – mental handicap/mental retardation

FROM PRECOGNITIVE TO COGNITIVE AND METACOGNITIVE RESOURCE INVENTORIES: LEARNING AND DECIDING

Table 11.2 is focused more squarely on the characteristic cognitive patterns for the Down syndrome population. The intent is to identify cognitive and metacognitive resources as likely to have value for programme construction. A most easily retrieved source of relevant data is found in psychometric profiles of Down syndrome subjects compared with their mentally handicapped peers (Part A). A second data source (Part B) is found in the debates over the two major dichotomies; in cognitive functioning for the syndrome. These are, successive versus simultaneous mental processing and visual processing as superior to auditory mental processing. The final section (Part C) attempts to isolate capacities for relearning, consolidation and attending particularly to the syndrome and a necessary part of instructional technology.

Part A, item 1, suggests that subjects with Down syndrome are more homogenous in ability patterns than other groups with mental handicaps (Clausen, 1968). The happy implication is that within-syndrome remediation can achieve a certain predictability and uniformity of application. There is disagreement, however on the nature of the maturational curve and on the different degrees of within- and between-subject variation along that curve (Henderson, 1985). The shape of the maturational phenomenon is easily imagined with an overall model of development of persons with Down syndrome across the life span that is curvilinear – a trajectory of initially rapid growth, slowing by late childhood and with deceleration evident by young to mid-adulthood. Developmental variability along the curve peaks in late childhood and the teenage period and at the point when the trajectory has flattened (the plateau) (Dykens *et al.* 1994a; Fowler, 1988; Gibson, 1966). If sketched, the combined trajectories and deviation patterns would be POD-like, with most variability at the plateau, and in a negative direction, and with the least variability at the two ends.

Item 2 notes a generally more stable Wechsler (Kaufman, 1979) test profile for Down syndrome than for exogenous mental handicap. A notable exception for persons with Down syndrome is the Block Design (BD) subtest where a rapid decline in scores is evident by the third and fourth decades of life. This exception is a vital one because Guilford and Merrifield (1960) consider BD to be the strongest measure of G while Kaufman (1979) rates BD as a comparatively pure test of abstraction powers. Accordingly, the decline of BD prowess over time is widely considered (Fuld, 1978, 1984) to be an indicator of a risk for dementia. The relative stability of the other Wechsler Performance (P) scale items is attributed to the visual/motor resources of those with Down syndrome (Pueschel *et al.*, 1987b) and to test items where verbal or abstract ability is secondary to success.

Items 3, 4, and 5 reflect test results that favour Down syndrome (over controls) in a number of performance domains. It can be supposed that more efficacious intervention might result from bonusing programme content in the direction of these resources (Dykens *et al.* 1994a; Silverstein *et al.*, 1982; Silverstein *et al.*, 1985). Greenspan and Delaney (1983), using a 12-variable scale, add 'niceness' to the psychometric advantage. A final item, attraction to symmetry or 'good form' (Stratford, 1979), is a mixed blessing for programme designers. Nakamura (1965) first observed that students with Down syndrome were best at circle drawing and form board completion. These tasks are not only visual/motor in skills required but also engage imitation and a drive to achieve symmetry. Weak lateralization is implicated to account for these preferences. So it is that students can and do make errors in their copying and other pencil work in the direction of creating symmetry. While this is perhaps a primitive or neuro-pathological tendency, its presence does help the teacher and programmer to work with these tendencies in positive ways.

Items 1 to 3 of Part B concern structure and choice in learning and teaching. The first two items are elaborated in Kopp *et al.*, (1983) and Landry *et al.*, (1994). The third item appears to be a deficit but is included here because Rietveld (1983) found that students with Down syndrome could learn in 'free choice' situations following some months of concentrated training. Item 4 returns to the value of program delivery timing. We noted (Berry *et al.*, 1984) in a cognitive enrichment experiment that better results from training were achieved during the third decade of Down syndrome adulthood. Similar training in the fourth decade of life was less beneficial. Perhaps intensive cognitive training for the population with Down syndrome could profitably be delayed to adolescence and young adulthood. Items 5 through 7 should not be difficult to incorporate in curricula. Elaboration of each can be located in Gibson and Fields (1984), Gibson (1978) and Zekulin *et al.*, (1974).

It is contended that the greatest potential for cognitive supplementation is realized by first building successive (v. simultaneous) mental encoding skills while employing visual/motor modes of learning (v. auditory/verbal encoding). If this is done it becomes more possible to reach the disability side of these equations (Berry *et al.*, 1984; Gibson *et al.*, 1988). Items 8 through 10 suggest training opportunities for building simultaneous cognitive processing skills. Das and his group have been the major players in this field of study (Das *et al.*, 1979; Snart *et al.*, 1982) noting, for example, that *appropriately timed* cognitive training in simultaneous encoding is the foundation of abstract thought. It can be supposed too that the appropriate, usually visual, modality be stressed. The work of Ashman (1982), Kerr and Blais (1988), and Lincoln, *et al.*, (1985) offers useful elaboration on expanding these more complex metacognitive functions.

The final two items in Part B of Table 11.2 stress the advantages, in early life especially, of making the visual modality the major teaching vehicle. Establishing the visual and motor systems pathways for cognitive encoding, storage and retrieval provides a foundation for later improvements in the auditory cognitive sphere. Readiness will also have advanced with time and general maturity. Pueschel *et al.*, (1987b) and Pueschel (1988) suggest the neurological foundations of this sequencing of intervention by modality. First, they contend that early auditory system teaching strategies could frustrate the child with Down syndrome and further retard learning. Secondly, Pueschel (1988, p. 209) suggests why:

> Myelination of nerve fibers occurs for specific neuronal tissues at different times in the development of the central nervous system. It is known that nerve fibers of auditory associations are myelinated late during development when an increase in peroxidative damage may occur. Thus, selective perturbations of oxygen-free radical metabolism will affect adversely myelin formation in nerve tracts concerned with auditory processing.

Further elaboration is offered by Courchesne (1988) and Lincoln, *et al.*, (1985).

Part C of Table 11.2 has two themes: 1) the identification of training tactics for attention generation and maintenance (items 1 to 8), and 2) the importance of relearning procedures for purposes of the consolidation of material taught. The first item is derived from the Anwar and Hermelin (1979) study on the distraction potential of kinesthetic 'after-effects' on spatial learning. Item 2 indicates that attention and comprehension of sequenced linguistic material improves when a supporting extra-linguistic context is part of instruction (Kernan, 1990). Item 3 is the general case, and item 4 tells us that attention is not served by the instructional manipulation of parallel tasks (Kopp, 1983). The mechanism appears to be a tendency of children with Down syndrome to pay excessive attention to one focus, such as a toy, or mother's face. Non-MH children can be closely task-engaged, learn and yet continue to monitor their environment – to simultaneously manage multiple tasks (Landry and Chapreski, 1990) (item 5). Or is it mere perseveration at work? Legerstee and Bowman (1989) might favour that claim, in their finding that attention is more productive and less perseverative if the task has animation or novelty. Task animation, however, cannot extend to motion as such and to where tactile and visual task attention is significantly reduced by the parallel use of a spatial element in the learning situation. Item 7 needs no elaboration.

Discovering the causes of attention problems in Down syndrome and other mental handicapping conditions is important because isolating the origins of distractibility leads more directly to prevention. Among the obvious sources are poor memory (storage and retrieval), faulty central processing of auditory inputs, defective vision and eye movement, hypotonus, defective hearing, impulsivity and perseveration (Gibson, 1978). Programmers will be aware of Rayner's (1992) treatments ranging from enhancing visual central processing to improved reading. Item 8, the last in the attention-distraction series, contends for a flexibility of approach by learners with Down syndrome in perceptual discrimination tasks (Stratford and Alban-Metcalfe, 1981). Or is it partly a matter of distraction consequent on structural defects of vision? Pesch *et al.*, (1978) followed 41 subjects with Down syndrome through five age groups (to age 23 years) to record 23 with strabismus, 14 having nystagmus, 24 hyperopes, and so on. Related behavioral shortfall was noted for motor skills, directionality recognition, auditory memory and body sense. Vietze (1983) interpreted the 'visual flexibility' as impulsivity. But if visual exploration is thus improved and learning with it, the source can be discounted. The reader will have taken the point that a biobehavioral resources and deficits registry for Down syndrome is not fixed and that some deficits can be manipulated as if assets.

The final three items address the need to employ a learning/relearning model of programme delivery. Item 9 stresses that the strategy works best when the learner with Down syndrome is in an accelerated stage of motivational progress and depending on modalities involved. Intensive relearning programmes applied during growth plateau stages would presumably be less effective and more stressful, doing little to alter a decelerative growth trajectory (Fowler, 1988; Gibson, 1966). Lastly (items 10 and 11), Wishart (1986, 1987, 1991, 1993) advises using a high-intensity relearning model to advance consolidation and generalization of even rote-learned material. She adds that the model is most effective if the tasks are visual/motor in content, at least in the early stages of instruction. For example, digit recall training (auditory/visual) didn't respond to a relearning strategy (Schroth, 1975; Schultz, 1983; Wishart, 1991) – a matter of poor timing?

RECONCILING COMPETING MANAGEMENT MODELS: THE BETTER TO BREACH THE 'DEVELOPMENTAL WALL'

The two tables of biobehavioral 'resources' for Down syndrome are necessarily limited. A more comprehensive accounting would necessarily include resource elements in the domains of memory, language, behavioural variation by chromosomal subtypes (translocations, mosaicisms for example), the arousal and drive properties of the syndrome, ability/disability pattern shifts with age (Rasmussen and Sobsey, 1994) and the risk elements for psychopathology. Add to this the more extensive 'deficits' record for the syndrome (Gibson and Fields, 1984) and the remediation programme possibilities are greatly magnified. The syndromic model of management is especially promising because: 1) the ability/disability particulars are structurally definable, 2) these particulars are therefore more readily manipulated for research and remediation purposes, and 3) will necessarily require the skills of a multidisciplinary team to effect such manipulations. There is ample evidence, too, that health and rehabilitation specialists – speech pathologists, physical and occupational therapists, and brain-behaviour experts, among others, prefer a bio-behaviorally oriented services delivery model (McWilliam and Bailey, 1994). Many educators and developmental psychologists opt, however, for the 'delay' model of management.

Valuable insights into why our service for those with mental handicaps and research assumptions and models vary so sharply is explored by Hodapp and Dykens (1994). They identify two main cultures of behavioral research and conse-quent service systems. One culture employs the syndromic approach. The second culture exploits the levels-of-impairment approach. The distinction parallels, generally, Zigler's delay-difference or developmental-deficit dichotomy (Hodapp *et al.*, 1990). While Hodapp and Dykens invite a reconciliation of these two cultures, the 'call' might be premature. For one, the disciples of the two cultures differ widely in discipline identification, training background and assumption about the nature and future of persons with mental handicaps. 'Difference' or deficit-oriented programmes treat specific biobehavioral artifacts, which, it is claimed, largely cluster by etiologies. Delay philosophies view all persons with mental handicaps as cut from the same cloth and whose common problem is slowness of development. Adherents advocate, and reasonably so, raising the intensity of generic manage-ment programmes. But, gains using omnibus stimulation tactics are not reliably in the cognitive domain (Garber *et al.*, 1991; Gibson and Harris, 1988; Piper and Pless, 1980). Life span studies by Carr (1992) on the durability of the effects of parenting practices on assets/deficits profiles are ongoing, however. The syndromic/cognitive intervention approach is yet to be as well tested.

Nor do the two cultures explored by Hodapp and Dykens tell the entire story. There are two possible additional management doctrines; one old and in rejuvena-tion and the other new and aggressive. These are the Care and Protection model and the Redefine and Deny model. As recently as 1977, Wunderlich's respected textbook on Down syndrome argued that children with Down syndrome can be helped to be healthier, the better to advance quality of life. However, comprehension, judgement and communication capacities are declared the least amenable to intervention and hence health and happiness are predicated on humane care and protection – in group homes, institutions, families and foster families. Venue matters little if the match between needs and service is a beneficial one. Exploitation, self-injury, abuse by others and simple deprivation are thus prevented. As the more seriously mentally handicapped survive longer and in improved physical condition, this previously abandoned care and protection model will contrive to acquire new life and new subscribers among parents as well as many professionals.

The second proposed addition to the 'two cultures' is the doctrine of Redefinition and Denial. This position is presently predominant in mental retardation manage-ment circles. It can be identified by its premises and practices. These include the re- and de-diagnosis of mental retardation (Luckasson, *et al.*, 1992; Reiss, 1994), banning IQ tests, the invention of numerous euphemisms for mental retardation/ mental handicap that tend to dissipate the parameters of the condition or to blend it in with more 'acceptable' handicapping conditions, redefining intelligence as mere survival skills (Sternberg and Wagner, 1986), legislating the paid assistant as prothesis, designing programmes to raise intelligence (IQ) – a fruitless enterprise we are told if IQ is to reflect the neuronal components of cognitive processes (Ginsberg 1972; Spitz 1986; Vernon 1979), designing school programmes with performance criteria to fit ability levels – and nobody fails (Perkins, 1994). Support for this fourth culture is found in a current trend to give feeling, compassion, friendship, helping and other subjective elements a more equal place with cold rationalism and the high-tech society. There is more to life than intellect and more to the citizen with mental handicaps than IQ (Saul, 1994).

All four management cultures have merits and shortcomings that tend collectively to balance and cancel. For example, a child with Down syndrome graduates from a first level developmentalist intervention experience to a more intensive biobehavioral and syndromic treatment regimen. In later years, he or she will benefit further from the Care and Protection culture – from the 'bad' side of society – and from the Re-define and Deny model – the 'good' society at work. In the fourth culture we need only take care that the server is not the one primarily served and that the citizen with mental handicaps is not prematurely shunted into the third or fourth culture as if these were exclusive models of management.

Put them all together and they spell comprehensive programming aimed at breaching the 'developmental wall' (Gibson, 1966) in competency growth, with resulting enrichment of life for all citizens with mental handicap of developmental origin.

REFERENCES

Anwar, F. (1981) Motor function in Down's syndrome. In N.R. Ellis (ed.) *International Review of Research in Mental Retardation*, vol. 10. New York: Academic Press.

Anwar, F. (1983) The role of sensory modality for the reproduction of shape by the severely retarded. *British Journal of Developmental Psychology*, **1**, pp. 317–27.

Anwar, R. and Hermelin B. (1979) Kinesthetic movement after-effects in children with Down syndrome. *Journal of Mental Deficiency Research*, **23**, pp. 287–97.

Ashman, A.F. (1982) Coding, strategic behavior and language performance of institutionalized mentally retarded young adults. *American Journal of Mental Deficiency*, **86**, pp. 627–36.

Barr, M.W. (1904) *Mental Defectives: Their History, Treatment and Training*, Philadelphia: Blakiston's.

Benda, C.E. (1946) *Mongolism and Cretinism*, New York: Grune and Stratton.

Belmont, J.M. (1971) Medical behavioral research in retardation. In N.R. Ellis (ed.), *International Review of Research in Mental Retardation*, vol. 5, New York: Academic Press.

Berry, P., Groeneweg, G., Gibson, D. and Brown, R.I. (1984) Mental development in Down's syndrome adults. *American Journal of Mental Deficiency*, **89**, pp. 252–56.

Bilovsky, D. and Share, J. (1965) The ITPA and Down syndrome: an exploratory study. *American Journal of Mental Deficiency*, **70**, pp. 78–82.

Blacketer-Simmonds, D.A. (1953) An investigation into the supposed differences existing between mongols and other mentally defective subjects with regard to certain psychological traits. *Journal of Mental Science*, **99**, pp. 702–19.

Blessing, K.R. (1959) The middle range mongoloid in trainable classes. *American Journal of Mental Deficiency*, **63**, pp. 812–21.

Carr, J. (1992) Assets and deficits in the behaviour of people with Down's syndrome: a longitudinal study. In B. Tizard and V.P. Varma (eds), *Vulnerability and Resilience in Human Development: a Festschrift for Ann and Alan Clarke*, pp. 57–71 London: Jessica Kingsley.

Clausen, J. (1968) Behavioral characteristics of Down's syndrome subjects. *American Journal of Mental Deficiency*, **73**, pp. 118–26.

Cornwell, A.C. and Birch, H.G. (1969) Psychological and social development in home-reared children with Down's Syndrome. *American Journal of Mental Deficiency*, **74**, pp. 341–50.

Courchesne, E. (1988) Psycho-anatomical considerations in Down Syndrome. In L. Nadel (ed), *The Psychobiology of Down Syndrome*, Cambridge, MA: MIT/Bradford.

Cratty, B.J. (1974) *Motor Activity and the Education of Retardates*, 2nd edn, Philadelphia: Lea and Febiger.

Crookshank, F.G. (1924) *The Mongol in Our Midst*, London: Kegan Paul.

Cunningham, C.C. (1983) Early support and intervention. In P. Mittler and H. McCanecine (eds) *Parents, Professionals and Mentally Handicapped People: Approaches to Partnership*, London: Croom Helm.

Das, J.P., Kirby, J. and Jarman, R.F. (1979) *Simultaneous and Successive Cognitive Processes*, New York: Academic Press.

Down, J.L.H. (1987) Observations on ethnic classification of idiots. *Mental Science*, **13**, pp. 121–28.

Dubowitz, V. (1980) *The Floppy Infant*, London: Heinemann.

Dykens, E.M., Hodapp, R.M. and Evans, D.W. (1994a) Profiles and development of adaptive behaviour in children with Down syndrome. *American Journal on Mental Retardation*, **98**, pp. 580–58.

Dykens, E.M., Hodapp, R.M. and Leckman, J.F. (1994b) *Behavior and Development in Fragile-X syndrome* Thousand Oaks: Sage.

Fennell, C.H. (1904) Mongolian imbecility, *Journal of Mental Science*, **50**, 32.

Fowler, A. (1988). Determinants of rate of language growth in children with Down syndrome. In L. Nadel (ed), *The Psychobiology of Down Syndrome*, Cambridge, MA: MIT Press.

Fuld, P.R (1978) Psychological testing in the differential diagnosis of the dementias. *Aging*, **7**, pp. 185–93.

Fuld, P.A. (1984) Test profiles of cholinergic dysfunction of Alzheimer's-type dementia. *Journal of Clinical Neuropsychology*, **6**, pp. 380–92.

Garber, H.L. (1991) The Milwaukee project and critique. Special book review section *American Journal on Mental Retardation*, **95**, pp. 477–525.

Gibson, D. (1966) Early developmental staging as a prophecy index in Down's syndrome. *American Journal of Mental Deficiency*, **70**, pp. 825–28

Gibson, D. (1978) *Down's Syndrome*, Cambridge: Cambridge University Press.

Gibson, D (1991a). Down syndrome and cognitive enhancement: not like the others. In K. Marfo. (ed), *Early Intervention in Transition*, New York: Praeger.

Gibson, D. (1991b) Searching for a life-span psychobiology of Down syndrome: advancing educational and behavioral management strategies. *International Journal of Disability, Development and Education*, **38**, pp. 71–89.

Gibson, D. and Fields, D.L. (1984) Early infant stimulation programs for children with Down syndrome: a review of effectiveness. In M.L. Woolraich and D.K. Routh (eds), *Advances in Developmental and Behavioral Pediatrics*, vol. 5, Greenwich, CT: JAI Press.

Gibson, D. and Harris A. (1988) Aggregated early intervention effects for Down syndrome persons: patterning and longevity of benefits. *Journal of Mental Deficiency Research*, **32**, pp. 1–17.

Gibson, D., Groeneweg, G., Berry, P. and Harris A. (1988), Age and pattern of intellectual decline among Down syndrome and other mentally retarded adults. *International Journal of Rehabilitation Research*, **11**, pp. 45–47.

Ginsburg, H. (1972) *The Myth of the Deprived Child: Poor Children's Intellect and Education*, Englewood Cliffs: Prentice-Hall.

de Grandement-Fortier, N. (1983) [The non-hierarchization of behaviour and creativity among Down's syndrome individuals] *Revue de Modification du Compartement*, **13**, pp. 117-28.

Greenspan, S. and Delaney, K. (1983) Personal competence of institutionalized adult males with or without Down Syndrome. *American Journal of Mental Deficiency*, **88**, pp. 218-20.

Guilford, J.P. and Merrifield, P.R. (1960) *The structure-of-intellect model: Its uses and implications*. Report from the Psychological Laboratory (No. 24), University of Southern California.

Harris, A.J. and Gibson, D. (1988) Syndrome-specific tactile performance proceedings, Canadian Psychological Association Annual Conference, Montreal.

Henderson, S.E. (1985) Motor skill development In D. Lane and B. Stratford (eds), *Current Approaches to Down's Syndrome*, London: Holt, Rinehart and Winston.

Hodapp, R.M., Burack, J.A. Zigler, E. (eds) (1990) *Issues in the Developmental Approach to Mental Retardation*, New York: Cambridge University Press.

Hodapp, R.M. and Dykens, E.M. (1994) Mental retardation's two cultures of behavioral research. *American Journal on Mental Retardation*, **98**, pp. 675-87.

Huffner, V. and Redlin, W. (1976) [Imitation responses in Mongoloid children] *Zeitschrift fur Klinische Psychologie*, **5**, pp. 277-86.

Kanner, L. (1964) *The History of the Care and Study of the Mentally Retarded*, Springfield: Thomas.

Kaufman, A.S. (1979) *Intelligence Testing with the WISC-R*, New York: Wiley.

Kernan, K. (1990) Comprehension of syntactically indicated sequence by Down syndrome and other mentally retarded adults. *Journal of Mental Deficiency Research*, **34**, pp. 169-78.

Kerr, R. and Blais, C. (1988) Directional probability information and Down syndrome: A training study. *American Journal on Mental Retardation*, **92**, pp. 531-38.

Kopp, C.B. (1983) Risk factors in development. In P.S. Mussen (ed.), *Handbook of Child Psychology*, vol. 2, New York: Wiley.

Kopp, C.B., Krakow, J.B. and Johnson, K.L. (1983) Strategy production by young Down syndrome children. *American Journal of Mental Deficiency*, **88**, pp. 164-69.

Landry, S.H. and Chapieski, M.L. (1990) Joint attention of six-month-old Down syndrome and pre-term infants: 1. Attention to toys and mother. *American Journal on Mental Retardation*, **94**, pp. 488-98.

Landry, S.H., Garner, P.W., Pirie, D. and Swank, P.R. (1994) Effects of social context and mother's requesting strategies on Down's syndrome childrens' social responsiveness. *Developmental Psychology*, **30**, pp. 293-302.

Lane, D. and Stratford, B. (1985) *Current Approaches to Down's Syndrome*, London: Holt, Rinehart and Winston.

LeBlanc, D., French, R. and Schultz, B. (1977) Static and dynamic balance skills of trainable children with Down's syndrome. *Perceptual and Motor Skills*, **45**, pp. 641-42.

Legerstee, M. and Bowman, T.G. (1989) The development of response to people and a toy in infants with Down syndrome. *Infant Behavior and Development*, **12**, pp. 465-77.

Lewis, V.A. and Bryant, P.E. (1982) Touch and vision in normal and Down syndrome babies. *Perception*, **11**, pp. 691-701.

Lincoln, A.J., Courchesne, E., Kelman, B.A. and Galambos, R. (1985) Neuropsychological correlates of information-processing by children with Down syndrome. *American Journal of Mental Deficiency*, **89**, pp. 403-14.

Luckasson, R., Coulter, D.L., Polloway, E.A., Reiss, S., Schalock, R.L., Snell, M.E., Spitalnik, D.M. and Stank, J.A. (1992) *Mental Retardation: Definition, Classification and Systems of Support*. 9th edn. Washington: American Association on Mental Retardation. (See also critiques, in *American Journal on Mental Retardation* (1994) **98**, pp. 539-49.)

McNeill, W.D. (1955) Developmental patterns of mongoloid children: a study of certain aspects of their growth and development. *Dissertation Abstracts*, **15**, pp. 86-87.

McWilliam, R.A. and Bailey, D.B. (1994) Predictors of service-delivery models of center-based early intervention. *Exceptional Children*, **61**, pp. 56–71.

Nakamura, H. (1965) An enquiry into systematic differences in the abilities of institutionalized adult mongoloids. *American Journal of Mental Deficiency*, **69**, pp. 661–65.

Neeman, R.L. (1971) Perceptual-motor attributes of mental retardates: a factor analytic study. *Perceptual and Motor Skills*, **33**, pp. 927–34.

Netley, C. and Rovet, J. (1982) Atypical hemispheric specialization of Turner syndrome subjects. *Cortex*, **18**, pp. 377–84.

Øster, J. (1953) *Mongolism*, Copenhagen: Danish Science Press.

Penrose, L.S. and Smith, G.F. (1966) *Down's Anomaly*, London: Churchill.

Perkins, K.P. (1994) No such thing as integration. *Chicago Tribune*, 18 October [From PBS programme Frontline: School Colors]

Pesch, R.S., Nagy, D.K. and Caden, B.W. (1978) A survey of the visual and developmental-perceptual abilities of the Down's syndrome child. *Journal of the American Optometric Association*, **49**, pp. 1031–37.

Piper, M.C. and Pless, I.B. (1980) Early intervention for infants with Down's syndrome: a controlled trial. *Pediatrics*, **65**, pp. 463–68.

Pueschel, S.M. (1984) *The Young Child with Down Syndrome* New York: Human Sciences Press.

Pueschel, S.M (1988) Visual and auditory processing in children with Down syndrome. In L. Nadel (ed.), *The Psychobiology of Down Syndrome*, Cambridge, MA: MIT/Bradford.

Pueschel, S.M., Gallagher, P.L., Zartler, A.S. and Pezzullo, J.G. (1987) Cognitive and learning processes in children with Down syndrome. *Research in Developmental Disabilities*, **8**, pp. 21–37.

Pueschel, S.M., Tingey, C., Rynders, J.E., Crocker, A.C. and Crutcher, D.M. (eds) (1987) *New Perspectives on Down Syndrome*, Baltimore: Brookes.

Rasmussen, D.E. and Sobsey, D. (1994) Age, adaptive behavior and Alzheimer disease in Down syndrome: cross-sectional and longitudinal analyses. *American Journal on Mental Retardation*, **99**, pp. 151–65.

Rayner, K. (1992) *Eye Movements and Visual Cognition*, New York: Springer-Verlag.

Reiss, S. (1994) Issues in defining mental retardation *American Journal on Mental Retardation*, **99**, pp. 1–7.

Rietveld, C.M. (1983) The training of choice behaviours in Down's syndrome and non-retarded preschool children. *Australia and New Zealand Journal of Developmental Disabilities*, **9**, pp. 75–83.

Rohr, A. and Burr, D.B. (1978) Etiological differences in pattern of psycholinguistic development of children of I.Q. 30–60. *American Journal of Mental Deficiency*, **82**, pp. 549–53.

Rovet, J. and Netley, C. (1982) Processing deficits in Turner's syndrome. *Developmental Psychology*, **18**, pp. 77–94.

Saqi, S.M. (1983) Reaction times and movement times of Down's syndrome children. Unpublished MSc thesis, University of London.

Saul, J.R. (1994) *The Doubter's Companion* New York: Viking. (See also his 1993 *Voltaire's Bastards*.)

Scheerenberger, R.C. (1983) *A History of Mental Retardation*, Baltimore: Brookes.

Schroth, M.L. (1975) The use of I.Q. as a measure of problem solving ability with mongoloid and non-mongoloid children. *Journal of Psychology*, **91**, pp. 49-56.

Schultz, E.E.J. (1983) Depth of processing by mentally retarded and MA- matched non-retarded individuals. *American Journal of Mental Deficiency*, **88**, pp. 307–13.

Share, J., Gralicker, B. and Koch, R. (1964) The predictability of Gesell development scales in Down's syndrome. In US Department of Health, Education and Welfare, Children's Bureau: *The Case of the Retarded Child. Therapy and Prognosis*, pp. 39–43, Washington: Government Printing Office.

Silverstein, A.B., Agena, D., Alleman, A.C. Derecho, K.T., Gray, S.B., and White, J.F.

(1985) Adaptive behaviour of institutionalized individuals with Down syndrome. *American Journal of Mental Deficiency*, **89**, pp. 555–58.

Silverstein, A.B., Legutki, G., Friedman, S.L. and Takayama, D.L. (1982) Performance of Down syndrome individuals on the Stanford-Binet intelligence scales. *American Journal of Mental Deficiency*, **86**, pp. 548–51.

Snart, F., O'Grady, M. and Das, J.P. (1982) Cognitive processing by subgroups of moderately mentally retarded children. *American Journal of Mental Deficiency*, **86**, pp. 465–72.

Spitz, H.H (1986) *The Raising of Intelligence: a Selected History of Attempts to Raise Retarded Intelligence*, Hillsdale: Erlbaum.

Stedman, D.J., and Eichorn, D.H. (1964) A comparison of the growth and development of institutionalized and home-reared mongoloids during infancy and early childhood. *American Journal of Mental Deficiency*, **69**, pp. 391–401.

Sternberg, R.J. and Wagner, R.K. (1986) *Practical Intelligence: Nature and Origins of Competence in the Everyday World* New York: Cambridge University Press.

Sternlicht, M. (1966) *A Talk to Parents of the Mongoloid Child*, New York: Staten Island Aid for Retarded Children.

Sternlicht, M. and Wanderer, Z.W. (1962) Nature of institutionalized adult mongoloid intelligence. *American Journal of Mental Deficiency*, **67**, pp. 301–02.

Stratford, B. (1979) Attraction to 'good form' in Down's syndrome. *Journal of Mental Deficiency Research*, **23**, pp. 243–51.

Stratford, B. and Alban-Metcalfe, J.A. (1981) Position cues in discrimination behavior of normal, Down syndrome and other mentally handicapped children. *Journal of Mental Deficiency Research*, **25**, pp. 89–103.

Strauss, A.A. and Kephart, N.C. (1955) *Psychopathology and Education of the Brain-Injured Child*, New York: Grune and Stratton.

Strauss, A.A. and Lehtinen, L.E. (1947) *Psychopathology and Education of the Brain-Injured Child*, New York: Grune and Stratton.

Tingey, C., Mortensen, L., Matheson, P. and Doret, W. (1991) Developmental attainment of infants and young children with Down's syndrome. *International Journal of Disability, Development and Education*, **38**, pp. 15–26.

Vernon, P.E. (1979) *Intelligence: Heredity and Environment*, San Francisco: Freeman.

Vietze, P.M. (1983) Attention and exploratory behavior in infants with Down syndrome. In T. Field and A. Sostek (eds), *Infants Born at Risk: Psychological, Perceptual and Cognitive Processes*, New York: Grune and Stratton.

Weiss, G. and Hechtman, L.J. (1986) *Hyperactive Children Grow Up*, New York: Guilford.

Wender, P.H. (1987) *The Hyperactive Child, Adolescent and Adult: Attention Deficit Disorder Through the Lifespan*, New York: Oxford University Press.

Wishart, J.G. (1986) The effects of step-by-step training on cognitive performance in infants with Down's syndrome. *Journal of Mental Deficiency Research*, **30**, pp. 233–50.

Wishart, J.G. (1987) Performance of young non-retarded children and children with Down syndrome on Piagetian infant search tasks. *American Journal of Mental Deficiency*, **92**, pp. 169–77.

Wishart, J.G. (1991) Taking the initiative in learning: a developmental investigation of infants with Down syndrome. *International Journal of Disability, Development and Education*, **38**, pp. 27–44.

Wishart, J.G. (1993) The development of learning difficulties in children with Down's syndrome, *Journal of Intellectual Disabilities Research*, **37**, pp. 389–403.

Wunderlich, C. (1977) *The Mongoloid Child: Recognition and Care*, Tuscon: University of Arizona Press.

Yessayan, L. and Pueschel, S.M. (1984) Neurological investigations. In S.M. Pueschel (ed.), *The Young Child with Down Syndrome*, New York: Human Sciences Press.

Zekulin, X.Y., Gibson, D., Mosley, J.L. and Brown, R.I. (1974) Auditory-motor channeling in Down syndrome subjects, *American Journal of Mental Deficiency*, **78**, 571–77.

12 Avoidant Learning Styles and Cognitive Development in Young Children

Jennifer G. Wishart

Children with Down's syndrome (Down's syndrome) face many problems in growing up. A substantial percentage have to cope with health complications of varying severity and nature, a great many have to manage with visual or hearing acuity that is far from perfect, and yet others have to put up with motor difficulties ranging from minor clumsiness to major problems with fine motor coordination. Undoubtedly however, the overriding challenge faced by the majority of children with Down's syndrome lies in mastering the key cognitive skills of childhood. Attaining academic milestones and problem-solving skills much beyond those of the average six- to eight-year old proves to be a very uphill task for most children; a great number reach adulthood without ever having developed even these relatively low levels of cognitive ability. Early progress is highly encouraging but all too often this promise fails to be realized in later years. It is essential to find out why this is the case and to try to identify ways to help children maintain their early rate of progress.

This chapter looks at how young children with Down's syndrome go about their learning. Rather than examining which specific abilities they acquire and at what age, it looks at some of the strategies they use when faced with learning new skills, how they respond to making mistakes, and what use they make of other people. It also looks at whether the learning style of children with Down's syndrome changes in any significant way as they grow older. In particular, it examines to what degree children might actually be adding to their already-existing difficulties by adopting counterproductive behaviour strategies when faced with opportunities to learn new, more advanced cognitive skills. Findings from a number of longitudinal research studies will be presented which provide evidence indicating that with increasing age and experience, children with Down's syndrome often change from being active and relatively able problem-solvers into progressively more reluctant learners. These studies indicate that motivational deficits may significantly inhibit the learning process in many children, not only delaying the acquisition and consolidation of new skills but also denying them the full benefits of those skills they do finally acquire. With judicious management of their learning experiences, these are problems which we might well be able to help them to overcome.

LEARNING TO LEARN: SOME INHERENT PROBLEMS

Any attempt to help must first recognize the very real obstacles standing in the way of children's progress. Children with Down's syndrome start out with a considerable number of biologically-determined disadvantages. Despite being the smallest of the human chromosomes, the extra copy or part copy of chromosome 21 present in Down's syndrome has a massive influence on how development unfolds – from conception, throughout the years of childhood and adolescence, and on into adult years. Down's syndrome influences the developmental process in many ways and at many levels. Surprisingly perhaps, some of its effects are beneficial. Children with Down's syndrome develop fewer dental caries than other children, for example, and although heart problems are strongly associated with the condition, certain diseases and abnormalities, such as aortic stenosis and arteriosclerosis, are very rare, occurring much less frequently in persons with Down's syndrome than in the general population (Cunningham, 1987; Marino *et al.*, 1990; Newton, 1992). Epilepsy is another example. Not only are children with Down's syndrome less prone to epilepsy than children with other kinds of mental handicap, but for those who do suffer infantile spasms the neurological prognosis is considerably better than in the general population (Howells, 1989; Stafstrom and Konkol, 1994).

The underlying causal mechanisms which act to protect certain aspects of development in children with Down's syndrome are not yet fully understood and unfortunately beneficial effects are in the minority. Most of the effects definitely are not beneficial. For a very small percentage of children, the condition may even prove life-threatening, for example, for those born with severe heart defects, with major abnormalities of the gastrointestinal system, or who contract leukaemia. The majority, however, enjoy good health and for them, the greatest problem stems from the effects that Down's syndrome has on development of the central nervous system and thus on their ability to learn.

These children enter life with an ability to learn which is already significantly impaired biologically. There is also evidence that further deceleration in brain growth occurs post-natally, with differences in brain size from normal being smallest at birth and increasing in post-infancy years. Electron microscopy studies suggest a pattern of arrested or delayed differentiation, with defects in neuronal migration and additional problems in postnatal synaptogenesis (Takashima *et al.*,1981; Sylvester, 1986; Kemper, 1988). Even in adults, the Down's syndrome brain can still be distinguished by its embryonic simplicity, with its lack of surface complexity, its reduced volume and weight, and its immature neronal connections (Uecker *et al.*, l993). Basic structural differences shown by pathological studies of adult brains include a smaller cerebellum and cerebellum and immaturity in the frontal and temporal lobes, with the size of the hippocampus reduced by as much as 30–50% in some cases.

Some of the more obvious consequences of these abnormalities in brain development are immediately discernible. The reduction in size of the cerebellum, for example, is likely to underlie poor muscle tone and motor sequencing deficiencies. Likewise, the immaturity in frontal and temporal lobes is implicated in the significant memory deficits and impairment in spatial representation and in temporal sequencing skills found in children and adults. Abnormal development in these areas might also be implicated in the accelerated ageing process reported (see Lott· and McCoy, 1992; Uecker *et al.*, 1993; Wisniewski, 1990). Findings from studies of prenatal and infant brains suggest that at least some of these abnormalities are already evident at birth, with function being impaired further by delayed myelinisation and the atrophy of dendritic spines in the first years of life, normally the most rapid – and vulnerable – period of brain growth (Sylvester, 1983; Takashima *et al.*, 1981).

Neurophysiological studies have shown how these structural and functional abnormalities produce widespread maladaptive changes in neural functioning – in sensory, memory and attention systems, and in auditory, visual and somatosensory modalities (Courchesne, 1988). Function is also adversely affected throughout development by the gene dosage effects which arise from the presence of the extra copy of all or part of chromosome 21. Chromosome 21 may be small but it is estimated to contain 1500 or so genes. Translocation studies have shown that trisomy of only the bottom third of chromosome 21 is sufficient to produce all of the anatomical and biochemical abnormalities associated with Down's syndrome and it now appears from genetic mapping studies that only a relatively small region within this, known as 21q22, may be specifically responsible for the pathogenesis. Only 50 to 100 genes may therefore be implicated but amongst those now identified as being on 21q22 – and therefore acting in triplicate – are a number of genes with profound implications for cognitive growth and physical health. These include the gene coding for the enzyme superoxide dismutase (SOD 1), which in excess is likely to cause lipoperoxidation and cell membrane malfunction, the Gart gene, which codes for 3 different enzymes involved in purine synthesis and is thus likely to underlie some of the disruption to CNS development seen in Down's syndrome, and the ETS-2 oncogene, which may be responsible for the elevated incidence of leukemia (Newton, 1992; Patterson, 1987). Dosage effects arising from the triplication of genes located outside the segments of chromosome 21 (considered critical for Down's syndrome) are also likely to compromise cognitive functioning.

Our knowledge of the direct – and indirect – consequences of the presence of an extra copy of each of the genes on chromosome 21 is still very limited but it is already clear that even first-order gene dosage effects are far from straightforward. The impact on development of overproduction of gene products is not always uniform nor is it always universally expressed. Some of the effects may also become evident only very late in life. One obvious example of this is the gene coding for the amyloid precursor protein mRNA, a gene now mapped to chromosome 21 and known to be associated with familial Alzheimer's disease and thus with the early onset of deterioration in cognitive functioning (St George-Hyslop *et al.*, 1987). Levels of this protein might have been expected to be elevated by a factor of 1.5 in Down's syndrome, as has been shown to be the case in investigations of other genes near the region considered critical (Epstein, 1986). In Down's syndrome fetal brains, however, APP levels have been shown to be 4.6 times greater than normal (Neve *et al.*, 1988). This overproduction is consistent with evidence that all adult Down's syndrome brains at postmortem show the senile plaques and neurofibrillary tangles characteristic of Alzheimer's disease. Although cognitive deterioration can be difficult to assess, a number of studies have failed to find the corresponding clinical evidence of dementia in many persons with Down's syndrome, however, even when highly sensitive neuropsychological testing has been used to assess changes in their cognitive functioning in later years (Schapiro *et al.*, 1989; Schapiro *et al.*, 1992; Thase, 1988; Wisniewski *et al.*, 1994). This fits with recent evidence showing that it may be variations in genes on chromosomes other than 21 which are important in determining who will and will not suffer dementia, both for persons with Down's syndrome and for the rest of the population (Roses *et al.*, 1994; Royston *et al.*, 1994).

Our understanding of the relationship between brain pathology and behaviour still has a very long way to go and the picture need not necessarily be as bleak as it at first might seem. It is obviously important to recognize all of the inherent limitations which Down's syndrome imposes on many aspects of children's development but future research in the neurosciences may also provide us with valuable information on those aspects of brain development which are relatively spared. With this information, we will be in a much better position to help children in their efforts to learn since we shall then be able to offset identified developmental strengths against existing developmental weaknesses.

HELPING CHILDREN WITH DOWN'S SYNDROME TO LEARN: EARLY INTERVENTION

It is clear from all of the above that Down's syndrome brings with it considerable biological disadvantages when it comes to cognitive development. This should not be taken as meaning that there is nothing that can be done to facilitate the learning process and indeed since the 1960s, a great deal of parental and teacher effort has been invested in trying to help them overcome some of the inherent difficulties they inevitably have to face when trying to learn new skills. The general consensus is that this extra educational input – and the much more positive attitude it reflects – greatly increases their chances of developing to their full potential and certainly many are now achieving skills rarely seen in their counterparts in earlier generations (Berry and Gunn, 1989). Much of the effort to assist children in their learning has been channelled into early intervention programmes. The content, methods and intensity of intervention may vary greatly from country to country but early intervention programmes are now the norm in virtually all developed countries. Once again, the general consensus is that these programmes are beneficial, giving the child the best possible start in life and providing encouragement and professional support to parents in the difficult early years.

One of the major byproducts of the introduction of early intervention has undoubtedly been the raising of parental, professional and public expectations of the progress that can be made in pre-school years. This has engendered a wider recognition of the need to provide appropriate educational support from birth throughout childhood and has opened the doors to all sorts of opportunities for learning which were previously closed. The more direct impact of early intervention is more difficult to establish. While those who design and implement programmes have often reported major gains in young children receiving early intervention (Dmitriev and Hayden, 1975), independent reviewers have generally been far less impressed by the measurable levels of success achieved by most programmes (Gibson and Harris, 1988; Spiker and Hopmann, 1995; Spitz, 1986). Advocates of early intervention often claim the credit for the higher levels of competence being seen today, but others would maintain that these advances are just as likely to stem from the better management of health problems in the present generation of children, from the more positive attitudes of parents and teachers towards them, and from their greatly increased access to education and a more normal lifestyle. There is some concern amongst professionals that we are in fact in danger of overestimating what is being achieved by today's children and that we should not lose sight of the fact that the majority continue to experience significant learning difficulties throughout their childhood years.

Assessing whether or not a specific programme of intervention is directly effective is far from straightforward (Marfo, 1991). Any attempt at evaluating or comparing the efficacy of different early intervention programmes is usually beset by major difficulties. A common problem is that programmes are often under constant revision during the period of intervention. Basic features of programmes – such as age of the child at entry, length of participation in the programme, frequency and content of sessions, input expected from parents – also tend to vary enormously, making it extremely difficult to compare their efficacy. Some programmes have to be evaluated on the basis of only very small numbers of participating children and even with widely-adopted programmes, such as Portage, there is often huge variability in how the programme has been implemented in different parts of the country and even by different professionals working within the same area. This variability makes evaluation a minefield, even if all relevant information on implementation of the programme and on family and child characteristics has been carefully documented throughout the intervention, which unfortunately usually turns out to be the exception rather the rule (Dunst, 1986).

Many of the ground-breaking early intervention programmes claiming high success rates made no use of concurrent control groups and assessed their impact only by comparing the progress of children in their programme against available developmental norms for children with Down's syndrome. These norms were typically based on earlier generations of children, almost all of whom would have been institutionalised from birth. It would indeed have been surprising if any group of children with Down's syndrome being brought up at home in the 1970s and 1980s had not exceeded norms from institutionalised children of the 1950s and 1960s, regardless of whether they had participated in an early intervention programme or not. This was, after all, a time when public and scientific interest in early childhood development was at a peak, with early stimulation being seen by many as holding the key to enhancing intelligence levels in children, both with and without learning disabilities. New 'educational' toys for babies and young children enjoyed enormous popularity and fathers as well as mothers were encouraged to provide as much and as varied stimulation as possible in these early formative years.

There can be little doubt that some early intervention programmes have had some notable successes, particularly in enhancing cognitive development in children from socially or economically disadvantaged backgrounds (White and Castmo, 1985). Thirty years on, however, the benefits of early intervention to children whose learning difficulties are biological rather than socio-economic in origin remains very much open to question. Many of the gains made by children who participate in early intervention programmes have proved to have very poor 'tenacity' and therefore little true developmental value, as Gibson (1978) was one of the first to point out. Frequently, early intervention succeeded only in bringing forward the age of acquisition of a rather limited range of motor or self-help skills, skills which would normally appear in due course even without the benefits of additional teaching. Programmes which aimed at encouraging cognitive skills fared little better when outcome measures were subjected to scientific scrutiny. Many of these focused directly on promoting acquisition of the sorts of skills usually targetted in formal tests of early intelligence and, not surprisingly, such programmes often did result in 'gains' in IQ scores over the course of the intervention. However, there was little evidence of generalization of the trained skills to other tasks and in many cases, the advantage gained proved to be very short-lived, with children not given any specific training soon catching up with programme children and performing at much the same level (Sloper *et al.*, 1986).

Although there are serious questions to be asked about whether early intervention programmes repay the effort invested in them, it is in fact now very likely that the opportunity to assess their true value may have been lost. Despite widespread acknowledgement that proper scientific evaluation is essential, it seems likely that future attempts at objective assessment will have little more success in providing definitive answers. No matter how many doubts are expressed by professionals and researchers about the efficacy and cost-effectiveness of early intervention programmes, they would seem to be here to stay since the consumers – parents – are convinced of their value. As a result, few would be likely to agree to their child being entered into the control group of any evaluation study if that meant their child receiving no intervention. Most of today's researchers would in any case find it ethically unacceptable to withhold intervention from any child for this purpose. Although the direct cognitive benefits likely to result from participating in intervention are questionable, it is widely accepted that there are indirect benefits to both child and family at many levels. At best, we are likely to be able to evaluate only the effects of more versus less intervention, comparing development in children whose parents are very active partners in professionally-directed interventions with that in children whose families choose to accept or have available only minimal outside help. Even here, disambiguating the different factors at work would be extremely problematic since the differences in parental choice underlying degree of participation would almost certainly reflect other important differences in the environments in which the two groups of children would be learning and growing up (Crombie, 1994).

One fairly recent exception to the otherwise limited and short-term success of early intervention deserves some attention here: this is in the teaching of basic literacy skills to very young children. While it has to be said that some of these programmes have often lacked sufficiently rigorous controls to allow proper evaluation, it is nevertheless undeniable that some are clearly succeeding in teaching reading and writing skills – sometimes at remarkably early ages (Buckley, 1985; Buckley and Bird, 1993; Johansson, 1993). As these skills were previously thought to be beyond the intellectual reach of most adults with Down's syndrome, attempts to teach them to children were few and far between prior to the 1980s. On the basis of results reported thus far, however, it now seems feasible that with teaching which is more sensitively-tailored to the specific educational needs of children with Down's syndrome – teaching which recognises their short-term memory problems, their deficits in auditory and visual sequential memory and the relative strength of visual over auditory processing ability (Bower and Hayes, 1994; Marcell and Armstrong, 1982; McDade and Adler, 1980; Snart, 1982; Varnhagen *et al.* 1987) – many more children may be able attain some level of these key skills in the future (Bird and Buckley, 1994). This could in turn conceivably unlock the door to the acquisition of other, more advanced cognitive skills. At present, however, many of these skills – and the language skills on which so much of cognitive development ultimately depends – are unfortunately still proving very elusive (Duffy and Wishart, 1994; Fowler, 1990, 1995).

NURTURING DEVELOPMENTAL POTENTIAL

The relative lack of impact thus far of many intervention programmes on cognitive development should not be taken to mean that children with Down's syndrome cannot be helped to achieve higher levels of understanding or to reach more advanced academic goals than is usually the case currently. It is widely accepted that the developmental progress in any child is determined by a complex interplay between genetic potential and the physical and psychological environment in which that potential unfolds. Presently, we have no ways of correcting for the adverse influence of the extra chromosome on brain development. We are now very close to a full biomedical understanding of Down's syndrome but each new advance makes it increasingly clear that it will be very difficult, if not impossible, to intervene genetically or biochemically to reduce the undesirable effect Down's syndrome has on the developmental process. Accepting that there may never be a biomedical 'cure' does not, however, remove the grounds for believing that children born with Down's syndrome can be helped to achieve more than they currently tend to do. The biologically-given tools they have for learning may be compromised from conception onwards, but this does not prevent the learning process itself from remaining open to amelioration using appropriately tailored psychological methods.

The presence of Down's syndrome will inevitably place upper limits on what can be achieved by this route, as would the genetic makeup of any child. With a working understanding of the inherent restrictions placed on development, however, and with a better knowledge of how their learning normally progresses, we should be able to ensure that each child makes full use of all of the cognitive skills that he or she is genetically capable of acquiring. The fact that early intervention has thus far had few successes in effecting real and lasting cognitive gains does not undermine this assertion in any way. Few intervention programmes to date have been grounded in an understanding of development in children with Down's syndrome. Most are directly based on theories and teaching methods derived from studies of how development proceeds in children who have none of the dis-advantages that children with Down's syndrome are born with. Their lack of impact is not therefore surprising.

SETTING REALISTIC GOALS

What should we expect children with Down's syndrome to be able to achieve and how can we best encourage each child to develop to his or her full potential? There are some signs that interventionists are beginning to accept that some goals perhaps need to be reset and that the inherent limitations on certain aspects of development need to be better acknowledged. The 'slow is fast enough' philosophy represented by Goodman (1992) reflects an important shift in thinking in this area while still stressing the considerable potential for development present in all but the most profoundly-handicapped of children. This potential for development is clearly still present in teenage years (Crombie, 1994), with a fair number of young adults continuing to add to their skills into their twenties and thirties (Carr, 1988; 1994; Shepperdson, 1994).

There are several reasons for believing that these children could be helped to achieve more than most of them currently do. The very wide range of ability levels found at all ages (Carr 1985; Gibson, 1978; Sloper *et al.*, 1990) indicates clearly that Down's syndrome, unlike many other mentally-handicapping conditions of genetic origin, does not in itself place an immutably low ceiling on the development of cognitive skills. Cognitive ability is actually relatively high in many young children with Down's syndrome, much higher than might be expected given the levels of achievement typically seen at older ages (Wishart, 1988, 1993a). For reasons that are not yet fully understood, this early potential is not usually realized in later years but it is nevertheless clearly there. Evidence that the learning process under-lying acquisition of early cognitive skills is responsive to structured interventions also provides reason for believing that many could achieve more, with a number of studies demonstrating that children can be helped to reach the next stage in their development more quickly than they might otherwise have done if given appropriately-tailored teaching (Broadley *et al.*, 1994; Duffy and Wishart, 1987).

Taken together, these three facts justify some degree of optimism about the scope for effective intervention. It would be pointless to deny that the size and longevity of the gains made thus far with early intervention and training studies have been disappointing. It is also true that to date ability to generalize newly-acquired cognitive skills to other tasks has proved to be unimpressive (Duffy and Wishart, 1994; Pitcairn and Wishart, 1995). In recent years, however, some individual children have undoubtedly made, and maintained, remarkable progress in some areas of their development. Although firm quantitative data are often hard to find and much of the evidence is anecdotal, the fact that even a small number of young people are doing so well demonstrates that higher levels of achievement are indeed possible at older ages and are not restricted to early stages in development or to skills at the bottom of the developmental ladder.

Those children and young adults who are high achievers often receive a disproportionate amount of media attention and it is important not to lose sight of the fact that such individuals are not representative of the average child or adult with Down's syndrome. The 'everything is possible' flag-waving which often accompanies accounts of their achievements is not always helpful. Teachers and parents can become disillusioned and disheartened when their best efforts to produce the superstars they read about and see on national television fail. What should be borne in mind is that while intervention can help each child to reach his or her full genetic potential, it can never remove the limits put on that potential by the presence of Down's syndrome (Newton and Newton, 1992). What *is* possible is to supplement a child's experience and support his or her attempts at learning in ways that will promote the maximum gain at whatever level of cognitive ability is potentially available to that child. Advocacy should not be allowed to replace objectivity when evaluating progress (Spitz, 1993) but exceptional individuals nevertheless set the terms of reference for interventionists and serve as a constant reminder of what could perhaps be achieved in more cases. However, we will need a much better understanding of how children with Down's syndrome normally go about the task of learning and a much more detailed knowledge of the developmental processes underlying that learning if this aim is to realised.

THE FIRST OBJECTIVE: MAINTAINING DEVELOPMENTAL RATE

We are now in the fourth decade of early intervention and expanded educational opportunities but the question of how to intervene most effectively is still unresolved. Despite a great deal of psychological research, we still lack any real understanding of why it is that some children manage to achieve so much while others, regardless of how much effort is put into helping them, do not. Intervening in developmental processes can pay exciting dividends but it is important to remember that it is not a risk-free endeavour. Any intervention, no matter how well-intentioned, runs the risk of having the opposite effect to that desired if the training methods adopted are not firmly grounded in an understanding of how the process of learning normally unfolds in any given group of children. There are many questions which still require answers when it come to understanding development in children with Down's syndrome. Not least of these is why IQ scores apparently decline as children grow older and whether it is possible to stem this decline.

Although there have been a great many studies, very few of these have focused attention on the process of development itself. As a result we are still no further forward in knowing why it is that the initially highly promising rate of development seen in so many children in their earliest years is continued only exceptionally into later years. A number of studies, both old and recent, confirm that rate of cognitive development tends to slow down as children get older. While average IQ (the intelligence quotient derived from a child's score on a standardised test of intelligence) is often just below the bottom of the 'normal' range in early infancy, by school age IQ levels are more likely to be within the moderate to severe range of mental handicap (Brown *et al.*, 1990; Carr, 1985; Gibson, 1978).

What does this decline in IQ represent in real terms? Some have suggested that there is in fact no real decline, attributing the apparent changes in IQ levels to differences in the types of test we use to assess intelligence at different age levels. On the one hand, the tests used in early infancy are accused of being insufficiently sensitive to pick up early signs of the cognitive difficulties whose presence will become all too obvious at later ages whilst, on the other, the tests used to assess ability at older ages are criticised for being too language-dependent and therefore putting children with Down's syndrome at a disadvantage because of the specific language problems they invariably experience. According to this view, development in actuality is slow but basically steady throughout childhood – the early tests overestimate capability while the later tests underestimate true ability levels.

It is important to stress that while there is evidence that IQ scores decline with increasing age (Carr, 1985), it does not follow that there is little further mental growth as children get older. This is very far from the case. For all but the most profoundly disabled of children, new skills continue to be acquired throughout childhood and as a result, mental age continues to increase steadily.

IQ tests are constructed in such a way that when skills are acquired at the normal rate, mental age increases while the IQ score remains at approximately the same level. This relationship also holds true when development progresses constantly but at a less than the normal rate. On any standardized test of intelligence, for example, a child developing at half the normal rate will score an IQ of around 50; provided this rate of development is maintained, IQ-level will remain constant, regardless of age at testing. A slip in a child' s IQ-level indicates that new skills are accruing slowly not only in comparison with children whose development is progressing normally but also in comparison with the child's own progress earlier in development. Why should this be?

POSSIBLE FACTORS UNDERLYING CHANGES IN DOWN'S SYNDROME DEVELOPMENTAL RATE

It would be all too easy to conclude that the slowing in Down's syndrome developmental rate is an inevitable consequence of the condition itself. Given our current knowledge of the genetic basis of Down's syndrome and of its effects on brain development, this might suggest that any amelioration would thus be beyond our control. This would seem an unduly pessimistic conclusion. Neurological deficits clearly underpin many of the cognitive difficulties experienced but there is good reason to believe that a number of psychologically-determined factors also contribute directly to their failure to maintain early developmental rates. If this is the case, the possibility of improving developmental outcomes through behavioural intervention becomes a viable prospect.

Learning, by its very nature, is a developmental process highly susceptible to the influence of psychological factors. One of the factors most likely to influence how any child will approach new learning is a child's developing perception of how 'good' a learner he or she is and therefore of how likely it is that any effort invested in learning will be repaid with success. Given the inherent difficulties they have in learning new skills, it would seem highly plausible that their belief in their own efficacy as learners would not be strong and that enthusiasm for learning might wane as age increases and experience of failure grows. A good number of authors in the past have emphasised the possible role of motivational deficits in depressing performance but surprisingly few experimental studies have been carried out in this area in recent years (Hodapp and Zigler, 1990). Even fewer of these have taken a developmental perspective or investigated the degree to which motivational deficits might directly undermine the growth of competence. In an attempt to fill this gap, our own longitudinal studies have used a number of experimental paradigms to look at the learning strategies used at different ages. The findings provide converging lines of support for the suggestion that children actively contribute to the decline in their own developmental rate in two important ways – by becoming increasingly passive learners and by side-stepping opportunities for new learning. This would be bad developmental news for any child but is of course especially unfortunate if that child is already burdened with significant learning difficulties of biological origin. Not only is performance on a day-to-day basis likely to be sub-optimal, but the whole process of building up a working repertoire of key skills is likely to be compromised and de-stabilized. This could have adverse implications for IQ test performance and also for the likely pattern of change in IQ test scores over time. Failure to maintain developmental rate would seem unavoidable, with a consequent drop in IQ scores over time. As we have seen, this is very much the developmental picture that comes from IQ studies of children with Down's syndrome.

IQ TESTING AS A MEASURE OF COGNITIVE ABILITY IN CHILDREN WITH DOWN'S SYNDROME

IQ testing has always played a central role in the study of cognitive development in Down's syndrome. Most normative studies have used IQ tests to assess competence at different age levels and in experimental studies IQ scores are often used as the basis for matching children with Down's syndrome with normally-developing control subjects. IQ tests measure a wide variety of key skills and many are capable of providing very rich quantitative and qualitative data on cognitive development in childhood. Few research studies take full advantage of this potential richness, however, with the result that some of the conclusions drawn from IQ-based studies of cognitive development in children with Down's syndrome may well be built on very shaky foundations, as we shall see.

In aiming to provide an accurate reflection of a child's competence, any kind of cognitive test is wholly dependent on the child's performance on the day being a reliable index of the presence or absence of the abilities the test is designed to measure. This distinction between overt performance and underlying competence is important and it is essential that the match between the skills demonstrated in any formal assessment and the skills actually acquired up to that point in development is close. It is widely agreed that IQ scores usually provide a reliable and valid measure of competence in children who are developing normally but there can be less confidence that they do so in the case of children with Down's syndrome. Our own data in fact suggest strongly that distinguishing 'can't do' from 'won't do' can be extremely difficult in this group of children, with the result that the mismatch between competence and how this is expressed in performance can at times be very large indeed. An IQ score from a single testing session may be providing a very valid measure of the level of efficiency with which a child *uses* his or her cognitive skills on a daily basis but may be giving a very inaccurate picture of the skills potentially available to that child. Evidence that motivational deficits may be obscuring the true developmental picture is brought together below. However, there is also a second factor which may also be directly impeding developmental progress and interacting with motivational deficits to compound the adverse effects on development – a basic instability in the developmental process itself.

Conventional IQ tests all make one major and very basic assumption about development – that it is a stable and steadily incremental process. This is reflected in the very method by which IQ tests are constructed and IQ scores calculated. By six years, for example, the average child is expected to have acquired most of the cognitive skills typical of this age level and to have retained all of the less advanced skills acquired over the preceding years; in most test procedures, this assumption is so strong that the continuing presence of these abilities is simply taken for granted rather than checked. This is widely believed to be a reasonable assumption for children who are developing normally. It may not be a justifiable assumption in the case of development in Down's syndrome, however, since a growing body of evidence suggests that the consolidation and retention of many skills may be far from perfect in many of these children.

Shapiro (1975) and others have maintained for some time now that instability may in fact be a major defining feature of the developmental process in children with Down's syndrome, affecting aspects of their physical as well as mental development. Our own recent research provides considerable support for this hypothesis. The degree to which this instability is biologically or psychologically determined is not yet clear but what is clear is that it must make the process of development radically different in children with Down's syndrome. The assumption that Down's syndrome development can be fully understood in terms of a slowed-down version of normal development underpins all IQ testing, as we have seen; the possibility that it might be fundamentally different in nature is not even considered. The same assumption underlies the use of terms such as 'developmentally delayed', 'slow developers' and 'mentally retarded', all of which are widely applied to children with Down's syndrome with little question. It also underpins much of current educational practice.

This chapter is not the place in which to go into the difference versus delay controversy in any great depth. It is a measure of the complexity of the issues that the same research findings are at times cited by supporters of both camps. Given the scale and the nature of the disruption to brain development now known to result from Down's syndrome, however, it seems implausible that there would *not* be major differences in how cognitive development proceeds in children with Down's syndrome, and that only a slower rate and lower final ceiling would distinguish Down's syndrome development from normal development. The view that this development can be understood fully in terms of normal developmental theory nevertheless has numerous supporters although the 'difference' viewpoint has recently become much better represented in the literature (Cicchetti and Beeghly, 1990; Gibson and Harris, 1988; Zigler and Balla, 1982). Some of the studies cited in support of slow development theory depend heavily on standardised psychometric tests, either as outcome measures or in matching procedures. This is problematic since such studies may have presupposed in their design the answers to the question they seek to address. The possibility of drawing inaccurate conclusions about development in Down's syndrome are perhaps even greater in those studies where only cross-sectional data have been collected. The impact of motivational deficits or of any instability in development are impossible to measure in single-session scores from individual children. The huge variability in ability levels also means that important developmental patterns may well be obscured in any analysis of data grouped by age; patterns may be consistent from child to child but this can easily be hidden if there are large differences in the timing of each phase in development from child to child (Gunn and Berry, 1989).

In the following sections, we shall look at how young children with Down's syndrome perform on a number of different cognitive tasks at different ages. Most of the findings are drawn from longitudinal studies and the data from the IQ studies in particular provide a good example of just how uninformative one-off test scores can be in trying to unravel developmental patterns. They also show just how misleading performance in any one testing session can be as an indicator of developmental status and of progress to date. All of the studies provided evidence of motivational deficits – of can't do' versus 'won't do' behaviour – in many of the children tested. The data also make it clear, however, that motivational deficits alone cannot account for all of the fluctuation in performance levels seen over the periods of development under study.

DISTINGUISHING 'CAN'T DO' FROM 'WON'T DO' BEHAVIOURS

In trying to establish what children with Down's syndrome can and cannot do at various stages in their development, we need to be confident that test performance is an accurate reflection of underlying competence. In the course of carrying out a series of studies on the development of cognitive ability, we were repeatedly struck by the similarity in a number of the responses produced during testing by many of the children under study. The various tasks made very different cognitive demands and different children produced different behaviours, but a number of these behaviours seemed to have the same intent – to divert the attention of the experimenter away from the task in hand. We described these as 'cognitive avoidance' behaviours (Pitcairn and Wishart, 1995; Wishart, 1988, 1991b, 1993a, 1993b). Children's strategies for avoiding specific cognitive challenges took many forms, with both positive and negative behaviours being produced. At the very youngest ages, avoidance behaviours were most likely to be negatively expressed – for example, by refusing to look, by struggling down the mother's lap, or by suddenly crying. Older infants, pre-schoolers and school-age children were much more likely to use their developing social skills to avoid participation. Instead of just protesting, they would find some way of drawing attention to something else in the room (usually present but sometimes invented); the youngest would simply smile engagingly or produce some sort of party trick, such as clapping hands or blowing bubble – literally turning on the charm to divert the adult's attention away from the task. Obviously none of these social behaviours are unique to children with Down's syndrome; all are commonly seen in other young children. The difference would seem to lie in the use to which these behaviours are put and the contexts in which they are produced. Rather than making productive use of the adult as a potential partner in a problem-solving setting, the children seemed in our studies to be using their social skills to change the very nature of the interaction (McTurk *et al.*, 1985). The other children we tested also often interacted engagingly with the experimenter during testing but the difference in the timing of these social interactions was very noticeable – it was much more likely to be between rather than during trials. As soon as initial suspicion of the experimenter or the test setting had subsided, most normally-developing children just got on with the task in hand, looking for approval, praise or help only after having first attempted to solve for themselves the problem being presented.

OPTING OUT OF LEARNING: EVIDENCE FROM OBJECT CONCEPT STUDIES

The clearest evidence of how cognitive avoidance strategies were being used to avoid difficult learning came from our longitudinal studies of what is commonly referred to as 'object concept development'. These studies investigated how children come to understand the nature of objects and the rules which govern simple events involving objects. We wanted to find out the age at which children with Down's syndrome, for example, would appreciate that a toy hidden inside a cup still exists even although it cannot be seen and that it will share in any movements of that cup and can still therefore be retrieved from it in its new location. Adults often find it difficult to believe that children have to acquire knowledge as basic as this but there are a great many studies showing that *all* children have to go through a fairly lengthy apprenticeship before they acquire a working concept of objects and their properties (Dunst, 1990; Morss, 1983, 1984; Piaget, 1955; Uzgiris and Hunt, 1975). Many psychologists consider the thinking processes required to solve object concept tasks to be protypical of all later thought; still others believe an understanding of the nature of objects to be a prerequisite for the development of symbolic thought and language (Gopnik and Meltzoff, 1986; Piaget, 1955).

Object concept tasks undoubtedly have a number of advantages when it comes to examining cognitive development in Down's syndrome. The first is that they require very little in the way of motor skills and therefore do not place young children at additional disadvantage because of poor muscle tone. In object concept tasks, the child typically has only to remove a small cup or cloth to find a toy which has been hidden; as long as it is clear where the child is trying to search, this search need not be skillfully executed. The second advantage is that this sequence in early cognitive development has been unusually well researched. We have norms for age of acquisition of each stage and detailed descriptions of the types of errors typically made prior to achieving each of these (Uzgiris and Hunt, 1975; Wishart and Bower, 1984). This makes it much easier to detect any differences in how children with Down's syndrome develop the understanding required for success on the tasks. It has also been shown that the age at which object concept tasks are first solved is related to later differences in IQ and adaptive functioning (Kahn, 1992; Wachs, 1975) and that the rate at which each stage is acquired is highly susceptible to differences in experience and upbringing (Hunt *et al.*, 1975; Wishart and Bower, 1985). We therefore know that this is a developmental process which is important to later developmental success and that it is influenced by environmental as well as genetic factors. For all of these reasons, object concept tasks provide an excellent background against which to assess whether cognitive development in children with Down's syndrome can be best described in terms of normal developmental processes or whether it is fundamentally different in its organization and structure.

In our studies, performance on four different levels of hiding task was regularly monitored in 30 children with Down's syndrome aged between 4 months and 3 years at onset of testing (see Wishart, 1990, 1993 a, b). Typically-developing children would be expected to succeed on the lowest level task by about five months and on the highest by about two years of age. The aim was to present four trials of each task in all testing sessions, irrespective of whether the child had passed or failed on any of the tasks in earlier sessions. The tasks were always presented in increasing order of difficulty, with a different toy being used on each of the four trials and site of hiding randomised over trials. The lowest level of task involved a single cup and a visible displacement of the toy; the most complex used two identical cups and an invisible displacement sequence (for a full description see Wishart and Bower, 1984).

Many children succeeded at surprisingly early ages on some of these tasks and yet most also produced avoidant behaviours in response to specific tasks at specific points in their development. Analyses relating production of avoidant responses in each of the four task contexts to the child's current developmental status indicated that avoidance or diversionary tactics were most likely to be employed when the child was faced with a task which was above his or her current stage in development. Interestingly, a task did not have to be much above the child's current level to lead to this type of counter-productive behaviour. Even more interestingly perhaps, one trial was sometimes enough for a child to arrive at a 'won't do' strategy, even although on the basis of age of acquisition subsequently demonstrated, success might well have been close had only just a little more effort been expended. This suggests that avoidance behaviours are not therefore always a direct consequence of experiencing repeated failure – in our studies, children would sometimes switch off very suddenly, as likely to do so after a run of successes as after a run of failures. The net result was that many had to be scored as failing on a given task although in actuality they had neither passed nor failed, simply avoided taking part in the required number of trials. Their production of avoidant strategies could not be put down simply to fatigue or boredom with either hiding games or with specific toys. Moving on to a different level of task more often than not led to renewed enthusiasm and eager search for the self-same toys – although this enthusiasm was not always sustained if the next task too was above their current developmental level.

Avoiding tasks which are still too difficult may seem an understandable enough response, particularly given the unfavourable balance of success to failure which must be experienced in everyday life by the average child with Down's syndrome. Other children generally do not react in this way in the same situation, however, and the developmental implications of avoidant behaviours are unlikely to be benign. The control children in our studies, children without Down's syndrome but at the same stage in their cognitive development, showed very few avoidance behaviours when presented with these four levels of task and if anything, seemed more often intrigued than put off by their mistakes on the more difficult tasks.

Clearly avoidant behaviours were most often associated with tasks that were 'difficult' in relation to the child's current developmental level. However, a rather different kind of opting-out strategy was also sometimes evident in response to tasks which had been fully mastered at younger ages, in earlier testing sessions. Although children still seemed sufficiently interested in these 'easy' tasks and would search for the hidden toy, they frequently made errors. They would look surprised by these errors and yet did not always bother to correct them. Their search strategies were often also very low-level – indiscriminate sweeping of the cups off the table or selection of the same cup on every trial, the latter a strategy bound to fail as often as it succeeds in any two-location hiding task. As a result, the success demonstrated at younger ages often proved to be short-lived and was not reliably re-produced at older ages. (See Figure 12.1 which compares the performance between six and eighteen months of two infants, one with and one without Down's syndrome, on one of the four object concept tasks, the AAB task, which is passed at around eight to ten months in normal development.) The poor performance of the infant with Down's syndrome in later sessions apparently reflected a deterioration in actual competence rather than merely inadequate motivation or insufficient attention to the task in hand. Hiding chocolate or a rusk instead of a toy would sometimes restore success but only in sessions fairly close to the age of initial success on that particular task; it was far less effective in later testing sessions.

If the behaviour of children with Down's syndrome on these object concept tasks mirrors how they respond to cognitive challenges in the real world, then clearly they must be denying themselves numerous opportunities to learn new skills and to build on existing ones. They must also be depriving themselves of much of the valuable information that comes from making mistakes, a process which may result in 'incomplete' learning, as Morss (1983) has suggested. This in turn could underlie the instability which appears to characterise the Down's syndrome learning process (see below). Errorless learning is quite often used in teaching children with Down's syndrome on the basis that it avoids having to unlearn the wrong responses made when first learning any new skill. Our own research on errorless learning suggests that while this strategy can be very helpful in teaching new tasks it is one which needs to used with caution. Skills learned in

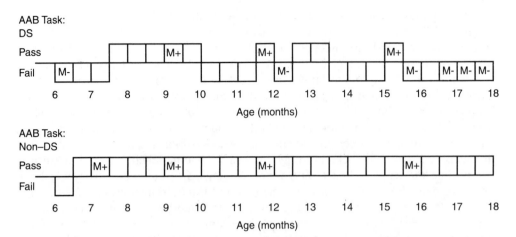

Figure 12.1 Performance on the AAB object concept task.
Passes marked M+ are those where choc or rusks were required for success and standard presentations failed. Fails marked M− are sessions in which the child failed to engage in the required number of trials, irrespective of what was hidden (adapted from Wishart, 1993b).

this way do not appear to transfer readily to new tasks, even when these are very similar in terms of content and task demands (Duffy and Wishart, 1994).

RELINQUISHING THE INITIATIVE IN LEARNING

Failure to make the most of learning opportunities and neglecting to consolidate new learning were also clearly demonstrated in our studies of operant learning in infants with Down's syndrome (see Wishart, 1990, 1991c, 1993b). This research was designed to look more directly at counter-productive behaviours in learning contexts and to investigate the degree to which this kind of behaviour might itself be a product of learning. This meant going right back to the beginnings of cognitive development to look at how very young babies with Down's syndrome approach problem-solving. Again, because of the hypotonia often present, a task requiring minimal motor skills was chosen for study. The babies sat securely in a padded infant seat. ɪf they kicked either foot, this broke a lightbeam resulting in a signal being fed into a microcomputer controlling the movements of a brightly-coloured acetate mobile projected on to a screen in front of them. This computer recorded both the mobile's turns and the baby's kicks. In an operant learning task like this, the aim is to find out how long it takes the baby to notice the connection between his or her activity and the movements of the mobile. Typically, once the contingency has been detected, rate of kicking quickly rises, often accompanied by excited vocalisations and smiles (Watson, 1972, 1984). Operant learning techniques have been widely used in studies of normal development and are particularly useful when working with a population with limited or delayed motor skills. It is therefore surprising how few studies have made use of this paradigm to investigate cognitive development in children with Down's syndrome (Brinker and Lewis, 1982; Glenn and Cunningham, 1984).

The computer programme allowed two main features of the task to be varied: whether the mobile turned every time or only some of the times the baby kicked; and whether it would turn independently of any effort on the part of the baby and, if so, how frequently and at which points in the session. The objective was to find out which ratio of success to failure in controlling the mobile's movements would encourage the most active exploration of the situation. We also wanted to investigate whether providing 'free' reinforcement was helpful or unhelpful to the learning process. This was done by looking at the effects on performance of both contingent and non-contingent mobile turning. In contingent sessions, the mobile would turn if, and only if, the child kicked through the beam. In some schedules, it would turn every time the child kicked (100% reinforcement). In others, kicking would be effective only 80% of the time, with the mobile turning four times out of five on average (the non-working trial being randomly inserted by the computer), a ratio closer to real life experience than perfect contingency between actions and their effects. In non-contingent sessions, a pre-determined number of additional 'free' rotations could be delivered at random intervals by the computer, even though the child had not kicked. Again, this mimics real life – sometimes something happens because of someone else's activity, not one's own. From these variations in conditions, we hoped to determine firstly, whether providing different levels of success (100% v 80%) had differential effects on how quickly the children learned that they could control the movements of the mobile, and secondly, to see whether providing 'free' turns assisted or hindered the learning process.

Fifty children with Down's syndrome aged between one month and two years helped with these studies, many coming in at several ages in order for us to be able to assess the effects of age and experience on response to this task. As would be expected, the children with Down's syndrome did less well than non-Down's syndrome children of the same age: they were generally slower to detect the relationship between their kicking and the turns of the mobile, were less active in their response to withdrawal of control in 'extinction' periods (when the computer turned off the mobile and kicking was no longer effective), and were less responsive to the introduction of non-contingent reinforcement. Using 100% reinforcement (where every kick worked) seemed more effective at younger ages than 80% reinforcement, suggesting that maximizing success rates in the early stages of learning can be beneficial; at older ages the pattern was less clear.

More interesting, however, were the age-related differences in response to non-contingent reinforcement in the two groups of children. With increasing age, the children with Down's syndrome came to rely on the computer to produce the mobile's movements – even though they provided clear evidence that they still knew how to control it and were still very interested in seeing it turn. The older children seemed happy to settle for the low rates of non-contingent reward over the higher levels potentially available to them through exerting their own control over its movements. The occasional 'free' turn, instead of providing encouragement, produced a decline in self-generated activity. This is the exact opposite of what might have been expected and was certainly the opposite of what had been intended in the original design of the experiments (see Figure 2 for a comparison of one child's performance at two age levels).

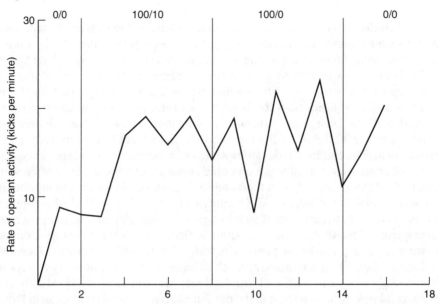

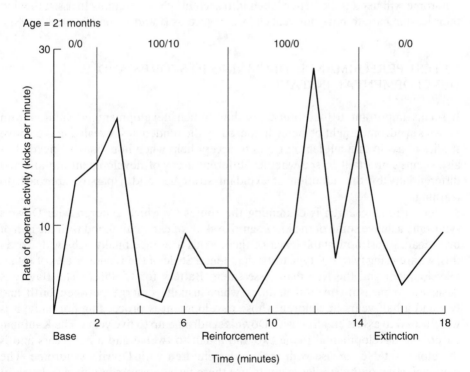

Figure 12.2 Performance of one child with Down syndrome at 9 months of age and one year later on the same operant task.
0/0 – 0%: reinforcement contingent on kicking, 0% non contingent ('free')
100/10: reinforcement is 100% contingent on kicking, 10% non-contingent
100/0: reinforcement is 100% contingent on kicking, 0% non-contingent
(adapted from Wishart, 1990).

Many studies have shown that being able to have some degree of control over what goes on around you is essential to psychological well-being. If this control is lost or removed, 'learned helplessness' often results (Kearsley, 1979; Peterson *et al.* 1993). There is no reason to assume that retaining a belief in self-efficacy and exercising some control over surrounding events is any less important for children with learning disabilities than for anyone else. Intuition alone would suggest that it could well be even more crucial, since further iatrogenic retardation could become a very real threat to children who fail to interact fully with what goes on around them. The children in our studies had every opportunity to experience a high degree of control over what was happening around them and yet they often simply relinquished this control. Given their continuing interest in seeing the mobile turn, this gives cause for concern. As Cunningham and Mittler (1981) have pointed out, the active contribution of the child himself is fundamental to the progress of development. This study is far from alone in finding evidence of low arousal, poor persistence, and passivity in young children with Down's syndrome. Deficits in exploratory behaviour and mastery motivation have also commonly been reported (Berry *et al.*, 1984; Cicchetti and Sroufe, 1976; McTurk *et al.*, 1985; Mundy *et al.*, 1988). Weaknesses such as these in the natural learning style of children with Down's syndrome will need to be better taken into account if our attempts to assist them in their learning are to have any real chance of success (Landry and Chapieski, 1989).

IQ TEST PERFORMANCE, DECLINING IQ SCORES AND DEVELOPMENTAL INSTABILITY

It seems important to determine just how much development in children with Down's syndrome might be being hindered by the tendencies revealed in the above studies to avoid difficult learning and to accept help when none may be needed. It also seems important to see whether different areas of development are affected differentially by the adoption of avoidant strategies and a passive approach to learning.

Our current research is examining the routes by which children with Down's syndrome achieve some of the key cognitive skills of early childhood with the aim of investigating just how stable each of these skills are once finally achieved. To do this, we are using two 'IQ'-type tests: the Mental Scale of the Bayley Scales of Infant Development and the Kaufman Assessment Battery for Children. The Bayley is designed to measure mental abilities which usually emerge between birth and two and a half years in children whose development is proceeding normally; it is widely used to assess children with Down's syndrome up to five years. The Kaufman covers the developmental range two and a half to twelve and a half years and is therefore suitable for use with most older children with Down's syndrome. The main objective of the studies is not to use these tests to assess intelligence levels at different ages. The intention is to use their controlled procedures and detailed norms to monitor developmental pathways in children with Down's syndrome and to see what use they make of differing components of their intelligence at different stages in their development.

Fifty-four children with Down's syndrome aged between three months and twelve years entered the study although final numbers will be somewhat lower. The children are being presented with the same set of Bayley or Kaufman tasks by the same tester on six separate occasions over a one-year period; only two testers will have been used throughout. At least 40 of these children will go on to be tested a further six times one year later, thereby giving a three-year window on their development.

As well as providing a detailed picture of strengths and weaknesses at different ages and at different developmental stages, these studies will establish whether scores from single session IQ testing provide a reliable measure of current cognitive status in children with Down's syndrome. They will also show whether IQ scores give any indication of individual children's potential for further development. This research is still in progress but it has been clear from a very early stage that the children often score very differently on two different occasions, even if these are separated in time by as little as a week. In some cases, IQ scores rise; in others they fall. Even in cases where scores stay fairly constant over sessions, a false impression of consistency in performance is sometimes be given, with variability in performance masked by some items improving while others decline, the net effect being no change in overall score.

If fluctuation proves to be a recurring feature of IQ-scoring profiles over time, this obviously raises great problems in interpreting the meaning of IQ scores in this group of children. More crucially, if it reflects an inherent instability in their cognitive development, the implications could be very serious indeed. Before coming to any overly pessimistic conclusion, however, these fluctuations in performance require very close examination. As we have already noted, the validity of any assessment procedure depends on there being a deep equivalence between overt performance and underlying competence. That is, for any assessment to be accurate, the child must be prepared to demonstrate to the tester on the day of testing whether or not he or she actually has, in his or her cognitive repertoire, the ability being tested. In real-life assessments (as opposed to research studies), IQ testing is usually carried out by an adult who is a relative stranger to the child, with testing often taking place in unfamiliar surroundings, typically without the parent present. To arrive at an IQ score, children have to be scored as passing or failing on every item presented and unless the child behaves so badly as to be considered 'untestable', the assessment is seldom repeated. It is important to remember that the items in IQ batteries in general allow little possibility for chance success – either the child has the particular ability required to solve a specific problem (e.g. to put two coloured geometric shapes together to match a given picture or to repeat five numbers in a given order) or the child does not. Interpreting failures is not always so easy.

Before embarking on the main longitudinal study, we first carried out a cross-sectional Bayley study with 35 children with Down's syndrome aged between three months and five years of age, followed by a small-scale test-retest study of 18 children aged between six months and four years. In the test-retest study, the two sessions were separated by a maximum of two weeks (Wishart and Duffy, 1990). The data from the initial crosssectional study appeared to provide confirming evidence of a developmental pattern of declining IQ in young children with Down's syndrome, with the gap between expected and observed achievement levels increasing with increasing age (Figure 15.3). Given that all of the children in this study had access to an educational home visiting service, these data at first glance seemed to quash hopes that early intervention can counteract the decline in developmental rate with age reported in so many earlier studies.

When individual scores were examined in-depth, however, there was encouraging evidence that the underlying basis for this apparent failure to maintain developmental rate might not be as straightforward as it at first seemed. What the individual data suggested was that motivational factors were responsible for many of the failures registered. A significant proportion of the children tested in fact responded to some Bayley items in ways which in a non-research setting might quickly have led to them being classified simply as 'untestable'. Test materials were cast aside, banged on the table, mouthed, or otherwise responded to in task-inappropriate ways; at other times, they were simply ignored as the child attempted to grab the experimenter's score sheet or anything else within range. Low levels of task-appropriate engagement were a common feature of children's performance and just as in the object concept studies described earlier, a variety of both positive and negative strategies were used to divert the experimenter from presenting the tasks. Favourite party-tricks – such as waving goodbye, blowing kisses, or pretend hiding games – were produced, sometimes in the same session as spectacular displays of bad temper, with both kinds of off-task behaviour often quickly subsiding as soon as a new test item was introduced. Not surprisingly, failures by default were a common feature of scoring profiles. Children were scored as failing on a given task, not because they had clearly demonstrated that they were not yet at the required developmental stage but simply because of their refusal to engage in the task at any meaningful level.

The test-retest study revealed some further interesting data. As can be seen from Table 1, mean raw scores varied very little over sessions at any of the six age levels tested. Closer examination of individual profiles revealed a very different picture, however. Even in cases where raw scores were very similar over the two sessions, pass/fail patterns had often changed on a substantial number of items (Table 1). One three-year old, for example, attained a raw score of exactly 128 on both occasions, giving her a mental age of 19 months. Item-item comparison of her passes and fails in the two sessions showed that her performance had nevertheless varied on six (26%) of the 23 items presented in both sessions. A minor drop of three points in raw score in the second session of one two-year old similarly proved on closer examination to be obscuring test-retest variation on 11 items – 31% of the 35 presented . There were in fact 74 instances in which performance on a given test item had improved on the second session and 91 instances in which performance had deteriorated, a total of 165 cases of instability (for a detailed analysis of these findings, see Duffy, 1990).

This degree of instability in performance was unexpected on a test which is described as 'unrivalled at determining a child's developmental status in relation to its age-mates' (Francis *et al.*,1987) and which has been very widely used in research studies of children with Down's syndrome. The reliability data provided

Table 12.1 Test-retest variation in performance on Bayley Scale items

Age (months)	Testing session 1 Mean raw score (AE)	2	Number of test items on which performance varied over sessions Fail-to-pass	Pass-to-fail
6	55.3 (4.5)	53.3 (4.5)	12	19
12	77.3 (7.0)	75.6 (7.0)	10	15
18	100.0 (11.0)	99.7 (11.0)	11	13
24	109.0 (13.0)	108.7 (13.0)	16	16
36	131.3 (19.0)	130.3 (19.0)	12	15
48	142.3 (22.0)	142.3 (22.0)	13	13
		Totals:	74	91

AE = age equivalent in months

for individual items in the Bayley Mental Scale are surprisingly thin. Although the standardization sample consisted of 1262 infants, item-item reliability figures are drawn from only a very small number of children (28), at only one age level (8 months) and on only 59 of the test items (Werner and Bayley, 1966). Reliabilities were reported only where very high or very low, with the added complication that some with low reliability were subsequently excluded in revisions of the test. Any attempt to compare reliability in our sample with Bayley norms was therefore greatly restricted. When we compared reliability on only those items which had achieved the highest reliability figures in the Werner and Bayley study, it was clear that the performance of the Down's syndrome children in our study was far less reliable than would be expected on the basis of their data. A further comparison made with Horner's (1980) data on test-retest reliability on 76 Bayley items in children of 9 and 15 months also showed the performance in our sample to be significantly less reliable over testing sessions than that of normally-developing children.

These comparisons highlighted the need to collect our own normative data on the reliability of the Bayley and this part of the investigation is currently coming to a close. While it is evident that a number of Bayley items do not always elicit the same level of performance from normally-developing children on repeat presentations, it is also very evident that this unreliability is much amplified in the case of children with Down's syndrome, being both more frequent and persisting over longer periods of time. These findings are in line with the developmental patterns seen in the studies of object concept development outlined above, where task avoidance and fluctuating performance levels were equally common.

By extending the period of test-retest data collection, we hope to be able to investigate the degree to which the instability in performance already evidenced might be contributing to any decline in IQ scores found with increasing age. Kaufman data collection is not yet complete but Bayley data are available on 24 children aged between three months and five years on entry to the study who were repeat-tested over periods of from nine to eighteen months. The number of failures by default showing up in these longitudinal data would seem to indicate a strong and persistent tendency in children with Down's syndrome to underperform on this kind of test. Task avoidance in fact accounted for over half (64%) of the 761 instances of reversals in performance we found over pairs of sessions at any given age level.

Distinguishing reversals in performance stemming from inadequately-motivated performance from those which reflect a genuine loss in competence is not easy. Lapses in success which persist into later sessions would seem more likely to represent true regression, however. This interpretation is supported by the finding that, in individual developmental profiles, failures by default contributed less to longer-term reversals in performance than to short-term instability. More detailed analyses also suggested that the degree of test/re-test unreliability manifested at the acquisition stage of certain skills might be related to the loss of these skills at older ages, since older children most commonly failed on those tasks requiring skills which they had experienced particular difficulty in acquiring.

Figure 12.3 illustrates the effect of unstable performance on individual developmental profiles over the longer term. The graph shows the relationship of mental age to chronological age for a child tested twice every three months between the 30th and 48th months. 'Session l' points give the score achieved in the first of the two testing sessions presented at each age level. 'Optimal' scores, by contrast, credit all items passed on either the first or second of these two closely-spaced sessions. 'Optimal-plus' scores credit all items passed up to and including that testing session, irrespective of any subsequent unreliability at ages beyond that of initial acquisition. On the basis of the 'one-off' Session l scores, it looks as if this child's development plateaued between 36 and 48 months, and that no developmental progress was made over this year. When 'optimal' scores are examined, however, it

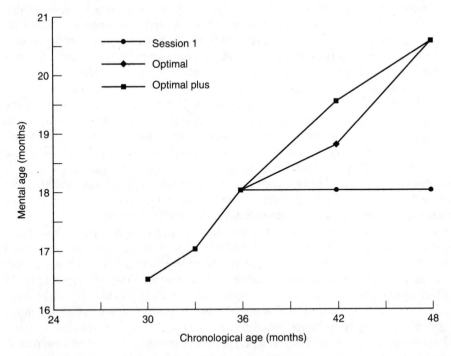

Figure 12.3 The effect of skills lost and gained over an 18 month period on mental age scores (adapted from Wishart 1993b)

is evident that new skills were being gained, but were not being reliably produced. What the 'optimal-plus' scores illustrate is the potential for steady progress if each new skill had been consolidated into the repertoire and used to the full.

Figure 12.4 shows the same pattern in another child with Down's syndrome regularly tested between the ages of 42 and 60 months. Developmental level is expressed in terms of an IQ-type score, as a Bayley Developmental Quotient. Again, the patterning of scores show an apparent decline when only single session performance is considered, a less rapid drop when all contemporaneous successes are credited, and evidence of the higher developmental quotient which might reasonably have been expected had she retained all new skills beyond the period of initial acquisition and reproduced them in subsequent sessions.

These data suggest that the developmental plateaux and failures to maintain developmental rate which characterize development in Down's syndrome deserve much closer examination (see Chapter 14, this volume). Failure to maintain developmental rate may derive as much from failure to make full use of each new ability as it is acquired, as from a slowing in the acquisition process itself. Plateaux may not represent periods of consolidation, as has been suggested (Cunningham, 1987) but may be disguising periods of flux; although new skills are still being acquired, any gain in IQ is cancelled out by the apparent loss of old skills. At the very least, the data indicate that the tests we currently use to assess cognitive competence in young children with Down's syndrome may not do so very well

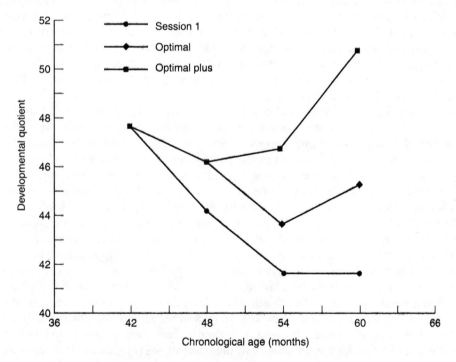

Figure 12.4 The effect of skills lost and gained over an 18–month period on the Bayley Scales Developmental Quotient (adapted from Wishart, 1993b).

and may be providing us with less-than-accurate estimates of children's current developmental status and with a poor indication of how their development may progress.

MAXIMIZING DEVELOPMENTAL POTENTIAL

All of the above evidence suggests that children with Down's syndrome do not make the best use of the cognitive abilities they develop. What can we do to encourage them to become more active and more efficient learners? One of the first things we have to acknowledge is that the effects the extra chromosome has on brain development and functioning will always makes learning a very uphill task for most of these children. Many of the learning problems they experience are a direct consequence of these effects and no amount of early intervention or gifted teaching can remove these limitations on their ability to process and retain information. If efforts to help the children in their learning are to have any chance of success, these inherent limitations need to be fully recognized and their specific educational needs addressed.

It would appear that development in children with Down's syndrome is not just a slower, less efficient version of normal developmental processes, and yet much of current teaching – and many early intervention programmes – make only very basic adaptations to teaching methods which have previously proved to be successful with ordinary children. Skills are usually taught in the order they appear in normal development, with little attention being paid to the different patterning of strengths and weaknesses in children with Down's syndrome, or to the different developmental pathways which this group of children follow. Little attention is paid to the different use they make of specific skills at differing points in their development (Franco and Wishart, 1995).

The developmental data outlined above suggest that not all of the learning problems that children with Down's syndrome experience are an inevitable consequence of Down's syndrome, however. Some of the difficulties they face stem as much from crucial differences in the psychological environment in which they grow and learn as from the biological disadvantages they carry from birth. The experience of learning is always going to be very different for the child with Down's syndrome. In comparison to children who are developing at the usual rate, most skills will take much longer to learn and inevitably a greater degree of failure is experienced over a longer period of time before success is finally achieved. This can hardly help the child with Down's syndrome to establish any great faith in his or her own learning ability. Low expectations on the part of parents and professionals of what they are likely to be able to achieve can only compound this problem (Foreman and Manning, 1993; Wishart and Manning, 1995). One of the broader ways in which we may therefore be able to help in reducing some of the children's difficulties is by paying much more attention to how they go about the task of learning and by looking more closely at the contexts we provide for that learning. If we are to find ways around the detrimental learning style that children with Down's syndrome would appear to adopt as they grow older, we shall obviously need a greater insight into how they interpret and respond to the successes and failures that they encounter during the learning process. We will also need to establish how we can best support their efforts to learn without creating a child–teacher partnership in which the child is able to relinquish much of the learning initiative to others.

The developmental patterns found in some of the studies outlined above provide considerable support for the view that the way that children with Down's syndrome come to perceive themselves as learners may play a large part in determining final developmental outcomes. The motivational deficits that many children show when faced with learning new skills – indeed the motivational deficits that they often show even when only asked to make use of skills that they already have – must surely undermine the progress of their development. From a very early age, it is evident that many avoid opportunities for learning new skills and make poor use of those skills that they do acquire, thereby failing to consolidate many of them into their repertoires. These behaviour patterns can only add to the learning difficulties that they already have.

It would seem then that at least some of the learning difficulties we see may not be an unavoidable consequence of Down's syndrome itself. Although it is an inescapable fact that many of the children's difficulties are biologically based and currently beyond biomedical intervention, the evidence that psychological factors also influence the rate and course of development means that there are still real prospects for ameliorating development through behavioural interventions. It has yet to be established exactly how open development may be to intervention but there would still seem reason to believe that children with Down's syndrome can be helped to find ways to compensate for the learning difficulties that they are born with and to become more confident, active learners. In this respect, we should perhaps begin to question whether the emphasis on acquisition of formal academic skills may not be in danger of going too far. Although recent studies indicate that many more children now attain some skill in reading, writing and arithmetic, final levels of achievement for most are still not very high (Shepperdson, 1994; Sloper *et al.*, 1990). It is important that they continue to be given every opportunity to learn basic academic skills throughout childhood – and indeed into adult years – but it is equally important that we do not neglect encouraging the development of other skills equally important to a successful transition into adult life. For many children, it is often the lack of adequate development in social and communication skills rather in formal academic skills that proves to be the limiting factor in how successfully they integrate into their local communities (Buckley and Sachs, 1987; Thomson, *et al.*, 1995).

One final point is worth emphasizing. Despite the very many research studies carried out, there is still a great deal that we do *not* know about cognitive development in Down's syndrome. The studies described here were specifically undertaken in order to attempt to fill in some of these gaps in our understanding of cognitive processes in children with Down's syndrome but further longitudinal studies are essential if we are to identify the teaching strategies best suited to the specific needs and skills at each stage in their development. The teaching methods which are designed on the basis of future findings may well prove to differ fundamentally from those currently in use and their success rate may be much improved. As pressure on funding bodies grows, it has sometimes been suggested that increasing availability of prenatal screening programmes will soon negate the need for research into the difficulties of children with Down's syndrome. This suggestion needs to be resisted. Even if the impact of screening on numbers of Down's syndrome births were as predicted – and epidemiological studies suggest that it may well turn out to be considerably less than has been predicted (Nicholson and Alberman, 1992) – this is irrelevant. There is a sufficiently large number of children already born with Down's syndrome whose learning difficulties deserve the continuing attention of researchers. There are good prospects that this kind of research will lead us to more effective teaching strategies. It would be ironic if research efforts were to tail off now, just as real dividends seem close.

ACKNOWLEDGEMENTS

This research was supported by the Medical Research Council of Great Britain. Many thanks are due also to the families and children who worked with the author on the studies and to the Scottish Down's Syndrome Association for advice and generous assistance. The collaboration of Dr Louise Duffy was also much appreciated, as was the advice of Dr Lynn Nadel.

REFERENCES

Berry, P., Gunn, P. and Andrews, R.J. (1984) The behaviour of Down's syndrome children using the 'lock box': a research note. *Journal of Child Psychology and Psychiatry*, **25**, pp. 125–31.

Bird, G. and Buckley, S. (1994) *Meeting the Educational Needs of Children with Down's Syndrome: A Handbook for Teachers*, Portsmouth: University of Portsmouth Press.

Bower, A. and Hayes, A. (1994) Short-term memory deficits and Down's syndrome: a comparative study. *Down's Syndrome: Research & Practice*, **2**, pp. 47–50.

Brinker R.P. and Lewis, M. (1982) Making the world work with microcomputers: a learning prosthesis for handicapped infants. *Exceptional Children*, **49**, pp. 163–70.

Broadley, I., MacDonald, J. and Buckley, S. (1994) Are children with Down's syndrome able to maintain skills learned from a short-term memory training programme? *Down's Syndrome: Research and Practice*, **2**, pp. 116–22.

Brown, F.R., Greer, M.K., Aylward, E.H. and Hunt, H.H. (1990) Intellectual and adaptive functioning in individuals with Down syndrome in relation to age and environmental placement. *Pediatrics*, **85**, pp. 450–52.

Buckley, S. (1985) Attaining basic educational skills: reading, writing and number. In D. Lane, and B. Stratford (eds), *Current Approaches to Down's Syndrome*, London: Holt, Rinehart and Winston.

Buckley, S. and Bird, G. (1993) Teaching children with Down's syndrome to read. *Down's Syndrome: Research and Practice*, **1**, pp. 34–39

Buckley, S. and Sachs, B. (1987) *The Adolescent with Down's Syndrome: Life for the Teenager and the Family*, Portsmouth: Portsmouth Down's Syndrome Trust.

Carr, J. (1985) The development of intelligence. In D. Lane and B. Stratford (eds), *Current Approaches to Down's Syndrome*, pp. 167–86, London: Holt, Rinehart and Winston.

Carr, J. (1988) Six weeks to twenty-one years old: a longitudinal study of children with

Down's syndrome and their families. *Journal of Child Psychiatry and Psychology*, **29,** pp. 407–31.

Carr, J. (1994) Long term outcome for people with Down's syndrome. *Journal of Child Psychology and Psychiatry*, **35,** pp. 425–39.

Cicchetti, D. and Beeghly, M. (1990) *Children with Down Syndrome: a developmental Perspective.* New York: Cambridge University Press.

Cicchetti, D. and Sroufe, L. (1976) The relationship between affective and cognitive development in Down syndrome infants. *Child Development*, **47,** pp. 920–29.

Courchesne, E. (1988). Physioanatomical considerations in Down syndrome. In L. Nadel (ed.), *The Psychobiology of Down Syndrome*, pp. 291–314, Boston: MIT Press.

Crombie M.P. (1994) Development of adolescents with Down syndrome: does early intervention have a long term effect? Unpublished PhD dissertation, University of Queensland.

Cunningham, C. (1987) Early intervention in Down's syndrome. In G. Hosking and G. Murphy (eds), *Prevention of Mental Handicap: A World Review*, pp. 170–82, London: Royal Society of Medicine.

Cunningham, C.C. and Mittler, P.J. (1981) Maturation, development and mental handicap. In K.J. Connolly and H.R. Prechtl (eds), *Maturation and Development: Biological and Psychological Perspectives*, London: Heinemann.

Duffy, L. (1990) The relationship between competence and performance in early development in children with Down's syndrome. Unpublished PhD dissertation, University of Edinburgh.

Duffy, L. and Wishart, J.G. (1987) A comparison of two procedures for teaching discrimination skills to Down's syndrome and non-handicapped children. *Journal of Educational Psychology*, **57,** pp. 265–78.

Duffy, L. and Wishart, J.G. (1994) The stability and transferability of errorless learning in children with Down's syndrome. *Down's Syndrome: Research and Practice*, **2,** pp. 51–58.

Dunst, C. (1986) Overview of the efficacy of early intervention programs. In L. Bickman and D.L. Weatherford (eds), *Evaluating Early Intervention Programs for Severely Handicapped Children and Their Families*, pp. 79–147, Austin: Pro-Ed.

Dunst, C. (1990) Sensorimotor development of infants with Down syndrome. In D. Ciccetti and M. Beeghly (eds), *Children with Down Syndrome: A Developmental Perspective*, pp. 180–230, New York: Cambridge University Press.

Epstein, C.J. (ed.), (1986) *The Neurobiology of Down Syndrome*, New York: Raven.

Foreman, P.J. and Manning, E. (1993) Paediatric management practices in Down's syndrome: a follow-up-survey. *Journal of Paediatrics and Child Health*, **29,** pp. 27–31.

Fowler, A. (1990) Language abilities in children with Down syndrome: evidence for a specific syntactic delay. In D. Cicchetti an M. Beeghly (eds), *Children with Down Syndrome: A Developmental Perspective*, pp. 302–28, New York: Cambridge University Press.

Fowler, A. (in press) Language learning. In L. Nadel and C. Epstein (eds), *Down Syndrome: Into the 21st Century*, (provisional title), New York: Wiley-Liss.

Frances, P.L., Self, P.A. and Horowitz, F.D. (1987) The behavioral assessment of the neonate: an overview. In J.D. Osofsky (ed.), *Handbook of Infant Development*, 2nd edn, New York: Wiley.

Franco, F. and Wishart, J.G. (in press) The use of pointing and other gestures by young children with Down's syndrome. *American Journal on Mental Retardation*.

Gibson, D. (1978) *Down's Syndrome: The Psychology of Mongolism.* Cambridge: Cambridge University Press.

Gibson, D. and Harris, A. (1988) Aggregated early intervention effects for Down Syndrome persons: patterning and longevity of benefits. *Journal of Mental Deficiency Research*, **32,** pp. 1–17.

Glenn, S.M. and Cunningham, C.C. (1984) Selective preference to different speech stimuli in infants with Down's syndrome. In K. Berg (ed.), *Perspectives and Progress in Mental Retardation, Vol. 1*, pp. 201–10, Baltimore: University Park Press.

Goodman, J.F. (1992) *When Slow is Fast Enough* New York: Guilford Press.

Gopnik, A and Meltzoff, A.N. (1986) Relations between semantic and cognitive development in the one word stage: the specificity hypothesis. *Child Development*, **57**, pp. 1040–53.

Gunn P. and Berry, P. (1989) Education of infants with Down syndrome. *European Journal of Psychology of Education*, **4**, pp. 235–46.

Hayden, A.H. and Dmitriev, V. (1975) The multidisciplinary preschool programme for Down's Syndrome children at the University of Washington Model Preschool Center. In B.Z. Friedlander, G.M. Sterritt and G.E. Kirk (eds), *The Exceptional Infant. Vol. 3. Assessment and Intervention*. New York: Brunner/Mazel.

Hodapp, R.M. and Zigler. E. (1990) Applying the developmental perspective to individuals with Down syndrome. In D. Cicchetti and M. Beeghly (eds), *Children with Down Syndrome: A Developmental Perspective*, pp. 1–28, New York: Cambridge University Press,

Homer, T.M. (1980) Test-retest and home-clinic characteristics of the Bayley Scales of Infant Development in 9- and 15-month old infants. *Child Development*, **51**, pp. 754–58.

Howells, G. (1989) Down's syndrome and the general practitioner. *Journal of the Royal College of General Practitioners*, **39**, pp. 470–75.

Hunt, J.McV., Paraskevoopouous, J., Schickedanz, D. and Uzgiris, I. (1975) Variations in the mean age of achieving object permanence under diverse conditions of rearing. In J.E. Rynders and J.M. Horrobin (eds), *The Exceptional Infant: Vol. 3*, New York: Brunner/Mazel.

Johansson, I. (1993) Teaching prereading skills to disabled children. *Journal of Intellectual Disability Research*, **37**, pp. 413–18.

Kahn, J.V. (1992) Predicting adaptive behaviour of severely and profoundly mentally retarded children with early cognitive measures. *Journal of Intellectual Disability Research*, **36**, pp. 101–14.

Kemper, T.L. (1988) The neuropathology of Down syndrome. In L. Nadel (ed.), *The Psychobiology of Down Syndrome*, pp. 269–89. Boston: M.I.T. Press.

Khan, I., Fisher, R.A., Johnson, K., *et al.* (1994) The SON gene encodes a conserved DNA binding protein mapping to human chromosome 21. *Annals of Human Genetics*, **58**, pp. 25–34.

Kearsley, R.B. (1979) Iatrogenic retardation: a syndrome of learned incompetence. In R.B. Kearsley and I.E. Sigel (eds), *Infants at Risk: Assessment of Cognitive Functioning*, Hillsdale: Erlbaum.

Landry, S.H. and Chapieski, M.L. (1989) Joint attention and infant toy exploration: effects of Down syndrome and prematurity. *Child Development*, **60**, pp. 103–18.

Lott, I.T. and McCoy, E.E. (1992) *Down Syndrome: Advances in Medical Care*, New York: Wiley-Liss.

McDade, H.L. and Adler, S. (1980) Down syndrome and short-term memory impairment: a storage or retrieval deficit? *American Journal on Mental Deficiency*, **84**, pp. 561–71.

McTurk, R.H., Vietze, P.M., McCarthy, M.E., McQuiston, S. and Yarrow, L.J. (1985) The organisation of exploratory behavior in Down syndrome and nondelayed infants. *Child Development*, **56**, pp. 573–81.

Marcell, M.M. and Armstrong, V. (1982) Auditory and visual sequential memory of Down syndrome and non-retarded children. *American Journal on Mental Deficiency*, **87**, pp. 86–95.

Marfo, K. (ed.), (1991) *Early Intervention in Transition: Current Perspectives on Programs for Handicapped Children*, New York: Praeger.

Marino, B., Vairo, U., Corno, A., Nava, S., Guccione, P., Calabro, R., and Marcelletti, C. (1990) Atrioventricular canal in Down syndrome: prevalence of associated cardiac malformations compared with patients without Down syndrome. *American Journal of Diseases of Children*, **144**, pp. 1120–22.

Morss, J.R. (1983) Cognitive development in the Down's syndrome infant: slow or different? *British Journal of Educational Psychology*, **53**, pp. 40–47.

Morss, J.R. (1984) Enhancement of object permanence in the Down's syndrome infant. *Child: Care, Health and Development*, **10,** pp. 39–47.

Mundy, P., Sigman, M., Kasari, C., and Yirmiya, N. (1988) Nonverbal communication skills in Down syndrome children. *Child Development*, **59,** pp. 235–49.

Neve, R.L., Finch, E.A. and Dawes, L.R. (1988) Expression of the Alzheimeret amyloid precursor gene transcripts in the human brain. *Neuron*, **1,** pp. 669–77.

Newton, R. (1992) *Down's Syndrome*, London: Optima

Newton, R.W. and Newton, J.A. (1992) Management of Down's syndrome. In T.J. David (ed.), *Recent Advances in Paediatrics*, Edinburgh: Churchill Livingstone.

Nicholson, A. and Alberman, E. (1992) Prediction of the number of Down's syndrome infants to be born in England and Wales up to the year 2000 and their likely survival rates. *Journal of Intellectual Disability Research*, **36,** pp. 505–18.

Patterson, D. (1987) The causes of Down syndrome. *Scientific American*, 257, pp. 42–48.

Peterson, C., Maier, S.F. and Seligman, E.P. (1993) *Learned Helplessness: A Theory for the Age of Personal Control*, New York: Oxford University Press.

Piaget, J. (1955) *The Construction of Reality in the Child*, London: Routledge and Kegan Paul (original French edition 1937).

Pitcairn, T.K. and Wishart, J.G. (1995) Reactions of young children with Down's syndrome to an impossible task. *British Journal of Developmental Psychology*, **12,** pp. 485–90.

Roses, A.D., Strittmatter, W.J. and Pericak-Vance, M.A. (1994) Clinical application of apolipoprotein E genotyping to Alzheimer's disease. *Lancet*, **343,** pp. 1564–65.

Royston, M.C., Mann, D, Pickering-Brown, S. *et al.* (1994) Apolipoprotein Ee2 allele promotes longevity and protects patients with Down's syndrome from dementia. *Neuroreport*, **5,** pp. 2583–85.

Schapiro, M.B., Haxby, J.V. and Grady, C.L. (1992) Nature of mental retardation and dementia in Down syndrome: study with PET, CT and neuropsychology. *Neurobiology of Aging*, **13,** pp. 723–34.

Schapiro, M.B., Luxenberg, J.S., Kaye, J.A., Haxby, J.V., *et al.* (1989) Serial quantitative CT analysis of brain morphometrics in adult Down's syndrome at different ages. *Neurology*, **39,** pp. 1349–53.

Shapiro, B.L. (1975) Amplified developmental instability in Down's syndrome. *Annals of Human Genetics*, **38,** pp. 429–37.

Shepperdson, B. (1994) Attainments in reading and number in teenagers and young adults with Down's syndrome. *Down's Syndrome: Research and Practice*, **2,** pp. 97–101.

Sloper, P., Cunningham, C.C., Turner, S. and Knussen, C. (1990) Factors relating to the academic attainments of children with Down's syndrome. *British Journal of Educational Psychology*, **60,** pp. 284–98.

Sloper, P., Glenn, S.M. and Cunningham, C.C. (1986) The effect of intensity of training on sensori-motor development in infants with Down's syndrome. *Journal of Mental Deficiency Research*, **30,** pp. 149–62.

Snart, F. (1982) Cognitive processing by subgroups of moderately mentally retarded children. *American Journal of Mental Deficiency*, **86,** pp. 465–72.

Spiker, D. and Hopmann, M.R. (1995) The effectiveness of early intervention for children with Down syndrome. In M.J. Guralnick (ed.), *The Effectiveness of Early Intervention: Directions for Second Generation Research*, Baltimore: Brookes (in press).

Spitz, H.H. (1986) Preventing and curing mental retardation by behavioral intervention: an evaluation of some claims. *Intelligence*, **10,** pp. 197–207.

Spitz, H.H. (1993) Early educational intervention research and Cronbach's two disciplines of scientific enquiry. *Intelligence*, **17,** pp. 251–5.

St George-Hyslop, P.H., Tanzi, R.E., Polinsky, R.J. *et al.* (1987) The genetic defect causing familial Alzheimer's disease maps on chromosome 21. *Science*, 235, pp. 880–84.

Stafstrom, C.E. and Konkol, R.J. (1994) Infantile spasms in children with Down syndrome. *Developmental Medicine and Child Neurology*, **36,** pp. 576–85.

Sylvester, P.E. (1983) The hippocampus in Down's syndrome. *Journal on Mental Deficiency Research*, **27,** pp. 227–36.

Sylvester, P.E. (1986) The anterior commisure in Down's syndrome. *Journal on Mental Deficiency Research*, **30,** pp. 19–26.

Takashima, S., Becker, L.E., Armstrong, D.L. and Chan, F. (1981) Abnormal neuronal development in the visual cortex of the human fetus and infant with Down's syndrome: a quantitative and qualitative Golgi study. *Brain Research*, **225,** pp. 1–21.

Thase, M. (1988) The relationship between Down syndrome and Alzheimer's disease. In L. Nadel (ed.), *The Psychobiology of Down Syndrome*, Cambridge, MA: MIT Press.

Thomson, G.O.B., Ward, K. and Wishart, J.G. (in press) The transition to adulthood for children with Down's syndrome. *Disability and Society*.

Uecker, A., Mangan, P.A., Obrzut, J.E. and Nadel, L. (1993) Down syndrome in neurobiological perspective: an emphasis on spatial cognition. *Journal of Clinical Child Psychology*, **22,** pp. 266–76.

Uzgiris, I. and Hunt, J.McV. (1975) *Assessment in Infancy: Ordinal Scales of Psychological Development*, Urbana: University Press.

Varnhagen, C.K., Das, J.P. and Varnhagen, S. (1987) Auditory and visual memory span: cognitive processing by TMR individuals with Down syndrome or other etiologies. *American Journal on Mental Deficiency Research*, **91,** pp. 398–405.

Wachs, T. (1975) Relation of infants' performance on Piaget scales between 12 and 24 months and their Stanford-Binet performance at 31 months. *Child Development*, **46,** pp. 929–35.

Watson, J.S. (1972) Smiling, cooing and 'the game'. *Merrill-Palmer Quarterly*, **18,** pp. 323–39.

Watson, J.S. (1984) Bases of causal inference in infancy: time, space and sensory relations. In L.P. Lipsitt and C. Rovee-Collier (eds), *Advances in Infancy Research: Vol. 3*, pp. 152–65, Norwood: Ablex.

Werner, E.E. and Bayley, N. (1966) The reliability of Bayley's revised scale of mental and motor development during the first year of life. *Child Development*, **37,** pp. 39–50.

White, K.R. and Castro, G. (1985) An integrative review of early intervention efficacy studies with at-risk children: implications for the handicapped. *Analysis and Intervention in Developmental Disabilities*, **4,** pp. 177–201.

Wishart, J.G. (1988) Early learning in infants and young children with Down's syndrome. In L. Nadel (ed.), *The Psychobiology of Down Syndrome*, pp. 7–50, Boston: MIT Press.

Wishart, J.G. (1990) Learning to learn: the difficulties faced by infants and young children with Down's syndrome. In W.I. Fraser (ed.), *Key Issues in Research in Mental Retardation*, pp. 249–61, London: Routledge.

Wishart, J.G. (1991a) Early intervention. In W.I. Fraser, R. MacGillvray and A. Green (eds), *Halla's Caring for People with Mental Handicap* (8th ed.), pp. 21–27, London: Butterworth Heinemann.

Wishart, J.G. (1991b) Taking the initiative in learning: a developmental investigation of infants with Down's syndrome. *International Journal of Disability, Development and Education* (formerly *Exceptional Child*), **38,** pp. 27–44.

Wishart, J.G. (1991c) Motivational deficits and their relation to learning difficulties in young children with Down's syndrome. In J. Watson (ed.), *Innovatory Practice and Severe Learning Difficulties*, pp. 80–100, Edinburgh: Moray House Press.

Wishart, J.G. (1993a) Learning the hard way: avoidance strategies in young children with Down's syndrome. *Down's Syndrome: Research and Practice*, **1,** pp. 47–55.

Wishart, J.G. (1993b) The development of learning difficulties in children with Down's syndrome. *Journal of Intellectual Disability Research*, **37,** pp. 389–403.

Wishart, J.G. and Bower, T.G.R. (1984) Spatial relations and the object concept: a normative study. In L.P. Lipsitt and C.K. Rovee-Collier (eds), *Advances in Infancy Research* (Vol. 3), pp. 57–123, Norwood: Ablex.

Wishart, J.G. and Bower, T.G.R. (1985) A longitudinal study of the development of the object concept. *British Journal of Developmental Psychology*, **3,** pp. 243–58. (Reprinted in: G.E. Butterworth and P.L. Harris (eds), (1985) *Infancy*, pp. 35–50, Leicester: British Psychological Society.)

Wishart, J.G. and Duffy, L. (1990a) Instability of performance on cognitive tests in infants and young children with Down's Syndrome. *British Journal of Educational Psychology*, **59,** pp. 10–22.

Wishart, J.G. and Manning, G. (in press) Trainee teachers' expectations of ability in children with Down's syndrome.

Wisniewski, K. (1990) Down syndrome children often have brain with maturation delay, retardation of growth and cortical dysgenesis. *American Journal of Medical Genetics*, **7,** pp. 274–82.

Wisniewski, K.E., Zimmerli, E. and Devenny, D.A. (1994) Cognitive changes related to normal aging in adults with Down syndrome. Poster presented at the 10th International Down Syndrome Research Conference, Charleston, South Carolina, April.

Zigler, E. (1969) Developmental versus difference theories of mental retardation and the problem of motivation. *American Journal on Mental Deficiency*, **73,** pp. 536–56.

Zigler, E. and Balla, D. (1982) *Mental Retardation: the Developmental-Difference Controversy*, Hillsdale: Erlbaum.

13 Early Intervention with Delayed Children: Policies and Pedagogy

Joan F. Goodman

The ancient educational dispute between freedom and restraint, between the view of educational progressives that children's natural interests should be supported and the behaviourist allegiance to a predetermined curriculum, is manifested today in the split between early childhood programmes for ordinary children and early intervention programmes for disabled children. Professionals concerned with the former stress the advantages of child-directed, teacher-supported play activities. They frown on 'finished products,' 'correct' solutions and adherence to adult ideas of achievement (Bredekamp, 1987). Special education professionals tend to enlist in the competing camp. Since its inception, the field of early intervention has been committed to a strongly diagnostic/prescriptive model under which instructors first identify and measure deficits in children's abilities and then establish and teach to specific behavioural objectives (Anastasiow, 1978; Bailey and Wolery, 1984; Carta *et al.*, 1991; Hanson and Lynch, 1989; Heshusius, 1982; Mahoney *et al.*, 1989; Mahoney *et al.*, 1992; Mowder and Widerstrom, 1986; Neisworth and Bagnato, 1987; Wolery *et al.*, 1992).

These two schools – labelled by Kohlberg *et al.* (1987) as progressive/developmental and cultural transmission – differ fundamentally on the purposes of education, the psychological nature of the child and the process of learning. The progressive model, often referred to as Developmentally Appropriate Practice (DAP) in preschool settings, holds that the object of education is to assist children achieve ever greater responsible autonomy by supporting their passage through the developmental stages. The natural motivation of children to understand their surroundings and create meaning must be fertilized through a dialectical interchange with the environment. The educator's task, therefore, is to provide challenging experiences that mesh with the child's natural proclivities, but not to impose learning – a strategy that is inevitably doomed because an unready, uninterested child will reject the adult's agenda. By contrast, the cultural transmission model, which is aptly called 'remedial' when applied to the mentally retarded, holds that the object of education is to bring children's behaviour into conformity with community standards, or to approximate those standards to the extent possible. Because children are motivated by parents' and teachers' expectations and approval, the educator's task is to select, order, instil, and reinforce an appropriate chronology of attainments (Kohlberg, 1968; Kohlberg *et al.*, 1987; Kohlberg and Mayer, 1972).

It is not surprising that educators of handicapped and non-handicapped children have tended to draw from separate traditions. It is easier to trust the natural evolving developmental processes in a child perceived to be 'intact' than one perceived to be 'damaged'. We can be relaxed with a normal child, confident that he or she will make use of ordinary experiences, that in time he or she will put aside the rattle and bottle and learn to talk with rather little effort on our part. Waiting out a retarded child's slow-paced growth is another matter. Following and reacting to his or her minimal overtures appears to waste valuable time – time we should use to correct his or her delay. The possibility that our forceful intrusion might be counter-productive, that supportive rather than directive intervention might actually better serve the child's welfare, appears cold-hearted, even negligent.

The effort to restore mental competence is an essential component of contemporary changes in social attitudes toward disabled children. In the last 20 years, we have witnessed a dramatic decrease in stigmatization and increase in mainstreaming children once rejected and excluded; the premise of our enlarged and publicly supported services, however, is that they will promote accelerated learning. The implication running through the educational laws is that respecting the handicapped child means attempting to remediate his or her deficiencies, not merely protecting or encouraging the child's natural developmental patterns. The legislation mandating public education for handicapped preschoolers, (Public Law 99–457, p. 1145) for example, is clear in its remedial intents:

> [T]here is an urgent and substantial need – (1) to enhance the development of handicapped infants and toddlers and to minimize their potential for developmental delay, (2) to reduce the educational costs to our society, including our Nation's schools, by minimizing the need for special education and related services after handicapped infants and toddlers reach school age, (3) to minimize the likelihood of institutionalization of handicapped individuals and maximize the potential for their independent living in society.

Our remedial attitudes toward the mentally retarded find a partial analogy in the experiences of the deaf. Harlan Lane (1992), a prominent expert on deaf education, argues passionately that the 'audist establishment' has failed to respect the integrity of deaf language and culture. Instead of accommodating to their special needs, 'benefactors' have pressed upon them the ways of the hearing world – oral speech and comprehension. Under the 'mask of benevolence', and the authority of medicine and psychology, educators have 'colonized' this minority group by suppressing their natural mode of communication. The result of the 'benevolence' has been an educational disaster. According to Lane (ibid.), the average 16-year-old deaf student reads at the level of the average 8-year-old hearing child. Thirty-five per cent of the deaf, after high school completion, cannot read at a second-grade level and 75 per cent are unable to read a newspaper. In their best subject, math., the deaf are four years behind the hearing. Of course, it can be argued that the comparison of the deaf to the retarded is faulty. The deaf have an alternative culture; the mentally retarded do not. Yet, in common, our interventions are designed to 'treat' existing 'pathologies'. Lane (1992, p. 181) argues that 'oralists' should 'move deaf education toward the deaf student . . . adopt student-centered education . . . and use what the deaf pupil brings to the learning process'.

In this chapter I argue that as with the deaf, so with the retarded. Rather than attempting to accelerate development, we could support their 'natural' developmental pace; as Lane would have us, appreciate their 'natural' language. Although remediation may be appropriate for *all* children to accomplish *certain* kinds of learning (such as the social proprieties of toileting and table manners) and in *some* children ·(perhaps the autistic) for *all* learning, generally speaking we should avoid the 'fix-up' demands of society and, instead, adopt the more developmental supportive form of education. In the long run, such an approach both respects retarded children, by not depriving them of the liberty rights we grant to the non-handicapped and, further, is likely to produce more self-reliant, expressive and autonomous individuals, without sacrificing skill achievement. On the other hand, acceding to acceleration pressures – attempting to bring 3 to 5-year-old children, functioning at half their chronological age, to the level of normal 5-year-olds – results in repressing developmentally productive toddler-like immaturities, in a curriculum that emphasizes drill on a narrow range of acceptable behaviours and required skills, in the regulation and control of spontaneous explorations and, inevitably, in excessive use of authoritarian control technologies that produce excessively docile and passive behaviour in children. My essential point is that instead of demanding more of the retarded child we should moderate our demands; we should meet the child on his or her own turf and support his or her evolving, albeit slow, development; we should construct environments especially designed for his or her rate of growth and level of interest rather than insisting that he or she makes it in our speeded-up environments; in short, we should uncouple respect and acceptance from a demand to conform.

To explore these matters I take the reader to a typical early intervention programme, Midwood, a prototype of the many I visited across the USA as part of an extensive field study on early intervention for preschool children (Goodman, 1992). A brief glance at the early morning activities will begin to give the reader a sense of how the acceleration imperative plays out in practice; how considerate care by attentive adults can also be repressive. The children on whom I focus fall into the moderate range of mental retardation (IQs roughly 40 to 60). That means their mental age, or functional level, is roughly half their chronological age. The following vignette does not apply to every programme, or any programme all the time, but it is representative of what I observed.

EARLY INTERVENTION PRACTICES

Doreen, a 3-year-old with Down syndrome, arrives on a school bus to join five other preschoolers with disabilities at Midwood, a regular elementary school. As the group proceeds down the corridor, Doreen drops the hand of her teacher Teresa, sits on the floor, and pulls at a diaper from her small backpack. Teresa, who needs to keep her group together and moving, bends over Doreen and says urgently but patiently, 'It's time to walk now Doreen.'

Shaking her head Doreen responds, 'Me sit.'

'Doreen,' entreats Teresa, 'I know you want to be a big girl and walk to class now. I will help you put away your diaper.'

Teresa, under increasing pressure from the other children who are breaking rank, reluctantly picks up a resistant Doreen, puts her into a wagon with another child, and the small group proceeds.

Once inside the classroom the children have a brief free play period. Doreen, troubles forgotten, proceeds to the doll corner where she puts on a large felt hat and preens in front of a head-to-foot mirror. She begins a game of tilting her hat so that it falls off, replaces it, and postures again at the mirror. At the fourth repetition, Teresa asks her aide Anita: 'Can you help Doreen find something more productive to do, perhaps with David' (a 5-year-old with Down syndrome)?

Anita asks Doreen to join her and David in putting a baby doll to bed. Doreen reluctantly approaches and David thrusts a baby bottle at her. She ignores it and, instead, puts her big felt hat on the doll. Anita says: 'Oh, that's too *big* for baby. You are *big* but she is *little*. Can you and David find a *little* blanket to cover her?' Anita's attention is then diverted by another child and Doreen walks back to the mirror dragging a blanket and the hat.

After ten minutes of free play the children are summoned to circle. Molly (age 4, diagnosis unknown, moderate retardation), who has been unloading blocks from a shelf, pays no attention and is told by Anita, 'It's time to be all done now.' No response. Anita then walks over to her and says, 'Molly, I guess you want Anita to help you clean-up.'

At circle, Doreen plays with Molly's long soft hair, while Molly, indifferent to Doreen's caresses, tries to get hold of her own shoe buckle. When Teresa notices, after the greeting song, she reminds the children, 'It is time to listen now. Doreen and Molly where do we keep our hands? Hands need to sit on our laps, remember?' Anita, seated behind the girls, reaches around and places the girls' hands on their laps. Teresa continues, 'I like the way you have your hands now.'

Teresa then proceeds with the calendar asking, 'What month is this?'

The answers come in: 'Winter', 'Monday', 'Thanksgiving'.

To the last, Teresa comments, 'Thanksgiving, that's close. Is Thanksgiving in November or December?'

'November,' responds David.

She then asks for the date. When no one responds she points to a posted calendar of the month and begins to count with the children, 'One, two, three . . . ' When they reach 11 she stops and says, 'Good counting, today is November 11th.'

During the calendar work, Molly, unsuccessful in reaching her shoes, slips away from the circle, crawls under a low table, and is finally able to remove them. Teresa, taking note, says to Anita, 'Molly wants you to help her sit.' After Anita restores Molly to the chair, Teresa compliments her for 'good sitting', and says, 'Now it's time for colours' – and the activities continue.

Even from this brief glance at a typical programme, we can see that the children have entered a culture, an order, that in its 'schoolishness' is alien to their 'toddlerishness' – a phenomenon common to our preschools more generally. It starts with the physical environment. Because Midwood is an elementary public school building, the adults must carefully monitor the movements of their special children down long corridors of classrooms and whenever they leave their own room for such activities as toileting, lunch, playground or gym. It is difficult for young children functioning as toddlers (18 months to two years in our example) to walk that distance without yielding to distractions, as Doreen does when she has a 'sit down' to play with her diaper.

The demands of a school culture continue inside the room where the children are expected to abide by group routines. Teresa, much like teachers of older non-disabled children, has partitioned her morning into periods for different activities: toileting, free play, circle, art, cognitive, gross motor, toileting again and departure. When it is 'time to', she expects the children to put away their activities and move on. Molly is in the thick of moving blocks about when called for circle. She is required to come and, after slipping away, required to return.

The accelerated preacademic curriculum, with its emphasis on colours, shapes, numbers, puzzles and size, is taught throughout the day, and often in a separate period devoted to 'cognitive' learning. Almost all programmes review daily the calendar (month, day and date) and the weather. Although constant exposure has familiarized children with the general vocabulary in these domains, their confusion is obvious from the answers: They offer 'Winter', 'Monday', 'Thanksgiving' as equivalent possibilities. Teresa 'helps' by seizing on 'Thanksgiving' and then by narrowing their choices to two alternatives: November (emphasized by voice tone) or December. She 'helps' with the date by seizing upon the right answer from the stream of their rote counting.

Because of the concern to accelerate development, teachers are averse to wasting time. Even during free play, therefore, they lead children away from activities that appear repetitive and unsocial. As we saw with Doreen, however, the adult suggestion (to play with the doll and David) is often disregarded, and the attempt may abort an activity that was meaningful and enjoyable to the child (preening at the mirror).

What teachers perceive to be 'off task' are the usual occupations of toddlers. A major interest of children at this stage is the body – theirs and others. Doreen moves a hat about her head and is fascinated by the changes it produces in her appearance; she lifts up her shirt to inspect her slightly protruding stomach and rubs her hand across its contours; she enjoys the feel of Molly's soft hair in her hands during circle time, while Molly is eager to gain access to her own feet. The children are interested in the relationship of objects to each other – experiences of in-out, on-off. Doreen likes to pull the diaper out of the bag, stuff it in, pull it out again. Molly likes to fill a wagon with blocks from a shelf and then replace them all. Collecting and depositing, throwing and retrieving are often attached to in-out actions. Children at this stage are forever filling baskets, purses and bags which they move about; they make piles of objects which they zealously guard and then disband. Molly collects forks, spoons, cups, plates and pans, and dumps them into the carriage. Moving and climbing are favoured – the physical enactment of in-out, up-down, under-over. Doreen does not use her blanket to cover the doll but tries to snuggle under it herself. Molly slips under the table; she also crawls into the coat cubbies and even into a toy oven.

The natural activities of these children can be described as circular rather than linear. In-out, on-off, open-close and up-down are repetitive rather than sequential.

They go nowhere, have no start or completion. However, as Piaget observed, small children delight in self-chosen repetition. Through such acts they learn the nature and function of the physical world and their role as causal agents. Through repetitive encounters with the environment children make the 'discovery and conservation of the new' (Piaget, 1952, p. 138). They sort out what they can do, what they can make other people and things do, and how the animate differs from the inanimate. Though a psychologist might see this as the essence of early mastery and the foundation for later learning and self-confidence, to others the repetition appears idle and unproductive, particularly when the child is 3 or 4 years old.

CONTROLLING CHILDREN

In order to press forward their demands upon reluctant children and avoid classroom malfunction, teachers have developed a set of powerful control techniques. Without doubt teachers are kind, gentle and patient with children. They offer unstinting praise and rarely criticize. But, for all the gentleness, teachers are operating very tight ships. Their use of authority takes a variety of forms.

Disguising the retardation

Because they are so thoroughly on the side of children, teachers do what we all do in relationships of affection – seek to avoid seeing the children fail. In practice, this means 'cheating' on the child's behalf by excessive shaping of responses. Favourite means of doing this are to limit the number of possible answers to two, extract the right response from children's familiar rote recitations, monitor children's responses closely and guide them physically when necessary, and sometimes simply supply the right answer. As a result, the children appear to be doing better than they really are, the retardation is masked. They become oriented to teacher-pleasing. Often, with no notion of the right answer, they guess wildly or search the teacher for hints rather than think independently. Teacher-pleasing, or teacher-appeasing, and wild guessing work against personal autonomy, integrity, self-reliance, independence core values of all educators.

When children do not respond to coaching or answer-shaping, teachers, unwilling to lower demands, have no alternative but to take control of the activity. The outcome of this domination is likely to be a complete role reversal with teachers planning and carrying out the bulk of a project, while children serve as helpers. The problem is that when there is no 'take' by the child, there is also no continuity; the children look impressive only while the teacher dominates the play. When the teacher quits so does the child.

Distorting intentions

Teachers disguise the motor restlessness, negativism and failures that are part of the children's immaturity by subtly distorting their feelings. They may put words of agreement in the mouth of a child who, in fact, wants to disagree. The denial of children's true intentions makes programmes look more harmonious and collaborative than they truly are.

Teresa says to Doreen, who is playing in the corridor with an excavated diaper, 'I know you want to be a big girl.' When Molly resists coming to circle, Anita says, 'I guess you want Anita to help you clean-up.' When Molly leaves circle during 'calendar' time, crawls under a table and removes her sneaker, Teresa says to Anita, 'Molly wants you to help her sit.' As Teresa and Anita know, Doreen does not want to be a big girl, she wants to play with her diaper; Molly does not want to help clean-up, she wants to keep unloading blocks; and she wants to be freed from, not helped in, sitting. These incidents have in common the projection of teachers' wishes upon children. It is the teachers who want the children to follow the rules – walk down the corridor, clean-up, sit in the circle.

Positive reinforcement also distorts children's feelings. 'Good sitting' may be delivered after a child has been bad (i.e., not sitting), so that the child hears approval in the context of a reprimand. The reinforcement is at odds with his or her own dejection and anger. Similarly, when a child is told 'good trying' after doing poorly, the comment conflicts with his or her own disappointment, which often is not acknowledged. Teachers do not say, 'That colouring job wasn't too good, was it?' They are so reluctant to be negative that many inhibit dispensing simple orders such as, 'You must sit, you must not run', and replace them with, 'I can help you sit' and 'good walking'.

Perhaps the distortions seem harmless – after all, they represent a manner of talking that adults use with children all the time. But, particularly with this population, they may erode a sense of self. If a teacher says, 'You must sit, like it or not', she is bluntly exercising adult authority while leaving the child free to oppose the demand, to be angry, sulky and resistant. The child knows the teacher disapproves and can nurse his or her wounds or resentment. Failure, disappointment and disapproval are part of life. However, to 'protect' children from negative feelings and reactions distorts their reality and, conceivably, makes coping with the inevitable negatives in life more difficult. When teachers mask their superior authority by complimenting a child for his or her unwilling submission ('That's nice sitting now') or distorting his intentions ('You want to help sitting'), they are in fact saying, 'You don't really feel what you feel, you will feel what I tell you to feel.' It is one thing to set limits, rules, and structure, and to enforce them with approval *and disapproval*; quite another to tell children they want to follow the rules when they do not, or that they are good and doing well when, in fact, they are bad and doing poorly. Denying a child the authenticity of his or her own drives is especially unfortunate when directed at children who are weak and rather easy to manipulate.

Schedules

The daily schedule is a powerful tool for teachers to modulate and regulate children's behaviour. Frequent prescribed changes of activity keep children's behaviour from exceeding carefully constructed boundaries. Although on paper periods generally extend from 15 to 30 minutes, in reality they are generally shorter because of transitions. In a two-and-a-half hour programme there are, typically, six to eight scheduled periods that include toiletting, free play, circle, eating, work, gross and/or fine motor.

Schedules serve many purposes. Most obviously, they give teachers a framework for ensuring that activities they want covered will be covered – that songs will be sung at circle time, learning objectives covered at work time. Schedules enable teachers to provide children a daily variety – a time to play, a time to work, a time to participate in large groups, a time to fly solo. Schedules make for predictability, consistency, structured expectations, familiarity, and a sense of security. Boundaries provide safe spaces that can encourage children to be more expressive than an unregulated unpredictable envjronment.

But as schedules become tighter and more rigid, they also restrict behaviour. They define an established order to which everyone must conform, and keep the teacher in a firm position of control. The periodic mandatory shifts in activities serve to break up any difficulty a teacher may be having with a child. If Molly cannot tolerate circle time and darts away, no matter; the start of another activity will put an end to this behaviour. A firm schedule can seriously limit children's freedom while making the teacher's job easier.

The schedules leave little time for trouble to develop, but little time also for a child to probe his or her own capacities and interests. Children are not usually finished with what they are doing when the lights flicker to indicate a period is ending. At Midwood, for example, Doreen was not satiated with mirror play when interrupted. She would have liked to linger, admiring herself in the glass. Molly gave no sign that she was through moving blocks from shelf-to-truck-to-floor-to-shelf when it was 'time to' come to circle. In all likelihood, the teacher's common practice of issuing warnings that a period is soon to end results from the children's reluctance to make the switch. It is curious that in a population where 'attention deficit' is a widely cited problem, the teacher so often interrupts the engrossed child to terminate an activity.

Praise

To understand the use of praise in early intervention centres we need to distinguish between praise that rewards a child's achievement and reinforces his or her pleasure in it, and praise, without achievement, that disguises a command. When praise acknowledges a genuine accomplishment, it not only reinforces the action, but resonates with a child's perceived sense of competence. Very different from this shared rejoicing is praise *prior* to any accomplishment, e.g. at the initial point in the chain of events ('good looking at the pictures'), or before the chain has started ('good sitting', 'good listening'). Heaping praise on a child when he or she is not feeling pleased, is not even looking for an adult judgement, undermines the child's personal authenticity. It only thinly masks the true message: 'Do what you're told, don't be disobedient.' In early intervention programmes teachers praise children for each step in a task, for the steps leading up to a task, and for not being out of step. They praise children for poor work ('Good trying to remember'), for simple compliance ('Good keeping your hands in your lap'), for cessation from naughtiness ('I like the way you've stopped hitting'). They give them bits of food, stickers, stamp their hands, add links in a chain just for not misbehaving.

At a certain threshold, the outpouring of praise works against what it is designed to promote – self-worth. The child is not given a chance to evaluate his or her own efforts, to move on from experiences of disappointment and discouragement, to differentiate on his or her own a good from an inferior production. Teacher approval becomes a substitute for child effectiveness. In this atmosphere of excessive non-discriminating evaluation, the child is deprived of neutral space to work or play as he or she is inclined, without the direction of adult commentary. It is as if the teacher were saying, 'Since you cannot do much, I'll praise your effort and compliance' – which explains why there appears to be so much less positive reinforcement in classrooms for traditional children, who nevertheless accomplish more (Stipek and Sanborn, 1985). When constant praise does work, the child becomes addicted, looking to the teacher for approval after each part-act and waiting for approval before making the next move.

Narrowing the permissible

Much of what toddlers do naturally and do in their homes is either forbidden or confined to special times and places in school. By limiting what is allowable at school, teachers have yet another device to minimize disruptions. Basically children are supposed to act a lot like teachers: curb their emotional and physical responses; maintain a positive, calm, patient manner; keep to the assigned task; abide by the rules of collective living with consideration and patience.

There are physical restraints: Children are not allowed to climb, kick, and run (except in gross motor or outdoor play); crawl under furnishings or into spaces (ovens, doll carriages, cradles, cubbies); climb on top of furnishings (tables, bureaus, chairs, shelves); touch themselves or one another. Children may not throw material (except balls and other objects made for throwing, and then only at certain times); wander without purpose; leave (circle, work, the room); shift objects from one place to another, particularly if they are removed to another section of the room; mouth or smell (except when it is snack time or there is a lesson in smells); yell, cry, or throw a tantrum. Even sitting on the floor, rather than in chairs, is often prohibited.

There are behavioural restraints: Children are not to make a mess (mix up toys, dump puzzles, spill); not to grab, but to use words rather than hands; not to invade the property rights of others – no taking another child's toy, no interrupting another child's play; not to ignore adult commands until the adult releases their attention. They are to sit and wait – for their turn at circle, for the group to leave the room, for a teacher to help; follow the daily routine and postpone preferred play. When playing, they must do so appropriately and with the toys specified. Sometimes the materials children like best – sand (rice, beans, water, whatever is in the tub), jungle gyms, slides, rocking boats, trampolines – will not be present or, if present, not available. The toys that are plentiful – toys with small pieces that stack, sort, nest, insert, designed to help children learn colours, shapes, sequences, part/whole relationships – may require adult supervision. Art material such as paint, crayons, paste, playdoh and, to a lesser extent, housekeeping equipment, also may require heavy adult supervision.

There are input restraints: The curriculum is very repetitious because teachers believe that without constant rehearsal the slow child will not learn. And so the same core curriculum items – colours, shapes, numbers puzzles, big/little – are reviewed day after day. What makes the instruction tedious is that these items do not admit of much variation. Teaching colours is not like teaching sand play. The child either knows or does not know the colour.

Altogether the management techniques add up to a lot of restriction and the 'choices' children have are fairly limited. When a teacher offers only two options to a question, the child cannot give a third. When a teacher takes over an activity, the child cannot invent a response. A child cannot contradict the teacher who tells him or her how he or she feels. When it is 'time to', the child must submit to the routine. The steady stream of reinforcement leaves a child without opportunities to learn from mistakes, and narrowly channelling the permissible deprives him or her of experiencing the possible. The techniques succeed not just in controlling and subduing children but in producing *seemingly* high levels of student attainment.

Both the difficult curriculum and the control systems erected to support it might be defensible if it were true – as many believe – that children with mental retardation learn by a different set of rules from those without retardation; that is, if in addition to being delayed, such children have defective minds. Then the pathology of the children provides a rationale for force-feeding development.

DELAYED OR DEFECTIVE?

Opinions about those with retardation have been remarkably steadfast. The ideas of professionals a century ago are very reminiscent of teachers today. Then, as now, the 'defect' view prevailed. For example, using a two-type defect typology, Tredgold (1908), an early expert whose text on the 'feeble-minded' went through nine editions, described 'aments' as: passive, inert, sluggish; *or* restless, mobile, impulsive, instinctive (animal like), inattentive. By 1952 he had reduced the list to stable/apathetic, or unstable/excitable. This dichotomy still prevails among contemporary experts, many of whom describe those with retardation as inert and unresponsive on the one hand, and as inattentive and restless on the other. Specifically, the children are considered to have diminished intrinsic motivation (Bailey and Wolery, 1984; Harter and Zigler, 1974; Haywood *et al.*, 1982; Zigler and Balla, 1982), to be relatively unresponsive and low in initiative (Brinker and Lewis, 1982; Hanzlik and Stevenson, 1986; Jones, 1978, 1980; Mundy *et al.*, 1988), to be poor at exploration (Garwood, 1983), play (Anastasiow, 1978), and spontaneous learning (Fewell and Kelly, 1983). They also show limited self-regulation and planning abilities (Naglieri, 1989; Whitman, 1990), and act impulsively (Kopp, 1990; Kopp *et al.*, 1983a; Kopp *et al.*, 1983b). The picture of an empty, drifting, unresponsive, impulsive organism, when combined with acceleration pressures, makes it clear why early intervention programmes resist developmental approach. Are they right?

At one cut, those with retardation are defective by definition. If they were not slow to learn they would not be retarded. Even if we match Doreen at age 4 with a younger normal child, say age 2, Doreen, because she is retarded (learning in one year what another child learns in six months) will respond more slowly. At the point of initial comparison, the two children may have achieved the same amount – that's what it means to have equivalent developmental ages – but they will be unequal in *processing* new material. After all, if Doreen learned like a normal child she would not stay retarded for long! That means, in any instructional situation with the 2-year-old, Doreen is unlikely to understand as quickly, be as responsive, see as many alternatives. It will take her twice the time to learn something new, she will be less alert, more will pass her by. Teresa, quite naturally, sees her endless preening at the mirror as 'non-productive', not crediting her need for extra time to complete her play. Researchers have actually documented the slower response times in those with mentally retardation (Kail, 1992; Lee *et al.*, 1987). Even at a biological level, it has been suggested that children with retardation have a less reactive central nervous system (Ganiban *et al.*, 1990).

Problems of attention manifested by distractibility and impassivity are less obviously true by definition, but plausible. Cognitive psychologists consider attentional control to be the highest aspect of intelligence; no wonder, then, that it should be weak in those with low intelligence. Here, too, in any given situation, the child with a 50 IQ should not be expected to have the attention, impulse control and interests even of the normal younger child who is at the same developmental level. But while distractibility is blatantly apparent in early intervention programmes, its causes are less so. It may be a consequence of the children's slow processing, a reaction to excessive school demands, or both.

We cannot completely disregard the 'environmentalist' argument that children acquire such qualities as passivity, rigidity and inattentiveness as a protective defence against environments poorly calibrated to their developmental level. Molly, for example, may be distractible at circle time because she has not completed her block play and cannot follow all the calendar talk, but Molly is not distractible when playing with the blocks or her shoes. When a teacher 'redirects' the children from these 'off task' activities to difficult tasks, they, overwhelmed, may narrow their foci and block out adult entreaties (appearing rigid or slow); or, without a good match for their interests, 'float' (distractible). If we keep in mind that these children are functioning at half their age, the possibility of overload seems plausible.

Researchers, by studying a broad range of characteristics in young children with retardation across situations, have attempted to answer the question: are children with retardation innately different from those of like mental age and, if so, how? Although the variability among children, as always, defies a clear response, the broad conclusion (largely but not entirely drawn from studies of children with Down syndrome) is that the child with retardation goes through the same stages in the same sequence as normal children and, from this perspective, is accurately described as developmentally delayed. More specifically:

> Delayed young children achieve major milestones in a similar order and with a similar organization as their normally developing peers, the main reliable differences being that the rate of development is slower and the appearance of achievements is later. This general finding applies to socioaffective development, selective attention, sensori-motor development, language and symbol formation, pretend play, and attachment behaviors.
>
> (Krakow and Kopp, 1983, p. 1143)

On the other hand 'differences appear in situations where (a) a primary task involves acquisition, encoding, retention, transformation, or transmission of selected information, and (b) the information is either not immediately obvious or there are competing stimuli from which the child must select' (ibid., p. 1144). The differences may produce 'a slow rate of development or increasing constriction of the repertoire of responses that are available', i.e., rigidity (ibid., p. 1144).

The growth of language and play illustrate the delay-only position. Children with Down syndrome, for example, like typical children, do not use language referents until they have a clear grasp of the conceptual category to which the word applies; that, in turn, requires understanding that objects are permanent even when not immediately visible (object permanency); early referents are to action and function words (Bruner, 1983; Mervis, 1988, 1990; Nelson, 1973; Warren and Rogers-Warren, 1982); symbolic play does not emerge until the child is 'preoperational' (can mentally represent experiences in which he or she has participated – Cicchetti and Beeghly, 1990; also Rondal, 1988, with severely retarded children). Further, there are strong play-language correspondences: children with retardation who have no language also have no symbolic play; at the one-word stage they manage single symbolic schemes; complex play combinations await word combinations (Spiker, 1990). The content of play and language in children with Down syndrome also parallels that of their mental-age peers. They use as many toys, play out as many roles with just as much imagination (Fewell and Kaminsky, 1988; Krakow and Kopp, 1983; Loveland, 1987; Motti *et al.*, 1983; Seibert *et al.*, 1984, in a diagnostically mixed population). Their first words come from the same categories, e.g. toys, food, clothing, animals, vehicles (though language acquisition is slower than one would predict, Mervis, 1990); and, when 'mean length of utterance' (MLU) is held constant, they produce very similar vocabularies (Leifer and Lewis, 1984).

The same parallelism characterizes their emotional development. They become attached to caretakers, fearful of strangers, and negativistic in the same sequence and at the same mental ages as non-retarded children. They laugh or smile at the same circumstances and in the same order – first to being touched, then to seeing incongruous situations, such as mother sucking on baby's bottle (Cicchetti and Beeghly, 1990).

But there is a hitch, a close look reveals differences between children with and without mental retardation functioning at similar levels. In the humour study, for example, children with Down syndrome smiled more and laughed less than the controls, presumably because they 'simply could not process the incongruity with sufficient speed to produce the tension ... required for laughter' (Cicchetti and Sroufe, 1976, p. 927). Their emotional expression was muted; both initial arousal and recovery from arousal were slower (Cicchetti and Beeghly, 1990; Emde *et al.*,

1978). Studies have shown that attention in the young child with retardation (at least in those with Down syndrome) is more poorly deployed, sustained or controlled than in children of the same mental age. Their play patterns are more stereotypic, repetitive and rigid, and they are less likely to monitor their environment (Kopp, 1990; Kopp *et al.*, 1983a; Kopp *et al.*, 1983b; Krakow and Kopp, 1983; Mundy and Kasari, 1990).

Despite these caveats, the research evidence is that most children with uncomplicated mental retardation develop similarly to the non-retarded. Their problem is in *rate* rather than *manner* of learning, and differences, when they appear, have more to do with slowness of processing than other mental defects. What this suggests educationally is that programmes for the slow child should, for the most part, be guided by the same developmental principles as programmes for any other child. I will note just three such principles which, if taken seriously, would cause considerable revamping of early intervention.

DEVELOPMENTAL PRINCIPLES

Early knowledge through action

Fundamental to the theories of both Piaget and Werner is that the young child's world is made up of 'things-of-action' (Werner, 1948), the natural movement of objects and the movement of the child upon objects. As Piaget (1964, p. 76) succinctly explains: 'To know an object, to know an event, is not simply to look at it and make a mental copy or image of it. To know an object is to act on it. To know is to modify, to transform the object, and to understand the way the object is constructed.' The growth of language, logico-mathematical concepts, causality, space, and time all emerge from early sensory-motor schemata. Jerome Bruner, in *Child's Talk* (1983), describes the process: little children do just a few things (e.g. reaching, holding, banging, looking); they then apply a single act to a wide range of objects (e.g. banging on everything in sight), or use their entire action repertoire on one object. Mimicking this pattern, early word combinations consist of a large assortment of words linked to a class of just a few words (open-pivot). More complex language, constrained by rules requiring the proper placement of an agent-action-object sequence, does not emerge until a child is goal-directed in his or her play and understands that he or she acts upon objects to make things happen.

The content of language also is function or action oriented. First words are of things that move independently (e.g. dog, cat, baby, car, truck, mama, dad), or things that can be manipulated (e.g. shoe, sock, hat, ball), not static and abstract qualities such as form, colour, and number (Nelson, 1973). Without the experiential base, the meaning of new words and concepts cannot be absorbed. The child truly takes in only that small portion of the linguistic environment that can be attached to the knowledge-of-action he already possesses (Mervis, 1988; Newport *et al.*, 1977).

Children in early intervention programmes are certainly active. In addition to their work periods, they have regularly scheduled times for indoor and outdoor play. These activities, however, tend to be seen either as either a break from 'work', or as another means for infusing the curriculum. And the curriculum is not generally the stuff of action. Consider how many times letters, numbers and shapes are removed from a child's experience: letters, for example, are abstracted from printed words, printed words from spoken language, spoken language from the representation of experience, finally the representation from the experience itself. Teachers committed to 'developmental' instruction would do the opposite: start with the child's activity and expand on (or abstract from) it as the child's mastery, curiosity, and personal timetable permit. From the experience comes the pretend enactment, from the enactment an elaboration through stories, from the story the words and finally, and not for a long time, the letters. As Bruner (1972) puts it, the natural course of learning is from 'knowing how' to 'knowing that'.

Stage progression

The child's movement towards a more differentiated and objective world occurs gradually and in an orderly fashion. Children cannot be rushed through the stages; an unready child rejects instruction, and attempts to skip or accelerate understanding in preschoolers have been unsuccessful (Hobbs and Bacharach, 1990; Kamii and Derman, 1971; Ravn and Gelman, 1984). Educators, eager for their diligent instruction to 'take', are deceived by children's mimicking and memorizing feats into believing that the rote recollection of answers to specific questions amounts to major progress. The child with a delay, for example, may be an excellent counter without understanding basic counting principles, i.e. each item in a series can be tagged only once (1-to-1 correspondence); the last item tagged represents the total (cardinal value); counting is the same regardless of the item (item indifference); and the order of counting is immaterial (order indifference) (Gelman and Cohen, 1988). Research has shown that an unready child will reject adult instruction until he or she has a prelinguistic base; the influence of adults in this growth is very modest (Brown, 1973; Bruner, 1983; Mervis, 1987; Nelson, 1973; Newport *et al.*, 1977). The teacher's stimulus for change is an effective prod 'only to the extent that it is significant, and it becomes significant only to the extent that there is a structure which permits its assimilation (Piaget, 1964, p. 182).

Preschool children with moderate retardation are functioning at the end of the sensori-motor stage (roughly mental age of 0 to 2) and the beginning of the pre-operational stage (roughly mental age 2 to 7). They are just beginning to represent experience in language and symbolic play but do not understand abstract concepts (e.g. 'more', 'small', even 'animal'). To do so requires the formation of a stable objective reality impossible for children who are still perceptually dominated, egocentric and preconceptual (Piaget, 1951/1962). Such children do not see the unity underlying multiple appearances, or the multiplicity in things that look the same. At ages 2 and 3, the image is all-consuming; concepts lacking constant perceptual referents – and that includes all words that are generalizations of specific instances – are not understood.

Even harder than concepts that unify objects with different appearances (e.g.

animal) are those that refer to attributes of things or relations between things. Such terms – including colours, antonyms and prepositions, all early intervention favourites – modulate meaning rather than making reference (Brown, 1973). Ordinary children do not consistently name colours accurately until ages 3 to 4 (Andrick and Tager-Flusberg, 1986; Bornstein, 1985a, 1985b; Nelson, 1985). Even at these ages children do not reliably distinguish 'more' from 'less' and 'same' from 'different'. The easiest of the antonyms, 'big' versus 'little', is not attained until age 4 and even then the discrimination is likely to be based on height alone (Clark, 1979; Maratsos, 1973; Ravn and Gelman, 1984). Small children see objects as absolutely big or little. They do not see how the same thing can be small in one context and big in another. That awaits a mental age of approximately 7 years when they move into the stage of concrete operations.

Play also cannot be advanced beyond the child's stage. At the end of the sensori-motor period, as they approach 2 years of age, children begin to pretend, but only to a limited extent. They will go through sleeping, eating, drinking routines with themselves or with a doll, they may even develop a few sequences (e.g. feed the doll and put her to bed), but they cannot take on roles of other people until they are more cognitively decentred and better able to grasp the lives of others (ages 3 to 5).

A teacher, acknowledging the limits set by developmental stage, may wish to modify much of the core curriculum. There is scant possibility that these children understand seriation and large time dimensions (both reviewed daily with the calendar), the relativism of size and objective spatial concepts. It is therefore diffi-cult to justify daily calendar drills, antonyms (like more and less, big and little), colours, counting, sequencing and shape-sorting exercises. Aside from the fact that this material is not embedded in any meaningful natural context, learning it requires a degree of objectivity that is a long way off for the preschool child with moderate retardation.

Intrinsic motivation

Because early intervention programmes tilt strongly toward extrinsic motivation (external reinforcement of external demands), we need to reconsider the nature and value of intrinsic drives. The Piagetian infant who bats a mobile and shakes a rattle, who later gets 'into everything' as he or she pulls, pushes, dumps and fills, is propelled by his or her own curiosity and drive for mastery. The infant repeats a simple action over and over just for the pleasure of making something happen, and does not wait for approval from the environment, indeed is not easily deterred by disapproval. Play, in the early years, is the ideal expression of intrinsic motivation. In its reliance on flexibility, divergent thinking, freedom from a specific objective, it is antithetical to external reinforcement which constrains behaviour. In fact, there is research to suggest that external reinforcement of play actually degrades invention (Deci, 1975; Deci and Ryan, 1982; Fein and Kohlberg, 1987; Lepper, 1981). Driving the child's growth of intelligence is the simple pleasure of following his or her own interest. As Whitehead (1929/1959, p. 48) put it: 'There can be no mental development without interest. Interest is the *sine qua non* for attention and apprehension' (italics in the original).

Intrinsic motivation must be encouraged, released, tapped, not commanded or coerced. This enticing approach towards learning, as Whitehead has beautifully described, is particularly important for the novice learner who requires consider-able freedom if he or she is to discover the effects of his or her own initiative, for-mulate questions, seek answers. Ideally, a teacher's guidance

> answers to the call of life within the child. In the teacher's consciousness the child has been sent to his telescope to look at the stars, in the child's consciousness he has been given free access to the glory of the heavens. Unless, working somewhere, however obscurely, *even in the dullest child*, there is this transfiguration of imposed routine, the child's nature will refuse to assimilate the alien material . . . My point is that a block in the assimilation of ideas inevitably arises when a discipline of precision is imposed before a stage of romance has run its course in the growing mind . . . Without the adventure of romance, at the best you get inert knowledge without initiative, and at the worst you get contempt of ideas – without knowledge.
>
> (Ibid. pp. 51–52, italics added).

Were teachers to give up substantial authority and support the 'transfiguration of imposed routine', they would have to back away from a heavily prescriptive achievement-oriented curriculum. Objectives for children would be constructed through reciprocal interactions between children and teachers. The responsibilities of teachers would shift from skill instruction to the stimulation and expansion of children's natural inclinations (except in so far as such inclinations were highly deviant, e.g. self-stimulating and self-destructive behaviours). A child's lost or absent interest in an activity would suggest suspension or alteration of the objec-tive, not persistence through increased directive teaching. Teresa, less burdened by acceleration demands, would permit Doreen to pull the diaper from her bag or preen in front of the mirror, Molly to skip circle time when busy unloading blocks, and the girls to play with each other's hair. Such behaviours would no longer be viewed as 'unproductive'.

This go-slow message should not be misinterpreted as an endorsement for benign neglect. Children with disabilities and their families need and deserve professional intervention in the preschool years. It takes self-conscious discipline to resist one's natural instinct to increase pressure on the slow-to-respond child. It takes understanding, sensitive and well-trained personnel to circumvent children's passivity and distractibility, to provide an environment that invites prolonged productive participation and to spot and enlarge upon nascent interests and skills. Rather than getting children prepared for the next environment, however, we must prepare present environments that intrigue and appeal. Decreasing educational demands will give these children, like other children, the opportunity for mastery and discovery, for fulfillment of their own drives while they gradually meet expec-tations set by adults. The burden of change, however, cannot rest on teachers alone. We will not allow the child with mental retardation to progress at his or her own rate unless we are comfortable with the delay. In gaining this acceptance, the words of Donna Williams (1992, pp. 206–07), once a child with autism, might prove helpful:

I do not believe that being sane or intelligent is superior to being insane or retarded ... In the end, it is not knowledge that matters but the nature of a person's spirit. Alone, it is not the mind that strives for knowledge but the spirit that guides it. Untouched purity, innocence, and honesty of one's own spirit make up possibly the highest stage any person could hope to reach.

REFERENCES

Anastasiow, N.J. (1978) Strategies and models for early childhood intervention programs in integrated settings. In M.J. Guralnick (ed.), *Early Intervention and the Integration of Handicapped and Nonhandicapped Children*, pp. 85–111, Baltimore: University Park Press.

Andrick, G. and Tager-Flusberg, H. (1986) The acquisition of color terms. *Journal of Child Language*, **13**, pp. 119–34.

Bailey, D.B. Jr and Wolery A. (1984) *Teaching Infants and Preschoolers with Handicaps*, Columbus: Merrill.

Bornstein, M.H. (1985a) Colour-name versus shape-name learning in young children. *Journal of Child Language*, **12**, pp. 387–93.

Bornstein, M.H. (1985b) On the development of color naming young children: data and theory. *Brain and Language*, **26**, pp. 72–93.

Bredekamp, S. (ed.), (1987) *Developmentally Appropriate Practice in Early Childhood Programs Serving from Birth through Age 8*, expanded edn, Washington, DC: National Association for the Education of Young Children.

Brinker, R.P. and Lewis, M. (1982) Discovering the competent handicapped infant: a process approach to assessment and intervention. *Topics in Early Childhood Special Education*, **2**, pp. 1–16.

Brown, R. (1973) *A First Language*, Cambridge, MA: Harvard University Press.

Bruner, J.S. (1972) Nature and uses of immaturity. *American Psychologist*, **8**, pp. 687–707.

Bruner, J.S. (1983) *Child's Talk: Learning to Use Language*, New York: Norton.

Carta, J.J., Schwartz, I.S., Atwater, J.B. and McConnell, S.R. (1991) Developmentally appropriate practice: appraising its usefulness for young children with disabilities. *Topics in Early Childhood Special Education*, **11**, pp. 1–20.

Cicchetti, D. and Beeghly, M. (1990) An organizational approach to the study of Down syndrome: contributions to an integrative theory of development. In D. Cicchetti and M. Beeghly (eds), *Children with Down Syndrome: A Developmental Perspective*, pp. 29–62, New York: Cambridge University Press.

Cicchetti, D. and Sroufe, L.A. (1976) The relationship between affective and cognitive development in Down's syndrome infants. *Child Development*, **47**, pp. 920–29.

Clark, E. (1979) *The Ontogenesis of Meaning*, Wiesbaden: Akademische Verlagsgesellschaft Athenaion.

Deci, E.L. (1975) *Intrinsic Motivation*, New York: Plenum.

Deci, E.L. and Ryan, R.M. (1982) Curiosity and self-directed learning: the role of motivation in education. In L.G. Katz (ed.), *Current Topics in Early Childhood Education*, vol. 4, pp. 71–85, Norwood: Ablex.

Emde, R.N., Katz, E.L. and Thorpe, J.K. (1978) Emotional expression in infancy: early deviations in Down's syndrome. In M. Lewis and L.A. Rosenblum (eds), *The Development of Affect*, pp. 351–60, New York: Plenum.

Fein, G.G. and Kohlberg, L. (1987) Play and constructive work as contributors to development. In L. Kohlberg with R. DeVries, G. Fein, D. Hart, R. Mayer, G. Noam, J. Snarey and J. Wertsch (eds), *Child Psychology and Childhood Education: a Cognitive Developmental View*, pp. 392–440, New York: Longman.

Fewell, R.R. and Kaminsky, R. (1988) Play skills development and instruction for young children with handicaps. In S. Odom and M. Karner (eds) *Early Intervention for Infants and Children with Handicaps*, pp. 145–58. Baltimore: Brookes.

Fewell, R.R. and Kelly, J.F. (1983) Curriculum for young handicapped children. In S.G. Garwood (ed.), *Educating Young Handicapped Children: a Developmental Approach*, pp. 407–33, 2nd edn, Rockville: Aspen.

Ganiban, J. Wagner, S. and Cicchetti, D. (1990) Temperament and Down syndrome. In D. Cicchetti and M. Beeghly (eds), *Children with Down Syndrome: a Developmental Perspective*, pp. 63–100, New York: Cambridge University Press.

Garwood, S.G. (1983) Special education and child development: a new perspective. In S.G. Garwood (ed.), *Educating Young Handicapped Children: a Developmental Approach*, pp. 3–37, Rockville: Aspen.

Gelman, R. and Cohen, M. Qualitative differences in the way Down syndrome and normal children solve a novel counting problem. In L. Nadel (ed.), *The Psychology of Down Syndrome*, pp. 51–99, Cambridge: MIT Press.

Goodman, J.G. (1992) *When Slow is Fast Enough*, New York: Guilford.

Hanson, M.J. and Lynch, E.W. *Early Intervention: Implementing Child.and Family Services for Infants and Toddlers Who Are At-Risk or Disabled*, Austin: Pro-ed.

Hanzlik, J. and Stevenson, M. (1986) Interaction of mothers with their infants who are mentally retarded, retarded with cerebral palsy, or nonretarded. *American Journal of Mental Deficiency*, **90**, pp. 513–20.

Harter, S. and Zigler, E. (1974) The assessment of effectance motivation in normal and retarded children. *Developmental Psychology*, **10**, pp. 169–80.

Haywood, H.C., Meyers, C.E. and Switzky, H.N. (1982) Mental retardation. In M.R. Rosenzweig and L.W. Porter (eds), *Annual Review of Psychology*, vol. 33, pp. 309–42, Palo Alto: Annual Reviews.

Heshusius, L. (1982) At the heart of the advocacy dilemma: mechanistic world view. *Exceptional Children*, **49**, pp. 6–13.

Hobbs, M. and Bacharach, V.R. (1990) Children's understanding of big buildings and big cars. *Child Study Journal*, **20**, pp. 1–17.

Jones, O.H.M. (1978) A Comparative study of mother-child communication with Down's syndrome and normal infants. In H. Schaffer and J. Dunn (eds), *The First Year of Life: Psychological and Medical Implications of Early Experience*, 175–95, New York: John Wiley.

Jones, O.H.M. (1980) Prelinguistic communication skills in Down's syndrome and normal infants. In T.M. Field, S. Goldberg, D. Stern, and A.M. Sostek (eds), *High-Risk Infants and Children: Adult and Peer Interactions*, pp. 205–25, New York: Academic Press.

Kail, R. (1992) General slowing of information-processing by persons with mental retardation. *American Journal on Mental Retardation*, **97**, pp. 333–41.

Kamii, C. and Derman, L. (1971) The Engelmann approach to teaching logical thinking: findings from the administration of some Piagetian tasks. In D.R. Green, M.P. Ford, and G.B. Flamer (eds), *Proceedings of the CTB/McGraw-Hill Conference on Ordinal Scales of Cognitive Development*, pp. 127–47, New York: McGraw-Hill.

Kohlberg, L. (1968) Early education: a cognitive-developmental view. *Child Development*, **39**, pp. 1013–62.

Kohlberg, L., with R. De Vries, G. Fein, D. Hart, R. Mayer, G. Noam, J. Snarey and J. Wertsch (1987) *Child Psychology and Childhood Education: a cognitive developmental View*, New York: Longman.

Kohlberg, L. and Mayer, R. (1972) Development as the aim of education. *Harvard Educational Review*, **42**, pp. 449–96.

Kopp, C.B. (1990) The growth of self-monitoring among young children with Down syndrome. In D. Cicchetti and M. Beeghly (eds) *Children with Down Syndrome: a Developmental Perspective*, pp. 231–51, New York: Cambridge University Press.

Kopp, C.B., Krakow, J.B. and Johnson, K.L. (1983a) Strategy production of young Down syndrome children. *American Journal of Mental Deficiency*, **88**, pp. 164–69.

Kopp, C.B., Krakow, J.B. and Vaughn, B. (1983b) Patterns of self-control in young handicapped children. In M. Perlmutter (ed.), *Development and Policy Concerning Children with Special Needs: Minnesota Symposia on Child Psychology*, vol. 16, pp. 93–128, Hillsdale: Erlbaum.

Krakow, J.B., and C.B. Kopp, (1983) The effects of developmental delay on sustained attention in young children. *Child Development*, **54**, pp. 1143–55.

Lane, H. (1992) *The Mask of Benevolence: Disabling the Deaf Community*, New York: Alfred Knopf.

Lee, J., O'Shea, L.J. and Dykes, M. (1987) Teacher wait-time: performance of developmentally delayed and non-delayed young children. *Education and Training in Mental Retardation*, **22**, pp. 176–84.

Leifer, J. and Lewis, M. (1984) Acquisition of conversational response skills by young Down syndrome, and nonretarded young children. *American Journal of Mental Deficiency*, **88**, pp. 610–18.

Lepper, M.R. (1981) Intrinsic and extrinsic motivation in children: detrimental effects of superfluous social controls. In W.A. Collins (ed.), *Aspects of the Development of Competence*, pp. 155–214. Hillsdale: Erlbaum.

Loveland, K.A. (1987) Behaviour of young children with Down syndrome before the mirror: finding things reflected. *Child Development*, **58**, pp. 928–36.

Mahoney, G., O'Sullivan, P. and Fors, S. (1989) Special education practices with young handicapped children. *Journal of Early Intervention*, **22**, pp. 261–68.

Mahoney, G., Robinson, C. and Powell, A. (1992) Focusing on parent-child interaction: the bridge to developmentally appropriate practices. *Topics in Early Childhood Special Education*, **12**, pp. 105–20.

Maratsos, M. (1973) Decrease in the understanding of the word 'big' in preschool children. *Child Development*, **44**, pp. 747–52.

Mervis, C.B. (1987) Child-basic object categories and early lexical development. In U. Neiser (ed.), *Concepts and Conceptual Development: Ecological and Intellectual Factors in Categorization*, New York: Cambridge University Press.

Mervis, C.B. (1988) Early lexical development: theory and application. In L. Nadel *The Psychobiology of Down Syndrome*, pp. 101–43, Cambridge, MA: MIT Press.

Mervis, C.B. (1990) Early conceptual development of children with Down syndrome. In D. Cicchetti and M. Beeghly (eds), *Children with Down Syndrome: A Developmental Perspective*, pp. 252–301, New York: Cambridge University Press.

Motti, F., Cicchetti, D. and Sroufe, L.A. (1983) From infant affect expression to symbolic play: the coherence of development in Down syndrome children. *Child Development*, **54**, pp. 1168–75.

Mowder, B.A. and A.H. Widerstrom, (1986) Philosophical differences between early childhood education and special education: issues for school psychologists. *Psychology in the Schools*, **23**, pp. 171–74.

Mundy, P. and C. Kasari, (1990) The similar-structure hypothesis and differential rate of development in mental retardation. In R.M. Hodapp, J.A. Burack, and E. Zigler (eds), *Issues in the Developmental Approach to Mental Retardation*, pp. 71–92, New York: Cambridge University Press.

Mundy, P., Sigman, M. Kasari, C. and Yirmira, N. (1988) Nonverbal communication skills in Down syndrome children. *Child Development*, **59**, pp. 235–49.

Naglieri, J.A. (1989) A cognitive processing theory for the measurement of intelligence. *Educational Psychology*, **24**, pp. 185–206.

Neisworth, J.T. and Bagnato, S.J. (1987) *The Young Exceptional Child: Early Development and Education*, New York: Macmillan.

Nelson, K. (1973) Structure and strategy in learning to talk. *Monographs of the Society for Research in Child Development*, **38**, 1–2, Serial No. 149.

Nelson, K. (1985) *Making Sense: the Acquisition of Shared Meaning*, Orlando: Academic Press.

Newport, E.L., Gleitman, H. and Gleitman, L.R. (1977) Mother, I'd rather do it myself: some effects and non-effects of maternal speech style. In C.E. Snow and C.A. Ferguson (eds), *Talking to Children: Language Input and Acquisition*, pp. 109–49, London: Cambridge University Press.

Piaget, J. (1951/1962) *Play, Dreams and Imitation in Childhood*, New York: Norton.
Piaget, J. (1952) *The Origins of Intelligence in Children*, New York: International Universities Press.
Piaget, J. (1964) Cognitive development in children: Piaget, development, and learning. *Journal of Research in Science and Technology*, **2**, pp. 176–86.
Public Law 99–457. *Education of the Handicapped Act, Amendments of 1986*, 100, Stat. 1145.
Ravn, K.E. and Gelman, S.A. (1984) Rule usage in children's understanding of 'big' and 'little.' *Child Development*, **55**, pp. 2141–50.
Rondal, J.A. (1988) Parent-child interaction and the process of language acquisition in severe mentally retardation: beyond the obvious. In K. Marfo (ed.), *Parent-Child Interaction and Development Disabilities*, pp. 114–25, New York: Praeger.
Seibert, J.M., Hogan, A. and Mundy, P. (1984) Mental age and cognitive stage in young handicapped and at-risk children. *Intelligence*, **8**, pp. 11–29.
Spiker, D. (1990) Early intervention from a developmental perspective. In D. Cicchetti and M. Beeghly (eds), *Children with Down Syndrome: a Developmental Perspective*, pp. 424–48, New York: Cambridge University Press.
Stipek, D.J. and Sanborn, M.E. (1985) Teachers' task-related interactions with handicapped and nonhandicapped preschool children. *Merrill-Palmer Quarterly*, **31**, pp. 285–300.
Tredgold, A.F. (1908) *Mental Deficiency (Amentia)*. New York: Wood.
Warren, S.F. and Rogers-Warren, A. (1982) Language acquisition patterns in normal and handicapped children. *Topics in Early Childhood Special Education*, **2**, pp. 70–79.
Werner, J. (1948) *Comparative Psychology of Mental Development*, New York: International Universities Press.
Williams, D. (1992) *Nobody Nowhere*, New York: Random House.
Whitehead, A.N. (1929/1959) *The Aims of Education and Other Essays*, New York: Macmillan.
Whitman, T.L. (1990) Self-regulation and mental retardation. *American Journal of Mental Deficiency*, **94**, pp. 347–62.
Wolery, M., Strain, P. and Bailey, D. (1992) Applying the framework of developmentally appropriate practice to children with special needs. In S. Bredekemp and T. Rosegrant (eds), *Reaching Potentials: Appropriate Curriculum and Assessment for Young Children*, vol. 1, pp. 92–112, Washington: National Association for the Education of Young Children.
Zigler, E. and Balla, D. Introduction: the developmental approach to mental retardation. In E. Zigler and D. Balla (eds), pp. 3–8, *Mental Retardation: the Developmental–Difference Controversy*, Hillsdale: Erlbaum.

14 Play

Anne Jobling

'So where to go from here?'

(McConkey, 1985, p. 300)

With this challenge, McConkey concluded a comprehensive review of play and its relationships within the lives of individuals with Down syndrome. He noted the long overdue recognition that play extended beyond the childhood years to become an aspect of leisure and friendship in adult life and he suggested that play be considered as both a tool of development and an ongoing, essential element in a quality lifestyle.

McConkey recommended that subsequent investigations should emphasize the value of play and he pointed his readers to several well-known definitions:

- play as an environment for learning
- play as a self-active representation of ones' self
- play as a feeling; an expression of joy and mastery
- play as the fool that might become king

(McConkey,1985, p. 300–02)

This chapter will present some of the more recent investigations about playing and the players with Down syndrome, and consider them in terms of McConkey's challenge.

PLAY AS AN ENVIRONMENT FOR LEARNING

What value does play have in the development of children with Down syndrome?

In early educational programmes for children with special needs, it seems that the value of play in learning has been developed and shaped by the integration of two sets of knowledge. First, educators have promoted the value of play and playing as essential for development and learning, especially in a child's early years. Play was viewed in Piagetian theory to be closely associated with the growth of intelligence and as such for children with intellectual disabilities it was quickly translated into intervention strategies and programmes with organized schedules, behavioural checklist and developmental sequences (Fewell and Vadasy, 1983; Garwood, 1982;

Rogers, 1988). The first curricula specifically devoted to play was developed by Fewell and Vadasy (1983). They developmentally sequenced play milestones into over 192 activities. By structuring programmes of play in this way educators considered that the cognitive, social and language deficits in the developmental progress of children like those with Down syndrome could be assessed and systematically addressed. These assumptions did not go unchallenged (Schwartzman, 1978; Sutton-Smith, 1979, 1987) and in 1991, Schwartzman decided that the seriousness of educators had transformed play.

Secondly, from snapshot-styled observations of players with intellectual disabilities, researchers and educators categorized their playing as asocial, with random low-level activity (Wade, 1973) and lacking in spontaneity (McConkey, 1985). This style of playing was said to require attention and an interventional style of educational programming was developed. As the players were considered to be 'trainable', play training or play therapy-styled instructional approaches were considered as means to achieve the necessary developmental ends (Christie, 1986; Schaefer and O'Connor, 1983; Wehman, 1977). In early childhood special education, this view seemed to persist even though Smith and Syddall (1978) and McConkey (1986) had challenged the basis and directions of this style of programme and a number of researchers had reported that children with intellectual disabilities were able to engage in playful activity (Li, 1981; Mogford, 1977; Tizard *et al.*, 1976).

As play, development, and the characteristics of children with intellectual disabilities such as Down syndrome became inextricably linked, an interest was developed in play 'as a causative and predictor variable' (Johnsen, 1991, p. 201). Early childhood educators seemed to consider the value of play for players with intellectual disabilities in terms of arresting deficits to facilitate learning. These children were at risk! Various organized styles of play training and tutoring (some more perilously close to drudgery than others) were viewed as a necessary part of the children's home and school programmes and these spawned a wide variety and range of didactic, formalized and teacher-directed curricula models (Bailey and Wolery, 1984; Day and Parker, 1977; Lerner *et al.*, 1987; Odom and Karnes, 1988; Pieterse *et al.*, 1988). Observations of the children's play in social settings such as preschools were seen as a good informal tool for the assessment of the child's ability (Guralnick, 1993; Guralnick and Weinhouse, 1984) and the duration of involvement in the programme and the level of parent–child interaction were seen as key variables to child's developmental progress (Mahoney *et al.*, 1992; Marfo and Kysela, 1988).

Did these educational interventions using play produce developmental gains?

Recent reports have been mixed and it seems that within the devised play programmes there are other variables associated with the play programme rather than the play *per se* that may influence the progress of development. These include time spent playing (Marfo and Kysela, 1988), parental involvement in the playing (Marfo, 1988, 1991; Tannock and Girolametto, 1992; Yawkey, 1982), and teaching strategies employed by the play programme (Yoder *et al.*, 1991).

In an intervention programme of play activities (Handicapped Children's Early Education Program for Preschoolers) where the instructional model proposed that teachers were to be specifically encouraged to teach those skills in which the children failed to show competency, Fewell and Oelwein (1991) reported on the progress of 92 children with Down syndrome. After the programme, there were no significant differences noted in the two motor (gross and fine) or the two language (expressive and receptive) areas of development, but 'useful' gains had been made in self-help and social skills development. Limited time in the programme was considered a reason for the lack of progress.

Developmentally appropriate practices (DAP) in early childhood education are seen to represent a revised direction for Early Childhood Special Education (ECSE) practices (Fox and Hanline, 1993). This approach to teaching children with special needs featured a naturalistic style of play interaction using less intrusive teaching methods and focused on the interests of the playing child. As some gains in the language and communication aspects of development for children with special needs have been reported (Warren and Reichle, 1992), Fox and Hanline (1993) applied this approach and reported two case studies. One of these was a boy with Down syndrome aged 4 years 8 months with an age equivalent score on the Battelle Development Inventory of 12 months and with hearing and visual problems. The target behaviours reported – puts objects in container, gives objects and manipulates objects with both hands – were 'embedded' in his playing, and there was an intervenor nearby to assist him. With this approach the target behaviours were shown to increase and there was some evidence of maintenance up to the sixty-fifth session, but the researchers were cautious about the long-term stability of the gains.

In another study, a group of six children (aged 47 to 66 months with a language age 19 months below normal) was used to compare the developmental effects of two different teaching approaches (Losardo and Bricker, 1994). The first was a play-activity style of instruction with varied communication patterns and the second was a direct style of instruction with adult-request type of communication. Tentatively, the study supported the activity-based instruction (playing) as more effective for continuing progress and generalization but less efficient during acquisition. However, there were no significant differential effects and the researchers suggested the child's interest in the interaction may be an important consideration.

In all these studies, researchers have emphasized the exploratory and tentative nature of their conclusions and it would seem that sensitive, well-planned and long-term research is needed to provide firm evidence of the value of using play in these specific approaches to early educational interventions. After conducting a meta-analysis of 46 play-training research studies, Fisher (1992) noted that the research was diverse, often ambiguous in its definitions and beset with methodological problems. Like Christie and Johnsen (1985) and Sloper *et al.* (1990), he questioned the effectiveness of intensive and adult-contrived play. He suggested as an alternative that intervention should adopt an approach to programming that valued play for its elements of fun and enjoyment and combined it with more formal teaching techniques.

Goodman (1992) from her wide range of field observational studies would seem to agree with this 'mixed approach'. She considered that direct teaching may be useful for self-help skill development but noted that in numerous programmes the playing in 'free' play time was focused on targeted objectives from the children's individual education programmes. She criticized the teaching approaches in Early Childhood Special Education which reflected an adherence to developmental checklists that made both the environment and the programme objectives too narrow, and failed to consider the abilities and interests of the child.

Finally, any consideration of using play to produce developmental gains, would be neglectful if it failed to consider the children themselves. Teachers need to help children construct their own play and not just repeat or reproduce the precise teacher-demonstrated or modelled play which may be irrelevant or too complex (Bromwich, 1985; Goodman, 1992). Also from the child's perspective, if they can only play under direction and supervision then the 'teaching of play' must be considered to have been ineffective (Gunn, 1982). Effective programming will develop independent players, not just remediate deficits (Cherkes-Julkowski and Gertner, 1989).

Although the importance of play and a range of philosophies about playing form the basis of many programmes in special education for those with Down syndrome, it is suggested that educators should abandon their anxious quest to stimulate development by manipulating play activities towards the next developmental milestone or functional skill. Instead, they should continue to remind themselves that development can be supported by the playful nature of playing as it creates good feelings within the players which motivates them to continue engaging in the activity (Jobling, 1988).

PLAY AS SELF-ACTIVE REPRESENTATION OF ONE'S INNER SELF: THE CHARACTERISTICS OF THE PLAYERS

Since programming in play settings for children with Down syndrome has yielded such a confusion of gains in the short term, and doubtful ones in the long term, there has been increasing advocacy for etiology-specific intervention programmes which may provide a better way to facilitate the children's developmental progress (Gibson, 1991; Hodapp and Dykens, 1991). Gibson (1991) suggested that the lack of effect from programming was due to its 'willy-nilly' approach in addressing the specific characteristics of children with Down syndrome. Specific characteristics required specific programmes he argued.

As play has been considered a child's experimental dialogue with the environment (Garvey, 1977), can observations of children with Down syndrome playing enable educators to understand the play as self-active representations and, as a consequence, value the play characteristics of these players?

Play characteristics in children with Down syndrome

Although there have been few studies after the preschool years, the reported achievements and differences in the playing of children with Down syndrome demonstrate that this group of children show a wide range abilities and disabilities across both chronological and developmental (Bromwich, 1985; Cicchetti and Beeghly, 1990; LaVeck and Brehm, 1978; McConkey, 1985).

It has been reported that the development of play in infants and toddlers with Down syndrome has a similar organizational structure to that of their peers (Beeghly *et al.*, 1989; Loveland, 1987), and that play continues to mature, though at a slower rate than normal (Beeghly *et al.*, 1990). The level and quality of the playing observed in children with Down syndrome is considered to be closely associated with both affective and cognitive development, demonstrating a coherence in development (Beeghly *et al.*, 1989, 1990; Motti *et al.*, 1983).

Particularly when playing with toys, the behavioural sequence in the play of children with Down syndrome reflects the child's developmental level (Gowen *et al.*, 1992; Jeffree and McConkey, 1976; Motti *et al.*, 1983). However, when performances are matched developmentally with non-handicapped children in this type of play, it must be taken into consideration that the children with Down syndrome are older and have had more experience with the functional manipulation of objects (Bromwich, 1985; Hogg and Moss, 1983). In a study of representational play in handicapped children (six of whom had Down syndrome) Bromwich (1985) reported that at a developmental age of 18 months, the children's chronological age ranged from 19 to 39 months and that both chronological age (CA) and mental age (MA) may have had differential effects on the playing and on any comparisons made with the developmental progress of non-handicapped children.

Although there is general developmental progress in the playing abilities of children with Down syndrome, it has been suggested that there are several distinctive player characteristics (Beeghly *et al.*, 1989). These appeared to be particularly related to a passive and neutral attitude when playing and a lack of responsiveness and change in the play, as well as a variable level of attentiveness to toys and social play interactions.

Passivity – responsiveness

A certain level of passivity and a general slowness to interact with objects, people and the environment seem to have been consistently considered as part of the interactional pattern or style of children with Down syndrome (Henderson, 1985; Mundy *et al.*, 1988; Wade, 1973). Even though Serifaca and Cicchetti (1976) reported that smiling and other interactive behaviours (such as showing things to mother) were similiar to other developing children, others have particularly noted a general 'neutrality' of expressions in infants and toddlers with Down syndrome (Gunn *et al.*, 1981; Jens and Johnson, 1982; Kasari *et al.*, 1990; Legerstee and Bowman, 1989, Loveland, 1987).

In a comparative observational study of the spontaneous play in infants (N=30 with Down syndrome), Mundy *et al.* (1988) reported that the children with Down syndrome made fewer requests for either objects or assistance and seemed to be less motivated to explore or to request information. This characteristic was also reported by Beeghly *et al.* (1990) for play sequences between mothers and infants or toddlers from 20 to 76 months of age.

Several reasons may be advanced for these passive characteristics and the generalized lack of explorative behaviour. The first reason can be found in the specific gross and fine motor abilities of children with Down syndrome. In a study designed to examine the exploratory behaviour of infants with Down syndrome, Vietze *et al.* (1983) reported a significant relationship between the involvement in effect-producing toys and problem-solving tasks and motor development as measured with the BSID. This was especially related to fine motor manipulation tasks. Hypotonia was seen to have negatively influenced the ability of the infants with Down syndrome to reach and make contact with a toy, and to manually play with it. This remained so, even though these infants are considered to have had more experiences than age-matched peers at manipulating objects (Hogg and Moss, 1983).

Playing for toddlers and preschoolers often involves vigorous physical activity and the use of developing gross motor skills. In particular, for participation in active games at preschool, 'one cannot underestimate the physical fitness level and combination of motor skills required' (Dalley, 1985, p. 14). Play in active games also affects the interaction of the preschooler with peers and when children's motor skills are delayed or different from other children, their playing may be devalued or rejected (Bergen, 1988). Children with Down syndrome often experience a delay in motor skill development (Harris and Shea, 1984; Henderson, 1985; Jobling and Gunn, 1995) and both Hulme and Lunzer (1966) and Krakow and Kopp (1983) have noted the effect of slower locomotion on social and explorative behaviours. The children may have difficulty keeping up with the others, fall more readily and be unsure when running, climbing or jumping. Games and equipment which require balance and co-ordination skills and rough-and-tumble play are often avoided (Watkinson and Muloin, 1988). So, in the playground (Titus and Watkinson, 1987; Watkinson and Muloin, 1988) and the classroom 'milieu' (Malone and Stoneman, 1990) the moment in the play may pass too quickly for them to make a contribution, or others may quickly do it for them, or their play may be redirected towards more passive activities. All this can have a negative effect on the children's efforts to play and they may give up and become onlookers.

Frequently, perhaps with cognitive or language gains in mind for the child with Down syndrome, the focus of early childhood programmes (both centre- and home-based) has been directed towards the more sedentary play activities such as puzzles, blocks, dough and computers, and physical development has been enhanced by a structured therapy programme. Young children (with or without Down syndrome) who like to be active can easily become bored and listless with the repetitive nature of such activities in highly directed play settings and this can lead to behaviours such as sitting passively, becoming resistant or running amok!

The observed neutral expressions and low responsiveness in children with Down syndrome may also be a reflection of hypotonia. In a 'stranger study' Serifaca and Cicchetti (1976) considered it as a physiological variable that may have caused the slower reaction of the children with Down syndrome to the stimuli and stress of the situation. But both Linford and Duthie (1970) and Eberhard *et al.* (1989) have demonstrated that inactivity in those with Down syndrome is likely to be a psychological rather than a physiological difficulty. Is passivity, then, a self-active representation or a reflection of expectations and programming approaches? Are these children bored?

Or as Gunn (1981) wondered, is it the enjoyment of the social praise (good girl/boy) that arouses the child in the play interaction rather than the success in the activity itself. She later considered whether the expected low arousal levels in infants with Down syndrome had lead to the intensive style of interaction promoted in some programmes (as reported by Brooks-Gunn and Lewis, 1982) which may have influenced the notion of 'mutual enjoyment' in the activity (Gunn and Berry, 1989).

Some support for this view comes from two studies. In a study of mother–infant interactions at home, Stevenson *et al.* (1985) observed low responsivity in both mothers and infants and concluded that this may have been the inadvertent result of intensive stimulation and training programmes. In another study, Fischer (1988, p. 141) noted that 'when mother failed to respond the children seemed surprised'. It was suggested that these toddlers with Down syndrome may have become accustomed to an interactional pattern that acted immediately and indiscriminately.

From these perspectives, the expectations of others and the experiences of children with Down syndrome when playing may have shaped a passive style demonstrated and in doing so, further limited the spontaneity of the children's play. And if this style of playing is developed early it may last a lifetime (Buckley and Sacks, 1987; Cherkes-Julkowski and Gerner, 1989; Cheseldine and Jeffree, 1981; Jobling, 1989).

Repetition of behaviours

It has been observed that children with Down syndrome engage in exploratory play behaviour that is repetitive (McConkey, 1985). This qualitative attribute of their playing was observed by Krakow and Kopp (1982) in a laboratory play session with toys. They reported that at both the infant and the toddler level, there were more stereotypical repetition of behaviours than would normally be expected, such as throwing toys as infants and reverting to banging and mouthing as toddlers. In a later study of home corner playing, these researchers once again reported that children with Down syndrome frequently repeated the same type of play with the same objects in the same sequence. The examples given were feeding the baby, combing hair and going shopping.

Some explanations may be advanced for this behaviour. First, Gunn (1982) in a pilot study of children with Down syndrome in preschool play settings noted this type of behaviour especially with puzzles, beads and family-type symbolic play, and suggested that the children seemed to reach a 'comfort level' where they felt secure and competent in their playing. She also wondered if this behaviour reflected their inability to initiate a new aspect or direction for an activity. While playing with mother (Gunn *et al.*, 1981) and the Goodman Lock Box (Berry *et al.*, 1984) these researchers commented that the infants and children with Down syndrome seemed either not to enjoy or even be interested in mastery-type activities. This observation that children with Down syndrome during play show less pleasure and were more likely to reject mastery-type toys has subsequently been made by Ruskin *et al.* (1994).

Secondly, Krakow and Kopp (1983) commented that children with Down syndrome seemed to lack an understanding of the properties and possibilities of a toy in symbolic play and therefore there was the necessity for them to repeat the same known idea over and over again. Also the variety and number of their object transformations or substitutions in symbolic play were limited (Beeghly *et al.*, 1990). This lack of creativity in the play and a seeming inability to organize and structure play was also noted by Sloper *et al.* (1990). However, by using colourful characters, and pictures of the children themselves playing outdoors with balls and on climbing frames, Katz and Singh (1986) demonstrated that when assisted to understand and gain knowledge of the properties and function of such play things, children with moderate to severe intellectual disability can increase their range and levels of involvement with the playthings.

Attending to the play

Attending to a play situation is a complex phenomen which involves not only focusing on the playthings but also monitoring the environment (Krakow and Kopp, 1982). For players with Down syndrome, it would seem that their predominant attending behaviour either for exploring objects or in social interactional situations is 'looking' (Krakow and Kopp, 1982; MacTurk *et al.*, 1985; Senapati, 1989; Vietze *et al.*, 1983).

A comparative study by Loveland (1987) on the looking behaviors of infants with and without Down syndrome (MA 16 to 32 mths) concluded that there were similarities in the developmental organization of the behaviour, but there seemed to be different tendencies and strategies in the attentional, motivational and explorative areas of development.

Researchers have developed an interest in this aspect of children's play as there appears to be an interrelationship between attention, persistence, exploratory behaviour, mastery and competence in development (Messer *et al.*, 1986; Yarrow *et al.*, 1983). In a group of handicapped infants aged 9 to 24 months (six with Down syndrome) Bromwich (1985) noted significant differences in the visual planning/ evaluation aspect of the children's play, such as interest in play, attention span characteristics and capacity, number of schema and schema sequencing actions and characteristics.

Attention to play things

When playing with toys in a contrived laboratory setting, infants and toddlers with Down syndrome were observed to interact with the toys for the same amount of time as the comparison group but focused solely on the toys and spent a limited time showing, seeking help or giving the toys to mother (Krakow and Kopp, 1982). Unlike the comparison children, the toddlers aged 3 to 4 years, with a mean developmental age of 29 months, attended to the same object throughout the session. It was also noted that both infants and toddlers with Down syndrome engaged in seemingly unoccupied looking.

Of particular interest with regard to this 'looking' behaviour are the results of studies into the organization of exploratory playing in children with Down syndrome (MacTurk *et al.*, 1985; Vietze *et al.*, 1983). With several groups of infants with Down syndrome (N = 7 at 6 months; N = 12 at 8 months and N = 3 at 12 months) some of which were included in two of the age samples, Vietze *et al.* (1983) reported that 'looking' tended to reach its peak at 6 months. Progressively, infants advanced to play that explored and they attempted to master objects rather than just look at them, although qualitative differences with normally developing infants were still noted.

In the MacTurk *et al.* (1985) study, exploratory behaviour while playing with toys was assessed over two laboratory sessions . It was observed that the children with Down syndrome (N = 11) looked a great deal and looking was considered the 'hub of their behavioural organisation' (MacTurk *et al.*, 1985, p. 580). There appeared to be transitional patterns in the 'looking' which were reflected in patterns that showed a tendency to return to 'look' after instances of 'off task' or 'explore' behaviour whereas other children returned to social behaviour after either 'off task or 'explore' behaviour.

With older children (mean CA 22.63 months) Ruskin *et al.* (1994) also reported a similar atypical pattern of task exploration in comparison to normally developing children, a backward and forward pattern between high and low levels of exploration. But they found no qualitative differences in the toy play, and particularly noted that children with Down syndrome had a tendency to reject mastery-type toys. With a more complex interaction and manipulation of playthings that could be used in a sequence (Goodman Lock Box), Berry *et al.* (1984) found that preschoolers with Down syndrome were motivated to unlock a door to obtain the toy but seemingly had no desire to relock the door. They speculated that locking the door gave the children no mastery value, or perhaps they had some difficulty with the 'mental representation of a plan of action' (Berry *et al.*, 1984, p. 130). Others had also considered this aspect (Elliott, 1990; Henderson, 1985; MacTurk *et al.*, 1985) and Wishart (1993) has reported that children with Down syndrome appear to have a problem not only in planning actions but also in maintaining and using existing skills to solve problems.

In playing, attention needs to be given not only to the toys but also to the social environment. A study by Landry and Chapieski (1990) examined the attentional patterns of 14 infants with Down syndrome playing with toys alone and then with toys and their mothers. In both situations, the infants demonstrated poor attentional skills which were considered less mature than normal infants and which limited their exploratory behaviour with toys. The researchers commented that the infants appeared to have difficulties in co-ordinating attention to mother and the toy. Cherkes-Julkowski and Gertner (1989) reminded educators of the difficulty of this task for a 'novice' and of the cognitively exhausting consequences of multi-faceted interactions for older children. Perhaps it is not surprising that in play alone at home children with intellectual disabilities have demonstrated more 'peak play' and superior abilities to those they show with others at school (Malone and Stoneman, 1990).

PLAY AS A FEELING; AN EXPRESSION OF JOY AND MASTERY: PLAYING WITH OTHERS

A significant part of children's play involves playing with others. Social play enables children to demonstrate their skills to others and to give expression to their feelings. Some research has indicated that in symbolic play, children with Down syndrome show a particular ability in its socially related aspects with affect 'the force behind play' (Beeghly *et al.*, 1990). Partners in social play can be family members, teachers and peers, and throughout a child's life each group plays an influential role.

Mothers

Mothers are usually an infant's first and most frequent social partner, so many studies have examined the interactional patterns of mothers as they played with their babies and toddlers with Down syndrome. These studies have noted differential responsiveness to the social play of mothers (Gunn *et al.*, 1982; Krakow and Kopp, 1982) a lack of signalling or searching for mother when placed in a stressful situation (Serifaca and Cicchetti, 1976), and problems in shifting attention between toys and people (Legerstee and Bowman, 1989; Kasari *et al.*, 1990).

However social play does progress. Gunn (1982) showed that social play for mothers and their babies with Down syndrome progressed through a variety and range of turn-taking and vocal games. Using Crawley's (1987) play codes in combination with codes for vocal games (raspberries etc.) the researcher demonstrated that tactile play diminished with age and by 13 months there was a marked increase in games with a motor/vocal component such as Peek-a-Boo. The mothers often imitated the child's vocalization and spent much time in teaching these games to their babies. In another study when mothers were asked to engage in four play and two caring sessions with their children (four groups of eight dyads and in the group aged 6 to 30 months, 3 of the dyads had a child with Down syndrome) at home, the researchers noted little difference in the role and style of interaction between teaching and play (McCollum and Stayton, 1988 cited by Marfo, 1991). However, although the mothers' combination style of teaching and playing produced no negative effects, Bray (1988) considered that if it continued, it could lead to feelings of incompetence for the child with Down syndrome during play.

Although for some time there has been a recognition of the importance of the home in early childhood special education (Bronfenbrenner, 1979), there is now a growing movement which incorporates the family into intervention programmes

(Beckman and Bristol, 1991; Garwood *et al.*, 1988; Marfo, 1991). Therefore, it may become increasingly necessary to understand and investigate social play interaction in relation to the styles of interaction and children's competencies. Studies of parents playing with their children with Down syndrome (McConachie, 1991; McConkey and Martin, 1983; Mahoney *et al.*, 1992; Marfo, 1991) and the observational work of preschoolers by Goodman (1992) has suggested that interactions can be positive and successful for the child when the mother's or teacher's play requests are within the child's capabilities. Even so, compliance to a request may still be difficult for the child with Down syndrome (Kopp, 1990). Findings from studies of self-regulation and control may help parents and teachers to facilitate the growth of self-regulating skills through play.

SIBLINGS

In general, sibling research has suggested that non-disabled siblings can gain satisfaction from their ability to play with and care for the sibling with a disability, and both mothers and siblings reported they were 'happy with the way they got along' (McHale *et al.*, 1986).

However, the social interactions of sibling play can often create situations of social dominance and control (Yeatman and Reifel, 1992). Who decides what to play? Who directs the continuation or changes in the play or terminates the play interaction? It has been established in play at home between dyads in which one member has Down syndrome that although the 'handicap did not seem to alter the general nature of sibling interactions ... it does seem to affect the within dimensions of the play' (Abramovitch *et al.*, 1987, p. 875). In particular it was the sibling without the disability regardless of birth order that controlled the play (Abramovitch *et al.*, 1987; Senatapi, 1989).

Using Bronfenbrenner's (1979) concepts of reciprocity, a study which particularly examined this 'balance of power and control' in play was conducted by Bray (1988). This study examined the daily play activities and experiences of ten children with Down syndrome in 40 hours of home observations (also comparison groups matched CA and MA). Bray, like Pepler *et al.* (1984), found that the interactional style of the sibling was adult styled and highly directive and unlike either CA or MA matched style of play. The play to which the child with Down syndrome was directed was often construction or dramatic type activities in order to encourage the perceived necessity of joint play (Pepler *et al.*, 1984).

There is a risk that a directive style of sibling play could produce for the children with Down syndrome an experience of play in which there was a high incidence of negative feeling and affect in power control interactions. They may also experience fewer responses to their infrequent initiations and find it difficult to initiate or counter-attack due to their limited language (Bray, 1988).

Such social interaction experiences for children with Down syndrome have also been reported by Senapati (1989). Her study was designed with two dyad groups, a sibling and a child with Down syndrome who was either older (aged 17 to 35 months) or younger (aged 15 to 26 months) than the sibling. She reported that the older and/or the more competent child generally controlled the play. However, it was interesting to note that within one dyad pair a high level of conflict was produced due to the fact that the older, more competent child was 'not happy' to play with the sibling with Down syndrome and engaged in a high percentage of independent play from which the sibling was excluded.

It would seem that children with Down syndrome interacting in social play settings with their siblings may have an impoverished and negative experience of play, in terms of Bronfenbrenner's transfer of power and control, unless they have a competent and willing partner who allows and encourages play that gives them feelings of control, competency and joy.

Peers and friends

As children progress through childhood, peer relationships and friendships grow and develop incorporating considerable amounts of sharing of knowledge, conversations and activities, as well as caring for each other (Hartup, 1983). Friendships can develop in a child's life as early as 12 months, and these early friendships have significance in a child's future social status. Within stable friendship relationships, children can develop social competencies and often such friendships protect them from the negative effects of peer rejection (Howes, 1983, 1988).

Investigations of children with Down syndrome interacting in play settings with their peers have produced a variety of findings. From videotaped playgroup interactions (Sinson and Wetherick, 1981, 1982) concluded a 'lack of the conventions of mutual gaze' as being responsible for the isolation of the children with Down syndrome. They reported that child after child attempted to interact with the children with Down syndrome and then gave up, leaving the child with Down syndrome physically and socially isolated. One child (Katy) was seemingly without play partners for two years! The researchers questioned the pursuit of integrated settings for children with Down syndrome.

Although it has been acknowledged that sometimes strained relationships and social isolation developed in play settings with their peers (Guralnick, 1990), it is believed that these setting are far more socially stimulating and responsive for children with disabilities than programmes in specialized settings (Beckman and Kohl, 1987; Demchak and Drinkwater, 1992; Field *et al.*, 1982; Guralnick, 1990; Shevin, 1987).

There is some evidence (although limited to structured dyads) that in social play non-disabled preschoolers can accommodate and modify their interactional patterns (especially verbally) to the disabled peer (Guralnick and Paul-Brown, 1980). However, in these dyads the interactional experience for the lower functioning child was that of behavioural requests, whereas the other children participated in questions, mutual interaction and information exchanges!

Expressive language, the use and interpretation of non-verbal expressions and gestures play a role in facilitating play interactions and in fostering friendships and peer relationships. Children with Down syndrome are known to have an expressive language difficulty and there is also doubt about their ability to 'read' the facial and gestural expressions of others.

Loveland (1987) suggested that there was a need for research in this area as there was some uncertainty for the child with Down syndrome in their interpretation of another person's affect, gesture and social behaviour. Given the continuous shifting of affect expressions during normal social interactions (Kasari *et al.*, 1990) and Down syndrome limitations in eye contact patterns (Sinson and Wetherick, 1982), the child with Down syndrome may have difficulty in appraising the people and the situation in which they are playing. Adults with intellectual disability have also been reported to have considerable difficulties in interpreting facial expressions in social contexts. Their recognition of particular affects such as anger and sadness were not accurate, they became confused (Maurer and Newbrough, 1987).

Teachers

Although friendships are a familar aspect of school life, they can not be quantified as commodities in a child's individual education programme (Strully and Strully, 1985) and the idea of social interaction through 'paid friends' limits an individual's experiences and community connections (Amado, 1993). However, peer play needs encouragement as the development of friendships are vital.

Teachers often use peers in teaching children with disabilities. However, using peers to teach social responses has been questioned except when the teaching is related to simple responses in social settings (McHale and Olley, 1982). The teaching of structured social play routines by playmate/s in one setting may not generalize to other play situations. Especially in preschool years, the child with Down syndrome often attends a variety of play setting, and within one week may be asked to cope with a confusing array of social interactional experiences with teachers and peers.

It may be preferable for teachers to provide support rather than to teach routines to students as they interact in playing. One such supports may be to teach *all* the children in the setting or settings a non-verbal signing system. Then their social and representative playing, requests, questions and informational exchanges could take place on a relatively equal footing. Another may be to support the interpersonal aspects of the play. It was demonstrated in a group interaction between low IQ (less than 30) adolescents and their non-handicapped peers that a teacher could facilitate and support the peer interaction by resolving some of the interactional difficulties such as social turn-taking. The play experiences were enhanced and 'yes!' was the answer given to the question, 'Is anyone having fun yet?' (Cole, 1986).

SO WHERE ARE WE NOW?

What is the value of play to players with Down syndrome?

There is considerable evidence that at home and school, children with Down syndrome experience a diminished range and variety of interactional play opportunities and experiences. In a study of 100 families with children under 5 years, Walsh and McConkey (1983) reported that play outside.the home was limited and that the chance to play regularly with other children was lacking for three out of every four children. Once at school, children with Down syndrome frequently played with younger children and relied on their parents to stimulate and maintain their social activities (Sloper *et al.*, 1990). As adults, their leisure tended to be solitary and passive with the family providing friendship (Buckley and Sacks, 1987; Cheseldine and Jeffree, 1981; Jobling, 1989; Reiter and Levi, 1980).

The loneliness that appears to develop in children with Down syndrome cannot be satisfactorily explained, however it must leave the child and young adult themselves with dubious feelings about the value of play as an expression of joy and mastery. Nevertheless, there has been very little research in this area, and many important personal and interpersonal questions with regard to play partners and individuals with Down syndrome need to be addressed (Serifica, 1990).

Unfortunately, it would seem that investigations of play for children with Down syndrome have met few of McConkey's value of play challenges. Play has continued to be 'a causative and predictor variable' (Johnsen, 1991, p. 201), either in research related to deficits in child characteristics or as a tool of intervention and assessment with a focus on the development of play skills, rather than on the play that the children want. As Schwartzman (1991) stated, play for the players has evaporated. In special school classrooms, Shevin (1987, p. 234) noted that play was not valued in its own right, 'Special education practices had been extremely effective in turning special settings into places where play is infrequent and un-relaxed', while unashamedly Sutton-Smith (1987, p. 281), in commenting on Shevin's chapter, suggested that special educators 'consider play as some form of addiction which children are so disposed to that it can be used for their control. The children are, thus, victims of their own need for play'.

Hopefully however, these depressing and pessimistic views of play and children with special needs are reversible. Some restoration may be possible if Smith's (1986, p. 1) suggestion for 'a more balanced and objective view of what play is, what its benefits are, and the role of play in development, education, training, therapy and recreation' can be translated into actions across children's various play environments.

Specifically, here it is considered that more 'balance' may be necessary when theories of play and their relationship to children's lives are translated into educational practices.

First, for the players, there needs to be better 'balance' between the skills required and the challenges presented in the playing. Skills as well as meaningful challenges are considered an important aspect of a player's motivation to continue the 'game'. When a person's skills are held in balance with the challenges of a situation, a behavioural state described as 'Flow' is said to have been reached (Csikszentmihalyi, 1975). Csikszentmihalyi saw the value of play as its potential ability to produce 'Flow' with cognitive abilities not necessarily being a part of this concept. According to Csikszentmihalyi (1988), when a person is involved in a challenging activity that totally involves their skills, there is a feeling of great exhilaration, and an increase in the person's skills enables progress towards other challenges. 'Flow' becomes a reflection of the person's being 'beyond boredom and anxiety' and gives that person a growing sense of fulfilment.

For children with disabilities both Goodman (1992) and Bricker (1992) have considered the necessity of a 'balance' between skills and meaningful challenges. No matter how many exciting possibilities the environment offers, unless the challenges are meaningful (i.e. the child can understand and gain information from them) and are within the child's ability to participate, playing for the child could lead to frustration and anxiety.

Second, there needs to be more 'balance' developed between the role of power and control within the play, as the sense of playing includes both feelings of reciprocity and autonomy. This issue has been discussed previously with regard to the relationships in sibling play but, even when playing more generally, children with Down syndrome must find the play satisfying because it calls upon their personal direction, invention and control (Goodman, 1992, p. 218). Playmates such as parents, teachers, siblings and peers must be prepared to share ideas or directions in the play in order that a balance can be achieved. Constructed involvement and developmental checklists may be too intrusive and controlling for the child to develop his or her interests. Teachers and parents may not be able to play dual roles of play partner as well as instructor and behavioural enforcer (McCollum and Stayton, 1988; Shevin, 1987). Adults, teachers and parents, have different perceptions to children as to what constitutes play and what makes an activity playful for the child (Cunningham and Wiegel, 1992; Sutton-Smith, 1989). Is it possible that children with Down syndrome alone or as onlookers might consider themselves to be playing? As Takhvar (1988, p. 238) aptly stated 'until we can know what the children themselves feel about the orientation of play activities firm conclusions cannot be drawn', and this is particularly pertinent when considering children with Down syndrome.

Third, particularly in educational settings, consideration needs to be given to more 'balance' between the teaching of play skills and the experiences of playing. For children with Down syndrome the 'tools' for gaining value from playing may be in the motor, language and social aspects of development. Yet play should involve more than a series of tasks to be mastered; the child needs to move towards an independence in play not just the next task on a list. Playing offers a wide range of opportunities, some lead to learning new skills, some encourage practice, while others provide novel and affective experiences (Yeatman and Reifel, 1992).

For many young children with Down syndrome, it is often difficult to maintain such a 'balance' as they have busy schedules of appointments and highly structured weeks, and time for playing is limited. However without this 'balance', programmes that provide children and adolescents with only skills training could be considered in play terms as 'instructional imprisonment' while programmes with just experiences (a sort of 'osmosis' approach to learning) could be considered as 'mere entertainment' (Paddick cited by Jobling and Hayes, 1991). It is therefore essential to hasten slowly, as skill development balanced with a range of experiences is worth while and should not be rushed.

Fourth, for the players, a better 'balance' needs to be developed between the demands of the programme and the family's activities. Sensitive thought and a longer-term view should be adopted with regard to playing for children with Down syndrome especially in early childhood settings. There seems to be some urgent need to cram the children's achievements into specific educational time frames and levels of programme expectations on families can be intense. Several educators are now beginning to view a more 'balanced' approach as worthy of serious consideration (Bricker, 1992; Goodman, 1992; Mahoney and Sullivan , 1990). For the family involved in their child's educational programme, some adaptation may be needed in order to achieve a balance between home play and school play as traditional models begin to give way to more family orientated practices (Hanes, 1985; Sloper *et al.*, 1983).

Finally, more 'balance' in playing needs to be restored to the players themselves. In looking beyond the deficit characteristics and the demands of the next developmental milestone acquisition, play has so much to offer for players with Down syndrome throughout their lives. Bruner (1977) advised for the sake of play and its players that in any discussions or investigations of play, it was important to fuse/balance the seriousness of play's role in human development with the enjoyment and hilarity observed in its database as children played. He used the 'play' of Popov the great Russian clown to illustrate his meaning and in this example showed that perhaps Sutton-Smith's (1979) 'fool that might be king' could become one and the same thing.

With these 'balances' in mind, is playing for players with Down syndrome that is directed, constructed, controlled and manipulated across a lifetime, disastrous to the value of play? As Sutton-Smith (1987, p. 289) has so aptly commented:

'What we are all saying to *educators* is that you may do without play but only at a cost to student motivation and vitality . . . these are going to be important resources for the child in the long run as far as their sense of the worthwhileness of life is concerned'.

So for children and adolescents with Down syndrome *do* begin to balance and preserve the excellence within the nature of play itself and let the players play!

REFERENCES

Abramovitch, R., Stanhope, L., Pepler, D. and Corter. C. (1987) The influence of Down syndrome on sibling interaction. *Journal of Child Psychology and Psychiatry*, **28,** pp. 865–79.

Amado, A.N. (ed.) (1993) *Friendship and Community Connections between People with and without Disabilities*, Baltimore: Brookes.

Bailey, D.B. and Wolery, M. (1984) *Teaching Infants and Preschoolers with Handicaps*. Columbus: Merrill.

Beckman, P.J. and Bristol, M.M. (1991) Issues in developing the IFSP: a framework for establishing family outcomes. *Topics in Early Childhood Special Education*, **11** (3), pp. 19–31.

Beckman, P.J. and Kohl, F.L. (1987) Interactions of preschoolers with and without handicap in integrated and segregated settings: a longitudinal study. *Mental Retardation*, **25,** pp. 5–11.

Beeghly, M., Perry, B.W. and Cicchetti, D. (1989). Structural and affective dimensions of play development in young children with Down syndrome. *International Journal of Behavioral Development*, **12,** pp. 257–77.

Beeghly, M., Weiss-Perry, B. and Cicchetti, D. (1990) Beyond sensorimotor functioning: early communication and play development of children with Down syndrome. In D.

Cicchetti and M. Beeghly (eds), *Children with Down Syndrome: a Developmental Perspective*, pp. 329–68 New York: Cambridge University Press.

Bergen, D. (ed.) (1988) *Play as a Medium for Learning and Development: a Handbook of Theory and Practice*. Portsmouth, NH: Heinemann.

Berry, P., Gunn, P. and Andrews, R.J. (1984) The behaviour of Down's syndrome children using the 'lock box': a research note. *Journal of Child Psychology and Psychiatry*, **25**, pp. 125–31.

Bray, D.A. (1988) Social interaction at home of young children with Down syndrome. Paper presented at the 8th World Congress, International Association for the Scientific Study of Mental Deficiency, Dublin, August.

Bricker, D. (1992) The changing nature of communication and language intervention. In S.F. Warren and J. Reichle (eds) *Causes and Effects in Communication and Language Intervention*, pp. 361–76, Baltimore: Brookes.

Bromwich, R.M. (1985) Play behavior of handicapped and non-handicapped infants between 9–24 months. In S. Harel and N.J. Anastasiow (eds), *The at Risk Infant: Psycho/Socio/Medical Aspects*, pp. 379–87. Baltimore: Brookes.

Bronfenbrenner, U. (1979) *The Ecology of Human Development*, Cambridge, MA: Harvard University Press.

Brooks-Gunn, J. and Lewis, M. (1982) Development of play behavior in handicapped and normal infants. *Topics in Early Childhood Special Education*, **2** (3), pp. 14–27.

Bruner, J.S. (1977) Introduction. In B. Tizard and D. Harvey (eds), *Biology of Play*, pp. v–xvi, London: Heinemann Medical.

Buckley, S. and Sacks, B. (1987) *The Adolescent with Down's Syndrome*, Portsmouth: Portsmouth Polytechnic.

Cherkes-Julkowski, M. and Gertner, N. (1989) *Spontaneous Cognitive Processes in Handicapped Children*, New York: Springer-Verlag.

Cheseldine, S.E. and Jeffree, D.M. (1981) Mentally handicapped adolescents: their use of leisure. *Journal of Mental Deficiency Research*, **25**, pp. 49–59.

Christie, J.F. (1986) Training in symbolic play. In P. Smith (ed.), *Children's Play: Research Developments and Practical Applications*, pp. 57–66, London: Gordon and Breach.

Christie, J.F. and Johnsen, E.P. (1985) Questioning the results of play training research. *Educational Psychologist*, **20** (1), pp. 7–11.

Cicchetti, D. and Beeghly, M. (eds) (1990) *Children with Down Syndrome: a Developmental Perspective*, New York: Cambridge University Press.

Cole, D.A. (1986) Facilitating play in children's peer relationships: Are we having fun yet? *American Educational Research Journal*, **23**, pp. 201–15.

Crawley, S.B., Parks Rogers, P., Friedman, S. Iaccobo, M., Citioos, A., Richardson, L. and Thompson, M.A. (1987) Developmental changes in the structure of mother–infant play. *Developmental Psychology*, **14**, pp. 30–6.

Crawley, S.B. and Spiker, D. (1983) Mother-child interactions involving two year olds with Down's syndrome: a look at individual differences. *Child Development*, **54**, pp. 1312–23.

Csikszentmihalyi, M. (1975) *Beyond Boredom and Anxiety*, London: Jossey-Bass.

Csikszentmihalyi, M. and Csikszentmihalyi, I.S. (eds) (1988). *Optimal Experiences: Psychological Experiences: Psychological Studies of flow in consciousness*. New York: Cambridge University Press.

Cunningham, B. and Wiegel, J. (1992) Preschool work and play activities: child and teacher perspectives. *Play and Culture*, **5**, pp. 92–99.

Dalley, M.L. (1985) Physical activity for the very young. *CAHPER Journal*, November/December, pp. 13–17.

Day, C.M. and Parker, R.K. (eds) (1977) *The Preschool in Action: Exploring Early Childhood Programs*, 2nd edn, Boston: Allyn and Bacon.

Demchak, M.A. and Drinkwater, S. (1992) Preschoolers with severe disability: a case against segregation. *Topics in Early Childhood Special Education*, **11**, pp. 70–83.

Eberhard, Y., Eterradossi, J. and Rapacchi, B. (1989) Physical aptitudes to exertion in children with Down's syndrome. *Journal of Mental Deficiency Research*, **33**, pp. 167–74.

Elliott, D. (1990) Movement control and Down's syndrome: a neuropsychological approach. In G. Reid (ed.), *Problems in Movement Control*, pp. 201–16, Amsterdam: North Holland.

Fewell, R.R. and Kaminski, R. (1988) Play skills development and instruction for young children with handicaps. In S.L. Odom and M.B. Karnes (eds), *Early Intervention for Infants and Children with Handicaps*, pp. 145–58, Baltimore: Brookes.

Fewell, R.R. and Oelwein, P.L. (1990) The relationship between time in integrated environments and developmental gains in young children with special needs. *Topics in Early Childhood Special Education*, **10,** pp. 104–16.

Fewell, R.R. and Vadasy, P.F. (1983) *Learning Through Play*. Allen, TX: Developmental Learning Materials.

Field, T., Roseman, S., De Stefano, L.J. and Koewler, J. (1982) The play of handicapped preschool children with handicapped and nonhandicapped peers in integrated and non-integrated situations. *Topics in Early Childhood Special Education*, **2** (3), pp. 28–38.

Fischer, M.A. (1988). The relationship between child initiation and maternal responses in preschool-age children with Down syndrome. In K. Marfo (ed.), *Parent-Child Interaction and Developmental Disabilities*, pp 126–44, New York: Praeger.

Fisher, E.P. (1992) The impact of play on development: a meta-analysis. *Play and Culture*, **5,** pp. 159–81.

Fox, L. and Hanline, M.F. (1993) A preliminary evaluation of learning within developmentally appropriate early childhood settings. *Topics in Early Childhood Special Education*, **13,** pp. 308–27.

Garvey, C. (1977) *Play*. Cambridge, MA: Harvard University Press.

Garwood, S.G. (1982) Piaget and play: translating theory into practice. *Topics in Early Childhood Special Education*, **2** (3), pp. 1–13.

Garwood, S.G., Fewell, R.R. and Neisworth, J.T. (1988) Public Law 94–142: you can get there from here. *Topics in Early Childhood Special Education*, **8,** pp. 1–11.

Gibson, D. (1991) Down syndrome and cognitive enhancement: nor like the others. In K. Marfo (ed.), *Early Intervention in Transition: Current Perspectives on Programs for Handicapped Children*, pp. 61–90, New York: Praeger.

Goodman, J. (1992) *When Slow is Fast Enough*. London: Guildford Press.

Gowen, J.W., Johnson-Martin, N., Goldman, B. and Hussey, B. (1992) Object play and exploration in children with and without disabilities: a longitudinal study. *American Journal on Mental Retardation*, **97,** pp. 21–38.

Gunn, P. (1982) Play and the handicapped child. In B.H. Watts, A.J. Andrews, L. Conrad and J. Calder.(eds), *Early Intervention Programs for Young Handicapped Children in Australia 1979–1980*, pp. 147–55, Canberra: Australian Government Publishing Service.

Gunn, P. and Berry, P. (1989) Education of infants with Down syndrome. *European Journal of Psychology of Education*, **4,** pp. 235–46.

Gunn, P., Berry, P. and Andrews, R.J. (1981) The affective response of Down's syndrome infants to a repeated event. *Child Development*, **52,** pp. 745–48.

Gunn, P., Berry, P. and Andrews, R.J. (1982) Looking behavior of Down syndrome infants. *American Journal on Mental Deficiency*, **87,** pp. 344–47.

Guralnick, M. (1990) Major accomplishments and future directions in early childhood mainstreaming. *Topics in Early Childhood Special Education*, **10** (2), pp. 1–17.

Guralnick, M. (1993) Developmentally appropriate practice in the assessment and intervention of children's peer relations. *Topics in Early Childhood Special Education*, **13,** pp. 344–71.

Guralnick, M. and Groom, J.M. (1988) Friendships of preschool children in mainstreamed playgroups. *Developmental Psychology*, **24,** pp. 595–604.

Guralnick, M.J. and Paul-Brown, D. (1980) Functional and discourse analyses of non-handicapped preschool children's speech to handicapped children. *American Journal of Mental Deficiency*, **84,** pp. 444–54.

Guralnick, M.J. and Weinhouse, E. (1984) Peer-related social interactions of developmentally delayed young children: development and characteristics. *Developmental Psychology*, **20,** pp. 815–27.

Hanes, M.L. (1985) Parent training: an overview and synthesis. In S. Harel and N.J. Anastasiow (eds), *The at Risk Infant: Psycho/Socio/Medical Aspects*, pp. 13–18, Baltimore: Brookes.

Harel, S. and Anastasiow, N.J. (eds), (1985) *The at Risk Infant: Psycho/Socio/Medical Aspects*, Baltimore: Brookes.

Harris, S. and Shea, A.M. (1984) Down syndrome. In S.K. Campbell (ed.), *Paediatric Neurologic Physical Therapy*, 2nd edn, pp. 131–68, Edinburgh: Churchill Livingstone.

Hartup, W.W. (1983) The peer system. In E.M. Hetherington (ed.), *Handbook of Child Psychology: Vol 4. Socialization, Personality and Social Development*, pp. 163–96, New York: Wiley

Henderson, S. (1985) Motor skill development. In D. Lane and B. Stratford (eds), *Current Approaches to Down's Syndrome*, pp. 187–218, London: Holt, Rinehart and Winston.

Hodapp, R.M. and Dykens, E.M. (1991) Towards an etiology-specific strategy of early intervention with handicapped children. In K. Marfo (ed.), *Early Intervention in Transition: Current Perspectives on Programs for Handicapped Children*, pp. 41–61, New York: Praeger.

Hogg, J. and Moss, S.C. (1983) Prehensile development in Down's syndrome and non-handicapped preschool children. *British Journal of Developmental Psychology*, **1**, pp. 189–204.

Holme, R.M. (1992) Play during snacktime. *Play and Culture*, **5**, pp. 295–304.

Howes, C. (1983) Patterns of friendship. *Child Development*, **54**, pp. 1041–53.

Howes, C. (1988) Peer interactions of young children. *Monographs of the Society for Research in Child Development*, **53** (1, Serial No. 217).

Hulme, I. and Lunzer, E.A. (1966) Play, language and reasoning in subnormal children. *Journal of Child Psychology and Psychiatry*, **7**, pp. 107–23.

Hunter, D. (1984) Social constraints on play behavior of the disabled person. *Leisurability*, **11** (4), pp. 8–12.

Jeffree, D.M. and McConkey, R. (1976) An observation scheme for recording children's imaginative doll play. *Journal of Child Psychology and Psychiatry*, **17**, pp. 189–97.

Jens, K.G. and Johnson. N.M. (1982) Affective development: a window to cognition in young handicapped children. *Topics in Early Childhood Special Education*, **2** (2), pp. 17–24.

Jobling, A. (1988) The 'play' focus in early intervention: Children with intellectual disabilities. *The Exceptional Child*, **35**, pp. 119–124.

Jobling, A. (1989) Leisure, recreation and residence. In P. Gunn and J. Bramley (eds), *Adolescent Girls with Intellectual Disabilities: School and Post-School Options*, pp. 89–110, St. Lucia: Fred and Eleanor Schonell Special Education Research Centre.

Jobling, A. and Gunn, P. (1995) The motor development of children and adolescents with Down syndrome. In A. Vermeer and W.E. Davis (eds), *Physical and Motor Development in Mental Retardation*, pp. 181–90, Basel: Karger AG.

Jobling, A. and Hayes, A. (1991) Integrating recreation into educational programmes for persons with Down syndrome. In C. Denholm (ed.), *Adolescents with Down syndrome: International Perspectives on Research and Programme Development*, pp. 175–82, Victoria, BC: University of Victoria.

Johnsen, E.P. (1991) Searching for social and cognitive outcomes in children's play: selective second look. *Play and Culture*, **4**, pp. 201–13.

Kasari, C., Mundy, P., Yirmiya, N. and Sigman, M. (1990) Affect and attention in children with Down syndrome. *American Journal on Mental Retardation*, **95**, pp. 55–67.

Katz, R.C. and Singh, N.N. (1986) Increasing recreational behavior in mentally retarded children. *Behavior Modification*, **10**, pp. 508–19.

Kim, T.Y., Lombardino, L.J., Rothman, H. and Vinson, B. (1989) Effects of symbolic play intervention with children who have mental retardation. *Mental Retardation*, **27**, pp. 159–65.

Knieps, L.J., Walden, T.A. and Baxter, A. (1994) Affective expressions of toddlers with and without Down syndrome in a social referencing context. *American Journal on Mental Retardation*, **99**, pp. 301–12.

Kopp, C. (1990) The growth of self-monitoring among young children with Down syndrome. In D. Cicchetti and M. Beeghly (eds), *Children with Down Syndrome: a Developmental Perspective*, pp. 231–51, New York: Cambridge University Press.
Krakow, J.B. and Kopp, C.B. (1982) Sustained attention in young Down syndrome children. *Topics in Early Childhood Special Education*, **2** (2), pp. 32–42.
Krakow, J.B. and Kopp, C.B. (1983) The effects of developmental delay on sustained attention in young children. *Child Development*, **54,** pp. 1143–55.
Landry S.H. and Chapieski, M.L. (1990) Joint attention of six month old Down syndrome and preterm infants: I. attention to toys and mother. *American Journal on Mental Retardation*, **94,** pp. 488–98.
LaVeck, B. and Brehm, S.S. (1978) Individual variability among children with Down's syndrome. *Mental Retardation*, **16**, pp. 135–37.
Legerstee, M. and Bowman, T.G. (1989) The development of responses to people and a toy in infants with Down's syndrome. *Infant Behavior and Development*, **12,** pp. 465–77.
Lerner, J., Mardell-Czudnowski, C. and Goldenberg, D. (1987) *Special Education for Early Childhood Years*, Englewood Cliffs: Prentice-Hall.
Li, A.K.F. (1981) Play and the mentally retarded child. *Mental Retardation*, **19,** pp. 121–26.
Linford, A.G. and Duthie, J.H. (1970) The use of operant technology to induce sustained exertion in young trainable Down's syndrome children. In G. Kenyon (ed.), *Contemporary Sports Psychology*, pp. 515–21; Chicago: Athletic Institute.
Lobato, D. (1983) Siblings of handicapped children: a review. *Journal of Autism and Developmental Disabilities*, **13,** pp. 347–65.
Lobato, D., Barbour, L., Hall, L.J. and Miller, C.T. (1987) Psychosocial characteristics of preschool siblings of handicapped and non-handicapped children. *Journal of Abnormal Childhood Psychology*, **15,** pp. 329–38.
Losardo, A. and Bricker, D. (1994) Activity-based intervention and direct instruction: a comparison study. *American Journal on Mental Retardation*, **98,** pp. 744–65.
Loveland, K. (1987) Behavior of young children with Down's syndrome before the mirror: Finding things reflected. *Child Development*, **58,** pp. 928–36.
McCollum, J.A. and Stayton, V. (1988) Gaze patterns of mothers and infants as indicators of role integration during play and teaching with toys. In K. Marfo (ed.), *Parent-Child Interaction and Developmental Disabilities*, pp. 47–63, New York: Praeger.
McConachie, H.R. (1991) Home-based teaching: what are we asking of parents? *Child: Care, Health and Development*, **17,** pp. 123–36.
McConkey, R. (1985) Play. In D. Lane and B. Stratford (eds), *Current Approaches to Down Syndrome*, pp. 282–314, London: Holt, Rinehart and Winston.
McConkey, R. (1986) Changing beliefs about play and handicapped children. In P.K. Smith (ed.), *Children's Play: Research Developments and Practical Applications*, pp. 91–106, London: Gordon and Breach.
McConkey, R. and Martin, H. (1983) Mothers' play with toys: A longitudinal study with Down's syndrome infants. *Child: Care, Health and Development*, **9,** pp. 215–26.
McHale, S.M. and Gamble, W.C. (1989) Sibling relationships of children with disabled and nondisabled brothers and sisters. *Developmental Psychology*, **25,** pp. 421–29.
McHale, S.M. and Olley, J.G. (1982) Using play to facilitate the social development of handicapped children. *Topics in Early Childhood Special Education*, **2** (3), pp. 76–86.
McHale, S.M., Sloan, J. and Simeonsson, R.J. (1986). Sibling relationships of children with autistic, mentally retarded and non-handicapped brothers and sisters. *Journal of Autism and Developmental Disorders*, **16,** pp. 399–413.
MacTurk, R.H., Vietze, R.M., McCarthy, M.E., McQuiston, S. and Yarrow, L.J. (1985) The organisation of exploratory behavior in Down syndrome and non-delayed infants. *Child Development*, **56**, pp. 573–81.
Mahoney, G., O'Sullivan, P. and Robinson, C. (1992) The family environments of children with disabilities: diverse but not so different. *Topics in Early Childhood Special Education*, **12,** pp. 386–402.
Mahoney, G., Robinson, C. and Powell, A. (1992) Focusing on parent-child interaction: the

bridge to developmentally appropriate practices. *Topics in Early Childhood Special Education*, **12**, pp. 105–20.

Mahoney, G. and Sullivan, P. (1990) Early intervention practices with families of children with handicaps. *Mental Retardation*, **28**, pp. 169–76.

Malone, D., and Stoneman, Z. (1990) Cognitive play of mentally retarded preschoolers: observations in the home land school. *American Journal on Mental Retardation*, **94**, pp. 475–87.

Marfo, K. (ed.) (1988) *Parent-Child Interaction and Developmental Disabilities*, New York: Praeger.

Marfo, K. (ed.) (1991) *Early Intervention in Transition: Current Perspectives on Programs for Handicapped Children*, New York: Praeger.

Marfo, K. and Kysela, G.M. (1988) Frequency and sequential patterns in mothers' interactions with mentally handicapped and non-handicapped children. In K. Marfo (ed.), *Parent-Child Interaction and Developmental Disabilities*, pp. 64–89, New York: Praeger.

Maurer, H. and Newbrough, J.R. (1987) Facial expressions of mentally retarded and non-retarded children: recognition by mentally retarded and non-retarded adults. *American Journal of Mental Deficiency*, **91**, pp. 505–10.

Messer, D.J., McCarthy, M.E., McQuiston, S., MacTurk, R.H., Yarrow, L.J. and Vietze, P.M. (1986) Relation between mastery behavior in infancy and competency in early childhood. *Developmental Psychology*, **22**, pp. 366–72.

Mogford, K. (1977) The play of handicapped children. In B. Tizard and D. Harvey (eds), *Biology of play*, pp. 170–84, London: Heinemann Medical.

Motti, F., Cicchetti, D. and Sroufe, L.A. (1983) From infant affect expression to symbolic play: the coherence of development in Down's syndrome children. *Child Development*, **54**, pp. 1168–75.

Mundy, P., Sigman, M., Kasari, C. and Yirmiya, N. (1988) Nonverbal communication skills in Down's syndrome children. *Child Development*, **59**, pp. 235–49.

Odom, S.L. and Karnes, M.B. (eds) (1988) *Early Intervention for Infants and Children with Handicaps*, Baltimore: Brookes.

Odom, S.L. and Warren, S.F. (1988) Early childhood special education in the year 2000. *Journal of the Division for Early Childhood*, **12**, pp. 263–73.

Pepler, D., Stanthorpe, L. and Crozier, K. (1984) Play with Down's syndrome siblings: what's the difference? *Leisurability*, **11** (4), pp. 19–26.

Pieterse, M., Bochner, S. and Bettison, S. (eds), *Early Intervention for Children with Disabilities: the Australian Experience*, Sydney: Special Education Centre, Macquarie University.

Reader, L. (1984) Pre-school intervention programmes. *Child: Care, Health and Development*, **10**, pp. 237–51.

Reiters, S. and Levi, A.M. (1980) Factors affecting social integration of noninstitutionalized MR adults. *American Journal of Mental Deficiency*, **85**, pp. 25–30.

Rogers, S.J. (1988) Cognitive characteristics of handicapped children's play: a review. *Journal of the Division for Early Childhood*, **12**, pp. 161–68.

Rubin, K.H. (1980) *New Directions for Child Development: Children's Play*, San Francisco: Jossey-Bass.

Ruskin, E.M., Mundy, P., Kasari, C. and Sigman, M. (1994) Object mastery motivation of children with Down syndrome. *American Journal on Mental Retardation*, **98**, pp. 499–509.

Rynders, J.E. and Horrobin, J.M. (1990) Always trainable? Never educable? Updating educational expectations concerning children with Down syndrome. *American Journal on Mental Retardation*, **95**, pp. 77–83.

Schaefer, C.E. and O'Connor, K.J. (eds) (1983) *Handbook of Play Therapy*, New York: Wiley.

Schlottmann, R.S. and Anderson, V.H. (1975) Social and play behaviors of institutionalized mongoloid and nonmongoloid retarded children. *Journal of Psychology*, **91**, pp. 201–06.

Schwartzman, H.B. (1978) *The Anthropology of Children's Play*, New York: Plenum.

Schwartzman, H.B. (1991) Imagining play. *Play and Culture*, **4**, pp. 214–22.

Senapati, R. (1989) Sibling relationship of disabled children: A study of play, prosocial and conflict behaviour, and teaching between siblings. Unpublished doctoral dissertation, Schonell Special Education Research Centre, University of Queensland, Brisbane.

Senapati, R. and Hayes, A. (1988) Siblings of handicapped children: a review. *Australian Journal of Early Childhood*, **13** (2), pp. 33–37.

Serafica, F.C. (1990) Peer relations of children with Down's syndrome. In D. Cicchetti and M. Beeghly (eds), *Children with Down Syndrome: a Developmental Perspective*, pp. 369–98, New York: Cambridge University Press.

Serafica, F.C. and Cicchetti, D. (1976) Down's syndrome children in a strange situation: attachment and explorative behaviors. *Merrill-Palmer Quarterly*, **22**, pp. 137–49.

Shevin, M. (1987) Play in special school settings. In J. Block and N. King (eds), *School Play: a Source Book*, pp. 219–51, New York: Garland.

Sinson, J.C. and Wetherick, N.E. (1981) The behavior of children with Down syndrome in normal groups. *Journal of Mental Deficiency Research*, **15**, pp. 113–20.

Sinson, J.C. and Wetherick, N.E. (1982) Mutual gaze in pre-school Down's and normal children. *Journal of Mental Deficiency Research*, **26,**, pp. 123–29.

Sloper, P., Cunningham, C.C. and Arnljotsdottir, M. (1983) Parental reactions to early intervention with their Down's syndrome infants. *Child: Care, Health and Development*, **9**, pp. 357–76.

Sloper, P., Turner, S., Knussen, C. and Cunningham, C. (1990) Social life of school children with Down's syndrome. *Child: Care, Health and Development*, **16**, pp. 235–51.

Smith, P.K. (ed.) (1986) *Children's Play: Research Developments and Practical Applications*, London: Gordon and Breach.

Smith, P.K. and Syddall, S. (1978) Play and non-play tutoring in pre-school children: is it play or tutoring that matters? *British Journal of Educational Psychology*, **48**, pp. 315–25.

Stevenson, H.W. and Siegel, A.E. (1984) *Child Development Research and Social Policy*, vol. 1, Chicago: University of Chicago Press.

Stevenson, M.B., Leavitt, L.A. and Silverberg, S.B. (1985) Mother-infant interaction: down syndrome case studies. In S. Harel and N.J. Anastasiow (eds), *The at Risk Infant: Psycho/Socio/Medical Aspects*, pp. 389–95, Baltimore: Brookes.

Stoneman, Z., Brody, G.E. and MacKinnon, C. (1984) Naturalistic observations of children's activities and roles while playing with their siblings and friends. *Child Development*, **55**, pp. 617–27.

Strully, J. and Strully, C. (1985) Friendship and our children. *Journal of the Association for Persons with Severe Handicaps*, **10**, pp. 224–27.

Sutton-Smith, B. (1979) *Play and learning*, New York: Gardner.

Sutton-Smith, B. (1987) School play: a commentary. In J. Block and N. King (eds), *School Play: a Source Book*, pp. 277–89, New York: Garland.

Sutton-Smith, B. (1989) Reversible childhood. *Play and Culture*, **2**, pp. 52–63.

Takhvar, M. (1988) Play and theories of play: a review of the literature. *Early Child Development and Care*, **39**, pp. 221–44.

Tannock, R. (1988) Mothers' directiveness in their interactions with their children with and without Down's syndrome. *American Journal on Mental Retardation*, **93**, pp. 154–65.

Tannock, R. and Girolametto, L. (1992) Reassessing parent-focused language intervention programs. In S.F. Warren and J. Reichle (eds), *Causes and Effects in Communication and Language Intervention*, pp. 49–80, Baltimore: Brookes.

Titus, J.A. and Watkinson, E.J. (1987) Effects of segregated and integrated programs on the participation and social interaction of moderately mentally handicapped children in play. *Adapted Physical Activity Quarterly*, **4**, pp. 204–19.

Tizard, B. and Harvey, D. (eds) (1977) *Biology of Play*, London: Heinemann Medical.

Tizard, B., Philips. J. and Plewis, I. (1976) Play in pre-school centres: 1. play measures and their relation to age, sex and IQ. *Journal of Child Psychology and Psychiatry*, **17**, pp. 251–64.

Vietz, P., McCarthy, M., McQuiston, S., MacTurk, R. and Yarrow, L.J. (1983) Attention and exploratory behavior in infants with Down's syndrome. In T. Field and A. Sostek (eds), *Infants Born at Risk*, pp. 251–68, New York: Grune and Stratton.

Wade, M.G. (1973) Biorhythms and activity of institutionalized mentally retarded persons diagnosed hyperactive. *American Journal of Mental Deficiency*, **78,** pp. 262–267.

Warren, S.F. and Reichle, J. (eds) (1992) *Causes and Effects in Communication and Language Intervention*, Baltimore: Brookes.

Watkinson, E.J. and Muloin, S. (1988) Playground skills of moderately mentally handicapped youngsters in integrated elementary schools. *The Mental Retardation and Learning Disability Bulletin*, **16** (2), pp. 3–13.

Wehman, P. (1977) *Helping the Mentally Retarded Acquire Play Skills*, Springfield: Thomas.

Wilson, J., Blacher, J. and Baker, B.L. (1989) Siblings of children with severe handicaps. *Mental Retardation*, **27,** pp. 167–73.

Wishart, J.G. (1986) Siblings as models in early infant learning. *Child Development*, **57,** pp. 1232–40.

Wishart, J.G. (1993) The development of learning difficulties in children with Down's syndrome. *Journal of Intellectual Disability Research* **37,** pp. 389–403.

Yarrow, L.J., McQuiston, S., MacTurk, R.H., McCarthy, M.E., Klein, R.P. and Vietze, P.M. (1983) Assessment of mastery motivation during the first year of life: contemporaneous and cross-age relationships. *Developmental Psychology*, **19,** pp. 159–71.

Yawkey, T.D. (1982) Effects of parents' play routines on imaginative play in their developmentally delayed preschoolers. *Topics in Early Childhood Special Education*, **2** (3), pp. 66–75.

Yawkey, T.D. and Pelligrini, A.D. (eds) (1984) *Child's Play: Developmental and Applied*, Hillsdale: Erlbaum.

Yeatman, J. and Reifel, S. (1992) Sibling play and learning. *Play and Culture*, **5,** pp. 141–58.

Yoder, P.J., Kaiser, A.P. and Alpert, C.L. (1991) An exploratory study of the interaction between language teaching methods and child characteristics. *Journal of Speech and Hearing Research*, **34,** pp. 155–67.

Zetlin, A. (1986) Mentally retarded adults and their siblings. *American Journal on Mental Retardation*, **91,** pp. 217–25.

15 Language and Speech

Pat Gunn and Mary Crombie

For many years, it has been reported that the language of individuals with Down syndrome is slow to develop, both in comparison with others and in comparison with other domains of their own development. (motor, social, cognitive). Nevertheless, the language is not unique or deviant and it seems to be a product of the same rules that govern normal language. It has also been observed that there is an inconsistency in the spontaneous use of a new structure. If this is regarded as an instability associated with a transition in development, this too seems not to be unique to the syndrome (see Thelen and Smith, 1994, for a dynamic systems view of development). Finally, considerable variability in competence has been reported.

Recent studies have been in general agreement with these conclusions although there is now a sharper focus on the asynchronies of development (between language and other domains of development, and within language itself). There is also some interest in individual variability with a recognition of the limitations in group results and the need for longitudinal case studies.

ASYNCHRONIES IN DEVELOPMENT

It has been reported that language skills do not develop in synchrony with other domains of development. There has been most interest in language-cognition comparisons, although slowness in comparison with motor and social development has also been investigated.

Typical findings include those by Smith and von Tetzchner (1986) who found that at 3 years chronological age (CA), their sample of 13 children with Down syndrome was significantly more delayed on the Gesell language subscales than the remaining subscales. In another study, children with Down syndrome with a non-verbal mental age of 2 years performed at the fiftieth to sixtieth percentile for the 2 year norms of Lee's Developmental Sentence Scoring procedure while those with MA 3 to 6 years performed at the tenth to fifteenth percentile for the 3 to 6 year age norms (Wiegel-Crump, 1981). Syntax less complex than expected for developmental level and lower standardized scores at higher mental ages suggests that the syntactic language skills of children with Down syndrome fail to keep pace with increasing cognitive development. Although this conclusion is weakened by the cross-sectional nature of the study, it is compatible with the results of other recent studies including those by Fowler (1990), Miller (1988), and Rondal (1988).

Researchers who have used comparisons between different assessment instruments include Miller (1988) who compared various receptive and expressive language scales with an MA on the Stanford Binet. These early studies were concerned with spoken language only and signed words were not included until later studies (Miller *et al.*, 1992). There was no typical profile of scores for all the children with Down syndrome (n = 56; CA 10 months to 5 years) but half the group were delayed (in comparison with the Stanford Binet scores) in productive but not receptive language. The delay between MA and productive vocabulary became progressively larger with age. In another cross-sectional study reporting a gap between MA and language which increased with age, Cunningham *et al.* (1985) used a play scale, the Stanford-Binet, and the Reynell language scales. There are psycho-metric difficulties in comparing scores on tests that have been standardized on different populations and there are limitations in the use of age equivalent scores to indicate an increased gap over time. The gap must necessarily increase if one measure develops at a consistent but slower rate than the other. Also, the necessity of including signed vocabulary with spoken words has been underlined by Miller *et al.* (1992).

Miller (1988) extended his previous study to undertake a series of comparisons which controlled either for mental age (MA) or mean length of utterance (MLU). In the first small sample study, children with Down syndrome, CA 24 to 36 months, matched to a control group on MA, produced significantly fewer words and only the children in the control group produced multiword sentences. In a second study of the conversational interactions of 12 children with Down syndrome (MA = 36 months), Miller applied Ingram's productivity index (a word had to be used in at least two different utterances, each with different words preceding and following the target word). He found that the children had lower productivity scores than a control group, matched on MA. The MLU for the group with Down syndrome at 1.6 was also much lower than the control group MLU of 3.6.

These results agreed with the lag between vocabulary and cognitive development which had been reported at the one-word stage by Cardoso-Martins *et al.* (1985). These researchers found that acquisition progress in both the production and comprehension of object names was slower for their Down syndrome group than for a non-delayed group even when the rate of sensori-motor cognitive develop-ment was considered. They pointed out that children need to acquire a considerable number of words before syntactic acquisition begins and concluded that a delay in vocabulary acquisition would impact on the development of syntactic skills.

Miller continued his previous investigations with a third study which did not match on MA but did instead on MLU. He matched 30 children with Down syndrome to a control group on three different MLU levels, 1.2, 1.4, 1.7. He now found no sig-nificant difference between the groups on the number of productive words at any MLU level. A more surprising finding was that the children with Down syndrome produced significantly more, different words. Although surprising, it confirmed Rondal's earlier conclusions of a higher type-token ratio (Rondal 1978).

Overall, these studies suggest that there is an asynchrony between cognitive development and the productive language of children with Down syndrome, and between the development of vocabulary and syntax in this language.

In another study which pointed to divergence between various components of language, Harris (1983) compared the language of ten Down syndrome with ten non-delayed children matched on MLU. At the start of the study, the children were using predominantly single-word utterances but some longer phrases. The group with Down syndrome ranged in age from 2 years 6 months to 2 years 9 months (boys) and 3 years 7 months to 4 years 11 months (girls). The language of the children with Down syndrome closely resembled the language of the non-delayed younger children of the same MLU with regard to primary semantic relations (e.g. agent and action, action and object) but Harris reported that there were several areas where the children with Down syndrome exhibited differences. He found a higher proportion of different words, agreeing with Rondal that the language at this stage of children with Down syndrome has a higher type token ratio. He also found other differences regarding self-repetition and rote utterances but concluded that 'These data point to variations in the extent to which the two groups were organizing and coordinating the various component skills of language, rather than to qualitative differences among the sub-skills themselves' (Harris, 1983, p. 163).

The previous studies were concerned with productive language but a similar conclusion was reached in a study of syntactic comprehension. Bridges and Smith (1984) matched children with Down syndrome to comparison children on the basis of verbal comprehension age on the Reynell Developmental Language Scale. The children used small toys to act out active or passive test sentences which the experimenter read to them. The results supported the proposition that there are no fundamental differences between children with Down syndrome and non-delayed children with respect to comprehension processes. However, there was evidence of a slight delay in the acquisition of syntactic strategies in comparison with receptive vocabulary development.

In discussing the possibility that some results are an artefact of the test used for matching comparison groups, Chapman *et al.* (1991) suggested that this delay would have seemed larger if the matching had been restricted to a vocabulary test rather than the Reynell which includes both vocabulary and syntactic items. These researchers used two subtests of the fourth edition of the Stanford-Binet, bead memory and pattern analysis, in order to match on a measure of non verbal development. The mean of these subtests was taken as an indication of mental age. Age equivalent scores on vocabulary (Peabody Picture Vocabulary Test – Revised) were found to be more advanced than scores on syntax comprehension tests (Test for Auditory Comprehension – Revised)for adolescents with Down syndrome. The advantage increased with age and was significantly greater than the difference in the scores of the control group who were matched on the Stanford Binet, 4th ed. scores and Socio-economic status. Multiple regression analyses showed that chronological age (CA) and MA accounted for about 80 per cent of the variance in both Peabody Picture Vocabulary Test–Revised and Test for Auditory Comprehension – Revised scores. Mild hearing loss accounted for another 4 per cent.

It was suggested that studies which match on a non-verbal test with minimum memory demands such as the Columbia Mental Maturity Test or the Leiter (e.g. Rosin *et al.*, 1988) may find a deficit in syntax comprehension but no evidence of vocabulary advanced for MA.

The delay in syntactic development has been the focus of several studies by Fowler and her colleagues (Fowler, 1990; Fowler *et al.*, 1994). In reporting a cross-sectional study of four moderately retarded adolescents (CA 10.9 to 13.0 yrs) and a longitudinal study of one young girl, Rebecca, from 51 to 89 months of age, Fowler *et al.*(1994) noted a slowdown at Stage III (Brown, 1973) of language development in both the adolescents and the younger child. At this stage of normal development, some closed class vocabulary (pronouns, prepositions, articles, inflectional morphemes) have been developed but more complex constructions are acquired later. Rebecca' s progress from Stage I (when children begin to use more than one word in their utterances) to Stage III was 'strikingly normal' but her progress then slowed and she made little and erratic progress.

Analyses of her language structures showed that these appeared to be similar to those of normally developing children at the same language stage (although as Lahey, 1994, reminded, we do not have normative morpheme acquisition data on a large enough sample of children). For both the four adolescents and Rebecca, syntactic development seemed to be internally coherent with consistency between the development of MLU, grammatical morphology and syntactic constructions. The researchers concluded that the same processes of acquisition are evident in the grammar constructed by children with Down syndrome but they emphasized that the absolute levels achieved are very low, with few attaining beyond the simple phrase-structure grammar of a normal 2-year-old.

Although their study assessed language production only, this conclusion is in agreement with Fowler (1990) who found that individuals with Down syndrome also show a problem with the comprehension of syntax and a ceiling in its development. She argued that the ceiling in syntactic development cannot be attributed to puberty as Lenneberg *et al.* (1964) had proposed but is due, rather, to an increasing complexity in the linguistic structures. There seems to be a hurdle over which only a few with Down syndrome can jump and the hurdle arises from new linguistic demands. As Fowler *et al.* (1994, p. 135) remarked, 'It is difficult to ignore the fact that the stopping point in this group of children precedes the dramatic growth in syntactic development that has captured the imagination of linguists'.

The proposal of a ceiling in grammatical competence has been refuted by Chapman *et al.* (1992) who argued that adolescents with Down syndrome do show an advance in grammatical skills and that these may not be found in the free play and conversational settings used in the Fowler studies. In addition to a six-minute conversation sample, these researchers collected a 12-minute narrative sample in which an interviewer asked 49 children and adolescents with Down syndrome, 5 to 20 years of age, about pictures, photos from home, video events etc. Instead of a plateau in MLU, Chapman *et al.* (1992) found that the older participants, 16 to 20 years of age, had a higher MLU than the younger adolescents for both narrative and conversation. If the study had collected only a conversation sample for the age range 5 to 16 years, they would have concluded (wrongly) that there had been no syntactic progress.

Chapman *et al.* (1992) then compared the language of the two older groups with MLU and SES matched normal controls. In agreement with earlier reports, they found some evidence of a grammatical morpheme deficit, particularly with respect to closed class categories. They argued that intervention would be beneficial for some adolescents with Down syndrome and that intervention should focus on the use of complex sentences and grammatical morphemes.

COMMUNICATIVE SKILLS

Because of the significance of language for communication with others, several studies have investigated the synchrony between communicative skills and developmental level. These studies have used structured tasks to elicit declarative and imperative responses or have observed the child during interactions with another person (usually the caregiver).

Smith and von Tetzchner (1986) reported that the frequency of prespeech vocalizations and performance on declarative tasks in 2-year-old children with Down syndrome was below that of younger children matched on MA and sensorimotor level. On the other hand, several studies of older children at the one-word stage of development have shown no significant differences from comparison children matched on Stage I of language development (MLU of 1 to 2 morphemes) with regard to their communicative intentions or clarification strategies (Coggins *et al.*, 1983; Coggins and Stoel-Gammon, 1982; Owens and MacDonald, 1982).

In one of the first studies to investigate early pragmatic behaviours in Down syndrome, Greenwald and Leonard (1979) found that the correspondence between these behaviours and sensorimotor abilities was influenced by chronological age. The older children in their study (mean age of 3 years 4 months) sometimes used words rather than gestures or vocalizations to encode their intentions despite being at a pre-symbolic stage of development.

It has been suggested that this asynchrony between communicative abilities and other aspects of development arises from the greater length of time the child with Down syndrome remains at the same stage of development. Pragmatic deficits may be evidenced at very young ages but older children with Down syndrome will have participated in communicative exchanges for much longer than MLU matched children. It is not uncommon to find that their exchanges cover a wider range of topics and conversational strategies although these may include gestures and signing as well as spoken words.

The acquisition of conversational response skills when responding to questions from mother was investigated by Leifer and Lewis (1984). There were three groups of children, one of non-delayed children (CA 18 to 23 months) matched with two MLU in the other (CA from 3.5 years to 4.5 years). As expected, the children with Down syndrome showed delayed response performance in comparison with the non-delayed children of the same CA. However, when matched on MLU, the children with Down syndrome demonstrated significantly greater response abilities than their matched peers. Miller (1987) queries the use of MLU at an early Stage I level of development (one word) and contended that, as a measure of production, it was not an appropriate match in a study of response performance. He interpreted the results as showing that the children had comprehension skills more advanced than their production skills.

The children's use of sign language was not considered but Wootton (1991) took signs into account when investigating the nature of child responses to parental offers. These included offering to give or get an object, or to perform an activity for the child (CA between 3 and 4 years). The research specifically distinguished an offer from a request and excluded non-verbal offers. In general, it was concluded that the repertoire of responses was similar to that of children of the same developmental age (Reynell comprehension age between 1,1 and 2,1 years) but that gaze patterns may be an important component of child responses.

A more recent study which matched on both the Vineland and Reynell scales reported that the children with Down syndrome (age 21 to 47 months) had poor expressive verbal language but they were competent in the use of declarative pointing (Franco and Wishart, 1995). They also made more visual checks as they grew older and they checked more with an age mate with Down syndrome than with their mothers. The authors suggested that this multichecking may be a consequence of the child's experience with failed messages but whatever the cause, it seems to indicate the child's recognition of the need to monitor a social partner. In particular, these children seemed to be more aware of this need with a less competent (or less familiar) partner.

Another finding from this study was that although children used declarative pointing they produced few request gestures. This agreed with Mundy *et al.*'s (1988) report that although 18 to 48 month old children with Down syndrome showed high frequencies of social interaction behaviours, they showed a significant deficit in non-verbal requesting skill relative to MA matched children. The results of that study also suggested that the deficit was related to the late development of expressive language. In discussing the possible reasons for the few requests for objects, the researchers suggested that children with Down syndrome may be less motivated than other children to obtain and explore objects. Franco and Wishart (1995) discussed the possibility that this low motivation results from repeated experiences of interactive failure which lead the child to believe that requests will be misunderstood or rejected.

A study by Beeghly *et al.* (1990) with slightly older children found that the deficit in requesting behaviour was also evident in speech acts. Fewer requests were made in comparison with an MA matched group.

The interpretation of these communication studies depends on whether groups are matched on MA or on a linguistic measure. Although Beeghly *et al.* (1990) noted a deficit in requesting speech acts in comparison with MA matched controls, there was no significant difference from the MLU matched group. Of importance is their finding that for both groups, MA and communicative skills improved as MLU increased from early Stage I (MLU 1.01 to 1.49) to late Stage 1 (MLU 1.50 to 1.99). However, apart from requests, the communicative skills of children with Down syndrome were more mature than the MLU matched controls at both MLU levels. These researchers concluded that their data indicated an asynchrony between syntactic and pragmatic development for children with Down syndrome that was not reflected in the development of the control children. Given the much older age of the children with Down syndrome, it seems that both cognitive development and experience have contributed to the development of their social communication skills.

Studies of adults with Down syndrome have also suggested that their communicative skills are greater than their verbal skills. Correct grammar may not be used but strategies such as the use of key words, such as yesterday or tomorrow, are implemented to cover an inability to encode tense (Sabsay and Kernan, 1993).

Delay in comparison with other domains of development and asynchrony between various aspects of language has encouraged interpretation in terms of models of modularity or isolable language subsystems (Shallice, 1988). There now seems to be some agreement that children actively construct their own language given the constraints (or parameters) of a biologically based substrate (or module) which is language specific but which interacts with cognitive (non-linguistic), social, and external information. A major question concerns the extent to which syntax can be considered in terms of a linguistic module which is autonomous of the functional aspects of language (Tager-Flusberg, 1994). The growth in vocabulary and communicative competence in comparison with children of the same MA seems to be associated with the more extensive experiences of the older child with Down syndrome but linguistic factors seem to be implicated in a slowdown in syntactic competence at Stage III. As Fowler commented, there are a few children with Down syndrome who break the barrier at Stage III, and they then show dramatic increases in performance level.

VARIABILITY

Although Fowler *et al.* (1994) have emphasized the apparent homogeneity regarding the low level of syntactic ability, there is considerable variability in the acquisition of vocabulary and communications skill (Miller *et al.*, 1992).

Adult case studies provided by Hunt (1967), Rondal (1994), Seagoe (1964) and Vallar and Papagno (1993) provide vivid contrasts with those of Sigafoos and his colleagues. These latter researchers have designed programmes to develop requesting and labelling behaviours in adults who are severely disabled, several of whom have Down syndrome. For example, Paul is mute. He can follow simple spoken directions and he gestures in an idiosyncratic fashion. Dave has three words and a few signs which are difficult to interpret (Sigafoos *et al.*, 1990). Carol's only vocal behaviours are loud, undifferentiated sounds but she can imitate 36 signs (Sigafoos *et al.*, 1989) and Mike is mute and has no sign language (Sigafoos and Kook, 1992). Some of these young people develop challenging behaviours because they have no alternative way of communicating (Sigafoos, 1995).

In contrast are cases of exceptional language ability. Two were reported several decades ago (Hunt, 1967; Seagoe, 1965) and presented the written diaries of two young men. The other two are recent descriptions of the expressive spoken language of two young women. Rondal (1994) described the 'quasi-normal language functioning' of Francoise, whose language was French and who was 33 to 34 years of age at the time of his study Her speech was fluent and of normal intonation. Her sentences were complete and of correct construction.

The other case study was provided by Vallar and Papagno (1993) who reported the language abilities of FF, a 23-year-old Italian woman who was fluent in Italian,

French and English. Her WAIS (Weschler Adult Intelligence Scale) IQ was 71 (verbal 80 and performance 63). Her vocabulary, synonym judgement, and performance on tasks testing phonological short-term memory was in the normal range but she was severely impaired in tasks assessing visuo-spatial perception, long-term memory and in a range of reasoning tasks.

Despite their achievements, the overall picture of the language development of the two women is uneven when receptive and expressive language is considered in its entirety (phonology, grammar, semantics, pragmatics). FF's vocabulary was remarkably good and her conversations were fluent but she was extremely slow in reading words and could not recall a short story accurately. Francoise overused idiomatic expressions and there tended to be a lack of cohesion in her discourse organization.

Vallar and Papagno (1993) concluded that phonological short-term memory plays an important role in the acquisition of vocabulary and that the acquisition of good vocabulary doesn't require the whole cognitive system but only some components. In similar vein, Rondal (1994) suggested that Francoise' s language demonstrated a dissociation of syntax from the lexicon and pragmatics (i.e. between the computational and conceptual aspects of language, in Chomsky's 1980 terms). He supported the view that language development could be explained in terms of modularity concepts (or even better by the isolable subsystems advocated by Shallice, 1988) and that the conceptual aspects of language were more likely to reflect non-linguistic cognitive limitations than the computational aspects.

PROCESSING LIMITATIONS

In both the previous case studies, the authors probed to determine whether special processing characteristics could be identified. Rondal (1994) considered the role of the left hemisphere in speech perception while Vallar and Papagno (1993) emphasized phonological memory.

An early investigation of speech perception and ear advantage in children with Down syndrome was conducted by Hartley (1985). She found that significantly more children with Down syndrome (7.6 to 13.6 years CA) showed left-ear advantage indicating a possible right hemisphere dominance for speech perception.

Elliot *et al.* (1987) reviewed the available evidence and concluded that this simple model is untenable. They proposed a left-right structural dissociation, with the left hemisphere dominant for complex movements (including speech) and the right dominant for speech perception. As a result, certain functions would be isolated from the neural mechanisms best equipped to handle that function.

On the other hand, not all persons with Down syndrome demonstrate right hemisphere dominance for speech perception (for example Francoise in Rondal's case study was left-hemisphere dominant for both speech reception and production). Although Rondal acknowledged that there were limitations both in our knowledge of the role played by the two hemispheres and in the technical methodology used in current studies (see Tannock *et al.*, 1984), he thought it was a 'logical interpretive necessity' to conclude that some parts of Francoise's brain had been spared the effects of the trisomy. Yet it may hasty to conclude that her language competence originated from normal hemispheric dominance. Evidence of an association does not prove the direction of influence and Piccirilli *et al.* (1991) suggested that atypical lateralization may depend more on a language deficit than on the syndrome. As Locke (1994, p. 609) argued, 'although in neurophysiological, neuroanatomical, and behavioral genetic studies one may seem to be viewing the bases of developmental language disorders, one may in fact be seeing the structural and functional *expression* of these problems'. He proposed that the analysis involved in establishing a grammar would not be activated until the child had learnt sufficient words. If these analytic mechanisms are not activated in the left hemisphere, the right hemisphere will tend to take over linguistic functions.

In addition to the interest in hemispheric processing, there has been research interest in the possibility of errors in the information input to the brain. Speech perception by infants and young children has been little researched but there are reports that infants and young children with Down syndrome find it difficult to process rapid spectral information, with steady-state vowel formants easier to process than the more rapidly changing consonant formants (see review by Lynch and Eilers, 1991).

Such perceptual difficulties would be magnified by the hearing impairments commonly reported for Down syndrome. Hearing loss is most often due to conductive impairment and has been attributed to a high incidence of recurrent otitis media with fluid accumulation in the middle ear. Several studies have investigated the effect of otitis media with effusion (OME) on language development.

A significant association was found between language functioning and a history of otitis media in a small group of adolescents with Down syndrome (11 to 21 years of age) by Whiteman *et al.* (1986). These authors also indicated that many cases of otitis media in young children with Down syndrome may go undetected in childhood unless ear health is monitored regularly.

Otitis media with effusion is not restricted to Down syndrome but is common in young children in the general population. Consequently, there have been several studies of its effect on child development. A review of 20 studies of the relationship between OME and children's academic achievement and related behaviour found conflicting results due mainly to poor research design (Roberts and Schuele, 1990). These authors, however, stressed the importance of the cumulative effects of OME, and the interactive effects of the teacher, caregiver, learning environment, medical care, language stimulation, general health and cognitive status. Wuest and Stern (1990) also concluded that despite the shortcomings of inconclusive research, chronic OME does appear to have an impact on the child's language development.

In a prospective study, Feagans *et al.* (1987) researched the relationship between attentional processes and later language development (narrative skills and discourse) in young day-care children who had experienced episodes of otitis media in the first three years of life. Their results indicated that MLU was not related to otitis media but that narrative skills were affected in children with a high frequency and duration of otitis media in the first three years of life. Since these children also exhibited a higher incidence of off task behaviour, the authors suggested that otitis media may produce attentional deficits which in turn affect specific aspects of language development, particularly discourse and narrative. These results appear to have significance for Down syndrome given reports concerning inattentiveness and distractibility (Gunn and Cuskelly, 1991) and limits in discourse organization (Rondal, 1994)

In addition to the possibility that the information is degraded by poor sensory encoding, individuals with Down syndrome face other sources of difficulty in processing speech. Children with Down syndrome are significantly impaired with regard to the speed of orienting to and processing auditory information and several studies have reported deficits in auditory short-term memory (Lincoln *et al.*, 1985; Mackenzie and Hulme, 1987; McDade and Adler, 1980; Marcell and Armstrong, 1982; Marcell *et al.*, 1988; Marcell and Weeks, 1988; Snart *et al.*, 1982; Varnhagen *et al.*, 1987).

The ability to hold information in working memory is an integral aspect of speech perception and there have been attempts to design intervention strategies which will improve memory skills in Down syndrome.

INTERVENTION

When Mackenzie and Hulme (1987) investigated memory span (using digit sequence recall) they concluded that the teenagers in their sample had not developed the cognitive strategies which helped the remembering of information. They attributed the poor performance to a failure to use the Articulatory loop to rehearse information in working memory. On the basis of this report, Broadley and MacDonald (1993) gave memory training in rehearsal and organization to 25 children with Down syndrome over a six-week period. An improvement in memory skills was found over both the short (six weeks) and medium (six months) term (Broadley *et al.*, 1994). These results were specific to the type of training and there was some uncertainty as to trainer and mainstreaming effects. Comblain (1994) undertook a similar training study and again reported a significant improvement at the first posttest with some improvement remaining six months later. Despite the uncertainty about the long-term efficacy, these are attempts to design and monitor an intervention programme geared to a syndrome-specific deficit (see Chapter 14, this volume).

In addition to the search for links between language development and processing characteristics within the syndrome, there has been consistent interest in the early communicative exchanges with the primary care-giver. These have been seen as important precursors of later communication skill and there has been much research into the characteristics of care-giver (especially mother) infant interaction. Many of these studies started with the assumption that interactions unhelpful for the development of the child's communicative competence could be identified and that effective interventions could then be planned. Some of the early studies have shown limitations in the vocal turn-taking of very young infants with Down syndrome and their mothers but they have been limited by the small sample size, a need to distinguish the qualitative aspects of vocal clashing (does it mark periods of high enjoyment or is it poor turn-taking on behalf of one partner rather than another?) or is the clashing no greater than the probability of joint vocalization given high vocalization on the part of either the mother or child? A detailed study of the nature of these overlaps in four older children aged between 3 years 4 months and 3 years 9 months showed that these overlaps were often similar to the kind of overlap which frequently occurs in adult talk. The more advanced children were better able to remedy the situation when an overlap did occur (Peskett and Wootton, 1985).

In general, studies of parental interactions with infants and young children with Down syndrome have been inconclusive. There are many factors which will affect the type and style of parent behaviours. These include the age, developmental level and temperament of the child, and the setting in which the interactions take place (free play or teaching). The style of interaction will also depend on the culture, the level of parental stress and whether it is with father or mother (Hanson, 1992; Girolametto and Tannock, 1994). In research studies there is the added difficulty of choosing a suitable comparison group. Should it match on CA, MA, receptive or expressive language level (syntax or vocabulary)?

In a study examining mother–child interactions involving 2-year-olds with Down syndrome, Crawley and Spiker (1983) did not use a comparison group, pointing out instead that neither the mothers nor the children with Down syndrome were a homogeneous group in relation to interactive style. They were interested in examining whether individual differences in patterns of mother–child interactions (free play) are related to child competence. There was wide variation between the mothers along such dimensions as directiveness and sensitivity although it was concluded that 'mothers who combine sensitivity and directiveness in ways that provide stimulation value may have more competent children' (Crawley and Spiker, 1983, p. 1320). Nevertheless, as has been noted, an unresponsive and passive child may need a higher level of directiveness (Cardoso-Martins and Mervis, 1985; Tannock, 1988; Tannock and Girolametto, 1992).

While investigating non-verbal communication skills in children with Down syndrome, Mundy *et al.* (1988) found the care-givers of these children appeared to be even more responsive to their child's acts than the care-givers of a non-delayed group of children. These researchers reported that although skill in non-verbal requesting may be a useful intervention target for the child, it was relatively independent of care-giver behaviour.

Fischer (1987, 1988) also found a higher level of maternal responsiveness to a child with Down syndrome but cautioned that this may reduce the frequency of spontaneous communications by the child. By using an ABA time series experiment, he demonstrated that two boys with Down syndrome (age 54 and 57 months) revised their messages significantly more often when the mother responded to the child's utterances less frequently. He stressed the need to provide time for children to repair their own failed messages. This may of course depend on the child's self-confidence and willingness to persist with the message.

In reviewing early communication and language intervention programmes, Warren (1993) concluded that optimal intervention is not feasible without an understanding of the way in which language and other domains of behaviour function as systems across different levels of development. For that reason, the research indicating the nature of the syntactic deficits in Down syndrome language and the role of experience in vocabulary and communicative development has implications for intervention.

As Peters (1994) pointed out, there has been little exploration of the effect of context on the acquisition of grammar. She cited the Griffiths study of the production of first words within routines and asked whether there were some circumstances in which context could also facilitate the emergence of closed class words. Her case study of a blind boy suggested that multiple contexts would stimulate generalization and she emphasized the need to discover the degree to which children's developing linguistic systems were sensitive to context.

Research with deaf children is also relevant to this question since their language reveals an incomplete grammar with missing functional elements (de Villiers *et al.*, 1994) . The significance for children with Down syndrome is that these elements are most often missing from their language too and there is an implication that despite the constraints of an innate linguistic substrate, a complete grammar is influenced by the nature of the language input. The question as to how to provide this early enough and in what form (written or signed) is relevant to both groups. De Villiers *et al.* speculated that children need to acquire a complete grammatical system before they can make use of the grammar they encounter in written material. They raised the question as to whether a sign language (which does have its own formal grammatical structure) would set the stage well in this respect.

There are several reports of children with Down syndrome who have learned to communicate through speech after being taught initially to sign (Clibbens, 1993). This concurs with our own experience. Also, we have observed the use of signing to remove ambiguity when articulation is poor and some parents have used the concurrent use of the sign to emphasize the articulation of a spoken word. Signing has also been used in conjunction with rebuses in some successful learning-to-read programmes.

Written language has the advantage of being less transient than signs or speech and there is some evidence that the relationship between speech and reading is not completely one-way. Buckley has argued that the development of reading skills will impact on speech and language (Buckley, 1993; Buckley and Bird, 1993; Chapter 19, this volume) and Farrell's discussion of the relationship between phonemic awareness and reading raises the possibility that phonemic awareness training would impact on both reading and speech. Meyers (1988, 1989) has reported that writing on computers with synthesized speech output can improve both the spoken and written language of the child with Down syndrome.

Chapman *et al.* (1992) took the optimistic view that missing syntactic elements, mainly closed class words, could be taught in intervention programs and Jenkins (1993) also suggested that it could be useful to target syntactic skills. She attributed the better performance on prepositions for her group of children with Down's syndrome to an emphasis in schools and therapy sessions. What kind of teaching is a moot question.

Intervention teaching methods have been characterized along a continuum from highly structured, behaviourally based methods to naturalistic social interactions with hybrid methods such as milieu teaching in the middle of the continuum (Yoder *et al.*, 1991). As Yoder *et al.* commented, there have been few treatment-by-aptitude studies involving language teaching methods. In practice, the highly structured approaches tend to be used with those who have the most severe disabilities (e.g. Sigafoos and Kook, 1992). The naturalistic programmes have been more common with very young children and often form the basis of programmes which use parents as the primary teacher. Yet as Tannock and Girolametto (1992) concluded, research on the efficacy of this type of programme is plagued by methodological weaknesses.

After an exploratory study, which compared the efficacy of a highly structured method of teaching language to handicapped preschoolers with milieu teaching, Yoder *et al.* concluded that whereas lower functioning children may best learn conversational skills and new vocabulary through naturalistic interactions, children who were functioning at a higher level may acquire new syntactic structures more quickly through highly structured interventions. Bearing in mind the need to generalize to other settings, however, they expected that conversationally based approaches would still be necessary to facilitate the use of new structures in conversation.

Conversational skill, however, depends on the intelligibility of the communication as well as the correct use of vocabulary and syntactic structures in the language. But because of the wider implications for the acquisition of language, more recent research has focused on the characteristics of Down syndrome language than on the intelligibility of the communication and the characteristics of the speech. Yet intelligibility is an important issue in the day-to-day life of the person with Down syndrome. For instance, Sabsay and Kernan (1993) found that deficits in syntax were less of an impediment to the communication of adults with Down syndrome than severe speech defects.

SPEECH

There are a number of speech disorders reported for Down syndrome. In various studies, the voice has been perceived as hoarse, hypernasal, gruff and low pitched. Others have reported on the prevalence of immature phonological patterns, disorders of rhythm and stammering (Devenny *et al.*, 1990; Van Borsel, 1988). Given the range of these difficulties and their effects on intelligibility, it is not surprising that adolescents with Down syndrome have difficulty in being understood by conversational partners. Familiarity with the context and the partner helps but in other situations, it has been found that intelligibility decreases and the adolescents lack the repair strategies necessary for communication to continue (Bray and Woolnough, 1988).

Buckley and Sacks (1987) found that adolescents with Down syndrome were often intelligible to their parents but not to strangers and Korbin (1986) described the frustration of Sarah, a 9-year-old child with Down syndrome, when her speech was not understood. By the time that Sarah was 14 years old, she started to withdraw from others and she refused to read aloud. Korbin attributed this to

Sarah's continued experience of not being understood and a greater awareness of her handicap.

It would not be unexpected for these effects to become magnified by the time the adolescent becomes an adult. Sabsay and Kernan (1993) noted that misunderstandings can use up considerable amounts of conversation time for adults with Down syndrome or, worse, lead to stressful communications. These researchers concluded that it would be more helpful to teach adults with Down syndrome to communicate with the skills they already have rather than attempt to improve and extend their syntactic skills. In this respect, it is of relevance that Bray and Woolnough found that the most successful repair strategy for the adolescents in their study was signing.

Several reasons have been advanced for speech difficulties in Down syndrome. These include impaired hearing, delayed or disordered phonological development and problems in planning and/or implementing the sequence of sounds necessary for speech. Low muscle tone and oral/facial anomalies affecting jaws, tongue and teeth may also contribute to difficulties in articulation. Surgical tongue reduction has been carried out but Parsons *et al.* (1987) reported that this surgery had no significant effect on articulation and no significant improvement in articulation was noted in a six-month post operative follow-up of 18 children with Down syndrome.

A recent thorough investigation of the articulatory patterns of three young adults with Down syndrome also contra-indicated the need for such surgery. Through the use of electropalatography (EPG) and a test of diadochokinetic rate, this study revealed impairment at all levels of speech production. There were phonological delays, motor programming problems and difficulties in co-ordinating the movements of tongue and lips. Hamilton (1993) suggested that her results lent some support to the theory of an articulatory impairment which could be the result of hypotonia. She emphasized the need for clinical interventions to focus on articulatory skills as well as phonological development. She also suggested that the EPG could be used effectively in treatment to provide visual feedback. Since an acrylic palate with electrodes has to be fitted for these measurements, the method is probably most suitable for older children and young adults.

Voice is another aspect of speech which may be affected by hypotonia and Pryce (1994) discussed the possibility that the gruffness in the voices of people with Down syndrome was associated with flaccidity in the extrinsic and intrinsic laryngeal muscles. A study of 30 adults with Down syndrome, which used electromyographic (EMG) biofeedback, showed that they needed greater levels of energy to activate their vocal cord vibrations than the adults in three comparison groups. These groups included adults with learning disabilities other than Down syndrome, adults who had been referred because of dysphonic problems, and a control group. Pryce made the interesting observation that the telegraphic style of communication which is usually considered to be a reflection of syntactic constraints may also be encouraged by problems in voice production. Individuals with Down syndrome may be unable to produce voice for long enough to sustain longer sentences. Her recommendations were very practical. Encourage people with Down syndrome to drink more water or water-based drinks (excluding those with caffeine or alcohol) as good fluid intake is important for the voice. She also commented on the strategies used by singing teachers to improve voice and remarked that few people with Down syndrome could sing. Perhaps this is another avenue for intervention.

Singing and drama seem to be ideal avenues for practising speech and communication skills in an enjoyable and non-threatening environment (see Chatterton and Butler, 1994, for one description). A decade ago Glenn and Cunningham (1984) reported that infants with Down syndrome would rather listen to sung nursery rhymes than listen to their mothers talking to them. These researchers suggested that these rhymes could have an important function in developing early vocabulary and communicative skills.

It may also be speculated that with older children and adults, music and drama activities provide a purpose for practice which is more meaningful to the individual than intervention goals which have more meaning to the therapist. Finally, if the ultimate goal of language or speech intervention is to help the person with Down syndrome have more self-confidence and to enjoy a range of communicative activities, more consideration might be given to these creative pursuits.

REFERENCES

Beeghly, M., Weiss-Perry, B. and Cicchetti, D. (1990) Beyond sensorimotor functioning: early communicative and play development of children with Down syndrome. In D. Cicchetti and M. Beeghly (eds), *Children with Down Syndrome: A Developmental Perspective*, pp. 329–68 Cambridge: Cambridge University Press.

Bray, M. and Woolnough, L. (1988) The language skills of children with Down's syndrome aged 12 to 16 years. *Child Language Teaching and Therapy*, **4**, pp. 311–24.

Bridges, A. and Smith, J.V.E. (1984) Syntactic comprehension in Down's syndrome children. *British Journal of Psychology*, **75**, pp. 187–96.

Broadley, I. and MacDonald, J. (1993) Teaching short term memory skills to children with Down's syndrome. *Down's Syndrome: Research and Practice*, **1**, pp. 56–62.

Broadley, I., MacDonald, J. and Buckley, S. (1994) Are children with Down's syndrome able to maintain skills learned from a short-term memory training programme? *Down's Syndrome: Research and Practice*, **2**, pp. 116–22.

Brown, R. (1973) *A First Language*. Cambridge, MA: Harvard University Press.

Buckley, S. (1993) Developing the speech and language skills of teenagers with Down's syndrome. *Down's Syndrome: Research and Practice*, **1**, pp. 63–71.

Buckley, S. and Bird, G. (1993) Teaching children with Down's syndrome to read. *Down's Syndrome: Research and Practice*, **1**, pp. 34–39.

Buckley, S. and Sacks, B. (1987) *The Adolescent with Down's Syndrome: Life for the Teenager and for the Family*. Portsmouth: Portsmouth Polytechnic.

Cardoso-Martins, C. and Mervis, C.B. (1985) Maternal speech to prelinguistic children with Down syndrome. *American Journal of Mental Deficiency*, **89**, pp. 451–58.

Cardoso-Martins, C., Mervis, C.B. and Mervis, C.A. (1985) Early vocabulary acquisition by children with Down syndrome. *American Journal of Mental Deficiency*, **90**, pp. 177–84.

Chapman, R.S., Kay-Raining Bird, E. and Schwartz, S.E. (1990) Fast mapping of words in event contexts by children with Down syndrome. *Journal of Speech and Hearing Disorders*, **55**, pp. 761–70.

Chapman, R.S., Schwartz, S.E. and Kay-Raining Bird, E. (1991) Language skills of children and adolescents with Down syndrome. *Journal of Speech and Hearing Research*, **34**, pp. 1106–21.

Chapman, R.S., Schwartz, S.E. and Kay-Raining Bird, E. (1992) Language production of older children with Down syndrome. Paper presented at the 9th World Congress of the

International Association for the Scientific Study of Mental Deficiency, Gold Coast, Australia.

Chatterton, S. and Butler, S. (1994) The development of communication skills through drama. *Down's Syndrome: Research and Practice*, **2**, pp. 83–84.

Chomsky, N. (1980) *Rules and Representations*, New York: Columbia University Press.

Clibbens, J. (1993) From theory to practice in child language development. *Down's Syndrome: Research and Practice*, **1**, pp. 101–06.

Coggins, T.E., Carpenter, R.L. and Owings, N.O. (1983) Examining early intentional communication in Down's syndrome and nonretarded children. *British Journal of Disorders of Communication*, **18**, pp. 99–107.

Coggins, T.E. and Stoel-Gammon, C. (1982) Clarification strategies used by four Down's syndrome children for maintaining normal conversational interaction. *Education and Training of the Mentally Retarded*, **17**, pp. 65–67.

Comblain, A. (1994) Working memory in Down's syndrome: training rehearsal strategy. *Down's Syndrome: Research and Practice*, **2**, pp. 123–26.

Crawley, S.B. and Spiker, D. (1983) Mother-child interactions involving two-year-olds with Down syndrome: a look at individual differences. *Child Development*, **54**, pp. 1312–23.

Cunningham, C.C., Glenn, S.M. Wilkinson, P. and Sloper, P. (1985) Mental ability, symbolic play and receptive and expressive language of young children with Down's syndrome. *Journal of Child Psychology and Psychiatry*, **26**, pp. 255–65.

de Villiers, J., de Villiers, P. and Hoban, E. (1994) The central problem of functional categories in the English syntax of oral deaf children. In H. Tager-Flusberg (ed.), *Constraints on Language Acquisition: Studies of Atypical Children*, pp. 9–47, Hillsdale: Erlbaum.

Devenny, D.A., Silverman, W., Balgley, H., Wall, M.J., & Sidtis, J.J. (1990) Specific motor abilities associated with speech fluency in Down's syndrome. *Journal of Mental Deficiency Research*, **34**, pp. 437–43.

Elliott, D., Weeks, D.J. and Elliott, C.L. (1987) Cerebral specialization in individuals with Down syndrome. *American Journal of Mental Retardation*, **92**, pp. 263–71.

Feagans, L., Sanyal, M., Henderson, F., Collier, A. and Appelbaum, M. (1987) Relationship of middle ear disease in early childhood to later narrative and attention skills. *Journal of Pediatric Psychology*, **12**, pp. 581–94.

Fischer, M.A. (1987) Mother-child interaction in preverbal children with Down syndrome. *Journal of Speech and Hearing Disorders*, **52**, pp. 179–90.

Fischer, M.A. (1988) Social communicative revision behaviors in children with Down syndrome. *Journal of Childhood Communication Disorders, 12*, pp. 1–10.

Fowler, A.E. (1990) Language abilities in children with Down syndrome: evidence for a specific syntactic delay. In D. Cicchetti and M. Beeghly (eds), *Children with Down Syndrome: a Developmental Perspective*, pp. 302–28, Cambridge: Cambridge University Press.

Fowler, A.E., Gelman, R. and Gleitman, L.R. (1994) The course of language learning in children with Down syndrome: longitudinal and language level comparisons with young normally developing children. In H. Tager-Flusberg (ed.), *Constraints on Language Acquisition: Studies of Atypical Children*, pp. 91–140, Hillsdale: Erlbaum.

Franco, F. and Wishart, J.G. (1995) The use of pointing and other gestures by young children with Down's syndrome. *American Journal on Mental Retardation* (in press).

Girolametto, L. and Tannock, R. (1994) Correlates of directiveness in the interactions of fathers and mothers of children with developmental delays. *Journal of Speech and Hearing Research*, **37**, pp. 1178–92.

Glenn, S.M. and Cunningham, C.C. (1984) Nursery rhymes and early language acquisition by mentally handicapped children. *Exceptional Children*, **51** (1), pp. 72–74.

Greenwald, C.A. and Leonard, L.B. (1979) Communicative and sensorimotor development of Down's syndrome children. *American Journal of Mental Deficiency*, **84**, pp. 296–303.

Gunn, P. and Cuskelly, M. (1991) Down syndrome temperament: the stereotype at middle childhood and adolescence. *International Journal of Disability, Development and Education*, **38**, pp. 59–70.

Hamilton, C. (1993) Investigation of the articulatory patterns of young adults with Down's syndrome using electropalatography. *Down's Syndrome: Research and Practice*, **1**, pp. 15–28.

Hanson, M.J. (1992) Ethnic, cultural, and language diversity in intervention settings. In E.W. Lynch and M.J. Hanson (eds), *Developing Cross-Cultural Competence*, pp. 3–18, Baltimore: Brookes.

Harris, J. (1983) What does mean length of utterance mean? Evidence from a comparative study of normal and Down's syndrome children. *British Journal of Disorders of Communication*, **18**, pp. 153–69.

Hartley, X.Y. (1985) Receptive language processing and ear advantage of Down's syndrome children. *Journal of Mental Deficiency Research*, **29**, pp. 197–205.

Hunt, N. (1967) The world of Nigel Hunt. the Diary of a Mongoloid Youth, London: Darwin Finlayson.

Jenkins, C. (1993) Expressive language delay in children with Down's syndrome: a specific cause for concern. *Down's Syndrome: Research and Practice*, **1**, pp. 10–14.

Korbin, J.E. (1986) Sarah: the life course of a Down's syndrome child. In L.L. Langness and H.G. Levine (eds), *Culture and Retardation*, Dorderecht: D. Reidel.

Lahey, M. (1994) Grammatical morpheme acquisition: do norms exist? *Journal of Speech and Hearing Research*, **37**, pp. 1192–94.

Leifer, J.S. and Lewis, M. (1984) Acquisition of conversational response skills by young Down syndrome and nonretarded young children. *American Journal of Mental Deficiency*, **88**, pp. 610–18.

Lenneberg, E.H., Nichols, I.A. and Rosenberger, E.F. (1964) Primitive stages of language development in mongolism. *Association for Research in Nervous and Mental Disease*, **42**, pp. 119–37.

Lincoln, A.J., Courchesne, E., Kilman, B.A. and Galambos, R. (1985) Neuro-psychological correlates of information-processing by children with Down syndrome. *American Journal of Mental Deficiency*, **89**, pp. 403–14.

Locke, J.L. (1994) Gradual emergence of developmental language disorders. *Journal of Speech and Hearing Research*, **37**, pp. 608–16.

Lynch, M.P. and Eilers, R.E. (1991) Perspectives on early language from typical development and Down syndrome. *International Review of Research in Mental Retardation*, **17**, pp. 55–90.

McDade, H.L. and Adler, S. (1980) Down syndrome and short-term memory impairment: A storage or retrieval deficit? *American Journal of Mental Deficiency*, **84**, pp. 561–67.

Mackenzie, S. and Hulme, C. (1987) Memory span development in Down's syndrome, severely subnormal and normal subjects. *Cognitive Neuropsychology*, **4**, pp. 303–19.

Marcell, M.M. and Armstrong, V. (1982) Auditory and visual sequential memory of Down syndrome and nonretarded children. *American Journal of Mental Deficiency*, **87**, pp. 86–95.

Marcell, M.M., Harvey, C.F. and Cothran, L.P. (1988) An attempt to improve auditory short-term memory in Down's syndrome individuals through reducing distractions. *Research in Developmental Disabilities*, **9**, pp. 405–17.

Marcell, M.M. and Weeks, S.L. (1988) Short-term memory difficulties and Down's syndrome. *Journal of Mental Deficiency Research*, **32**, pp. 153–62.

Meyers, L.F. (1988) Using computers to teach children with Down syndrome spoken and written language skills. In L. Nadel (ed.), *Psychobiology of Down Syndrome*, pp. 247–65, Cambridge, MA: MIT Press.

Meyers, L.F. (1989) Language development and intervention. In D. Van Dyke, D.J. Lang, F. Heide, S. van Duyne and M.J. Soucek (eds), *Clinical Management Considerations in Down Syndrome*, pp. 153–64, New York: Springer-Verlag.

Miller, J.F. (1987) Language and communication characteristics of children with Down syndrome. In S.M. Pueschel, C. Tingey, J.E. Rynders, A.C. Crocker and D.M. Crutcher (eds), *New Perspectives on Down Syndrome*, pp. 233–62, Baltimore: Brookes.

Miller J.F. (1988,) The developmental asynchrony of language development in children with Down syndrome. In L. Nadel (ed.), *The Psychobiology of Down Syndrome*, pp. 167–98, Cambridge, MA: MIT Press.

Miller, J., Sedey, A., Miolo, G., Murray-Branch, J. and Rosin, M. (1992) Vocabulary acquisition in young children with Down's syndrome. Paper presented at the 9th World Congress of the International Association for the Scientific Study of Mental Deficiency, Gold Coast, Australia, August.

Mundy, P., Sigman, M., Kasari, C. and Yirmiya, N. (1988) Non verbal communication skills in Down syndrome children. *Child Development*, **59**, pp. 235–49.

Owens, R.E. and MacDonald, J.D. (1982) Communicative uses of the early speech of non delayed and Down syndrome children. *American Journal of Mental Deficiency*, **86**, pp. 503–10.

Parsons, C.L., Iacona, T.A. and Rozner, L. (1987) Effect of tongue reduction on articulation in children with Down syndrome. *American Journal of Mental Deficiency*, **91**, pp. 328–32.

Peskett, R. and Wootton, A.J. (1985) Turn-taking and overlap in the speech of young Down's syndrome children. *Journal of Mental Deficiency Research*, **29**, pp. 263–73.

Peters, A.M. (1994) The interdependence of social, cognitive, and linguistic development: Evidence from a visually impaired child. In H. Tager-Flusberg (ed.), *Constraints on Language Acquisition: Studies of Atypical Children*, pp. 195–219, Hillsdale: Erlbaum.

Piccirilli, M., D'Alessandro, P., Mazzi, P., Sciarma, T. and Testa, A. (1991) Cerebral organization for language in Down's syndrome patients. *Cortex*, **27**, pp. 41–47.

Pryce, M. (1994), The voice of people with Down's syndrome: an EMG biofeedback study. *Down's Syndrome: Research and Practice*, **2**, pp. 106–111.

Roberts, J.E. and Schuele, C.M. (1990) Otitis media and later academic performance: The linkage and implications for intervention. *Topics in Language Disorders*, **11** (1), pp. 43–62.

Rondal, J.A. (1988) Language development in Down's syndrome: a life-span perspective. *International Journal of Behavioral Development*, **11**, pp. 21–36.

Rondal, J.A. (1994) Exceptional cases of language development in mental retardation: The relative autonomy of language as a cognitive system. In H. Tager-Flusberg (ed.), *Constraints on Language Acquisition: Studies of Atypical Children*, pp. 155–74, Hillsdale: Erlbaum.

Rosin, M.M., Swift, E., Bless, D. and Vetter, D.K. (1988) Communication profiles of adolescents with Down syndrome. *Journal of Childhood Communication Disorders*, **12** (1), pp. 49–63.

Sabsay, S. and Kernan, K.T. (1993) On the nature of language impairment in Down syndrome. *Topics in Language Disorders*, **13**, pp. 20–35.

Seagoe, M.V. (1964) *Yesterday Was Tuesday, All Day and All Night: The Story of a Unique Education*. Boston: Little Brown.

Seagoe, M.V. (1965) Verbal development in a mongoloid. *Exceptional Children*, **31**, pp. 269–73.

Shallice, T. (1988) *From Neuropsychology to Mental Structure*. Cambridge: Cambridge University Press.

Sigafoos, J. (1995) Challenging behaviour: communication intervention to replace and prevent challenging behaviour. In N. Butterfield, M. Arthur and J. Sigafoos (eds) *Partners in Everyday Communicative Exchanges*. Sydney: MacLennan and Petty.

Sigafoos, J., Doss, S. and Reichle, J. (1989) Developing mand and tact repertoires in persons with severe developmental disabilities using graphic symbols. *Research in Developmental Disabilities*, **10**, pp. 183–200.

Sigafoos, J. and Kook, A. (1992) Obtaining a correspondence between requesting and selecting preferred objects. *Developmental Disabilities Bulletin*, **20** (1), pp. 1–12.

Sigafoos, J., Reichle, J., Doss, S., Hall, K. and Pettitt, L. (1990) 'Spontaneous' transfer of stimulus control from tact to mand contingencies. *Research in Developmental Disabilities*, **11**, pp. 165–76.

Smith, L. and von Tetzchner, S. (1986) Communicative, sensorimotor, and language skills of young children with Down syndrome. *American Journal of Mental Deficiency*, **91**, pp. 57–60.

Snart, F., O'Grady, M. and Das, J.P. (1982) Cognitive processing by subgroups of moderately mentally retarded children. *American Journal of Mental Deficiency*, **86**, pp. 465–72.

Steffens, M.L., Oller, D.K., Lynch, M. and Urbano, R.C. (1992), Vocal development in infants with Down syndrome and infants who are developing normally. *American Journal on Mental Retardation*, **97**, pp. 235–46.

Tager-Flusberg, H. (ed.) (1994) *Constraints on Language Acquisition: Studies of Atypical Children*, Hillsdale: Erlbaum.

Tannock, R. (1988) Mothers' directiveness in their interactions with their children with or without Down syndrome. *American Journal of Mental Retardation*, **95**, pp. 154–65.

Tannock, R. and Girolametto, L. (1992) Reassessing parent focused language intervention programs. In S. Warren and J. Reichle (eds), *Causes and Effects in Communication and Language Intervention*, pp. 49–80, Baltimore: Brookes.

Tannock, R., Kershner, J.R. and Oliver, J. (1984) Do individuals with Down's syndrome possess right hemisphere language dominance? *Cortex*, **20** (2), pp. 221–31.

Thelen, E. and Smith, L.B. (1994) *A Dynamic Systems Approach to the Development of Cognition and Action*, Cambridge, MA: MIT Press.

Vallar, G. and Papagno, C. (1993) Preserved vocabulary acquisition in Down's syndrome: the role of phonological short-term memory. *Cortex*, **29**, pp. 467–83.

Van Borsel, J. (1988) An analysis of the speech of five Down's syndrome adolescents. *Journal of Communication Disorders*, **21**, pp. 409–21.

Varnhagen, C.K., Das, J.P. and Varnhagen, S. (1987) Auditory and visual memory span: cognitive processing by TMR individuals with Down syndrome or other etiologies. *American Journal of Mental Deficiency*, **91**, pp. 398–405.

Warren, S.F. (1993) Early communication and language intervention: challenges for the 1990s and beyond. In A.P. Kaiser and D.B. Gray (eds), *Enhancing Children's Communication*, pp. 376–95, Baltimore: Brookes.

Whiteman, B.C., Simpson, G. and Compton, W.C. (1986) Relationship of otitis media and language impairments in adolescents with Down syndrome. *Mental Retardation*, **24** (6), pp. 353–56.

Wiegel-Crump, C.A. (1981) The development of grammar in Down's syndrome children between the mental ages of 2–0 and 6–11 years. *Education and Training of the Mentally Retarded*, **16**, pp. 24–30.

Wootton, A.J. (1991) Offer sequences between parents and young children with Down syndrome. *Journal of Mental Deficiency Research*, **35**, pp. 324–38.

Wuest, J. and Stern, P.N. (1990) Childhood otitis media: the family's endless quest for relief. *Issues in Comprehensive Pediatric Nursing*, **13**, pp. 25–39.

Yoder, P.J., Kaiser, A.P. and Alpert, C.L. (1991) An exploratory study of the interaction between language teaching methods and child characteristics. *Journal of Speech and Hearing Research*, **34**, pp. 155–67.

16 Reading Acquisition by Young Children

Sue Buckley, Gillian Bird and Angela Byrne

INTRODUCTION

The study of reading development in young children with Down syndrome is still in its infancy. There are very few published studies in the literature and these consist of single case studies (e.g. Carter, 1985; Duffen, 1976), surveys of the reading skills of small samples of children (e.g. Lorenz *et al.*, 1985), our own review articles describing our practical experience, case studies and discussion of the practical and theoretical significance of learning to read (e.g. Buckley, 1985; Buckley *et al.*, 1986; Buckley and Bind, 1993; Buckley and Bird, 1993, 1994) and articles addressing the issue of the cognitive strategies that the children are using to read (e.g. Cossu *et al.*, 1993; Evans, 1994).

One reason for the limited amount of information available on the reading abilities of children with Down syndrome is that until recently it was assumed that most of the children were not able to learn to read and, consequently, the majority of teenagers and adults with Down syndrome alive in the world today have never had the opportunity to learn to read. In some countries, the USA, Australia and the UK for example, there has been an awareness of the potential for literacy development for the children for at least 20 years (Hayden and Dmitriev, 1975; Pieterse and Treloar, 1981) and some children in experimental intervention and education programmes have benefited but the special education or care facilities available to most children have been slow to introduce literacy teaching into the curriculum.

Even when literacy has been introduced, it has been too little and too late. In the UK for example, until the last five years, the majority of children with Down syndrome were educated in special schools for children with severe learning difficulties. In these schools literacy teaching was usually limited to teaching a social sight vocabulary to teenagers; that is, a sight vocabulary of the words that may be useful in getting about their environment such as 'ladies', 'gents', 'exit', 'bus stop', 'police'. Introducing literacy teaching at the usual age in the UK of five years was not considered appropriate for children with Down syndrome.

During this time there have been children with Down syndrome learning to read and write, as the individual case studies illustrate, but in all these cases the main teaching has been provided by the child's parents, before they entered the school system and the continued involvement of parents has been essential to the child's progress.

Fortunately this situation is changing rapidly in the UK and in many other countries. In the UK over the past five years, increasing numbers of children with Down syndrome are being mainstreamed. This means that they are attending the same neighbourhood primary schools as the typically developing children in their community from five years of age, with appropriate additional support, and having the same access to literacy teaching from five years of age as all other children.

In the area of the UK local to the Sarah Duffen Centre, almost all the children with Down syndrome are being mainstreamed with support from the psychologists from the centre who have actively promoted this change in educational practice. For the first time, it has become possible to study the literacy development of truly representative population samples of children with Down syndrome and a longitudinal study of 24 children is under way (Byrne *et al.*, 1995). The first results from this study are discussed later in this chapter.

In our view, for children with Down syndrome, the benefits of learning to read go beyond simply acquiring a functionally useful level of reading and writing skill. We will argue that progress in reading can develop speech and language skills, auditory perceptual skills and working memory function; all areas where children with Down syndrome usually display difficulties (Fowler, 1990; Hulme and Mackenzie, 1992).

Drawing on the limited amount of published research and our own experience of teaching children with Down syndrome, this review will therefore address four questions:

1. What levels of literacy skills can we expect children with Down syndrome to achieve?
2. How should they be taught to read and write?
3. Are they using the same cognitive strategies to read as other typically developing children?
4. Will the activity of learning to read develop other cognitive skills?

WHAT LEVELS OF LITERACY SKILLS CAN WE EXPECT CHILDREN WITH DOWN SYNDROME TO ACHIEVE?

For the reasons outlined in the introduction, it is not possible to give an accurate answer to this question. Reading is a skill that needs to be taught and until all children with Down syndrome have access to appropriate literacy teaching it is not possible to determine what proportion of the population can achieve a functional level of literacy nor the range of achievement that may be possible. However a review of the existing data may give some indications to guide parents and educators and serve as a baseline against which future achievements can be compared.

In a survey in which 154 parents completed questionnaires in the USA (Pueschel and Hopmann, 1993), the parents of 31 17 to 21-year-olds reported that 50 per cent could read more than 50 words, 67 per cent could read sentences, 53 per cent could 'sound out' new words, 50 per cent read books and 45 per cent enjoyed reading. Their survey showed that few children under 7 years old had any reading skill. In the 33 4 to 6-year-olds no child could read more than 50 words though two could 'sound out' new words and one read sentences. At 7 to 10 years, 20 per cent of 31 children could read more than 50 words, 47 per cent read sentences, 27 per cent read books, 47 per cent enjoy reading and 21 per cent use phonics to sound out new words. At 11 to 16 years, the figures for the same levels of achievement for 34 children were 47, 61, 56, 58, and 44 per cent respectively. This study suggests that about half of the population had achieved a useful level of literacy and enjoyed reading, by the time they were young adults.

Two studies published in the UK in the 1980s indicate very limited reading progress in the first years at school. Casey *et al.*, (1988) followed the progress of 36 children with Down syndrome, 18 in mainstream placements and 18 in schools for children with moderate learning difficulties. The children did not differ in cognitive development at the start of their schooling. After two years, 90 per cent of the girls and 67 per cent of the boys in the mainstream classrooms could achieve scores on both the accuracy and the comprehension components of the Neale Reading Test. The children in the special schools were lagging behind with 90 per cent of the girls and 33 per cent of the boys scoring on accuracy and only 44 per cent of the girls and 33 per cent of the boys scoring on comprehension. As the children were equally able at the start of the study, it is likely that the difference in reading progress two years later is due to differences in the teaching of reading in the two school types.

In a study of 58 children with Down syndrome in Manchester, Lorenz *et al.* (1985) report that at 5 years of age 47 per cent of the children could read their own name and 19 per cent read 5 to 10 words, at 6 years the figures for these two levels of attainment were 63 per cent and 32 per cent, at 7 years, 75 per cent and 44 per cent. In a later survey of 117 children, age range from 6 to 14 years, also from this Manchester cohort, only 20 children could achieve a score on a standardized reading test (Sloper *et al.*, 1990).

In a survey of 90 teenagers in the UK (Buckley and Sacks, 1987), parents reported that 66 of the teenagers could read at least a 'social sight' vocabulary. Of these 66 readers, just half could read more than 50 words and 15 (16 per cent of the total group) could be described as quite good readers and enjoyed reading books, including adventure stories and books on sport or nature. In this study, many parents commented that their teenagers attempted to master the TV, sport and pop pages of the newspaper and that even those unable to read, enjoyed looking at books and being read to. Carr and Hewitt (1982), reporting on a group of 43 16 year olds, state that seven could read quite well, about the same proportion of the group as that in the Buckley and Sacks study.

The reader is reminded that the data from all these surveys is difficult to interpret as many of the children studied will not have been taught to read. We certainly cannot assume that all the children and young people had reached the upper limit of their reading ability.

Individual case studies

The functional literacy skills of individual children with Down syndrome were being reported as early as 1961 by Butterfield and 1964 by Seagoe. The young men described in these papers had been taught by their parents as had Nigel Hunt, who had his diary, *The World of Nigel Hunt*, published in 1966 The foreword to the book, written by Nigel's father, describes the difficulties he experienced when trying to convince the educators of the time that Nigel could actually read and write!

It was the progress of Sarah Duffen as described by her father Leslie (Duffen, 1976) that first drew our attention to the possibility that children with Down syndrome could achieve functional levels of literacy and that reading might accelerate speech and language acquisition. Sarah's progress suggested that it might be valuable to start teaching children to read from as early as 2 or 3 years of age. Since 1981, we have been exploring this approach and have accumulated a number of case studies of which the following are examples of early readers who continued to have good teaching.

Daniel was introduced to reading at 2 years and 4 months when he had a production vocabulary of about 50 single words. He learned to read ten words in two months and these were chosen to build two-word phrases for him to read at 2 years 8 months. These were rapidly transferred to his speech, according to the observations recorded by his home visiting teacher (Norris, 1989). By 2 years 11 months Daniel was reading six three-word phrases, which again he rapidly began to use in his speech. At 3 years 4 months he could read 66 flashcards and many two- and three-word combinations of these. The next month he was reading simple books and the words 'and' and 'a' appeared in his speech. At 3 years 6 months he was reading four-word sentences and at 3 years 8 months he could read 116 words and was speaking in six-word sentences. Daniel's rapid progress continued and, at 8 years of age, his reading age was 12 years 4 months and spelling age 9 years 9 months on the school assessment. Daniel is now 9 years and 6 months of age and the following is an example of his free writing:

> When we arrived at the villa it was more like a swimming pool to me but as I got closer I saw it was a villa. I thought it was very good at first. When we got in there was a wooden building with staff in it and I thought what is this building doing in the middle of the villa. Then next to it was the ruins of a Roman villa. I wanted to explore so we spilt up in our groups I was in Mrs Blacks group. First we worked on the arch way then we moved on to the cellar then my favourite part the dining room. Then we met Stephen he was just about to go upstairs then Mrs Gilbert said if I was afraid of heights then Katie and Hannah could go upstairs with them. I did a wonderful picture of a Roman farm. Then we had lunch and then me and Stephen went to choose a postcard but it was to busy and Stephen had to go and finish his pictures. I bought a postcard of a Roman Castle I loved it very much so I paid for it. Then it was time to go back to school. The other coach went off without us but we followed it and got back to school and we found a short cut.

Daniel finds handwriting difficult and is still printing. He prefers to use a word processor for writing and wrote the above story on his computer. He reads punctuation correctly but leaves much of it out when writing. He is being educated in a mainstream school and is average in his class for all subjects.

Louise was introduced to reading at 3 years 2 months when she learned to read her family names, 'Mummy', 'Daddy', 'Stephen' and 'Louise' by playing matching games. Two months later, she learned 'car', 'book', 'shoe', 'teddy', 'ball' and 'dolly'.

At 3 years 7 months 'walking', 'sleeping' and 'drinking' were added and she read two-word phrases such as 'Louise walking', 'Mummy sleeping'. Louise's mother and a speech and language therapist worked together, making simple books and a dictionary of pictures into which Louise had to slot the words into the correct pages. At 4 years 4 months she could read 35 single words on flashcards and some two-word sentences. She could also pick out known words in storybooks. Two months later, she could read more than 60 words and short phrases, in games, in full sentences and in books. She was also able to memorize and say whole sentences that she had previously read. Louise is now 8 years 8 months and has a reading accuracy age of 7 yrs 4 months and reading comprehension age of 6 yrs 8 months on the Neale Reading Test. She is progressing well with both reading and writing, forming capitals as well as lower case letters in joined handwriting.

Alistair learned to read in the same way as Daniel and Louise. At 10 years 8 months he has a reading accuracy age of 7 years 11 months and comprehension age of 6 years 9 months on the Neale. At 9 years he wrote the following in cursive script:

> Christmas story I am the shepherd
> one very cold night I was looking after my sheep. My friends told me about a special baby that had just been born. Some of the shepherds were fast asleep. I woke them up and told them about the baby. An angel said you must go to Bethlehem and find the baby. He will be wrapped in a warm cloth and lying in a manger. I found the baby Jesus and it made me feel very happy.

Writing and spelling progress shows considerable variation among the children. In the UK the children begin to have spellings to learn and spelling tests from their third year in school, at age 7 years. Our observations indicate that early on the children are 'visual' spellers. For example, Catherine's teacher reports that at 6 years she writes the word, looks at it to see if it looks right and if not corrects it. At 7 years, Daniel was still a 'visual' speller but at 9 years is a 'phonic' speller.

While case studies such as these are valuable, they do not allow us to generalize about the potential for literacy for all children with Down syndrome. The children described have benefited from early intervention at home, continuous teaching from their parents and mainstream schooling.

We have worked with other children who made the same preschool progress but who received no further literacy teaching in their special schools so can read no more as teenagers than they could as 5-year-olds. In order to advance our understanding, we need to be able to study representative population samples of children with Down syndrome longitudinally, collecting the same data on all the children and keeping detailed records of the teaching that they are receiving. With one of our graduate students, we have just embarked on such a study (Byrne *et al.*, 1995). We are following the progress of 24 children with Down syndrome and comparing their progress with a group of their mainstream classmates who are matched with them on reading age, as well as classmates who are average readers for their age.

The study will chart the reading, writing and spelling progress of the children, look at the cognitive strategies they are using to read and the links between reading, language and memory skills. Table 16.1 illustrates the reading ability for the children with Down syndrome at the start of the research and their scores on language and cognitive tasks at this time, compared with the children matched with them on reading age and the average readers from the same classes.

The figures in Table 16.1 illustrate the uneven cognitive profile of the children with Down syndrome. The children in this group are typically in a mainstream class of children who are one year younger in chronological age, hence the age difference for the two comparison groups of children who were their classmates. All the children with Down syndrome are learning to read and their reading ages range from 5 years to 8 years 5 months. The typically developing children identified by their teachers as average readers for their age demonstrate even cognitive profiles over all the measures, whereas the slower readers for their age in the same classes turn out to be significantly delayed relative to the average readers on all these measures. The children with Down syndrome, while matched with the slower readers on the reading measures, are significantly behind them on the number, language and memory measures. In other words, the children with Down syndrome show advanced reading ability compared to all their other cognitive skills at this time.

Table 16.1 Cognitive profiles of three groups of children from the same school classes. The measures are scales from standardized tests and the results are expressed as age related scores in years and months (Adapted from Byrne *et al.*, 1995)

Group	N	mean age	read age BAS	read age KAB	read comp KAB	spell age BAS	numb age BAS	vocab age BPVS	gram age TROG	digit span BAS
Down syndrome	24	8.2	6.3	6.3	6.6	6.4	4.1	4.5	4.3	6.7
Average readers	42	7.3	7.3	7.6	7.6	7.6	7.3	7.9	8.0	17.9
Reading matched	31	7.1	6.4	6.6	6.6	6.9	6.4	6.3	5.9	15.4

Key:
BAS – British Ability Scales
KAB – Kaufman Assessment Battery
BPVS – British Picture Vocabulary Scale
TROG – Test for Reception of Grammar

Table 16.2 shows the scores for the children with Down syndrome when they are divided into three groups according to their age and school year. The figures in this table illustrate steady progress in every measure with age for the children with Down syndrome, though it must be remembered that this is cross-sectional not longitudinal data. We will have longitudinal data for all these children in due course. For most measures, the gains made by Group 3 compared to Group 2 are much larger than those made by Group 2 compared to Group 1. On all but one of the reading and number measures the children in Group 3 show at least a 12-month gain and their mean age is 16 months older than Group 2. There seems to be a spurt in development here which could be linked to progress in reading and we will explore this later in the chapter.

Table 16.2 Cognitive profiles of children with Down syndrome divided into three groups on the basis of age and school year (Adapted from Byrne *et al.*, 1995)

Children with Down syndrome	Group 1 N = 8	Group 2 N = 9	Group 3 N = 5
Mean age – months	6yrs 8m	8yrs 3m	9yrs 7m
1 BAS – reading	5.25 (5y5m)	14.44 (6y2m)	38.60 (7y2m)
2 KAB – reading	6.00 (5y3m)	12.00 (6y3m)	20.60 (7y6m)
3 KAB – understand	0.00 (6y3m)	0.56 (6y6m)	4.20 (7y0m)
4 BAS – spelling	0.75 (6y1m)	1.00 (6y1m)	5.50 (7y2m)
5 BAS – number	6.00 (3y8m)	8.78 (3y11m)	16.20 (4y11m)
6 BAS – digits	5.13	5.89	10.60
7 BAS – visual recall I	2.63	4.13	4.8
8 BAS – visual recall D	0.38	2.5	1.75
9 BPVS – vocabulary	8.25 (3y7m)	9.75 (4y5m)	12.00 (5y4m)
10 TROG – grammar	3.75 (<4y0m)	6.33 (4y3m)	7.80 (5y0m)

HOW SHOULD THEY BE TAUGHT TO READ AND WRITE?

In addressing the question of teaching methods, the relevant issue is whether there are any differences in the way one should teach a child with Down syndrome to read compared with the teaching methods used for typically developing children. In our view, the same methods should be used for all children but teachers will need to take account of the relative delay in language knowledge and memory skills of the children with Down syndrome when teaching them to read.

We would teach all children by establishing a small sight vocabulary first, choosing words and sentences that the children use every day in their speech and encouraging them to build their own phrases and sentences with this sight vocabulary. Next, while continuing to expand their sight vocabulary, we would be teaching letter-sound correspondences using the words the children can already read in order to do this in a way which shows them from the start how the letter-sound knowledge can help them to read an unfamiliar word. We would be encouraging the children to write from the start, tracing over words and sentences with fingers and pens, then moving on to copying and free writing. This approach fits in with the research on children's reading development which indicates that all children move from a logographic stage (when words are recognized by 'sight' only) to an alphabetic stage (when words can be 'sounded out' letter by letter) and then to an orthographic stage (Frith, 1985; Gathercole and Baddeley, 1993a). Frith emphasizes that it is the activity of writing and spelling that develops the child's use of an alphabetic strategy.

Three reading strategies

Research shows that there are three strategies that can be used when reading, 'visual', 'phonological' and 'context'. First, as printed words become familiar to the reader, they are stored in a visual word store in the brain and then recognized directly when reading by comparison with the stored visual image. This is called the direct visual route for reading. Secondly, once letter-sound rules are known then an unfamiliar word can be read by 'sounding it out' to identify its spoken form from the store of spoken word forms that have been established in the brain during learning to talk. This is called the 'phonological' route to reading. When faced with an unfamiliar word in a sentence, a third strategy for decoding it can be used, that of 'context'. The word can be guessed as one which will be grammatically correct and fit the story. Here the reader is drawing on their language knowledge to find the word rather than decoding it visually or phonologically.

In reality, more than one strategy may be in use simultaneously. For example, if using 'context' to guess an unfamiliar word in a sentence, several words might fit in semantically and grammatically, but only one of these synonyms will match the letters on the page phonically, so a final correct choice will depend on letter-sound knowledge. Young children at the logographic stage, with little phonic knowledge, may be quite happy to guess and insert a word that is semantically correct, but not orthographically correct, so, for example reading 'shut' when the printed word is 'closed' (Buckley, 1985; Seymour and Elder, 1986).

Children with Down syndrome seem to often be good 'visual' readers, finding it relatively easy to establish a sight vocabulary from as early as two years of age. Using the 'phonological' route and the 'context' strategy depend on any child having an adequate knowledge of vocabulary and grammar. The word can only be decoded by 'sounding out' if the word is in the child's spoken vocabulary. The word can only be guessed as one that will fit in the sentence if it is a known word and if the child is able to understand the whole sentence, both syntactically and semantically. This will require the sentence structure to be at a grammatical level that the child has mastered, and then the ideas conveyed will only be understood if they are within the child's experience. Children with Down syndrome will usually have considerably less language knowledge than other children at their reading level, so be less able to use context and phonological recoding strategies to access words and meaning. Further, to be good at phonological recoding, a child must be able to hear all the sounds in the words and, given the hearing loss and auditory processing problems that the children often have, they are likely to be less able to use this route with ease than their typically developing peers.

Our observations however, suggest that despite these very real additional difficulties experienced by the child-with Down syndrome compared to typically developing children, they do progress to being able to use phonological recoding for reading and spelling, and they are able to use context. For the teacher, it is essential that he or she understand the level of skills that the child brings to the task and that he or she helps the child to progress slowly but steadily in using all three strategies. It is particularly important that teachers know how much language knowledge a child has in order to avoid exposing the child to material that he or she can read aloud but cannot decode for meaning. Further, all children learn new language from reading (Garton and Pratt, 1989) so it is very important that the teacher appreciates that reading can be a powerful way to help the child expand language knowledge. Evidence presented in the case histories and elsewhere in this chapter suggests that learning new language from reading may be more effective for the child with Down syndrome than learning from listening, as they have significant auditory processing and memory difficulties which visual learning may help to overcome.

ARE CHILDREN WITH DOWN SYNDROME USING THE SAME COGNITIVE STRATEGIES TO READ AS OTHER TYPICALLY DEVELOPING CHILDREN?

Our observational data to date suggests that children with Down syndrome are using the same strategies as typically developing children when learning to read, though they may progress from one stage to the next rather more slowly. We have records of children making both visual errors (e.g. confusing 'this' and 'shoe' or 'hair' and 'rain') and semantic errors (e.g. reading 'closed' for 'shut' or 'flannel' for 'bath') characteristic of the logographic stage in the early stages of their reading development, when they have no knowledge of letter-sound rules. Later they progress to an alphabetic stage and are able to use phonic knowledge for reading and spelling. As their vocabulary and knowledge of grammar grow, they are increasingly able to use context to identify new words.

Our longitudinal study will provide more adequate information as we are assessing their strategy use and progress over time using a variety of computerized tasks based on Seymour and Elder (1986).

WILL THE ACTIVITY OF LEARNING TO READ DEVELOP OTHER COGNITIVE SKILLS?

Research on the links between typically developing children's reading progress and other aspects of cognitive development suggest reciprocal interactions. The more language knowledge and the better the phonological awareness and working memory skills children bring to the task of reading, the faster they will learn to read in the first year of reading instruction. In the second year, reading success appears to develop working memory and phonological awareness skills (Ellis and Large 1988; Gathercole and Baddeley, 1993b). Being able to read opens up access to knowledge and the biggest vocabulary explosion for children is between the ages of about 7 and 16, when children are typically learning on average 3,000 words every year (Nagy and Herman, 1987). Reading and writing also teach children correct grammar (Hutt, 1981).

While we are as yet unable to support the argument that reading will have the same benefits for children with Down syndrome with sufficient data, the figures in Table 16.2 illustrate significant gains in reading scores for Group 3 compared to Group 2 and in digit span scores (a working memory measure). The language measures and all the other measures with the exception of visual memory show significant gains between Groups 1 and 3. This is suggestive of functional links between the abilities measured that show significant gains over the same period, but of course cannot demonstrate the direction of any possible causal links. It is hoped that the longitudinal data on these children will increase our understanding of the issues. We would contend that these skills, reading, language and working memory, are likely to be reciprocally interactive and that progress in any one may 'bootstrap' progress in another. In children with specific learning difficulties such as the children with Down syndrome the direction of this 'bootstrapping' between skills may not be the same at any one developmental point as that seen in typically developing children.

One area where we do have some data is on the effect of reading on speech and language skills. For the young children, case study records suggest that reading encourages progress to longer utterances and improved grammar in speech. They also suggest that reading improves articulation and speech intelligibility. For most children with Down syndrome, there is a well-documented lag between comprehension and expressive speech skills, probably due to a variety of difficulties which may include problems with word retrieval, sentence structuring and speech-motor control. The limited development of working memory may also be implicated so that reading may provide the opportunity to practise saying sentences which the child is unable to generate spontaneously even though he or she understands them. This hypothesis is supported by the results of work with adolescents with Down syndrome (Buckley, 1993, 1994, 1995). In a study designed to improve the productive syntax of a group of 12 teenagers, teaching which used print to support the learning was more effective in teaching correct production over six different sentence structures than speech and picture only teaching. All the teenagers did better in the reading condition (see Buckley, 1993), but there were large individual differences. The teenagers who gained the most were those with no reading ability and the smallest digit spans. At the end of the training year, the teenagers demonstrated a significant gain in comprehension of grammar compared to a previous baseline year of no intervention beyond ordinary school practice and a significant increase in the length of the utterances that they used in everyday conversation (Buckley, 1995).

CONCLUSION

We hope that we have convinced the reader that most children with Down syndrome are able to achieve a useful level of literacy ability and that all the children should have an opportunity to learn to read, as even a small sight vocabulary will help their speech and language skills and may improve their auditory discrimination and working memory function. Reading instruction should be considered as soon as the child has single-word comprehension as the earlier the child is able to establish a sight vocabulary, the greater the benefit for his or her language and cognitive development.

ACKNOWLEDGEMENTS

The authors would like to express their thanks to all the schools, parents and children without whom this work would not have been possible.

REFERENCES

Buckley, S.J. (1985) Attaining basic educational skills: reading, writing and number. In Lane. D and Stratford B. *Current Approaches to Down's Syndrome*, London: Holt, Rinehart and Winston.

Buckley, S.J. (1993) Developing the speech and language skills of teenagers with Down's syndrome. *Down's Syndrome: Research and Practice*, **1** (2), pp. 63–71.

Buckley, S.J. (1994) Improving the expressive grammar of teenagers with Down's syndrome. In J. Clibbens and B. Pendleton (eds), *Proceedings of the Child Language Seminar*, Plymouth: University of Plymouth.

Buckley, S.J. (in press) Increasing the conversational utterance length of teenagers with Down's syndrome. *Down's Syndrome: Research and Practice*.

Buckley, S.J. and Bird, G. (1993) Teaching children with Down syndrome to read. *Down's Syndrome: Research and Practice*, **1** (1), pp. 34–41.

Buckley, S.J. and Bird, G. (1994) *Meeting the Educational Needs of Children with Down Syndrome*, Portsmouth: University of Portsmouth.

Buckley, S.J., Emslie, M., Haslegrave, G and LePrevost, P. (1986) *The Development of Language and Reading Skills in Children with Down's Syndrome*, (new edition, 1993), Portsmouth: Portsmouth Polytechnic.

Buckley, S.J. and Sacks, B.I. (1987) *The Adolescent with Down Syndrome: Life for the Teenager and for the Family*, Portsmouth: Portsmouth Polytechnic.

Butterfield, E.C. (1961) A provocative case of overachievement by a mongoloid. *American Journal of Mental Deficiency*, **66**, pp. 444–48.

Byrne, Buckley, MacDonald and Bird (1995) Investigating the literacy, language and memory skills of children with Down's syndrome and their mainstream peers. *Down's Syndrome: Research and Practice*, (in press).

Carr, J. and Hewitt, S. (1982) Children with Down syndrome growing up. *Association for Child Psychology and Psychiatry News*, **10**, pp. 10–13.

Carter, S. (1985) Darings world of books. *Exceptional Parent*, May, pp. 23–25.

Casey, W., Jones, D., Kugler, B. and Watkins, B. (1988) Integration of Down syndrome children in the primary school: a longitudinal study of cognitive development and academic attainments. *British Journal of Educational Psychology*, **58**, pp. 279–86.

Cossu, G., Rossini, F. and Marshall, J.C. (1993) When reading is acquired but phonemic awareness is not: a study of literacy in Down syndrome. *Cognition*, **46**, pp. 129–38.

Duffen, L. (1976) Teaching reading to teach language. *Remedial Education*, **11** (3), pp. 139–42.

Ellis, N. and Large, B. (1988) The early stages of reading: a longitudinal study. *Applied Cognitive Psychology*, **2**, pp. 47–76.

Evans, R. (1994) Phonological awareness in children with Down syndrome. *Down's Syndrome: Research and Practice*, **2** (3), pp. 102 – 05.

Fowler, A. (1990) Language abilities in children with Down's syndrome: evidence for specific syntactic delay. In D. Cicchetti, and M. Beeghly (eds), *Children with Down's Syndrome: a Developmental Perspective*, Cambridge: Cambridge University Press.

Frith, U. (1985) Beneath the surface of developmental dyslexia. In K.E. Patterson, J.C. Marshall and M. Coltheart (eds), *Surface Dyslexia*. Hove: LEA.

Garton, A and Pratt, C. (1989) *Learning to be Literate*, Oxford: Blackwell.

Gathercole, S. and Baddeley, A. (1993a) *Working Memory and Language*. Hove: LEA.

Gathercole, S. and Baddeley, A. (1993b) Phonological working memory: a critical building block for reading development and vocabulary acquisition. *European Journal of the Psychology of Education*, **8**, pp. 259–72.

Hayden, A.H. and Dmitriev, V. (1975) The multidisciplinary Preschool Programme for Down syndrome children at the University of Washington Model Preschool Centre. In B.Z. Friedlander, G.E. Kirk and G.M. Sterritt, *Exceptional Infant*, vol 3.

Hulme, C. and Mackenzie, S. (1992) *Working Memory and Severe Learning Difficulty*, London: LEA.

Hunt, N. (1966) *The World of Nigel Hunt*, London: Darwen Finlayson.

Hutt, E.L. (1981) *Teaching Language Disordered Children: A Structured Curriculum*, London: Edward Arnold.

Lorenz, S., Sloper, P. and Cunningham, C. (1985) Reading and Down syndrome. *British Journal of Special Education*, **13** (2), pp. 65–67.

Nagy, W.E. and Herman, P.A (1987) Breadth and depth of vocabulary knowledge: implications for acquisition and instruction. In M.G. McKeown and M.E. Curtis (eds), *The Nature of Vocabulary Acquisition*. Hillsdale: Lawrence Erlbaum.

Norris, H. (1989). Teaching reading to help develop language in very young children with Down's syndrome. Paper presented at the National Portage Conference, Peterborough.

Pieterse, M. and Treloar, R. (1981) *The Down Syndrome Program: Progress Report 1981*, Sydney: Macquarie University.

Pueschel, S.M. and Hopmann, M.R. (1993) Speech and language abilities of children with Down's syndrome. In Kaisen, A.P. and Gray, D.B. (eds), *Enhancing children's Communication: Research Foundations for Intervention*, pp. 335–62, London: Brookes.

Seagoe, M.V. (1964) *Yesterday Was Tuesday, All Day and All Night: the Story of a Unique Education*, Toronto: Little Brown.

Seymour, P.H.K. and Elder, L. (1986) Beginning reading without phonology. *Cognitive Neuropsychology*, **3** (1), pp. 1–36.

Sloper, P., Cunningham, C., Turner, S. and Knussen, C. (1990) Factors related to the academic attainments of children with Down's syndrome. *British Journal of Educational Psychology*, **60**, 284–98.

17 Continuing Literacy Development

Margaret Farrell

This chapter considers some of the issues related to continuing literacy-learning for older children, adolescents and adults with Down syndrome. It is assumed that such learning is for personal and social development, as well as for work skills and functional needs for living in the community.

We know children with Down syndrome can successfully learn basic reading and writing skills (Chapter 16). Much less is known about continuing literacy development in older children and adolescents. This is perhaps because less, one might even say *little*, has been systematically tried (Carr, 1994; Sloper *et al.*, 1990). There are two possible explanations of this. Because we are so used to thinking in terms of normal development, teachers, and perhaps many parents, may have assumed that if certain educational benchmarks are not attained by early adolescence they *never* will be attained. Second, teachers may have been influenced by the idea that children with Down syndrome reach a learning plateau, and therefore may have regarded academic goals as a waste of time for older students. At upper primary and secondary levels, and particularly in special education, this belief has led to an emphasis on practical living-skills and a neglect of continuing development in literacy and numeracy.

Language and general cognitive development are the most serious casualties of this self-fullfilling prophecy. Because their growth in language and basic literacy skills takes longer, young people with Down syndrome are being denied the very educational experiences they need in order to develop these skills further. Practical living-skills instruction seldom includes the intentional development of social concepts, general knowledge, problem-solving and thinking skills which are the basis of the regular upper primary and secondary school curriculum, although there is no logical reason why this should be so. Moreover, even though it can be demonstrated that people with intellectual handicaps have a great deal to gain from continuing opportunities to learn, comparatively few of them have access to further appropriate education after secondary school. This is true even in communities in developed countries, where the need for postsecondary and further education is generally acknowledged and provided for. It must be argued that provision of this extra time for students with intellectual disabilities is an equity issue.

Further, this issue is not simply one of extra educational time. The appropriateness of the educational plan is also important, and significant concerns related to educational setting remain unresolved (Chapter 23, this volume). With legislative support for community participation and normalization for persons with disabilities, educational rhetoric has tended to favour instruction in mainstream, or so-called inclusive, settings rather than in special education. Yet, in spite of the many appealing philosophical arguments put forward, many of the practical aspects of this ideal have not been addressed. There is a need for empirical research about the efficacy of inclusive education and its ability to provide systematic instruction for individuals with intellectual disabilities. Research also needs to be undertaken related to the skills, attitudes and concerns of teachers, and to the transfer of resources from special education to the special needs sector of regular classes. In many situations, the implementation of inclusive education appears to have been associated with cost-cutting, and conditions are created in classrooms which may affect all students adversely.

INSTRUCTIONAL APPROACHES

Instructional approaches depend to a large extent on the educational context. Traditionally, students who have intellectual disabilities have been thought to benefit from the individually based, structured techniques possible in small classes in special educational settings, but these approaches may not be so easy to implement in regular classrooms where there are many students to consider. In classrooms in regular education the majority of students are operating at a more advanced cognitive level, dealing with more complex content, and learning at a much faster rate than the child with special needs. Because teachers have to distribute their time and attention equitably, those students who take longer to learn, who require simpler tasks because they lack prerequisite skills, who need more carefully sequenced subject materials and who require more supervised practice, may be severely disadvantaged. Given the faster learning of normal children, the attainments of the slower-achieving students can seem to be more incompatible with the general classroom level with each passing year. By about Year 4, for example, in almost every subject area for which the teacher plans, the prerequisite knowledge and skills of the child with Down syndrome may seem inadequate.

Even with the best intentions, unless teachers have recourse to adaptive techniques, as well as to appropriate resources and generous provision of classroom aid, the slower achievers are likely to be able to participate less and less easily in whole-group instruction and to fall further and further behind. They are usually quite aware that they are not coping, and just like other discouraged children with special needs, including very bright children who experience specific learning difficulties, they may become either passive spectators or troublesome students who act out their frustration in non-compliance and maladaptive behaviours.

Special education too has come in for its share of criticism. In the past, students with intellectual disabilities have been largely segregated from normal peers. Often they have had few opportunities to play, talk and interact socially with non-disabled children other than their siblings. That is, they have fewer positive peer models, receive less interactional feedback from non-disabled peers about how they are doing in work and play, and have little practice in understanding and meeting the social and linguistic expectations of the wider community. The cynics suggest that special education teaches children *how* to be intellectually disabled.

Others have argued that the structured teaching techniques and smaller class numbers which appear to help slower students achieve specific learning goals may themselves have a downside, particularly if behavioural methods are employed. Such instruction has often relied on rote, or drill and skill approaches (Roehler and Duffy, 1991), with tasks broken down and divided into separate skills to be mastered one at a time. Although the intention is to simplify the learning, students taught by such methods frequently have difficulty in generalizing and applying it (Ballard, 1987). This may be because the discrete components learned do not relate, from the learner's point of view, to any useful purpose. Although the teacher knows why a specific skill is being taught, it is not always self-evident, nor clearly conveyed, to the student. A well-known example of this is the phenomenon of reading words without any attempt at understanding. The reading is regarded by the student as a performance rather than a search for information and ideas.

Further, subskills may be taught in a conceptual void, the learner having no overview of how complex processes like reading and writing actually work. They may not even recognize that print is speech or thought written down. Consequently, students taught by these methods may not apply their oral language skills to reading. That is, they do not have the opportunity to learn how to use their understanding of speech and their control of phonology and syntax, to monitor meaning, to problem-solve, or to use self-help strategies. Recognition of the importance of conceptual development in early reading and writing has been growing in the last three decades (Clay, 1972; Downing, 1979; Durkin, 1966; Dyson, 1982; Ferriero, 1985; Francis, 1982; Sulzby and Teale, 1991; Teale, 1982). All students need to understand how the skills they are learning are interrelated, and how they fit with what they already know. Students need to know the purposes for which they are learning skills, and how, when and where to use them.

A related concern is that strong adult direction may not always be the best way to promote students' self-motivation and initiative. Gunn (1993) suggested that learners are more likely to initiate practice and maintain and generalize skill when they see an activity as enjoyable and of personal use. Arousing interest and sponteneity, and offering students opportunities for choice, may be as important in academic work as in leisure activities. Our enthusiasm for early intervention and systematic instruction ought not to be imposed on slower-developing children as a tedious series of 'tasks to be mastered almost from the day that they are born' (ibid., p. 9).

Overemphasis on individual teacher-directed instruction also limits opportunities for spontaneous interactions with teachers and classmates. It provides little practice of participatory skills such as turn-taking, attending, responding to the contributions of others, and gaining and maintaining adult and peer attention (Ballard, 1987). Independence and motivation can be enhanced when students are given opportunities to select and control learning materials, and when they are assisted to self-pace, self-monitor and self-correct (Turner, 1992). It is clear that for all children the right to learn has to be balanced by the right to become a self-managing learner.

In literacy education the emphasis in special education has most often been on teaching reading vocabulary associated with functional life-skills, such as cooking, using public transport or following written instructions about household chores and appliances. Less often has there been an emphasis on using print for pleasure and social purposes or as a medium for improving listening, speaking, thinking and learning. Persons with Down syndrome, and those of us who would like to assist them to read and write, need to be in no doubt of the importance of literacy in getting what we need and want in our world, and in becoming who we want to be. While trying to devise effective ways of teaching the skills of literacy, it is important to let these young persons share our experience of the power and magic of literacy and our appreciation of its utility for individual expression, communication, amusement, intellectual stimulation and social participation. In high-quality educational settings these experiences are offered long before the children begin to read and write for themselves, and continue throughout the long learning process.

Neither regular nor special education settings in their present forms may be able to provide everything needed to help students with intellectual disabilities. The ideal setting may need to include the best features of both. While it is more difficult to maximize some learning outcomes for the slower learners in regular classrooms, the very experience of interactive, self-motivated learning is important in itself. We do not need new magical solutions, but we will have to use the well-tried principles of good teaching practice. For models, we need to look to those classroom teachers who are efficient organizers, expert problem-solvers and resourceful and meticulous planners, and who are considerate and persistent in collaborative settings. Certainly, teachers will need supportive, flexible administrative policies within their schools, which include provision of time to consult about, plan and organize co-operative teaching with colleagues. They will need adequate material resources, ready access to information, relevant in-service training and above all adequate staffing levels.

PLANNING FOR STUDENTS WITH DOWN SYNDROME

To choose appropriate goals and to programme adaptively for exceptional students, teachers need an understanding of those students' attainments and of their learning strengths and difficulties. What can be expected of young people with Down syndrome in middle-to-upper primary school and secondary school? This is not an easy question, because the Down syndrome population includes a wide range of abilities, as does the rest of the population. There are high achievers who attain some skill levels close to the average range, and there are some who are severely retarded. As Perera (1994) pointed out, it is important to recognize this range, lest parents feel disappointed or in some way responsible when differences in ability among persons with Down syndrome become apparent. On the other hand, shared family characteristics and environment have been found to be quite significant predictors of children's development (Crombie, 1994; Sloper *et al.*, 1990). For example, being involved in interesting family conversations and social activities, sharing books and seeing other family members reading and writing at home are just as important for children with Down syndrome as they are for other children. But when comparing students who have Down syndrome with non-disabled children, the important thing to remember is the difference in chronological milestones. Children with Down syndrome develop intellectually at a much slower rate. Although 12-year-old students with Down syndrome may be as mature physically as their age peers, and share similar social interests, they are likely to be functioning cognitively and linguistically at a much lower level – perhaps within the same range as non-disabled 6 or 7-year-olds.

READING SKILLS IN PERSPECTIVE

When evaluating work and planning individual instructional goals, it is helpful to consider the errors, difficulties and cognitive strategies of an intellectually disabled student in the light of what we know about younger non-disabled students at a similar cognitive, linguistic and conceptual level. Comparisons might also be usefully made, with students with specific reading and writing disabilities who have received the same amount and type of teaching as the children with intellectual disabilities. It should be remembered that (for all learners) effective use of learning strategies depends on prerequisite knowledge and skill (Brown, 1982; Chi, 1981). For example, most reading instruction for children with intellectual disabilities has been based on whole-word or sight methods of word recognition (Connors, 1992; Hoogeveen and Smeets, 1990), the assumption presumably being that such children do not make use of phonological cues.

Work with older children with Down syndrome suggests that this is not the case (Farrell and Elkins, 1994/95). It may simply be that they do not have the prerequisite skills and knowledge to do so. Although there are a number of reports of students with Down syndrome learning rudimentary phonics at the one-letter/one-sound level (cat, dog, bun), few such children appear to have received long-term, systematic instruction in phoneme/grapheme correspondences at the letter-cluster level (for example, ir, spr, igh, tion, old, dge, air, ace), even though 'English is quite regular' when analysed in these ways (Mason, 1977). There are hardly any reports of students with intellectual disabilities being systematically shown how to use analogy, word structure, inflections, syllabification or suffixes and prefixes in decoding. Further, although we know that for all literacy-learners, one of the most significant sources of difficulty in decoding is lack of phonemic awareness (the ability to perceive and manipulate sounds in words), there are very few studies reporting phonemic awareness training for children with intellectual disabilities (Hoogeveen and Smeets, 1990). The attempts of intellectually disabled students to pronounce unknown words are, therefore, very like those of non-disabled youngsters in the early stages of reading who have still to learn a wider range of word-analysis strategies. They seem, as Mason (1977) put it, to rely on 'a word memorizing strategy to pronounce words'.

Research with non-disabled children has shown that an extensive automatic sight vocabulary facilitates access to text meanings (Adams and Huggins, 1985), so acquisition of a sight vocabulary is an important beginning skill. We also know from the general literature that acquisition of sight vocabulary is more rapid when readers can use phonemic and orthographic knowledge to identify unknown words (Adams, 1990; Chall, 1983; Gough *et al.*, 1992; Stanovich, 1986). Conners (1992, p. 591), noting the 'sparse' research on reading instruction for students with moderate mental retardation, reported that 'word analysis, or phonic analysis, has been shown to be superior to word-supply methods in the long run for oral reading-error correction'. Bateman (1991) stressed the importance of phonological instruction in word recognition for all children who 'need good instruction', including children labelled slow learners, learning disabled, specific reading retarded, reading backward, and dyslexic. Research related to teaching non-disabled children also emphatically endorses this view (Adams, 1990; Gough *et al.*, 1992; Nicholson, 1992; Perfetti, 1985; Stanovich, 1986; Tunmer and Chapman, 1993).

We know that students with intellectual disabilities, including children with Down syndrome, can be taught sight vocabulary at a very early age by using flash cards in conjunction with spoken words and phrases (Buckley, 1985; Buckley and Bird, 1993). We also know that they can be effectively instructed in a variety of other word-recognition strategies which can draw on this sight-word knowledge, including using analogies of known sight words (Guthrie and Cunningham, 1982); using onset and rhyme (Buckley and Bird, 1993); and phonemic decoding (Bateman, 1991; Conners, 1992; Hoogeveen and Smeets, 1990; Meyers, 1990; Pieterse and Treloar, 1981). Past debates about reading (particularly in relation to hard-to-teach children) have centred on which of these skills should be given instructional precedence. It would be more useful to look at their compatibility and interdependence (Conners, 1992).

But as Bateman (1991, p. 13) pointed out, 'the application of phonics skills is only one of the ways children use to recognize words', albeit an important part. Although a vast amount of the general reading literature is devoted to the use of context and prediction skills in reading comprehension and word recognition, it would seem nothing has been reported about teaching comprehension strategies and thinking skills to children with intellectual difficulties, or about teaching semantic and syntactic cueing skills which would help them monitor their reading accuracy and understanding, and provide an additional support for letter-based and word-based decoding strategies.

MEDIATING LITERACY

Although learning words is an essential part of the early reading process, there is a lot more to literacy than learning about letters and words. Learning to read and write is a long and quite difficult process for most students, and entails gradual acquisition of many complex interdependent skills and understandings. Although a number of non-disabled children appear to pick up literacy skills effortlessly and without apparent explicit instruction, it is by no means a natural process (Reid, 1993). Cazden (1992) wrote of the necessity of 'a continuum of experiences with print that are mediated for the learner by different kinds of social assistance'. One kind of assistance involves what Cazden (1992, p. 306) terms the 'socialization of attention', the role of assistance – given less consciously by parent to child, more deliberately by teacher to student or class – is to focus attention on the most significant features, or those features that particular learners seem to be ignoring. The teacher both selects examples and focuses attention at the moment of encounter.

A second kind of assistance, described sometimes as 'scaffolding' (Greenfield, 1984; Wood, 1988) or 'assisted performance' (Tharp and Gallimore, 1989), provides support-in-action, which allows learners to perform and practise tasks, with adult assistance, which they could not do alone. In favoured circumstances in our culture, development in literacy for non-disabled children accompanies the development of speech and cognitive functioning. Children with intellectual disabilities also learn from both spontaneous and intentional socially mediated experiences. Understandings about literacy can begin in infancy and continue through life (see also Ferriero, 1985; Feuerstein, 1985; Reid, 1993; Snow, 1983; Sulzby and Teale, 1991; Teale, 1982; Vygotsky, 1978).

LANGUAGE

It is usually assumed that language skills are a prerequisite for literacy. Traditionally, literacy instruction has taken children's abilities in speaking, listening and understanding rather for granted, perhaps because of the seemingly effortless competence of most non-disabled children. The relationships between certain aspects of language, and difficulties in learning to read and write, are now being more closely studied (Catts, 1991). Children who come from a disadvantaged (Fox, 1990) or different (Delpit, 1988) language environment appear more likely to experience difficulty. Children with Down syndrome generally experience so much difficulty with receptive and expressive language that they may, in fact, be helped to learn language through literacy instruction (Buckley and Bird, 1993).

The delay in language development of students with Down syndrome is usually apparent in spoken language, and difficulties may be experienced in word recall, articulation, syntax, and the formulation and expression of ideas. Understanding the speech of others appears somewhat less difficult for them, although middle ear disorders, such as conductive deafness, quite often interfere with receptive processes, and may further inhibit the development of articulation, vocabulary and grammar. Oral comprehension can also be affected by auditory memory difficulties, for example, in relation to processing sentences or instructions. Verbal instruction is more effective when combined with visual or activity-based information, and it is wise to seek some feedback during spoken communication, such as asking a student to repeat a question or to rehearse instructions. Processing written sentences may also be more difficult for persons experiencing auditory memory deficits, particularly if the decoding process is laboured. On the other hand, written language is less transient than speech and allows time for reflection and discussion through rereading. Given that language is the basis for most learning, it is extremely important for teachers to understand the factors affecting language processing, particularly in the case of students with learning or intellectual disabilities.

Provided the auditory stimulus is clearly heard, the main factors involved in oral comprehension are language processing skills (word recall, working memory and memory strategies); control of grammar and syntax; general and linguistic knowledge (concepts and vocabulary which have been acquired through experience and learning); and the students' general level of intellectual functioning. Achievement in these areas can be improved through mediated experiences, instruction and assisted performance. Many important aspects of actively listening for information can be taught (Brown, 1980; Feuerstein, 1980; Snow, 1983; Tharp and Gallimore, 1989; Vygotsky, 1968).

Auditory perception, understanding and remembering are interdependent processes. For example, we can often compensate for missing or unclear auditory information if we know, in general, what to expect. Comprehension is also easier when we are familiar with the context and the content of the language, and when we have some expectation of what the purpose of the communication may be. Also we usually remember better if we see what new information and procedures have to do with what we already know. Teachers can help children by encouraging comparison, review and prediction, and by linking new learning with familiar ideas and situations.

COMPREHENSION

Literacy cannot contribute to continuing, lifelong learning unless it is based on effective comprehension. Some important ways of helping students with intellectual disabilities improve their oral and written comprehension skills in the classroom would therefore be: providing flexible control of noise levels; arranging seating so that the students who need it have easy access to help and information; gaining students' attention (including eye contact) before speaking to them; focusing students on the object or topic under discussion (using such means as pointing, intonation, highlighting, underlining or coloured chalk); controlling the length of questions and instructions; eliciting frequent feedback from listeners and readers to ensure they have understood; waiting while students ask and respond to questions, and encouraging other students to do likewise; modelling appropriate responses so that other students can learn to assist the students who are having difficulty listening and speaking; providing for, and encouraging, support from peers; and providing a variety of alternative modes of communication, such as visual aids, video, manipulative and concrete materials, dramatic enactments and signing. It would also be important to help these students to recognize when they were not understanding and to encourage them to ask for assistance or additional information.

Expressive and receptive language and growth in world knowledge are mutually facilitative. The care adults take in mediating language and ideas is important for all students who experience memory and language difficulties, but immensely so for children with Down syndrome.

PEER INTERACTIONS

Students with intellectual disabilities may not know how to initiate and sustain conversations, or how to seek help from more able peers. Specific instruction, including modelling, feedback and practice, may be needed to make them aware of the social graces, language conventions and timing involved in successfully enlisting support, and in working and playing with others. These skills are important in all contexts, and their acquisition cannot be taken for granted. Cullinan *et al.* (1992, p. 348), stressed that

> social mainstreaming needs are too important to be left solely to informal interaction and the serendipitous 'teachable moment'. On the contrary, social mainstreaming goals and objectives should be explicit, and activities should be systematic, with specific activities allocated to particular time periods . . . The beauty of teaching social skills lies in their importance in the day-to-day life functioning of students – in school, on the playground, on the bus, in the home and neighbourhood, immediately as well as throughout the school career and thereafter.

Related to this, because work in small co-operative groups may be very valuable, explicit instruction and guided practice in how to work co-operatively would be necessary, not only for the student with Down syndrome, but for the whole class. Gillies (1994) has shown that, with such guidance, learning for the lower achievers in mixed ability co-operative groups is more likely, be enhanced. The same has been shown to apply with peer tutors (Heward *et al.*, 1982; Topping, 1989). Both tutors and students appear to benefit from interactions when care is taken with implementation. For example, Cooke *et al.* (1982) described how peer tutors helped a 7-year-old child with Down syndrome in a Year 1 classroom improve her sight vocabulary.

Peter

The importance of well orchestrated assistance from peers is illustrated vividly in *Educating Peter* (Goodwin and Wurzburg, 1992), a video documentary about a third-grader with Down syndrome who transferred from a special school to a fully inclusive classroom. Peter seemed not well prepared for the social demands of this new context and initially engaged in a number of challenging behaviours. The teacher and the school counsellor wisely enlisted the aid of his classmates, and together they studied the situations in which Peter's unacceptable behaviour usually occurred. Since challenging behaviours are for the most part learned and not necessarily associated with Down syndrome, together they were able to devise and implement strategies which helped them respond promptly and firmly during troublesome episodes. This problem-solving approach, carefully guided and monitored by the teachers, elicited responsible support from his classmates and eventually helped Peter become an accepted and valued class member. The camera candidly recorded Peter's initial difficulties and documented his social and educational gains. The value to the class of their experiences is reflected in the remarks of one young class commentator: 'You think that you're teaching Peter things, but really Peter's teaching you things. We might be teaching him stuff like how to do things, but he's teaching us more how to think and how to react to other problems.'

Differences in social adjustment among children with Down syndrome depend on a variety of personal, family and environmental factors. So too do differences in academic attainments. Reading skills vary according to aptitude, intellectual maturity, home experiences with literacy, and the amount and type of formal teaching the children have received. Many reports have documented early educational attainments achieved when expectations of success are combined with opportunities to learn, and systematic, appropriate instruction.

Nigel Hunt

Probably the best-known instance of literacy in a person with Down syndrome is the 1967 publication *The World of Nigel Hunt: the Diary of a Mongoloid Youth*. This delightful book, often quoted, but perhaps too seldom read, has much to tell us. The first surprise is the realization that this is indeed Nigel's own work. In the preface, Nigel's father explains how their son, thought by contemporary experts to be 'quite ineducable', was taught to read and spell, largely through the efforts of his mother. Mrs Hunt, with unfailing confidence in her son's capacities, and, according to her husband, an 'almost incredible patience and persistence', playfully introduced Nigel to the principles of print, or what we would now refer to as phonemic awareness and concepts about words and letters. Mr Hunt (ibid., pp. 23–24) wrote:

> Almost as soon as he could talk, Grace started to spell short words to him phonetic-ally ... While she was doing her washing Grace would show Nigel a packet of 'Daz' and say, 'This is my Der, A, Zer – Daz.' In this way she exploited the echolalia which is so typical of mongolism. Nigel would repeat what she had said. And so it would go, with 'Ker, A, Per – cap,' 'Ker, O, two F's make Fer, Two E's make an EEE – coffee.'

From about the age of five years, as Nigel played with plastic letters, Grace encouraged him to say the appropriate letter sounds. Eventually Nigel learned to do this and then one day she heard 'some intriguing goings-on in the kitchen'. Nigel was seated on the floor rearranging the grocery cupboard. As he put each tin and packet carefully back in place he enthusiastically applied his letter sound skills to the pronunciation of the label. 'Ker, O, Er Ker, O, Er – ah! Cocoa! You go in there,' (ibid., pp. 24–25). From there it was but a short step to reading a simple storybook – and Nigel was on his way. This story will no doubt please proponents of phonic approaches to reading, but Mr Hunt was interested in a much more important aspect of Nigel's learning. He noted:

> This illustrates one point which is typical of Nigel and may well be typical of other Mongoloids: he always knows a great deal more than he will let on. Every now and then he suddenly comes out with some new accomplishment of which we have been unaware. He is, however, extremely wary of attempting anything before he is confident that he can do it properly (ibid., pp. 25–26).

Nigel's own prose reads fluently and displays a use of technical literacy skills (including typing) which few had previously thought possible. His ideas are not abstract or particularly sophisticated but his diary writings touchingly describe events and places important to him. Mr Hunt admitted that perhaps Nigel's abilities were in the superior range for persons with Down syndrome, but it is also significant that he grew up in an environment, at home and for the most part at school, that did not place limits on what might be expected of him. Nigel is important, because he is an inspiration.

As we enlarge our knowledge of what persons with intellectual disabilities may achieve, it is essential that curriculum include continuing, systematic opportunities for them to learn to read and write, particularly during adolescence and early adulthood, when, developmentally, they may be best able to profit from formal instruction. We are also beginning to understand that literacy learning is fundamentally similar for everyone and that the literature related to good teaching practice in all educational settings is relevant to students with intellectual disabilities. Many teachers feel they don't know enough about the various sources of difficulty and delay, but they have only to look to the approaches and teaching skills which work for non-disabled beginning and developing readers. These provide useful models for adult literacy and for fostering literacy in slower developers (Bateman, 1991; Kitz, 1988). It is well documented that many non-disabled school children and adults have difficulty acquiring literacy skills, and it would appear that all instruction in literacy education needs to be adapted to individual needs. Therefore teachers at all levels and across all disciplines need to be well informed about key factors in literacy development.

THE READING PROCESS

A helpful way to understand the complexity of reading is to think about it as a process of reconstructing a writer's meanings from print, a process which requires written-word identification plus linguistic comprehension (Gough *et al.*, 1992; Perfetti, 1985). The reading begins with the visual perception and recognition of words and the subsequent or, some would argue, simultaneous allocation of meanings to these words from semantic memory. This is similar to the process of hearing, identifying and giving meaning to spoken words (Reid, 1993). In both speech and reading, as this lexical access occurs, a further synthesis of meaning takes place. The reader or listener integrates the words into phrases and sentences, constructing understanding in terms of previous paragraphs, knowledge of the topic and the purpose of the communication. Whereas listeners rely a lot on contextual and personal cues from a speaker, such as intonation, pauses, gestures and facial expressions, an efficient reader is helped, in his construction of meaning, by punctuation, pictures, prior knowledge about the subject-matter, figures of speech such as similes and metaphors, and perhaps by knowledge about the author. Various types of predictable text may also assist readers and listeners, such as rhyme in a poem or familiar phrases such as 'once upon a time'. Interpretations are influenced further by predictions about the intentions of the speaker or writer as signalled by the use of a particular communication structure, such as in a recipe, a letter or an announcement, or as in familiar sequences of events such as in fairy stories or cowboy movies. However, even non-disabled children do not always spontaneously use these cues in spoken and written language, and need to be specifically taught.

Reading comprehension, then, involves the use of many sources of information, together with a variety of problem-solving strategies based on efficient language skills, vocabulary, world knowledge and fast access to the literal meaning of the printed text, that is, automatic word recognition. Each of these factors has its own prerequisites and developmental trajectory. As learners advance in literacy, the relationships between the component skills change. For example, as fluency increases, the attention and problem-solving skills which are initially needed for word recognition in reading, and for spelling and letter formation in writing, can be reallocated to reflective and imaginitive processes. Teachers have to understand which skills need to be developing at any given stage of competence, so that they can assist the student by focusing attention, by clearly showing and telling, and by providing sufficient opportunities for successful practice. Above all, it is important to remember that language acquisition is largely driven by its utility and use in practice (Halliday, 1975; Perera, 1994). Unless students are convinced that written language serves personal and social needs in the same way that oral or signed language does, the motivation to use and practise it will be largely absent. Instruction has to involve a lot of real, purposeful reading and writing, and a lot of discussion, thinking and enjoyment.

DEFINING AND MEASURING READING

Reading attainments are usually expressed in terms of assessment of one or more of the reading components. That is, constructs such as reading age are artefacts of the criteria of reading and of the standardized assessment instruments used. Some reading levels are defined in terms of children's ability to recognize a sample of sight words (word recognition tests). Although this is a necessary and important skill to measure, it does not necessarily mean that continuous text containing those words will be read with understanding. Nor do the scores alone indicate whether a student can read new words independently. The testees' skills in using letter-sound and orthographic knowledge can be observed, however, and they can be asked also about the meanings of the words they can pronounce. There is no opportunity to see whether the students can use sentence context or other text features to monitor meaning.

A holistic view of reading accuracy and comprehension can be gained through instruments based on reading and understanding unseen continuous text. Such tests give an estimate of reading age, but they also afford the opportunity to observe how the reader integrates various strategies such as whole-word sight-recognition, phonemic decoding, use of spelling knowledge and word structure, use of semantic and syntactic cues, and use of illustrations, prior knowledge, text structure and inference. For instructional purposes these processes can be observed and monitored when children are reading familiar books, by using Running Record observations (Clay, 1980), or by using informal reading inventories (Holdaway, 1980). For research and comparison, a standardized record of independent, reading is necessary. Pieterse *et al.* (1988), for example, reported reading ages based on the Neale Analysis of Reading Ability. Eight children with Down syndrome (CA 7.2 to 9.3), who had entered mainstream classes following an early intervention programme, attained reading ages (RA) on the Neale test close to their chronological age (RA 6.1 and 9.3 years). On the other hand, Carr (1994) reported that only 16 of a group of 41 21-year-olds read well enough to attain a reading age score on the Neale reading test, the average being 7.5 years. She suggested they may have had little teaching in reading in the schools for children with severe learning disabilities which they had attended.

Sloper *et al.* (1990) based literacy attainment scores of 181 students with Down syndrome on teachers' responses to checklists. In the reading checklist, teachers were asked to rate each student's attainments at each of 17 levels of increasing difficulty, ranging from picture-matching to getting information in newspapers. The writing checklist included scribble to imaginative writing. Interestingly these authors found that 'type of school' was an important indicator of success for children with Down syndrome. They noted that 'children in mainstream schools were likely to have higher academic attainments than those in special schools, even after allowing for the mental ages of the children in different schools' (ibid., p. 292).

More of this sort of information is needed, so that the developmental literacy range of children with Down syndrome and the relationships between the various test results and aspects of instruction can be better understood. Some of the 15- to 17-year-olds we are monitoring at the Schonell Special Education Research Centre are clearly in emergent phases of literacy, just beginning to show an active interest in books and writing. Others have attained reading accuracy ages up to 12 years and comprehension ages to 11.5 years, as measured by the Neale Analysis of Reading Ability. These more advanced students are able to write coherent sentences and use writing for personal and functional purposes such as letters, lists, diaries and class reports. However, even when their word-recognition skills are sound and their reading accuracy is quite high, these students often find it difficult to remember details, especially when text sentence structure is more complex than their personal speech, or when the passages are long. This may reflect memory difficulties reported by Broadley and MacDonald (1993) and Meyers (1990), but such difficulties might also occur because the text involves unfamiliar situations and concepts, or words which are not in the reader's spoken vocabulary. When allowed to refer to the text, these students are usually able to answer literal comprehension questions but still have difficulty dealing with questions which require inference. This also probably reflects a lack of general knowledge and experience of the topics, and again suggests that one of the highest curriculum priorities is to develop oral language skills and provide an environment where students can use and improve them.

WRITING

The research literature does not appear to include any reports of qualitative assessment of the writing of students with Down syndrome. In regard to handwriting, Hoffman *et al.* (1990) summarized several studies of the fine motor skills and hand functions of children with Down syndrome and reported general difficulty with fine motor tasks, compared with normal children. The children with Down syndrome had significantly lower grip strength and slower development of efficient pencil grasp. For example, the norm for the static tripod grip is 3 to 4 years but was attained by the Down syndrome population between 4 and 8 years. Compared with the norm of 4 to 6 years, the more desirable dynamic tripod grip was attained between 5 and 12 years by the children with Down syndrome. However there was a wide variability within the population, and grip strength appears to increase with chronological age. So, in addition to the cognitive delay and auditory difficulties expected, teachers need to compensate for likely delays in the fine motor skills associated with proficiency in drawing, writing and other fine motor tasks. Motor difficulties can also affect other general learning skills such as focusing attention and visual-motor co-ordination. Since students with Down syndrome may find potentially valuable fine motor activities frustrating and tiring, care should be taken to provide short, appropriate and interesting tasks, easy-to-use instruments and very positive feedback. (See Bird and Buckley, 1994; Ziviani and Elkins, 1993 for suggestions which might be helpful if adapted for older students.)

Writing and reading instruction appear to be mutually facilitative(Clay, 1985; Frith 1985; Raphael and Englert, 1989), and curiosity and experimentation with writing often lead to the acquisition of concepts essential to learning to read (Chomsky, 1971; Durkin, 1966; Dyson, 1982). Some approaches to teaching literacy (for example, language experience, process writing and whole language) aim to help children develop reading and writing together, and sensibly advocate providing students with many opportunities to do 'real' reading and writing, based on interests, literature and other subjects in the curriculum. However, in the past, some teachers using these approaches have overestimated the 'naturalness' of learning to be literate (Reid, 1993), and have not provided sufficient explicit explanation of the workings of print, or systematic provision for practice (Mather, 1992; Spiegel, 1992;). Aspects of beginning literacy which cannot be taken for granted and which need to be carefully taught include concepts about how print relates to speech (Clay, 1980), phonemic and metalinguistic awareness (Tunmer and Hoover, 1992), letter formation (Sassoon, 1993), letter-sound knowledge (Adams, 1990), and orthographic knowledge (Peters, 1993).

Students need to be systematically guided through the process of co-ordinating these elements as they read for understanding and try to put their ideas into writing. Such complex operations require assistance from the teacher through modelling, scaffolding, and careful control of difficulty factors. The latter, which makes the experience and exercise of independent learning possible, might include: requiring only a small amount of unfamiliar material at a time; carefully sequencing learning so that new knowledge and skills build on what has been already mastered; providing time for guided practice with new text; and selecting tasks and materials which can be successfully completed, given the amount of teacher, aide or peer assistance available. In other words, teachers need to structure learning activities to ensure that the students will be able to use some initiative and experience success. This need for structured learning applies for most children, but particularly in the case of children who have learning difficulties. Systematic and structured instruction should not be confused with rote-teaching skills out of context or with neglect of meaning or self-direction. It merely ensures that students have the knowledge, skills and assistance they need to engage productively with the task and be active learners.

THE READING RECOVERY MODEL

Providing assisted-practice with reading and writing is an effective and integral aspect of the Reading Recovery Programme (Clay, 1987; Lyons *et al.*, 1993). During one-to-one tutoring sessions, youngsters are helped to read familiar and new books, and to formulate and write sentences of interest. They are guided, as they read and write, to use concepts, skills and strategies which will lead to independent reading and writing. The teacher carefully promotes the student's ability to monitor the meaning in print, while at the same time developing concepts about words and letters, phonological awareness skills, and self-help use of letter-sound knowledge, word structure and familiar vocabulary. Although this programme is used with Year 1 students who are not succeeding as well as they should in class, it includes many instructional features which are particularly suited to helping older students who are experiencing difficulty, or, as in the case of students with Down syndrome, who attain an appropriate cognitive level later in life. Lyons *et al.* (1993), gave a comprehensive description of this process and its theoretical base, and provided insights which might also be useful for parents and teachers of children with intellectual difficulties. Successful Reading Recovery teachers understand students and the learning-to-read process very well, but, in addition, they have been meticulously educated in the art of providing the right prompt at the right time. One of the problems to be solved in teaching children with intellectual handicaps in inclusive settings, is providing sufficient quality individual learning sessions of this kind, to ensure a sound foundation as well as continuing progress in literacy. A second challenge is to engage students in similar beneficial learning interactions during performance-based instruction in whole-class settings.

CATERING FOR OLDER STUDENTS IN INCLUSIVE SETTINGS

Many upper-primary and secondary programmes for students with intellectual difficulties tend to be based on the assumption that inclusive education is only possible in practical subjects such as woodwork, home economics, physical education and technical drawing. Even in these lessons, lower achieving students are often monitored by an aide and are not involved in interactions with peers or class teachers. But literature, the social sciences, health education and the practical sciences also provide skills and insights relevant to independent living, especially if there are opportunities to be really involved in practical activities, related literacy activities, video, and group discussions. As Perera (1994, p. 37) noted:

> Persons with Down syndrome of any age and condition can work:
> IF: we study their specific capabilities and abilities.
> IF: we train them correctly.
> IF: we adapt the jobs to their specific abilities.
> IF: we give them the opportunity to do so.

These principles apply equally to work in school. Although students with intellectual disabilities would find unadapted content, concepts and tasks difficult to work with, teachers can learn to modify lesson objectives, work procedures and at least some of the talk, to cater for the needs of individuals (Collicott, 1991). Multilevel planning for classroom instruction is always good teaching practice, and when the range of abilities is extended it becomes rather like teaching a multiage group in a small rural school. For example, the teacher might include all the children in one social studies lesson, but have different goals, interactions, activities and evaluation criteria for a 14-year-old and a 7-year-old student. Good teachers make these kinds of adjustments all the time. Where students with intellectual difficulties are concerned, it just requires more persistence, resourcefulness and imagination.

Multilevel planning certainly takes a great deal of time, and teachers need to be very familiar with individual student attainments to match lesson goals with existing knowledge and skills. This is where collaboration with other teachers and understanding administrative support become important. When planning (perhaps jointly with special education personnel), teachers need to be able to select appropriate aspects of the lesson content, translate these to a suitable conceptual level, and devise modified activities, materials and evaluation. Planning should include not only content and activities but also how to keep the slower student interested and involved during whole-class discussions. Interactional aspects of the lesson should aim to enhance the experience of inclusion – for all students. Non-disabled peers can benefit from helping less able students understand ideas, follow routines and complete activities. Alternative activities could be tactfully arranged during more complex instruction with advanced learners. Planning for multilevel instruction would cover whole-group, co-operative group and peer-tutor activities. Such planning and teaching cannot and will not be done unless school policy and administrators recognize the expertise and time that it takes, and give support and encouragement to teachers to do it. Like all quality processes, it comes at a price.

Teachers need to understand the operational level and the basic literacy and numeracy attainments of students if they are to plan coherently for growth. Further, it would assist the students with Down syndrome if teachers, carers and even peers have some understanding of the ways in which language development can be enhanced in informal settings through personal social exchanges (Snow, 1983). One of the best ways for most children to assimilate new ideas and information is through discussion and instructional conversations (Goldenberg, 1993). It is especially important that teachers and carers learn to use written language to help older students with Down syndrome extend their vocabulary and give them greater control of language forms such as syntax, idiom and figures of speech. Although it is easier to arrange assisted performance and practice in one-to-one settings, teachers need to learn how to include these elements in whole-class settings, whatever the developmental range. Even more difficult, they need to be able to assist the non-disabled children to share knowledge and to talk productively with the children who experience difficulties with language. Such skills are an important aspect of work in co-operative groupings.

CONCLUSION'

In summary, until quite recently literacy instruction for persons with Down syndrome has most often been considered in terms of the language deficits and learning difficulties characteristic of the syndrome rather than from the point of view of what is known about how other children and adults learn to read and write. Research as well as teaching approaches have reflected limited assumptions about what persons with Down syndrome might achieve. Studies have tended to discuss literacy acquisition in terms of whether students can master particular discrete skills, and for the most part, to bypass questions about what part literacy might play in the lives of students, especially as they move into adolescence and adulthood. No doubt researchers and teachers do see skills and techniques in perspective and in terms of overall purpose, but it seems that a consistently narrow focus on isolated skill outcomes, particularly where behavioural techniques are employed, can lead to situations where the pupils, and sometimes even the teachers, lose sight of what literacy is for. For regular school children, literacy instruction is regarded as a major aspect of lifelong intellectual growth, fundamentally related to the development of oral language and thought. Why not also for children with Down syndrome?

REFERENCES

Adams, M.J. (1990) *Beginning to Read: Thinking and Learning about Print. (A Summary)*, prepared by S.A. Stahl, J. Osborne, and F. Lehr, Urbana-Champaign: University of Illinois.

Adams, M.J. and Huggins, A.W.F. (1985) The growth of children's sight vocabulary: a quick test with educational and theoretical applications. *Reading Research Quarterly*, **20**, pp. 262–81.

Ballard, K.B. (1987) The failure of behavioural strategies as a model of teaching. Paper presented at the annual conference of the Australian Behaviour Modification Association, Surfers Paradise.

Bateman, B. (1991) Teaching word recognition to slow-learning children. *Reading, Writing and Learning Disabilities*, **7**, pp. 1–16.

Bird, G. and Buckley, S. (1994) *Meeting the Educational Needs of Children with Down's Syndrome: a Handbook for Teachers*, Portsmouth: University of Portsmouth.

Brent, R. and Anderson, P. (1993) *The Reading Teacher*, **47**, pp. 122–26.

Broadley, I. and MacDonald, J. (1993) Teaching short term memory skills to children with Down's syndrome. *Down's Syndrome Research and Practice*, **1**, pp. 56–62.

Brown, A.L. (1980) Metacognitive development in reading. In R. Spiro, B. Bruce, and W. Brewer (eds), *Theoretical Issues in Reading Comprehension: Perspectives from Cognitive Psychology, Linguistics, Artificial Intelligence and Education*, Hillsdale: Erlbaum.

Brown, A.L. (1982) Learning and development: the problem of compatability, access and induction. *Human Development*, **25**, pp. 89–115.

Buckley, S. (1985) Attaining basic educational skills: reading, writing and number. In D. Lane and B. Stratford (eds) *Current Approaches to Down's Syndrome*. London: Cassell.

Buckley. S. and Bird, G. (1993) Teaching children with Down's syndrome to read. *Down's Syndrome: Research and Practice*, **1**, pp. 34–39.

Carr, J. (1994) Annotation: long term outcome for people with Down's syndrome. *Journal of Child Psychology and Psychiatry*, **35**, pp. 425–39.

Catts, H.W. (1991). Early identification of reading disabilities. *Topics in Language Disorders*, **12**, pp. 1–16.

Cazden, C. (1992) Revealing and telling: the socialization of attention in learning to read and write. *Educational Psychology*, **12**, pp. 305–13.

Chall, J.S. (1983) *Stages of Reading Development*, New York: McGraw-Hill.

Chi, M.T.H. (1981) Knowledge development and memory performance. In N. Friedman, J.P. Das and N. O'Connor (eds), *Intelligence and Learning*, pp. 221–29, New York, Plenum.

Chomsky, C. (1971) Write first, read later. *Childhood Education*, **47** (6), pp. 296–99.

Clay, M. (1972) *Reading: The Patterning of Complex Behaviour*, 2nd edn, Portsmouth, NH: Heinemann.

Clay, M. (1980) *The Early Detection of Reading Difficulties: a Diagnostic Survey with Recovery Procedures*, Auckland: Heinemann.

Clay, M. (1987) Implementing Reading Recovery: systematic adaptations to an educational innovation. *New Zealand Journal of Educational Studies*, **22**, pp. 35–58.

Clay, M. (1985) *The Early Detection of Reading Difficulties* (3rd ed.) Auckland: Heinemann.

Collicott, J. (1991) Implementing multi-level instruction: strategies for classroom teachers. In G.L. Porter and D. Richler (eds), *Changing Canadian Schools: Perspectives on Disability and Inclusion*, pp. 191–218, Toronto: Roeher Institute.

Conners, F.A. (1992) Reading instruction for students with moderate mental retardation: Review and analysis of research. *American Journal on Mental Retardation*, **96**, pp. 577–97.

Cooke, N., Heron, T., Heward, W. and Test, D. (1982) Integration of a Down's syndrome child in a classwide peer tutoring system: a case report. *Mental Retardation*, **20**, pp. 22–5.

Crombie, M.P. (1994) Development of adolescents with Down syndrome: does early intervention have a long term effect? Unpublished PhD thesis, University of Queensland.

Cullinan, D., Sabornie, E.J. and Crossland, C.L. (1992) Social mainstreaming of mildly handicapped students. *The Elementary School Journal*, **92**, pp. 339–51.

Delpit, L.D. (1988) The silenced dialogue: power and pedagogy in educating other people's children. *Harvard Educational Review*, **58**, pp. 280–98.

Downing, J. (1979) *Reading and Reasoning*. Edinburgh: Chambers.

Durkin, D. (1966) *Children Who Read Early*. New York: Random House.

Dyson, A.H. (1982) Reading, writing and language: young children solve the written language puzzle. *Language Arts*, **59**, pp. 829–39.

Farrell M. and Elkins, J. (1994/95) Literacy for all? The case of Down syndrome. *Journal of Reading*, **38** (4), pp. 2–13.

Ferriero, E. (1985) The relationship between written and oral language: the children's viewpoints. In M.M. Clark (ed.), *New Directions in the Study of Reading*, pp. 83–94, London: Falmer.

Feuerstein, R. (1980) *Instrumental Enrichment: an Intervention Program for Cognitive Modifiability*, Baltimore: University Park Press.

Fox, B.J. (1990) Antecedents of illiteracy. *Social Policy Report: Society for Research in Child Development*, **14** (4), pp. 1–19.

Francis, H. (1982) *Learning to Read*. London: Allen and Unwin.

Frith, U. (1985) Beneath the surface of developmental dyslexia. In K.E. Patterson, J.C. Marshall and M. Coltheart (eds), *Surface Dyslexia: Neuropsychologic and Cognitive Studies of Phonological Reading*, pp. 301–30, Hillsdale: Erlbaum.

Gillies, R.M. (1994) The effects of structural and unstructured cooperative learning groups on students' behaviours, interactions, and learning outcomes. Unpublished PhD thesis. University of Queensland.

Goldenberg, C. (1992/93) Instructional conversations: promoting comprehension through discussion. *Reading Teacher*, **46,** pp. 316–26.

Goodwin, T.C. (Producer) and Wurzburg, G. (Director) (1992) *Educating Peter* [Videorecording], Santa Monica: HBO Direct Cinema.

Gough, P.B., Juel, C. and Griffith, P.L. (1992) Reading, spelling, and the orthographic cypher. In P.B. Gough, L.C. Ehri and R. Treiman (eds), *Reading Acquisition*, Hillsdale: Erlbaum.

Greenfield, P.M. (1984) A theory of the teacher in the learning activities of everyday life. In B. Rogoff and J. Lane (eds), *Everyday Cognition: Its development in Social Context*, pp. 117–38, 292–93, Cambridge, MA: Harvard University Press.

Gunn, P. (1993) Characteristics of Down syndrome. In Y. Burno and P. Gunn (eds), *Down Syndrome: Moving Through Life*. London: Chapman & Hall.

Guthrie, F.M. and Cunningham, P.M. (1982) Teaching decoding skills to educably mentally handicapped children. *The Reading Teacher*, February, pp. 554–59.

Heward, W.L., Heron, T.E. and Cooke, N.L. (1982) Tutor huddle: key element in a class-wide tutoring system. *Elementary School Journal*, **83,** pp. 115–23.

Halliday, M. (1975) *Learning How to Mean: Explorations in the Development of Language*. New York: Arnold.

Hoffman, M.N., Peterson L.L. and Van Dyke, D.C. (1990) Motor and hand function. In D.C. Van Dyke, D.J. Lang, F. Heide, S. van Duyne and M.J. Soucek (eds), *Clinical Perspectives in the Management of Down Syndrome*, pp. 93–101, New York: Springer-Verlag.

Holdaway, D. (1980) *Independence in Reading*, Ashton Scholastic.

Hoogeveen, F.R. and Smeets, P.M. (1990) Establishing basic reading skills in moderately retarded children. In W.J. Fraser (ed.), *Key Issues in Mental Retardation Research: Proceedings of the Eighth Congress of the International Association for the Society of Mental Deficiency (IASSMD)*, London: Routledge.

Hunt, N. (1967) *The World of Nigel Hunt: The Diary of a Mongoloid Youth*. London: Darwin Finlayson.

Kitz, W.R. (1988) Adult literacy: a review of the past and a proposal for the future. *Research and Special Education*, **9** (4), pp. 44–50.

Lyons, C.A., Pinnell, G.S., and de Ford, D.E. (1993) *Partners in Learning: Teachers and Children in Reading Recovery*, New York: Teachers College Press.

Mason, J.M. (1977) *The Role of Strategy in Reading by the Mentally Retarded*, Technical Report No. 58, Urbana-Champaign: University of Illinois.

Mather, N. (1992) Whole language reading instruction for students with learning disabilities: caught in the cross fire. *Learning Disabilities Research & Practice*, **7,** pp. 87–95.

Meyers, L.F. (1990) Language development and intervention. In D.C. Van Dyke, D.J. Lang, F. Heide, S. van Duyne and M.J. Soucek (eds), *Clinical Perspectives in the Management of Down Syndrome*, pp. 153–64, New York: Springer-Verlag.

Nicholson, T. (1992) Reading wars: a brief history and an update. *International Journal of Disability, Development and Education*, **39,** pp. 173–84.

Perera, J. (1994) It is never too late to learn to work: an experience with adults with Down's syndrome developed in Majorca, Spain. *Down's Syndrome Research and Practice*, **2** (1), pp. 36–39.

Perfetti, C.A. (1985) *Reading Ability*, New York: Oxford University Press.

Peters, M. (1993) The teaching of spelling. In R. Beard (ed.), *Teaching Literacy: Balancing Perspectives*, pp. 176–86, London: Hodder and Stoughton.

Pieterse, M., Bochner, S. and Bettison, S. (eds) (1988) Early Intervention for Children with

Disabilities: The Australian Experience. Sydney: Special Education Centre, Macquarie University.

Pieterse, M. and Treloar, R. (1981) *The Down's Syndrome Program: Progress Report.* Sydney: Macquarie.

Raphael, T.E. and Englert, C.S. (1989) Integrating writing and reading instruction. In P. Winograd, K.K. Wixson and M.Y. Lipson (eds), *Improving Basal Reading Instruction,* (pp. 231–55), New York: Teachers College Press.

Reid, J. (1993) Reading and spoken language. In R. Beard (ed.), *Teaching Literacy: Balancing Perspectives,* pp. 22–34, London: Hodder and Stoughton.

Roehler, L.R. and Duffy, G.G. (1991) Teachers' instructional actions. In R. Barr, M.L. Kamil, P. Mosenthal and P.D. Pearson (eds), *Handbook of Reading Research,* vol. 2, pp. 861–83, New York: Longman.

Sassoon, R. (1993) Handwriting. In R. Beard (ed.), *Teaching Literacy: Balancing Perspectives,* pp. 187–201, London: Hodder and Stoughton.

Sloper, P., Cunningham, C., Turner, S. and Knussen, C. (1990) Factors related to the academic attainments of children with Down's syndrome. *British Journal of Educational Psychology,* **60,** pp. 284–98.

Snow, C.E. (1983) Literacy and Language: relationships during the pre-school years. *Harvard Educational Review,* **53,** pp. 165–89.

Spiegel, D.L. (1992) Blending whole language and systematic direct instruction. *The Reading Teacher,* **46,** pp. 38–44.

Stanovich, K.E. (1986) Matthew effects in reading: Some consequences of individual differences in the acquisition of literacy. *Reading Research Quarterly,* **21,** pp. 360–406.

Sulzby E. and Teale, W. (1991) Emergent literacy. In P.D. Pearson, R. Barr, M.L. Kamil and P. Mosenthal (eds), *Handbook of Reading Research,* 2nd edn, pp. 35–48, New York: Longman.

Teale, W H.(1982) Toward a theory of how children learn to read and write naturally. *Language Arts,* **59** (6), pp. 555–70.

Tharp, R.G., and Gallimore, R. (1989) The social context of cognitive functioning in the lives of mildly handicapped persons. In D.E. Sugden (ed.), *Cognitive Approaches in Special Education,* pp. 51–81, London: Falmer.

Topping, K. (1988) *The Peer Tutoring Handbook: Promoting Cooperative Learning.* London: Croom Helm.

Tunmer, W.E. and Chapman, J.W. (1993) To guess or not to guess, that is the question: metacognitive strategy training, phonological recoding skill, and beginning reading. *Reading Forum N.Z.,* **1,** pp. 3–14.

Tunmer, W.E. and Hoover, W.A. (1992) Cognitive and linguistic factors in learning to read. In R.B. Gough, L.C. Ehri and R. Treiman (eds), *Reading Acquisition,* pp. 175–214, Hillsdale: Erlbaum.

Turner, J.C. (1992) A motivational perspective on literacy instruction. Paper presented at the annual meeting of the National Reading Conference, San Antonio, Texas.

Vygotsky, L.S. (1968) *Mind in Society: The Development of Higher Psychological Processes,* Cambridge, MA: Harvard University Press.

Wood, D. (1988) *How Children Think and Learn.* Oxford: Blackwell.

Ziviani, J. and Elkins, J. (1993) Fine motor skills in the classroom. In Y. Burns and P. Gunn (eds), *Down Syndrome: Moving Through Life.* London: Chapman & Hall.

18 Teaching Addition to Children

James Hanrahan and Tina Newman

Since the early 1970s, there has been considerable research conducted on how non-handicapped children learn arithmetic (Gelman and Gallistel, 1978; Ginsburg, 1986; Groen and Parkman, 1972; Kamii and DeClark, 1985). However, few investigations have involved children with Down syndrome. Yarmish (1988) has suggested that this lack of attention to the arithmetic achievement of children with Down syndrome may reflect a widely held belief by researchers that these children are unable to understand number concepts. The few studies conducted on this topic indicate that children with Down syndrome have very limited number skills and few progress to the point where they are able to demonstrate competence on the most fundamental of the four operations, addition.

There is evidence that many children with Down syndrome can learn skills such as number recognition, rote counting to ten and the addition of small numbers when concrete manipulatives are available (Irwin, 1991). A debate currently exists in the literature on the issue of whether the children learn such skills differently from their non-handicapped peers. Several researchers have suggested that few children with Down syndrome are capable of the spontaneous use of such numerical skills to solve problems in a meaningful way (Cornwall, 1974; Gelman, 1982; Gelman and Cohen, 1988). However, a study by Caycho et al. (1991) demonstrated that when a developmental age of approximately 5 years is reached, children with Down syndrome are capable of more than the rote learning of arithmetic skills and it has been reported that some children at this developmental level have learned the basic rules that govern counting (Caycho et al., 1991; Gelman and Cohen, 1988).

Given the dearth of research on how children with Down syndrome learn arithmetic, it is not surprising that there is even less information on how to teach arithmetic to these children. Indeed, Irwin (1991) was unable to identify a single study that focused primarily on arithmetic instruction with children with Down syndrome. Baroody and Snyder (1983) have reported that researchers have used a variety of behavioral techniques to teach developmentally delayed children to count and add small sets of objects. Brown and DeLoache (1978) have suggested that such behavioral procedures may produce only rote learning and may not change the cognitive structure of these children. However, Yarmish (1988) has pointed out that the inability to develop a strategy doesn't rule out the ability to apply the strategy once taught. Whether learned by rote or rule, basic number skills such as counting sets of objects are a prerequisite for learning many life skills. For example, instructional programmes based on the rote counting of objects have been designed for skills such as money management for developmentally delayed children (Langevin *et al.*, 1994; McDonnell *et al.*, 1984). Such programmes may be suitable for use with those children whose numerical skills are limited to counting or adding small sets of objects by rote.

Several researchers have recommended more cognitively based approaches to arithmetic instruction which stress such activities as the partitioning of sets and the co-ordination of oral counting with pointing for children with Down syndrome (Caycho *et al.*, 1991; Gelman and Cohen, 1988; Yarmish, 1988). It has been suggested that such instruction should facilitate learning of the rules that underlie such activities as counting and adding numbers. This in turn would permit children to advance beyond instructional programs based on the rote application of number skills.

DOT NOTATION INSTRUCTION

One instructional approach that appears to have something to offer both rote and rule learners is a method that applies dots to each numeral from 1 to 9. This dot notation system was first developed for use in special education classrooms (Kramer and Krug, 1973). These researchers were primarily interested in finding a method that would allow developmentally delayed children to add numbers without having to rely on cumbersome concrete representations such as fingers or blocks. Kramer and Krug (1973) suggested that their dot notation system provided the child with a method of addition that would eventually result in the memorization of addition facts. This early attempt at a dot notation system was extended through the work of Bullock *et al.* (1977) and Bullock *et al.* (1989) into a broadly applied programme called 'Touch Math' which focuses on early number concepts and the four operations: addition, subtraction, multiplication and division. In the Touch Math programme, each numeral from 1 to 9 is superimposed with a fixed pattern of reference points or dots that the learner can touch and count in sequence (Figure 18.1). With practice, these patterns are memorized and the dots are gradually removed. In time, the student memorizes the position of the dots and continues to count them as if they were still marked on the numbers. After learning to count numbers in this way, students are taught to transfer this knowledge to help them master the four operations.

ADVANTAGES OF A DOT NOTATION APPROACH

Several researchers have found that children with Down syndrome can learn to add numbers using a count-all procedure (Buckley and Sachs, 1987; Irwin, 1989, 1991). As with non-handicapped children, this strategy is most often performed by counting physical manipulatives such as blocks or fingers. For example, a child counting 2+3 using the count-all strategy would hold up two fingers on one hand and count 'one, two' and hold up three fingers on the other hand and count 'one, two, three' and finally count all the fingers 'one, two, three, four, five'.

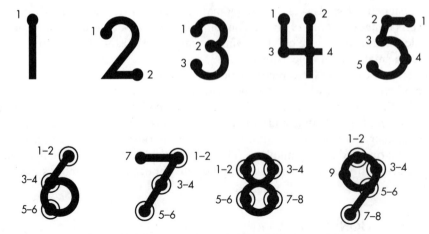

Figure 18.1 Sequence of counting Touch Math numerals

Prerequisites
- Counting.
- Numeral identification 1–9.

Key instructions
- Single touchpoints are touched and counted one time and double touchpoints (dots and circles) are touched and counted twice.
- Students touch with pencil tips and count aloud.
- The correct sequence of touching and counting should be consistently followed.
- Students should not be asked to draw their own touchpoints.

Helpful hints for young students
- The single touchpoints for 7 and 9 may be called a nose.
- The numeral 8 looks like a robot. Count the head first, and then the body.

A dot notation approach appears to offer several advantages to children who have not progressed beyond the rote application of the count-all strategy. One significant advantage is that this approach eliminates the need to rely on fingers or other physical manipulatives. Physical manipulatives are not very portable and when children use their fingers, sums are usually limited to a total of ten. However, with a dot notation approach, children can add all possible pairs of single digit addenda which extends their addition range to 18. Moreover, when single digit numerals are presented in a column or row, children can add sums as high as they can count.

Some developmentally delayed children appear embarrassed when using fingers or other obvious means of representation and prefer to guess incorrectly rather than use concrete referents , when adding (Hanrahan *et al.*, 1993). However, with a dot notation method, children can use the count-all strategy without fingers as the dots on the numerals act as a concrete referent. To an observer, it appears that the child is adding without the use of concrete objects. Consequently, developmentally delayed children appear much more like their non-handicapped peers when engaged in simple counting and addition tasks. This should facilitate their integration into regular classes.

A second advantage with a dot notation method is that it provides children with an orderly, concrete method that consistently leads to a correct sum. With practice, children can be expected to memorize many basic addition facts. If a particular combination is forgotten, the child can easily generate the fact by counting all the dots. If sums are incorrect, the child is either counting or touching incorrectly. In either case, such errors are easy to identify and correct (Bullock, 1991).

In the Touch Math programme the dots are presented in a multisensory context as the children not only see the touch points on the numerals but they are also taught to touch the dots with their pencil tip as they count out loud. In this way the students are receiving the same information through three different channels, thus allowing for the learning styles of visual, auditory and tactile-kinaesthetic learners. As pointed out by Scott (1993) this may be particularly important for children with special needs as they have a greater opportunity to grasp information when it is presented through multiple channels.

The mechanistic nature of the dot notation method suggests that this approach may be appropriate for the instruction of children who have learned to count or add objects primarily by rote. However, the Touch Math programme (Bullock *et al.*, 1989) is not limited to use with such learners and contains some of the activities recommended for children with Down syndrome who are capable of a more conceptual understanding of arithmetic. With the Touch Math method students are able to rely on the rote counting sequence, but are provided with the opportunity to think about the numbers and their relationships to each other, as there is a concrete representation of each number in the touchpoints.

Finally, the organization of the Touch Math programme is based, to a large extent, on the developmental stages followed by non-handicapped children as they learn to count and master the four operations. For example, initial activities involve training in those areas identified by Gelman and Cohen (1988) as crucial for counting and the addition component matches the count-all, count-on and number fact strategy sequence typically followed by non-handicapped children (Carpenter and Moser, 1984).

RESEARCH SUPPORTING THE DOT NOTATION SYSTEM

The dot notation approach has not generated much research since its introduction by Kramer and Krug (1973) and refinement by Bullock *et al.* (1977) with the exception of an article by Kokaska (1975) who recommended the method for developmentally delayed students. Flexer and Rosenberger (1987) have criticized the use of the dot notation approach with non-handicapped children, suggesting that children become too dependent on the method. This may not be an issue for children with Down syndrome. Most recently, Scott (1993) used the Touch Math programme with a sample of three mildly developmentally delayed students. She reported that the method was suitable for teaching both addition and subtraction to these children. Pupo (1994) also employed the method successfully to instruct three developmentally delayed children in addition.

We (Newman and Hanrahan) have recently investigated the effectiveness of the Touch Math programme with a small group of children with Down syndrome.

Their study was conducted to determine if the children could learn simple addition with addenda one to five using the Touch Math method. As indicated in Figure 21.1, dot representation for numerals above 5 is more complex than that for the numerals from 1 to 5. Consequently, this experiment was designed to determine if children with Down syndrome could learn the most basic elements of the Touch Math programme.

Four Trisomy-21 children with Down syndrome aged 8, 9, 10 and 15 were chosen for the study. All attended a special school in the Greater Montreal area. All children were able to recognize numerals from 1 to 10 and were able to count ten objects. The results of the study suggested that the Touch Math programme was an effective instrument for the instruction of simple addition with these students. Students took from five to 16 instructional periods lasting from 20 to 30 minutes to master this simple addition strategy as applied to number pairs with addenda up to five. Touch Math was introduced as a replacement for the ineffective strategies that the children were using prior to intervention and proved to be successful in significantly improving the results from pretest to posttest of all four children. Students' scores on a multiple probe measure rose from an average of 16.2 per cent correct prior to intervention to an average of 95.6 per cent correct following intervention. The students also demonstrated success in maintaining these improved results with simple addition problems.

In follow-up probes ranging from one to five months, all the children were successful in maintaining their improved results. This maintenance was facilitated for the three youngest children through a classroom math programme that was implementing the Touch Math approach. These three students were introduced to this class at the beginning of their intervention and participated with the class during and following the Touch Math experiment. It was observed that although all three of these children continued to maintain high results for the examiner, two of them had some difficulty adjusting to the classroom setting. This was evident when the students were consistently demonstrating for the examiner skills that they were not using or were not using as successfully when placed in the classroom. This difficulty with generalizability may be the result of a change in the instructor or a change from a one-on-one instruction to a group setting. One child had no difficulty with maintenance and generalized well to the group setting and a different instructor. He continued to demonstrate mastery of single digit addition with the touchpoints faded with both the examiner and the classroom teacher and continued to develop new skills.

The oldest subject was not placed in the Touch Math class and was not exposed to the Touch Math programme for one month following intervention. A maintenance probe at this time demonstrated strong results. In a test of generalizability, however, this subject failed to use the Touch Math approach when presented with single digit addition problems on a computer screen, with a different examiner, during the course of a separate experiment. He had been presented with Touch Math materials on the same day as this experiment and was placed in the same room, at the same desk in order to complete the problems. The different mode of presentation and the new examiner are possible reasons for the lack of generalizability.

The potential of using this programme to teach all of the basic math facts is an important characteristic of the method and each of the four students in this study has the possibility of advancing further with their addition skills. Two children have already developed skills beyond those taught for the purposes of the study. In their Touch Math class they have been taught to solve addition problems with addenda up to nine and they have also been learning to add using a count-on approach. The count-on approach has been found to follow the count-all approach with non-handicapped children (Carpenter and Moser, 1984) and it was the next step in the Touch Math addition kit. The children are instructed to 'touch the larger number, say its name, and continue counting' the touchpoints on the smaller number. Only the smaller number has touchpoints initially and eventually those are also faded. The ability of children with Down syndrome to count-on has also been demonstrated in a different context by Irwin (1991) who was able to teach a group of eight children with Down syndrome aged 11 to 13 to use the count-on strategy by adapting a procedure designed for use with non-handicapped children by Secada *et al.* (1983). The children in her study mastered the count-on strategy with one week of instruction and most were able to generalize this strategy to materials other than those used for instruction six months after the experiment ended.

In the Newman and Hanrahan study, some of the touchpoint configurations were found to be easier to learn than others. The numerals 1 to 3 appeared to be the easiest to learn and retain for all the children. As indicated in Figure 18.1, each of these numerals is counted from the top down and the touchpoints are at corners or ends of the lines. The numeral 4 was often counted out of order, but always counted the correct number of times. The children had no difficulty remembering the location of the touchpoints of 4, perhaps because they are located at the corners of the numeral. However, they had a problem remembering the sequence recommended in the programme, possibly because the order moves around the numeral and not from top to bottom. The number 5, when it was miscounted, was always miscounted in the same way. The children would miss the touchpoint placed on the rounded curve of the numeral, the only touchpoint not on a corner or the end of a line. These observations suggest that it may be useful to investigate which touchpoint patterns are best remembered by children with Down syndrome in order to improve the effectiveness of the programme for this population.

Gelman and Cohen (1988) suggest that non-handicapped children are more likely to self-correct than their peers with Down syndrome when counting. However, in the Newman and Hanrahan study, two of the children were observed self-correcting when counting the touchpoints which suggests that these students are capable of understanding some of the principles underlying counting. This finding is consistent with results reported by Caycho *et al.* (1991). One child in the Newman and Hanrahan study also demonstrated self-correction skills when solving addition problems. He spontaneously recounted questions when he had miscounted on either addenda, either directly following the miscount or at the end of the problem. This self-correction suggests an ability to attend to the relevant relationships between numbers, a progression beyond rote skill learning that has been found with other developmentally delayed students (Hanrahan *et al.*, 1993). This skill was not evident with any of the other children who would occasionally miscount addition problems and have to be encouraged to correct themselves.

SUGGESTION FOR IMPLEMENTATION AND FURTHER STUDY

The one-on-one instruction provided to students who participated in our study is not the general mode of instruction available in special or regular schools. Although many children with Down syndrome are taught in small group settings, often the resources needed for the intense one-on-one instruction that was available in this experiment cannot be provided. Observations of the Touch Math class in which the children participated suggest that this programme is effective in a group setting; however, a more thorough investigation of this question is needed.

Observations made during our study also raised questions of generalizability that should be investigated more thoroughly. The possibility that some children with Down syndrome may not generalize the use of this method to different settings or with different instructors is very important when determining the effectiveness of the approach. The ability to implement the method when the children are presented with the numbers in a different mode or in a different setting is essential if the programme is going to be worth while to the student. The children in this study did demonstrate some generalizability, and investigating ways of increasing this generalization is important.

It is possible that dot placement could be altered to meet the individual or group needs of different students. The preliminary finding that touchpoints on corners and ends of lines and top to bottom counting patterns are easier to remember provides a focus for further study. The touchpoints may be moved around to determine if there are configurations that are easier to remember for some or all students. It may be that individuals will have their own personal configurations that they find easiest to recall or there may be one configuration for each numeral that is easiest for all students.

Finally, as a multisensory approach, the Touch Math method may be supplemented with a variety of sensory experiences. For example, instructors may want to augment the touchpoints on the numerals with fabrics or perforations that students can feel when they touch the dots. This can be done on number lines or wall-posters for an additional sensory pathway for the student. This tactile-kinaesthetic experience may be especially effective in meeting the learning styles of some students.

In conclusion, the signs of progress in our study and in other reports (Pupo, 1994; Scott, 1993) suggest that the Touch Math method may be used or adapted for use with children with Down syndrome. Certainly, further investigation of this programme seems warranted.

REFERENCES

Baroody, A.J. and Snyder, P.M. (1983) A cognitive analysis of basic arithmetic abilities of TMR children. *Education and Training of the Mentally Retarded*, **18**, pp. 253–59.

Brown, A.L. and DeLoache, J.S. (1978) Skills, plans, and self-regulation. In R.S. Seigler (ed.), *Children's Thinking: What Develops?*, pp. 3–55, Hillsdale: Erlbaum.

Buckley, S. and Sachs, B. (1987) *The Adolescent with Down's Syndrome: Life for the Teenager and for the Family*, Portsmouth: Portsmouth Polytechnic.

Bullock, J.K. (1991) *Touch Math Addition Kit*, 4th edn, Colorado Springs: Innovative Learning Concepts.

Bullock, J.K., Pierce, S. and McClelland, L. (1989) *Touch Math*, Colorado Springs: Innovative Learning Concepts.

Bullock, J., Pierce, S., Strand, L. and Branine, K. (1977) *Touch Math Teachers Manual*, Colorado Springs: Touch Math.

Carpenter, T.P. and Moser, J.M. (1984) The acquisition of addition and subtraction concepts in grades one through three. *Journal for Research in Mathematics Education*, **15**, pp. 179–202.

Caycho, L., Gunn, P. and Siegal, M. (1991) Counting by children with Down syndrome. *American Journal on Mental Retardation*, **95**, pp. 575–83.

Cornwall, A.C. (1974) Development of language, abstraction, and numerical concepts in Down's syndrome children. *American Journal of Mental Deficiency*, **79**, pp. 179–90.

Flexer, R.J. and Rosenberger, N. (1987) Beware of tapping pencils. *Arithmetic Teacher*, January, pp. 6–10.

Gelman, R. (1982) Basic numerical abilities. In R.J. Sternberg (ed.), *Advances in the Psychology of Intelligence: Vol. 1*, pp. 181–205, Hillsdale: Erlbaum.

Gelman, R. and Cohen, M. (1988) Qualitative differences in the way Down's syndrome and normal children solve a novel counting problem. In L. Nadel (ed.), *The Psychobiology of Down's Syndrome*, pp. 51–99, Cambridge: MIT Press.

Gelman, R. and Gallistel, C.R. (1978) *The Child's Understanding of Number*, Cambridge, MA: Harvard University Press.

Ginsburg, H. (1986) *Children's Arithmetic: How They Learn It and How You Teach It*, Austin: ProEd.

Groen, G. and Parkman, J. (1972) A chronometric view of simple addition algorithms. *Psychological Review*, **79**, pp. 329–43.

Hanrahan, J., Rapagna, S. and Poth, K. (1993) How children with learning problems learn addition: a longitudinal study. *Canadian Journal of Special Education*, **9**, pp. 101–09.

Irwin, K.C. (1989) The school achievement of children with Down's syndrome. *New Zealand Medical Journal*, **102**, pp. 11–13.

Irwin, K.C. (1991) Teaching children with Down Syndrome to add by counting-on. *Education and Treatment of Children*, **14**, pp. 128–41.

Kamii, C. and DeClark, G. (1985) *Young Children Reinvent Arithmetic*. New York: Teachers College Press.

Kokaska, S.M. (1975) Classroom techniques: a notation system in arithmetic skills. *Education and Training of the Mentally Retarded*, **10**, pp. 96–101.

Kramer, T. and Krug, D.A. (1973) A rationale and procedure for teaching addition. *Education and Training of the Mentally Retarded*, **8**, pp. 140–45.

Langevin, J., Drouin, C. and Hanrahan, J. (1994) Teaching a prudent strategy of payment to children with learning problems. *Journal of Practical Approaches to Developmental Handicap*, **18** (2), pp. 20–23.

McDonnell, J.J., Horner, R.H. and Williams, J.A. (1984) Comparison of three strategies for teaching generalized grocery purchasing to high school students with severe handicaps. *Journal of the Association for Severe Handicaps*, **9**, pp. 123–33.

Pupo, M. (1994) Teaching intellectually disabled students addition through a multisensory approach. Unpublished Master's thesis, McGill University, Montreal.

Scott, K.S. (1993) Multisensory mathematics for children with mild disabilities. *Exceptionality*, **4,** pp. 97–111.

Secada, W.G., Fuson, K.C. and Hall, J.W. (1983) The transition from counting-all to counting-on in addition. *Journal for Research in Mathematics Education*, **14,** pp. 47–57.

Yarmish, R. (1988). Numerical equivalence and the developmentally impaired. *Focus on Learning Problems in Mathematics*, **10** (4), pp. 31–50.

19 Motor Development and Physical Education

Greg Reid and Martin E. Block

Scholars of Down syndrome argue that movement skills affect cognitive and social functioning, as well as subsequent motor development (Ulrich *et al.*, 1992). More specifically, motor competence and physical fitness are related to vocational (Coleman *et al.*, 1976) and recreational opportunities, self-care adequacy (Jobling and Gunn, 1995), and reduction of morbidity and obesity (Rimmer *et al.*, 1993). In fact, a recent volume on Down syndrome devoted entirely to movement through the life span (Burns and Gunn, 1993), underscores the value that professionals hold for movement competence and physical activity.

In order to reap the benefits noted, it is necessary to participate in physical activity and to practice motor skills. While this may seem obvious, some research suggests that this might be problematic for individuals with Down syndrome. People with an intellectual disability tend to lead sedentary lives (Cheseldine and Jeffree, 1981; McConkey *et al.*, 1981; Watkinson and Wall, 1981). In fact, inactivity may begin as early as age 5 for children with Down syndrome (Canada Fitness Survey, 1983; Levinson and Reid, 1991; Sharav and Bowman, 1992). Moreover, Putnam *et al.* (1988) found that almost a third of 71 persons with Down syndrome lacked the skill to participate in a leisure activity. Insufficient skill, and a lack of intrinsic interest in physical activities are likely to result in a sedentary lifestyle, which may place the person at risk in terms of adult health (Pitteti and Campbell, 1991).

This scenario is not described to be alarmist or pessimistic, for many people with Down syndrome enjoy an active lifestyle. Rather, our purpose is to highlight the need for careful, thoughtful and competent physical activity programming. Motor development is one area, in addition to others covered in this volume, which impacts on programming and instruction. Hence, the objectives of this chapter are 1) to summarize the motor development literature on Down syndrome from the perspective of gross motor functioning and physical fitness, and 2) to outline principles of physical activity programming which augment their movement skills and participation patterns.

MOTOR DEVELOPMENT

Motor development in Down syndrome will be affected by the health and medical concerns described in other chapters of this volume, as well as by the support, encouragement, and stimulation provided by care-givers. Cardiac, visual, hearing and kinaesthetic problems are often noted (Block, 1991). Obesity is common in Down syndrome from early childhood (Chumlea and Cronk, 1982) and its effect will be described below. In addition, hypotonia and skeletal development influence movement skills and physical fitness.

Hypotonia is one of the most frequently cited conditions associated with Down syndrome. Dubowitz (1980) described hypotonia as a) an increase in the joint range of motion, b) diminished resistance of the joints to passive movements, and c) unusual postures such as the frog-like position of the legs in the supine position. Infants are often described as floppy or like a rag doll, although hypotonia does decrease with age. Not surprisingly perhaps, the lack of muscle tone is related to lack of strength in children and adolescents (Morris *et al.*, 1982). Yet the exact influence of hypotonia on neuromuscular control remains elusive. As Anson (1992) observed, normal stretch reflex activity (Shumway-Cook and Woollacott, 1985) indicates that the muscles are showing electrical activity, hence they are not without tone. Also, research by Davis and Kelso (1982) suggests that it is not hypotonia *per se* which is the major muscular problem in Down syndrome, but a lack of control of muscles stiffness. Thus, hypotonia remains a clinical reality of Down syndrome, but more research will be necessary to elucidate its precise role in motor development.

The skeletal development associated with persons with Down syndrome has several unique facets. First, there is evidence that their short stature is a product of a slow and uneven rate of long bone development. It seems that the rate of growth is particularly slow in early childhood but more normal in preadolescence and adolescence (Cronk, 1978; Rarick *et al.*, 1965; Thelander and Pryor, 1966). Secondly, the growth of the legs appear to be particularly effected (Rarick and Seefeldt, 1974). Third, joint laxity is common although not often disabling (Dugdale *et al.*, 1986). A specific case of joint laxity has had a pronounced effect on physical activity programming, that is, atlanto-axial instability. It is an increased laxity of the transverse ligaments between the atlas and axis of the cervical spine, which could damage the spinal cord if the neck was dislocated by forceful flexion. It is usually recommended that all persons with Down syndrome have a radiograph of the cervical spine to confirm this instability and that participation in sports which put pressure on the neck be avoided (*Official Special Olympics Sports Rules*, 1992). Estimates for the condition vary, often between 12 per cent and 20 per cent (Pueschel, 1987). Yet, there are recent data which suggest the radiograph may be unreliable at detecting the condition (Selby *et al.*, 1991). Also, it has been argued that the instability may not predict dislocation, and that the lack of real evidence of accidents may have needlessly excluded individuals with Down syndrome from participating in some sports (Davidson, 1988). Atlanto-axial instability is likely to remain an important point of debate and research in the years to come. Until the issues are resolved, however, we recommend a conservative approach.

Following Gallahue (1989) and Block (1991), we will discuss motor and physical fitness development in Down syndrome according to four age categories: Infancy, 0–2 years; childhood, 2–10 years; adolescence, 10–18 years; and young adulthood, 18–40 years.

Research describing the motor behaviour of individuals with Down syndrome usually compares their performance with other children or adults. It is apparent they do not acquire motor skills at the same rate as their non-handicapped peers. The more interesting question is how they perform compared to others with intellectual disabilities of similar chronological and mental age. If they are inferior (or superior) in this regard, different programming principles or practices might be advanced. In addition, investigating these differences allows us to begin to separate the impact of general intellectual difficulties, from specific neuromotor impairments associated with Down syndrome. We will highlight these comparisons.

The research is not without its share of methodological weaknesses, most of them noted previously by Henderson (1985) and Block (1991). Rather than repeat this discussion, we will stress the findings from the more effectively designed research.

We will emphasize research from an applied perspective or using tasks that are ecologically valid, since our purpose is to relate this knowledge to physical activity programming. There are excellent reviews of research exploring the underlying factors influencing motor behaviour, thus attempting to explain how and why individuals with Down syndrome differ from typical development (e.g. Anson, 1992; Anwar, 1981; Elliott, 1990; Elliott and Weeks, 1993; Henderson, 1985). However, the applicability of this research to programming is not always apparent in its early stages (see Reid, 1993, for a discussion of these issues).

Finally, we build upon Henderson (1985) in suggesting that three points characterize the motor development of individuals with Down syndrome. First, they do not perform generally as well as their non disabled peers. Second, there are large individual differences within the syndrome. Third and tentatively, there appears to be a number of areas in which individuals with Down syndrome are qualitatively or quantitatively different from peers of similar intellectual functioning and chronological age.

Infancy, 0–2 years

The first two years of human life are largely characterized by reflexive and spontaneous behaviour, and the attainment of postural control. Not surprisingly, therefore, the Down syndrome literature on infancy has dealt with these topics.

Infants with Down syndrome exhibit several reflexes such as the Moro, palmar and plantar grasp, and automatic stepping, beyond the typical time of termination (Cowie, 1970). Other reflexes are abnormal both in terms of the degree of response or time scale. Recently, Harris (1985) has demonstrated that their head-righting reflexes and equilibrium reactions occur with marked delays. These disturbances in reflexive behaviour, then, signal some unusual neuromotor functioning in Down syndrome within the first year.

Body rocking and head rolling are examples of spontaneous, quantifiable, rhythmical movements that usually occur in the first year of life. Developmentalists now view these behaviours as early signs of motor development (Thelen, 1979, 1985). MacLean *et al.* (1991) investigated these spontaneous movements in infants with Down syndrome, infants with a variety of motor impairments and infants without disability. The overall amount of rhythmical activity was not different between the children with Down syndrome and those with no disability, although those with Down syndrome demonstrated more mouth and foot subtypes of motor behaviour. The authors concluded that the rhythmical and spontaneous movements were apparent at similar developmental periods across the three groups. The average age at the start of the study was about 6 months for the infants without a disability and 14 months for those with Down syndrome. While the authors did not determine the presence of the spontaneous movements in the infants with Down syndrome at 6 months, their appearance in the second year of life certainly indicates an early delay in motor development.

A number of pioneering studies (e.g. Carr, 1970; Cowie, 1970) showed that the emergence of motor milestones such as rolling or sitting during the first six months of life were only slightly delayed in infants with Down syndrome while the delays were greater for later developing skills such as standing and walking. Yet, Rast and Harris (1985) tested 15 infants with Down syndrome and 15 without disabilities from 3 to 4 months of age for four postural reactions. They found the postural reactions of the youngsters with Down syndrome to be significantly less effective than their peers. These data, coupled with the findings of MacLean *et al.* (1991) suggest that the motor development of infants with Down syndrome is delayed, when compared to children without Down syndrome, from the first few months of life. Since children with Down syndrome will generally develop more slowly, the gap between them and other children will necessarily increase with age.

The early delay in motor development might be related to ineffective postural reactions. Haley (1986) demonstrated delays with righting, equilibrium and protective postural reactions in infants with Down syndrome compared to children without disabilities. Interestingly, once the infants with Down syndrome acquired the necessary postural reaction, they soon achieved the related motor milestone. Moreover, Butterworth and Cicchetti (1978) found delays in the development of the visual-postural system of infants with Down syndrome, either too little or too much postural reaction to visual stimulation. Finally, Shumway-Cook and Woollacott (1985) assessed the muscular responses of the legs to postural perturbations. They found that the children with Down syndrome showed a muscle pattern identical with non-disabled controls, but their responses were slower, more variable and less adaptive to changing task conditions. It seems apparent that the postural reactions of infants with Down syndrome are slow to develop.

Ulrich *et al.* (1992) speculated that the delay in acquiring independent walking may be related to lack of postural control or strength. They held seven, 11-month-old babies with Down syndrome upright over a small treadmill and showed that the infants produced alternate stepping patterns on the moving belt. None of the children had attempted to walk or even to stand alone at the time of the testing. The authors argued that the basic neural network for walking was intact, but independent walking was likely delayed by inadequate postural control or strength.

While children with Down syndrome appear to follow the same sequence of development as infants without disabilities (Carr, 1970; Cowie, 1970; Hogg and Moss, 1983), there may be qualitative differences or atypical movement patterns.

It is possible that these children assume unique positions or exhibit unusual movements in order to maintain postural stability (Block, 1991; Burns, 1993). For example, Lydic and Steele (1979) reported parental accounts of children with Down syndrome sitting with legs spread extremely far apart, walking with a wide base, and coming to a sitting position by spreading the legs in a prone position and pushing up with the hands until they sit upright.

Despite delays or unusual patterns of movement (which of course can be viewed positively as adaptive responses to biological or physiological constraints) most children with Down syndrome will learn to sit, walk, run, climb, grasp, dress themselves and participate in a host of physical activities. While children without disabilities, on average, will sit independently, stand alone, walk alone and run at 7, 11, 12 and 18 months respectively, youngsters with Down syndrome will accomplish these tasks at 9, 18, 18 and 48 months (Henderson, 1985). In addition, their range acquisition is larger than that of children without Down syndrome. For example, walking independently will usually occur between 9 and 17 months, but in Down syndrome the variability is 13 to 48 months. The milestones of standing and walking which seem to depend on strength and balance are particularly delayed compared to reaching and grasping (Dyer *et al.*, 1990). Clearly, any intervention that is attempted in the first few years of life must be conducted with these enormous individual differences in mind.

Henderson (1985) and Block (1991) have reviewed the motor behaviour intervention research. The findings are clearly mixed, some studies providing support for early intervention while others indicating no accelerated motor development. It is possible that certain intervention strategies (e.g. to improve muscle tone) may be effective only at a certain age, or for a highly specific aspect of motor development. Despite the equivocal nature of the research, writers still recommend early therapeutic intervention, as well as play and movement exploration to assist normal muscle tone, reflex behaviour, sensory integration, postural control and movement patterns (e.g. Diamond, 1986; Mercer, 1993; Niman-Reed and Sleight, 1988).

Childhood, 2–10 years

Posture, stability and walking have been investigated in studies of young children with Down syndrome, not surprisingly, since the infant research pointed to immaturity in these areas.

The postural responses of four children with Down syndrome, aged 3 to 6 years were found to be both similar and different from children without Down syndrome (Shumway-Cook and Woollacott, 1985). When they unexpectedly swayed forward or backward, all children responded with similar muscle activation patterns. However, the children with Down syndrome were slower to react and considerably more variable in the response. A generally slowness in movement has been observed in children with Down syndrome (e.g. Anson, 1992; Henderson, 1985; Jobling and Gunn, in press; Latash and Corcos, 1991). Shumway-Cook and Woollacott concluded that children with Down syndrome exhibit similar co-ordination patterns but have problems in the refinement or control of this co-ordination.

Parker *et al.* (1986) investigated the walking patterns of ten, 5-year-old children with Down syndrome. They reported a wide range of development, some showing extreme immaturity and others walking with a pattern expected of his or her age. As a group, the children walked with increased flexion in the hip and knee, a wide base of support, and a shortened step length, possibly indicating compensation for instability.

Fundamental motor patterns such as running, jumping, skipping, climbing, catching, throwing and striking will also develop through the childhood years. These are crucial for children with Down syndrome to function on the playground with peers (Jobling, 1993). In addition, these patterns become the building blocks of specific movement skills required for sport, dance and recreation competence. It is clear that children with an intellectual disability do not perform as well as children without an intellectual disability on a variety of movements, whether measured as qualitative motor patterns (Holland, 1987) or quantitative motor skills and abilities (Rarick *et al.*, 1976). With regard to children with Down syndrome, Block (1991) states that this comparison with non-disabled peers is no longer of any practical interest to either researchers or practitioners. The more interesting comparison is between individuals with Down syndrome and peers with a similar intellectual disability (Block, 1991; Reid, 1985).

This latter comparison is included in several studies, but the conclusions are not clear. Connolly and Michael (1986) found differences favouring girls without Down syndrome, when compared to girls of similar age and IQ with Down syndrome, on the Bruininks-Oseretsky Test of Motor Proficiency. The boys of both groups did not differ. Henderson *et al.* (1981) used the Cratty Six-Category Gross Motor Test and showed that the 10-year-old children with Down syndrome were inferior to a chronological and mental age-matched group on balance and locomotor agility. Cratty (1974) had previously described the performance of individuals with Down syndrome as inferior to others with an intellectual deficit on the same test. In contrast, LeBlanc *et al.* (1977) did not demonstrate overall differences on the Cratty balance test between children with and without Down syndrome who were matched on age. Certainly more research is necessary to clarify the issue of differences between children with and without Down syndrome who have similar intellectual functioning.

The physical fitness literature does not shed significant light on these comparisons either. Wang and Eichstaedt (1980) evaluated the fitness of children with moderate intellectual disabilities, including those with Down syndrome. The test items included the flexed arm hang, sit-ups, shuttle run, standing long jump, 50-yard (46m) dash, softball throw and endurance runs. No consistent differences were produced between the subgroup with Down syndrome and the other subjects. Contrary results were found in a cross-Canada assessment of the physical fitness of children with moderate intellectual disability, using similar items, (Canada Fitness Award, 1983). The standards for receiving one of the four awards (Excellent, Gold, Silver, Bronze) are different for the children with Down syndrome with the exception of the endurance run. At most ages, and on most fitness items, the students with Down syndrome can reach a given level (e.g. Bronze) with a score that is less than that of the child without Downs syndrome. Thus, the Canadian children with Down syndrome did not appear to be as physically fit as children of similar age and intellect.

Obesity is related to physical fitness as well as overall health in Down syndrome (Barham, 1993). In addition, parents and professionals are concerned with its relationship to social prejudice, aesthetics and limitations in activity (Chad *et al.*, 1990; Sharav and Bowman, 1992). Obesity is more common in girls than boys in Down syndrome (Cronk *et al.*, 1985) with the tendency towards gaining excess weight beginning in late infancy (Chumlea and Cronk, 1982). Thus, studying factors associated with obesity in Down syndrome has been an active area of inquiry. They appear to have a normal basal metabolic rate as adults, that is, the energy expenditure for normal body maintenance at rest (Schapiro and Rapoport, 1989). While hypothyroidism may contribute to obesity in some individuals with Down syndrome, a low level of physical activity may be a significant influence for many others.

Sharav and Bowman (1992) compared 30 sibling pairs, each with one child with Down syndrome, on dietary practices and physical activity. The children ranged in age from 2 to 14 years, with an average age of about 4 years 6 months for children with Down syndrome and 6 years 6 months for siblings. The caloric intake was not significantly different for the two groups, but parents reported that the children with Down syndrome were less active than their siblings and spent more time indoors. The authors noted that the parents in their study were a select population, having a high educational level. Notwithstanding this, the tendency toward a sedentary lifestyle began in early childhood. This has clear implications for parent and professionals concerned with the well-being of individuals with Down syndrome.

Evaluating the motor development of children with Down syndrome is not a trivial task. Motor tests such as the Cratty Six-Category Gross Motor Test and the Bruininks-Oseretsky have been criticized as static and unrelated to real play and games situations (Reid, 1985), and for questionable validity (Henderson *et al.*, 1981) and underlying theoretical assumptions (Davis, 1984). They are likely of limited used today, rather than no use at all. We recommend that the assessment techniques outlined in the programme planning section of this chapter be considered in future motor development research with Down syndrome.

Adolescence, 10–18 years

It is imperative that the movement needs of adolescents with Down syndrome are addressed by parents and professionals, for it is during this period that further improvement in fundamental skills may be realized, specific sport and recreation skills developed, and physical fitness becomes a concern. As Barham (1993, p. 151) argues, movement limitations 'can become barriers to integration ... and thwart attempts ... to become active participants in employment, leisure and recreational settings'. Yet, there are only a few studies exploring the motor behaviour of adolescents with Down syndrome.

One such study, from Australia (Jobling and Gunn, 1995), is unique because it is longitudinal. This research design is more appropriate than cross-sectional studies to determine if youngsters with Down syndrome become increasingly proficient or deficient in motor skills at certain ages compared to their age- or age and IQ-matched peers. That is, if a 5-year-old child with Down syndrome lags behind his or her peers, does the difference increase, decrease or remain constant during childhood, adolescents and young adulthood? There are some suggestions that differences in motor development increase with age (Carr, 1970; Henderson, 1985) while others argue that the differences are an artefact of measurement (Rast and Harris, 1985).

Jobling and Gunn (1995) assessed the motor behaviour of 74 children with Down syndrome over a period of 4 years, from ages 9 years 6 months to 13 years 5 months, using the long form of the Bruininks-Oseretsky Test of Motor Proficiency. In addition, a smaller group was reassessed at 16 years of age. The mean IQ for the youngsters at each of the four years varied only from 47 to 50. Performance was substantially below age expectations for all items, a continuation of slow motor development evident from infancy. In particular, these young adolescents had difficulties with balance, consistent with earlier postural reactions and stability problems (e.g. Shumway-Cook and Woollacott, 1985) and with speed of response, again in concert with the general slowness associated with Down syndrome (e.g. Anson, 1992). There was significant improvement across ages 10 through 13 on three of the eight test items. When the effect of age was analysed for 20 subjects tested at 10, 12 and 16 years all items exhibited improvement, save balance. On the balance subtest, 12 of the 16-year-old subjects did not reach the standard for children without disabilities at 4 years 2 months. The overall improvement in performance to 16 years of age suggests that the lag between individuals with Down syndrome and their age peers is essentially a reflection of a slower rate of development associated with Down syndrome. There was no compelling evidence in the longitudinal data set to suggest that the rate of motor development in Down syndrome is appreciably unique, that is, showing plateaus or accelerations at unusual periods.

Eichstaedt *et al.* (1991) administered a number of motor performance and physical fitness items to three groups of individuals: those with mild intellectual disability, moderate intellectual disability and Down syndrome. This was a cross sectional study of children and adolescents from 6 to 20 years of age. The motor performance of the boys and girls with a mild intellectual disability were generally superior compared to Down syndrome. The group with moderate intellectual disability were only superior to Down syndrome on two items, the stork stand, a balance measure, and the shuttle run (boys only). The difficulty with balance is consistent with the data from Jobling and Gunn. However, it is difficult to conclude from these data that youngsters with Down syndrome are generally inferior to peers with similar age and IQ because the groups were not matched on these variables. Yet, one might conclude tentatively that the motor skills associated with Down syndrome are similar or slightly inferior to those associated with moderate intellectual disabilities.

Muscle tone and strength have not been extensively studied. Clausen (1968) reported similar grip strength measures from subjects with Down syndrome and from those with comparable intellectual disability. Morris *et al.* (1982) found that children with Down syndrome, aged 4 to 17 years had lower muscle tone and inferior grip strength compared to children without disability, but did improve with age. Eichstaedt *et al.* (1991) demonstrated that individuals with Down syndrome had lower upper body strength as measured by the flexed arm hang compared to those with mild intellectual disability but only the boys scored lower than a comparison group with moderate intellectual disability. Finally, these researchers also showed that their subjects with Down syndrome were not as proficient in muscular endurance (assessed by sit-ups and push-ups) as a group with mild intellectual disability but they did not differ from those with moderate intellectual disability. One can conclude, again tentatively, that the muscle tone and strength of adolescents with Down syndrome is comparable to those with moderate intellectual disabilities but generally inferior to those with mild intellectual disabilities.

Parker and James (1985) supported the common observation that individuals with Down syndrome have remarkable flexibility. Their subjects, aged 5, 10 and 15 years of age, were more flexible than a comparison group of age-matched peers but showed a similar decrement in joint range of movement with age. A group of individuals with Down syndrome were also more flexible than groups with mild or moderate intellectual disability (Eichstaedt *et al.*, 1991).

Cardiovascular fitness, important for sustained physical exertion, has been, perhaps, the most frequently measured variable of physical fitness in the last 20 years. It has been suggested that this fitness variable may be particularly important for individuals with an intellectual disability because of the relationship between cardiovascular functioning, and health, longevity and productivity (Fernhall *et al.*, 1989; Fryers, 1986; Pitetti and Campbell, 1991; Pitetti and Tan, 1991). Fernhall *et al.* (1989) were the first to assess a group of adolescents with Down syndrome with an oxygen uptake protocol of cardiovascular fitness, previous workers having used field tests such as distance running to predict cardiovascular fitness. They reported that their subjects could participate safely in exhausting work, after screening for contraindications to exercise. However, cardiovascular fitness was very low and the subjects did not reach age expected maximum heart rates. Thus, with both field tests and direct measures of oxygen uptake, it is apparent that the cardiovascular fitness of adolescents with Down syndrome is not as efficient as age peers, but there are no studies that have compared them with peers of similar age and IQ. There has been some effort to improve their performance through training. Millar *et al.* (1993) divided 14 adolescents into exercise (n = 10) and control (n = 4) groups. The exercise group participated in a 10 week walk/jog programme. There was no significant change in oxygen uptake, the most valid physiological variable for cardiovascular functioning. However, the exercise group did spend more time walking on the treadmill during the posttest, it simply did not translate into a higher value for oxygen uptake.

The simplest explanations of these disappointing findings is a lack of motivation to train and insufficient time devoted to the programme. Certainly more training studies with adolescents are required. However, Eberhard and co-workers (Eberhard *et al.*, 1989; Eberhard *et al.*, 1991) have investigated physiological factors which may limit performance and training effects in adolescents with Down syndrome. Their research suggests that these individuals have similar biochemical responses to exercise but somewhat different endocrine responses. There has also been some discussion that individuals with Down syndrome may have a lower maximum heart rate, thus limiting their exercise potential. While Pitetti *et al.* (1992a) reported low maximum heart rates, more recent data from Portugal indicated levels commensurate with age (Varela and Pitetti, in press). Studies in the next few years will no doubt unravel the complex set of motivational, training and physiological variables that may explain their low cardiovascular functioning.

Finally, although adults with Down syndrome may have a typical basal metabolic rate, some preliminary evidence may prevent this generalization to adolescents. Chad *et al.* (1990) did not include a control group without Down syndrome, but compared their results to previously published data. The basal metabolic rate was lower in Down syndrome, leading the authors to suggest that it may be a contributing factor to obesity. They correctly point out that exercise will be an important prevention and treatment of obesity along with nutritional awareness.

Young adulthood, 18–40 years

There appears to be no published motor development studies of adults with Down syndrome. The few investigations in the wider field of motor behaviour that have recently been completed focus on physical fitness and obesity. Professionals are now strongly advocating physically active lifestyles for adults with Down syndrome for health, recreational and vocational reasons (James, 1993).

As previously noted, the basal metabolic rate of adults with Down syndrome does not differ from that of adults without a disability (Schapiro and Rapoport, 1989). None the less, obesity of adults with Down syndrome remains a major concern of health professionals. Individuals with an intellectual disability carry more adipose tissue than people without a disability, the women more frequently than men being classified as obese (Pitetti *et al.*, 1993). The short stature associated with Down syndrome gives the impression that obesity may be more prevalent in this population than in the larger group of individuals with an intellectual disability. In fact, some research bears this out (Climstein *et al.*, 1992). Yet, data from Pitetti *et al.* (1992a) indicated that only the males with Down syndrome had a higher percentage of body fat than the control subjects with an intellectual disability. Moreover, Rimmer *et al.* (1992) did not demonstrate any differences for either gender. However, 42 per cent of the men and 61 per cent of the women were classified as obese. They also found no differences between the groups with regard to total cholesterol, low- and high-density lipoprotein cholesterol, and triglycerides, although previous research has classified a large percentage of adults with an intellectual disability in the moderate- to high-risk category for coronary heart disease on the basis of total cholesterol (Rimmer and Kelly, 1991). Notwithstanding the value of comparing individuals with Down syndrome to other groups, the need to address their problem with obesity is evident.

Pitetti *et al.* (1993) reviewed the studies aimed at modifying the weight and body composition of people with intellectual disabilities. Some research reported no change while others indicated modest improvements only. Investigations were as short as eight weeks, but it is clear that dealing with obesity is likely a lifelong challenge. Combinations of diet, exercise, nutritional education and behavioural therapy (e.g. reinforcement, self-monitoring) will likely be necessary (Pitetti *et al.*, 1993). Engaging in an active lifestyle is critical, since some professionals (Emes *et al.*, 1990) have argued that inactivity is the most important factor in obesity for individuals with an intellectual disability.

Flexibility and strength are important for ageing adults, in part to maintain independence in living. The hypermobility of youngsters with Down syndrome likely decreases in adulthood because of the improvement in hypotonia. There is minimal published data on adult flexibility in Down syndrome but normal ageing processes are no doubt occurring. Yet, it is likely that adults with Down syndrome enjoy a level of flexibility that is conducive to active and independent living. The picture is not quite so positive for strength. The low muscle tone of infancy (Cowie, 1970) and the reduced level of strength in childhood and adolescence (Morris *et al.*, 1982) precedes the strength exhibited by adults. Three groups of 18 adults were assessed for isokinetic leg and arm strength, including a group with Down syndrome, one with intellectual disability but without Down syndrome and, a final group without disability (Pitetti *et al.*, 1992b). The two groups with an intellectual disability had the lowest levels of strength and those with Down syndrome were inferior to peers with an intellectual disability on leg strength. Pitetti *et al.* (1992b) cogently argue that strength must be considered as an important fitness variable since it is related to vocational pursuits, recreation and activities of daily living.

Cardiovascular fitness has been at the forefront of the exercise boom of the past two decades. Pitetti and Campbell (1991) argued that people with intellectual disabilities may be at a significant health risk due to low levels of cardiovascular functioning, their sedentary lifestyles, and the finding that cardiovascular disorders are the most common form of disease among elderly people with an intellectual disability. A number of fitness reviews outline testing and assessment issues, the fitness levels associated with intellectual disability, and the results of the training studies (e.g. Fernhall *et al.*, 1988; Lavay *et al.*, 1990; Pitetti *et al.*, 1993; Seidl *et al.*, 1987).

Adults with Down syndrome might be in a particular state of health risk. The limited research indicates that their cardiovascular fitness is inferior to that of peers with an intellectual disability but without Down syndrome (Pitetti *et al.* 1992a). One of the factors involved in this low level of cardiovascular fitness may be a lower peak or maximum heart rate than would be expected on the basis of age (Pitetti *et al.* 1993). It is not yet clear if the heart rates reported in the literature are a reflection of our inability to coerce the participants to push themselves to near exhaustion, or a biological/physiological limitation inherent in intellectual disabilities and Down syndrome. Future research will resolve this issue like the most recent data on Down syndrome showing age-expected heart rates (Varela and Pitetti, in press).

Readers interested in promoting cardiovascular fitness should become conversant with the latest discussion of testing techniques and training methods. For example, using some existing regression equations to predict the maximum oxygen uptake of individuals with Down syndrome may overpredict their true capacity (Climstein *et al.*, 1992) This discussion has been well presented by Pitetti *et al.* (1993).

PROGRAMME PLANNING

With a basic understanding of the physical and motor characteristics of children with Down syndrome, the next step is to develop and implement a comprehensive programme to help these individuals improve their motor skills and develop functional, lifetime leisure skills. Programme planning is the process of determining what content to target for instruction, what the student's present level of performance is on the targeted content, and what to teach and how to teach it. Once the programme has been developed, a physical educator can then implement the programme and conduct ongoing assessment to make sure the programme is effective.

While children with Down syndrome share some common characteristics, each individual child will display unique attributes in terms of movement patterns, rate of motor development, fitness levels, health, ability to follow directions and levels of motivation. Thus, programme development has to be individualized to meet the unique needs of each child. This section will focus on programme development with information in the following three areas: selecting content for instruction, assessment to facilitate programme development and implementation, and instructional, curricular, and equipment modifications to facilitate the acquisition of critical motor skills.

Selecting content for instruction

One of the most important considerations in programme planning for children with Down syndrome is selecting appropriate activities for instruction. Since children with Down syndrome will have motor delays and learn and refine new skills slower than their peers without disabilities, it is critical to select skills that are the most important for each child. In the past, a developmental or 'bottom up' approach has been used to develop programmes. More recently, an ecological or 'top down' approach has been suggested for programme development. It is important to understand each of these approaches when determining content.

Developmental approach

A developmental approach traditionally has been used to determine the appropriate content for children with disabilities, including children with Down syndrome (Auxter *et al.*, 1993; Brown *et al.*, 1979; Kelly, 1991; Rainforth *et al.*, 1992; Sherrill, 1993). This approach is based on a normal model of development with a focus on key milestones that children are expected to achieve at certain ages. Those who follow a developmental approach argue that development follows a relatively set sequence, and this sequence should be taught to children with disabilities in order to correct and prevent further delays (Rainforth *et al.*, 1992). Children typically are tested using a developmental assessment with markers or milestones indicating critical skills at various ages. The content that would be targeted for any child after assessment would be the next milestone on the developmental progression (Sherrill, 1993).

While at first glance a developmental approach seems to make sense, this type of approach has many drawbacks. Rainforth *et al.* (1992) outlined three specific concerns with a pure developmental approach. The first and perhaps the greatest concern is the possibility that the child will be 'stuck' at lower levels of the continuum and thus only be given instruction on these lower level skills. This is particularly critical as children get older and are preparing for life away from school (Brown *et al.*, 1979). For example, what content would be targeted for a student with Down syndrome who is 15 years old yet still functions like a 5-year-old? Following a developmental approach, teachers and specialists would target skills at the next developmental level, i.e., skills expected at the 5+ year level (e.g., prereading, colouring, body awareness, locomotor patterns). Critical skills that this student needs to be successful at work, in the community, at home, and during leisure time are more or less ignored because these types of skills are thought to be beyond the skill level of the student (Brown *et al.*, 1979; Rainforth, *et al.*, 1992). In addition, adaptations that could help students perform more functional skills are not provided and students will eventually graduate from this type of programme with very few functional skills, skills that will help them be successful in work and community settings (Block, 1994; Brown *et al.*, 1979; Kelly, 1991).

A second and related concern with the developmental approach is that many of the skills that are listed on developmental sequences are not necessarily skills that children need to learn (Campbell and Stewart, 1986; Rainforth, *et al.*, 1992). For example, it might be important to note that a child with Down syndrome can only balance on one-foot for two seconds. Does this mean that we should target the specific skill of balancing on one foot for five seconds, or could we incorporate balance activities into more functional skills such as walking up and down stairs, learning how to kick a ball in a soccer unit, or learning how to step and throw in a softball unit?

A final concern noted by Rainforth and her colleagues was that teachers and specialists who follow a developmental approach might view children as 'developmentally young'. The problem here is that these adults then interact, use activities, and present materials that are more appropriate for the developmental age rather than the chronological age of the student. This makes children seem even more delayed than they really are. In addition, it does not allow students the opportunity to work with materials or demonstrate social skills critical for working and living in the community (Brown *et al.*, 1979; Krebs and Block, 1992).

The developmental approach is fine for normally developing children. In addition, the developmental approach might be appropriate for very young children with Down syndrome such as toddlers and preschoolers. However, for school-age children with Down syndrome, what inevitably happens is that they remain at the lower end of the developmental scale. By age 5 they function like a 2-year-old, by age 10 they may function like a 4-year-old, and by 20 they may function like an

8-year-old. If all we have given them are activities appropriate for younger children, they will never acquire independent lifetime leisure skills.

Ecological approach

An ecological approach (also known as a functional, community-referenced, or top-down approach) has proven to be an effective way of prioritizing appropriate goals and activities for instruction while overcoming the problems associated with the developmental approach (Auxter, *et al.*, 1993; Block, 1994; Brown and Snell, 1993; Rainforth, *et al.*, 1992; Wessel and Kelly, 1986). The focus of planning is on what skills a student will need upon graduation from school to be as independent and successful as possible in work, home, community and recreation endeavours (Brown *et al.*, 1979; Falvey, 1989; Rainforth, *et al.*, 1992). In terms of physical education, the targeted post-graduation goal is having the necessary motor, fitness, cognitive and social skills needed to participate in community-based lifetime leisure skills such as bowling, swimming, tennis, golf, aerobic dance and weight training (Block, 1992; 1994; Kelly, 1991; Krebs and Block, 1992)

Rainforth *et al.* (1992) and Brown (1979) noted that it is not enough to simply pick functional, lifetime skills at random. To make this approach truly ecological or 'community-referenced' (Brown *et al.*, 1979), prioritized long-term goals must be relevant to the student in terms of where he or she lives, what he or she likes to do, and what is available in the community. How then does one determine which lifetime leisure skills make it to the top of the top-down model? Many factors need to be considered before making this decision. Most importantly, the child's skills and interests should be evaluated in relation to what is popular and available in the community (Block, 1994; Rainforth, *et al.*, 1994; Schleien *et al.*, 1993). This inter-action between the student and his or her environment is critical and provides social validity to the choice of skills. In addition, it is important to determine the availability of certain activities in the community in terms of cost and transportation requirements and accommodations these community facilities are able to make for persons with disabilities. Table 19.1 presents a list of factors to consider when determining which goals to prioritize for a particular student.

For example, Billy, a 13-year-old with Down syndrome, might be interested in softball as the long-term goal for his motor/recreation programme. Billy is a big baseball fan. He has his own baseball mitt, and he often plays catch or hits a ball off a tee with his dad's help. Softball is popular in Billy's community with several leagues for young adults. These leagues range from highly competitive to more recreational where virtually anyone is welcome. In addition, Special Olympics has a Unified Softball League (both players with and without mental retardation play on the same team) in the community for teenagers. Thus, there will be opportunities for Billy to practise and play baseball well into adulthood. Tennis also is popular in the community where Billy lives, and would seem to be a functional, lifetime leisure skill to target for someone with Down syndrome. However, tennis would not be targeted for Billy because a) neither Billy nor his parents are interested in tennis, b) people in Billy's community who play tennis are skilled players, c) Billy's eye-hand co-ordination and strength are very limited making even adapted tennis

Table 19.1 Factors to consider when prioritizing goals and objectives

Student's strengths and weaknesses referenced to current and future needs (severity of disability)	What are student's abilities, referenced to regular physical education activities and community play/recreation activities?
How much time do you have to teach skills, and what is the chance student will acquire skills?	Younger students can be 'exposed' to more variety of skills, while older students should begin to focus on skills needed to participate in specific lifetime leisure activities.
Student's interests	What recreational/sport activities does the student prefer?
Parent's interests	What recreational/sport activities do the student's parents prefer?
Peer interests	What activities do peers play on the playground, in the neighborhood and in community recreation?
What recreation facilities are available in the community?	Prioritize activities that will be available to the student in the community, e.g. are there bowling alleys, recreation centres, etc.? Are they accessible?
What equipment/transportation is available?	Does the student need special equipment, e.g. bowling ramp, flotation devices? Is transportation to community recreation facilities available?
What support services (in terms of personnel) is available?	Who will be available to assist the student in physical education and recreation? Do you need specially trained persons to work with student, e.g. for signing to non-verbal students?

Adapted from Block, M.E. (1994). Reprinted with permission.

activities difficult, and d) the community has only a handful of tennis courts that are used almost every night during the summer and fall. Thus, tennis may be deemed functional in general terms, but it would not be ecologically appropriate for Billy.

Time plays a big factor in developing top-down programmes. While children without disabilities can learn a variety of skills during school, many children with disabilities, including children with Down syndrome, will learn skills at a much slower rate. As Brown *et al.* (1979) noted, teachers and parents do not have the luxury of exposing children with disabilities to the same variety of activities as their peers. Typically developing children can learn and forget hundreds of things and still acquire the skills needed to be successful, independent adults. This is not true for individuals with intellectual disabilities. Programmes that focus on exposure inevitably cause these students to graduate with a smattering of skills in different areas but no real functional skills. With the top-down approach, the goal is to make sure that students graduate from the programme with at least a few of the critical functional skills related to work, shopping, self-help, household care and lifetime leisure skills (Block, 1994; Brown *et al.*, 1979; Kelly, 1991; Krebs and Block, 1992).

Thus, a factor to consider when determining how many top-down plans to develop for a particular student is how long this student takes to learn and master motor skills. If it takes a student a great deal of time to master critical skills, then this student might have only two lifetime leisure goals targeted for graduation. On the other hand, if the student learns and masters skills at a faster rate, then perhaps three or even four lifetime leisure skills can be targeted. The critical point is that students should not simply be exposed to activities. Rather, they should be involved in activities that they have a high likelihood of mastering. This may mean that some students with Down syndrome might only have two top-down plans. However, with proper instruction, we can expect the student to graduate with an ability to participate in a functional, lifetime leisure activities. This is much better than exposing a student to a variety of activities that he or she will never master.

Once long-term goals are outlined, then specific skills needed for the student to achieve these goals are delineated. In addition, skills that are not needed to reach the long-term goals can be eliminated from the programme. This may mean that many skills seen in a typical developmental model are eliminated because they have no direct bearing on the targeted goals. For example, a child with Down syndrome may have golf, aerobic dance and softball as lifetime leisure skills as the top of her top-down plan. The team can then delineate critical skills needed to help her reach these goals. For golf, skills such as striking, walking, twisting, bending, body awareness, knowing the basic rules of golf, and functional levels of fitness to play golf such as strength (enough to hold the club and hit the ball with some force), flexibility (to do a golf swing), and endurance (to walk the course and hit the ball repeatedly) would be included in the top-down plan. Many other skills would not be needed for this student to learn how to play golf, so these skills are not taught. These skills include kicking, throwing, catching, jumping, hopping, skipping, walking a balance beam, doing a somersault, doing a pull-up and running the mile. These are skills that would traditionally be taught in a developmental approach but have no relation to this student's top-down plan (note that throwing and catching would be included in the top-down plan for softball).

Kelly (1991) conceptualized the ecological approach as a pyramid with the top of the pyramid constituting the targeted lifetime leisure activity and lower levels of the pyramid describing skills needed to successfully participate in the targeted lifetime leisure activity (Figure 19.1). Skills build upon each other such that the lowest part of the pyramid focuses on body awareness and control skills that are needed to acquire locomotor and manipulation skills. In turn, these underpin combined skills needed to successfully participate in the targeted lifetime leisure activity. Note that many of the skills at the lower part of the pyramid are a part of typical elementary physical education programmes Thus, preschool and elementary-aged children with Down syndrome will probably work on many of the same skills as their peers without disabilities (e.g. body awareness and control, basic locomotor patterns).

As the child gets older and begins to focus on skills needed for the targeted lifetime leisure skill, differences between the programme for the child with Down syndrome and his or her peers will become more evident. In such cases, students

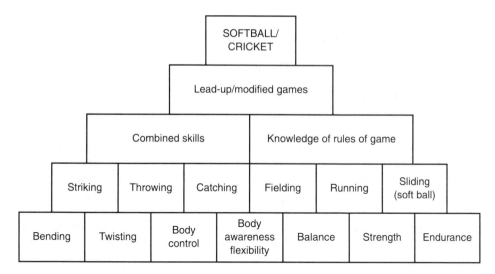

Figure 19.1 Top down pyramid (adapted from L.E. Kelly, 1991, *Achievement-based curriculum: Teaching manual*, Charlottesville, VA: University of Virginia)

may either work on different skills than their peers during regular physical education (e.g. work on the overhand throw and hitting a ball off a tee for softball to peers who work on picking the ball up and tossing it with lacrosse sticks), or work on targeted skills at community-based facilities such as swimming pools, health clubs, bowling alleys and golf courses. The key is that students with Down syndrome are focusing on critical skills they need in order to be successful in the targeted lifetime leisure skill upon graduation.

In summary, children with Down syndrome learn skills at a slower rate than their peers. Thus, instructional time cannot be wasted by simply exposing these children to activities and skills that they will never master. The ecological approach to programme planning is believed to be the most effective way of making sure only critical, functional skills, that will help the student be as independent as possible upon graduation, are targeted for instruction.

Assessment to facilitate programme development and instruction

Once the top-down plan has been outlined, it is important to assess the student on critical skills needed to reach the top of the plan. Again, in order to make this assessment truly ecological, environments where the student is expected to use these skills should be identified and analysed (Brown *et al.*, 1979; Brown and Snell, 1993; Falvey, 1989; Rainforth, *et al.*, 1992). For example, if soccer has been targeted for a particular student, all of the skills needed to play soccer in the student's community are identified and analysed. Certainly skills such as kicking, trapping, passing, dribbling and running would be analysed. However, more than just analysing specific soccer skills, other factors to successful participation are delineated and analysed, including getting dressed for the activity, transportation to and from the field, and appropriate social skills.

The most recommended ecological assessment strategy for students with disabilities including students with Down syndrome is the process know as *ecological inventories* (Brown *et al.*, 1979; Brown and Snell, 1993; Krebs and Block, 1992; Rainforth, *et al.*, 1992) These informal inventories focus on the important domains (vocational, community, domestic, leisure) that are needed for successful adult functioning. Each domain is then broken down into critical activities and skills that the student needs to be successful within the targeted environments. The student is assessed on his or her competency on these critical activities and skills, and then appropriate objectives and instructional plans are developed and implemented. Brown *et al.* (1979) outlined the following five stages (listed hierarchically) of the ecological inventory process: identify curricular domain; identify and survey current and future natural environments; divide the relevant environments into subenvironments; inventory these subenvironments for relevant activities; and determine skill required for performance of the activities.

Identify curricular domain

Rather than focusing on developmental hierarchies and physical education curricula, in ecological inventories curricular domains represent major life areas, lead to selection of practical skills, and emphasize functional goals of self-sufficiency. In addition, traditional areas such as motor, communication and social skills are embedded within these functional domains (Brown and Snell, 1993).

Current and future natural environments

The next stage of the process is to identify specific environments where the student will participate in the targeted activity. In the case of soccer, current and future environments would include the school playgrounds where soccer is played during physical education and recess, neighbourhood fields where soccer is played after school, and local community fields where soccer is played in community leagues and in Special Olympics programmes.

Subenvironments

Subenvironments that make up the larger environment are then identified. Thus, subenvironments would be delineated for school fields, the neighbourhood and community fields. Take for example the case of soccer during physical education. Subenvironments include the hallway, locker room, the gym and the soccer field. For community-based soccer, subenvironments might include dressing at home, transportation to and from the community field, locating the correct field, warming up with teammates, sitting on the bench and playing the game. Many sub-environments afford skill training on related skills such as dressing and grooming in the locker room and at home, communication skills in the gym or while sitting on the bench, and social skills during skill work, playing the game, and while being transported back and forth to the field.

Relevant activities

With subenvironments identified, the next step is to determine what activities take place within each subenvironment. These activities describe essential skills that a student needs to be able to be successful within each subenvironment. While there are many skills that can be found within each subenvironment, only those skills that are truly essential should be targeted for instruction (Block, in press; Brown and Snell, 1993). For example, skills within the subenvironment of the locker room include various grooming skills such as dressing and undressing, taking a shower, combing hair, shaving, brushing teeth, putting on deodorant, etc. Yet, the most essential skills for a student with Down syndrome might simply be dressing and undressing, taking a shower and combing hair. The other skills are not essential for the student to be successful. In terms of gross motor skills, the subenvironment of game play might include such skills as dribbling, passing, trapping (using various body parts), chipping, shooting, juggling, faking, changing speed, changing directions, etc. Again, while these skills all fit under the subenvironment of 'soccer game', for a student with Down syndrome who has limited skills and who takes a long time to learn a skill, the most essential to focus on might be passing, trapping balls passed on the ground and dribbling.

Skills required

The final step in the process is to break down or task analyse each activity into teachable components. These teachable components then become the specific focus of instruction. For example, passing a soccer ball can be broken down into the following teachable components:

1. locate teammate
2. approach the ball
3. plant non-kicking foot next to ball
4. rotate hip outward so that inside of foot is facing ball
5. bring kicking leg back
6. bring kicking leg forward
7. contact ball with inside of foot
8. follow through towards teammate
9. performs all components smoothly

The teacher can then provide instruction and practice opportunities to the student that focus on the components of the skills that the student needs to improve. For example, a teacher notes that her student with Down syndrome is having difficulty with rotating his hip outward so that the inside of the foot is in position to kick the ball. The teacher can then provide specific instructional feedback and teaching cues as well as activities that promote hip rotation.

It should be noted that there are many prepackaged curriculums that already have task analyses and instructional programme for a variety of motor development and sport skills. Three in particular that are very good and have been specifically designed for students with mental retardation (including students with Down syndrome) are the ICAN Program (Wessel, 1976), the Special Olympics Sports Skills Guides (Special Olympics, 1993), and Stepping Out for Fitness (Reid *et al.*, 1990).

In addition to teachable components, teachers should determine how much of a particular skill is needed for a student to be successful. For example, a student might be able to demonstrate all the components of a skilful side-of-the foot pass, yet not pass the ball accurately or put enough force into the kick to get the ball to team-mates. Learning the technique is not alone sufficient but the student now needs to work on using more force and passing the ball more accurately. This notion of 'how much' should be functionally referenced. That is, how far a student should be expected to kick a soccer ball should not be based on some arbitrary number but rather on some specific, functional criteria such as 5 metres (the typical distance between team-mates).

Again, ecological inventories provide teachers with a clear understanding of the critical environments and essential skills within each of these environments that are needed for a student to be successful in a particular activity. By using the step-by-step approach outlined above, teachers can keep track of what skills a student needs to work on and how well the student is progressing towards short-term instructional objectives and long-term goals.

Teaching motor skills to students with Down syndrome

With content delineated and a student's specific goals and objectives in place, the next step in programme planning is actually helping students acquire motor skills. Some of the key strategies to consider when teaching students with Down syndrome include ecological task analysis, curricular adaptations, and instructional adaptations.

Ecological task analysis

Davis and Burton (1991) developed a new type of task analysis that extended previous task analytical models, most notably Herkowitz's Developmental Task Analysis Model (1978). Herkowitz's developmental task analysis described a skill such as throwing or striking and then listed a variety of factors related to equipment and presentation of the task that could affect performance. For example, factors that could affect striking include size and weight of the bat, distance the ball is tossed, speed of toss and trajectory of toss. These factors were then matched to particular students so that a teacher would know that one child did best with a particular bat when the ball was tossed from 10 feet away while another child did better with a different bat and the ball tossed from a different distance.

Davis and Burton noted that, while a great beginning in skill analysis, Herkowitz's model has several flaws. Specifically, Herkowitz's model does not consider either the goal of the given task or the attributes of the mover. The goal of the task can have a tremendous influence on the movement pattern a mover might display and movers with different capabilities and physical characteristics respond quite differently to changes in task factors.

For example, Herkowitz listed ball size as a factor that can affect throwing performance. However, the size of a mover's hand in relation to the ball size taken together will determine performance. Children with large hands may be unaffected by subtle changes in ball size, while children who have smaller hands, including students with Down syndrome, may be forced into a completely new pattern as ball size is increased. For example, Block and Provis (1992) found that changes in ball size caused children with Down syndrome to change from a one-handed to two-handed throwing pattern while similar changes in ball size only caused subtle changes in age-matched children without disabilities. Similarly, balance requirements in the task might not negatively affect a student who has good balance, yet such requirements could have a dramatic affect on children with Down syndrome who have difficulty with even simple balance tasks. Performer characteristics, like the goal of the task, are critical determinants to performance, yet performer characteristics are absent from previous task analysis models.

In an effort to correct flaws found in Herkowitz's model, Davis and Burton proposed the ecological task analysis model (ETA). The major tenets of ETA are as follows:

1. Actions are the result of the complex relationship between the task goal, the performer, and the environment. ETA includes a description of the task goal and the performer as critical factors in movement outcome.
2. Tasks should be categorized by function and intention rather than movement pattern or mechanism of performance. The same function can be achieved through very different movement patterns. While a particular pattern might be most efficient for a group of movers who have similar abilities and physical characteristics, other movers with different abilities and characteristics might find a different movement pattern more efficient. This is particularly true for students with Down syndrome who have unique physical characteristics (e.g. smaller stature, smaller hands) and limited balance and motor control. Rather than describing a movement pattern such as running or kicking, ETA utilizes a functional task category that describes the general intent of the movement. Running becomes one form of the function: *locomotion*, to move from one place to another, and kicking becomes one form of the function: *propulsion*, to propel a stationary or moving object or person. Within each functional task category is criteria for performance. For example, under locomotion to move from one place to another, criteria include to move with efficiency, precision, accuracy, speed and/or distance. Each mover might use a different pattern to accomplish a given function and criteria.
3. Invariant features of a task and variations within a task may be defined in terms of essential and non-essential variables, respectively. Essential variables describe the invariant characteristics of the movement. Basically, essential variables refer to the underlying patterns that organize and define a movement. Relative timing

between the two lower limbs in walking or galloping are examples of an essential variable. For practical purposes, broader descriptors of patterns of co-ordination such as arm action in throwing also can be viewed as essential variables. Non-essential variables refer to dimensions or control parameters that, when scaled up or down, may cause the mover to change to a new, qualitatively different pattern of co-ordination (new essential variable) (see Davis and Burton, 1991, for more a detailed description). These control variables can include physical dimensions of the mover such as limb length or weight, body proportions, or postural control; or they can refer to task factors such as ball size, weight of striking implement or size of target. For example, striking a ball off a tee to a small target 5 feet away would result in a pattern of co-ordination (essential variable) that is characterized by no stepping, no preparatory backswing, and no trunk rotation. As the student move farther away from the target and the target gets bigger (less demand on accuracy, scaling up the non-essential variable of force production), the throwing pattern change to a qualitatively different striking pattern that includes, transferring weight by stepping, trunk rotation and preparatory backswing.

4. A direct link should be established between the task goal and the constraints of the mover and environment. In traditional task analyses, we measure the environment (ball size) without reference to the mover's characteristics (hand size). ETA uses a 'performer-scaled' measure which links the dimensions of the environment and the mover. What results is a specific boundary condition in which the mover-environment relationship affords one type of movement but not another. For example, we can measure ball size as a ratio of a mover's hand size. The mover–ball size ratio for a mover who has a hand span of 8 inches and a ball size of 9 inches would be equal to 9–8 = 1.125 performer-scaled ratio. Recent research suggests that when the ball to hand size ratio is slightly greater than 1.0 (ball is slightly larger than person's hand size), the student will change to a different throwing pattern (Burton *et al.*, 1992). As noted above, while changes in ball size often result in subtle changes in children without disabilities, such changes can have dramatic effects with children who have Down syndrome (change from one-hand to two-hand throwing) (Block and Povis, 1992).

According to Davis and Burton, some of the advantages of using the ETA is that a teacher can more accurately determine under which set of conditions the student is able to achieve the task, the set of conditions that elicit the most efficient and effective pattern (optimal performance), and the dimension values at which the student chooses to use a different skill to perform a skill (e.g. changes from galloping to running). ETA appears to be a viable approach to understanding how movers, including children with Down syndrome, prefer to move and how changes in task variables affect movement (see Table 19.2 for a sample checklist of curricular adaptations that follow the ETA model).

Table 19.2 Sample curricular modifications for students with Down Syndrome

Does the student have limited strength?

Things to consider	*Selected modifications (if any) and comments*
Shorten distance to move or project object	
Use lighter equipment (e.g., balls, bats)	
Use shorter striking implements	
Allow student to sit or lie down while playing	
Use deflated balls or suspended balls	
Change requirements (a few jumps, then run)	

Does the student have limited speed?

Things to consider	*Selected modifications (if any) and comments*
Shorten distance (or make it longer for others)	
Change locomotor pattern (running v. walking)	
Make safe areas in tag games	

Does the student have limited endurance?

Things to consider	*Selected modifications (if any) and comments*
Shorten distance	
Shorten playing field	
Allow 'safe' areas in tag games	
Decrease activity time for student	
Allow more rest periods for student	
Allow student to sit while playing	

Does the student have limited balance?

Things to consider	*Selected modifications (if any) and comments*
Provide chair/bar for support	
Teach balance techniques (e.g. extend arms)	
Increase width of beams to be walked	
Use carpeted rather than slick surfaces	
Teach students how to fall	
Allow student to sit during activity	
Place student near wall for support	
Allow student to hold peer's hand	

Does the student have limited co-ordination and accuracy?

Things to consider	*Selected modifications (if any) and comments*
Use stationary balls for kicking/striking	
Decrease distance for throwing/kicking/shooting	
Make targets and goals larger	
Use larger balls for kicking and striking	
Increase surface of the striking implements	
Use backstop	
Use softer, slower balls for striking and catching	
In bowling-type games, use lighter pins	
What can you do to optimize safety	

Note: Suggestions listed above should be matched to meet the unique physical and motor characteristics of each individual child.
Source: Block, M.E. (1994). Reprinted with permission.

Instructional adaptations

Another teaching consideration when working with students with disabilities is how to present information so that students pick up the critical elements. Block (1994), Eichstaedt and Lavay (1992), Seaman and DePauw (1989) and Sherrill (1993) outlined several instructional factors that could be manipulated to facilitate learning in children with disabilities including children with Down syndrome. Two key instructional factors are described in the following list (see Table 19.3 for a more comprehensive list of potential modifications):

1. *Teaching style.* According to Mosston (1981), a common teaching style adopted by physical education teachers is the command approach. In this approach, the teacher controls when, how, and how often students take their turns. In most cases, there is very little room for creativity with everyone expected to do a particular movement the same way. This can be particularly effective with those students with Down syndrome who have difficulty in unstructured, open environments. This approach provides many opportunities for practice with specific instructional feedback.

    In contrast to the command approach, the exploration approach or 'movement exploration' allows students to take a more active role in their programme. The teacher presents a general challenge, and students then choose how they will meet the challenge. There is no right or wrong way to move, rather each student chooses the type of movement that works best for him or her. Children problem-solve, become more active in the process of discovery and, theoretically, have more meaningful learning and skill acquisition. Note how this type of approach matches the ecological task analysis. Although this style allows for greater individuality and creativity, it does take longer for students to master critical skills and this can be a limitation for children with Down syndrome, who often need more instruction and extra feedback.

2. *Instructional prompts.* Instructional prompts refer to the many forms and types of assistance a teacher can provide to a student to facilitate learning (Snell and Brown, 1993). Prompts can take a variety of forms including verbal cues and instruction, gestures (e.g. pointing), visual cues (e.g. markers on the wall), modelling or demonstrations, and various amounts of physical assistance. Students with Down syndrome often need extra cues other than verbal cues to understand how to correctly perform motor skills. Verbal instructions and even demonstrations might get students to generally imitate a critical component of a skill, but gestures, touching key body parts, and even physical manipulations, are often needed facilitate learning. Physical assistance is particularly useful for students with Down syndrome who do not understand how properly to position their body and perform complex movements such as throwing and striking. However, at some point the student will have to experience how the movement should be executed or how it 'feels' on their own if they are going to repeat the performance. Some cues that are particularly useful for children with Down syndrome are markers or footprints placed on the floor that signify correct starting and movement positions. Similarly, tape markings placed on key parts of the body that designate such things as side orientation to target, which foot to step with, which hand goes on top of the bat, etc. can be effective.

In summary, there are many curricular and instructional adaptations that can be implemented to facilitate motor skill learning in children with Down syndrome. Curricular modifications, particularly within the ecological task analysis model, can

Table 19.3 Checklist to determine instructional modifications to accommodate students with disabilities

Student's name: _____

PE Class/Teacher: _____   Who will implement modifications? (circle one) reg. PE teacher classmates peer tutor teacher assist. specialist

Instructional component	Things to consider	Selected modifications (if any) and comments
Teaching style	Command, problem-solving, discovery	_____
Class format and size of group	Small/large group; stations/whole-class inst.	_____
Level of methodology	Verbal cues, demonstrations, physical assist.	_____
Starting/stopping signals	Whistle, hand signals, physical assistance	_____
Time of day	Early a.m., late a.m., early p.m., late p.m.	_____
Duration of instruction	How long will student listen to instruction?	_____
Duration of expected participation	How long will student stay on task?	_____
Order of learning	What order will you present instruction?	_____
Instructional setting	Indoors/outdoors; part of gym/whole gym	_____
Eliminate distractions	Lighting, temperature, extra equipment	_____
Provide structure	Set organization of instruction each day	_____
Level of difficulty	Complexity of instructions/organization	_____
Levels of motivation	Make setting and activities more motivating	_____

Source: Block, M.E. (1994). Reprinted with permission.

help students improve performance by matching equipment and task requirements to the abilities and characteristics of the mover. Instructional modifications can help students with Down syndrome understand exactly what is expected of them in terms of when and how to perform critical movement skills.

EXTRACURRICULAR AND POST-SCHOOL ACTIVITIES

There are other physical fitness and recreation outlets besides school-based motor development and physical education for children and adults with Down syndrome. Regular community recreation and sports programmes are available in many communities and these will accept persons with Down syndrome if they have the necessary skills.

On the other hand, many individuals with Down syndrome have disabilities that limit their motor and cognitive skills making participation in the regular community recreation programmes difficult. In such instances, many recreation programmes can be modified. For example, different divisions in cross-country and downhill skiing programmes will accommodate skill levels from beginner to advanced. Bowling leagues have a built-in handicapping system that allows for individual differences. With this handicapping system, an individual with Down syndrome could join a local bowling league and participate without the burden of negatively affecting his or her team.

Other recreation programmes that offer various levels of competition or participation to accommodate different abilities include swimming, hiking/walking programmes, aerobics and fitness classes, weightlifting, golf, tennis, cross-country skiing and softball. For example, many communities offer recreational and instructional swimming programmes for adults who are not proficient swimmers. This type of programme provides extra instruction, practice in the shallow end where adults can stand up, and the use of various teaching aids and flotation devices. These accommodations would allow an adult with Down syndrome to participate in a community swimming programme.

Participation in fitness activities and classes is also common for adolescents and adults. Beyond health-related benefits, there are opportunities for social interaction. Although motivation is sometimes a problem for fitness participants with intellectual disabilities, Barham (1993) and Reid *et al.* (1990) provide practical suggestions.

Even community-wide team sport programmes such as softball and basketball leagues often accommodate individuals with limited skills. For example, a young person with Down syndrome might be interested in joining the local softball league in his or her community. Fortunately, the community where this person lives offers three levels of softball and he or she would fit nicely into the 'C' division since most of the players are not very skilled and are learning how to play the game. In addition, the players in this division may be less competitive, more interested in making sure everyone is having fun and more accepting of the limited motor, cognitive and social skills of this player.

Special Olympics

Finally, Special Olympics, a sports training and competition programme designed specifically for persons with mental retardation (including persons with Down syndrome), is available in many communities around the world. Special Olympics equalizes competition such that persons with similar abilities compete against each other in both individual and team sports.

The mission of Special Olympics is to provide year-round sports training and athletic competition in a variety of Olympic-type sports for all individuals with mental retardation age 8 years and older (Single, 1992, p. 27). Originally started in 1968 with three countries, Special Olympics has grown to be a world-wide programme with more than 100 countries in the programme including many former eastern block countries and new republics of the former Soviet Union. Special Olympics now provides training and competition in 23 official winter and summer sports, three senior sports, six Unified Sports, and Motor Activities (modified sports for persons with very severe disabilities).

In summary, there are many extracurricular recreation opportunities for individuals with Down syndrome. Some of the activities can take place while the individual is still in school, other opportunities are available after graduation. Since the ultimate goal is to help those with Down syndrome master lifetime leisure skills, it important to provide community-based recreation opportunities as often as possible. Ideally, some training would take place in these community-based environments so that children with Down syndrome can make the transition on leaving school from school-based motor and physical education programmes to community-based recreation.

REFERENCES

Anson, J.G. (1992) Neuromotor control and Down syndrome. In J.J. Summers (ed.) *Approaches to the Study of Motor Control and Learning*, pp. 387–412, Amsterdam: Elsevier Science.

Anwar, F. (1981) Motor function in Down's syndrome. *International Review of Research in Mental Retardation*, **10,** pp. 107–38.

Auxter, D., Pyfer, J. and Huettig, C. (1993) *Principles and Methods of Adapted Physical Education*, St Louis: Mosby.

Barham, P. (1993) Development of skills throughout adolescence and early adult life. In Y. Burns and P. Gunn (eds), *Down Syndrome: Moving through Life*, pp. 151–68, London: Chapman and Hall.

Block, M. (1991) Motor development in children with Down Syndrome: a review of the literature. *Adapted Physical Activity Quarterly* **8,** pp. 179–209.

Block, M.E. (1992) What is appropriate physical education for students with profound disabilities? *Adapted Physical Activity Quarterly*, **9,** pp. 197–213.

Block, M.E. (1994) *A Teacher's Guide to Including Students with Disabilities in Regular Physical Education*, Baltimore: Brookes.

Block, M.E. (in press) All kids can have physical education the regular way. In M.S. Moon (ed.) *Just for the Fun of It: Community Physical Education Leisure Programs*, Baltimore: Brookes.

Block, M.E. and Provis, S. (1992) Effects of ball size on throwing patterns in children with Down Syndrome. Paper presented at the North American Federation of Adapted Physical Activity Symposium, Montreal, October.

Brown, L., Branston, M.B., Hambre-Nietupski, S., Pumpian, I., Certo, N. and Gruenewald, L. (1979) A strategy for developing chronological-age-appropriate and functional curricular content for severely handicapped adolescents and young adults. *The Journal of Special Education*, **13**, pp. 81–90.

Brown, F. and Snell, M.E. (1993) Meaningful assessment. In M.E. Snell (ed.), *Instruction of Students with Severe Disabilities*, 4th edn, pp. 61–98, New York: Merrill.

Burns, Y. (1993) The development of movement: the basis of effective performance and life skills. In Y. Burns and P. Gunn (eds) *Down Syndrome: Moving Through Life*, pp. 19–36, London: Chapman and Hall.

Burns, Y. and Gunn, P. (eds), (1993). *Down Syndrome: Moving Through Life*, London: Chapman and Hall.

Burton, A.W., Greer, N.L. and Wiese Bjornstal, D.M. (1992) Variations in grasping and throwing patterns as function of ball size. *Pediatric Exercise Science*, **5**, pp. 25–41.

Butterworth, G. and Cicchetti, D. (1978) Visual calibration of posture in normal and motor retarded Down syndrome infants. *Perception*, **7**, pp. 513–25.

Campbell, P.H. and Stewart, B. (1986) Measuring changes in movement skills with infants and young children with handicaps. *Journal of The Association for Persons with Severe Handicaps*, **11**, pp. 153–61.

Canada Fitness Award (1983) Adapted for use by trainable mentally handicapped youth. Fitness and Amateur Sport, Canada.

Canada Fitness Survey (1983) *Physical Activity among Activity-Limited and Disabled Adults in Canada*, Ottawa: Fitness Canada.

Carr, J. (1970) Mental and motor development in young mongol children. *Journal of Mental Deficiency Research*, **14**, pp. 205–20.

Chad, K., Jobling, A. and Frail, H. (1990) Metabolic rate: a factor in developing obesity in children with Down syndrome? *American Journal of Mental Retardation*, **95**, pp. 228–35.

Cheseldine, S.E. and Jeffree, D.M. (1981) Mentally handicapped adolescents: their use of leisure. *Journal of Mental Deficiency Research*, **25**, p. 49–59.

Chumlea, W.C. and Cronk, C.E. (1982) Overweight among children with Trisomy 21. *Journal of Mental Deficiency Research*, **25**, pp. 275–79.

Clausen, J. (1968) Behavioral characteristics of Down's syndrome in subjects. *American Journal of Mental Deficiency*, **73**, pp. 118–26.

Climstein, M., Pitetti, K.H., Barrett, P.J. and Campbell, K.D. (1992) Accuracy of predicting treadmill VO_2max in Down syndrome and non-Down syndrome mentally retarded adults: abstract no. 212. *Medicine and Science in Sports and Exercise* **24**, s36.

Coleman, E., Ayoub, M.M. and Friedrich, D. (1976) Assessment of physical work capacity of institutionalized mentally retarded males. *American Journal of Mental Deficiency*, **80**, pp. 629–35.

Connolly, B.H. and Michael, B.T. (1986) Performance of retarded children, with and without Down syndrome, on the Bruininks-Oseretsky test of motor proficiency. *Physical Therapy*, **66**, pp. 344–48.

Cowie, V.A. (1970) *A Study of the Early Development of Mongols*, Oxford: Pergamon.

Cratty, B.J. (1974) *Motor Activity and the Education of Retardates*, 2nd edn, Philadelphia: Lea and Febiger.

Cronk, C.E. (1978) Growth of children with Down syndrome: birth to age 3 years. *Pediatrics*, **61**, pp. 564–68.

Cronk, C.E., Chumlea, W.C. and Roche, A.F. (1985) Assessment of overweight children with Trisomy 21. *American Journal of Mental Deficiency*, **89**, pp. 433–36.

Davidson, R.G. (1988) Atlantoaxial instability in individuals with Down's syndrome: A fresh look at the evidence. *Pediatrics*, **81**, pp. 857–65.

Davis, W.E. (1984) Motor ability assessment of populations with handicapping conditions: challenging basic assumptions. *Adapted Physical Activity Quarterly*, **1**, pp. 125–40.

Davis, W.E. and Burton, A.W. (1991). Ecological task analysis: translating movement behaviour theory into practice. *Adapted Physical Activity Quarterly*, **8**, pp. 154–77.

Davis, W.E. and Kelso, J.A.S. (1982) Analysis of 'invariant characteristics' in motor control of Down's Syndrome and normal subjects. *Journal of Motor Behavior*, **14**, pp. 194–212.

Diamond, L. (1986) Teaching your baby with Down syndrome: an introduction to early intervention. In K. Stray-Gunderson (ed.), *Babies with Down Syndrome: a New Parents Guide*, pp. 133–58, Kensington: Woodbine House.

Dubowitz, V. (1980) *The Floppy Infant*, 2nd edn, Clinics in Developmental Medicine No. 76. Spastics International Publications, London: Heinemann.

Dugdale, T.W., Renshaw, T.S. and Newington, C. (1986) Instability of the patellofemoral joint in Down syndrome. *Journal of Bone and Joint Surgery*, **68**, pp. 405–13.

Dyer, S., Gunn, P., Rauh, H. and Berry, P. (1990) Motor development in Down syndrome children: an analysis of the motor scale of the Bayley Scales of Infant Development. In A. Vermeer (ed.) *Motor Development, Adapted Physical Activity and Mental Retardation*, pp. 7–20, Basel: Karger.

Eberhard, Y., Eterradossi, J. and Rapacchi, B. (1989) Physical aptitudes to exertion in children with Down's syndrome, *Journal of Mental Deficiency Research*, **33**, pp. 167–74.

Eberhard, Y., Eterradossi, J. and Therminarias, A. (1991) Biochemical changes and catecholamine responses in Down's syndrome adolescents in relation to incremental maximal exercise. *Journal of Mental Deficiency Research*, **35**, pp. 140–46.

Eichstaedt, C. and Lavay, B. (1992). *Physical Activity for Individuals with Mental Retardation: Infant to Adult*, Champaign: Human Kinetics.

Eichstaedt, C., Wang, P., Polacek, J. and Dohrmann, P. (1991) Physical fitness and motor skill levels of individuals with mental retardation, ages 6–21. Normel: Illinois State University.

Elliott, D. (1990) Movement control and Down syndrome: a neuro-psychological approach, in G. Reid (ed.), *Problems in Movement Control*, pp. 201–16, Amsterdam: Elsevier Science.

Elliott, D. and Weeks, D.J. (1993) A functional systems approach to movement pathology. *Adapted Physical Activity Quarterly*, **10**, pp. 312–23.

Emes, C., Velde, B., Moreau, M., Murdoch, D.D. and Trussell, R. (1990) An activity based weight control program. *Adapted Physical Activity Quarterly*, **7**, pp. 314–24.

Falvey, M.A. (1989) *Community-Based Curriculum: Instructional Strategies for Students with Severe Disabilities*, 2nd edn, Baltimore: Brookes.

Fernhall, B., Tymeson, G., Millar, L. and Burkett, L. (1989) Cardiovascular fitness testing and fitness levels of adolescents and adults with mental retardation including Down syndrome. *Education and Training in Mental Retardation*, **24**, pp. 133–38.

Fernhall, B., Tymeson, G.T. and Webster, G.E. (1988) Cardiovascular fitness of mentally retarded individuals. *Adapted Physical Activity Quarterly*, **5**, pp. 12–28.

Fryers, T. (1986) Survival in Down's syndrome. *Journal of Mental Deficiency Research*, **30**, pp. 101–10.

Gallahue, D.L. (1989) *Understanding Motor Development*, 2nd edn, Indianapolis: Benchmark.

Haley, S.M. (1986) Postural reactions in infants with Down syndrome: Relationship to motor milestone development and age. *Physical Therapy*, **66**, pp. 17–22.

Harris, S.R. (1985) Neuromotor development of infants with Down syndrome. *Developmental Medicine & Child Neurology*, **27**, pp. 99–100.

Henderson, S.E. (1985) Motor skill development. In D. Lane and B. Stratford (eds), *Current Approaches to Down's Syndrome*, pp. 187–218, London: Holt, Rinehart and Winston.

Henderson, S.E., Morris, J., Ray, S. (1981) Performance of Down syndrome and other related children on the Cratty gross-motor test. *American Journal of Mental Deficiency*, **85**, pp. 416–24.

Herkowitz, J. (1978) Developmental task analysis: the design of movement experiences and evaluation of motor development status. In M. Ridenour (ed.), *Motor Development: Issues and Applications*, pp. 139–164, Princeton: Princeton Book.

Hogg, J. and Moss, S.C. (1983) Prehensile development in Down's syndrome and non-handicapped preschool children. *British Journal of Developmental Psychology*, **1**, pp. 189–204.

Holland, B.V. (1987) Fundamental motor skill performance of non-handicapped and educable mentally impaired students. *Education and Training in Mental Retardation*, **22**, pp. 197–204.

James, B. (1993). The elderly person with Down Syndrome: the benefits of an active life. In Y. Burns and P. Gunn (eds), *Down Syndrome: Moving Through Life*, pp. 169–90, London: Chapman and Hall.

Jobling, A. (1993) Play and movement education. In Y. Burns and P. Gunn (eds), *Down Syndrome: Moving through Life*, pp. 109–34, London: Chapman and Hall.

Jobling, A. and Gunn, P. (1995) The motor proficiency of children and adolescents with Down Syndrome. In A. Vermer and W.E. Davis (eds) *Physical and Motor Development in Mental Retardation*, New York: Karger, pp. 181–90.

Kelly, L.E. (1991) *Achievement-Based Curriculum: Teaching Manual*, Charlottesville: University of Virginia.

Krebs, P.L. and Block, M.E. (1992) Transition of students with disabilities into community recreation: The role of the adapted physical educator. *Adapted Physical Activity Quarterly*, **9**, pp. 305–15.

Latash, M.L. and Carcos, D.M. (1991) Kinematics and electromyographic characteristics of single-joint movements of individuals with Down Syndrome. *American Journal of Mental Retardation*, **96**, pp. 189–201.

Lavay, B., Reid, G. and Cressler-Chavez, M. (1990) Measuring the cardiovascular endurance of persons with mental retardation. a critical review. *Exercise and Sport Sciences Reviews*, **18**, pp. 263–90.

LeBlanc, D., French, R. and Shultz, B. (1977) Static and dynamic balance skills of trainable children with Down syndrome. *Perceptual and Motor Skills*, **45**, pp. 641–42.

Levinson, L.J. and Reid, G. (1991) Patterns of physical activity among youngsters with developmental disabilities. *CAHPER Journal*, **57** (3), pp. 24–28.

Lydic, J.S. and Steele, C. (1979). Assessment of the quality of sitting and gait patterns in children with Down syndrome. *Physical Therapy*, **59**, pp. 1489–94.

MacLean, W.E. Jr, Ellis, D.N., Galbreath, H.N., Halpern, L.F. and Baumeister, A.A. (1991) Rhythmic motor behavior of perambulatory motor impaired, Down syndrome and nondisabled children: a comparative study. *Journal of Abnormal Child Psychology*, **19**, pp. 319–92.

McConkey, R., Walsh, J. and Mulcahy, M. (1981) The recreational pursuits of mentally handicapped adults. *International Journal of Rehabilitation Research*, **4**, pp. 493–99.

Mercer, L. (1993) The active preschooler. In Y. Burns and P. Gunn (eds), *Down Syndrome: Moving Through Life*, pp. 95–108, London: Chapman and Hall.

Millar, A.L., Fernhall, B. and Burkett, L.N. (1993) Effects of aerobic training in adolescents with Down syndrome. *Medicine and Science in Sports and Exercise*, **25**, pp. 270–64.

Morris, A.F., Vaughan, S.E. and Vaccaro, P. (1982) Measurements of neuromuscular tone and strength in Down syndrome children. *Journal of Mental Deficiency Research*, **26**, pp. 41–46.

Mosston, M. (1981) *Teaching Physical Education*, Columbus: Merrill.

Niman-Reed, C. and Sleight, D.H. (1988) Gross motor development in young children with Down syndrome. In C. Tingey (ed.), *Down Syndrome: A Resource Handbook*, pp. 95–118, Boston: College Hill Press.

Official Special Olympics Sports Rules (1992) Washington, DC: Special Olympics International.

Parker, A.W., Bronks, R. and Snyder, C.W. (1986) Walking patterns in Down syndrome. *Journal of Mental Deficiency Research*, **30**, pp. 317–30.

Parker, A.W. and James, B. (1985) Age changes in the flexibility of Down syndrome children. *Journal of Mental Deficiency Research*, **29**, pp. 207–18.

Pitetti, K.H. and Campbell, K.D. (1991) Mentally retarded individuals: a population at risk? *Medicine and Science in Sports and Exercise*, **23**, pp. 586–93.

Pitetti, K.H., Climstein, M., Campbell, K.D., Barrett, P.J. and Jackson, J.A. (1992a) The cardiovascular capacities of adults with Down syndrome: a comparative study. *Medicine and Science in Sports and Exercise*, **24**, pp. 13–19.

Pitetti, K.H., Climstein, M., Mays, M.J. and Barrett, P.J. (1992b) Isokinetic arm and leg strength of adults with Down syndrome: a comparative study. *Archives of Physical Medicine and Rehabilitation*, **73**, pp. 847–50.

Pitetti, K.H., Rimmer, J.H. and Fernhall, B. (1993) Physical fitness and adults with mental retardation: an overview of current research and future directions. *Sport Medicine*, **16**, pp. 23–56.

Pitetti, K.H. and Tan, D.M. (1991) Effects of a minimally supervised exercise program for mentally retarded adults. *Medicine and Science in Sports and Exercise*, **23**, pp. 594–601.

Pueschel, S.M. (1987) Health concerns in persons with Down Syndrome. In S.M. Pueschel, C. Tingey, J.E., Rynders, A.C. Crocker and D.M. Crutcher (eds), *New Perspectives on Down Syndrome*, pp. 113–34, Baltimore: Brookes.

Putnam, J.W. Pueschel, S.M. and Gorder-Holman, J. (1988) Community participation of youths and adults with Down syndrome. In S.M. Pueschel (ed.), *The Young Person with Down Syndrome: Transition from Adolescence to Adulthood*, pp. 77–92, Baltimore: Brookes.

Rainforth, N., York, J. and Macdonald, C. (1992) *Collaborative Teams for Students with Severe Disabilities*, Baltimore: Brookes.

Rarick, G.L., Dobbins, D.A. and Broadhead, G. (1976) *The Motor Domain and Its Correlates in Educationally Handicapped Children*. Englewood Cliffs: Prentice Hall.

Rarick, G.L., Rapaport, I.F. and Seefeldt, Y. (1965) Age of appearance of ossification centres of the hand and wrist in children with Down's disease. *Journal of Mental Deficiency Research*, **9**, pp. 24–30.

Rarick, G.L., Seefeldt, V. (1974) Observations from longitudinal data on growth in stature and sitting height of children with Down's Syndrome. *Journal of Mental Deficiency Research*, **18**, pp. 63–78.

Rast, M.M. and Harris, S.R. (1985) Motor control in infants with Down syndrome. *Developmental Medicine & Child Neurology*, **27**, pp. 675–85.

Reid, G. (1985) Physical activity programming. In D. Lane and B. Stratford (eds), *Current Approaches to Down Syndrome*, pp. 219–41, London: Holt, Rinehart and Winston.

Reid, G. (1993). Motor behavior and individuals with disabilities: linking research and practice. *Adapted Physical Activity Quarterly*, **10**, pp. 359–70.

Reid, G., Montgomery, D.L. and Seidl, C. (1990) *Stepping Out for Fitness: A Program for Adults Who Are Intellectually Handicapped*, Ottawa: CAHPER.

Rimmer, J.H., Braddock, D. and Fujiura, G. (1992) Blood lipid and percent body fat levels in Down syndrome versus non-DS persons with mental retardation. *Adapted Physical Activity Quarterly*, **2**, pp. 123–29.

Rimmer, J.H., Braddock, D. and Fujiura, G. (1993) Prevalence of obesity in adults with mental retardation: implications for health promotion and disease prevention. *Mental Retardation*, **31**, pp. 105–10.

Rimmer, J.H. and Kelly, L.E. (1991) Effects of a resistance training program of adults with mental retardation. *Adapted Physical Activity Quarterly*, **8**, pp. 146–53.

Schapiro, M.B. and Rapoport, S.I. (1989) Basal metabolic rate in healthy Down's syndrome adults. *Journal of Mental Deficiency Research*, **33**, pp. 211–19.

Schleien, S.J., Green, F.P. and Heyne, L.A. (1993) Integrated community recreation. In M.E. Snell (ed.), *Instruction of Students with Severe Disabilities*, 4th edn, pp. 526–45, New York: Merrill.

Seaman, J.A. and DePauw, K.P. (1989) *The New Adapted Physical Education*, 2nd edn, Mountain View: Mayfield.

Seidl, C., Reid, G. and Montgomery, D.L. (1987) A critique of cardiovascular fitness testing with mentally retarded persons. *Adapted Physical Activity Quarterly*, **4**, pp. 106–16.

Selby, K.A., Newton, R.W., Gupta, S. and Hunt, L. (1991). Clinical predictors and radio-logical reliability in atlantoaxial subluxation in Down's Syndrome. *Archives of Disease in Childhood*, **66**, pp. 876–78.

Sharav, T. and Bowman, T. (1992) Dietary practices, physical activity, and body-mass index in a selected population of Down Syndrome children and their siblings. *Clinical Pediatrics*, pp. 341–44.

Sherrill, C. (1993) *Adapted Physical Activity, Recreation and Sport: Crossdisciplinary and Lifespan*, 4th edn, Madison: Brown and Benchmark.

Shumway-Cook, A. and Woollacott, M.H. (1985) Dynamics of postural control in the child with Down syndrome. *Physical Therapy*, **65**, pp. 1315–22.

Single, D. (1992) *Skill, Courage, Sharing, Joy: The Stories of Special Olympics*. Washington: Special Olympics International.

Snell, M.E. and Brown, F. (1993) Instructional planning and implementation. In M.E. Snell (ed.), *Instruction of Students with Severe Disabilities*, 4th edn, pp. 99–151, New York: Merrill.

Special Olympics (1993) *Special Olympics: Soccer Sports Skill Guide*. Washington: Special Olympics.

Thelander, H.E. and Pryor, H.B. (1966) Abnormal patterns of growth and development in mongolism: an anthropometric study. *Clinical Pediatrics*, **5**, pp. 493–501.

Thelen, E. (1979) Rhythmical stereotypes in normal human infants. *Animal Behavior*, **27**, pp. 699–715.

Thelen, E. (1985) Developmental origins of motor coordinator: leg movements in human infants. *Developmental Psychobiology*, **18**, pp. 1–22.

Ulrich, B.D., Ulrich, D.A., and Collier, D.H. (1992) Alternating stepping patterns: hidden abilities of 11-month-old infants with Down Syndrome. *Development Medicine and Child Neurology*, **34**, pp. 233–39.

Varela, A.M. and Pitetti, K.H. (in press) Heart rate responses to two field exercise tests by adolescents and young adults with Down syndrome. *Adapted Physical Activity Quarterly*.

Wang, P. and Eichstaedt, C.B. (1980) *A Study of Physical Fitness Levels of Mentally Handicapped Children and Adolescents in Illinois*, Normal: Illinois State University.

Watkinson, E.J. and Wall, A.E. (1981) *The PREP Play Program*, Ottawa: CAHPER.

Wessel, J.A. (1976) *ICAN*. Northbrook: Hubbard.

Wessel, J.A. and Kelly, L. (1986) *Achievement-Based Curriculum Development in Physical Education*, Philadelphia: Lea and Febiger.

20 School and Integration

Adrian F. Ashman and John Elkins

It is a scorching day. The temperature is over 40°C in the shade of the trees in the school yard. Some people refer to this area as part of the Australian Outback, and it's not hard to accept the description when you look beyond the trees which shelter most of the buildings in this western plains town, across the shimmering, flat, brown land.

It's lunch-time and the children are playing in much the same way as they do in many other schools, almost oblivious to the heat and, certainly, to the drone of the ever-present grasshoppers. One boy stands out in the group of playing children if only because he is a little taller and, unlike the others, is wearing eyeglasses. He's running and laughing like the rest, intent on winning the game which seems to be a local version of touch football. The children call his name when he has the ball; he passes it with a little less finesse than others, but then calls out encouragement to the boy who now runs with it toward the goal-line.

It makes one wonder why there is a need to note that Bryson has Down syndrome. If there *is* a need to make any comment at all, it is how fortunate he must be when compared to many other school-aged children who have Down syndrome. He is accepted by his school mates, the teachers, and the members of the remote community where his family has been grazing cattle for four generations. For many others, it is not quite so rewarding to be integrated.

In this chapter, we consider the education of young people like Bryson and, in particular, the positive and negative aspects of policies which advocate for their integration into regular schools and regular classes. We first discuss the meaning of the terms 'integration' and 'inclusion' and discuss the needs of students in terms of current policies and practices. We also discuss the importance of the context (political, cultural and economic) in which children are educated, and consider the practical aspects and implications of schooling undertaken in integrated settings.

INTEGRATION, MAINSTREAMING AND INCLUSION

The term integration has different meanings in different countries. In the USA, integration usually refers to educating children from majority and minority ethnic groups in the same schools. In New Zealand, integration has referred to the unification of parochial and government schools into a common system (Chapman, 1988). Integration also implies the notion of a journey or process, so that it is possible to regard movement from any isolated setting toward regular classroom as integration. For example, a child living in an institution who attends a special school has experienced some integration.

Mainstreaming is often considered to be synonymous with integration. In the USA, mainstreaming implies placement within the mainstream of education, that is, the regular classroom and it is a guiding philosophy for the placement of children with special education needs. Some writers, however, have suggested that relatively few children with special needs have been truly mainstreamed in American public schools (Danielson and Bellamy, 1989) despite the rhetoric surrounding the theory and practice.

To add to the confusion, the term 'inclusion' has become popular as a way to describe educational provisions for students who are different. Some writers refer to schools having an inclusive curriculum, which can recognize the needs of girls, of students from minority cultures and of those who have disabilities. A new term, 'full inclusion', has now come into use as a way of emphasizing the view that students with disabilities should participate in *all* the activities of their classmates.

Because terminology changes over time, and from place to place, we will use *integration* throughout this chapter but the reader needs to be aware that it is the actual practice of teaching which matters, not the label that is used.

CONTEMPORARY POLICIES AND PRACTICES

Integration has not become a universally accepted education policy throughout the world, but it is a prominent principle in most western countries. In the UK, since the Warnock Report was presented some 25 years ago, the role of professionals in making educational decisions has been stressed although parents do have certain rights. Since the adoption of PL 94–142 in the USA two decades ago, there has been a substantial growth in integration, with the courts occasionally being used to settle disputes between parents and school board about the suitability of integrated or non-integrated placements for some children. In countries where class sizes in regular schools are very high, such as Japan and Hong Kong, or in China where there are traditional barriers to integration, relatively few students with disabilities are in regular classes. Also in places where the education system is highly competitive, those who have an intellectual disability will probably attend special schools. Several books and articles give a more detailed account of social, political and economic influences on integration (e.g. Ashman, 1995; Barton, 1989; Lewis, 1993; Lipsky and Gartner, 1992).

SYSTEM POLICY AND INTEGRATION

Developments in the USA have, perhaps, been the most significant international stimulus for changes to educational provisions for students with special needs. The US constitution contains a Bill of Rights which enables citizens to seek redress against the government if they believe discrimination has occurred. The powerful and effective civil rights campaigns for ethnic minorities during the 1960s provided a model for advocacy on behalf of children with a disability, such as Down syndrome. The federal government, through its Education for All Children legislation (PL 94–142) and more recent laws, established guidelines that state departments of education and local school districts needed to address when providing appropriate educational experiences for students with serious learning problems.

Legislation requires that children in public schools to be educated in the least restrictive environment. However, integration practices are not consistent across the USA and may reflect the financial circumstances of local districts, since federal funding is insufficient to provide all the extra costs of special education. Exemplary practices can certainly be found and while such examples are not uncommon, they are certainly not universal. Special schools and classes continue, although they now enrol mostly children with more severe disabilities who previously might have been excluded from school. In fact, the number of special class settings have remained almost unchanged since before the introduction of PL 94–142 (Danielson and Bellamy, 1989).

Sweden's approach to integration is one of the most progressive and, since 1980, there has been a trend toward 'one school for everybody' (Fex, 1987). In that country, the local education authority is progressive and reflects local opinion. National funding supports schooling and a proportion is devoted to students with learning difficulties. Unlike the USA, there are few regulations about the expenditure of funds, although there has been a trend toward reducing class sizes at the expense of employing special support teachers. National curriculum development has led to the use of special education methods as far as possible in regular schools on the basis that such adaptations will make integration easier.

Flexible organization within Swedish schools can allow teachers to meet many of the students' teaching and learning requirements. For example, small groups containing students with special needs can be formed within schools to satisfy short-term objectives. Students can spend more time than is normal studying particular topics and during the time allotted for free activities, students can also be given special support in proficiency subjects over and above the periods allotted for Swedish and mathematics.

A revised national curriculum is the foundation for the Swedish approach to special education. Efforts have been made to create school environments where all can succeed. In the context of schools recognizing their responsibility to meet student needs, integration becomes a matter of flexible organization and resource allocation to deal with the practical issues as they arise.

In New Zealand, the education system has undergone many changes in recent years (Ballard, 1991; Mitchell, 1991). Instead of being controlled by a centralized education department, schools now have great autonomy and responsibility within guidelines established by the Ministry of Education and a Special Education Service exists to provide advice and support for students with special educational needs.

There are various types of day and residential schools for students with disabilities, as well as units in regular schools and itinerant support services for students in regular classes. Through systematic in-service in mainstreaming, many schools have had staff skills increased through courses such as 'Individualised Educational Planning' (Thomson *et al.*, 1991). It is unclear whether further decentralization or privatization of education will occur, and whether contestability will change the central support role for the Special Education Service (Mitchell, 1991). As the situation in New Zealand concerning the provision of services to children with special needs remains dynamic, it is likely that further changes in the pattern of service delivery may continue into the next century.

In Australia, the state of Victoria was the first to establish a practical commitment to integration following upon the Ministerial Review of Educational Services for the Disabled. Its report, *Integration in Victorian Education* (1984), signalled the intention of the Victorian Education Department to increase the involvement of children with special needs in the education programmes, and social life of regular schools. The review committee recognized that some children would continue to need special programmes in segregated settings but that resources should be directed to support integration with co-ordination of services being seen as a high priority. Co-ordination was seen as being important at regional and school levels and special efforts were necessary to increase the awareness of integration within the school community.

Some evidence exists on the implementation of the Victorian review. Tarr (1988) examined progress since the report was adopted. He reported that, in 1988, there were about 250 integration teachers and 1,220 integration aides (many part-time) employed with the teaching service. Approximately $20 million was devoted to supporting nearly 3,000 students in over 1,000 regular schools, representing an average cost per student of over $6,000 per annum. On the negative side, the deprofessionalization of the Enrolment Support Group meant that many people with experience and expertise have been excluded from the planning of integration services for particular children. In recent years, other reviews of implementation have been made which suggest that the gap between principle and practice is difficult to close (Cullen and Brown, 1992).

Prior to the early 1960s, Italian special education was typical of that in many countries. However, at the beginning of 1968 revolutionary changes in the fabric of Italian society began and both education and health care systems were extensively criticized, in part because of their past alignment with the established political forces. In 1971 National Law 118 established the right of compulsory education for children with disabilities in regular public school classes, and in 1977 another law (NL517) strengthened the position of integration by removing severity of disability as a cause for segregating children. The resources needed were in part guaranteed by a ruling that integrated classes must not exceed 20 students, with not more than two students with disabilities in each. Almost overnight, special schools and classes were closed and the students who attended them were placed in regular schools. This tumultuous change was not without its advocates and detractors (Berrigan, 1987). There are claims and some admission that socialization of children with disabilities has benefited but learning has generally suffered. A further problem stems from the fact that Italian schools operate only four hours per day, and there is limited time for individual help. Teachers also have limited training in specialist skills, notably those needed to work with students with disabilities.

PRAGMATIC CONSIDERATIONS

In many western countries, governments at national or state levels have embraced the notion of equity and justice when considering the education of children with special needs. How they have done this has varied considerably. As a basic starting-point, however, most governments have accepted the view that integration derives from the principle of normalization which stresses the importance of life experiences for people with a disability which are as close as possible to those of others who do not have a disability. In the case of education, this means moving toward a situation where children can receive their education in situations which are the cultural norm, that is, regular classes in regular schools. Advocates of integration often criticize special class and special school placements because children with a disability have little opportunity to mix with, and learn from, peers without a disability.

Special schools, however, may not be such negative places, and some integration settings may be more restricting than advocates of integration describe. Not only do education contexts differ in their receptivity to students with special needs, but there is also variability in the extent to which parents seek regular class placements for their child with a disability. If parents have initially obtained a regular preschool placement for their child at preschool level, there is an understandable desire and expectation that the child will later attend a regular school. Thus, enrolment in a special school may only occur if the regular school setting proves unsatisfactory or if the school declines the child's continued enrolment. From the parents' perspective, the most important issue is likely to be the child's academic and social development.

From the teacher's perspective, however, aggressive or non-compliant behaviour may be the major reason for seeking the transfer of a child, with failure to learn being important only when the gap between the child's needs and the main class curriculum becomes great. Teachers who use more flexible teaching methods and who can adapt the standard curriculum to suit the needs of a child with a serious learning problem are likely to find it easier to manage.

Some special schools attempt to overcome common criticisms of segregated schooling, such as not providing opportunities for interaction with non-disabled peers. As Hegarty and Pocklington (1981) and others have shown, it is possible to make very strong links between regular and special schools. While there is potential for difficulties to arise, many positive examples of such co-operation have been documented. For example, Elkins and Atkinson (1985) noted very effective links between a technical high school and the senior section of an adjacent special school, both of which had students with similar curricular needs. The physical resources of both schools were shared and staff worked co-operatively to develop links.

If a parent chooses to enrol a child with a severe disability in a regular school, in most states the principal and teacher are likely to respond in terms of the practicality of accepting the child, rather than immediately recognizing the right of the child to be educated in their school. In recent years, policy statements have strengthened parental rights to choose educational placements, but there is still likely to be some variability in the approach taken to enrol students with a disability such as Down syndrome. At present, it is probably true to say that educators generally affirm the right of the child to regular class placement, whether or not this is clearly recognized in legislation. However, few would expect successful integration without careful planning and preparation, and additional resources.

While the debate about the effectiveness of integration versus segregation has been extensive (see Elkins, 1994, for a general overview), the major issue of concern is generally not a belief in the principle of integration, but how it is operationalized by school communities and systems (Bird and Buckley, 1994; Griffin, 1992). Griffin's (1992, p. 6) comments are salient here:

> You cannot do research to determine whether integration is good or bad. Integration is a philosophical issue. Once it is accepted it is served by empirical questions such as, 'To what extent does it occur?' 'How successful is it?' 'How can it be made to work more effectively?' 'For whom does it work best?' 'How much does it cost?' What level of resourcing is required?' And so on.
>
> It is sensible to consider comments like, 'Integration doesn't work,' very carefully. They may well be statements about practice rather than statements about philosophy. The resource issue, for example, is a practical issue, not a philosophical one. Some service providers would dearly like to support high levels of integration but recognise that integration does not seem to be working. They feel compelled to argue – albeit quietly – against integration. I argue that it is important to keep an open mind about the possibilities offered by integration. Parents' and advocates' concerns about practice must not be confused with philosophies. Philosophies provide the guiding principles. How the principles are operationalised is the real issue and this, in turn, is what makes integration work, or not work, for some people.

PROBLEMS WITH INTEGRATION POLICIES AND PRACTICES

Few nations keep adequate statistics on special education, and it is difficult to know how extensive the practice of integration is in various countries or even in states or regions within countries. In the USA the National Council on Disability reported on a number of important issues such as whether students with disabilities are achieving satisfactorily, are staying in school, are obtaining employment and able to live competently in society. The information presented covers the whole range of disabilities, but most is pertinent to Down syndrome such as the following:

- Parent-professional relationships too often are strained and difficult, and parents and professionals frequently view one another as adversaries rather than as partners.
- Some parents have difficulty finding appropriate services for their children.
- Parents and students report that some schools have low expectations for students with disabilities and establish inappropriate learning objectives and goals.
- Services often are not available to meet the needs of disadvantaged, minority, and rural families who have children with disabilities.
- There is a perception that the outcomes of due process hearings are biased in favour of the schools.
- There is no national database that includes the routine collection of data regarding due process hearings.

- Most school reform initiatives appear to be a response to declining academic achievement rather than efforts to find ways for schools to meet the diverse needs of all students.
- Evaluation procedures, disability classifications, and resulting placement decisions vary greatly among school districts and States, and they often are not related to students' learning characteristics.
- In practice, special education has been defined more as an organisational approach to delivering instruction – as part of a placement continuum – than as a specific body of professional expertise.
- Effective transition planning for high school students with disabilities can facilitate their success in adult life.
- School graduates with disabilities are more likely to be employed following school if comprehensive vocational training is a primary component of their high school program and they have a job secured at the time of graduation.

(National Council on Disability, 1990)

These findings for the USA may not apply everywhere, but may help parents and teachers to think through some issues as they make decisions about the education of students with Down syndrome.

CAN ALL STUDENTS WITH DOWN SYNDROME BE INTEGRATED?

Students with Down syndrome have been the subject of some large group studies, but the majority have used small numbers of participants. Sloper *et al.* (1990) reported data on the academic attainment of 123 students with Down syndrome. Using a composite index based on reading, number and writing, it was found that students attending regular schools performed better than those in special schools even after adjustment for their higher mental age. Interestingly girls scored higher than boys. It is not clear what factors influenced the placement of students, and whether the differences in academic attainment were evident prior to deciding where they should go to school, but at least it seems safe to conclude that a regular class setting is likely to assist academic growth.

The authors of this study suggest that in regular schools there is greater attention to academic growth, while in special schools the curriculum focuses on social and practical skills. Some American data on academic achievement has been published by Rynders and Horrobin (1990). They followed up 15 children with Down syndrome who had spent 7 years in regular classrooms. Their reading ability was mostly at second grade level for comprehension and even higher for word recognition. Complex arithmetic, however, was very difficult and only two made significant gains in learning mathematics.

Social development has also been an important issue for researchers into the effectiveness of integration. In a study of eight children with Down syndrome aged 6 to 7 years, Rietveld (1986) found few differences between them and a group of contrast children in attention, compliance, social integration and disruptive actions. However, their teachers believed that there were major differences in social development between the children with Down syndrome and the contrast children, despite the lack of empirical evidence to support such views. It was interesting to see that teachers often sat the child with Down syndrome close to them, and directed approvals, commands and questions to them at three times the frequency to other children.

Peck *et al.* (1988) studied four preschool children, three of whom had Down syndrome, and ten normally developing peers in regular preschool classrooms on a part-time basis. While no differences were noted in rates of negative social interaction or imitation, the students with disabilities had less interaction with non-disabled peers than the latter did among themselves. The authors suggest that more needs to be known about part-time integration in order to decide whether it is an appropriate model.

Budgell (1986) commented upon the drift toward segregation in the UK that has been noted with children with Down syndrome who begin their school life in regular classes but eventually are relocated to special schools as they grow older. Six students receiving preschool education were integrated while only one in the 13 to 16 years age group was still in a regular class. Budgell suggested that there are persisting assumptions about children with Down syndrome that they are quali- tatively different from other children and, as they cannot be cured, there is little that can be done to assist their learning and development. He suggested that there are a number of conceptual frameworks which influence teachers' views and practices with children with Down syndrome, based upon humanistic, cognitive develop- ment, behavioural and interactionist views. These interact with school structures to affect how children with special needs are served.

In primary schools, for example, teachers generally stay with the same children for a school year (if not longer) and operate more on an integrated day approach than one tied to a timetable. In primary school, teachers get to know their students well and, because of flexibility in classroom organization and in presenting the curriculum, students with Down syndrome present few challenges. In secondary school, classrooms are less interactive and thus, give teachers fewer opportunities to learn about their students than in primary classrooms. Classroom organization is less flexible and there are fewer opportunities to modify the curriculum for students who are having learning problems.

Budgell (1986) also suggested that problems are encountered whenever students with Down syndrome change schools. As they get older, it is the inflexibility of the organization of schools which appears to create problems rather than help to ameliorate the learning difficulties being experienced by the students.

In Australia, schools operate on much the same principles and organizational structure as in Great Britain. Pieterse and Center (1984) provided one of the earlier reports of the integration of eight students with Down syndrome into regular schools. They suggested that the process of integration appeared to be most successful when the senior administrative staff of the school was convinced of the benefit of integration for both the child and the non-disabled peers. When the principal and class teachers were familiar with the early education process which the children had experienced, special services were more readily employed in the school. When the child's teacher was ambivalent about accepting support within the classroom and the principal less committed to providing resources, the integration process presented difficulties. The separation of primary from secondary schools in Australia presents a similar difficulty as in Great Britain. Secondary schools are 'driven' by the curriculum and children experiencing learning problems have fewer opportunities to develop learning processes and basic competencies than in the earlier school years.

Few studies have examined the effectiveness of integrated versus segregated settings for children with Down syndrome. One study by Fewell and Oelwein (1990) stands out. They examined the impact of degree of integrated education on the rate of children's development across several domains. The participants in their study were 58 students with Down syndrome who were in segregated settings full-time, in regular classes up to five hours per week and in regular classes more than five hours per week. Differences were not significant except in communication where children in special classes full-time performed better, perhaps due to the smaller class size.

The question of how best students with Down syndrome can be integrated is a matter of some debate. Some evidence in favour of the proposition that integration is possible for all students comes from settings where segregation is not possible, like the vignette which opened this chapter. In isolated rural areas, for example, there are limited opportunities for special school placement and children with a disability must be educated along with their peers or provided their educational experiences through distance education programmes. However, this does not always produce successful outcomes (Hayes and Livingstone, 1986) and, indeed, some children living in isolated areas may rarely gain the educational experiences that would enable them to develop intellectually to the extent that may be possible.

In provincial towns and cities where community cohesion is often less than in rural settings, it is easy for teachers and parents to expect that others (i.e. specialists) should provide services for those who have special needs. Indeed, some might argue that children with serious learning problems are better served in segregated classes and schools where their needs can be addressed more effectively than in regular classrooms. Some writers have suggested, therefore, that it may never be possible to eliminate all segregated special education (Brown *et al.*, 1989a; Brown *et al.*, 1989b; Brown *et al.*, 1991).

INTEGRATION: A CASE BY CASE APPROACH

Much of the literature dealing with the schooling and the integration of children with Down syndrome is based upon case studies. In many of these, the children's abilities, the enthusiasm and dedication of parents, and system reactions to the integration of the children are described in detail. What emerges from these various case studies, is a diverse set of interactions and interrelationships which exemplify the heterogeneity of children with Down syndrome and of the preparedness of teachers to accommodate them in their classrooms.

Reports by Allen (1987) and Bookbinder (1986) are two case studies that high-light system reactions against including children with Down syndrome in regular schools. In Britain, the 1981 Education Act required formal assessment to establish an appropriate placement for children with special education needs. In the case reported by Bookbinder, the boy had successfully attended a regular primary school for four years and was headed for a local comprehensive school. The local education authority (LEA) however, had the boy assessed in compliance with the Act and it was concluded that the secondary school would not be able to accommodate his needs. The only option was for the boy to travel away from his neighbourhood to attend a special unit designed to cater for children with learning difficulties.

As the boy formerly had attended regular schools and was, largely, no different from other children, the parents appealed the decision. The LEA claimed that the secondary school would need extra staff and equipment at a cost thought to be excessive and defended the appeal. The parents gained the support of people who had known the boy for some time and, against evidence from others (an educational psychologist, medical officer, school administrators), were successful. The boy has continued his education in the comprehensive school and was eventually provided with additional equipment by the LEA.

Many writers have included case studies of the integration of students with Down syndrome, each of which provides an insight into the problems that are encountered and sometimes resolved.

Another report, of the part-time placement of Peter – a 7-year-old boy with Down syndrome – in a regular first grade classroom, focused upon the perspectives of his classmates (Schnorr, 1990). He was not regarded as a true member of the class even though he had his own desk. He was seen as a student who 'belonged to' the resource room; his learning tasks were different (e.g. colours not numbers); and the activities that he undertook were seen as play rather than school work. Socially, the first graders neither engaged in play with Peter, nor was he identified as a friend by any of them.

A similar situation was described by Bruni (1982) who conducted a detailed study of Faye, a girl with Down syndrome, who was placed in a Grade 1 classroom whose teacher, Karen, had 15 years experience. Faye had a special programme for an hour each day and speech therapy for half an hour. In Karen's room, Faye's desk was centrally placed, and the other 17 children are seated according to control techniques, typically using girls to separate boys.

While Faye was present most of the day, and appeared to participate in activities, closer examination revealed that she did different worksheets, and always joined the low progress groups for reading activities.

The classroom was well organized with many opportunities for children to manage themselves on certain tasks or activities. However, Karen often related to Faye in ways which were different to other children, particularly anticipating that Faye would need help on simple tasks that other children can manage either unaided or with peer assistance. As Bruni (1982, p. 14) reports it 'Faye is seen as usually needing help and incapable of working out problems for herself or calling for help when she needs it'. Furthermore, there seem to be different standards expected of Faye than other children, and her classmates are sometimes expected to behave like 'good' older siblings, and to adopt preventive strategies to avoid problems such as Faye taking pencils from other children.

Karen was not fully comfortable with having Faye in her classroom in that she was a group of one and not part of the social structure. Despite the statement that the primary objective of Faye's being in the classroom was socialization, she did not belong, and was somewhat overprotected, thus not having many chances to have real interactions and gain experience leading to better social skills.

Karen's attempt to explain how Faye was different was only partially successful. Although she was able to indicate that Faye learned more slowly and needed extra support, the children still seemed to regard her with some puzzlement. This was probably aggravated by Faye's attempts to initiate social interaction by teasing or playing tricks. Those children who have most interactions with Faye did so as older to younger children, particularly in authoritarian ways. It seems as if adults, particularly the teacher, Karen, do not attempt to regulate the social interaction of the class so as to benefit Faye.

Magazines such as *The Exceptional Parent* also provide useful information from which parents can glean guidance and optimism. Lois Elias, for example, described her experiences with her son, Jason, as did his teacher, principal and aide (Elias *et al.*, 1983). It is clearly evident that each contributed important elements to Jason's education. This informal team noted the following factors:

- The aide is excellent;
- Suitable educational materials were found;
- The teacher is interested in Jaco and is a master teacher;
- Jason was able to participate in regular class activities for half the regular school day;
- Space was found for quiet one-to-one instruction;
- The other children accepted Jason;
- Jason is well-behaved and happy;
- The parents were available when needed.

(Ibid., p. 58)

WHAT EFFORT IS NEEDED TO MAKE INTEGRATION SETTINGS SUCCESSFUL?

Many of the case studies that have reported successful integration experiences have demanded considerable effort from parents, as a recent publication of the Australian Institute on Intellectual Disability (Bowman and Virtue, 1993) attests. It contains accounts by two mothers of children who have Down syndrome. Ingrid has a 7-year-old son, Paul, who attends a local primary school. As a teacher, she had much experience with children before Paul was born. She took an active part in parent committees at Paul's school with a particular focus upon integration which was a high priority of the government. She noted that ignorance of Down syndrome by other parents and some teachers was an impediment. She also found that teachers tended to have lower expectations than she did, yet were unable or unwilling to work harder with Paul in order to have him attain what Ingrid believed he could. She noted also that the rigorous behavioural approach followed in his early intervention was not used at school where more holistic curricula were followed. Before long there were major problems in the school, including his teacher taking stress leave and threats of action by the Teachers' Union. The union was striving for a full-time integration aid. Paul was shared among teachers, so that he was expected to cope with several sets of classmates. She also experienced opposition from some parents.

When Ingrid considered placing Paul at a special school, she found that the principal argued strongly for segregation (i.e. opposed the government policy). Ingrid found that she and her parent advocate had extensive interaction with Education Department advisers. She believed that there was so much opposition to Paul's attending a regular school that she might have to capitulate. However, by repeating the first grade with a new teacher a much improved experience resulted. Ingrid still carried a number of extra burdens such as driving Paul to therapy sessions (which would have been provided in a special school). Ultimately Ingrid hopes that Paul will learn to read and write and negotiate the adult world with reasonable independence. She recognizes that a special school may be a better option when he is older and needs prevocational training.

Peg's story has some points of similarity with Ingrid's. Also a teacher, she has both a son, Gary, and a foster daughter, Sophie, who joined the family when Gary was 4 years old, both of whom have Down syndrome. Gary attended a special school, while Sophie went to a local primary school, mainly because of their different abilities. A supportive teacher was able to include Sophie very well for a few years. Later teachers did not manage as well. Tension grew, especially on days when no integration aide was available, and Sophie was moved to the special education setting. Peg's devotion as both a mother and a foster parent was very intense, yet despite her professional background, she fought many struggles, particularly in attempting to secure an appropriate education for Sophie. Clearly, all case studies are not unequivocal successes, nor are they wholly failures. Each needs to be taken on board for what it may say about the challenge of educating children who have Down syndrome.

Another story of a parent's efforts on behalf of a child with Down syndrome is told by noted special educator, Bud Fredericks (1986). He explained the nature of his son's disability to a fifth grade class into which he was transferring. Fredericks believes that most parents can do the same and thereby create a better context for their child's education.

PRACTICAL ISSUES THROUGH ADOLESCENCE AND ADULT LIFE

While much of the literature on students with Down syndrome has focused on those in the earlier grades of school, interest has also been shown in those at the secondary level.

The secondary school years

The secondary school offers a number of potential advantages for educating students with Down syndrome, and also presents particular problems. There are important issues to be considered, such as peer relationships and socialization, and matters relating to the application and/or adaptation of the secondary curriculum for students who experience learning difficulties.

FIynn and Kowalczyk-McPhee (1989, p. 39) for example, described how a 17-year-old boy was accepted by the football players at his high school which led to greater social involvement in the school and acceptance.

> T.D. came to St. Jerome's High School with the label 'trainable retarded.' In his first year at St. Jerome's he was given a full course load of history, mathematics, physical education, drama, instrumental music, religion, and English. His work placement was in the school library. One lunch hour T.S.'s usual lunch friend was absent and so T.D. walked up to the table where the football team ate. Approaching the biggest football player he asked, 'Can I eat with you guys?' An over 6 foot-tall player stood up, carried a chair over for T.D., and put it on his immediate left. As a result of the peer support system and the level of commitment between students that this event generated, T.D. is genuinely part of school events.

Because high schools are usually large, they may offer not only full inclusion but also placement in a special class for part or all of the curriculum. Also, a large school is likely to have one or more specialist teachers who can provide additional support to subject teachers. But such large schools often prove overwhelming to new entrants, and a student with Down syndrome might need careful induction into school life.

Ward (1991) sets out a very useful checklist of information, covering issues which might concern any parents of any student entering high school, such as transport, facilities, general characteristics of the school, its ethos. Other issues of particular relevance to the education of students with Down syndrome include attitudes towards disability, school policies, staff skills, support staff, openness to parent input, curriculum options and/or adaptation, and preparation for work.

A recent report from the UK (Lincoln *et al.*, 1992) reported that with increasing pressure from parents, students with Down syndrome are being included successfully in comprehensive secondary schools. Parents have sought the advantages of a broad curriculum and recognize that while some negative incidents are inevitable, there are many positive benefits which will outweigh the problems. The benefit to oral language facility from interaction with other students is also considered to be a strong argument in favour of inclusion. Lincoln *et al.* note that having three students with Down syndrome in the one large secondary school has served to illustrate their variability so that a stereotypic perspective is undermined.

Determination by the school to make integration work seems to be more important than expertise, though special support is very helpful, perhaps essential in the beginning stages when the problems have become evident and the solutions not yet achieved. Working backwards from desired adult outcomes, it is evident that many young people with Down syndrome would benefit from the social contact of regular schools in order to participate in the wider society. In the past, special schooling was the norm since sheltered workshop and residential institutional services were the predictable course for those who did not live with their parents.

It is reasonable, however, to recognize that neither a special setting nor the mainstream are likely to offer the ideal preparation for life. Indeed, parents who have chosen regular schooling have needed either to supplement the curriculum by their own deliberate intervention, or to agitate vigorously to ensure that such special programming as may be needed is actually provided.

Schools can make things much more pleasant and successful by recognizing that simple assumptions about what is true of all adolescents are not necessarily so. Each student with Down syndrome will have some areas which teachers or peers need to accommodate.

Of course one reason why parents are reluctant to choose a mainstream school is that there are risks of exposure to undesirable behaviour. The support of a group of parents and professionals may be crucial for the success of an integrated placement. Also, within limits, for adolescents with Down syndrome to have similar experiences to those of their peers may be important to acquiring robust self-concepts in adult life.

Beyond the school years

One difficulty faced by parents who have to decide on the type of school their child with Down syndrome should attend is how that choice will affect long-term outcomes. Unfortunately there is little evidence to illuminate such decision-making. A study conducted in France by Diederich (1994) indicates that if children's intellectual disabilities are not too severe, they will be able to achieve normal adult life patterns if family and social support systems are provided. Thus whether children attend a regular or special school may be less important than whether their family and community are accepting and supportive throughout their lives.

CONCLUSION

Integration for students with Down syndrome presents a confusing picture. In western countries with small to moderate class sizes, and awareness of human rights issues, there have been many attempts – some successful – to educate these students in their local schools. Additional support is usually provided through expert consultation and additional aide time. However, where class sizes are large or the education system is highly competitive, special schooling will be the norm.

Advocates of integration are tending to argue that what is needed is the restructuring of regular school (Ballard, 1991; Stainback *et al.*, 1989; Vlachou and Barton, 1994; West and Cummins, 1990). While teachers generally support this view they are being stressed by issues such as the National Curriculum in the UK, and National Education Goals (America 2000) in the USA. We, therefore, conclude that it has been demonstrated that some students with Down syndrome can be integrated but success has many necessary conditions which often will not all be present without considerable effort from parents, teachers and school administrators.

Students such as Bryson, to whom we referred at the beginning of this chapter seem fortunate indeed. However, the challenge for all those involved in the education of children with Down syndrome is to remain vigilant of changing circumstances that might limit the students' opportunities to learn and their enthusiasm to do so.

REFERENCES

Allen, L. (1987) *Like Other Children*. Purley: Surrey Centre for Studies of Integration in Education.

Ashman, A.F. (1995) The education of students with an intellectual disability in the People's Republic of China. *European Journal of Special Needs Education*, **10**, pp. 46–56.

Ballard, K.D. (1991) An ecological analysis of progress toward non-restrictive environments in New Zealand. In A.F. Ashman (ed.), *Current Themes in Integration (The Exceptional Child Monograph No. 2)*, pp. 23–35, St Lucia: Fred and Eleanor Schonell Special Education Research Centre.

Barton L. (1989) *Integration: Myth or Reality?*, London: Falmer.

Berrigan, C. (1987) Integration in Italy: a dynamic movement. Paper presented at the annual conference of the Association for the Severely Handicapped, Chicago, October [ERIC document no. ED294341].

Bird, G. and Buckley, S. (1994) *Meeting the Educational Needs of Children with Down's Syndrome*, Portsmouth: University of Portsmouth.

Bookbinder, G. (1986) Professionals and wrong predictions. *British Journal of Special Education*, **13**, pp. 6–7.

Bowman, D. and Virtue, M. (1993) *Public Policy, Private Lives*, Canberra: Australian Institute on Intellectual Disability.

Brown, L., Long, E., Udvari-Solner, A., Schwarz, P., VanDeventer, P., Ahlgren, C., Johnson, F., Gruenewald, L. and Jorgensen, J. (1989a) The home school: why students with severe intellectual disabilities must attend the schools of their brothers, sisters, friends, and neighbours. *Journal of The Association for Persons with Severe Handicaps*, **14** (1), pp. 1–7.

Brown, L., Schwarz, P., Udvari-Solner, A., Frattura Kampschroer, E., Johnson, F., Jorgensen, J. and Gruenewald, L. (1989b) Should students with severe intellectual disabilities be based in regular or in special education classrooms in home schools? *Journal of The Association for Persons with Severe Handicaps*, **14** (1), 8–12.

Brown, L., Long, E., Udvari-Solner, A, Davis, L, VanDeventer, P., Ahlgren, C., Johnson, F., Gruenewald, L., and Jorgensen, J. (1991) How much time should students with severe intellectual disabilities spend in regular education classrooms and elsewhere? *Journal of The Association for Persons with Severe Handicaps*, **16** (1), pp. 39–47.

Bruni, S.L. (1982). *The class and Faye: social interaction of a handicapped child in an integrated first grade class*, Syracuse: Syracuse University (ERIC document ED271905).

Budgell, P. (1986) Drifting towards segregation. *British Journal of Special Education*, **13**, pp. 94–95.

Chapman, J.W. (1988) Special education in the least restrictive environment: mainstreaming or maindumping? *Australia and New Zealand Journal of Developmental Disabilities*, **14**, pp. 123–34.

Cullen, R.B. and Brown, N.F. (1992) Integration and special education in Victorian schools: a program effectiveness review. Unpublished paper, Directorate of School Education, Victoria.

Danielson, L. C. and Bellamy, G. T. (1989) State variation in placement of children with handicaps in segregated environments. *The Exceptional Children*, **55**, pp. 448–55.

Diederich, N. (1994) The future and conditions of social and professional integration for adults leaving a special school. *European Journal on Mental Disability*, **1**, pp. 5–12.

Elias, L., Goble, G., Schefer, B. and Jaco, J. (1983) Jason goes to kindergarten. *Exceptional Parent*, **13** (1), pp. 55–58.

Elkins, J. (1994). The school context. In A. Ashman and J. Elkins (eds.), *Educating Children with Special Needs*, (2nd edn.) Sydney: Prentice Hall.

Elkins, J. and Atkinson, J.K. (1985) *Comparative Study of Three School Programs: OECD/CERI Project on the Transition of Handicapped Youth*, St Lucia: Fred and Eleanor Schonell Educational Research Centre.

Fewell, R.R. and Oelwein, P.L. (1990) The relationship between time in integrated environments and developmental gains in young children with special needs. *Topics in Early Childhood Special Education*, **10**, pp. 104–16.

Fex, B.-I. (1987) Special education in Sweden. In C.R. Reynolds and L. Mann (eds), *Encyclopedia of Special Education*, vol. 3, New York: Wiley.

Flynn, G. and Kowalczyk-McPhee, B. (1989) A school system in transition. In S. Stainback, W. Stainback, and M. Forest (eds), *Educating All Students in the Mainstream of Regular Education*, Baltimore: Brookes.

Fredericks, B. (1986). I helped my son into the mainstream. *Exceptional Parent*, **16** (5), pp. 14, 16–17.

Griffin, T. (1992) Do we really need a Couchman? *Intellectual Disabilities*, **5** (1), pp. 4–6.

Hayes, A. and Livingstone, S. (1986) Mainstreaming in rural communities: an analysis of case studies in Queensland schools. *Exceptional Child*, **33**, pp. 35–48.

Hegarty, S. and Pocklington, K. (1981) *Educating Pupils with Special Needs in the Ordinary School*, Windsor: NFER-Nelson.

Lewis, A. (1993). Integration, education and rights [1]. *British Educational Research Journal*, **19**, pp. 291–302.

Lincoln, J., Batty, J., Townsend, R. and Collins, M. (1992) Working for greater inclusion of children with severe learning difficulties in mainstream secondary schools. *Educational and Child Psychology*, **9**, pp. 46–51.

Lipsky, D.K. and Gartner, A. (1992) Achieving full inclusion: placing the student at the centre of education reform. In W. Stainback and S. Stainback (eds), *Controversial Issues Confronting Special Education*, pp. 3–12, Boston: Allyn and Bacon.

Ministerial Review of Education Services for the Disabled (1984) *Integration in Victorian Education: Report*. Melbourne: Government Printer.

Mitchell, D.R. (1991) Special education in New Zealand: Perspectives on the coming decade. Country report prepared for the 11th APEID Regional Seminar on Special Education, Yokosaka, Kanagawa, Japan, 14–19 October.

National Council on Disability (1990) The education of students with disabilities: where do we stand? A report to the President and the Congress of the United States, September 1989. *Journal of Disability Policy Studies*, **1**, pp. 103–32.

Peck, C.A., Palyo, W.J., Bettencourt, B., Cooke, T.P. and Apolloni, T. (1988) An observational study of 'partial integration' of handicapped students in a regular school. *Journal of Research and Development in Education*, **21**, pp. 1–4.

Pieterse, M. and Center, Y. (1984) The integration of eight Down's syndrome children into regular schools. *Australia and New Zealand Journal of Developmental Disabilities*, **10**, pp. 11–20.

Rietveld, C.M. (1986) The adjustment to school of eight children with Down's syndrome from an early intervention program. *Australia and New Zealand Journal of Development Disabilities*, **12**, pp. 159–75.

Rynders, J. and Horrobin, J. (1990). Always trainable? Never educable? Updating educational expectations concerning children with Down's syndrome. *American Journal on Mental Retardation*, **95**, pp. 77–83.

Schnorr, R.F. (1990)' Peter? He comes and goes . . . ': first graders' perspectives on a part-time mainstream student. *Journal of the Association for Persons with Severe Handicaps*, **15**, pp. 231–40.

Sloper, P., Cunningham, C., Turner, S. and Knussen, C. (1990) Factors related to the academic attainments of children with Down syndrome. *British Journal of Educational Psychology*, **60**, 284–98.

Stainback, S., Stainback, W. and Forest, M. (1989) *Educating All Students in the Mainstream of Regular Education*, Baltimore: Brookes.

Tarr, P. (1988) Integration policy and practice in Victoria: an examination of the Victorian Government's educational provisions for students with impairments, disabilities and problems in schooling since 1984. In A.F. Ashman (ed.), *Integration: 25 Years on. (Exceptional Child Monograph No. 1)*. St Lucia: Fred and Eleanor Schonell Special Education Research Centre.

Thomson, C., Brown, D., Chapman, J., Benson, A. and Pine, T. (1991) *Individualized Educational Planning: a Guide for Meeting Learners' Needs*, Palmerston North: Massey University.

Vlachou, A. and Barton, L. (1994) Inclusive education: teachers and the changing culture of schooling. *British Journal of Special Education*, **21**, pp. 105–07.

Ward, J. (1991) Integrating students with Down syndrome into secondary school. In C. Denholm (ed.), *Adolescents with Down Syndrome: International Perspectives on Research and Programme Development*, pp. 39–50, Victoria, BC: University of Victoria.

West, R.F. and Cummins, P. (1990) Personal and professional change associated with the integration of children with Down syndrome into the public schools. Paper presented at the annual meeting of the Mid-South Educational Research Conference, New Orleans, Louisiana, November.

Families

21 Families and Siblings: A Response to Recent Research

Ann Gath and Jane McCarthy

The principal aims driving the research into families, and brothers and sisters in particular, are unanimously agreed by researchers over the past 25 years (Lobato, 1983; Cuskelly, Chapter 13 in this volume) to be to answer two main questions:

1. Do family members, especially siblings, show problems in psychological adjustment?
2. What factors mediate the adjustment? Why do some individuals seem vulnerable and others resilient?

DOES HAVING A CHILD WITH DOWN SYNDROME IN ITSELF HAVE ADVERSE PSYCHOLOGICAL EFFECTS UPON OTHER CHILDREN IN THE FAMILY?

The first of these questions was driven by the debate in the 1950s and 1960s about whether children with major disabilities should be brought up in the family or placed out of the home in schools and institutions. Before 1950, it was the usual practice for doctors to advise parents not to take home a child with Down syndrome but to allow such a child to be cared for in what was usually a hospital environment. The reasons for the advice was that hospital care was better for the child, who certainly had a short expectation of life, and better too for the other children in the family who were considered likely to be deprived of their due share of love and attention. In their work, Tizard and Grad (1961) had referred to the 'burden of care' and others had suggested that a family with a handicapped child was a 'handicapped family' (Goldie, 1966).

Subsequent research, such as that of Stedman and Eichorn (1964), showed that being put 'with others of their own kind', as was often said, was not in the best interest of the children with disability. This was the state of knowledge at the outset of our own series of studies (Gath, 1978). That work was prompted by the questions of the parents who were then anxious to find out if bringing up their disabled child at home would be to the detriment of the other children. What those parents said was, 'It is all very well for me to make the choice for Mary to be brought up at home, but how can I make the choice on behalf of my other children? Will she be a blight on their lives throughout childhood and maybe even beyond?' No one had the answers.

The first idea was to compare families of a child with Down syndrome with those of another condition also recognizable at birth, but one which was regarded as treatable. The chosen comparison group was cleft lip with cleft palate, (Gath, 1972). Surgeons would come within days of delivery armed with photographs of children before and after corrective surgery. This pilot study looked at the situation ten years later when half of the Down syndrome group had significant problems of management, but only two of those with cleft palate were still much involved with hospitals. In this small study with 20 families in each group, few differences were found between the two groups of siblings. A decision was then made to use a two-pronged attack in the attempt to answer the question 'Did bringing up a child with Down syndrome at home have a deleterious effect on the other children in the family?' One method involved a postal survey of 20 families with a Down syndrome child in a geographical area, (Gath, 1973, 1974), and the second method was a contrasting approach following in detail over two years, families to which a child with Down syndrome had been born. The latter became the basis of the longitudinal study in which the children were revisited at the ages of 8 and 14, whilst the survey, a more superficial study, prompted questions about family functioning and structure that required an extension of the interview techniques used in the longitudinal study to a larger cross-section of families collected at the same time as the second follow-up at the age of 8.

The studies that have been reported in the ensuing years have confirmed the finding that there is no evidence that brothers and sisters are necessarily adversely affected by having a sibling with Down syndrome. However, no family with or without a child with a major disability is immune from many other sorts of family difficulty. Certain sorts of family problems may be associated indirectly with the event of the birth of a child with disability, but both may bear a relationship to some common factor.

One such family factor is family size. In the 1960s when the children in the earlier studies were born, contraception was by no means universally reliable. In the postal survey referred to above there were a number of families, more often but not exclusively, in the lower socio-economic groups, where the Down's child had arrived at the end of a family with a large number of children.

Life did appear to be distinctly hard for such families and much of the mother's responsibilities were shared with the older girls in the family. Such large families were much more rare in the groups where the index child had been born in 1970 or later. Where they did occur, and there was one such in the detailed prospective study, a large family was much more a matter of deliberate choice. Parenting though hard work was evidently enjoyed and the task of rearing a child with extra problems was approached with confidence although not without grief.

More and more anecdotal evidence supported the suggestion that many brothers and sisters found that having a brother or sister with Down syndrome or within a similar range of disability had brought enrichment rather than impoverishment. Their eyes were opened to different values from an early age and their choice of career was often influenced. Many spoke of wanting to be a teacher in a special school or to be a scientist discovering the cause of various disabilities. In every class of medical students, there appears always to be at least one who asks the searching questions and then explains they have a brother or sister at home with Down syndrome.

Comparison groups

There have been clear changes in the methodology in the past 30 years, particularly the use of appropriate control groups, (Stoneman, 1989). Since the subject at the start was in many ways virgin territory, ideas had to be tried out, experiments had to made in research design, and mistakes inevitably were made. The enormous variation between ordinary families throughout the general population is attributable to differences in family style and functioning which remain even after the closest matching for the more obvious variables of family size and socio-economic group. Real differences are not easily detected in small groups, yet detailed study of numbers large enough to make statistics meaningful become unwieldy and prohibitive in terms of expense. It was necessary first to do a trawl of all siblings to detect particular vulnerability and this was followed by focusing down on one sibling in the family, closest in age to the child with Down syndrome. As well as being investigated in their own right, the siblings were a useful yardstick by which parents could judge the differences in the quality and quantity of parental tasks which the disability posed. Ideally, the brothers and sisters should be individually matched holding constant all socio-demographic factors with another individual. This degree of matching proved impossible for two reasons. First, as it was agreed school reports for the sibling and the control should be completed by the same teacher, such detailed matching within one school class is unlikely to be achieved on all or even most accounts. Second, public attitudes towards reports on children had sharpened and ethical committees too were concerned about collecting data on non-clinical samples. Teachers were even more concerned. Co-operation was only achieved by allowing the control child to remain anonymous with no identifying data sought.

Consensus of research findings

Direct observation of siblings, (Brody *et al.*, 1991; Stoneham *et al.*, 1991) have substantiated many of the conclusions formed by the other studies. Despite naïve methodology in the earlier years, the research studies have largely been able to provide a helpful answer to the parents' urgent question. There is no evidence to support the notion that the presence of a child with Down syndrome, or with any other other major handicap, must of its essence adversely affect the lives of the other children brought up in that home. This is not to say that children are in any way immune from the ill effects of other social and family influences or that deprivation of reasonable, accessible services will harm not just the child with a disability, what ever that may be, but the other members of the family too.

WHAT ARE THE FACTORS THAT CAN MEDIATE THE ADJUSTMENT OF BROTHERS AND SISTERS OF CHILDREN WITH DOWN SYNDROME?

The answers to this question are required before effective services can be designed and to assist in targeting the points of greatest need.

Variation from family to family

Families with a child with Down syndrome vary widely, beautifully pointed out in the title of the book on the Manchester cohort, *One Feature In Common* (Byrne *et al.*, 1988), despite all being recruited in the same geographical area and within a certain specified time. It is also clear that the experience families encounter varies over time according to changes in attitudes, educational practice as well as medical practice and in the characteristics of the population at large. Some of the changes are evident in the studies carried out in the Oxford region, but are particularly clear in the two cohorts in South Wales, reported by Billie Shepperdson, (1988). Over ten years there had been a dramatic rise in the divorce rate in the general population, making data on marital breakdown in the 1970s difficult to reconcile with that gathered in the 1980s. Education for all children regardless of disability in the UK only dates from the early 1970s and the right to education until the age of 19 came much later. Later still, the wave of normalization made educational provision within mainstream schools an issue in some areas and for some families. The pattern of delinquency had changed with more girls exhibiting conduct disorders, which might provide some clue to the disparity between findings concerning conduct disorder in some British and some Australian studies.

Detailed study of family functioning

The meticulous time sampling study of Dupont (1980) on families with a child with disability emphasized the much greater physical work that parenting a child demands. The 'burden of care' from the Tizard and Grad study is still there. It is also clear in Dupont's work, that by far the greater burden is carried by the mother. Harris and McHale (1989) found that a detailed review of one day showed that much more time was spent in child care duties than originally had been estimated and that even outings, meant to be pleasurable for the whole family, were also extremely hard work. How does this affect interpretation of the work on brothers and sisters? Some attempt was made to look at siblings' share of chores in the Oxford study reported in 1986. The section in the Isle of Wight interview (Rutter *et al.*, 1970) dealing with 'Expectations and prohibitions' was used to see what work and what restrictions were put upon siblings. Great variation within the sample of families was found in the chores expected of the children and in the rules imposed. There was no significant difference between siblings of Down syndrome children and those of other handicapped children.

There may be too much focus on the issue of care responsibilities for the siblings which could be a red herring, as excessive domestic roles for siblings was the explanation postulated for the excess in conduct disorders in older siblings, an idea arising from clinical intuition but not tested until later studies when the findings regarding the older sisters were not replicated. Certainly there was no sign of the older siblings, boys or girls, doing any more child care or domestic work in those families in the prospective study in the first years when the babies were very much the mother's work, and in the toddler years were actually less of a nuisance than the control children.

Techniques of family measurement

The past 20 years has seen a growth of far more sophisticated family measurements, (Moos and Moos, 1981). Classification of family lifestyles (Mink *et al.*, 1988) has led to further understanding of both normal family functioning and of the modes of adaptation families have to make to meet the needs of different levels of learning disability.

Gallimore *et al.* (1989, 1993) of the 'ecocultural' niche to describe the adaptation made by the family. His model is useful when considering how one system producing a cohesive family can prove inadequate and even collapse if either the family itself moves on to another stage, as when siblings, of necessity, leave home or an outside adversity such as unemployment strikes.

Factors within the family

Family size has been discussed above in relation to the first apparently confusing results. Now, large families are very much more a matter of choice, the disadvantage for children is minimal if present at all. Indeed, there is evidence (Gath and Gumley, 1986), that the support of a selection of siblings is beneficial when the family has an additional task to cope with, such as in the case of a child with Down syndrome.

Place within the family or ordinal position has also been widely discussed. There is now no compelling evidence that being older than the child with Down syndrome is more or less stressful than being younger. What usually happens is that the older child does adopt a teaching or quasi-parental role quite early, but the younger sibling catches up developmentally, may have some months of strife during the period of overtaking, but then also adopts the same role as the older one.

The health of the other children

Few families can cope with a multiplication of problems. Two Down syndrome babies born to the same family is a very rare occurence, but adoptive parents have successfully reared two such children, often with natural-born normal siblings.

In other syndromes, particularly with known genetic implications, two severely handicapped children can be catastrophic. Other disasters, such as a severe illness or accident to another child also most understandably puts the family seriously off balance.

The health of the parents

The health, particularly the mental health, of parents is crucial to the well-being of children. It has been demonstrated that both the normal sibling and the child with Down syndrome may develop behaviour or emotional disorders in relation to parental ill health, but the latter shows a much greater vulnerability.

Marital strife

Discord within the family has a similar effect on children, but also shows the much greater sensitivity of the child with a disability. Marital discord and parental mental ill health often coexist, but is has also been seen from the group of families seen over at least two points in time that for some women, the ability to break out of a destructive relationship was followed by a marked improvement in not only their mental health but in the welfare of all their children, (Gath, 1990).

Factors operating from outside the family

Poor socio-economic circumstances, including poverty, inadequate housing and disordered or aggressive neighbourhoods severely impede children's optimal development. Children with Down syndrome and their siblings are no exception, but there is no reason why Down syndrome should be more common in such an environment, although other causes of learning disability often are.

Political and economic considerations

Changes in the funding and organization of schools, of social welfare and of medical services are undoubtedly influential for families, including siblings. Thirty years ago, a child with Down syndrome could be considered as a stigma and many were still being brought up in institutions rather than in families. As public attitudes change, brothers and sisters can regard their Down syndrome sibling with pride, visit his or her school and see his or her achievements.

On the other hand, recent moves all over the world have emphasized 'market values'. Some of the ideas and many of the cut-backs have not been to the benefit of unusual citizens.

THE WAY AHEAD

More work has been carried out looking at brothers and sisters of children with different disabilities, particularly autism, (Bolton *et al.*, 1994; Piven *et al.*, 1991). All this research on families with a child with a disability or who presents particular problems in parenting, has become involved in the dialogue with those engaged in more general family research, particularly that on brothers and sisters (Hayes, Chapter 12 in this volume). Judy Dunn (Dunn *et al.*, 1994) in her work on sibling relationships has found that the quality of relationship in early childhood and adolescence is linked to mother's current mood and report of hassles, echoing the findings discussed here. In addition, the continued debate of genetic and environmental influences on the development of children (Plomin, 1995) is highly relevant to the work on families where siblings differ by the presence or absence of one extra chromosome.

REFERENCES

Bolton, P., Macdonald, H., Pickles, A., Rios, P., Goode, S., Crowson, M., Bailey, A. and Rutter, M. (1994) A case-control family history of autism. *Journal of Child Psychology and Psychiatry*, **35**, pp. 877–900.

Byrne, E.A., Cunningham, C.C. and Sloper, P. (1988) *Families and their Children with Down's Syndrome: One Feature in Common*, London: Routledge.

Dunn, J., Slomkowski, C., Beardsall, L. and Rende, R. (1994) Adjustment in middle childhood and early adolescence: links with earlier and contemporary relationships. *Journal of Child Psychology and Psychiatry*, **35**, pp. 491–501.

Dupont, A. (1980) A study concerning the time-related and other burdens when severely handicapped children are reared at home. In *Epidemiological Research as a Basis for Organisation of Extra Mural Psychiatry*. Acta Psychiatrica Scandanavia, *62*, Suppl. **285**, pp. 249–57.

Gallimore, R., Weisner, T.S., Kaufman, S.Z. and Bernheimer, L.P. (1989) The social construction of ecocultural niches: family accommodation of developmentally delayed children. *American Journal of Mental Retardation*, **94**, pp. 216–30.

Gallimore, R., Weisner, T.S., Bernheimer, L.P., Guthrie, D. and Nihira, K. (1993) Family responses to young children with developmental delays: accomodation activity in ecological and cultural context. *American Journal of Mental Retardation*, **98** (2) pp. 185–206.

Gath, A. (1972) The mental health of siblings of congenitally abnormal children. *Journal of Child Psychology and Psychiatry*, **13**, pp. 211–18.

Gath, A. (1973) The school-age siblings of mongol children. *British Journal of Psychiatry*, **123**, pp. 161–67.

Gath, A. (1974) Sibling reactions to mental handicap: a comparison of the brothers and sisters of mongol children. *Journal of Child Psychology and Psychiatry*, **15**, pp. 187–98.

Gath, A. (1978) *Down's Syndrome and the Family*, London: Academic Press.

Gath, A. (1990) Down syndrome children and their families. *American Journal of Medical Genetics Supplement*, **7**, pp. 314–16.

Gath, A. and Gumley, D. (1986) Retarded children and their siblings. *Journal of Child Psychology and Psychiatry*, **28**, pp. 715–30.

Goldie, L. (1966) The psychiatry of the handicapped family. *Developmental Medicine and Child Neurology*, **8**, p. 456.

Harris, V.S. and McHale, S.M. (1989) Family life problems, daily caregiving activities, and psychological well-being of mothers of mentally retarded children. *American Journal on Mental Retardation*, **94**, pp. 231–39.

Lobato, D. (1983) Siblings of handicapped children: a review. *Journal of Autism and Developmental Disabilities*, **13**, pp. 347–65.

Mink, I.T., Blacher, J. and Nihira, K. (1988) Taxonomy of family life styles: iii Replication with families with severely mentally retarded children. *American Journal on Mental Retardation*, **93**, pp. 250–64.

Moos, R.H. and Moos, B. (1981) *Family Environment Scales*, Palo Alto: Consulting Psychologists Press.

Piven, J., Chase, G.A., Landa, R., Wzorek, M., Gayle, J., Cloud, D. and Folstein, S. (1991) Psychiatric disorders in the parents of autistic individuals. *Journal of American Academy of Child and Adolescent Psychiatry*, **30**, pp. 471–78.

Plomin, R. (1995) Genetics and children's experiences in the family. *Journal of Child Psychology and Psychiatry*, **36**, pp. 33–68.

Rutter, M., Tizard, J. and Whitmore, K. (1970) *Education, Health and Behaviour*, London: Longman.

Shepperdson, B. (1988) *Growing up with Down's syndrome*, London: Cassell Educational.

Stedman, D.J. and Eichorn, D.H. (1964) A comparison of the growth and development of institutionalised and home reared mongoloids during infancy and childhood. *American Journal on Mental Deficiency*, **69**, 391–401.

Stoneman, Z. (1989) Comparison groups in research on families with mentally retarded members: a methodological and conceptual review. *American Journal of Mental Retardation*, **94**, pp. 195–215.

Stoneman, Z., Brody, G.H., Davis, C.H., Crapps, J.M. and Malone, D.M. (1991) Ascribed role relations between children with mental retardation and their younger siblings. *American Journal on Mental Retardation*, **95**, pp. 537–50.

Tizard, J. and Grad, J.C. (1961) The Mentally handicapped and their Families, London: Maudsley Monograph 7.

22 Family Life in Community Context

Alan Hayes

Perhaps the single most influential factor in improving the quality of life for persons with Down syndrome has been the rapid movement away from institutional care to life within their family and its community. While it is entirely appropriate to focus on the new knowledge accumulating about the bio-genetic, medical, developmental and educational characteristics of persons with the syndrome, it is equally important to place such study in the context of the changes that have occurred in their life circumstances, particularly related to increases in opportunities and greater access to experiences of family and community life (Ludlow and Allen, 1979). In western nations the majority of persons with Down syndrome now live at home (Carr, 1994; Shepperdson, 1985). Life in the community stands in stark contrast to institutionalization (Rosen et al., 1976). Institutions, by their nature, do much to homogenize. Importantly, these change have allowed the individual differences among persons with the syndrome to be expressed (Crombie et al., 1991). Despite these major changes in living conditions, life expectancy and access to opportunity that have accompanied de-institutionalization, too many persons with Down syndrome still live very restricted lives (Carr, 1994).

This chapter explores a new approach to the study of families in which there is a member who has Down syndrome. It seeks, in particular, to move away first, from solely researching those with the syndrome to a complementary focus on their families and communities (Stone, 1973) and second, from focusing on the pathology that has typified much of the previous literature on persons with Down syndrome and their families (Byrne and Cunningham, 1984; Wright et al., 1984). Instead, it explores a new set of questions concerning the family and community contexts of contemporary life for persons with Down syndrome. These can be summarized as follows:

1. How is living in a family where there is a child with Down syndrome similar to, and different from, life in other families?
2. To what extent does the presence of a person with Down syndrome have differential effects within and between families?
3. Why are some families with a child who has Down syndrome vulnerable to major problems, while others appear resilient?

The answers to these questions are important to understand the nature of life in families with a child with Down syndrome. They are also of value for designing appropriate programmes to support those experiencing problems and to maintain those who are resilient. While there has been a steady increase in knowledge concerning the development of persons with disabilities, and the responses of their families, there still is a tendency to interpret disability as the cause of the reported patterns of family functioning and to seek evidence of group differences rather than focusing on the variations that occur between and within families (Hayes, 1994).

As such, the present chapter describes an approach to the study of families where there is a member with Down syndrome, grounded in the literature from the wider field of developmental psychology. It adapts conceptual frameworks that have developed in the study of families and extends these to the largely unexplored areas of child care, parenting, employment decisions and life accommodations in families with a child with Down syndrome. It also moves away from the perspective that the child with the disability is central to all major family decisions, characteristics and outcomes. The study of families where there is a child with Down syndrome is set in the context of the historical changes that have occurred in policy and practice, particularly focusing on the impact of policies of de-institutionalization, inclusion and the new emphasis on community life. A review of the literature on the impact of the presence of a person with a disability, such as Down syndrome follows. This review demonstrates the inappropriateness of the focus on pathology that has characterized the field in the past. The variation and variability of family reactions is explored by examining three sets of possible mediating and moderating factors: the disability and its characteristics; family characteristics; and the balance of family problems and resources. A discussion of issues concerning support for families then outlines some of the areas in which professionals can offer assistance, explores some of the reasons that families gravitate to alternative, unconventional treatments, and some of the benefits, as well as the costs, of the contemporary emphasis on family involvement in intervention. The emergent focus on the wider community context and the interconnections among families and their communities is described, before sketching the implications of the new orientation for research, service and training and, finally, providing a concluding summary of the elements of this new approach. Before turning to these topics, I would first like to share a personal insight into life in one family with a member with Down syndrome, that illustrates the value of examining family life in community context.

A PERSONAL PERSPECTIVE ON THE IMPORTANCE OF FAMILY LIFE FOR PERSONS WITH DOWN SYNDROME

Across my childhood and into early adult life, I glimpsed the impact on my extended family of Uncle Arthur, my mother's youngest brother, who had Down syndrome. The opportunity to live with his family for most of his life had a great influence on his health and well-being, and enabled him to give much to his family in return. Before she died, my grandmother had asked her children to promise to care for Arthur, at home, and he lived first with his widowed eldest sister and her family. On this sister's death, he went to live with another sister who lived next door to his sole surviving brother, and together they cared for him. When that brother died, Uncle Arthur was placed in a nursing home where he died four months after admission, at 64 years of age.

Within our family there seemed little awareness that he had Down syndrome. It was certainly a term that was never associated with him (nor was he ever referred to as mongoloid or retarded). Whenever I asked about him, I was told that he was 'just different'. To me he was simply 'my Uncle Arthur'.

I had realized, of course, that he was not like my other uncles and aunts, but that did not seem to be very important. It was not until I went to university that I realized that the label Down syndrome actually applied to my uncle. The family mythology was that his problems had arisen from meningitis in early life. In fact, he had almost succumbed on many occasions in the first year of his life and, eventually the nurse, having reached the conclusion that the situation was hopeless, told my Grandmother to 'let him go'. Contrary to the nurse's advice, my grandmother stayed with him all night, moistening his lips with brandy from a teaspoon. He survived and actually became quite a robust young boy, renowned for his mischief.

As a member of the family, he was included in everyday activities and was clearly much loved by his brothers, sisters, nieces and nephews, and took great pride in them. Like all of us, he had his foibles. He lived a life dominated by routine. Every Thursday evening he would obsessively organize his wardrobe. With equal obsessiveness he would count the number of times that he swept the front path or would arrange and rearrange his shoes, or would visit the same shop, almost every working day, to buy a soft drink and one headache powder. While he had a good sense of humour, Uncle Arthur was not always happy and, again like all of us, occasionally could be quite difficult. As he grew older, he became quite stubborn and increasingly difficult to manage. Ensuring that he attended to his personal care and hygiene became a source of considerable conflict in the family.

He had very little formal education, largely because my grandmother felt that it would 'overtax' him, given his early frailty. In fact, one of his brothers had tried to teach him to write, with some success, but my grandmother had put a stop to this. Despite such limited formal education, he managed his own money and had part-time jobs throughout most of his adult life.

The family lived near a racecourse and my uncle worked for farriers, stable owners and trainers, among others, and was largely accepted as part of the community. He occasionally encountered rejection, but learned to manage this with the support of his family and friends. In so many ways, his life reflects the benefits of having a loving and caring family and a supportive community. As one of my cousin's put it, after my grandmother's death 'he was treated well, but never cosseted'. The loving experiences in his family throughout life made it difficult for him to cope when in the last year of his life he had to move away from home, and his death soon after entering a nursing home, in part, may have been the result of the emotional trauma of leaving his home and those he loved.

The remarkable fact is that he survived into his mid-sixties, when the survival age for his cohort was less than ten years. The influence of chance, in giving him a family that chose to keep him at home, in an era when placing him in an institution was commonplace, would seem to have played a large role in his longevity and in the quality of his life, generally.

A NEW APPROACH: THE IMPORTANCE OF SOCIAL CONTEXT

In recent years there has been an increasing focus on the importance of social contexts and the experiences they afford for the development of children (Hayes, 1984; Meyer-Probst *et al.*, 1991). After a long history of focus on the child in isolation, throughout the 1970s and 1980s attention increasingly turned to the examination of the interaction between children and the salient people in their social worlds. With this came the recognition among researchers and special educators that people with a disability have the same emotional needs for social interaction that we all share. In fact, like all children, much of their development is dependent on the quality of the contact they have with other human beings.

For many years now, the mainstream of developmental psychology has recognized the importance of the family as a key context for development. The contemporary interest in the ecology of child development (Bronfenbrenner and Crouter, 1983) and the re-emergence of interest in the exploration of the developmental sources of individual differences (Asendorpf and Valsiner, 1992) are now themes that are being addressed routinely by those researching families. Consistent with this emphasis, it is now acknowledged that while there may be some broad similarities in families, even within the same family each person's experience family life is unique and the family is the crucible of individual differentiation (Dunn and Plomin, 1990; Plomin and Daniels, 1987). The work of researchers such as Dunn and Plomin has highlighted the extent to which one's brothers and sisters actually have had quite individual experiences of family life, because each has experienced a different set of interactions and knows the family across different periods of its life cycle.

Just as biologists stress the importance of studying life forms in their habitats, the ecological perspective in psychology views the developing person in the context of family, neighbourhood, community and societal systems (Bronfenbrenner, 1977; Bronfenbrenner and Crouter, 1983; Dunst and Trivette, 1990; Hayes, 1994; Simeonsson and Bailey, 1990). Researchers working within an ecological paradigm are exploring the many interconnections between families and their social networks (Cochran and Brassard, 1979), such as the extended family, the neighbourhood, school and community (Hayes, 1994; Senapati and Hayes, 1988).

The intensive study of the impact of family life on individuals with disabilities is, however, a relatively recent research emphasis (Simeonsson and Bailey, 1990). In the era of widespread institutionalization and lowered life expectancy, family life was not an issue. After a long tradition of studying the commonalities in the development of groups of individuals sharing the same diagnostic label, attention has turned to the study of within-group differences and the influence of key social contexts, such as the family, school, community or workplace on the development of persons with disabilities and those around them.

The recent work of Gallimore *et al.* (1993) has provided some particularly important directions for the field. Their work on families where there is a child with a disability or delay is set in the framework of ecocultural theory. This theory 'emphasizes that a major adaptive task for each family is the construction and maintenance of a daily routine through which families organize and shape their children's activity and development' (p. 186). They underscore the need to focus on the key issue confronting families of creating 'a sustainable and meaningful daily routine of family life' and label this process 'family accommodation' (p. 186). Among the areas of accommodation they list are: child care, domestic tasks and household jobs, social support, financial resources and parental roles. Finally, they highlight the importance of a model of family accommodation that 'takes account of *all* family members, not just the child with delays' (p. 187).

Until recently, the experiences of people with disabilities and their families have been paid scant attention in the literature on special education (Korbin, 1986), despite a rapidly growing literature on family members' perceptions of their experiences (Goodnow and Collins, 1990). The accelerating impact of movements for de-institutionalization, integration and inclusive education, reflect a more general recognition of the extent to which previous eras in special education have de-humanized people with Down syndrome by focusing on the disability rather than on the person. It is now recognized that the static diagnostic characteristics, while important, mask the 'realities' of life for those with Down syndrome. Equally, the shifts in attitudes that have resulted in greater access to the opportunities that the able-bodied take for granted have meant that more people with Down syndrome now live longer, more fulfilled lives with their families than previously was the case. As Carr (1994) concluded, however, there is still quite a distance to go. It is still the case that for many adults with a disability such as Down syndrome their families *are* their social networks, with restricted friendship and peer contact outside of home (Krauss *et al.*, 1992). For many, life at home may also restrict their social and life skills and make the transition from home to independent life in the community a difficult one (Cattermole *et al.*,1988). Their parents also face a longer life span and the difficult issues that must be faced when they are no longer able to care for their child with Down syndrome. Their other children are likely to be faced with the care both of their sibling with Down syndrome and their ageing parents. These are difficult issues that service providers and communities increasingly need to address.

HISTORY OF RESEARCH

The history of research on the social relationships and experiences of people with a disability is interesting to trace. A landmark in the study of the influence of social factors on the development of children was the work of Skeels, undertaken in the 1930s (Kirk, 1982). Skeels demonstrated that early social experiences could overcome the effects of the developmental disabilities associated with growing up in impoverished environments.

> The consistent element seemed to be existence of a one-to-one relationship with an adult who was generous with love and affection, together with an abundance of attention and experiential stimulation from many sources. Children who had little of these did not show progress; those who had a great deal, did.
>
> (Skeels, 1966, p. 7)

Over the last 20 years, the changes in ideas about the life possibilities for persons who are disabled, or at risk for developmental problems, have been revolutionary.

Of particular salience has been the move away from institutional, residential care to community or home living (Rosen *et al.*, 1976; Shonkoff and Meisels, 1990). As argued at the beginning of this chapter, this change probably more than any other has been responsible for the improvement in the developmental outlook for persons with disabilities (Ludlow and Allen, 1979).

Another set of changes gave rise to a range of movements advocating for individuals and their rights. In the USA advocacy on behalf of the intellectually disabled led first to reforms in institutional care and ultimately to the passage of PL 94–142 the Education of All Handicapped Children's Act 1975. The provisions of PL 94–142 cover the age range from 3 to 21 years (Bailey and Wolery, 1984). In October, 1986 the US Congress passed PL 99–457, amending PL 94–142 (Safer and Hamilton, 1993; Sheehan and Sites, 1989). The new act places particular importance on the assessment of families and the development of an Individual Family Service Plan detailing both the family's needs and resources to cope (Sheehan and Sites, 1989). These legislative changes in the USA have had considerable impact on policy and practice throughout the western world.

A third influence which has changed community views of persons with disabilities grew out of the movement to change environmental and living conditions for people with intellectual disabilities. The debate on whether development is the product of heredity or environment generally was resolved by the adoption of some form of 'interactionism' which states that inherited and environmentally experienced factors interact to bring about development (Wachs and Plomin, 1991). Researchers and practitioners alike realized, however, that while both inherited and environmental factors produce development, in the current state of knowledge the environmental factors are more amenable to intervention (Baumrind, 1993).

While the focus on families has been an important shift for the field, it is possible to discern a new phase of research and policy. In this case, the impetus for the shift comes from the fields of sociology and political science. The evocative title of Etzioni's (1993) volume, *The Spirit of Community*, captures the essence of this movement. Labelled, rather awkwardly, 'communitarianism', it has engendered lively, and at times heated, debate in the USA.

Adherents to the movement 'are dedicated to working with our fellow citizens to bring about the changes in values, habits, and public policies that will allow us to do for society what the environmental movement seeks to do for nature: to safeguard and enhance our future' (ibid., p. 3). Strengthening and supporting families is a central part of the agenda. As Etzioni puts it: 'The best place to start is where each new generation acquires its moral anchoring: at home, in the family' (ibid., p. 256). In part, the movement has grown out of a recognition that governments alone cannot solve the complex problems confronting contemporary communities. Further, it is recognized that as governments assumed responsibility for an ever more extensive range of services, some of the non-government organizations and agencies disappeared or lost their support bases within the community. In the field of disability the progressive shift of services to government agencies was largely a result of the movement for normalization (Elkins, 1994).

Before examining the trends toward community-focused research and service, the literature on families will be reviewed, in particular that on families with a child with Down syndrome. The move to a focus on families represents a key transition from past work emphasizing the individual. In future, the approach seems most likely to be oriented towards deeper understanding of the importance of community contexts and their inter-connections with individuals and their families.

IMPACT OF DOWN SYNDROME ON FAMILIES

Families are complex social systems and vary individually in their characteristics, beliefs, values psychological and material resources (Senapati and Hayes, 1988). Despite this, there has been a tendency to discuss people with a disability and their families as if all were alike (Stoneman and Brody, 1982).

Cunningham and Glenn.(1985) have described three broad approaches to the study of families and the impact of disability. The first seeks to identify which members of a family are vulnerable. The second focuses on needs of families, arguing that the presence of a child with the disability is a less central determinant of family functioning than the needs that remain unmet. The final approach explores the factors that influence different patterns of family coping and adaptation. They conclude, however, that these approaches do not capture the complexity and multifactorial nature of the impact of disability on families. In the place, they argue that what is needed for the field to advance are 'transactional' perspectives, where the factors are complexly interactive and influence each other reciprocally (Singhi *et al.*, 1990; Wright *et al.*, 1984).

In contemporary societies, families are experiencing unparalleled change in their structures roles, and responsibilities (Singer and Powers, 1993). The birth of any child represents a major perturbation of many aspects of family life (Lichtenstein, 1993). When that child has a disability, such as Down syndrome, considerable distress is the usual response (Wright *et al.*, 1984).

Reactions to the experience, however, vary widely (e.g., Wright *et al.*, 1984; Dunst and Trivette, 1990). Nevertheless, families typically go through a process of grieving which may never be entirely resolved (Cavanagh and Ashman, 1985; Seligman and Darling, 1989). Grief is a normal, if complex, human response (Powers, 1993). Eden-Piercy *et al.* (1986) have shown that successful adjustment, recovery and acceptance are related to the specific early feelings of shock, confusion, guilt, anger, despair, depression and disorganization that may follow the child's birth, with refusal and denial generally impeding the process of acceptance (Powers, 1993).

Addressing the grief is an important task for parents, as unresolved grief may engender other feelings such as guilt and anger which can be very difficult to resolve. Nixon (1993) describes the types of guilt that may ensue. He identifies three main types. The first is causation guilt, which sees parents attributing the birth of their child to their own actions as they search for 'the cause', often erroneously putting the blame on some imagined defect that may have no basis in fact. The second type, parental role guilt, typically takes the form of a deeply held belief that they have not met the societal expectation of a good parent and, as a result, are responsible for their child's developmental problems. The final type is moral guilt.

Here the parents may believe that they are being punished for transgressing some moral or religious standard by the birth of a child with Down syndrome.

While it is difficult to generalize, it appears that many families typically experience grief for two to three years although for some grieving is a life-long state, with particular associations (seeing the hospital where the child was born, or the doctor who attended) or anniversaries (such as the child's birthday or the couple's wedding anniversary) triggering the grief response (Powers, 1993). As Powers (ibid., p. 135) observes: 'some people have extraordinary difficulty assimilating their losses', and grief may become dysfunctional, impairing parental functioning and well-being, resulting in feelings of despair, apathy and hopelessness.

The alternative is coping that signifies adjustment to the reality of life with a child with Down syndrome, a return to equilibrium and the restoration of hope. It is the ability to sustain, or at least regain, hope that is so important in surviving the life crisis of the birth of a child with Down syndrome (ibid.). For many families the path to adjustment may involve learning to cope with the unexpected stressful situations that life with a child with Down syndrome may present.

While some researchers have concluded that there is no significant difference in the stress levels of families where there is a child with a disability, and families generally (Salisbury, 1987), others point to the debilitating effects of disturbed sleep, poor health (Dupont, 1988), psychiatric problems (Gath and Gumley, 1986), greater caretaking burden (Cunningham and Glenn, 1985), reduced time for self (Erickson and Upshur, 1989), restriction of leisure (Cunningham and Glenn, 1985), social isolation (Chetwynd *et al.*, 1986), and constraints on parental roles (Krauss, 1993; Waddington and Busch-Rossnagel, 1992) that may be experienced by such families, most particularly by mothers (Bright and Wright, 1985; Singhi, 1990). Mothers also report greater fluctuations than fathers in their moods and their feelings concerning having a child with Down syndrome (Damrosch and Perry, 1989). Fathers, however, appear to experience more stress related to difficulties in their attachment relationship with the child with a disability and their stress seems to be strongly related to the child's temperament and rewardingness (Krauss, 1993). Although the mean overall levels of depression have been shown to be not significantly different from the norms for the general population, there is considerable individual variation in lability of mood, for both groups (Gowen *et al.*, 1989). Parental stress, however, may show considerable stability over time (Dyson, 1993). Interestingly, this finding applied both to the families with a child with Down syndrome and to comparison families from the general population. Finally, added these factors is the often considerable financial burden to be borne by families (Burden and Thomas, 1986; Chetwynd, 1985; Chetwynd *et al.*, 1986).

Apart from the emotional impact, the birth of a child with Down syndrome may also lead the family to make major changes in their living situation and work. One of the earliest studies of families and disability was undertaken in what is now the Schonell Centre by Schonell and Watts (1956). They found that 28 per cent of families had been forced to relocate as a result of their disabled child, that fathers' work decisions had been affected, and that many reported a deterioration in the quality of family life.

Social isolation and the pressures of family life, out of synchrony with the normative stages of the family life cycle, may adversely affect health and well-being. Parents of children with disabilities may be at greater risk for stress-related illnesses and psychological problems such as chronic anxiety (Turnbull and Turnbull, 1986). Relationship breakdown may also result from the stresses placed on the family by the presence of the child with Down syndrome, although whether this occurs to a greater extent than in the general population has been a subject of contention among researchers (Gallagher and Bristol, 1989). For some time it has been asserted that the rate of divorce is higher in families with a child with a disability (Turnbull and Turnbull, 1986). In contrast, Gath (1978) found that the rate of divorce in her sample of families where there is a child with Down syndrome was half the rate expected for the general population. Limitations in current research and a lack of comparability, however, make a clear conclusion on the risk of family breakdown difficult at this time (Gath and Gumley, 1984, 1986). Further, the risk may be related to the presence of several factors in addition to the impact of disability, *per se*. For example, the strength of the marriage prior to the birth of the child seems to be a key factor in the risk of marital breakdown (Darling, 1987) and the risk of breakdown may be greater in the years immediately following the birth of the child than later (Gath, 1985b). After reviewing the current literature, Gallagher and Bristol (1989, p. 300) concluded that many factors may influence the couple's risk of a relationship breakdown

> it does appear that marital breakdown may be more likely to occur in families which were experiencing personal or financial difficulties before the birth of the child . . . in those in which the child was conceived premaritally . . . , in those in which the care of a defective child is not a shared value, or in those in which the demands of the handicapped child outstrip the available resources of the family and the services found in the community.

Beyond the impact on their relationship, the possible impact on the child's siblings may be another source of stress and anxiety for parents (Cuskelly, Chapter 23 in this volume). The manner in which other family members react to the birth of the child also may influence parental stress and coping. It is not uncommon for some members of one side of the extended family to blame the other, arguing that it must have been the mother's (or father's) 'fault' because there has never been a child with such a condition on their side. The fact that, in the majority of cases of Down syndrome, there is no inherited cause escapes them. Managing these family reactions may become an added source of stress for the family.

In the 40 years that separate the pioneering work of Schonell and his co-workers from recent research on the impact of disability on family life, the focus has shifted to the exploration of the social processes in families with handicapped children. Recent work at the Schonell Centre (Cuskelly and Gunn, 1993; Hayes, 1994; Hayes *et al.*, 1987), for example, has investigated some of the variations in social processes in families with a child with a disability. These have been related to differences in family structural variables, such as the position of the child with a disability in the family (first or later born) and the developmental spacing between children and their siblings (Hayes, 1994; Senapati and Hayes, 1988). To date, however, comparatively little attention has been paid to the systematic exploration of the linkages between families and their communities.

Several factors influence family reactions to their child with a disability. Turnbull and Turnbull (1986) describe three main sets of factors: first, the disability and its characteristics; second, the characteristics of the family; and third, the balance of individual problems and resources to cope (i.e. the balance of vulnerability and coping).

The disability and its characteristics

The specific condition

The specific condition the child has may influence the impact on the family, although the picture is far from clear. Comparisons of measures of parents stress and family functioning showed no differences between families with a child with Down syndrome, hearing impairment or developmental disability of unknown aetiology (Krauss, 1993), however, a comparison of stress levels in families where there is a child with Down syndrome or autism found significantly higher levels for the autistic group (Donovan, 1988).

Severity of the disability and its associated problems

The severity of the problem and the extent of dependency of the child with a disability may be related. The families of children with severe disabilities may need to provide extensive care for a much longer time than would normally be the case. The relationship between degree of severity and family stress levels and functioning again is not a simple one.

The severity of the disability may not have a strong relationship to family reactions and outcomes (Gath and Gumley, 1986; Krauss, 1993; Van Riper *et al.*, 1992). Byrne and Cunningham (1984, p. 849), in reviewing the research literature stated that 'in most studies, the severity and nature of the child's intellectual as opposed to physical impairments or behaviour problems are unrelated to reported levels of stress'. Adaptive behaviour, rather than overall level of severity of the disability, may bear a stronger relationship than degree of severity of intellectual disability to the stress experienced, particularly by mothers of young children (Hanson and Hanline, 1990). Finally, temperamental characteristics and the level of behavioural problems also seem to have a stronger influence on family stress levels than the degree of severity of the intellectual disability, *per se* (Beckman, 1983).

There is some evidence that professionals may perceive the impact of the presence of a child with a disability more negatively than parents, perhaps explaining why so much of the early work in this area focused on family pathology (Blackard and Barsh, 1982). Parental perceptions of their child may differ depending on the particular condition involved. As one would expect, a comparison of mothers' perceptions of their child with Down syndrome or motor impairment showed that the former group were particularly concerned about their child's communicational competence, the latter about motor proficiency, and that these concerns seemed to persist throughout the child's life (Hodapp *et al.*, 1992). The parents' perceptions of their child may also influence their behaviour, with parents of children with Down syndrome engaging in more direct teaching and behaviour management than parents of children without developmental problems (Stoneman *et al.*, 1983).

In addition, the behavioural problems of some children with disabilities may be a continuing source of stress for families. The behavioural problems often highlight the difficulties that parents have when interacting with their child, whose behaviour may be difficult to manage and may be seen as unrewarding (Pearl, 1993). In part, the problem may be related to the difficulty that parents (and professionals) have in coming to terms with the fact that what the children are doing is appropriate for their developmental age. It is a natural tendency to compare, however, and to expect the behaviours that are typical of the chronological, rather than the developmental, age. The extent to which each child with Down syndrome is out of synchrony with 'typical' children of that age may be difficult to grasp.

Age of the child with Down syndrome

The age of the child has been seen as an important determinant of family stress, with stress increasing as the child gets older (Gallagher *et al.*, 1983). In infancy and early childhood, the child with Down syndrome may be less rewarding for the parents because of limited responsiveness, or alternatively because of irritability and lack of routine (Beckman, 1983; Krauss, 1993). Older children, particularly those with physical or multiple disabilities may still require considerable assistance with feeding, toiletting, bathing and lifting in and out of bed or a wheelchair (Turnbull and Turnbull, 1986).

The stage of family life, however, may be more important than simply the age of the child, with transitions occurring on the initial diagnosis, or when parents recognize the faster developmental rate of younger siblings of the child with Down syndrome, or on entry to school, or at puberty, or when residential or other adult life issues become central (Cunningham and Glenn, 1985). Many of the problems encountered by families may also reflect the mismatch between the life cycle in families with a child with a disability and the community 'norms'. The gap may become particularly marked when in adulthood the person with a disability continues to produce behaviours that are usually associated with childhood, such as tantrums or aggressive outbursts. In later life, elderly parents may find that they lack the personal and physical resources to cope with these problems. Their situation may be exacerbated by the lack of residential placements options.

Early versus late detection

Down syndrome is an exception among disabling conditions in that it can be diagnosed so early in life, with great accuracy (Cooley and Moeschler, 1993). For most other conditions that result in developmental delay or intellectual disability the process of identification is more protracted and there may be no specific diagnosis available. It is easy to assume that conditions, such as Down syndrome, that are identifiable early in life might be more difficult for families to accept, as so soon after birth parents are confronted with the fact that their child is so different from the one they expected, in appearance and behaviour (Pearl, 1993). Some children with Down syndrome may provide less rewards for parental efforts in the areas of care, communication and social interaction (ibid., 1993). All these reactions are intertwined with the already emotionally charged period following the birth. It is little wonder that the period immediately following the birth of a child with Down syndrome is so difficult for many parents.

With prenatal diagnosis increasingly available (Cooley and Graham, 1991; Selikowitz, 1990) the impact of the news that their child has Down syndrome may occur before birth. There is little consideration of the longer-term psychological effects of prenatal diagnosis, particularly for those who elect to terminate the pregnancy.

But the issues surrounding early identification are not simple. When and how parents are told seems to be of crucial importance in influencing parental reactions (Burden, 1991). A study comparing the reactions of mothers of young children with Down syndrome, hearing impairment or neurological disorders indicated that there were more concerns related to the mother's perception of the social acceptability of a child with Down syndrome than for the other two groups (Hanson and Hanline, 1990). The initial trauma experienced by parents on being informed of their child's condition may become an enduring source of problems (Gath, 1985b; Stone, 1973). The availability of appropriate supports, as soon as possible after the birth, is to be recommended (Burden, 1991). Studies of parents who adopt a child with a disability provide further insight into the trauma of being informed that one's child has Down syndrome. Glidden (1991) and Glidden and Pursley (1989) have found that parents who adopt a child with a disability, such as Down syndrome, show more positive adjustment than biological parents, and continue to do so, over time. Again, however, early reactions seem to have a strong relationship with later outcomes (such as whether the parents elect to keep the adopted child) (Glidden, 1991).

The early identification of the disability and its visibility may mean that the family has less difficulty in gaining access to supportive services than families in which the child's disability is less easily identified (McNaught, 1988). Some evidence for this is provided by Krauss (1993) in a study comparing three groups of mothers with children with Down syndrome, or motor impairment or developmental disability of unknown aetiology. She found that the mothers of Down syndrome children reported higher satisfaction with the services provided to their child and family. Hanson and Hanline (1990) report a similar result.

In summary, the degree to which the presence of a child with a disability influences key family decisions remains unclear, and is likely to depend on several mediating factors such as the type of condition; the severity of the disability; the degree of behavioural disturbance; the extensiveness of each child's needs; the time of diagnosis; how parents are informed; the ages of that child and any siblings; and the stage of family life. None of these factors in isolation seems to be simply linked to the impact of Down syndrome on families. In part, this reflects the fact that it is not just a matter of the factors related to the child, but of equal importance are the characteristics of the family.

Family characteristics

Family form

In any family, size, form (nuclear, single parent or blended) and cultural background may have an influence on the impact of life events. With regard to the impact of disability, in larger families the siblings seem to be better adjusted, provided the family has adequate financial resources (McHale *et al.*, 1984; Powell and Ogle, 1985). While the precise explanation for this finding is not clear, it may reflect the ability of larger families to distribute the load across a larger number of persons. In the case of Down syndrome, if the child is one of the younger members of the family, parents and older siblings may be more experienced in caring for children.

Single parent families may experience more stress (Flynt and Ward, 1989; Salisbury, 1987) and have greater difficulty in coping than intact families (Beckman, 1983). Gallagher and Bristol (1989), however, caution that there has been little systematic research to support this conclusion. Again, it is most likely that there will be considerable variation across single parent families, both in the type and number of problems encountered and in their resources to cope.

The presence and involvement of fathers in caring for their child with a disability also seems to reduce the impact on the family (Turnbull and Turnbull, 1986) although this conclusion must be accepted with caution, given the limited research involving fathers (Pearl, 1993). Bristol and Gallagher (1986, p. 95) concluded that 'The limited data presently available suggest that two of the father's most critical roles may be supplying support to the child's mother and communicating to the family that their burden of care is worthwhile'.

One interesting finding is that in families with a child with Down syndrome, both parents tended to interact less with the child when the other parent was present, although the reduction in the father's level of interaction was greater than the reduction in the mother's in the father's presence (Stoneman *et al.*, 1983). While the limited research base has produced some interesting results, an accurate picture of the role of the father in families with a child with a disability must await further research (Bristol and Gallagher, 1986).

Ethnicity and cultural characteristics

Ethnicity and cultural background influence a family's daily life and value systems and are reflected in the beliefs parents hold about their role in the development of their children (e.g., Frey *et al.*, 1989; Goodnow, 1988; Turnbull and Turnbull, 1986). Professionals from the majority culture may need to be especially sensitive to the differences in values, customs and practices of families from a minority group background (Turnbull and Turnbull, 1986). One study has found that Afro-American mothers of children with moderate intellectual disability reported less stress than their Anglo-American peers (Flynt and Wood, 1989).

Socio-economic status (SES) also may influence family reactions to their child with a disability, although again the relationship is complex. For example, it cannot be assumed that the family from an upper SES background is automatically better equipped to cope with a child with a disability than the family of lower SES. Once again, the picture is not that simple. Farber and Ryckman (1965) highlighted the fact that upper SES families with a strong orientation to achievement may suffer what they labelled a 'tragic crisis' when their aspirations for their child are dashed by the news of the child's disability. In support of this conclusion, it has been found that parents from higher socio-economic groups were more likely to reject a child with Down syndrome than those from less advantaged groups (Shepperdson, 1985). At the other end of the spectrum, low SES families may be so beset with problems and have such limited resources to overcome their difficulties that it becomes extremely difficult to cope with the additional demands of a child with a disability (Meyer-Probst *et al.*, 1983; Sameroff and Seifer, 1983; Werner and Smith, 1982).

In addition, factors such as parental educational levels (Coon *et al.*, 1992), the number of children in the family (Fisman and Wolf, 1991), the health of the family members (Horwitz and Kazak, 1990) and the behavioural problems of the siblings of the child with Down syndrome (Cuskelly and Dadds, 1992) may be continuing sources of stress for some families, and mediate family functioning and developmental outcomes.

Family characteristics as mediating and moderating variables

Several mediating factors may have a particular impact on families and their levels of stress and ability to cope, although the recent comprehensive review by Beresford (1994) found the results to be equivocal. Not all families will be vulnerable and many will prove themselves remarkably resilient (Cunningham and Glenn, 1985). Gath (1985a) found that half the parents in her study were very positive about their family life. Similarly, Gath and Gumley (1984, p. 506) reported finding considerable evidence of 'fun and enjoyable family life'. Singer *et al.*, (1993, p. 69) go further, concluding in their review of the literature on stress and coping that 'a majority of parents of children with disabilities are [*sic*] not demoralized'. This echoes Byrne and Cunningham's (1985, p. 852) conclusion that 'stress is not an inevitable consequence for families'. Further, families that cope successfully seem to be characterized by addressing the range of tasks that families generally undertake (Singer and Powers, 1993). As Singer *et al.* (1993, p. 69) conclude, 'parents learn from their experiences and form normal bonds of love and enjoyment with their children. However, this positive acceptance does not exempt parents from a variety of everyday stressors that are often experienced when their child has a disability'.

Vulnerability and coping: The balance of family problems and resources

The balance of stress and problems, on the one hand, and fulfilment and fun, on the other, depends on each family's resources to cope and the supports available to them. In turn, these resources are also dependent upon the extent of other pressures on the family. Gallagher and Bristol (1989) cite four major crisis periods for families. These include the time when the parents are first informed of the child's disability, when the family first comes in contact with the service delivery system, when the child makes a transition to living away from home and when the parents realize that they are too old to care for their child. Gallagher and Bristol (1989) conclude that developmental delay or intellectual disability may place the family out of synchrony with the normative sequences of family life stages, and this may make interaction with other families with children of a similar age very difficult, leading to feelings of social isolation.

Factors contributing to resilience

Resilience, the obverse of vulnerability, depends on both the individuals' coping resources and the supports provided by those around them. Availability of supports outside the family appear to be very important in ameliorating the stress experienced by parents (Shapiro, 1989). Clearly, the tasks of parents of a child may be made much more difficult when supports are limited or not available (Hornby and Seligman, 1991). Kazak (1987) found that many mothers coped by having larger social networks outside the family than mothers in a comparison group for the general population, complementing the supports available from their immediate family. Seltzer and Krauss (1989), however, found that rather than social support, the overall family climate was a better predictor of maternal well-being.

The extent to which families can 'retain a sense of control over their households despite the need for intrusive involvements with a variety of professionals' (Singer and Powers, 1993, p. 11) is referred to as maintenance of family boundaries, and is an asset for coping. Enmeshed, insular families may have greater levels of problems and show less resilience. Resilience also seems to be related to the communication skills that family members possess, their capacity to be flexible, their degree of commitment to maintaining the family unit, their problem-solving abilities, the extent to which they maintain their social networks and develop sound working relationships with professionals (Singer and Powers, 1993). Powers (1993) concluded that the members of families that cope effectively demonstrate an ability to respond both to their family's and their own needs. Structured programmes can increase the range of coping skills that families have in areas such as monitoring and identifying stressors, using relaxation techniques, problem-solving and addressing counter-productive modes of thought (such as pessimism, negativity and inappropriate attributions, such as self-blame or guilt) (Singer *et al.*, 1993).

Variation in the impact of Down syndrome on families

The literature reviewed in the above three subsections shows that the effects of disability are complexly determined by multiple factors. The characteristics of child, family and their supports, as well as the personal resources of family members to cope all mediate and/or moderate the impact of the presence of a child with Down syndrome. This approach is anchored in systems theory, with its emphasis on the scope for change in systems and the potentially mutual influence of all elements in the system and its context. The dynamic relationship of vulnerability and coping is best understood in terms of the tendency for living systems, such as families, to return to a stable state (or homeostasis, to use the technical term) (Pearl, 1993).

> Some amount of disequilibrium is conducive for adjustment, and may be healthy in the face of a major change in the family system, such as the diagnosis of developmental delays in a young child. The best outcome from a systems theory perspective is that the family will experience some disequilibrium, leading to problem solving in areas of concern, while still maintaining homeostasis in routines. Many of the situations that families with a young delayed child must face are new to them. Sometimes old coping styles may not be effective.
>
> (ibid., p. 85)

SUPPORT FOR FAMILIES

Faced with the complex and diverse needs of all members, as discussed above, professionals are increasingly involved in the development and implementation of a range of family-centred services (Pearl, 1993; Thurman, 1993). Responsibility for meeting the needs of parents, as well as their children, may be difficult for many specialists to accept, but is another example of the need to move beyond 'treating' the child to supporting the family as a unit (Stone, 1973). There is still a gulf, however, between the supports advocated for families and those actually received, and many parents feel that professionals are not sufficiently sensitive to parental needs (Baxter, 1987).

The need for services offering multiple supports

Families of children may require several types of support across the years following the identification of their child's disability. These may include the following factors identified by Cunningham and Glenn (1985): assistance in coping with their emotions and handling the reactions of family and friends, provision of information about the child's disability and life prospects, advice on the services and benefits available, and help in facilitating their child's development and managing behaviour problems.

For some, the most important need may be to meet other families who have experienced the birth of a child similar to their own. Others may want to come to terms with the situation in the privacy of the immediate family. Still others may see provision of practical assistance such as home help, respite care or transport as their most essential or immediate needs.

Numerous programmes and services have been developed and implemented by government and voluntary agencies to assist and support families in which there is a child with Down syndrome. Some programmes focus on meeting the parents needs, while others focus on the siblings and others on the family as a unit. The Pilot Parents' Scheme is one approach that is used by associations for the families of children with Down syndrome (Hayes, 1984). In this scheme, a parent of a child with Down syndrome makes contact with another family soon after the birth of their child and acts as a resource for information about their day-to-day experience and as a source of emotional support. A similar approach is the Parent-to-Parent programme (Pearl, 1993; Santelli *et al.*, 1993).

Another service that is extensively used is a play group (Hayes, 1994). Play groups are an informal setting for parents to meet and discuss issues of common concern and for professionals to make contact with each child and family to familiarize them with the available services. As such, the play group may provide a useful transition from the home to involvement in a more formal intervention programme. Irrespective of the specific type of support to be provided, the provision of supportive social networks for families is an increasing priority in services for children with disabilities (Guralnick, 1988).

Respite care

The availability of respite care has been identified as one of the most requested areas of service in the field of disability (Singer *et al.*, 1993). A survey by Marc and McDonald (1988) found that respite care was more likely to be used by larger families, with higher levels of involvement with professional support services, and with children who had more severe disabilities and/or behavioural problems. Again, one of the key moderator variables appears to be the presence of behaviour problems. Access to respite care enables parents to gain access to recreation time, devote time to the other children in the family, and to reduce their stress and facilitate coping, particularly when their child requires considerable care or is difficult to manage. A study by Harris and McHale (1989) found that the greater the time spent with their child with an intellectual disability the higher the level of maternal depression. But respite care may not be a panacea. As Bowman and Virtue (1993, p. 10) observed, 'respite care might be likened to an intermission; in isolation, it does nothing to alleviate the ongoing stress of caring'.

Advocacy

Another way in which professionals can provide support is as advocates for families with a child with Down syndrome (Thurman, 1993). Families vary in the extent to which they feel comfortable interacting with professionals and service systems. A professional 'ally' can lobby for the services appropriate to their needs. Organizations such as the Down Syndrome Associations also play a vital role in advocacy and may do much to provide parents with the strategies required to present their case and communicate their needs more effectively. This may start with developing a deeper understanding of the professionals and the service systems within which they work and then formulating strategies for addressing some of the issues that may impede access to the required service (Shields, 1987).

Emotional support

But it should not only be a matter of parent support and provision of information. Professionals need training to be sensitive to the major adjustments that families have to make to the birth of a child with Down syndrome. The anger that many families express may be a very difficult emotion to handle, particularly as it is often manifested as criticism of the unhelpful, uncaring or unsupportive behaviour of professionals. For other families, anger may be difficult to express (Powers, 1993), and it may require considerable skill on the part of professionals to assist them to come to talk about this and their other powerful emotions. It is too easy for professionals to misinterpret the significance of emotions such as anger. Cunnnigham and Glenn (1985, p. 350) put it well:

> Many professionals interpret [parental criticisms of professionals] as an inevitable consequence of parental anger or guilt at having a child with Down's syndrome. But to do so is to use a pathological framework to interpret parental behaviour in much the same way as it was years ago when the child's condition was used to explain the lack of development or bizarre behaviour.

Psychological support services

For some family members, their problems may be sufficiently concerning to warrant more structured intervention. This may be focused on development of coping skills or alternatively, may take the form of cognitive-behavioural, counselling or psychotherapeutic programmes designed to address parents feelings of stress, anger or depression, for example. Using such techniques, families can be assisted to identify unresolved issues, to come to terms with their feelings, to cope at those times when they experience (or re-experience) severe grief, and to recognize personal and family strengths (Powers, 1993).

Cognitive-behavioural therapies

A recent emphasis in the field is on what has been labelled 'cognitive coping'. Turnbull and Turnbull (1993, p. 11) provide the following definition: 'Cognitive coping means thinking about a particular situation in ways that enhance a sense of well-being'. They list several strategies that are used in this mode of coping, including comparing one's situation to that of others in similar circumstances ('compared to others we're not that badly off . . . '), focusing on the positives and choosing to ignore the negatives ('things may be difficult but at least we have a strong relationship/a lot of support/a doctor who really cares/an easy child to manage . . . '), discovering a meaningful and personally enhancing interpretation of their situation ('Sue may have Down syndrome but she can give the world a lot, and that makes us proud to be her parents . . . '), exercising control ('through lobbying we can do a lot to improve the school and get the services John needs . . . ') or, finally, by seeing the humour in situations ('she actually thought that it was possible to catch Down syndrome . . . '). Psychoeducational Instruction (Singer *et al.*, 1993) is an example of an approach based on cognitive-behaviour theory. In this approach, a skills instructor assists parents to acquire and practise new coping skills. More effective coping and reduction in stress may also be an outcome of approaches that focus on imparting skills of child behaviour management to parents. These include STEP (Systematic Training in Effective Parenting) and PET (Parent Effectiveness Training) programmes (Cunningham, 1985), and Behavioural Parent Training (Singer *et al.*, 1993).

Counselling

A second type of specialist support is counselling, which can be focused on information provision, assistance with decision-making or provision of therapy. The issues addressed in counselling will vary, depending on the time at which the counsellors meet any family, for example, at or after diagnosis (Cooley and Moeschler, 1993). Any counselling intervention should start from the family's present concerns and counsellors should be careful not to presume what information is appropriate for a given family to hear at any stage. Like other intervention techniques, supportive counselling is often needed at key transition points in the life of families, such as on provision of a diagnosis, on entry to school, or on leaving home (Thurman, 1993). The timing of provision of information is important, and requires sensitivity to parents' needs. Having said that, it is equally important that information is presented in a manner that enables parents to understand and use it, that information overload is avoided and that professionals are sensitive to the feelings and perceptions of their clients, at that time (Trout and Foley, 1989). It also requires considerable skill in conveying technical information, for example, in a manner that makes it accessible to parents, who often report anger at being given information, but in a manner that made no sense to them or was not what they needed at that particular time (ibid., 1989).

Psychotherapy and psychiatric services

There is a range of specialist psychotherapeutic and psychopharmacological interventions to enable parents to address severe problems, such as anxiety or depression. It is beyond the scope of this chapter to describe these in detail, however, referral to such services is a matter that should be handled carefully. As argued above, the research on stress and coping clearly indicates that professionals should not presume that because a family has a child with Down syndrome there will necessarily be psychological problems requiring therapeutic intervention. It is not appropriate to assume that a family experiencing grief, anxiety or anger is pathological. Further, if pathology is present it is equally inappropriate to assume that it is caused by the presence of the child with Down syndrome. Its origins may lie elsewhere. Clearly professionals should not attempt to force psychotherapy on families (Trout and Foley, 1989) but should provide access to these services when family members recognize the dysfunctional and debilitating effects of personal problems (Powers, 1993).

Support for parental relationships

Another area in which support may be needed is in addressing any difficulties the parents have in their relationship following the birth of their child with Down syndrome. Again, many difficulties may respond well to the supportive involvement of family and friends, or non-specialist professionals, such as general practitioners, psychologists or social workers, but others may require the involvement of specialist supports. It has been reported that Behavioural Marital Therapy can be used to good effect in improving the quality of the relationship between the partners (Lichtenstein, 1993).

Family-centred approaches

The movement for family support and empowerment that has emerged in recent years in the USA has focused attention on the importance of identifying the needs of each family and providing supports that are appropriate to that family, that is a family-centred approach (Thurman, 1993). As Dunst and Trivette (1990, p. 345) argue:

> It is not just a matter of whether needs are met but rather the manner in which mobilization of resources and support occurs that is a major determinant of enabling and empowering families. To be both enabling and empowering in a way that promotes a family's capabilities and competencies, the family must be actively involved in the process of identifying and mobilizing resources . . .

The key element of this approach is to provide the supports that families identify as needed to increase their resilience and prevent problems becoming entrenched (Singer and Powers, 1993). In so doing, it seeks to strengthen the competence of family members in handling the situations and issues that arise in daily life (Pearl, 1993). Mobilization of community resources is a key element. To do this, professionals may need to be skilled at identifying these resources and in encouraging community participation in support programmes (Singer *et al.*, 1993).

The appeal of alternative, 'unconventional' treatments

It is easy to understand the appeal of alternative, unconventional treatments. When confronted by a disease or disorder that cannot be cured, it is understandable that people grasp any other option, even if of unproven efficacy, and not without risk. One of my parents' early recollections is of hearing the stories following the First World War of alternative, or to use their word 'quack', treatments for the soldiers who had been so massively maimed. These included immersion in animal urine or coating mustard gas victims in lettuce leaves, among others.

Over the years, the advocates of a wide range of unconventional therapies have promised dramatic improvement in the development, growth and well-being of persons with Down syndrome. Among these approaches Pueschel (1992) lists treatments involving pituitary extract, glutamic acid, thyroid hormone, 5-hydroxytrypophan, dimethyl sulfoxide, sicca cells, as well as a range of vitamin, mineral, hormone and enzyme therapies. Several general conclusions emerge from reviews of the evidence for the efficacy of these treatments. First, parents and professionals concerned with each treatment typically report very positive effects on the development of children with Down syndrome, following the treatment (see for example the reviews by Cooley and Graham, 1991). Second, the evidence for efficacy is often anecdotal or based on studies with major design and/or methodological flaws. Third, controlled studies usually have not supported the original claims. Finally, most of the treatments are not without significant risk, and yet adherents to these treatments appear to overlook the possibility that involvement in the treatment may have deleterious effects.

With regard to efficacy, several reviews have focused on the range of mega-vitamin therapies (e.g. Bidder *et al.*, 1989; Cooley and Graham, 1991; Foreman and Ward, 1986; Kozlowski, 1992; Pruess *et al.*, 1989; Pueschel, 1992). All report that there is no evidence from controlled trials to support the claimed gains on developmental measures. The study by Bidder *et al.* (1989), for example, found that children with Down syndrome who received a placebo actually made greater gains than those who were given a vitamin and mineral supplement for a period of three months. Children in the vitamin supplementation group showed frequent disturbing side effects (such as sleeplessness, flushing and changes in skin texture. Foreman and Ward (1986) point to the possible neurotoxic effects of megavitamin therapy and express concern that the doses prescribed are often 2,000 times the recommended daily intake.

Sicca cell therapy, involving the injection of dried cells from foetal lambs, in conjunction with vitamin mineral and enzyme supplementation, and educational and developmental interventions, has been advocated enthusiastically as a means of enhancing the growth, learning abilities and general development of persons with Down syndrome. Again, reviews of controlled trials fail to support these claims and warn of the potentially deleterious side-effects, such as allergic or anaphylactic reactions and the possibility of transmission of slow viruses (Foreman and Ward, 1986; Pueschel, 1992).

The Doman-Delacato Program is another approach that has attracted wide-spread interest among parents of children with Down syndrome. It involves intensive periods of motor patterning to re-establish the lower-level functions of the brain, in order for the higher level functions that are missing to be acquired (Zigler and Hoddap, 1986). Again, the consensus is that the claims of efficacy are unproven 'and the demands on families may be so great that harm could result from its use' (Foreman and Ward, 1986, p. 16).

Other treatments, such as facial plastic surgery have been widely advocated but, again, their efficacy remains to be established (Pueschel, 1992). There are important questions as to whether the pain and discomfort of the procedure are warranted and for whose benefit the procedure is undertaken (child, parent or the society at large?) (ibid.). Spinal manipulation also is often recommended, but again the efficacy has not been satisfactorily demonstrated and the risk of damage, particularly for those children with atlantoaxial instability, is a real concern (Selikowitz, 1990).

For some families, involvement in alternative programmes unites the parents and gives a sense of hope. The balance, however is a sensitive one as the search for a 'cure' may also perpetuate denial (Eden-Piercy *et al.*, 1986). For professionals, the issue of unconventional therapies may be a source of considerable concern. On the one hand, they have a responsibility to respond to parental questions about efficacy honestly. On the other, they have to realize that the appeal of such treatments is very powerful, especially as current approaches to treatment of Down syndrome do not offer the promise of a cure that the advocates of alternative approaches typically claim.

FAMILY INVOLVEMENT IN INTERVENTION

The benefits of family involvement

Families increasingly are seen as the focus of the intervention effort, and are often referred to as partners in the intervention (Dunst and Trivette, 1990). There are many sound reasons for involving families. The intervention can be delivered throughout the children's time at home, and in a context that is often more comfortable and secure for them. Cunningham (1985) suggests that parent involvement may be an economical and efficient way to deliver services, with increased chance of generalization of the skills and behaviours gained, as well as increased effectiveness given the greater opportunities parents have to influence their child, in a wide range of everyday situations. Skills can be transferred more extensively throughout the community to have a greater impact (ibid.). It has the further advantage of shifting the parental role from one of patient to that of active partner in the intervention effort with recognition of their rights to be involved in the key decisions about their child's life. For parents, involvement in intervention may require learning the skills required to communicate with professionals, to act as the advocate for their child and to take on the role of intervener. Parents, in turn, can act to train other parents (Rodger, 1986). Preparation of parents to assist in intervention can be either through individual or group training sessions. Group sessions may offer opportunities for greater social contact and vicarious learning, but individual training, while more expensive, may address each parent's individual concerns, needs or skill development areas (Cunningham, 1985). Group training may also offer an opportunity to compare life experiences with others who face similar circumstances, and this can play a valuable part in reducing self-blame as well as overcoming some of the feelings of isolation often reported by parents (Nixon, 1993). For the professionals involved, specialized skills may be required beyond those traditionally associated with their profession.

The cost of family involvement

Stimulated by the new legislation (PL 99–457) in the USA, parent support and involvement now are key features of the intervention programmes for the disabled. While training parents to be 'teachers' is a common approach it is not without its problems. The cost may be alteration of the interaction between parents and children with unanticipated negative consequences for their relationship (McConachie, 1991). Just as play can lose its enjoyment for children if too highly formalized, family life can become strained if the 'teaching role' detracts from the 'parent role' and may impede the development of appropriate parent–child relationships. Additionally, professionals may focus too narrowly on training parents to be their child's teacher and overlook the family's emotional needs (Guralnick, 1988; Honig, 1985). Furthermore, parents may not be comfortable with the role of teacher. Alternatively, they may be unable to take on the added responsibility of the teaching role, either because of the pressures of factors outside the home, at work or in the extended family, or as a result of circumstances within the family at the time. Finally, there is a danger that the demands of the teaching role may actually de-sensitize parents to their child's current interests, as they slavishly try to follow the home programmes. Wright *et al.* (1984, p. 63) put it succinctly:

> Parents who become successful teachers may have done so at the cost of becoming less of a parent. An additional cost may be a change in the structure of a family system or its overall functioning. By focusing on the parent as a teacher, professionals influence the parent–child interaction and may change the source of pleasure for parents of handicapped children.

Cunningham and Glenn (1985, p. 359) have highlighted the problems which may flow from parental responsibility for programme delivery: 'We need to move away from the notion of parents as trainers of the child and as extensions of the therapist, towards a model of a consumer partnership in which parents are active participants exercising control over the nature of the partnership'.

Parent involvement should not represent an abrogation of professional responsibility nor should it become a factor that overloads families and adds to their stress (Rodger, 1986). Partnerships of parents and professionals can have bidirectional influences, not only providing better supportive services to parents, but changing the ways in which professionals perceive these services and their delivery (Lucyshyn and Albin, 1993).

In other words, for many parents, sensitivity and emotional security may be much more important factors in their child's early development than provision of elaborate intervention programs. As McConachie (1991, p. 134) urged 'what we ask parents in helping their children must make sense in terms of their individual goals, energies and philosophy'. This the essence of a family centred approach. It should put the family first (Rodger, 1986).

COMMUNITY CONNECTIONS: CARING AND WORKING

Throughout the western world, there has been a dramatic increase in the rate of participation of women with dependent children in the workforce (Etzioni, 1993). These changes in participation, together with other recent societal changes, have had an impact on how households function and define parental roles (Goodnow and Bowes, 1994; Maas, 1990).

Although there is a relative lack of empirical work related to the nexus between the parenting and employment decisions in families where there is a child with Down syndrome, there is an extensive literature on the parenting, child care, and work decisions of families in the wider community. For example, Hock *et al.* (1988) have drawn attention to the complex relationships among parent–child attachment and decisions about employment and substitute care. DeMeis *et al.* (1986) had found that mothers who returned to paid employment showed an earlier decline in separation anxiety than mothers who delayed their return. In addition, their previous history of employment has been found to be more strongly associated with women's decisions to return to the workforce than their expressed beliefs about parenting and work or their family characteristics (Avioli and Kaplan, 1992). Gordon and Kammeyer (1980, p. 327) concluded, however, that economic need is 'the most prominent influence' on mother's decisions to return to the workforce.

Whatever the reasons for choosing to re-enter the paid workforce, or not, parental employment decisions have personal, family, and social ramifications that may require extensive accommodation. The decision is likely to reflect a dynamic interplay of factors specific to each family and community. This is the feature of particular heuristic value in Gallimore *et al.* (1993) concept of accommodation.

The adjustments that families must make are complex. For women who elect to work, they are faced with balancing the multiple competing demands on their time, and this may take considerable skill in accommodating to the various needs that they feel must be met Powell and Mainiero, 1992). Having a child with Down syndrome may add yet another set of factors to the already complex equation.

In this society, parenting and employment, and the accommodations they require, represent central issues for families. The burden of child care still falls heavily on women and is a major issue for them in making the decision to re-enter the workforce, or not (Maas, 1990). It is now more widely recognized, however, that the community needs to provide the supports to enable women to exercise their right to pursue a career, while also contributing to the rearing of children. The decision as to whether the mother will return to the workforce may be a particularly difficult one (Gallagher and Bristol, 1989). Community policies for de-institutionalization of children with disabilities, and the consequential press for family care, however, may have made it more difficult for these families to exercise the choices available to their peers (Bright and Wright, 1985). There is, however, some evidence that mothers of children with disabilities who re-enter the workforce show lower levels of depression than those who elect to stay at home and, in turn, there is a relationship between maternal depression and the level of behavioural problems of their child (Walker *et al.*, 1989). As Barling has shown, work and family life are interdependent and have a complex influence on parental well-being (Barling, 1990).

In families with a child with a disability, such as Down syndrome, both parents may be forced to adjust their contributions to care-giving, employment plans and other aspects of life to accommodate the particular needs of their child with a disability. The press for de-institutionalization and family care also may have led to a need for greater community support and understanding of parents of children with a disability, such as Down syndrome. How communities provide and organize work, child care and schools has an impact both on work and family life (Voydanoff, 1989). The availability of parental leave, flexibility in working hours, availability of long day care, and after-school care are all important in making it possible for parents to balance their work and family responsibilities. For those with a child with Down syndrome this balance may be much more difficult to achieve.

IMPLICATIONS

Implications for the study of families and the development of their members

As has been argued, the first and foremost implication of contemporary under-standing of the development of families with children with Down syndrome is that there is a greater need to acknowledge their individuality and to come to terms with the uniqueness of each family's experiences, stresses, coping mechanisms and supports. In the past, people often used the shorthand 'disabled family'. A colleague recounts the experience following the birth of her baby of a well-meaning hospital visitor opening the conversation with the phrase 'now that you are a Down's Mum'. This may be a completely inappropriate label, although it is sometimes applied by parents, as a reflection of their identity. The problem with it is that it uses the presence of the child with Down syndrome to define the family, in its entirety, and this may perpetuate inappropriate stereotyping and labelling. Moreover, it may provide a ready, though inappropriate, explanation for all the problems of the family. To the contrary, the evidence reviewed in this chapter points to the rich diversity of the children, their families and their impact on their families.

A second implication is that the impact of the presence of a child with a disability changes over the family life span and as a function of the other pressures and life events the family encounters. A third implication is that it is not necessarily the child with the disability who may be the most problematic member of the family. For example, many of the problems such families face are like those faced by other families, as children start school or pass through adolescence, or contemplate leaving home and endeavouring to enter the world of work. The problems that a sibling faces may not necessarily be at all related to the presence of a brother or sister with a child with a disability. It is tempting to attribute all the problems in a family to the presence of a child with a disability. Again, however, this may be quite inappropriate. From a practical perspective, it is a 'trap for young players' to no look beyond the easy, and perennial, explanation that the problem occurred because the child happens to be a member of a family with a child with a disability. In many families, the subsystems may vary greatly in the extent to which children are actually directly involved or affected by the person with special needs. Finally, it is important to recognize the other, diverse personal, relational and psychological needs that family members have. Respecting the individual starts with recognition that the person is comparable to yourself in complexity and uniqueness.

Implications for educators

The policies of integration, community living and inclusive education discussed above have profound implications for all members of society, but particularly for educators. Teachers now face pressures to perform a much wider set of roles than in previous generations. Schools now have a much closer relationship with families and teachers are expected to develop the skills required to provide support, not only to students, but also to their families. There may be a danger of these expectations becoming an unrealistic burden for individual teachers to shoulder. In times of economic stringency, some of the support services offered by other professionals, such as counsellors, guidance personnel, social workers and school psychologists may also be stretched to the limit. It is important that the teaching team in a school form effective networks to provide support for children with special needs who are enrolled in regular schools. It is also important that teachers identify the other sources of support available to families in their local communities. Some of these will include counsellors and other professionals in agencies or private practice, church and community groups and service clubs. At times the problem is not lack of available supports, but rather lack of knowledge of some of the resources upon which school personnel can draw. The school–community partnership needs to be just that, a reciprocal, mutually supportive relationship. In addition, teachers need to be aware of the resources available to conduct school-based programmes to support children with special needs and their families.

Along with changes in policy, such as integration and inclusive education, education systems have undergone considerable administrative change across the 1980s. Educational services now tend to be administered regionally, with devolution of greater financial, curriculum and administrative responsibilities to the schools. As Dimmock and Bain (1991) point out, however, there is a risk that children with special needs and their families may receive lower quality services from schools unless policy explicitly (and in legally binding ways) enshrines their rights to receive the particular services required to meet their special needs.

Implications for professional training

Finally, new approaches are needed to training and retraining to equip professionals to work in a family-centred fashion (Trout and Foley, 1989). Professionals are now increasingly called on to deliver parent training and advocacy services (Cunningham, 1985), and such services require that professionals demonstrate particular sensitivity to individual differences in the families they serve (McConachie, 1991). As such, they must be sensitive to the needs, resources and limitations of the families with whom they work and that they value the parent–professional partnership (Walker and Singer, 1993). There is also a need to know more about what makes a good group leader, and how these can be most appropriately trained (Cunningham, 1995). Greater awareness is also needed of the factors that promote coping and how these might be enhanced (Powers, 1993). This requires at least basic training in counselling and a sound awareness of the appropriate procedures for identification of problems and referral to relevant specialist services. Finally, the importance of interagency collaboration and the need for structures for communication should be highlighted in training programmes, given that involvement of multiple professionals, from a range of agencies, is an increasingly common mode of service delivery (Bruder and Bologna, 1993).

SKETCHING THE ELEMENTS OF A NEW APPROACH

It is now possible to summarize the key features of the new approach that is needed to family research and service development in this area. These include the need for:

- a sharper focus on the similarities and differences, both in children and in their families units;
- a more careful consideration of changes which occur over the life cycle of the family;
- a recognition that much of what happens within families is greatly influenced by their community context and the factors that connect them to it.

Exploring the sources of individual differences

With regard to the first implication, future research needs to continue to focus on the sources of the similarities and differences in children, in the structure of their family systems, and in the outcomes of growing up with a handicapped brother or sister. As argued above, families and the members within them do not form a homogeneous group (Byrne and Cunningham, 1985). To reiterate, in studies of people with intellectual disabilities it is, however, often assumed that they are a homogeneous group (Stoneman and Brody, 1982).

In addition, the differences between family subsystems largely have been overlooked. Greater attention also needs to be paid to the interconnections between families and their social networks, such as the extended family, the neighbourhood, school and community (Cochran and Brassard, 1979).

Exploring change across the family's life cycle

Second, there is a need to develop a better understanding of the changing characteristics of children and their families. Instead of focusing only on the effects on family members of life with a person with a disability, researchers need to give greater consideration to the dynamic processes which characterize the interactions and relationships in such families throughout their life cycle.

By providing a more accurate picture of the individuality of families and the dynamic nature of family systems, services can be developed which take account of the diversity of needs, resources and values of their clients. Kaiser and Hemmeter (1989) recently made an eloquent plea for moving beyond simplistic needs assessments, constructed from the professionals' perspective, to the analysis of the match between the needs and the values held by the members of each family.

Research

The approach outlined in this chapter requires a shift in research designs in this area. New designs and methodologies are needed to focus on some of the key linkages between families, and their communities and to explore issues related to child care, parenting and employment decisions, and their impact on life in families with a child with Down syndrome. Clearly, there is a need for a sharper focus on the influences of wider, contextual factors in determining patterns of family functioning and life accommodation, as mediated by those characteristics that are specific to each family.

Most importantly, however, there is a need for research designs that gauge the extent to which patterns of functioning in families where there is a child with Down syndrome are similar to those that are normative in any community, before exploring disability-specific explanations. The key issue is to determine those patterns of functioning that relate to Down syndrome as opposed to those that do not, in order to provide a balanced analysis of the variation and changes in life style that result from the presence of a child with Down syndrome. As such, it should be framed within the conceptual frameworks that have developed in the study of families, more generally, and extend these to the largely unexplored areas of child care, parenting, employment decisions, and life accommodations in families with a child with Down syndrome. Again, in so doing, it represents a movement away from the perspective that the child with the disability is central to all major family decisions, characteristics and outcomes.

Community connections

This chapter has argued the need to recognize the rich diversity of families of people with Down syndrome. While families may be similar in some ways, there are many differences among them. In fact, the differences extend to the experiences of individual members within the same family as a function of their birth order and roles at each point in the life of the family. Their differences, however, also reflect the diversity of the communities in which they live and the range of ways in which families connect to these. In short, future research in this area needs to recognize, explicitly, that much of what happens in families is a product of influences beyond the family. For services, the orientation should be widened to embrace a community perspective, in order to place family needs and resources in an appropriate context.

In writing this chapter I have had a sense of ill ease as to the validity of focusing specifically on families and Down syndrome. As the literature reviewed indicates, there seem to be few issues that can be regarded as specific to families with a child with Down syndrome. The challenge for the future is to move beyond the syndrome and to celebrate the rich diversity of children, their families and the communities within which they now live, in order to acquire the knowledge and to develop the services that are needed to strengthen those that are vulnerable while maintaining those that are resilient.

The brief account that I have provided of my own family's experience of life with my uncle, though only one personal anecdote, illustrates some of the key issues. Clearly, his birth, early fight for life and presence in the family were causes of great concern at the time, and to a varying extent remained so, throughout his life. The decisions concerning his care towards the end of his life become particularly difficult as his ageing siblings became incapable of caring for him, at home. His impact on the family was, however, far from the whole story. He was but one member of a large family and, from the reports of surviving relatives, by no means the most problematic. It seems that one of his older brothers, who had no identifiable disability was, by dint of a wild life style, a much greater worry to the family. It was also very clear that members of our family had very different views of him and of his impact, in part as a function of their differing contact with him. There was so much more to his life than Down syndrome. And there was certainly more than just his impact on the family. It is tempting to recite a litany of the negative impacts, but that would neither be easy nor honest, for what I remember most is all the fun of that small house in the suburbs, with so many people that I knew simply as 'my family'. Yes, I recall discussions about 'what would happen to Arthur' after his sister with whom he lived died, but I also remember the hushed discussions of how his disability pension had helped the family through a difficult period. Most of all, I recall a photograph taken some time in the late 1920s, of the family on holidays, formally posing for the photographer and to one side my uncle, slingshot in hand, wicked grin on his face, taking aim and revelling in life! Whither Down syndrome?

ACKNOWLEDGEMENTS

This chapter was prepared with the assistance of a grant from the Australian Research Council. Several people are to be thanked for their contributions: Mrs Joyce Madden offered invaluable assistance in filling in some of the gaps in my knowledge of family history. Margaret Beckman, Linda Gilmore and Ruth Way assisted in identifying and obtaining some of the relevant literature for the review. Brian Stratford, Pat Gunn and Pam Dix were long suffering as I obsessed over the draft. Karen and Sarah Hayes lovingly supported my efforts, in so many ways, and forgave my 'absence' while researching, writing and rewriting. My special thanks, however, is reserved for two groups of people. The first are the many families that have contributed so much to my education about Down syndrome and family life. The second is my Uncle Arthur and his family. I count the contact with them as among the richest of family experiences.

REFERENCES

Asendorpf, J. and Valsiner, J. (1992) Editors' introduction: Three dimensions of developmental perspectives. In J. Asendorpf and J. Valsiner (eds), *Stability and Change in Development: a Study of Methodological Reasoning*, pp. ix–xxii New York: Sage.

Avioli, P. and Kaplan, E. (1992) A panel study of married women's work patterns. *Sex Roles*, **26,** pp. 227–42.

Bailey, D.B. and Wolery, M. (1984) *Teaching Infants and Preschoolers with Handicaps*, Columbus: Merrill.

Barling, J. (1990) *Employment Stress and Family Functioning*, Chichester: John Wiley.

Baumrind, D. (1993) The average expectable environment is not good enough: a response to Scarr. *Child Development*, **64,** pp. 1299–1317.

Baxter, C. (1987) Professional services as support: perceptions of parents. *Australia and New Zealand Journal Developmental Disabilities*, **13** (4), pp. 243–53.

Beckman, P.J. (1983) Influence of selected child characteristics on stress in families of handicapped infants. *American Journal of Mental Deficiency*, **88,** pp. 150–56.

Beresford, B.A. (1994) Resources and strategies: How parents cope with the care of a disabled child. *Journal of Child Psychology and Psychiatry*, **35** (1), pp. 171–209.

Bidder, R., Gray, P., Newcombe, R., Evans, B. and Hughes, M. (1989) The effects of multivitamins and minerals on children with Down syndrome. *Developmental Medicine and Child Neurology*, **31,** pp. 532–37.

Blackard, M. and Barsh, E. (1982) Parents' and professionals' perceptions of the handicapped child's impact on the family. *Journal of The Association for the Severely Handicapped*, **7,** pp. 62–70.

Bowman, D. and Virtue, M. (1993) *Public Policy, Private Lives*, Canberra: Australian Institute on Intellectual Disability.

Bright, R. and Wright, J. (1985) Community-based services: the impact on mothers of disabled children. Paper presented at the third joint AGSSOMD/AAMR National Conference, Brisbane, Queensland, September.

Bristol, M.M. and Gallagher, J.J. (1986) Research on fathers of young handicapped children: Evolution, Review, and some future directions. In J.J. Gallagher and P.M. Vietze (eds), *Families of Handicapped Persons: Research, Programs, and Policy Issues*, Baltimore: Brookes.

Broman, S., Nichols, P.L., Shaughnessy, P. and Kennedy, W. (1987) *Retardation in Young Children*, Hillsdale: Erlbaum.

Bronfenbrenner, U. (1977) Toward an experimental ecology of human development. *American Psychologist*, **32,** pp. 513–31.

Bronfenbrenner, U. and Crouter, A.C. (1983) The evolution of environmental models in developmental research. In P. Mussen (ed.), *Handbook of Child Psychology*, 4th edn, New York: Wiley.

Bruder, M. and Bologna, T. (1993) In W. Brown, S. Thurman and L. Pearl, *Family Centred Early Intervention with Infants and Toddlers: Innovative Cross-Disciplinary Approaches*, pp. 103–27, Baltimore: Brookes.

Burden, R. (1991) Psycho-social transitions in the lives of parents of children with handicapping conditions. *Counselling Psychology Quarterly*, **4** (4), pp. 331–43.

Burden, R. and Thomas, D. (1986) Working with parents of exceptional children: the need for more careful thought and positive action. *Disability, Handicap and Society*, **1** (2), pp. 165–71.

Byrne, E. and Cunningham, C. (1985) The effects of mentally handicapped children on families: a conceptual review. *Journal of Child Psychology and Psychiatry*, **26** (6), pp. 847–64.

Carr, J. (1994) Long-term outcome for people with Down's syndrome. *Journal of Child Psychology and Psychiatry*, **35** (3), pp. 425–39.

Cattermole, M., Jahoda, A. and Markova, I. (1988) Leaving home: the experience of people with a mental handicap. *Journal of Mental Deficiency Research*, **32,** pp. 47–57.

Cavanagh, J. and Ashman, A.F. (1985) Stress in families with handicapped children. *Australia and New Zealand Journal of Developmental Disabilities*, **11,** pp. 151–56.

Chetwynd, J. (1985) Some costs of caring at home for an intellectually handicapped child. *Australia and New Zealand Journal of Developmental Disabilities*, **11** (1), pp. 35–40.

Chetwynd, J., Calvert, S. and Boss, V. (1986) Caring and coping: life for mothers of intellectually handicapped children. *The New Zealand Nursing Journal*, **79** (8), pp. 20–23.

Cochran, M. and Brassard, J. (1979) Child development and personal social networks. *Child Development*, **50** (3), pp. 601–16.

Cooley, W. and Graham, J. (1991) Down syndrome: an update and review for the primary pediatrician. *Clinical Pediatrics* **30** (4), pp. 233–53.

Cooley, W. and Moeschler, J. (1993) Counseling in the health care relationship: a natural source of support for people with disabilities and their families. In G. Singer and L. Powers (eds), *Families, Disability and Empowerment: Active Coping Skills and Strategies for Family Interventions*, pp. 155–74, Baltimore: Brookes.

Coon, H., Carey, G. and Fulker, D.W. (1992) Community influences on cognitive ability. *Intelligence*, **16** (2), pp. 169–88.

Crombie, M., Gunn, P. and Hayes, A. (1991) A longitudinal study of two cohorts of children with Down syndrome. In C. Denholm, (ed.), *Adolescents with Down Syndrome: International Perspectives on Research and Programme Development*, Victoria, BC: University of Victoria.

Cunningham, C. (1985) Training and education approaches for parents of children with special needs. *British Journal of Medical Psychology*, **58,** pp. 285–305.

Cunningham, C. and Glenn, S. (1985) Parent involvement and early intervention. In D. Lane and B. Stratford (eds), *Current Approaches to Down's Syndrome*, pp. 347–62, London: Cassell.

Cuskelly, M. and Dadds, M. (1992) Behavioural problems in children with Down's syndrome. *Journal of Child Psychology and Psychiatry*, **33,** pp. 749–61.

Cuskelly, M. and Gunn, P. (1993) Maternal reports of behavior of siblings of children with Down syndrome. *American Journal on Mental Retardation*, **97** (5), pp. 521–29.

Damrosch, S. and Perry, L. (1989) Self-reported adjustment chronic sorrow, and coping of children with Down syndrome. *Nursing Research*, **38** (1), 25–30.

Darling, R. (1987) The economic and psychosocial consequences of disability: family-society relationships. In M. Ferrori and M. B. Sussman (eds) *Childhood Disability and Family Systems*, pp. 45–61. New York: Haworth Press.

DeMeis, D.K. Hock, E. and McBride, S. (1986) The balance of employment and mother-hood: longitudinal study of mothers' feelings about separation from their first-born infant *Developmental Psychology*, **22,** pp. 627–32.

Dimmock, C. and Bain, A. (1991) Providing services to special needs students in a decentralised education system: an Australian perspective. *Australasian Journal of Special Education*, **15,** pp. 3–9.

Donovan, A. (1988) Family stress and ways of coping with adolescents who have handicaps: maternal perceptions. *American Journal on Mental Deficiency*, **92** (6), pp. 502–09.

Dunn, J. and Plomin, R. (1990) *Separate Lives: Why Siblings Are So Different*, New York: Basic Books.

Dunst, C.J. and Trivette, C.M. (1990) Assessment of social support in early intervention programs. In S.J Meisels and J.P. Shonkoff (eds), *Handbook of Early Childhood Intervention*, pp. 326–49, Cambridge: Cambridge University Press,

Dupont, A. (1988) A study concerning the time-related and other burdens when severely handicapped children are reared at home. *Acta Psychologica Scandinavica*, suppl. **285,** 62, pp. 249–57.

Dyson, L. (1993) Response to the presence of a child with disabilities: parental stress and family functioning over time. *American Journal on Mental Retardation*, **98,** (2), pp. 207–18.

Eden-Piercy, G., Blacher, J. and Eyman, R. (1986) Exploring parents' reactions to their young child with severe handicaps. *Mental Retardation*, **24** (5), pp. 285–91.

Elkins, J. (1994) The school context. In A. Ashman and J. Elkins (eds), *Educating Children with Special Needs*, pp. 71–103, New York: Prentice Hall.

Erickson, M. and Upshur, C. (1989) Caretaking burden and social support: comparison of mothers of infants with and without disabilities. *American Journal on Mental Retardation*, **94** (3), pp. 250–58.

Etzioni, A. (1993) *The Spirit of Community*, New York: Simon and Schuster.

Farber, B and Ryckman, D.B. (1965) Effects of severely mentally retarded children on family relationships, *Mental Retardation*, **2**, 1–17.

Fisman, S. and Wolf, L. (1991) The handicapped child: psychological effects of parental, marital, and sibling relationships. *Psychiatric Clinics of North America*, **14**, pp. 199–217.

Flynt, S. and Wood, T. (1989) Stress and coping of mothers of children with moderate mental retardation. *American Journal on Mental Deficiency*, **94** (3), pp. 278–83.

Foreman, P. and Ward, J. (1986) Treatment approaches in Down's syndrome: a review. *Australia and New Zealand Journal Developmental Disabilities*, **12** (2), pp. 111–21.

Frey, K., Fewell, R.R. and Vadasy, P. (1989) Parental adjustment and changes in child outcome among families of young handicapped children. *Topics in Early Childhood Special Education*, **8**, pp. 38–57.

Gallagher, J., Beckman, P. and Cross, A. (1983) Families of handicapped children: sources of stress and its amelioration. *Exceptional Children*, **50** (1), pp. 10–19.

Gallagher, J.J. and Bristol, M. (1989) Families of young handicapped children. In M.C. Wang, M.C. Reynolds and H.J. Walberg (eds), *Handbook of Special Education: Research and Practice: Low Incidence Conditions*, pp. 295–317. Oxford: Pergamon.

Gallimore, R., Weisner, T.S., Bernheimer, L.P., Guthrie, D. and Nihira, K. (1993) Family responses to young children with developmental delays: accommodation activity in ecological and cultural context. *American Journal on Mental Retardation*, **98** (2), pp. 185–206.

Gath, A. (1978.) *Down Syndrome and the Family*, London: Academic Press.

Gath, A. (1985a) Family factors in the development of behaviour disorders in retarded children. In J. Berg (ed.), *Science and Service in Mental Retardation*, pp. 124–131, London: Methuen.

Gath, A. (1985b) Parental reactions to loss and disappointment: the diagnosis of Down's syndrome. Developmental Medicine and Child Neurology, **27**, pp. 392–400.

Gath, A. and Gumley, D. (1984) Down's syndrome and the family: follow-up of children first seen in infancy. *Developmental Medicine and Child Neurology*, **26**, pp. 500–08.

Gath, A. Gumley, D. (1986) Family background of children with Down's syndrome and of children with a similar degree of mental retardation. *British Journal of Psychiatry*, **149**, pp. 161–71.

Glidden, L. (1991) Adopted children with developmental disabilities: post-placement family functioning. *Children and Youth Services Review*, **13**, pp. 363–77.

Glidden, L. and Pursley, J. (1989) Longitudinal comparisons of families who have adopted children with mental retardation. *American Journal on Mental Retardation*, **94** (3), pp. 272–77.

Goodnow, J.J. (1988) Parents' ideas, actions, and feelings: models and methods from developmental and social psychology. *Child Development*, **59**, pp. 286–320.

Goodnow, J.J. and Bowes, J.M. (1994) *Men, Women and Household Work*, Melbourne: Oxford University Press.

Goodnow, J.J. and Collins, W.A. (1990) *Development According to Parents: The Nature, Sources and Consequences of Parents' Ideas*, Hillsdale: Erlbaum.

Gordon, H. and Kammeyer, K. (1980) The gainful employment of women with small children. *Journal of Marriage and the Family*, **42**, pp. 327–36.

Gowen, J., Johnson-Martin, N., Goldman, B., and Appelbaum, M. (1989). Feelings of depression and parenting competence of mothers of handicapped and nonhandicapped infants: a longitudinal study. *American Journal on Mental Retardation*, **94** (3), pp. 259–71.

Guralnick, M.J. (1988). Efficacy research in early childhood intervention programs. In S.L.

Odom and M.B Karnes (eds), *Early Intervention for Infants and Children with Handicaps: An Empirical Base*, Baltimore: Brookes.

Hanson, M., and Hanline, M. (1990). Parenting a child with a disability: a longitudinal study of parent stress and adaptation. *Journal of Early Intervention*, **14** (3), pp. 234–48.

Harris, V. and McHale, S. (1989). Family life problems, daily caregiving activities, and the psychological well-being of mothers of mentally retarded children. *American Journal on Mental Retardation*, **94** (3), pp. 231–39.

Hayes, A. (1984). Interactions, engagements, and the origins and growth of communication. In L. Feagans, C. Garvey and R. Golinkoff (eds), *The Origins and Growth of Communication*, Norwood: Ablex.

Hayes, A. (1994). Disabilities and Families. In A. Ashman and J. Elkins (eds), *Educating Children with Special Needs*, 2nd edn, Sydney: Prentice-Hall.

Hayes, A., Senapati, R. and Gunn, P. (1987). Down syndrome children and their siblings: perspective-taking, teaching and caregiving. Paper presented at the Society for Research in Child Development Conference, Baltimore.

Hock, E., DeMeis, D., and McBride, S. (1988). Maternal separation anxiety: its role in the balance of employment and motherhood in mothers of infants. In A. Gottfried and A. Gottfried (eds), *Maternal Employment and Children's Development*, pp. 191–230, New York: Plenum.

Hodapp, R., Dykens, E., Evans, D., and Merighi, J. (1992). Maternal emotional reactions to young children with different types of handicaps. *Developmental and Behavioral Pediatrics*, **13** (2), pp. 118–23.

Honig, A.S. (1985). Reflections on infant intervention programs: What have we learned? In M. Frank (ed.), *Infant Intervention Programs: Truths and Untruths*, New York: Haworth Press.

Hornby, G. and Seligman, M. (1991). Disability and the family: current status and future developments. *Counselling Psychology Quarterly*, **4** (4), pp. 267–71.

Horwitz, W.A. and Kazak, A.E. (1990). Family adaptation to childhood cancer: sibling and family systems variables. *Journal of Clinical Child Psychology*, **19**, pp. 221–28.

Kaiser, A.P. and Hemmeter, M.L. (1989) Value based approaches to family intervention. *Topics in Early Childhood Special Education*, **8**, pp. 72–86.

Kazak, A. (1987) Families with disabled children: stress and social networks in three samples. *Journal of Abnormal Child Psychology*, **15** (1), pp. 137–46.

Kirk, S.A. (1982) Evolution and present status of early education of the handicapped. *The Exceptional Child*, **29**, pp. 71–78.

Korbin, J.E. (1986) Sarah: The life course of a Down's syndrome child. In L.L. Langness and H.G. Levine (eds), *Culture and Retardation*, pp. 19–32, Dordrecht: D. Reidel.

Kozlowski, B. (1992) Megavitamin treatment of mental retardation in children: a review of effects on behavior and cognition. *Journal of Child and Adolescent Psychopharmacology*, **2** (4), pp. 307–20.

Krauss, M. (1993) Child-related and parenting stress: differences between mothers and fathers of children with disabilities. *American Journal on Mental Retardation*, **97** (4), pp. 393–404.

Krauss, M., Seltzer, M. and Goodman, S. (1992) Social support networks of adults with mental retardation who live at home. *American Journal on Mental Retardation*, **96** (4), pp. 432–41.

Lichtenstein, J. (1993) Help for troubled marriages. In G. Singer and L. Powers (eds), *Families, Disability, and Empowerment: Active Coping Skills and Strategies for Family Interventions*, pp. 259–83, Baltimore: Brookes.

Lucyshyn, J. and Albin, R. (1993) Comprehensive support to families of children with disabilities and behavior problems: keeping it 'friendly'. In G. Singer and L. Powers (eds), *Families, Disability, and Empowerment: Active Coping Skills and Strategies for Family Interventions*, pp. 365–407, Baltimore: Brookes.

Ludlow, J.R. and Allen, L.M. (1979) The effect of early intervention and pre-school stimulus on the development of the Down's syndrome child. *Journal of Mental Deficiency Research*, **23**, pp. 29–43.

Maas, F. (1990) Child care needs of working families in the 1990s. *Family Matters*, **26,** pp. 59–63.

McConachie, H. (1991) Home-based teaching: what are we asking of parents? *Child: Care, Health and Development*, **17,** pp. 123–36.

McHale, S., Simeonsson, R.J. and Sloan, R.L. (1984) Children with handicapped brothers and sisters. In E. Schopler and G.B. Mesibov (eds) *The Effect of Autism on the Family*, pp. 327–42, New York: Plenum.

McNaught, M.E. (1988) Families and learning disability: the mother's perspective. Unpublished doctoral thesis, Macquarie University.

Marc, D-L. and MacDonald, L. (1988) Respite care: Who uses it? *Mental Retardation*, **26** (2), pp. 93–96.

Meyer-Probst, B., Rosler, H.D. and Teichmann, H. (1983) Biological and psychosocial risk factors and development during childhood. In D. Magnusson and V.L. Allen (eds), *Human Development: An Interactional Perspective*, New York: Academic Press.

Meyer-Probst, B., Teichmann, H., Hayes, A. and Rauh, H. (1991) Follow-up of a cohort of risk children from birth into adolescence: the Rostock longitudinal study. *International Journal of Disability, Development and Education*, **38,** pp. 225–46.

Nixon, C. (1993) Reducing self-blame and guilt in parents of children with severe disabilities. In G. Singer and L. Powers (eds), *Families, Disability and Empowerment: Active Coping Skills and Strategies for Family Interventions*, pp. 175–201, Baltimore: Brookes.

Pearl, L. (1993) Providing family-centred early intervention. In W. Brown, S. Thurman and L. Pearl (eds), *Family Centred Early Intervention with Infants and Toddlers: Innovative Cross-Disciplinary Approaches*, pp. 81–101, Baltimore: Brookes.

Plomin, R. and Daniels, D. (1987) Why are children in the same family so different from one another? *Behavioral and Brain Sciences*, **10,** pp. 1–60.

Powell, G. and Mainiero, L. (1992) Cross-currents in the river of time: conceptualizing the complexities of women's careers. *Journal of Management*, **18** (2), pp. 215–37.

Powell, T.H. and Ogle, P.A. (1985) *Brothers and Sisters: A Special Part of Exceptional Families*, Baltimore: Brookes.

Powers, L. (1993) Disability and grief: from tragedy to challenge. In G. Singer and L. Powers (eds), *Families, Disability, and Empowerment: Active Coping Skills and Strategies for Family Interventions*, pp. 119–49, Baltimore: Brookes.

Powers, M. (1991) Intervention with families of young children with severe handicaps: Contributions of a family systems approach. *School Psychology Quarterly*, **6** (2), pp. 131–46.

Pruess, J., Fewell, R. and Bennett, F. (1989) Vitamin therapy and children with Down syndrome: a review of research. *Exceptional Children* **55** (4), pp. 336–41.

Pueschel, S. (1992) General health care and therapeutic approaches. In S. Pueschel and J. Pueschel (eds), *Biomedical Concerns in Persons with Down Syndrome*, pp. 259–300, Baltimore: Brookes.

Rodger, S. (1986) Parents as therapists: A responsible alternative or abrogation of responsibility? *The Exceptional Child*, **33** (1), pp. 17–27.

Rosen, M., Clark, G. and Kivitz, M. (1976) *The History of Mental Retardation: Collected Papers*, vols 1 and 2, Baltimore: University Park Press.

Safer, N. and Hamilton, J. (1993) Legislative context for early intervention services. In W. Brown, S. Thurman and L. Pearl (eds), *Family Centred Early Intervention with Infants and Toddlers: Innovative Cross-Disciplinary Approaches*, pp. 1–19, Baltimore: Brookes.

Salisbury, C. (1987) Stressors of parents with young handicapped and nonhandicapped children. *Journal of the Division of Early Childhood*, **11** (2), pp. 154–60.

Sameroff, A. and Seifer, R. (1983) Familial risk and child competence. *Child Development*, **54** pp. 1254–68.

Santelli, B., Turnbull, A., Lerner, E. and Marquis, J. (1993) Parent to parent programs. In G. Singer and L. Power (eds), *Families, Disability, and Empowerment: Active Coping Skills and Strategies for Family Interventions*, pp. 27–57, Baltimore: Brookes.

Schonell, F.J. and Watts, B.H. (1956) A first survey of the effects of a subnormal child on the family unit. *American Journal of Mental Deficiency*, **61**, pp. 210–19.

Seligman, M. and Darling, R.B. (1989) *Ordinary Families, Special Children*, New York: Guilford.

Selikowitz, M. (1990) *Down Syndrome: The Facts*, Oxford: Oxford University Press.

Seltzer, M. and Krauss, M. (1989) Aging parents with adult mentally retarded children: family risk factors and sources of support. *American Journal on Mental Retardation*, **94** (3), pp. 303–12.

Senapati, R. and Hayes, A. (1988) Sibling relationships of handicapped children: a review of conceptual and methodological issues. *International Journal of Behavioral Development (Special Edition)*, **11**, pp. 89–115.

Sexton, D., Thompson, B., Perez, J. and Rheams, T. (1990) Maternal versus professional estimates of developmental status for young children with handicaps: an ecological approach. *Topics in Early Childhood Special Education*, **10** (3), pp. 80–95.

Shapiro, J. (1989) Stress, depression, and support group participation in mothers of developmentally delayed children. *Family Relations*, **38**, pp. 169–73.

Sheehan, R. and Sites, J. (1989) Implications of P.L. 99–457 for assessment. *Topics in Early Childhood Special Education*, **8**, pp. 103–15.

Shepperdson, B. (1985) Changes in the characteristics of families with Down's syndrome children. *Journal of Epidemiology and Community Health*, **39**, pp. 320–24.

Shields, C. (1987) *Strategies: A Practical Guide for Dealing with Professionals and Human Service Systems*, Richmond Hill, ON: Human Services Press.

Shonkoff, J.P. and Meisels, S.J. (1990) Early intervention: the evolution of the concept. In S.J. Meisels and J.P. Shonkoff (eds), *Handbook of Early Childhood Intervention*, pp. 3–31, Cambridge: Cambridge University Press.

Simeonsson, R.J. and Bailey, D.B. Jr (1990) Family dimensions in early intervention. In S.J. Meisels and J.P. Shonkoff (eds), *Handbook of Early Childhood Intervention*, pp. 428–44, Cambridge: Cambridge University Press.

Singer, G., Irvin, L., Irvine, B., Hawkins, N., Hegreness, J. and Jackson, R. (1993) Helping families adapt positively to disability: overcoming demoralization through community supports. In G. Singer and L. Powers (eds), *Families, Disability, and Empowerment: Active Coping Skills and Strategies for Family Interventions*, pp. 67–83, Baltimore: Brookes.

Singer, G. and Powers, L. (1993) Contributing to resilience in families: an overview. In G. Singer and L. Powers (eds) *Families, Disability, and Empowerment: Active Coping Skills and Strategies for Family Interventions*, pp. 1–25, Baltimore: Brookes.

Singhi, P., Goyal, L., Pershad, D., Singhi, S. and Walia, B. (1990) Psychosocial problems in families of disabled children. *British Journal of Medical Psychology*, **63** pp. 173–82.

Skeels, H.M. (1966) Adult status of children with contrasting early life experiences. *Monographs of the Society for Research in Child Development, Serial No. 105*, **31** (3).

Stone, H. (1973) The birth of a child with Down's syndrome: a medico-social study of thirty-one children and their families. *Scottish Medical Journal*, **18**, pp. 182–87.

Stoneman, Z., Brody, G. and Abbott, D. (1983) In-home observations of young Down syndrome children with their mothers and fathers. *American Journal on Mental Deficiency*, **87** (6), pp. 591–600.

Stoneman, Z. and Brody, G.H. (1982) Strengths inherent in sibling interactions involving a retarded child: a functional role theory approach. In N. Stinnett, B. Chesser. J. DeFrain and P. Knaub (eds), *Family Strengths. Vol. 4: Positive Support Systems*. Lincoln: University of Nebraska Press.

Thurman, S. (1993) Some perspectives on the continuing challenges in early intervention. In W. Brown, S. Thurman and L. Pearl (eds), Family Centred Early Intervention with Infants and Toddlers: Innovative Cross-Disciplinary Approaches, pp. 303–16, Baltimore: Brookes.

Trout, M. and Foley, G. (1989) Working with families of handicapped infants and toddlers. *Topics in Language Disorders*, **10** (1), pp. 57–67.

Turnbull, A. and Turnbull, H. (1993) Participatory research on cognitive coping: from concepts to research planning. In A. Turnbull, J. Patterson, S. Behr, D. Murphy, J. Marquis and M. Blue-Banning (eds), *Cognitive Coping, Families and Disability*, pp. 1–14, Baltimore: Brookes.

Turnbull, A.P. and Turnbull, H.R. III. (1986) *Families, Professionals and Exceptionality: A Special Partnership*, Columbus: Merrill.

Van Riper, M., Ryff, C. and Pridham, K. (1992) Parental and family well-being in families of children with Down syndrome: a comparative study. *Research in Nursing & Health*, **15**, pp. 227–35.

Voydanoff, P. (1989) Work and Family: A review and expanded conceptualization. *Journal of Social Behavior and Personality*, **3** (4), pp. 1–22.

Wachs, T.D. and Plomin, R. (1991) Overview of current models and research. In T.D. Wachs and R. Plomin (eds) *Conceptualization and Measurement of Organism–environment Interaction*, pp. 1–8, Washington: American Psychological Association.

Waddington, S. and Busch-Rossnagel, N. (1992) The influence of a child's disability on maternal role functioning and psychological well-being: genetic, social and general. *Psychology Monographs*, **118** (3), pp. 293–311.

Walker, B. and Singer, G. (1993) Improving collaborative communication between professionals and parents. In G. Singer and L. Powers (eds), *Families, Disability, and Empowerment: Active Coping Skills and Strategies for Family Interventions*, pp. 285–315, Baltimore: Brookes.

Walker, L., Ortiz-Valdes, J. and Newbrough, J. (1989) The role of maternal employment and depression in the psychological adjustment of chronically ill, mentally retarded , and well children. *Journal of Pediatric Psychology*, **14** (3), pp. 357–70.

Werner, E.E. and Smith, R.S. (1982) *Vulnerable but Invincible*, New York: Wiley.

Wright, J., Granger, R., and Sameroff, A. (1984) Parental acceptance and developmental handicap. In J. Blacher (ed.), *Severely Handicapped Children and their Families*, Orlando: Academic Press.

Wynn, M. and Wynn, A. (1979) *Prevention of Handicap and the Health of Women*, London: Routledge and Kegan Paul.

Zigler, E. and Hodapp, R. (1986) *Understanding Mental Retardation*, Cambridge: Cambridge University Press.

23 Siblings

Monica Cuskelly

The sibling relationship has been identified as the longest lasting relationship an individual is likely to experience (Bank and Kahn, 1982). Except for those who are the first born it begins at the same time as the relationship with parents, and lasts longer, as parents usually die before their children. Friends and partners are met as we progress through life, but many do not persist with us until the end. Brothers and sisters, then, have the potential to play a unique role in the lives of their siblings.

This role is more salient in some families rather than others, perhaps more in families that are isolated by geography, social disadvantage or culture and perhaps more in families when a sibling is disabled. Although there has been interest for some years in the siblings of children with disabilities, research into the nature of the sibling relationship seems to have been limited by a prevailing viewpoint that a child with a disability will place a great strain on the family and disrupt normal family functioning (e.g. Schild, 1971). This view has been buttressed by reports based on anecdotal evidence (for example, Kaplan, 1969; Poznanski, 1969; San Martino and Newman, 1974).

These early reports often lacked empirical evidence but were uncritically accepted by many writers and researchers. It is surprising that the results of these studies are still cited with authority, although later investigations have often failed to support their conclusions (for example, Breslau, 1982; Dyson, 1989; Lobato *et al.*, 1987; McHale and Gamble, 1989; Roe and Plummer, 1987).

There appear to be two main questions that are currently engaging the interest of researchers working with the brothers and sisters of children with a disability and these are relevant to the siblings of children with Down syndrome. The first relates to the psychological adjustment of siblings: do the siblings of children with disabilities show more problems in their psychological adjustment than siblings of other children? The second question focuses on the identification of factors which may act to protect children or make them more vulnerable to psychological problems: what are the factors that mediate the psychological adjustment of these siblings?

DO THE SIBLINGS OF CHILDREN WITH DOWN SYNDROME SHOW PROBLEMS IN PSYCHOLOGICAL ADJUSTMENT?

Table 23.1 contains a list those papers which have reported on the adjustment of siblings of children with Down syndrome and have included a comparison group or normative data. It should be noted that the comparison groups were formed differently for each study. Only one study collected information from the siblings themselves and most collected information from teachers, usually in addition to maternal reports.

The Gath series of studies provides a unique set in this literature as they cover a 15-year time span using the same instrument. These studies examined a range of issues relating to the development of children with Down syndrome and to the functioning of their families. In all studies Ann Gath used the Rutter scales (Rutter *et al.*, 1970). These scales have a parent version (Rutter A) and a parallel form for teachers (Rutter B). Her earliest report, in 1972, was based on parental and teacher reports of problem behaviour in 36 school-aged siblings of 22 children with Down syndrome. Two other groups were included in the study, one group of 35 school-aged siblings of 21 children with cleft palate, and a comparison group of 71 children who had been individually matched to the siblings in the two disability groups on age, sex, family size and position, type of school, school class and residential area.

Both parents and teachers completed the Rutter scales. One or both parents of all children in the study were interviewed and teachers received the questionnaires in the mail. There were no differences between either sibling group in the numbers who exceeded the clinical cut-off point on parental or teacher reports when compared to their matched comparisons. There were also no differences when the type of problem experienced by those rated as deviant were compared. It is interesting that rather more siblings of children with cleft palate were in the deviant range (43 per cent) than were siblings of children with Down syndrome (23 per cent). Proportionally twice as many first-born children in the sibling groups were rated as deviant in contrast to the comparison groups.

Gath (1972) pointed out that all the study families had their child with Down syndrome in the family home, which may have meant that the families were not typical of families with a child with Down syndrome at that time. Another proviso regarding the research came from Lobato (1983) who criticized this study and Gath's 1973 and 1974 studies on the basis that they included more than one sibling from some families. When more than one child from a family is included in a sample, it is possible that some families who are at the extremes may unduly influence the results.

In a further study, Gath (1973) identified 122 families with a child with Down syndrome who had a school-aged sibling. Families were posted the Rutter questionnaire with a request for permission to approach the siblings' teachers for further information. One hundred and four families with 174 non-disabled siblings participated in the study. Teachers were asked to complete the teacher version of the Rutter scale with respect to both the sibling and to the child next to the sibling on the class list. Schools were then asked to send the parent questionnaire to the

Table 23.1 Results of comparison studies which Investigated the psychological adjustment of the siblings of children with Down syndrome (DS)

Author (Place)	Sibling group	Comparison group	Age of sibling with disability (years)	Age of child	Instruments	Group effects
Gath (1972) (Oxford)	DS n = 36 Cleft palate n = 35	Individually matched n = 71	School age	8.6–12	Rutter A Rutter B	*Mother:* ns *Teacher:* ns
Gath (1973) (Oxford)	DS n = 174	Next child on class list n = 106	5–19	2–25	Rutter A Rutter B	*Mother:* ns *Teacher:* Sibs more problems. Female sibs more problems than males
Gath (1974) (Oxford)	DS n = 174	Compared to normative sample	5–19	2–25	Rutter B	*Teacher:* Sibs had more problems
Gath (1978) (Oxford)	DS n = 17	Matched at infancy to child with DS and family n = 16	school age	infants	Rutter A Rutter B	*Mother:* ns *Teacher:* ns
Gath and Gumley (1984) (Britain)	DS n = 19	Matched at infancy to child with DS and family n = 20	school age	8–10	Rutter A Rutter B	*Mother:* More sibs above clinical cutoff *Teacher:* More sibs above clinical cutoff
Gath and Gumley (1987) (Britain)	DS n = 95	Next child on class list n = 95	$M = 10.8$	$M^{\female} = 11.2$ $M^{\male} = 10$	Rutter B	*Teacher:* ns
Carr (1988) (Britain)	DS n = 20–27	Matched with child with DS n = 34–29	not known	4 11 21	Informal disc. Rutter A Rutter B Informal disc.	*Mother:* Comp. children more problems *Mother:* Comp. children more problems *Teacher:* ns *Mother:* Sibs more problems
Rodrigue, Geffken and Morgan (1993) (USA)	DS n = 20 Autism n = 19	Individually matched	$M = 11.05$	$M = 11.93$	CBCL Perceived Competence Scale	*Mother:* ns *Sibling:* ns
Cuskelly and Dadds (1992) (Brisbane, Australia)	DS n = 21	Compared to normative sample	5–16	4–15	RBPC	*Mother:* Sibs more CD. Female sibs more CD than male *Father:* Sibs more CD. Female sibs more CD than male *Teacher:* ns. Female sibs more CD than male
Cuskelly and Gunn (1993) (Brisbane Australia)	DS n = 70	group match for n = 67	$M^{\female} = 9.3$ $M^{\male} = 9.0$	Within 4 yrs of sib age	RBPC CD subscale	*Mother:* Sibs more CD. Female sibs more CD than male

parents of the comparison children. Seventy-four per cent of the comparison families returned the questionnaire and 84 and 82 per cent of teachers returned the forms for the siblings and the comparison children respectively.

The age ranges of both the siblings and the children with Down syndrome in the study were very wide (5 to 19 years for the siblings; 2 to 25 years for individuals with Down syndrome). The paper gave no information about the comparison group. As the comparison children came from the same classes as the siblings, it is probably safe to assume that the ages of the children were similar but there is a possibility that the groups differed on other demographic variables (Stoneman, 1989).

Twenty per cent of the siblings had scores above the clinical cut-off point on either the parent or the teacher rating with only 10 per cent of the comparison children being above this level. The Rutter scale has two subscales: Neurotic and Antisocial. There was no difference between groups in the children classified as Neurotic, but siblings were classified as Antisocial significantly more often than comparison children. Teachers were strikingly more likely to rate a child as deviant than were parents and the difference between the two groups stemmed primarily from teachers' reports of antisocial problems in the female siblings. There are some problems in using the Rutter scales to compare rates of problem behaviour across the sexes, however, as there are no separate sex norms.

Although there was no significant difference between the number of siblings born before or after the child with Down syndrome who were rated as deviant there was an interesting effect in terms of the type of problem reported. All children born *after* the child with Down syndrome who were rated as deviant were in the antisocial category while the children who were born *before* the child with Down syndrome were evenly divided between the Antisocial and Neurotic categories. Gender of the child with Down syndrome had no impact on siblings' reported problems. Family size appeared to contribute to sibling deviancy with children in families of two children or those with seven or more children having most problems.

Using the same sample described above, Gath (1974) compared the results with those found by Rutter *et al.*, (1970) in the Isle of Wight study. Large differences were apparent. Brothers of children with Down syndrome were twice as likely to be rated as deviant as boys in the comparison sample and an even larger increase occurred for sisters. Twenty-six per cent of boys and 16 per cent of girls were rated as deviant by either parents or teachers. There was apparently very little overlap between the children rated by parents and teachers as deviant – only one boy and one girl scored above the cut-off point on both parent and teacher reports. At primary school there were significantly more boys than girls rated as deviant whereas in the secondary group 24 per cent of female siblings scored above the cut-off point compared to 19.5 per cent of male siblings.

Both girls and boys were disadvantaged by coming from a large family, with the effect of family size being independent of social class. Birth order did not affect boys, but deviant girls were found to be either the oldest child or to be a middle child of a large family. Position relative to the child with Down syndrome was also important for girls. Girls were likely to be reported to have problems if they were older than the child with Down syndrome, particularly if they were more than three years older. Relative position had no impact on boys. Gath (1974) attributed the increased problem behaviour in female siblings to the demands placed upon them for increased responsibilities in the home, although no data was gathered to support this hypothesis.

In a two-year prospective study Gath (1978) followed 30 families with an infant with Down syndrome who was brought up in the family home, and 30 comparison families. The comparison families were matched as closely as possible on the birth date of the infant, the infant's ordinal position in the family, sex, socio-economic status (SES), maternal age and neighbourhood characteristics. At the first interview, undertaken as soon as possible after the birth of the child, parents completed the Rutter scale for all children who were attending school. Seventeen siblings and 16 comparison children were included. The questionnaires were completed on the basis of the child's behaviour over the previous 12 months. Two siblings and four comparison children were rated by their parents as deviant on the Rutter scales. Teachers were also asked to complete the Rutter scales, and questionnaires were returned for 13 siblings and 12 comparison children. There were two children in each group who were rated by their teachers to be above the clinical cut-off point. Only one sibling was regarded as having serious problems by both parents and teacher.

The teacher measures were repeated at the end of the two-year study. At this time, teachers of 18 siblings and 20 comparison children completed the questionnaire. Five siblings and four of the control group were rated as deviant. There were no differences in the scores of those children who were rated on both occasions. No differences existed between the two groups on maternal report. Gath (1978) interpreted this data as evidence that those siblings who had behaviour problems had them before the birth of their brother/sister with Down syndrome, however the direct link between those children rated deviant at the initial and the follow-up phases was not clearly made.

In 1984 Gath and Gumley followed up the families of 22 children with Down syndrome who had participated in the earlier two-year prospective study (Gath, 1978). Although there was no difference in the mean problem behaviours on the Rutter scales, both parents and teachers reported more siblings to be above the clinical cut-off point than comparison children. Parents reported 32 per cent of siblings and 26 per cent of comparison children to be above this point, and teachers' rating put 20 per cent of siblings and 10 per cent of comparison children in this group. This disparity suggests that, as the means of the two groups were not significantly different, there was greater variance among siblings than among the comparison group, i.e., while some siblings were reported to have a larger number of problems than comparison children, some were reported to have fewer problems.

Parents' ratings at this time certainly suggest an increase in problem behaviour on both sets of children since the earlier study (Gath, 1978). The lack of developmental norms for the Rutter scales makes it difficult to judge the clinical significance of these changes. The proportion of children rated as deviant by teachers decreased slightly for both groups. It is not possible to ascertain, from the published report, the overlap between parents' and teachers' reports in the sibling group. Two comparison children were rated by both parent and teacher to be in the clinical group. Behaviour problems in the child with Down syndrome were related to behaviour problems in the sibling, however the direction of that relationship is unknown.

In a study comparing the siblings of children with Down syndrome and siblings of children with an intellectual disability, Gath and Gumley (1987) found there was no difference between the two sibling groups on the proportion of children rated as deviant by their parents. Teachers reported on the siblings and on the next child down on the class list. On teacher reports, siblings of children with Down syndrome had no more problems than their classmates. The siblings of the children with an intellectual disability, on the other hand, had twice as many behaviour problems as their controls. These children were likely to have more difficulties with reading than their controls, unlike the siblings of the children with Down syndrome who did not differ from their controls. No direct comparison of teacher reports of the sibling groups was made, although they appeared to be quite different. Eighteen per cent of the siblings of children with Down syndrome were above the cut-off point on the Rutter scale (comparison = 20 per cent) in contrast to 29 per cent of the other sibling group (comparison = 13.6 per cent). The two comparison groups also appear to be quite different with respect to the level of behaviour problems but the authors did not examine their equivalence or that of any of the possibly influential demographic variables.

Emotional disorders were reported to be the most common type of problem (Gath and Gumley, 1987). There was no difference in the proportion of sisters and brothers rated as having either an emotional or a behavioural problem, however conduct disorders were more common in boys in both sibling groups. Therefore girls were more likely than boys to be reported to have an emotional problem. Relative position made no difference to adjustment in either sibling group, and the sex of the child with the disability was immaterial. Siblings of children with Down syndrome were more likely to have difficulties if they were the same sex as the child with Down syndrome, whereas this made no difference for the siblings of children with an intellectual disability. Again, siblings were more likely to be reported to be experiencing difficulties if the child with Down syndrome had behaviour problems. Siblings were less likely to exhibit problems if the adaptive functioning of the child with Down syndrome was high.

Another longitudinal study in the UK was undertaken by Janet Carr (1988) in a project that followed families with a member with Down syndrome for 21 years. Although this study focused primarily on the child with Down syndrome, some data about sibling adjustment were collected when the child with Down syndrome was 4 years old, 11 years old, and 21 years old. Unfortunately, the reports give no information about the age, sex, relative position of the sibling, nor of the match with the comparison siblings. There were more comparison brothers and sisters at each stage of the study than there were siblings of children with Down syndrome. These data were based on parents' replies to questions concerning the behaviour of the non-index children in the comparison families, i.e. those who were *not* matched to the child with Down syndrome. When the children with Down syndrome were 4 years of age, siblings were less likely to be reported as having problems than were comparison children (14 per cent v 31 per cent). The same difference occurred at 11 years of age (22 per cent v 45 per cent) but was reversed at 21 years of age (22 per cent v 10 per cent). Carr suggested that the result at 21 years may be due to the loss of four comparison families who had previously reported problems in their children. These studies included more than one child per family and so have the same interpretative problems as the early Gath reports.

In addition to the informal data gathered about problem behaviour, parents and teachers completed the Rutter questionnaires for all school-aged siblings when the child with Down syndrome was aged 11 years. At this time there were 18 families with a child with Down syndrome (and 23 school-aged siblings) and 25 control families (with 36 non-index comparison school-aged children) remaining in the study. No school-aged sibling scored above the clinical cut-off point on parental rating whereas three comparison children did. On teacher report, four siblings and six comparison children were in the clinical range.

In the only study found to examine the psychological adjustment of siblings of children with Down syndrome conducted in the USA, Rodrigue *et al.* (1993) compared the adjustment of this group with that of the siblings of children with autism and a well-matched comparison group. This is the only study to use information gathered from the siblings themselves. Siblings completed either the Perceived Competence Scale for Children (Harter, 1982) or the Pictorial Scale of Perceived Competence and Social Acceptance for Young Children (Harter and Pike, 1981) depending on their age. Mothers completed the Child Behavior Checklist (Achenbach and Edelbrock, 1983). The siblings of children with Down syndrome did not differ significantly from either of the other groups on either measure. No sex or birth order effects were found.

In an Australian study which collected information from mothers, fathers, and teachers, Cuskelly and Dadds (1992) reported that siblings of children with Down syndrome, particularly the female siblings, were at high risk for developing conduct disorder. In contrast to the UK report by Gath and Gumley (1987), all three raters agreed that the sisters of children with Down syndrome had more of these problems than brothers. These authors used an instrument which had both age and sex norms, and compared standardized scores, rather than raw scores. This enabled them to take account of the expected differences between boys and girls in the frequency of aggressive behaviours. Their contention that sisters were more vulnerable was undermined by the fact that the study on which it was based did not have a comparison group and the norms that were used to support this claim were from an instrument (the Revised Behavior Problem Checklist, RBPC, Quay and Peterson, 1983) that had been developed and standardized in a different country, the USA.

On the basis of the finding that female siblings were reported to have more conduct disorders than both brothers and the RBPC normative sample, Cuskelly and Gunn (1993) undertook a study which focused on conduct disorder and incorporated a comparison group. Information was collected from mothers and the results agreed with those reported by Cuskelly and Dadds (1992) – sisters of children with Down syndrome were reported to have more conduct problems than were brothers, and they also had more problems than girls in the comparison group.

After the Cuskelly and Gunn (1993) study was reported, follow-up data was collected on some of the original sample from the Cuskelly and Dadds (1992) study. This study employed an instrument which has Australian norms, the Child Behavior Checklist (CBCL) (Achenbach and Edelbrock, 1983) in addition to the the Conduct Disorder subscale of the RBPC. Almost all the girls who had been identified five years earlier as conduct disordered continued to exhibit a high level of problem behaviours, providing evidence that these problems were not transient.

Although these studies found some female siblings with long-term conduct disorders, it may be unwise to conclude that siblings of children with Down syndrome show more of these problems than other siblings. Cuskelly (1993) continued to investigate this issue and compared older siblings in a study with a more stringently designed comparison group (children individually matched on such variables as child age, gender of each child in the dyad, position in family, SES, family size). In this study, the difference between the groups regarding both internalizing and externalizing behaviours was no longer significant for either boys or girls.

WHAT FACTORS MEDIATE THE ADJUSTMENT OF SIBLINGS?

Although there is no compelling evidence that siblings of children with Down syndrome, as a group, are likely to have adjustment problems, it is apparent that some siblings are vulnerable to these problems and the question as to which factors contribute to that vulnerability becomes critical. Some authors have attempted to identify the variables that may act as mediators for these problem behaviours but most have investigated what have been labelled static variables (McHale *et al.*, 1984; Vadasy *et al.*, 1984) or social address variables (Bronfenbrenner, 1979). These static variables include such factors as age, relative position, same or opposite gender to the child with the disability, severity of the disability, number in family, and gender. Some of these studies have been discussed in the previous section. Studies which focus on the role of more dynamic variables such as family responsibilities and parental expectations are now being published. It is probable that these investigations will prove more fruitful than those which focused on static variables as the latter attain their impact through the operation of the former.

Farber (1960) was one of the first authors to find that the sisters of a child with a disability were reported by parents to exhibit more problem behaviours than were brothers. He assumed that parental dissatisfaction with the sisters arose from demands for the children to take on more responsibilities and to display more mature behaviour than would be usual. Farber's work was pivotal in identifying sex of the sibling as a potentially important variable in the adjustment of the sibling of a child with a disability. Sex has usually been considered as a static variable, however Farber (1959) clearly saw the impact on girls as being directly linked to their role within the family. Gender roles are and have been changing for some decades in many western societies and it seems highly probable that the differential impact on the sexes will have changed over that period. What it means to be a boy or a girl and within a family has been changing. Except in more traditional cultures and families, it would be illogical to expect that the relationships which existed in the late 1950s would be the same today (Skrtic *et al.*, 1984).

Although the age of the child with disabilities has been associated with poor sibling adjustment, many studies have included siblings from a large age range. Such a practice does not recognize the usual developmental changes that occur in children and may act to suppress or to artificially enhance the outcomes of interest. Severity of disability, family size and birth order are other static variables that have been implicated in the expression of problem behaviour in siblings of children with disabilities. The severity of the disability may have less impact in countries which have allocated more resources to families with a child with a disability or in areas in which there is an effective voluntary agency. Simeonsson and McHale (1981) suggested that the effects of birth order may be confounded by the age of the handi- capped child. A more meaningful comparison may be of relative developmental spacing. This is a dynamic variable that would enable exploration of the effects of the cross-over that occurs as younger siblings become more competent than their older, intellectually disabled brother or sister (Hayes, 1994; O'Connor and Stachowiak, 1971) and would require a longitudinal study.

Although the current trend toward smaller families may mean that family size is no longer a relevant variable, the discussion in the literature about the impact of family size may contribute to our understanding of some processes that make siblings more or less vulnerable to psychological disturbance. Early studies indicated that children in families of moderate size, with the exception of the oldest girl, appeared to be less vulnerable to developing adjustment problems than those in small families (Gath, 1973). It may be that the smaller families put more pressure on non-disabled children to achieve and that larger families protected the siblings against the effect of disability in their brother/sister (Fisman and Wolf, 1991; Gath, 1973; Grossman, 1972; Trevino, 1979), although if the families were too large, problems might arise, particularly for girls (Gath, 1973, 1974).

The explanation for the greater vulnerability of girls to the presence of a child with disability in the family has been the assumption that girls have had to shoulder more of the additional burden of care such a child presents (Farber, 1959, 1960; Featherstone, 1980; Gath 1973, 1974). There is ample evidence that children with a disability require more care-giving than children who are developing normally (Harris and McHale, 1989) and some evidence that for mothers, who are the primary care-givers, the caretaking demands of children with a disability are related to maternal stress (Beckman, 1983). There has long been a belief that some of that 'burden of care' (Mercer, 1966) has been shared with the non-disabled children in the family, particularly with the sisters of the child with the disability. Although there was not a great deal of direct evidence for this belief, it was an attractive one as it explained the recurrent findings that girls, in particular the oldest girl, had most difficulty in adjusting to the presence of a child with a disability (Farber, 1960; Gath, 1974; Grossman, 1972). Some support for the propo- sition could be found in Farber's (1960) study which reported that sisters who were more involved with their brother or sister with a disability were those with most role tension. 'Involvement' was not clearly defined, however, and as the same relationship did not apply to brothers the connection between responsibility and problem behaviour remained unclear. The potential for extra responsibilities to be associated with psychological disturbance has continued to attract support (Skrtic *et al.*, 1984; Stoneman and Brody, 1982) although there has been little empirical research of this association.

In addition to the proposed connection between high levels of responsibility and sibling problem behaviour, there is also an argument that poorer relationships between the sibling and the child with the disability are associated with increased responsibility because of the increased tension and conflict. These speculations remain, despite some evidence that siblings benefit from, and express satisfaction in, being involved in the management of their brothers' or sisters' behaviour (Chinitz, 1981; Craft *et al.*, 1990; Laviguer, 1976; Schreibman *et al.*, 1983). Some authors also argue that taking on more responsibility may benefit a child as it may lead to cognitive advancement (Bargh and Shul, 1980) and be helpful in developing a wide range of social roles (Bronfenbrenner, 1979). Providing assistance to parents with household tasks and care-giving may also give the siblings more opportunities for positive interactions with parents (Bryant and Litman, 1987).

Cuskelly and Gunn (1993) asked mothers about the domestic activity and self-care tasks undertaken by the siblings of children with Down syndrome and by a comparison group of children, 6 to 13 years of age. Age was related to responsibility, with older children in both groups undertaking more tasks. There were, however, no significant differences between boys and girls or between the two groups regarding these responsibilities. Contrary to the relationship which the literature predicts, there was a significant inverse relationship between involvement in such tasks and conduct problems for the sisters of the children with Down syndrome. The girls who provided more assistance were regarded by their mothers as showing fewer conduct problems. In a further study with siblings older than the child with Down syndrome, Cuskelly (1993) explored the nature of domestic tasks and their relationship to sibling adjustment and found that these siblings were more likely to be involved in tasks which involved responsibility for their younger brother or sister whereas comparison children were more likely to undertake routine domestic tasks. The sequelae of involving children in family tasks needs further exploration as this study suggested that sibling sex may influence the relationship between adjustment and responsibilities.

It may be not only with respect to household responsibilities and care-giving that parents of disabled children expect a high standard of performance from their non-disabled children. Retrospective studies of adult siblings of intellectually disabled persons have found that a proportion of those interviewed believed that their parents expected them to compensate for the disabled child by performing at an above-average level (Cleveland and Miller 1977; Kirkman, 1984). A number of authors have suggested that increased parental expectations have a deleterious impact of the psychological well-being of siblings of children with disabilities (Crnic and Leconte, 1986; Featherstone, 1980; Seligman, 1987), although there is no firm evidence to support this claim. In responding to the disability in one of their children, it is possible that parents increase their expectations of the other children in the family. They may develop an idealized view of what a 'typical' child is like and when the real child fails to live up to these enhanced expectations, he or she is judged to be deviant. Cuskelly and Gunn (1993) examined this possibility and found no significant differences in the reports of expected problems in 'typical' children from mothers of children with Down syndrome and comparison mothers. Mothers in both groups found it difficult to separate their responses about typical children from their experiences of their own children, so it is possible that the method used by these authors failed to address this issue adequately.

Other variables which may be important contributors to sibling adjustment include temperamental characteristics of the sibling, the child with Down syndrome and the parents. The sibling relationship, which may itself be influenced by the temperamental characteristics of the participants, may also have some bearing on the development of problem behaviour. Other important issues which have attracted recent family research interest are parental favouritism, children's perceptions of such favouritism, parental discipline strategies and the relationships between family members and their community.

CONCLUSION

The changes over time in sibling problems, as chronicled by the Gath studies, may be due to changing circumstances for families who have a child with Down syndrome and/or to broader social changes. In some countries, important changes for families include increased resources for the education of children with disabilities and for respite services. It has also been suggested that attitudes to persons with a disability have shown some changes (Rees *et al.*, 1991) which may make family life less difficult.

Gath pointed out that the families she studied in 1972 may have been atypical as they decided to keep their child with Down syndrome at home. It is nowadays usual for children with Down syndrome to remain with their natural families but the way these families conduct their day-to-day lives may be very different from their 1970s' counterparts. Social changes concerned with families, women's role within families and the broader society make it unlikely that research findings one or two generations ago have total applicability today. Possible cultural differences must not be overlooked either, as the contradictions between Gath's recent results and those from Australia demonstrate.

Despite such inconsistencies, it is clear that a perception of the child with Down syndrome as a disruption to normal family functioning and the cause of poor sibling adjustment is not tenable. The search for those variables which act to mediate and/or moderate sibling adjustment is worth while, however it must be recognized that definitive relationships will never be established. For individual siblings, adjustment is likely to be ever-changing as it is the product of personal characteristics, life stage, and the dynamic interaction of these with family characteristics all of which are embedded in social and cultural contexts which also change over time.

REFERENCES

Achenbach, T.M. and Edelbrock, C. (1983) *Manual for the Child Behavior Checklist and Revised Child Behavior Profiles*, Burlington: University of Vermont.

Bank, S. and Kahn, M.D. (1982) *The Sibling Bond*, New York: Basic Books.

Bargh, J.A. and Shul, Y. (1980) On the cognitive benefits of teaching. *Journal of Educational Psychology*, **72**, pp. 593–604.

Beckman, P.J. (1983) Influence of selected child characteristics on stress in families of handicapped infants. *American Journal of Mental Deficiency*, **88**, pp. 150–56.

Breslau, N. (1982) The psychological study of chronically ill and disabled children: are healthy siblings appropriate controls? *Journal of Abnormal Child Psychology*, **11**, pp. 379–91.

Bronfenbrenner, U. (1979) *The Ecology of Human Development*. Cambridge, MA: Harvard University Press.

Bryant, B.K. and Litman, C. (1987) Siblings as teachers and therapists. In F.F. Schachter and R.K. Stone (eds), *Practical Concerns about Siblings: Bridging the Research Practice Gap*, pp. 185–205. New York: Haworth Press.

Carr, J. (1988) Six weeks to twenty-one years old: a longitudinal study of children with Down's syndrome. and their families. *Journal of Child Psychology and Psychiatry*, **29**, pp. 407–31.

Chinitz, S.P. (1981) A sibling group for brothers and sisters of handicapped children. *Children Today*, November–December, pp. 21–23.

Cleveland, D.W. and Miller, N. (1977) Attitudes and life commitments of older siblings of mentally retarded adults: an exploratory study. *Mental Retardation*, **15**, pp. 38–41.

Craft, M.J., Lakin, J.A., Oppliger, R.A., Clancy, G.M. and Vander Linden, D.H. (1990) Siblings as change agents for promoting the functional status of children with cerebral palsy. *Developmental Medicine and Child Neurology*, **32**, pp. 1049–57.

Crnic, K.A. and Leconte, J.M. (1986) Understanding sibling needs and influences. In R.R. Fewell and P.F. Vadasy (eds), *Families of Handicapped Children: Needs and Supports Across the Lifespan*, pp. 75–98. Austin: Pro-Ed.

Cuskelly, M. (1993) Psychological adjustment of the siblings of children with Down syndrome. Unpublished PhD thesis, University of Queensland.

Cuskelly, M. and Dadds, M. (1992) Behavioural problems in children with Down's syndrome and their siblings. *Journal of Child Psychology and Psychiatry*, **33**, pp. 749–61.

Cuskelly, M. and Gunn, P. (1993) Maternal reports on behavior of siblings of children with Down syndrome. *American Journal on Mental Retardation*, **97**, pp. 521–29.

Dyson, L. (1989) Adjustment of siblings of handicapped children: a comparison. *Journal of Pediatric Psychology*, **14**, pp. 215–29.

Farber, B. (1959). Effects of a severely mentally retarded child on family integration. *Monographs of the Society for Research in Child Development*, **24** (2), (Serial No. 71).

Farber, B. (1960) Family organization and crises: maintainence of integration in families with a severely mentally retarded child. *Monograph of the Society of Research in Child Development*, **25** (1), (Serial No. 75).

Featherstone, H. (1980) *A Difference in the Family: Life with a Disabled Child*, New York: Basic Books.

Fisman, S. and Wolf, L. (1991) The handicapped child: psychological effects of parental, marital, and sibling relationships. *Psychiatric Clinics of North America*, **14**, pp. 199–217.

Gath, A. (1972) The mental health of siblings of congenitally abnormal children. *Journal of Child Psychology and Psychiatry*, **13**, pp. 211–18.

Gath, A. (1973) The school-age siblings of mongol children. *British Journal of Psychiatry*, **123**, pp. 161–67.

Gath, A. (1974) Sibling reactions to mental handicap: a comparison of the brothers and sisters of mongol children. *Journal of Child Psychology and Psychiatry*, **15**, pp. 187–98.

Gath, A. (1978) *Down's Syndrome and the Family: The Early Years*, London: Academic Press.

Gath, A. and Gumley, D. (1984) Down's syndrome and the family: follow-up of children first seen in infancy. *Developmental Medicine and Child Neurology*, **26**, pp. 500–08.

Gath, A. and Gumley, D. (1987) Retarded children and their siblings. *Journal of Child Psychology and Psychiatry*, **28**, pp. 715–30.

Grossman, F.K. (1972) *Brothers and Sisters of Retarded Children: An Exploratory Study*, Syracuse: Syracuse University Press.

Harris, V.S. and McHale, S.M. (1989) Family life problems, daily caregiving activities, and the psychological well-being of mothers of mentally retarded children. *American Journal on Mental Retardation*, **94**, pp. 231–39.

Harter, S (1979) *Manual for the Perceived Competence Scale for Children*, Denver: University of Denver.

Harter, S. (1982) The Perceived Competence Scale for Children. *Child Development*, **53**, pp. 87–97.

Harter, S. and Pike, R. (1981) *The Pictorial Scale of Perceived Competence and Social Acceptance for Young Children*. Denver: University of Denver.

Hayes, A. (1994) Families and disabilities. In A Ashman and J. Elkins (eds) *Educating Children with Special Needs*, 2nd edn, pp. 37–70, New York: Prentice Hall.

Kaplan, F. (1969) Siblings of the retarded. In S.B. Sareson and J. Doris (eds), *Psychological Problems in Mental Deficiency*, 4th edn, pp. 186–208, New York: Harper and Row.

Kirkman, M. (1984) The effects of a handicapped child on schooling, friendships and social life of the normal sibling. Paper presented at the 13th annual meeting, Australian Social Psychologists, Adelaide, Australia.

Lavigeur, H. (1976) The use of siblings as an adjunct to the behavioral treatment of children in the home with parents as therapist. *Behavior Therapy*, **7**, pp. 602–13

Lobato, D. (1983) Siblings of handicapped children: a review. *Journal of Autism and Developmental Disabilities*, **13**, pp. 347–65.

Lobato, D., Barbour, L., Hall, L.J. and Miller, C.T. (1987) Psychosocial characteristics of preschool siblings of handicapped and nonhandicapped children. *Journal of Abnormal Child Psychology*, **15**, pp. 329–38.

McHale, S.M. and Gamble, W.C. (1989) Sibling relationships of children with disabled and nondisabled brothers and sisters. *Developmental Psychology*, **25**, pp. 421–9.

McHale, S.M., Simeonsson, R.J. and Sloan, J.L. (1984) Children with handicapped brothers and sisters. In E. Schopler and G.B. Mesibov (eds), *The Effects of Autism on the Family*, pp. 327–42, New York: Plenum.

Mercer, J.R. (1966) Patterns of family crises related to reacceptance of the retardate. *American Journal of Mental Deficiency*, **71**, pp. 18–32.

O'Connor, W.A. and Stachowiak, J. (1971) Patterns of interaction in families with low adjusted, high adjusted, and mentally retarded members. *Family Process*, **10**, pp. 229–41.

Poznanski, E. (1969) Psychiatric difficulties in siblings of handicapped children. *Clinical Paediatrics*, **8**, (4), pp. 232–34.

Quay, H.C. and Peterson, D.R. (1983) *Interim Manual for the Revised Behavior Problem Checklist*, Published by the authors at 59 Fifth, Highland Park, New Jersey, 08904.

Rees, L.M., Spreen, O. and Harnadek, M. (1991) Do attitudes towards persons with handicaps really shift over time? Comparison between 1975 and 1988. *Mental Retardation*, **29**, pp. 81–86.

Rodrigue, J.R., Geffken, G.R. and Morgan, S.B. (1993) Perceived competence and behavioral adjustment of siblings of children with autism. *Journal of Autism and Developmental Disorders*, **23**, pp. 665–74.

Roe, D. and Plummer, S. (1987) Siblings of disabled children: A report of an investigative study. Paper presented at the 22nd annual conference of the Australian Psychological Society, Canberra.

Rutter, M., Tizard, J. and Whitmore, K. (1970) *Education, Health and Behaviour*, London: Longman.

San Martino, M. and Newman, M.B. (1974) Siblings of the retarded: a population at risk. *Child Psychiatry and Human Development*, **4**, pp. 168–77.

Schild, S. (1971) The family of the retarded child. In R. Koch and J.C. Dobson (eds), *The Mentally Retarded Child and his Family*, pp. 197–205, New York: Bruner.

Schreibman, L., O'Neill, R.E. and Koegel, R.L. (1983) Behavioral training for siblings of autistic children. *Journal of Applied Behavior Analysis*, **16**, pp. 129–38.

Seligman, M. (1987) Adaptation of children to a chronically ill or mentally handicapped sibling. *Canadian Medical Association Journal*, **15,** pp. 1249–52.

Simeonsson, R.J. and McHale, S.M. (1981) Review: research on handicapped children: sibling relationships. *Child: Care, Health and Development*, **7,** pp. 153–71.

Skrtic, T.M., Summers, J.A., Brotherson, M.J. and Turnbull, A.P. (1984) Severely handicapped children and their brothers and sisters. In J. Blacher (ed.), *Severely Handicapped Young Children and their Families: Research in Review*, pp. 215–46, New York:Academic Press.

Stoneman, Z. (1989) Comparison groups in research on families with mentally retarded members: a methodological and conceptual review. *American Journal on Mental Retardation*, **94,** pp. 195–215.

Stoneman, Z. (1990) Conceptual relationships between family research and mental retardation. *International Review of Research in Mental Retardation*, **16,** pp. 161–202.

Stoneman, Z. and Brody, G.H. (1982) Strengths inherent in sibling interactions involving a retarded child: a functional role theory approach. In N. Stinnett, J. De Frain, K. King, H. Lingren, J G. Rowe, S. Van Zandt and R. Williams (eds), *Family Strengths: Positive Support Systems*, pp. 113–29, Lincoln, NE: University of Nebraska Press.

Trevino, F. (1979) Siblings of handicapped children: identifying those at risk. *Social Casework*, **60,** pp. 488–93.

Vadasy, P.G., Fewell, R.R., Meyer, D.J. and Schell, G. (1984) Siblings of handicapped children: a developmental perspective on family interactions. *Family Relations*, **33,** pp. 155–67.

Living in the Community

24 Living in the Community

Trevor R. Parmenter

The following three chapters trace the journey of a person with Down syndrome through the transitions from school to young adulthood and beyond.

One of the basic assumptions throughout each of the chapters is that people with Down syndrome can live and work in the community, enjoy normal human relationships and an enhanced quality of life compared to that which was predicted by professionals in earlier decades.

Research in the area of Down syndrome in the 1970s and 1980s typically concentrated upon early intervention and educational programs, demonstrating, in the main, that early sensory and cognitive stimulation enhanced the overall functioning of young children with Down syndrome. Gains made in these early programs were shown to be maintained into the junior school years, provided on-going support was provided.

There has not been the same concentration of research on this specific population, however, in their later school years and beyond. While Vivienne Riches' chapter *Transition from School to Community* describes an approach being used in a school system for all adolescents with a disability it is suggested that the basic principles are nevertheless relevant for young people with Down syndrome.

The essential features of this approach are somewhat similar to those recommended by Roy McConkey in his chapter *Living in Developing Countries*, especially his section on mobilizing existing supports in the community.

The steps in effecting a smooth transition from school to work and adult living are basically those one should use with all young people – early planning at the secondary school level involving the teachers, the student and their families. The planning involves a consideration of the range of options the young person might choose upon leaving school. This process helps the school and the families appreciate the fact that a young person with Down syndrome will become an adult with the same needs and aspirations of his/her non-disabled peers. This process is especially important to combat the 'eternal child' syndrome which so often accompanies this population throughout their lives.

As the young student progresses through secondary schooling increasing attention should be given to how other agencies or supports in the community may be used to help this transition process. Disappointingly, in many countries, these young people leave school and return home to spend their lives in an un-stimulating environment, leading to a 'wash out' of the skills and competencies gained throughout their school life. This situation occurs so often because neither the school nor the families has given sufficient attention to post school planning.

While special education programs have quite properly focussed upon building skills and competencies, a different set of interventions are necessary to complement them throughout their lives. These involve natural supports that might be marshalled from within the community. Here it is necessary to define what is meant by *community*, for there are many interpretations.

In the discussions surrounding the movement of people with disabilities out of institutional living, it was assumed that living in a group home in an ordinary neighbourhood would ensure they were part of a community. However, many of these people were destined to lead lonely, solitary lives with few support networks except those provided by paid staff.

We need to help these young people build a community in which they establish friendships, mutual support networks and intimate relationships which people in general enjoy. For much of their younger lives we have concentrated solely upon building *independent living* skills. Now we need to emphasise the *interdependence* of living in a community where reciprocal relationships should be the major feature. Here we can learn lessons from developing countries.

We are becoming increasingly aware that in order to reduce the handicaps brought about the chromosomal impairment, there is a need both to develop basic skills and competencies within the person as well as making environmental adaptations which can ease their entry into normal community living. Of course we are still confronted with the handicapping attitudes of the community toward people with disabilities generally. But here, too, there have been promising improvements.

Of paramount importance is that we do not allow powerful ideological and philosophical factors to move us too far ahead of our capacity to deliver satisfying and secure lifestyles to these people. Each of the authors in this section make a plea that we view each individual as being unique. Therefore, we need a range of approaches in supporting people with Down syndrome in their communities.

For all parents it is hard to 'let go' and allow our adolescent children to develop a new life where family is not the sole focus of their relationships. For parents of children with a disability this is especially difficult. What we are now seeing, however, are large numbers of aging parents who have not 'let go' and who are now no longer able to care for their disabled son or daughter whom they have cared for at home.

In many countries supported employment in the general workforce has been a successful alternative to sheltered workshops. This development has an important implication for school programs which need to prepare the students for the general work environment, especially those social and interpersonal skills which are critical for job success.

For personnel who provide support in finding a job and subsequent on-the-job training, there is a challenge to transfer this support to more natural supports within the work environment; for instance co-workers. As Roy Brown points out in the chapter *Living in the Community as an Adult* work is only a part of one's total life and having a job alone does not ensure that the person will have a satisfactory quality of life. However, a significant finding by Knox (1994) is that a job in the community provides a person with a disability a valued identity, surely a contributing factor to one's quality of life (Parmenter, 1988, 1991).

There is a special need to ensure that there are supports which can be accessed at those periods in a person's life when significant changes occur. These situations may include changing jobs, getting married, retiring, or losing a close friend or relative.

The following three chapters provide a rich array of helpful suggestions for parents and carers of adolescents and adults with Down syndrome of ways in which these people may have a life that is self fulfilling. Neither author is suggesting that the process of growing into adulthood is going to be easy and without trials and anxieties.

It is being strongly suggested, however, that we must give adults with Down syndrome the opportunities and support which will provide them with a life that has a real purpose. We do not, as yet, have all the answers, but we must continue to combat the negativism which in former years resulted in many of these people having a fairly empty and sterile lifestyle.

REFERENCES

Knox, M. (1994). Workplace relationships – an insider's view. Paper presented to Joint National Conference of the Australian Society for the Study of Intellectual Disability and the National Council on Intellectual Disability, Fremantle, Western Australia.

Parmenter, T.R. (1988). An analysis of the dimensions of quality of life for people with physical disabilities. In R.I. Brown (Ed.) *Quality of life for handicapped people*. London: Croom Helm.

Parmenter, T.R. (1991). Quality of life for people with developmental disabilities. *International Review of Research in Mental Retardation*, **18**, 247–287.

25 Transition from School to Community

Vivienne Riches

Parents, professionals and policy-makers have been concerned about the poor outcomes achieved and the difficulties encountered by all students with disabilities, including those with Down syndrome, as these young people make the crucial transition from secondary schooling to life in the adult community. Research results over several decades had revealed a bleak picture for youth with disabilities postschool, affecting all areas of life from employment and education and training to living arrangements, social networks and relationships, leisure and recreation, interests and satisfaction. The evidence showed that students with disabilities were not making the transition from schooling to community adjustment and adult life as successfully as had been expected, with outcomes falling far short of those being achieved by peers without disabilities (Bellamy, 1985; Edgar, 1987, 1988; Ford *et al.*, 1992; Halpern, 1992; Hasazi *et al.*, 1985; Hasazi *et al.*, 1982; Horrocks, 1991; Knox and Parmenter, 1993; Krupinski *et al.*, 1973; Limbrick, 1977; Roessler *et al.*, 1990; Wagner, 1989).

Such findings contributed to an increasing awareness of the importance of the transition years, and the need to make definite plans, to co-ordinate services and to support students with disabilities during this challenging time, before they leave the school system. A range of transition initiatives have therefore been started and are now being implemented in various countries. These initiatives seek to empower students and families, so that students with disabilities can make more informed choices for the future, secure more satisfying living and working arrangements, enjoy a better quality of life in the community and gain access to appropriate generic and specialist adult services as and when necessary.

THE NEW SOUTH WALES TRANSITION INITIATIVE

In Australia, an OECD-sponsored inquiry resulted in the development of a national strategy for assisting students with disabilities in transition (Australian Steering Committee, 1985). Stimulated by this work, New South Wales (NSW) began a transition initiative in 1989, which brought together the government school sector, the NSW Technical and Further Education (TAFE) Commission and the Unit for Community Integration Studies, Macquarie University. Funded as an initiative of the Special Education Plan of the NSW Department of School Education, opportunity was provided to introduce and evaluate a system that was based on the principles identified in the national strategy and that could meet the unique needs of all students with disabilities who were in government special and mainstream secondary educational settings.

The aims were to build a strong foundation during the secondary school years, to assist students to plan for the future through the individual planning or future planning process, to assist students and families to identify and liaise with post-school options and services before school exit, and to facilitate and co-ordinate entry into the community, including post-secondary education and training, and other services as required.

Since transition is an outcome-oriented process, a transition process model was adopted, based on Halpern's work (Halpern, 1985; Halpern and Nelson, 1988), which acknowledged that a number of areas had to be addressed, rather than employment alone, if meaningful transition from school to community was to occur. Most educators and researchers now agree with this stance, and argue that transition planning and activity should include post-compulsory education and training, employment, financial security, residential arrangements, individual competence in community living, recreation and leisure and quality of life issues such as friendships, satisfaction and choice (Clark and Kolstoe, 1990; Edgar, 1987, 1988; Halpern, 1985, 1992; Halpern *et al.*, 1986; Parmenter, 1988, 1992; Riches *et al.*, 1993; Wehman, 1990, 1992; Wehman *et al.*, 1986)

The process of team building, needs assessment, planning, implementation and evaluation (Figure 25.1) has been applied at a number of levels, resulting in individual transition planning teams being established within schools to assist and support individual students, school-based teams being developed to address curriculum and school-related issues, community-based teams being formed to facilitate co-operation and collaboration at the community level and improve adult service provisions, and an Interdepartmental Committee on Transition being established to co-ordinate and collaborate on policy and practices at the central level (Glenday and Riches, 1990; Ling *et al.*, 1993; NSW Department of School Education, 1991; Parmenter, 1993; Parmenter and Riches, 1991; Riches and Parmenter, 1991).

Stodden (1991, 1994) has contended that the transition initiative should not be viewed as an add-on programme, but should provide a way or restructuring the very core activities of education to ensure desired outcomes are identified and addressed effectively. Smith *et al.* (1992) warned that, despite increased attention being given to the development and implementation of transition planning in special education, there are various pitfalls that can adversely effect the actual success of transitional processes for students with specific needs, such that practitioners must become good strategic planners. The NSW transition initiative has tried to be mindful of these issues, and although success varies across and within regions and areas, the transition process has emerged as a significant agent of change, affecting the way transition services for many students with disabilities are planned, delivered and evaluated for and by individuals, schools, communities and education authorities, working in partnership.

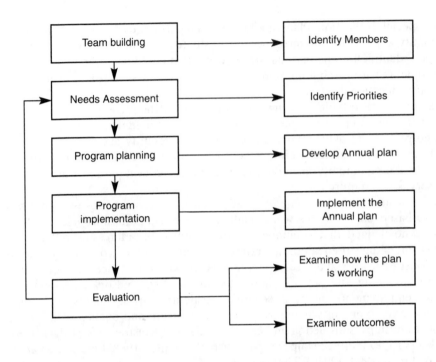

Figure 25.1 Transition process model (Halpern and Nelson, 1988)

CRITICAL FEATURES

A number of features have been identified as critical for ensuring the process is effective and that students with disabilities do make a smooth and effective transition. Many of these features had been identified by researchers before the commencement of the NSW initiative and had therefore been incorporated from the very start (CERI, 1988; Edgar, 1987; Halpern, 1989; Moon *et al.*, 1990; Patton and Browder, 1988; Wehman, 1990; Wehman *et al.*, 1985). However, experiences over the past six years have provided additional insights as well as ratifying the importance and the contribution that each of these elements plays in the Australian context. Critical features have been identified as:

- commitment and support at the central policy and funding level;
- individual transition planning involving all key stakeholders (students, parents/care-givers, advocates, teachers and relevant community agency personnel) as the central driving force for all planning and activity;
- the provision of relevant and appropriate school curricula and instruction, that enable students to gain valued credentials;
- access to and provision of a range of appropriate adult services in the local community, including meaningful training and employment options post-school;
- liaison with and linkage of students to post school options and opportunities before leaving school;

- ongoing professional development for teachers and service providers;
- community involvement and local planning;
- interagency co-operation and collaboration at all levels.

CENTRAL POLICY AND SUPPORT

Commitment from government and educational sectors at the policy and planning levels have been significant, contributing to the success of the transition initiative. Education and TAFE NSW policy support the Commonwealth and NSW Disability Services Acts of 1986 and 1993. Furthermore, the NSW Department of School Education (DSE), through its *Special Education Policy* (NSW Department of School Education, 1993a) has promoted principles of individual planning, parent and family involvement in decision-making, and interagency co-operation and collaboration, and in response to research findings, transition from school to post-school options was identified as a strategic outcome under the *Special Education Plan 1993–1997* (NSW Department of School Education, 1993b, p. 2). The aim is 'to provide the most educationally effective transition from school to community for students with disabilities'. Policy and commitment have been ratified and supported through staffing and resource provisions, and the initiative was rapidly expanded from pilot status in 1989 to a recurrent programme encompassing all regions in the state.

Previously educational sectors, government departments and non-government agencies tended to work in isolation. Increasingly, however, co-operation and collaboration are occurring centrally through the Interdepartmental Committee on Transition, and through co-operative cross-sectoral efforts. Both the Association of Independent Schools and the Catholic Education Commission have shown a commitment to transition policy and processes being implemented in schools, and co-operative efforts between all sectors, TAFE and Macquarie University have resulted in additional federal resources being won for specific projects, including the development and delivery of an open learning, distance education, National Professional Development course for teachers of students with disabilities in transition, and additional staffing in the form of Transition/School Liaison Officers who are able to further extend the transition initiative to students with disabilities in mainstream settings across the educational sectors, in areas not previously accessed or resourced.

Collaborative work contributed to additional State funding being granted to establish and run post-school provisions for students who have severe disabilities and high support needs, while a user-friendly document, outlining, under broad categories, the range of post-school options and services provided by government agencies in NSW has been developed. This document is to be disseminated to families and schools, while at a later stage, gaps, overlaps and anomalies in service provision are to be examined at the central level. National networks are being established and information and strategies are being shared at a national level.

INDIVIDUAL TRANSITION PLANNING

Individual transition planning (ITP) is an essential feature of the transition process. Comprehensive procedures and sample ITP pro formas have been developed and disseminated to teachers to assist in the preparation, implementation, management and monitoring of ITPs. Staff in participating schools are trained in the principles and practices involved. They are then encouraged, and initially assisted, to help establish ITPs for each student with a disability. A review of the implementation of the ITP system in the schools (Parmenter and Riches, 1990) confirmed the value of individual planning but resulted in some modifications and adaptations to the way in which the system was implemented. The involvement of other educational sectors has further highlighted the need for flexibility, and some schools now use a personal future or lifestyle planning approach in preference to the more structured ITP system (O'Brien, 1987). Where schools already have individual education plans (IEPs), the transition plan may be a separate section that is attached to the IEP, while in other cases, schools have preferred to integrate all instructional planning and additional support strategy planning under the one ITP format. Regular reviews and adaptations are required to keep the system dynamic and relevant to all key stakeholders, especially students, parents, advocates and school personnel.

Whatever individual planning approach is taken, preparation of teachers, students and parents and/or advocates before the ITP meeting has proved vital. Easy-to-follow checklists, written in plain English for students with intellectual disabilities, the use of videos, role-plays and other methods to prepare students and parent/carers and ensure increased and effective participation, choice and decision-making are increasingly being investigated and developed. The use of interpreters, Aboriginal Liaison Officers or other specialist support persons has proved beneficial for certain students, both in the preparation stage and at the planning meeting. The location of the planning meeting may also need to be negotiated, as a neutral or even home location can reduce some of the barriers that otherwise can occur in the school setting.

CURRICULUM AND INSTRUCTION ISSUES

It is now increasingly recognized that curriculum options are required that lead to quality learning outcomes and recognized and valued credentials for all students. The initial introduction of the NSW DSE Transition Initiative occurred principally in special education settings (special schools and special classes) where it became evident that few courses were available for students with intellectual disabilities, and many students were failing to gain any credential for their years of schooling. Several alternative functional curriculum packages, covering functional academics, vocational training, personal and social skills, daily living skills, recreation and leisure and travel training were developed and shared between schools involved in transition planning. Unfortunately, this meant that transition was incorrectly viewed by many teachers as a programme, and as an alternative programme to mainstream schooling, rather than a process applicable to all students. This misconception has gradually been corrected.

However, the choice of appropriate curriculum pathways and the achievement of credentials remain significant issues for all students, and especially for those students with disabilities who do not satisfy requirements for widely recognized credentials. Students have the option of choosing to study the regular curriculum, with the hope of gaining a credential, or of choosing an alternative and relevant but non accredited pathway. The inclusion movement encourages students and families to opt for social integration that necessitates studying the regular academic curriculum, aiming at accreditation at Year 10, (School Certificate) and Year 12 (Higher School Certificate) levels. Increasingly, students are opting for integration but, sadly, very few students with intellectual disabilities are able to successfully complete courses leading to Higher School Certificate credentials, formal credentials that are recognized and valued in the community. Junior students taking alternative courses can now earn a School Certificate credential in which courses are designated 'life skills'. These courses have a strong emphasis on practical and vocational training, with work experience provided either at school or in the community, so students can, through this mechanism, gain skills training for employment and later life.

The dilemma of choosing the most appropriate pathway faces many students and families, as well as teachers, and the choice is not always an easy one. Early planning and the provision of relevant information to students and families is essential for informed decision-making. Negotiations have been occurring with the credentialling body, the NSW Board of Studies, both centrally and through regional liaison officers, to ensure students do gain correct information and, wherever possible, accreditation for courses studied.

VOCATIONAL TRAINING

Secondary school vocational education has now been identified as a positive educational intervention on school performance and post-school outcomes for students with disabilities (Riches *et al.*, 1993; Wagner, 1989, 1991). Several vocational training programmes were established and funded as joint ventures under the NSW DSE Transition Initiative. The aim was to provide more systematic and occupationally oriented vocational training to students with disabilities in government school settings during their final school years. These community-based training programmes built upon school work experience programmes, and include job coaching, enclaves, work crews and TAFE transition courses. These are specialist programmes that have, nevertheless, been viewed very positively by students, families, schools and communities. ITPs consistently identify vocational training as a top priority, while evaluations reveal that these vocational training provisions have increased school retention rates, improved student and parent satisfaction, improved participation in post-secondary education and training, and contributed to better post-school employment outcomes for many students, particularly those with mild and moderate intellectual disabilities (Riches and Parmenter, 1990, 1993; Riches *et al.*, 1993; Watters *et al.*, 1993).

Increasingly, senior secondary education is introducing dual accredited courses with vocational training components, and the challenge for teachers is to ensure these generic courses are available to all students, such that those with special needs gain the assistance and support necessary to enable them to complete the courses successfully.

POST-SCHOOL OPTIONS AND OPPORTUNITIES

While secondary schooling should lay the foundation for a successful transition, a major concern for school personnel, students with disabilities and their families has been the lack of information on just what services are available post-school, as well as an inadequate number of appropriate, high-quality adult services to which students can make the transition from school.

Increasingly, provisions are being made to assist students with disabilities in higher education and training, and a range of opportunities and options are also available in the areas of accommodation, housing and support, respite care, advocacy, self-help groups and family support, legal services, health, social, recreation and leisure facilities and programmes, and transportation.

Although a number of programmes and facilities may exist, they may not always be available or accessible to individuals with disabilities due to entry criteria, waiting lists and/or geographic and distance factors. When there is a lack of availability of opportunities and options in the post-school arena, then, no matter how effective the foundation education and training may be, or how much planning may occur, transition will ultimately fail because there is nowhere to transition to. A major role of school-based and community-based transition teams, therefore, has been the identification, collection and dissemination of information to students with disabilities and their families about the availability of local and state adult services in a range of areas.

Gaps in service provision are being documented. In a number of cases, these service gaps have become the focus for concerted action at central and local levels. Concern over the lack of appropriate adult programmes for students who have severe disabilities and high support needs was highlighted by the follow-along study of the first cohort of students in transition (Riches *et al.*, 1993). Since 1993, the NSW Government has funded the Post School Options Program to assist school-leavers with disabilities who have high to moderate support needs who are making the transition from school to independent living in the community, through the provision of community access and other training and support.

LINKAGES

Effective communication and liaison with students and parents, school staff, other participating schools, regional and central office personnel, relevant adult agencies and training providers such as TAFE, and the local community has proved essential. Initially, project funding and structures did not provide for co-ordination functions. Since then, classroom teachers and relevant school executives have been trained and assisted in planning for the introduction and implementation of transition processes within their various schools.

Evaluations of various aspects of the NSW DSE transition initiative have all confirmed the importance of having specifically identified personnel to ensure these linkages are put in place, rather than leaving them to chance (Parmenter and Riches, 1990; Riches, 1993a; Riches and Parmenter, 1990, 1991, 1993; Watters *et al.*, 1993; Unit for Rehabilitation Studies, 1992). The provision of co-ordinator or liaison officer positions who can perform these important functions has therefore been identified as critical for success.

PROFESSIONAL DEVELOPMENT

One of the most critical facets identified for schools newly embarking on transition, and for ongoing implementation in those schools already involved, has been the in-service and professional development needs of staff. Specific priority areas identified by staff for professional development include skills and tools for practical and functional assessment across a number of curriculum areas; the development of appropriate and effective curricula in key learning areas; training in writing goals and behavioural objectives; the development of skills in individual planning as distinct from individual instruction; strategies to effectively involve parents and students in choice and decision-making; administration, timetabling and programming skills to accommodate student needs; meeting and negotiation procedures; ongoing training and support in ITP implementation and evaluation procedures; implementation and evaluation of data-based instruction; and training in student follow-up and follow-along procedures.

Field-based staff training and written guidelines and support documents have proven effective, while local workshops, State and National Transition Conferences have been popular. It is hoped that the addition of the university accredited National Professional Development course in transition will assist further in meeting the significant professional development needs that have been identified.

PARTNERSHIPS

The partnerships now operating between schools, communities and government departments are contributing to improved outcomes for students with disabilities who are in transition. Twenty Community Transition Teams now exist in NSW, enabling interagency co-operation and planning to occur at the local level. These teams have planned and carried out a range of activities to improve community attitudes and to assist people with disabilities in the areas of employment, residential provisions, recreation and leisure, transportation and advocacy (Riches, 1993b; Riches and Parmenter, 1991).

Many teams have developed and disseminated information directories, and the majority have held successful information expositions and information days.

Several new services have been established and/or extended through co-operative efforts of team members, including the establishment of a competitive employment, training and placement service in one community and an innovative co-worker model of supported employment for people with high support needs in another. A number of teams have developed strategies to promote community inclusion and social integration, and to foster more positive community attitudes towards people who have a disability. Databases are being developed that will assist in future planning and service provision. Students with disabilities, parents and families, teachers and service agency personnel have all benefited by these collaborative efforts, particularly through better information, streamlined referral procedures, additional and improved services, and direct liaison and networking within and between teams.

Technical assistance has been supplied by university staff at the state, regional, community and local-school levels, on various aspects of the project. This has proved essential to support structural rather than superficial change, and to assist in the translation of theory to practice. Other universities and professional bodies should be encouraged to contribute their expertise and support to schools, departments, agencies and communities at whatever level can be provided.

CONCLUSION

Working together can be difficult as trust has to be developed and agreement will not always be automatic or healthy. Working together at all levels to resolve problems can be challenging but can result in positive and productive outcomes for all players. Overall, the partnerships now forged through the NSW transition initiative have created a more dynamic and student-responsive service delivery system, enabled student needs to be more effectively met, assisted in empowering students and families during the important transition years, and contributed to better outcomes for students with disabilities. In addition, collaboration has fostered friendships and support networks among staff who previously felt isolated and vulnerable, and strengthened commitment among the various partners, who are now working together in new and exciting ways.

REFERENCES

Australian Steering Committee, (1985) *Project on Handicapped Youth in Transition: A Strategy for Disabled Youth in Transition*, Canberra: OECD/CERI.

Bellamy, G.T. (1985) Transition progress: comments on Hasazi, Gordon and Roe. *Exceptional Children*, **51**, pp. 474–77.

CERI (1988) *A Strategy for Disabled Youth in Transition*. Project on Handicapped Youth in Transition, National Steering Committee Report, Paris: OECD.

Clark, G.M. and Kolstoe, O.P. (1990) *Career Development and Transition Education for Adolescents with Disabilities*, New York: Allyn and Bacon.

Edgar, E. (1987) Secondary programs in special education: are many of them justifiable. *Exceptional Children*, **53**, pp. 555–61.

Edgar, E. (1988) Employment as an outcome for mildly handicapped students: current status and future directions. *Focus on Exceptional Children*, **21** (1), pp. 1–8.

Ford, J., Parmenter, T.R. and Koop, A. (1992) A qualitative study of social interactions in supported employment settings. Paper presented at 9th world congress of the International Association for the Scientific Study of Intellectual Disability, Broadbeach, Queensland, Australia, 5–9 August.

Glenday, S. and Riches, V. (1990) Transition for students with disabilities. *Australian Achievements in Special Education*. Conference proceedings of the 14th National Conference of the Australian Association of Special Education, Canberra, September.

Halpern, A.S. (1985) Transition: a look at the foundations. *Exceptional Children*, **51**, pp. 479–86.

Halpern, A.S. (1989) A systematic approach to transition programming for adolescents and young adults with disabilities. *Australian and New Zealand Journal of Developmental Disabilities*, **15** (1), pp. 1–13.

Halpern, A.S. (1992) Quality of life as a conceptual framework for evaluating transition outcomes. Keynote address at the University of Illinios Transition Research Institute's Seventh Annual Project Director's Meeting, Washington.

Halpern, A.S., Nave, G., Close, D.W. and Nelson, D. (1986) An empirical analysis of community adjustment for adults with mental retardation in semi-independent living programs. *Australian and New Zealand Journal of Developmental Disabilities*, **12**, pp. 147–57.

Halpern, A.S. and Nelson, D.J. (1988) *Secondary Special Education and Transition Teams Procedures Manual*, Eugene: University of Oregon, for the Oregon Department of Education.

Hasazi, S., Gordon L., Roe, C., Hull, M., Finck, K. and Salembier, G. (1985) A statewide follow-up of post high school employment and residential status of students labelled 'Mentally Retarded'. *Education and Training of the Mentally Retarded*, **20**, pp. 222–34.

Hasazi, S., Preskill, H., Gordon L. and Collins, M. (1982) *Factors Associated with the Employment Status of Handicapped Youth*. Cited in Wehman, P. Kregel, J. and Barcus, J.M. (1985) From school to work: a vocational transition model for handicapped students. *Exceptional Children*, **52**, pp. 25–37.

Horrocks, C. (1991) Isolation and security: transition process and outcomes for graduates with mental handicaps. Conference Paper Focus 91: The British Columbia Conference Emphasising Co-operative Approach Towards the Integration of Children with Disabilities into Regular Classrooms, Victoria, BC, Canada.

Knox, M. and Parmenter, T.R. (1993) An examination of the social networks and social support mechanisms for people with a mild intellectual disability in competitive employment. *International Journal of Rehabilitation Research*, **16**, pp. 1–12.

Krupinski, J., Mackenzie, A., Meredith, E. and Stoller, A. (1973) *A Follow Up of Mentally Retarded Young Adults*, Melbourne Mental Health Authority of Victoria, Special Publications No. 3.

Limbrick, D.N. (1977). Preparing intellectually handicapped people for work: a lifetime placement? Paper presented at the AAMR Seminar on Pensions or Progress, Melbourne, July.

Ling, A, Morris, C. and Riches, V.C. (1993) Transition for students with disabilities: the first five years. *Quality and Equity in Intellectual Disability*. Proceedings of the 29th ASSID National Conference, 30 November– 5 December Newcastle, NSW.

Moon, S.M., Diambra, T. and Hill, M. (1990) An outcome oriented vocational process for students with severe handicaps. *Teaching Exceptional Children*, Fall, pp. 47–50.

NSW Department of School Education (1991) The NSW transition model. *From School to What?* Proceedings of the First National Conference on Transition Education for Students with Disabilities, Gazebo Hotel, Sydney, 27–28 June.

NSW Department of School Education (1993a) *Special Education Policy*, Directorate of Special Education.

NSW Department of School Education (1993b) *Special Education Plan 1993–1997*, March, Sydney: School Education News.

O'Brien, J. (1987) A guide to lifestyle planning: using the activities catalogue to integrate services and natural supports. In B. Wilcox and G.T. Bellamy (eds), *The Activities Catalogue: an Alternative Curriculum for Youth and Adults, with Severe Disabilities*. Baltimore:. Brookes.

Parmenter, T.R. (1988) An analysis of the dimensions of quality of life for people with physical disabilities. In R. Brown (ed.), *Quality of Life for Handicapped People*, London: Croom Helm.

Parmenter, T.R. (1992) Quality of life of people with developmental disabilities. *International Review of Research in Mental Retardation*, **18**, pp. 247–87.

Parmenter, T.R. (1993) Strategies for young people with disabilities in transition Where have we been? Where are we going? Paper presented at the Association of Special Education Conference, Melbourne.

Parmenter, T.R. and Riches, V.C. (1990) *Establishing Individual Transition Planning for Students with Disabilities within the NSW Department of School Education*, Sydney: School of Education, Macquarie University.

Parmenter, T.R. and Riches, V.C. (1991) Transition education: pilot program for student with disabilities in transition in the NSW Department of School Education. *Australian Disability Review*, **1**, pp. 1–9.

Patton, J.R. and Browder, P.M. (1988) Transitions into the future. In B.L. Ludlow, A.P. Turnbull and R. Luckasson (eds) *Transitions to Adult Life for People with Mental Retardation: Principles and Practices*, pp. 293–311, Baltimore: Brookes.

Riches, V.C. (1993a) *Coordination: a Vital Key to Successful Transition for Students with Disabilities*, Sydney: School of Education, Macquarie University.

Riches, V.C. (1993b) NSW community transition teams as a forum for change. Paper presented at the NCID Conference on Building Better Communities, Canberra, October.

Riches, V.C. and Parmenter, T.R. (1990) *Evaluation 1989 TAFE Transition Courses*, Sydney: School of Education, Macquarie University.

Riches, V.C. and Parmenter, T.R. (1991) *Community Transition Teams: a Research and Development Report*, Sydney: School of Education, Macquarie University.

Riches, V.C. and Parmenter, T.R. (1993) *NSW TAFE Transition Courses for Students with Disabilities: a Research and Development Report*, Sydney: School of Education, Macquarie University.

Riches, V., Parmenter, T.R., Fegent, M. and Bailey, P. (1993) *Secondary Education: a Follow-Along Study of Students with Disabilities in Transition in NSW*, Sydney: School of Education, Macquarie University.

Roessler, R.T., Brolin, D.E. and Johnson, J.M. (1990) Factors affecting employment success and quality of life: a one year follow up of students in special education. *Career Development for Exceptional Children (CDEI)* Fall, **13**, pp. 95–107.

Smith J.G., Edelen-Smith, P.J. and Stodden, R.A. (1992). Seven pitfalls to avoid in systematic transition program planning and improvement: a school/community team response. Keynote address presented at the NSW State Transition Conference *Pathways to the Future*, Parramatta, 14–15 August.

Stodden, R. (1991) *A Re-Assessment, or Exploring the Sediment of Old Wine in New Bottles Labelled Transition*. 1st National Conference on Transition Education for Students with Disabilities, Sydney: Department of School Education, Special Education Directorate.

Stodden R.A. (1994). School to adult transition what does it mean for secondary school educators. Keynote address presented at the Transition '94 Conference on After the Classroom: Options for Youth, 19–20 March, Townsville, Queensland.

Unit for Rehabilitation Studies (1992) Transition project for students with disabilities: report and recommendations to the Department of School Education. Unpublished report, October.

Wagner, M. (1989) *The Transition Experiences of Youth with Disabilities: a Report from the National Longitudinal Transition Study*, Menlo Park: SRI International.

Wagner, M. (1991) *The Benefits of Secondary Vocational Education for Young People with Disabilities*. Findings from the National Longitudinal Transition Study of Special Education Students. Menlo Park, CA: SRI International.

Watters, M., Riches, V. and Parmenter, T.R. (1993) *NSW Transition Project: Secondary Vocational Education Job Coach Service*, Sydney: Macquarie University.

Wehman, P. (1990) School-to-work: elements of successful programs. *Teaching Exceptional Children*, Fall, pp. 40–50.

Wehman, P. (1992) *Life Beyond the Classroom: Transition strategies for young people with disabilities*, Baltimore: Brookes.

Wehman, P. Kregel, J. and Barcus, J.M. (1985) From school to work: a vocational transition model for handicapped students. *Exceptional Children*, **52** (1), pp. 25–37.

Wehman, P., Moon, M.S. and McCarthy, P. (1986) Transition from school to adulthood for youth with severe handicaps. *Focus on Exceptional Children*, **18,** pp. 1–12.

26 Growing Older: Challenges and Opportunities

Roy I. Brown

INTRODUCTION

It is only in recent years that people have started to contemplate the challenges of Down syndrome in relation to adult needs including sexuality and partnership. This arises almost entirely because of two factors. The first is the increase in longevity of people with Down syndrome which brings new possibilities for lifestyle. At the beginning of the century, the life expectancy of a new-born person with Down syndrome was nine years, but today, the average life span is beyond 50 years and one in ten live to 70 or more years. (Baird and Sadovnik, 1987). This phenomenal change is due, at least to a considerable degree, to medical intervention but social and environmental contributors also appear to be important. The second factor is environmental location because the vast majority of people with Down syndrome remain in society from birth onwards and therefore receive a range of stimulation, which was previously denied through institutionalization. For the first time, teachers and more particularly parents, no longer need view children with Down syndrome as people who will spend a few years at school and die at an early age, but rather as individuals who need to learn as much as possible in order to gain social, vocational and allied skills to compete as adults in the community.

ADULT LIFE: ITS RANGE AND EXPECTATION

Adult life is not made up of work alone and includes social living, such as developing friendships (Firth and Rapley, 1991), leisure and home making (Brown and Hughson, 1993), which form part of building a complex lifestyle. This at its best, has the possibilities of partnership, often through marriage, and sometimes the desire for parenthood (Brown, 1995; Selikowitz, 1990). The more normal the lifestyle of the developing youngster, the more opportunities exist for societal success in all dimensions of functioning.

For the first time, parents will be outlived by their offspring with Down syndrome. The prospect, for the developing adult is either one where society assumes that people with Down syndrome need care and protection and shelter as adults – one recent book (Gilbert, 1993) suggests adults with Down syndrome can expect to go to sheltered workshops for vocational training – or a far more enlightened and releasing path can be taken where people are helped to gain skills and experience, enabling them to live as independently as possible (Brown, 1994a,b). This can often involve employment, and in many instances independent or semi-independent social living and partnership and, eventually, retirement can be achieved.

There seems little doubt that the reasons for longevity are first found in the early years of life for people with Down syndrome. The ability to detect and correct adverse physical problems such as circulatory defects, makes a marked difference to health. Correction of such problems can lead to increases of energy and motivation for behavioural growth. The fact that individuals do not live in institutions and can function in the parental home means they are less likely to face hazards that exist in congregate care, but even when disease does occur the use of penicillin and recent advances in pharmacology increase the prospects for longevity. But there are reasons to believe that it is not just the developments in physical medicine and community living which have led to this change. Other possible factors include the interactive lifestyle which individuals with Down syndrome can now lead. Opportunities for inclusive education, the growth of positive self-image through physical recreation and leisure activities, and attempts to promote a higher activity level probably interact with these other factors to increase adult life span. We know that such factors are relevant to the non-disabled population and there is no reason to suspect the same factors do not apply here. Because it is likely that such factors will continue to increase, it seems more than likely that people with Down syndrome will in the end approach the life span of the rest of society. If this occurs we can expect higher energy levels, greater motivation and activity, along with increased success and, therefore, more positive self-image – each factor interacting with the other to produce a more effective and better quality lifestyle.

LIFE SPAN AND LIFESTYLE: THE INTERACTING EFFECTS

But some of this development is for the future. Today we find patterns, some negative, which have previously been set by segregated or limited education, lack of up-to-date knowledge among general practitioners and, sometimes, concerns among parents that care, rather than enrichment and structured intervention, is required. There is good evidence that major progress has been made, and our understanding of some of the special characteristics of persons with Down syndrome is now more broadly recognized (Pueschel, 1988; Selikowitz, 1990). Intervention and monitoring often needs to continue into adult years. The issues are multidisciplinary. They involve such concerns at hypothyroidism, poor vision, heart conditions but also, and importantly, assistance with speech and encouragement to explore and maintain physical, social and community activities (see conference reports of Brown, 1993; Denholm, 1989, 1991a, 1991b; Field, 1994).

But there is also evidence that increasing age may bring other new challenges. Gibson (1991) has summarized some of the issues surrounding early ageing and Brown (1994b) has noted the early adult decline in recreational activity levels. Not only do we see behavioural changes in people's twenties but evidence also suggests changes in the brain structure akin to that in Alzheimer patients. Although not all people with Down syndrome will demonstrate Alzheimer's disease, neurone tangles (a feature of the brain in person's with Alzheimer's disease) are found in pathology examinations of most people with Down syndrome. But the above is a general statement and it is important to note the wide variability in performance among people who have Down syndrome. The variabilities arise from inherited factors and their interaction with a wide range of social and physical environmental variables. They not only influence physical well-being but affect the way that people with Down syndrome perceive themselves and how they feel able to perform.

It is perhaps worth recognizing that a small minority of persons with Down syndrome are of average or low average cognitive ability (Cant *et al.*, 1953; Gibson, 1978). The majority of people with Down syndrome tend to function at severe to moderate levels of cognitive performance, and a reasonable percentage are mildly disabled. It seems possible, as Gibson has pointed out, that with early enrichment and more positive environments, higher levels of cognitive functioning may now be expected in adult years. If other factors are positive the individuals, as adults, should be able to be competent a wide range of jobs in the community. Although many still attend sheltered workshops, the advent of integration and inclusion within the school system makes this a less acceptable or unnecessary alternative as they grow older. We, therefore, must consider Down syndrome as a complex syndrome where better health and educational patterns and social opportunities will improve lifestyle, though each advance is likely to unearth new challenges. Past experience suggests the possibility of positive developments provided we recognize that intervention is a continuous process and requires multidisciplinary and family co-operation.

ASSOCIATIONS AND PARENT SOCIETIES

Many parent associations, such as the Canadian Down Syndrome Association, help parents, their offspring and interested professionals promote knowledge, expertise and practice. Until fairly recently, most of these associations concerned themselves primarily with the early and school years of people with Down syndrome. There is no doubt that this action was extremely relevant, but it is equally important to ensure that parents who have young people with Down syndrome orient their views to the future and the likely development of their child in later years.

For example, the author undertook a series of interviews with young adults with Down syndrome who had married. Some of these interviews were set up in Canada by members of the Ups and Downs Association. A young mother with a new-born child with Down syndrome asked if she could accompany him on one of the interviews. The people seen, two adults, one a woman with Down syndrome, the other a male with physical disabilities, gave an impressive account of life in their apartment and local community. They had some support, not least, their landlords, who described them as the most happy couple they knew. After the interview, the mother who accompanied the author, said that she found the interview exciting because, for the first time, she had some idea of what might be possible for her own child with Down syndrome.

It is important that parents, medical practitioners and teachers have a positive and future-orientated view of life for people with Down syndrome. Still we find teenagers and young adults with Down syndrome dressed more like young children, wearing clothing prescribed by parents. Dressing like other teenagers or as young adults, means that individuals are more likely to mingle with their age-appropriate peers. Modelling, which is based on the normal young person promotes normality. Chris Burke (Burke and McDaniel, 1993) who has Down syndrome often gives talks about his role as an actor, and at conferences is surrounding by young women without Down syndrome who regularly want his autograph, wish to dance with him and wish to talk with him. They see him as someone who is a successful actor not someone who has Down syndrome. It is not Down syndrome which is important in this context, but the behaviour of the person who has Down syndrome. In other words we need to continue to recognize the importance of physical health and medical intervention, but must also understand and promote effective social behaviour.

PEOPLE WITH DOWN SYNDROME PROMOTING PEOPLE WITH DOWN SYNDROME

In Canada, attempts have been made through the Canadian Down Syndrome Society to provide adults with a more positive lifestyle by helping them cope with a wide range of emotional events. They have been encouraged to set up their own organization and develop their own discussion groups leading to personal empowerment. Indeed they are beginning to link up across the country through annual and regional meetings. They are beginning to represent themselves. In the early stages most did not see this as possible but gradually through their own effective role models such as David MacFarlane, who is a Canadian actor with Down syndrome, they are taking charge of their own lives. Sometimes this is through imaginative support of a parent, helped by joint planning which involves parents and professionals and also, and importantly, friends. Support and guidance gradually develops (Lawrence *et al.*, 1993) and the young adult is the active focus of the group and makes the social choices. But there is also a need to learn how to speak out, how to problem-solve, and how to deal with the emotional and social issues which arise.

QUALITY OF LIFE

Many of these issues fall collectively under the concept of Quality of Life (Brown *et al.*, 1992; Goode, 1994; Parmenter, 1988) an issue which is coming to the fore in the field of adult rehabilitation both in terms of philosophy and practice. One of the major challenges involves an appreciation of people's attitudes about care and protection, and the development of emotional maturity among adults with Down syndrome.

In the vocational area, many people with Down syndrome now hold part-time or full-time jobs. Several of them in North America are actors appearing in live theatre and television. Others have jobs at hotels or at supermarkets where their work ranges from collecting trolleys, to serving, sorting, cleaning and carrying out a wide range of allied activities. Some have more than one part-time job. Although the above may not represent the norm, there are a sufficient number of examples to suggest that for most people with Down syndrome, these represent realistic possibilities. But studies relating to quality of life (Brown *et al.*, 1992) now identify emotional development with its implications for social behaviour and self-image as a high priority.

THE NEED FOR CHANGE

Most of today's parents of adults with Down syndrome have grown up in a society which provided few opportunities for young people with Down syndrome. Many of the parents have had to find their own way through 'the system', sometimes feeling that basic care, special classes and special schools were all that could be hoped for. Many other have been told that their child would not live long and would be best placed in an institution. That will not be the case for the next generation of children who are now being born with Down syndrome. Sadly however, for the few, the same messages will be put about. It is critical that medical practitioners, paediatricians, nurses and teachers gain a much more positive idea of the development that can take place supported by professional and social intervention.

Many people with Down syndrome have been nurtured in an environment where, understandably, care and protection have been the major practices. Very often, parents and professionals are unaware of the effects of care and protection unmodified by challenge and stimulation (Brown, 1994a). It is important to understand that the caring mode, desirable as it may be at times, can result in a less stimulating environment, depriving the individual of challenges and opportunities to learn new skills. In meeting with hundreds of parents with Down syndrome children over the years and discussing this issue with them, many indicate that the challenge of having a child with Down syndrome means, through force of habit and sometimes circumstance, that positive parents may not always provide appropriate stimulation. This is understandable because as the years pass, people with Down syndrome tend to fall increasingly behind their age peers, and this eventually results in parents feeling that they must carry out activities for the child, or they no longer wish to be heavily involved as parents. Some begin to think that change cannot possibly occur. Yet growth means new challenges.

SELF-EXPRESSION AND EMOTIONAL DEVELOPMENT

At a meeting of the Canadian Down Syndrome Society with young adults in Moncton in 1992, it became apparent that several young people had lost a parent over the previous year. In the meeting the author was holding with them (with parents as observers), several of the young people broke into tears describing their experience of grief and loss at the death of their parent. Empathy and suggestibility among the group, resulted in considerable signs of emotional distress. After the meeting, several parents asked why I had not called the meeting to a halt. I indicated that I did not believe that expressing grief was unprofitable, nor did it lead to harm, but to expressions of feelings from which individuals could learn and grow. Indeed within the meeting, several of the young adults began to comfort one another through verbal support and touching or holding each other. Afterwards, two women parents, who applauded the sessions, said they had lost their spouses and wanted to know why it was not possible for society to offer them similar support through the bereavement process! Yet, time and again, in the study undertaken by Brown *et al.* (1992), the authors came across individuals who were not allowed to go to funerals with relatives, or were left out of family mourning or consultation. Other adults felt the young people with Down syndrome were not capable of expressing appropriate emotions or understanding the implications of emotional situations.

Well-meaning parents may avoid dealing with emotional issues because they themselves have difficulty in coping under stress. They are being asked to suddenly treat individuals as mature adults when all along they and society have regarded their children as immature and disabled. It is critical that young and growing adults have opportunities to mediate these emotional experiences. Unfortunately, we have confused disability with the effects of handicap which largely result from society's perceptions, education and behaviours. Again opportunities to mix with adult society, the development of support networks, and working through emotional experiences tend to lead to growth. Where individuals have control over choices and can be provided with expert counselling, opportunities for further development are optimized (Brown, 1993).

FRIENDSHIP

One of the major challenges for people with Down syndrome is the need to develop a network of friends which can enable them to build relationships for later years. To date, most young people with Down syndrome will have gained their friendships on a restricted basis, largely, though not entirely, through contacts in special educational circles and later in sheltered workshops. Frequently, unlike the non-disabled population, they will tend to regard their professional contacts as friends.

There are a variety of ways in which friendship networks can be built and expanded, but they all entail immersion in society. Such networks, as they develop will lead, at times, as many parents have noted (see Lawrence *et al.*, 1993), to rejection. Yet many parents talk of the positive gains made when children learn to adapt and cope with social relations. Lawrence *et al.* have suggested that young adults with Down syndrome should have a support group made up of positive contacts in the community. It is essential under these circumstances that the individual with Down syndrome selects people with whom they feel comfortable. Such a group can help to plan balanced activities, friendship links and allied networks and also help develop leisure, social and employment networks.

The point is that people with Down syndrome need opportunities to express their ideas and to see them put into effect. This is one of the cornerstones of quality of life models and, although it may be argued by some, that people with Down syndrome are not in a position to choose, studies suggest that the majority of them are capable of making effective choices, although not always the ones which parents like (Brown *et al.* 1992). Their choices seem not dissimilar to their non-disabled peer group (Denholm, 1993). Although they may not always make appropriate choices, within a structured situation these choices can be explored in the way that people without disabilities make choices, some of which are also inappropriate. Growing adults need to explore and test their social environment! Certain activities and environments tend to foster friendships. The list of activities promoting and discouraging friendships, provided by Firth and Rapley (1991) indicates that many of the activities in which young adults with disabilities become involved, such as bowling, tend to discourage friendship. Employment and interactive social activities with age peers tend to promote it.

GROWING AWAY FROM PARENTS

Generally, people with Down syndrome have learnt to be accommodating and non-confrontational, yet normal adolescents learn to separate from their families, often through confrontational behaviour, and much of this does not meet with unanimous parental approval. Of course, such behaviour is more difficult to cope with if the individual goes on living at home, which is often the case for the young person with Down syndrome. Perceptually it is important to think of this confrontation as a step towards a time when the individual has his or her own apartment, or shares with friends. Indeed some parents have made a point of seeing that part of their house is physically separate, and this allows their son or daughter to have an individual lifestyle in his or her own living space but can still be provided with support when necessary.

Denholm (1993), makes it clear that teenagers and young adults have very specific concerns and wishes and that those with Down syndrome are not very different. Yet we do not often provide adults with Down syndrome with the means to explore such opportunities. Indeed we limit the environment from an early age. Brown and Timmons (1994) show that teenagers with disabilities have many fewer choices than teenagers without disabilities. The former go to bed earlier, contact less by phone, more frequently eat meals alone and obtain pocket money more haphazardly than teenagers without disabilities. Inclusion is needed at home and in the community as well as in school and employment. Whether society is ready for this and whether parents can take advantage of this are other matters.

LEISURE TIME

One key aspects of quality of life is the role played by leisure and recreation in an individual's lifestyle. Data suggests (Beck-Ford *et al.*, 1984; Brown *et al.*, 1992) that many people with intellectual disabilities have problems when it comes to maintaining or even attaining an effective leisure and recreation schedule. In their early years, people with Down syndrome may not have been encouraged or allowed to experience broad-ranging recreation. The role played by activities such as cycling, picnics with friends and family, going to football matches, being a member of a netball team, have often been denied with the result that in later life these experiences cannot be used as a transfer base. Leisure and recreation, though important in their own right, provide a learning and emotional base from which other skills develop. These include social and communication skills, physical fitness, positive self-image and motivation. It is not just that the adult with Down syndrome has a different leisure lifestyle from his or her non-disabled adult peers, but that the individual may never have experienced broad-based leisure experience during the developing years. Indeed people with intellectual disabilities, and particularly people with Down syndrome, tend to have an undue amount of leisure time moulded around sedentary activities, while relatively few of their activities can be regarded as social, physical or creative and actualizing leisure. This may account, in part, for the early ageing process, indeed earlier than in other people with similar cognitive levels of disability.

One can only conjecture what the impacts of this are likely to be, but some possibilities come to mind. A more sedentary lifestyle is going to fit in with a tendency to develop obesity and heart conditions in later life. It may, in part, be the interaction between lifestyle and physical changes which precipitates the rather earlier ageing process that is seen in many people with Down syndrome. Of course there are some other factors which might precipitate this, not least the fact that some of the genetic aspects of Alzheimer's disease are associated with Chromosome 21 (see Wizniewski, 1992). In other words there may be a predisposition to neural decay in people with Down syndrome. But even if this is the case, an ability to develop a normal range of leisure activities may delay the effects of any genetic predispositions – an argument which has now surfaced in the Alzheimer debate itself, for lifestyle may account for the fact that Alzheimer's disease is observed more frequently in people of lower abilities and poorer social economic development than with people of professional and active lifestyles. It is worth exploring whether highly developed leisure activities over a range of physical social and creative areas may increase life span and quality of life. Further, Beck-Ford *et al.* (1984) point out, recreational levels are linked to motivation, physical health and positive self-image which can in turn be used as means of enhancing other aspects of development, including employment.

SPORTS AND COMPETITION

Sporting activities may move from leisure status to more formal recreation. Some communities, by providing various levels of competition for people with disabilities including those with Down syndrome, offer them opportunities for success. These opportunities include sports and fitness programmes that can help individuals maintain and/or improve their overall fitness and motor skills. While many of these programmes are very competitive and require certain prerequisite motor, cognitive and social skills, many others can be accommodated to meet the needs of lesser skilled individuals including persons with Down syndrome. For example, bowling leagues have a built-in handicapping system that allows for individual differences. That is, the individual's average score is computed and weighted so that a person can compete equally with more or less skilled bowlers. This handicap allows a person with Down syndrome who averages 50 pins per game, for example, to compete equally with bowlers who average 150 pins or more per game.

Simlarly, many communities offer recreation programmes that do not require special prerequisite skills or offer various levels of competition/participation to accommodate different abilities. Swimming programmes for novices, aerobics and fitness classes, and weight lifting are some examples (see Reid and Block, this volume).

Further opportunities are offered by Special Olympics programmes. These provide training and competition in a variety of Olympic-type sports for individuals with intellectual disability (Single, 1992). Rules closely follow the official rules established by the international governing body of each sport. In addition, skill competitions and modified games are used to help athletes with more significant motor and cognitive delays learn and practise the fundamental skills of the sport. Training and competition are available for both individual and team sports.

Special Olympics accommodates athletes by assigning them to compete in divisions based on their age and gender as well as their abilities as measured by scores from pervious performances. Efforts are made to make sure that individual athletes or teams compete against other athletes or teams of equal ability. That way, all athletes have a reasonable chance of winning or placing in the event and being successful.

While some equate Special Olympics with one big competition at the end of the programme, Special Olympics prides itself in the training aspect of the programme as well. Athletes are required to train in their sport of interest for a minimum of eight weeks before competing. Training programmes are conducted by certified Special Olympics coaches who have gone through sport-specific coaching programmes. In addition, Special Olympics has developed comprehensive sports-skills training guides for each sport as a resource for coaches and volunteers. Thus, athletes get the most up-to-date information and coaching.

A relatively new programme offered by Special Olympics is the Unified Sports Program. This integrated programme pits even numbers of athletes with and without intellectual disabilities on the same team (Krebs and Cloutier, 1992). These teams compete in Unified Sports Leagues sponsored by Special Olympics or in regular community leagues. One of the advantages of Unified Sports is that it offers more opportunities for interaction between persons with and without disabilities than traditional Special Olympics.

THE ARTS AND DOWN SYNDROME

In recent years it has been recognized that the Arts have much to offer adults with Down syndrome. There are many examples of people with Down syndrome who paint, act and dance. A few reach professional standards and obtain employment at national and international levels. But the Arts also allow for the development of self-expression and modelling of behaviour. They provide opportunities to explore ideas and imagine the future. They also provide opportunities for dealing with anger and other emotions, and can encourage positive self-image, including rehearsal for real-life events. Warren (1984) and Warren and Nadeau (1988) have provided examples of workshops and study groups which can enhance such opportunities. In addition such resources can enrich the leisure times of people with Down syndrome and with such skills developed by early adult life, they provide resources for later life and retirement.

MARRIAGE AND PARTNERSHIP

Many adults who have Down syndrome are placed in a care situation even though their actual performance scores in intelligence, social skills, and home living skills are sufficiently high that they do not need to be in such situations. There is good evidence to suggest that the opportunities provided are unduly limited. Such limitations appear to occur, in particular, to young women with Down syndrome, for the records indicate that such women function in many skill areas at a higher level than their male counterparts though their opportunities in society are no greater and often less (Brown, 1994b). One restricted opportunity concerns making close relationships with other adults, including partnership and marriage. Opportunities for mating, bonding and sexual behaviour are particularly the subject of parental and professional concerns. Some have spoken on issues of care and protection, and what they have seen as gullible behaviour. They have particularly noted concerns about females who have Down syndrome. Some of the concerns are justified as both physical and sexual abuse are higher among people with disability, including Down syndrome, than in the rest of the community (Patterson, 1991; Sobsey and Varnhagen, 1989).

There seems little doubt that people with Down syndrome are capable of making long and positive relations with people of the same and opposite sex. They have a normal range of sexual needs (Pueschel, 1988), are capable of sexual enjoyment and fulfilment and can, with appropriate experience and opportunity, develop a keen awareness of the boundaries of exploitation in contrast to mutual enjoyment and satisfaction (Brown, 1995). But maturity of judgement is based on experience in the community. Such judgement requires the use of this experience and modelling to project into the future. Thus individuals need to develop skills in future planning. If an individual is overprotected he or she will be understimulated and unable to make appropriate judgements in adult social situations.

Although there are not, as yet, many young adults with Down syndrome, who have married, the numbers are increasing. Those marriages, like the marriages in the normal population, are varied. Some are successful, some are not, but those who have married often enjoy positive relationships and find mutual support in those relationships. Indeed, it can be argued that people with greater needs may be more supportive to one another in partnership, and bring about more positive gains than people who are more self-sufficient. Observations indicate that shopping, budgeting, home-making, decorating, friendship circles, can all be enhanced by marriage or partnership. Experience and modelling makes these possibilities even greater, since through these means they can empathize and develop a range of skills including emotional stability. Some of the partnerships are physically non-sexual yet are emotionally intimate and supportive. Interviews undertaken by the author illustrate that expressions of mutual love and support are strongly verbalized (Brown, 1995). Love and affection have been seen by the partners as predominant aspects of such relationships and, by the same token, the individuals are often highly rewarded by the relationship, leading to growth of self-image. The status of marriage is seen as an enhancement to life and paves the way from adolescence to maturity. As Gow (1994) indicates, people with disabilities are often denied rites of passage thus adding to rejection and status of maturity – marriage and sexual relationship constitute rites and entry to an adult world, a world which makes further demands and provides further opportunities for growth.

At times parents regret the development of such relationships. The author has come across examples where parents have refused to go to wedding ceremonies and, in one case, the church minister was asked not to officially certify the marriage ceremony so the event was one of drama and modelling rather than reality! Yet this was not seen as abnormal or a contradiction of the rights and emotional develop-ment of the persons concerned. It was assumed the individuals were not likely to find out!

A number of partnerships are between people who have some form of disability. Some interpret the arguments put forward by Wolfensberger (1972) about deviancy juxtaposition as indicating this is a retrograde step. If a quality of life model is accepted, choice is viewed as an essential feature, and such relationships viewed as desirable and supported. Given the types of environment in which people with Down syndrome mix and meet, it seems likely that people will tend, at this time, to make partnerships with other people who have disabilities, and this is the case with all the partnerships interviewed by the author.

Given society's tendency to non-assortative mating such behaviour should be regarded as normal. The individuals themselves see such relationships as appropriate and desirable. Their partnerships represent growth and frequently lead to greater inclusion in other aspects of society. As people with Down syndrome experience wider environments so wider partnership possibilities will come about.

Pregnancy among women, with Down syndrome is uncommon but has occurred (both males and females probably have lowered fertility). There is increased likelihood that the mother will have a child with Down syndrome, theoretically 10 per cent (Selikowitz, 1990). Issues relating to pregnancy should be discussed with the partners involved, and the potential implications shared. Issues of pregnancy, contraception and general sexual behaviour are issues which should be discussed during the developing years and not after waiting for partnerships to develop. Again future planning and the dignity of choice encourage mature decision-making. Some parents may find this too anxiety promoting! Certainly, this is a fear voiced by many potential grandparents. Here again, counselling and advice should be available on an ongoing basis and it is recommended that Down Syndrome

Associations develop professional advisory committees which act as a resource for people with Down syndrome and their parents and siblings.

AGEING AND RETIREMENT

People with Down syndrome age on the whole rather more quickly than people without Down syndrome. This is the status of Down syndrome now, but as we gain knowledge and apply it over the life span this will change. Thus the expectations for a child born with Down syndrome today are much more optimistic than for those who are now adults. At present people with Down syndrome still tend to die younger than many others with intellectual disability, although approximately one in ten will reach 70. It is likely that during their development they will reach fewer high peaks and start to decline in a variety of functions at earlier ages than other people. This is certainly true of leisure and physical skills, and there is evidence to suggest it may also be true of a wide range of cognitive skills (Gibson, 1978). It is not surprising, therefore, that when employed they may express a desire to retire earlier than other people.

There is a tendency in society to think that once people have gained independence, that they will lastingly keep independence. However, support may be needed as they age, and this is likely to occur at an earlier stage for people with Down syndrome. They may experience a need for a variety of health, social, physical and allied supports. Careful monitoring in adult life by knowledgeable general medical practitioners who recognize not only the usual symptoms of ageing but their higher frequency and earlier occurrence within the life span of people with Down syndrome is critical. The adult with Down syndrome should be monitored, for example, for specific diseases such as hypothyroidism and Alzheimer's disease. Treatment can alleviate many of the symptoms of the former including physical symptoms such as hair loss, and behavioural concerns including low energy level. It is unfortunate, to say the least, that adults with Down syndrome can be found who are bald, obese and lacking in energy who should have been treated for hypothyroidism.

CONCLUSIONS

The life span of people with Down syndrome has greatly increased, but opportunities for an adult lifestyle are often lacking. Given the variety of behaviour and health needs among adults with Down syndrome, opportunities in society need to be more wide ranging. Behaviourally, it is important to recognize that variability in behaviour and health needs is immense. The label 'Down syndrome' should not force one to think that the person will behave in a particular manner, yet there are some trends. People with Down syndrome, though having a greater life span than previously, on average will not live as long as the general population. Yet they are now likely to outlive their parents. Many people with Down syndrome, and in increasing numbers, will attain full-time or part-time employment and these jobs range from skilled to unskilled work. Many take on unskilled or semi-skilled work on a part-time basis. It is not unusual for a person to have more than one part-time job. In most cases there should not be a need for vocational workshops, but there should be opportunities for social support, and greater opportunities for individuals to develop friendships and social networks.

Opportunities to experience emotional development, including learning how to deal with emotional situations should be encouraged. In the past education and society have restricted such development. With the development of inclusive education and with, hopefully, greater understanding by adults, including parents and professionals, of the need to develop positive self-image, personal expression and motivation, quality of life can be enhanced. But effective adult life is dependant on normal and structured experience during childhood.

Partnership and marriage are now increasing among people with Down syndrome and represent a further aspect of normal and desirable development. Even so we can expect that people, partly for genetic, but also for social reasons, will decline in skills at rather earlier ages than most people. Therefore society must be ready and able to provide support, must recognize early retirement, but must also encourage as active a lifestyle as possible. It may be expected that the frontiers of ageing will be pushed back, and a near normal life span will eventually be attained. Partnership and self-fulfilment in work, community living and leisure need to be developed if quality of life rather than a simple increase in life span is to be attained (see Lawrence *et al.*, 1993 for a reading list on adult issues, and see Pueschel, 1988; Pueschel *et al.*, 1987; Selikowitz, 1990).

This chapter has not dwelt particularly on physical aspects of the adult. However it should be stressed that with increasing age, problems such as hypothyroidism can be expected. Much of the necessary monitoring of health can be carried out by general health practitioners provided they are alerted to such concerns. Challenges relating to eyesight, hearing and physical movement will occur and persons with Down syndrome are particularly vulnerable to these developments.

Although employment prospects are improving for people with Down syndrome, the experience of partnership, vocation (not just employment) and fulfilling leisure times enhance life. The role of the Fine Arts have brought increased self-image for many adults with Down syndrome – examples include painting, acting and dancing at professional as well as amateur levels.

Finally, society should have increasing optimism about the possibilities for quality lifestyles for people with Down syndrome. But to ensure this occurs, a life-span approach must develop with parents and professionals collaborating with the young person to ensure he or she develops as much control as possible over their life in the general community.

ACKNOWLEDGEMENT

I am grateful to Reid and Block (personal communication) for the section on Sports and Competition.

REFERENCES

Baird, P.A. and Sadovnik, A.D. (1987) Life expectancy in Down syndrome. *Journal of Pediatrics*, **110**, pp. 849–54.

Beck-Ford, V. and Brown, R.I., in collaboration with Gillberry, M. and Bolt, C. (1984) *Leisure Training and Rehabilitation: a Program Manual*, Springfield: Thomas.

Brown, R.I. (1995) Social life, dating and marriage. In L. Nadel and D. Rosenthal (eds), *Down Syndrome: Living and Learning in the Community*. New York: Wiley-Liss.

Brown, R.I. (1991) Some challenges to counselling in the field of disabilities. In S.E. Robertson and R.I. Brown (eds), *Rehabilitation Counselling: Approaches in the Field of Disability*, New York: Chapman and Hall.

Brown, R.I. (ed.), (1993) *Building Our Future*. Report of the 1992 National Conference of the Canadian Down Syndrome Society. Calgary: The Society.

Brown, R.I. (1994a) Life and living with Down syndrome: accepting the challenge. In D. Field (ed.), Proceedings of the *National Conference of the Canadian Down Syndrome Society Moncton 1993*. Fredericton: Psychology Department, University of New Brunswick and The Society.

Brown, R.I. (1994b) Down syndrome and quality of life: some challenges for future practice. *Down's Syndrome: Research and Practice*, **2** (1), pp. 19–30.

Brown, R.I., Bayer, M.B. and Brown, P.M. (1992) *Empowerment and Developmental Handicaps: Choices and Quality of Life*, Toronto: Captus Press.

Brown, R.I. and Hughson, E.A. (1993) *Behavioural and Social Rehabilitation and Training*, Toronto: Captus Press.

Brown, R.I. and Timmons, V. (1994) Quality of life: adults and adolescents with disabilities. *Exceptionality Education Canada*, **4**, p. 1–11.

Burke, C. and McDaniel, J.B. (1991) *A Special Kind of Hero*, New York: Doubleday.

Cant, W.H.P., Gerrard, J.W. and Richards, B.W. (1953) A girl of mongoloid appearance and normal intelligence. *Journal of Mental Science*, **99**, pp. 560–63.

Denholm, C. (ed.), (1989) *Preparing for the Year 2000*. Proceedings of the National Conference of the Canadian Down Syndrome Society. Calgary: The Society.

Denholm, C. (1991a) (ed.), *Learning Together, 1991 National Conference Proceedings. Halifax*, Calgary: Canadian Down Syndrome Society.

Denholm, C. (1991b) (ed.), *Adolescents with Down Syndrome: International Perspectives on Research and Programme Development. Implications for parents, researchers and practitioners* Victoria, BC: University of Victoria.

Denholm, C.J. (1993) Developmental Needs of Adolescents: Application to Adolescents with Down Syndrome. In R.I. Brown (ed.), *Building our Future*, Proceedings of 1992 National Conference of the Canadian Down Syndrome Society, Calgary, Canada.

Field, D. (ed.), (1994) *Proceedings of National Conference of Down Syndrome Society*, Moncton, 1993. Fredericton: Psychology Department, University of New Brunswick and The Society.

Firth, H. and Rapley, M. (1991) *From Acquaintance to Friendships: Issues for People with Learning Disabilities*, Kidderminster: BIMH.

Gibson, D. (1978) *Down's Syndrome*, London: Cambridge University Press.

Gibson, D. (1991) Adolescents with Down syndrome at risk for premature mental aging: a parent and teacher guide. In C. Denholm (ed.), *Adolescents with Down Syndrome: International Perspectives on Research and Programme Development. Implications for parents, researchers and practitioners*. Victoria, BC: University of Victoria.

Gilbert,(1993) *The A-Z Reference Book of Syndromes and Inherited Disorders*, London: Chapman and Hall.

Goode, D. (1994) *Quality of Life for Persons with Disabilities, International Perspectives and Issues*, Cambridge, MA: Brookline.

Gow, L. (1994) Enhancing Work and School of Adults with Intellectual Disabilities. Paper presented at the 18th Annual Conference of the Australian Association of Special Education, Adelaide, September.

Krebs, P.L. and Cloutier, G. (1992) Unified Sports: I've seen the future. *Palaestra*, **8** (2), pp. 42–45.

Lawrence, P., Brown, R., Mills, J. and Estay, I. (1993) *Adults with Down Syndrome: Together We Can Do It*, Calgary: Canadian Down Syndrome Society.

Parmenter, T.R. (1988) An analysis of the dimensions of quality of life for people with physical disabilities. In R. Brown (ed.), *Quality of Life for Handicapped People*, London: Croom Helm.

Patterson, P.M. (1991) *Doubly Silenced: Sexuality, Sexual Abuse and People with Developmental Disabilities*, Madison: Wisconsin Council on Developmental Disabilities.

Pueschel, S.M. (1988) *The Young Person with Down Syndrome*, Baltimore: Brookes.

Pueschel, S.M., Tingey, C., Rynders, J.E., Crocker, A.C. and Crutcher, D.M. (eds) (1987) *New Perspectives on Down Syndrome*, Baltimore: Brookes.

Selikowitz, M. (1990) *Down Syndrome: the Facts*, Oxford University Press.

Single, D. (1992) *Skill, Courage, Sharing Joy: the Stories of Special Olympics*, Washington: Special Olympics International.

Sobsey, R. and Varnhagen, C. (1989) Sexual abuse and exploitation. In M. Csapo and L. Gougen (eds), *Special Education Across Canada*, Vancouver: Vancouver Centre for Human Development and Research.

Warren, B. (1984) *Using the Creative Arts in Therapy*, London: Croom Helm.

Warren, B. and Nadeau, R. (1988) Enhancing the quality of life: the role of the arts in the process of rehabilitation. In R.I. Brown (ed.), *Quality of Life for Handicapped People*, London: Croom Helm.

Wisniewski, H.M. (1992) Aging, Alzheimer Disease & Mental Retardation. Paper presented at 9th World Congress, International Association for the Scientific Study of Mental Deficiency, Queensland, Australia.

Wolfensberger, W. (1972) *Normalization: the Principle of Normalization in Human Services*, Toronto: National Institute of Mental Retardation.

27 Down's Syndrome and Developing Countries

Roy McConkey

Down's syndrome occurs in every society of the world and throughout all the continents. Indeed there are hundreds of thousands more children and adults with this syndrome living in Africa, Asia and South America than in Europe, North America and Australasia. But the accumulated experience in helping these folk and their families is not shared equally. Well over 90 per cent of children and adults with Down's syndrome will receive special assistance in the affluent West whereas in the developing world, at best only one in 20 can expect any form of help (World Health Organization, 1985).

In this chapter, we review the prospects of children and adults with Down's syndrome in the 'third world', benefiting from the insights reported in the earlier chapters of this volume, and describe the most likely strategies as to how this could come about. As we shall see, there are many lessons to be gained for first world countries too as they strive for more cost-efficient, community-based services.

ANOTHER WORLD

People with Down's syndrome have only one thing in common – trisonomy 21. Thereafter their physical characteristics, personalities, intellectual abilities, family circumstances and life histories can be as varied as for any other human grouping based on a genetic characteristic, such as ginger hair. The danger of making simplistic generalizations is compounded by grouping nations under the label of developing countries. Despite the common term, such nations vary greatly in terms of cultures, social customs, politics and government spending on health, education and social services. Indeed similar variations are often apparent across different regions of the same country. Hence the prognosis for an infant born with Down's syndrome in one country or region could be very much better than in a neighbouring state.

With these reservations in mind, we can draw a number of contrasts between the developing and the developed world:

- *Among people with recognized disabilities in developing countries, there are proportionately fewer children and adults with Down's syndrome.* Many infants born with Down's syndrome do not survive beyond the first two years of life (Kuo-Tai, 1988; Rubin and Davis, 1986). Equally the life expectancy of adults is much lower due to a dearth of medical services. But as primary health care services develop and improved medical resources become available, the numbers of people with Down's syndrome will increase; this is a world-wide phenomena (Nicholson and Alberman, 1992).

- *People with Down's syndrome are unlikely to be treated as a distinct group; rather they tend to be grouped with others according to their functional handicap.* Most surveys of disability in developing countries have rightly concentrated on recording the handicaps presently experienced by the child or adult, e.g. inability to walk or to talk, rather than on the aetiology of the disability (Thorburn *et al.*, 1992). Likewise service provision, if it exists at all, often does not discriminate its users by aetiologies. However people with intellectual disabilities are often the least likely to be helped.

- *Children with Down's syndrome are unlikely to receive any special schooling.* In common with most children in developing countries who have disabilities, very few will receive any form of special education; the exception being those from rich, urban families who can afford to pay for private education. Most are also excluded from the local primary schools but, as the teachers are unlikely to have received any training in special education, those children who do attend may be neglected (Hegarty, 1993).

- *Superstitions and myths make it harder for people with Down's syndrome to integrate into their community.* Beliefs about the cause of the disability can reflect ill on families. Hence families may be inclined to 'hide' the child and neighbours may discourage contact in case the disability is contagious (Ingstad, 1988). Consequently children and adults with Down's syndrome may not be given the same opportunities to join in the life of the community and of learning to be a productive member of their family.

THE WAY AHEAD IN THE DEVELOPING WORLD

How then are we to create a better life for people with Down's syndrome in the developing world? First we need to be clear on what we are trying to achieve. Table 27.1 lists the core achievements which we might work towards. The experiences recounted in this volume suggest that these are attainable by most people with Down's syndrome.

Already there are examples from developing countries of young people with Down's syndrome who have attained these and many other competencies. But for millions more the prognosis is much bleaker. As one Asian father explained to me:

When our son was born we had never heard of a word called mongolism, never heard of Down's syndrome. We were shocked, psychologically shocked. It took us around six months to get over it. After that we said, 'let's go; there is a mission here'. We come from Asia where there are a lot of superstitions about why you have this sort of child, But we managed to get over it. My main advice to parents is to get over it as soon as possible, then do something about it, don't sit back. With Fang Fang we did not develop him in one day or two days, we have been developing him since the last nine years. We will continue.

Table 27.1 Core achievements for people with Down's syndrome

Nearly all people with Down's syndrome

- should have any additional sensorial or physical impairments recognized and if possible treated;
- should be independently mobile;
- should be able to take care of their self-care needs, especially feeding, toiletting and washing;
- should be able to communicate their basic needs, preferably through speech but with manual signs if needed;
- should be productive members of the family; assisting with chores around the home or farm, or helping with income generation.
- should behave in socially acceptable ways in public;
- should have a network of friends with whom they can spend time;
- should be involved in ordinary communities actvities, such as religious celebrations.

In urban settings, the lifestyle of an adult with Down's syndrome will be enhanced if they

- can use public transport independently;
- can earn an income;
- can shop and cook for themselves;
- have a network of friends and/or relatives who can offer help and advice.

A three-fold strategy is proposed for attaining these goals. First, by mobilizing existing health and educational resources within local communities to assist families who have children with Down's syndrome. Particular attention needs to be given to primary health care workers and to teachers in nursery and primary schools. Second, by empowering families – parents and siblings – to promote the physical, social, intellectual and emotional well-being of infants born with Down's syndrome. The role of home support workers – either paid or voluntary – will be emphasized along with group-based approaches. Third, by educating communities about the causes of disability and creating a willingness to involve children and adults with disabilities into the life of the community.

Handicaps to development

The outcomes and the strategies are easily stated but realizing them means counteracting powerful forces which bedevil developing nations (UNICEF, 1990). To ignore them is foolishness. Rather our strategies for helping the family with a disabled member must take full account of them.

- *Poverty* The struggle to find enough food is exhausting enough for families, and mothers especially, without having to contend with the extra demands of a sickly infant. Malnutrition among mothers and infants is endemic in many developing countries.
- *Health care* The economies of developing countries will never be able to sustain the levels of health care needed by persons with biological impairments. Infant mortality and increased morbidity will long continue to feature in third world statistics.
- *Universal education* Many countries are still unable to provide free primary education for all their children. Priority will be given by both families and educators to those who are can best benefit from it.

- *Unemployment* The growth of industrialization and the drift to the cities has increased competition for jobs. People with disabilities are more likely to be discriminated against by employers or they risk exploitation with poor wages and substandard working conditions (Tse, 1993).
- *Dependency on overseas donors* Many projects designed to assist people with disabilities and their families are funded by overseas aid agencies. The dilemma with such initiatives is that they create a dependency which prevents local communities and national governments from taking on the responsibility of caring for all their citizens (Mendis, 1993).
- *Corruption and injustices* Although not unique to developing nations, the effects of political corruption and social injustices are all the more striking there and affect more powerfully the most vulnerable members of society.

This depressing analysis had led some to question the wisdom of focusing our intervention efforts solely on people with disabilities while ignoring the wider social context in which the recipients live. Rather, the solution they espouse, is to empower communities to manage and direct their own development and in so doing to help all their members (Coleridge, 1993). This is new and radical thinking, for which western-style disability specialists have little experience or indeed sympathy, sheltered as they are by professional status and job security.

But I am convinced that the seeds of this thinking must permeate all the strategies we employ to create a better tomorrow for the world's children. At the very least this means that:

- change has to come from within families and communities. If imposed from outside these systems, it is unlikely to be sustained or to flourish (Hope and Timmel, 1984);
- the leaders who will instigate and nurture new developments are already present in every community but they need to be equipped with the skills and knowledge needed to function as effective leaders and given a vision of how things could improve for their community;
- development has to start with the present reality within communities and shaped according to their needs; hence there is no one universal 'treatment' or approach that can be immediately applied.

MOBILIZING EXISTING SUPPORTS IN THE COMMUNITY

The first line of help for families could come from existing workers in local communities. In this way many more people could receive at least some help within the foreseeable future rather than the alternative strategy of creating specialist services which will take many years before national coverage is attained.

However, in reality the options among existing workers are limited to two groups – primary health workers (either paid or voluntary) and nursery and primary school teachers. Neither group will have had any experience or training in identifying or remediating disabilities. A priority therefore is to include in their training information about disabilities.

Primary health workers

In many developing countries, primary health care is provided through minimally trained community-based health workers. Although their role varies from country to country the core tasks usually involve health and nutrition education, instigating community activities to improve hygiene and sanitation and referral to higher level services. Family planning, prenatal care, monitoring children's growth and encouraging the uptake of vaccinations also feature in many programmes (Berman *et al.*, 1987).

In theory then, such workers could fulfil a number of functions in relation to Down's syndrome:

- advising parents to complete their family before the mother is 35 years of age; thereby reducing the likelihood of the baby being born with Down's syndrome (Hosking, 1987);
- ensuring the baby with Down's syndrome receives adequate nutrition preferably through supporting the mother in breast-feeding and during the transition to solids;
- referring these children at an early stage for medical help if they develop colds and coughs.

With additional training and appropriate support, these workers could also undertake a number of other key functions:

- *Screening all children for possible sensorial and physical disabilities* The incidence of hearing problems in infants with Down's syndrome can easily go unrecognized and their communication competence will be severely impeded. The Guyana Community Based Rehabilitation Programme have recently produced a multimedia training package on screening for disabilities – including locally recorded video, an illustrated manual and record forms (O'Toole and McConkey, 1994). Children who test positively will need to be referred onwards although simple guidance can be given to the health workers to impart to families when an impairment is suspected.
- *Advising families on activities and routines which promote the infant's physical, social and intellectual development* Such information will benefit all infants but it is even more crucial for babies with Down's syndrome. Health workers' expertise must extend beyond the physical well-being of the child yet the intervention programmes presently available have been created for western cultures and the content should be adapted to local circumstances. Fortunately this is becoming more common in developing countries (see Appendix).

However, these high ambitions can be easily frustrated unless particular care is taken on the following points:

- *Selection of community health workers* The motivation and performance of workers is increased if trainees are chosen by their fellow-villagers, and after training they live and work among their own people (Haraldson, 1988).
- *Identification of key functions* The effectiveness of community health workers is impaired if they are expected to undertake too many diverse tasks. This risk

is high with disabilities as the needs of children vary so much according to their impairments.

- *Ongoing support and supervision is provided* The network of local workers must be supported by personnel who have training and expertise in coping with disabilities. Extra resources are therefore needed to provide such backup and a new style of professional worker is required, as we shall discuss, later (Berman *et al.*, 1987).

Primary teachers

With the growth of universal education throughout the world, teachers in primary or nursery education provide a second group of potential supporters to families with a child who has a disability. They could make three valuable contributions: opinion formation, school entry and family support.

Opinion formation

Headteachers especially are powerful leaders of local opinion, hence it is crucial that they are well informed about the causes of disability and how children and families can be helped. Such basic information should feature in all initial teacher training courses as well as in comparable courses for other professionals such as doctors and nurses (Mittler, 1992). Simple factual booklets describing disabilities and how children can be helped have proved useful (O'Toole and Maison-Halls, 1992).

School entry

Accepting the child into the local school provides opportunities for social integration and communication as well as the chance to learn new skills. However this is not an ideal solution given the large class sizes in most developing countries, the directive teaching style which is usually adopted and the inappropriateness of the curriculum for children with special needs. Not surprisingly many children with disabilities 'drop out' even if they are accepted in the first place.

Many diverse solutions have been proposed, the most radical involving a shift of focus from the child with special needs to reformulating the curriculum and organization of the school for the benefit of all children (Ainscow, 1993). As with community health workers, there is widespread agreement on the need for regular in-service training and specialist support for teachers which focuses on assessing pupils with disabilities and modifying the curriculum and teaching approaches to suit their needs (Hegarty, 1993). Arguably the biggest problem in the developing world is the dearth of suitable personnel to undertake these roles; a theme which we shall explore later.

Family support

A child's educational development is enhanced when families and teachers work in partnership. Mittler *et al.* (1986) have spelt out the practical implications of this – joint assessments of needs; home visits by teachers; explanations of educational goals and methods; shared activities at home and school and joint participation in training and policy-making. These ideals have proved difficult to attain in western countries and the prospect of their implementation in developing countries remains slim. But when such partnerships do emerge, many benefits accrue, not only to the child and family in question but also to others within that community and beyond.

Two formidable obstacles remain. In many developing countries teachers are paid such low wages that they have to undertake supplementary employment in order to support themselves and their families; hence they have limited time and no incentive to undertake 'extra' responsibilities. Secondly, the better teacher often seeks promotion to schools in cities and towns leaving the rural schools even more disadvantaged. For the foreseeable future, families with a child who has a disability will require special assistance over and above that which is presently provided in most communities.

EMPOWERING FAMILIES

Two strategies have proved uniformly successful across the world in empowering families, namely the provision of a home-visiting service by a trained worker who may be paid or unpaid; and the opportunity to participate in parent groups. In this section we explore the feasibility of making both approaches more widespread in developing countries.

Home visiting

One of the success stories of modern disability services in western countries has been the advent of home-visiting schemes in which a trained worker regularly visits the family from soon after the child's birth to advise on ways of promoting the child's development. With experience their role has widen considerably often providing emotional support to mothers as well as acting as an advocate for the family. Among the best-known schemes are those based on a model originating in Portage, USA but now in use in many other countries (Gartner *et al.*, 1991).

Around the same time, the concept of Community-Based Rehabilitation (CBR) was being promulgated by the World Health Organization as means of helping people with disabilities in the developing world (Helander, 1993). Here too, a trained worker, who may be paid or unpaid, visits the person with a disability at home to show the families – usually mothers, older sisters or grandmothers – what they can do to help their disabled member and to offer the family support and encouragement.

Although the evidence remains equivocal as to the impact such home-based programmes have on the development of the child with Down's syndrome (e.g. Farran, 1990) there is widespread agreement that they are valued highly by families (e.g. Thorburn, 1992). Gallagher (1992) attributes this to 'a new spirit of optimism and encouragement within the family of the affected child'.

O'Toole (1991) has identified a number of key factors in successful home-based services.

Home visitors

Personal qualities matter more than professional qualifications: empathy with the family; willingness to listen and consult; reliable and discreet; and nurturing the belief that the child is capable of learning and worth helping. Volunteers from local communities – often professionals such as nurses and teachers but also retired people and mothers of children with disabilities – have successfully fulfilled the role of home visitor. Other projects work through existing paid personnel such as health workers, or they have redeployed paid staff who previously worked solely in specialist centres or they have created new paid positions in CBR services.

Co-ordinators of services

The major task of the co-ordinator is not as a rehabilitation specialist but rather as a facilitator of human relations. They need to have a good understanding of local conditions and personalities and a visible presence in the field as they visit homes of clients to monitor and support the work of the home visitors. Co-ordinators are a major determinant of the home visitor's commitment and dedication. Perhaps the most crucial attribute of co-ordinators is the humility and wisdom to know when to stand back and allow local groups to take charge.

Sharing knowledge

Detailed attention to the initial and ongoing training of the home visitors is essential. As we have argued elsewhere (McConkey and Bradley, 1991) such training must be geared to the needs of the recipients, many of whom may be unable to read. Ideally the training should be:

- practical and relevant to the local situation not theoretical;
- based around learning by seeing and doing rather than from talks and books;
- available locally and easily accessible rather than in distant cities;
- directed at changing attitudes, planning service goals and at enabling trainees to forge partnerships with others as well as making them more skilled in coping with disabilities.

This analysis led us to promote a new style of ready-made training package based around locally produced video programmes and accompanying handbooks for tutors and participants. Such packages can also compensate for the dearth of experienced trainers often found in developing countries.

Information resources

Home visitors also need to have access to reference materials which will guide their inputs to families. In recent years a growing number of guides have been produced for use in developing countries, which are written in simple language with copious illustrations. Among the most popular are those produced by the World Health Organization (Helander *et al.*, 1989) and Werner's (1987) *Disabled Village Children*. A common criticism of both productions is the relative dearth of information about helping children with intellectual disabilities, but other authors have filled the gap (see Appendix).

The future role of rehabilitation professionals

The development of community-based services and their growing success at empowering families and communities to cope with disabilities demands a reappraisal of the training and functions of rehabilitation specialists – therapists, teachers and psychologists – within developing countries. Indeed some would argue that a similar exercise is urgently required in western societies now that new styles of services are becoming the norm (Schwartz, 1992).

In particular, specialists need to become adept at communicating their skills and expertise to others so that the 'therapy' can be applied by families or intermediate helpers. Invariably this means leaving the comfort of the clinic or hospital and adopting an itinerant role as they provide training courses in villages and towns for CBR workers, primary health personnel and teachers. Another feature of their role is the production of local information resources (Dowling, 1988).

Secondly, specialists need to integrate their advice and treatments so that the wasteful duplication or contradictory advice inherent in many multidisciplinary teams can be reduced. The likely outcome are new forms of generic training for professional workers in community-based services with correspondingly fewer specialists in disability services. Their role will be more confined to handling referrals of problematic cases, research into new techniques, and the teaching and training of front-line workers.

Third, disability specialists must become adept at understanding communities and the processes involved in community development. Leadership training, managing people and delegation of responsibilities are essential to their job.

Given the power and influence wielded by long-established and well-organized professional bodies in the affluent West; one might despair of changes like these happening quickly. But the winds of change which are blowing in disability services throughout the world could alter the landscape quicker than we might think. A formidable obstacle is the dearth of training opportunities in the developing world for this new style of disability specialist.

Parent groups

Another effective way of empowering families is through the establishment of parents' groups. The rationale for working with parents in groups can be easily summarized:

- *Reaching more families*   Thorburn *et al.* (1992) estimate that in Jamaica, only 2 per cent of children needing help receive CBR services; a finding common to many developing countries. Group work offers the potential to provide some help to many more families with the same or fewer resources than could be achieved through individual-based provision.
- *Building solidarity*   group work provides opportunities for parents to provide mutual support to one another. Such 'self-help' groups can lead to community action, such as the development of a special provision for children with marked disabilities (O'Toole, 1991).
- *Sharing experiences*   professionals workers no matter how experienced are not the fount of all wisdom. The advice (and admonitions) provided by other parents is often more credible than that given by professionals who may be perceived as having an incomplete understanding of family circumstances; hence the growth of parent-to-parent schemes internationally (Gartner *et al.*, 1991).
- *Understanding why*   In the past two decades a wealth of knowledge has been gained on promoting the well-being and development of children with special needs. Such knowledge must be accessible to families and communities but often this has not happened (UNICEF, 1990). Instead the prescriptive approaches which dominate disability services perpetuate a dependency on professional expertise rather than equipping families to become effective promoters of their children's development.

A strategy for working with parent and community groups

While working in Ireland in the early 1980s we began to explore the use of specially produced video courses as a way of working with groups of parents, an approach also used by other services (e.g. Rimmerman *et al.*, 1990). Later with assistance of Irish Foreign Aid we were able to extend this work to Zimbabwe and there I had the privilege of working alongside Lilian Mariga and Sally Templer (McConkey, 1989). These experiences demonstrated the effectiveness of this approach but left questions about its wider applicability to developing countries.

In 1990, the Special Education Unit of UNESCO launched a new initiative in parent and community education. The aim was to test the feasibility of producing video programmes in developing countries which could be used to inform families and communities about ways of overcoming children's disabilities. Partner agencies were identified in three developing countries – Uganda, Sri Lanka and Malawi – and each produced their own video-based training packages which they later field-tested with over 1,000 people in each of the participating countries. The packages are now available to others either to use directly or as examples for the creation of their own parent education packages (McConkey, 1993).

The value of this approach was confirmed by the reports from the field-testers. Families particularly appreciated:

- the range of activities which children with disabilities could perform successfully;

- the services available to help families and children;
- the love, patience and enthusiasm of the workers;
- the socialization of children with disabilities in the family and local communities;
- the change of attitude it provoked towards people with disabilities.

Among the changes which tutors and viewers wanted were:

- commentaries in local languages
- improved access to video equipment and transport
- similar programmes on other topics, such as toilet-training and reading.

In Malawi the package is now being used in nine CBR programmes, and in Sri Lanka there are plans to use the package in the training of public health workers. In Uganda and Sri Lanka the packages are being used in teacher-training programmes. In all countries, personnel are enthusiastic to produce further video programmes (see McConkey, 1993 for further details).

The value of the packages may extend beyond the benefits they bring to individual families. They provide local personnel, such as CBR workers, with a ready-made tool for working with groups and hence an opportunity for them to practise the skills and techniques of handling groups as well as gaining the confidence needed for this type of work.

Moreover, video provides an attraction for families to attend group meetings and therefore presents an opportunity for the formation of parent associations. Such groups have been instrumental in many countries for initiating their own services, such as local resource centres, and for persuading governments and other agencies to provide families with the help they need.

Of course, many of these outcomes could be attained without using video packages. Groups need leaders who have a vision of how life can be better for their community and a willingness to ensure that the group continues to meet the needs of all its members. We have much to learn about how such leaders can be nurtured in the field of disability but we can take consolation that often they have come to the fore in even the most deprived of societies when the opportunity is presented to parents or communities.

EDUCATING COMMUNITIES ABOUT DISABILITIES

The third strategy for creating a better future for people with Down's syndrome revolves around an informed and involved community, one which is disposed to 'making allowances' for the person's disabilities and to provide the extra help they may need to participate in community events.

A generation ago, unsympathetic communities would have been a feature of many so-called developed countries. The forces for change which have been at work in these societies over the past 30 years give us some indication of how change might come about in the developing world, although economic and political circumstances may require readjustments. Four major influences can be identified in addition to those already noted above.

1 *The formation of parent associations* Downs' Syndrome Associations have done much in developed countries to raise the public's awareness of this disability and to dispel myths and superstitions. Parent associations have also provided solidarity in lobbying for new services and in highlighting discriminatory practices (Shearer, 1985). Latterly the self-advocacy of young people with Down's syndrome has proved a potent influence also. In developing countries, the growth of similar associations is at a embryonic stage although there are notable exceptions, such as the Down's Syndrome Association of Zimbabwe.

2 *Opinion formers* Every community has its influential figures, be they local chiefs, religious leaders or political activists. Gaining their understanding and support can prove decisive in altering local opinion. A common way is by inviting their participation in any planning groups who are developing local services.

3 *Equal opportunities* Encouraging people with Down's syndrome to participate in many of the same pursuits as their able-bodied peers enables the community to dispel many of their myths and fears through personal experience. The recurring experience is that people with Down's syndrome are often their own best ambassadors (McConkey, 1994).

4 *Legislation* Changes in parental, professional and, ultimately, public opinion need to be reflected in new legislation which eliminates discrimination and requires government to expend money on services for people with disabilities (Mittler, 1993). The Convention on the Rights of the Child (UNICEF, 1990) signed by the largest ever gathering of the world's leaders provides a specific 10-point programme to protect the rights of children and to improve their lives.

A NEW TOMORROW

As has become abundantly clear in this chapter, the solution to better services for people with Down's syndrome in developing countries does not lie in promoting the technologies of disability but rather in the transformation of relationships. Therein lies the greatest lesson for the developed world. Despite the millions of pounds spent in the first world on disability services, we have not succeeded in removing the loneliness of many young adults with Down's syndrome providing them with productive employment and making them integral members of their society.

Nor will we ever achieve these ordinary ambitions if we concentrate solely on treating their disabilities. As we now realize, the quality of all our lives is determined primarily by our relationships with others. The biggest handicap which a disability can bring is a fracturing of the relationships which otherwise would naturally occur. Hence the thrust of all our interventions must be to build, or rebuild, the social networks which can be so easily taken for granted. This endeavour is as new for the affluent West as it is for the poorer nations. Money, as they say, cannot buy you friends.

Hence the nations of the world face a common challenge; do we share a common humanity with people who have an extra chromosome or do we see them as a different defective race? The future of millions of people with Down's syndrome, most yet unborn, depends ultimately on such a simple choice.

APPENDIX: TRAINING RESOURCES FOR THE DEVELOPING WORLD

This appendix gives details of video-based training packages and printed materials which have been produced in developing countries and around which training courses for families and community workers could be organized.

Video-based training packages

Nurturing Children's development

Living and Learning
Preschoolers and children with multiple handicaps
Enquiries to: Cheshire Homes Far Eastern Region
515Q Jalan Hashim
Tanjong Bungah
Penang, Malaysia
The course aims to develop an understanding of children with disabilities and how they can be helped. The course consists of five video programmes, recorded in Malaysia, totalling over 100 minutes along with a 90-page manual. The course covers a five-point teaching plan, activities for learning to move, learning about people, learning to think and learning to be independent. The course is available in English, Bahasa Malaysia and Mandarin.

Step-by-step
Enquiries to: Guyana CBR Programme
c/o EC Commission
PO Box 10847
Georgetown, Guyana
The course illustrates activities which families and volunteer helpers can use at home to further the development of children with disabilities. The course consists of five video programmes recorded in coastal Guyana (Caribbean) along with an 80-page illustrated manual. An overview of the Guyana CBR Programme is given along with programmes on learning to move, learning to talk, learning to think and learning to be independent. The course is available in English and Spanish.

A new tomorrow
Nurturing the development of babies and preschoolers
Enquiries to: Guyana CBR Programme
c/o EC Commission
PO Box 10847
Georgetown, Guyana

Aimed at primary health workers and families, this course illustrates how the physical, social and intellectual development of all children can be nurtured. The course consists of eight video programmes recorded in the Amerindian regions of Guyana along with a 40-page illustrated handbook. The course covers mobility, early cognitive skills, language acquisition, early literacy and numeracy skills as well as child–child activities. The course is available in English and Spanish.

One of the family
A training package for families with young children who have a disability
Enquiries to: UNESCO Special Education Unit
7, place de Fontenoy
Paris 75700
France
Produced by National Institute of Education, Sri Lanka, the course consists of eight video programmes, totalling around 100 minutes along with a 60-page handbook. Among the topics which the course covers are ways of helping children to learn, identifying disabilities, socialization, self-care skills, school readiness and household and vocational skills. The course is available in Sinhala, English and Tamil.

Learning Together
A series of programmes for use in parent and community education
Enquiries to: UNESCO Special Education Unit
7, place de Fontenoy
Paris 75700
France
Produced by the Ugandan Task Force on Educating Communities about Disability, this course consists of six video programmes, totalling 60 minutes in all, plus a 60-page handbook. The contents include programmes aimed at making communities more aware of the abilities of people with disabilities, on helping the development of all children through common play activities and on identifying disabilities and finding help. The course is available in English.

Getting Together
For education and integration of the mentally handicapped in Malawi
Enquiries to: UNESCO Special Education Unit
7, place de Fontenoy
Paris 75700
France
Produced by the Working Group for Mental Handicap in Malawi, this course consists of four video programmes, totalling nearly 50 minutes, plus a 40-page handbook. The contents include play activities to prevent developmental delays, to encourage mobility, communication and language and to develop self-care skills. The course is available in English.

Observing Children Playing
Enquiries to: Save the Children Fund
Middle-East Section
17, Grove Lane
Camberwell
London SE5

This 30-minute video and accompanying manual was produced in Morocco and aims to help parents, CBR workers and primary health personnel assess a child's level in play, and illustrates ways of furthering their development through play. The package is available in Arabic, French as well as English.

Other video-based training packages

A Better Life
For people with a Mental Handicap
Enquiries to: Cheshire Homes Far Eastern Region
515Q Jalan Hashim
Tanjong Bungah
Penang, Malaysia

The course focuses mainly on adult persons and aims to change viewers' expectations of these people by giving examples of good practice and encouraging them to evaluate good provision,and to identify new opportunities which could be started locally. A further aim is to build networks of helpers. The course consists of eight video programmes, around 100 minutes in all, and a 56-page handbook. It is available in English, Bahasa Malaysia and Mandarin.

Disability and Community
Enquiries to: Cheshire Homes Far Eastern Region
515Q Jalan Hashim
Tanjong Bungah
Penang, Malaysia

This six-unit course describes how the needs of children and adults with disabilities can be met in their local communities. Filmed mainly in the Asia-Pacific region but also in Morocco and the Caribbean, the aim is to show how families can be helped at home, how children with disabilities can be helped to attend ordinary schools, the ways in which they might gain productive employment and the living arrangements that are possible if families are no longer able or available to care. The course is available in English.

Community Action on Disability
Enquiries to: Guyana CBR Programme
c/o EC Commission
PO Box 10847
Georgetown, Guyana

This video course provides resource materials for trainers conducting introductory courses in CBR. Among the topics covered are identifying handicaps' involvement of families, ideas for influencing community attitudes and strategies for integrating children with disabilities into the regular school. The course consists of eight programmes, totalling around 120 minutes. A 50-page tutor's guide accompanies the video programmes. The course is available in English and Spanish.

Approaches to CBR
Enquiries to: Cheshire Homes Far Eastern Region
515Q Jalan Hashim
Tanjong Bungah
Penang, Malaysia
Filmed in the Philippines, Sri Lanka, the Caribbean and Morocco, this seven-unit course explores the various options for developing community based rehabilitation projects. It describes the role of field-workers and co-ordinators, the training resources which are available and how links can be made with existing services. The course is available in English.

Training for Work
A video course for people working with adolescents and adults who have disabilities
Enquiries to: Cheshire Homes Far Eastern Region
515Q Jalan Hashim
Tanjong Bungah
Penang, Malaysia
This package is designed for use with service staff and community helpers, and illustrates strategies and methods whereby people with disabilities can become gainfully employed in their local communities. It consists of five video programmes, totalling around 100 minutes; plus a 50-page illustrated manual and activity sheets. Also included is a compendium video showing over 80 different jobs being done by people with disabilities. This is designed to help viewers with intellectual disabilities to determine their job preferences. This packages is available in English.

Teaching Skills
Enquiries to: 515Q Jalan Hashim
Tanjong Bungah,
Penang, Malaysia
This course aims to illustrate five basic teaching techniques that can be used in a range of settings – home, school, work and recreation – with children and adults who have a disability, primarily in learning. The course consists of six video programmes and a handbook but includes guided practice sessions with a tutor. The course is available in English, Bahasa Malaysia and Mandarin.

Books and training manuals

Disabled Village Children: a Guide for Community Health Workers, Rehabilitation Workers and Families (1987)
Contact: Hesperian Foundation, PO Box 1692, Palo Alto, California 94302, USA

Training in the Community for People with Disabilities (1989)
Contact: Medical Rehabilitation, World Health Organisation, 1211 Geneva, Switzerland
Personal Transport for Disabled People; Simple Aids for Daily Living (1987) (and other publications)
Contact: Teaching Aids at Low Cost, PO Box 49, St Albans, Herts AL1 4AX, UK
Toys for Fun: a Book of Toys for Pre-School Children (easy to make playthings based around pictures)
Contact: Teaching Aids at Low Cost, PO Box 49, St Albans, Herts AL1 4AX, UK
Handbook for Teachers of Mentally Handicapped Children in Uganda (1987)
Contact: Special Education Dept., Ministry of Education, PO Box 7063, Kampala, Uganda
An Early Intervention Programme for Children with Mental Retardation (1991)
Contact: Malaysian Care, 21 Jalan Sultan Abdul Samad, Brickfields, 50470 Kuala Lumpur, Malaysia
Distance Training Packages for Parents
Contact: Bangladesh Protibondhi Foundation, 12 New Circular Road, West Mailbag, Dhaka 17, Bangladesh
Introduction to Developmental Disabilities: A booklet for community workers (1987) (and other publications)
Contact: NARCOD, PO Box 220, Kingston 10, Jamaica
Special Education for Mentally Handicapped Pupils (1986)
Speech, Language and Communication with the Special Child (1988) (and other publications)
Contact: Mental Health Centre, Peshawar, N.W.F.P., Pakistan
Pictostory leaflets on various topics for early childhood education
Contact: Community Rehabilitation Unit (Speech Therapy), Harare Hospital, PO Box ST 14, Southerton, Harare, Zimbabwe
Communicating with Children: A Language Training Manual (1991) (available in English and Nepali)
Contact: Teaching Hospital, Speech and Hearing Clinic, Kathmandu, Nepal
Jamaican adaptation of the Portage Kit (and other materials)
Contact: 3D Projects, 14 Monk Street, Spanish Town, Jamaica, West Indies

REFERENCES

Ainscow, M. (1993) Teacher development and special needs: some lessons from the UNESCO project 'Special needs in the classroom'. In P. Mittler, R. Brouillette and D. Harris (eds), *World Yearbook of Education 1993: Special Needs Education*, London: Kogan Page.
Berman, P.A., Gwatkin, D.R. and Burger, S.E. (1987) Community based health workers: head start or false start towards health for all?. *Social Science and Medicine*, **25**, pp. 443–59.
Coleridge, P. (1993) *Disability, Liberation and Development*, Oxford: Oxfam.
Dowling, M.A.C. (1988) How to make manuals for health workers. *World Health Forum*, **9**, pp. 414–19.
Farran, D.C. (1990) Effects of intervention with disadvantaged and disabled children: a

decade review. In S.J. Meisels and J.P. Shonkoff (eds), *Handbook of Early Childhood Intervention*, Cambridge: Cambridge University Press.

Gallagher, J.J. (1992) Longitudinal interventions: virtues and limitations. In T. Thompson and S.C. Hupp (eds), *Saving Children at Risk: Poverty and Disabilities*, London: Sage.

Gartner, A., Lipsky, D.K. and Turnbull, A. (1991) *Supporting Families with a Child with a Disability: an International Outlook*, Baltimore: Brookes.

Haraldson, S.S.R. (1988) Community health aides for sparse populations. *World Health Forum*, **9**, pp. 235–38.

Hegarty (1993) Education of children with disabilities. In P. Mittler, R. Brouillette and D. Harris (eds), *World Yearbook of Education 1993: Special Needs Education*, London: Kogan Page.

Helander, E. (1993) *Prejudice and Dignity: an Introduction to Community Based Rehabilitation*, Geneva: UNDP.

Helander, E., Mendis, P., Nelson, G. and Goerdt, A. (1989) *Training Disabled Persons in the Community*, Geneva: WHO.

Hope, A. and Timmel, S. (1984) *Training for Transformation: a Handbook for Community Workers*, Gweru: Mambo Press.

Hosking, G. (1987) *The Prevention of Mental Retardation from Bio-Medical Causation*, Brussels: ILSMH.

Ingstad, B. (1988) Coping behaviour of disabled persons and their families: cross cultural perspectives from Norway and Botswana. *International Journal of Rehabilitation Research*, **11**, pp. 351–60.

Kuo-Tai, T. (1988) Mentally retarded persons in the People's Republic of China: review of epidemiological studies and services. *American Journal on Mental Retardation*, **93**, pp. 193–99.

McConkey, R. (1989) Educating all parents: an approach based on video. In K. Marfo (ed.), *Parent-Child Interaction and Developmental Disabilities*, New York: Praeger.

McConkey, R. (1993) *Training for All: Developing Video-Based Training Packages for Parent and Community Based Education*, Paris: UNESCO.

McConkey, R. (1994) *Innovations in Educating Communities about Disability*, Chorley: Lisieux Hall.

McConkey, R. and Bradley, A. (1991) Videocourses: a modern solution to an age-old problem. In G. Upton (ed.), *Staff Training and Special Educational Needs*, London: David Fulton.

Mendis, P. (1993) CBR: where are you going?, *CBR News*, **15**, p. 8.

Mittler, P. (1992) Preparing all initial teacher training students to teach children with special educational needs: a case study from England. *European Journal of Special Needs Education*, **7**, pp. 1–10.

Mittler, P. (1993) Political and legislative conditions for the successful education of children with special educational needs. *International Journal of Rehabilitation Research*, **16**, pp. 289–98.

Mittler, P., Mittler, H. and McConachie, H. (1986) *Working Together: Guidelines for Partnership between Professionals and Parents of Children and Young People with Disabilities*, Paris: UNESCO.

Nicholson, A. and Alberman, E. (1992) Predictions of the number of Down's Syndrome infants to be born in England and Wales up to the year 2000 and their likely survival rate. *Journal of Intellectual Disability Research*, **36**, pp. 505–18.

O'Toole, B.J. (1991) *Guide to Community Based Rehabilitation Services*, Paris: UNESCO Guides for Special Education.

O'Toole, B.J. and McConkey, R. (1994) *Identification of Disabilities: a Guide for Primary Health Care Workers*, Georgetown: Guyana CBR Programme.

O'Toole, B.J. and Maison-Halls, (1992) *An Introduction to Disabilities*, Georgetown: Guyana CBR Programme.

Rimmerman, A., Levy, J.M., Levy, P.H. and Zeger, J. (1990) The use of videotapes in parent group education sessions. *International Journal of Rehabilitation Research*, **13**, pp. 171–74.

Rubin, I.L. and Davis, M. (1986) Etiology of developmental disabilities in Soweto, South Africa. *American Journal of Public Health*, **76,** pp. 1112–14.

Schwartz, D.B. (1992) *Crossing the river: Creating a conceptual revolution in community and disability*, Cambridge, MA: Brookline.

Shonkoff, J.P. and Meisels, S.J. (1990) Early childhood intervention: the evolution of a concept. In S.J. Meisels and J.P. Shonkoff (eds), *Handbook of Early Childhood Intervention*, Cambridge: Cambridge University Press.

Shearer, A. (1985) *Looking Forward: Report on an LSMH Symposium on the Future role of Voluntary Associations*, Brussels: International League of Societies for Persons with Mental Handicap.

Thorburn, M.J. (1992) Parental evaluation of community based rehabilitation in Jamaica. *International Journal of Rehabilitation Research*, **15,** 170–76.

Thorburn, M.J., Desai, P. and Paul, T.J. (1992) Service needs of children with disabilities in Jamaica. *International Journal of Rehabilitation Research*, **15,** pp. 31–38.

Tse, J.W.L. (1993) Employers' attitudes towards employing people with mental handicap. *International Journal of Rehabilitation Research*, **16,** pp. 72–76.

World Health Organization (1985) *Mental Retardation: Meeting the Challenge*, Geneva: WHO.

UNICEF (1990) *First Call for Children*, New York: UNICEF.

Werner, D. (1987) *Disabled Village Children*, Palo Alto: Hesperian Foundation.

Index